DATE DUE			
JUL 8 '83			
FEB 11 1994			

Under the general editorship of

CLAUDE E. BUXTON
Yale University

Readings for Introductory Psychology

RICHARD C. TEEVAN

Bucknell University

ROBERT C. BIRNEY

Amherst College

HARCOURT, BRACE & WORLD, INC.
New York · Chicago · Burlingame

Library of Congress Catalog Card Number: 65-11018

Printed in the United States of America

Preface

THIS BOOK OF READINGS is designed to acquaint the beginning student with the empirical base on which psychology rests. Because introductory textbooks cannot include full reports of experiments (space limitations alone militate against it), the beginning student may tend to overlook both the extensive efforts of psychologists to ground their generalizations on concrete empirical observation and the methods available to them for doing so. *Readings for Introductory Psychology* should prevent such oversights: it complements the knowledge of psychology that the student gains from his basic textbook with a knowledge of psychology as it is actually practiced by research psychologists.

The fifty-one articles (many of them reports of experiments designed to test particular hypotheses) have been selected with a view toward their interest and clarity for the beginning student. None of them is annotated or simplified, though a few are somewhat abridged; the original authors' reference lists appear at the end of each article. The selections provide empirical support for various important positions and theories discussed in the basic textbooks; they indicate the goals and the methods of psychological research; and they will give the student a sense of what the practice of psychological research is like.

The book is divided into ten sections, each introduced by a brief essay indicating the relationship between the individual selections and the section topic. Within each section, we have arranged the selections to help the student understand the topic covered. In Section VII (Motivation and Conflict), for example, the eight articles are grouped around three questions: How are the motives that establish behavior patterns acquired? How do motives, once acquired, help create new motives and behavior patterns? In what ways does an organism resolve conflicting motives? The selections—and the sections—need not, however, be read in the order in which they appear. We urge the instructor to assign them in whatever order seems most appropriate to his own teaching plan and to his basic textbook.

We want to thank Claude E. Buxton of Yale University and Ernest R. Hilgard of Stanford University for reviewing *Readings for Introductory Psychology* in manuscript and for making many helpful suggestions; to express our appreciation to the research staff and librarians of the Bucknell University and Amherst College libraries for their assistance and to Barry Smith and Ross Hartsough for their help in finding references and addresses; and, finally, to thank the authors and publishers of the articles included here for their kind cooperation in making them available to us.

RICHARD C. TEEVAN
Bucknell University

ROBERT C. BIRNEY
Amherst College

September 7, 1964

Contents

Readings for Introductory Psychology

SECTION I

Psychology as a Science

ALTHOUGH *psychologists use many different methods in their study of behavior and experience, in every case their goal is the same. Like other scientists, they try not only to observe, measure, and report isolated natural events, but more importantly, to establish verifiable statements about the relationships among them. This requires strict experimental and statistical controls; however, strict controls can be risky (for they can blind the scientist to valuable discoveries he might make while carrying on an experiment with a quite different aim) and difficult to achieve (for they require a high degree of objectivity). Yet in recent years psychologists have, despite these obstacles, made remarkable progress in using scientific controls properly and, through them, in establishing hypotheses as facts.*

In the first article in this section, "Introduction to Experimental Method," John Townsend discusses the relationships between psychology and science, reasoning and scientific explanation, and theorizing and experimentation, and shows the high level of sophistication that psychology can achieve through the use of scientific techniques. Arthur Bachrach, in "Psychological Research: An Introduction," points out that what can happen in the course of research, "accidental discovery," is often quite different from—and more valuable than—what the scientist set out to discover when he began his experiments.

Many factors can interfere with the objectivity that the scientist tries to maintain. Some of them, for example, egoism and the intellectual atmosphere of a scientist's time and culture, are discussed by Edwin Boring in "Psychological Factors in the Scientific Process."

The final article in this section, Joseph Royce's "Psychology in Mid-Twentieth Century," reviews the progress that has been made to date in many areas of psychology (such as experimental psychology, comparative and physiological psychology, and social psychology) through the application of scientific methods to problems that were once thought beyond the scope of science.

JOHN C. TOWNSEND

1. Introduction to Experimental Method

Psychology and Science

SINCE the earliest recorded event in history, man has attempted to inquire into the what, how, and why of not only his existence, but also the existence of almost all things with which he has come in contact. From man's experience, driven by insatiable curiosity, has come the bundle of facts we call knowledge.

SCIENCE AND MYSTICISM

The most exacting, direct, and efficient means by which facts have been collected and organized is by the use of tools of thinking and acting which have come to be known as scientific methods. But man has not always been scientific in the way he went about attempting to explain phenomena in nature. He has often, when baffled as to the cause of an event, resorted to attributing power over natural events to pagan gods.

If a primitive man saw lightning strike a tree and a fire result, he would be at a loss to explain the phenomenon in terms of the source of lightning and the chemistry of combustion. Because of lack of knowledge, he would not be able to explain the event satisfactorily in terms of the factors involved in the event itself. Instead, to find the cause, he would turn away from the event and go outside it to some hypothesized external agent. He would probably invent a god of lightning and a god of fire as the cause of the occurrence.

As man has progressed in his knowledge of the relationships of nature, he has felt less and less need to hypothesize mystical external agents as causes of natural phenomena. It is through the gaining of more and more facts of nature that man has slowly replaced ignorance, governed by superstition, with systematic scientific knowledge. A further discussion of this line of thought is to be found in the writings of Zilboorg and Henry (24, p. 27).[1]

Let us notice FIG. 1. The scientist works only within areas I and II. When he attempts to deal with area III, he becomes a mystic and a scientific renegade. Science attempts to enlarge area I and eliminate areas II and III. Since the work of the scientist is to find answers to problems by the method of determining the truth or falsity of testable hypotheses, he spends most of his time in area II.

The following example may further clarify the concept of the legitimate areas of scientific endeavor. Suppose a scientist's attention is called to an unexplained event which we will name event X. He is asked to find an acceptable scientific explanation for event X. Just where is event X located in the chart, FIG. 1? Event X cannot be in area I, for this area contains only that knowledge which has been gathered through the technique of validating hypotheses, and we said we have no known scientific explanation for event X. Event X cannot be located in area III, for this area contains only nontestable hypotheses or mystical explanations for events. The scientific explanation of event X must rest in area II, for this area is reserved for problems in need of scientific explanation and whose explanation is to be discovered by the process of testing the validity of hypotheses.

1 Numbers in parentheses throughout . . . refer to the bibliography found at the end of each [selection].

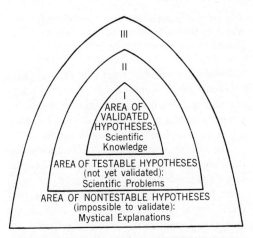

FIG. 1. The relationship of scientific knowledge, scientific problems, and mystical explanations.

During the history of mankind and his search for meaningful explanations of events, area I has increased in size while area III has decreased. Area II has also expanded. Although area II represents man's ignorance of the causes of events, it has become larger for two reasons: (*a*) area I, our present knowledge, has made us more conscious of the need of looking for explanations in terms of testable hypotheses, and (*b*) the answer to one problem most often suggests another problem. Northrop's (19) discussion of the analysis of the problem facing the scientist is relevant here.

DEFINITION OF SCIENTIFIC PSYCHOLOGY

Psychology itself grew from a varied background. It progressed from the mystical to the scientific stage during its long history. One of psychology's most prominent ancestors was philosophy. It was not until 1879 that psychology became dignified by having a laboratory dedicated to psychological research. See Bartley (2, p. 3) for a good, short history of psychology.

Regardless of the strides made by scientific psychology there are many today who would deny that psychology is a science. *Psychology is a science,* but only under certain conditions. Let us see when psychology is and when it is not a science.

Almost no one will disagree with you if you affirm that chemistry, physics, and biol-

ogy are sciences. Now it is obvious that the subject matter of each of these sciences is different. Chemistry treats of the composition of substances and their changes. Physics deals with the phenomena of inanimate matter involving no changes in chemical composition, and biology is the science which treats of living organisms. Therefore, we can say that science, whatever it is, is not defined in terms of the subject matter with which it deals. What, then, is a science?

The definition of science does not rest on what is accomplished, but how it was accomplished. The important factor present when science is present and absent when science is absent is the factor, scientific thinking. To define science as "any body of organized knowledge which has been gathered through the use of systematic methods of investigation" is close to the true definition, but only if the emphasis is placed on the method of investigating and not the materials investigated.

Scientific thinking is a particular kind of thinking. It has two major characteristics. These are *direction* and *control*. Above all, scientific thinking represents organized, orderly, methodical thought concerning the issues at hand. The common factor, then, running through all accepted sciences, is the method by which facts concerning a certain class of phenomena are gathered. If this is so, then there is no reason for excluding psychology from the list of sciences just because its subject matter is often of an intangible nature. So long as facts concerning the consciousness and behavior of organisms are gathered in accordance with the rules of scientific methodology, then such facts form an organized body of knowledge that meets every specification of a science. Conversely, psychology is not a science when its data are gathered and evaluated by unorthodox methods which break the rules of logic. Ruch (21, p. 3), Munn (18, p. 3), Cruze (9, p. 6), and Bugelski (5, p. 3) discuss psychology as a science.

COMMON SENSE AND SCIENTIFIC THINKING

The layman when presented with a problem will often attempt to answer it by "common sense," while the scientist would prefer to use scientific methods. Is the common-sense approach really different from the scientific approach? The answer is that the scientific methods grew out of the common-sense approach. In the growing process, Stebbing (22, p. 235) believed two major changes took place. First, common sense became organized to a high degree, and, second, there was a change in the type of order with which it dealt. The common-sense approach is usually an attempt to solve a problem by simply ruling out those factors which do not form an acceptable answer and taking as the answer that factor or circumstance which most completely accounts for the incident. The following is an example used by Stebbing (22) in a discussion of common-sense thinking:

Suppose that a man, having left his flat empty, returns in the early evening to find his front door bolted. He knows that he left no one in the flat. How, then, account for the bolted door? That burglars have broken into the flat is the first idea likely to occur to a Londoner. The suggestion springs into his mind almost before he has had time to reflect. But then a difficulty arises to check the acceptance of this idea. How could a burglar have left the door bolted on the inside? The flat is on the third floor of a straight-faced block, so that it is improbable that the entry should have been made through a window. Perhaps the bolt has slipped. But that idea is immediately rejected, since it is a stiff, horizontal bolt rarely used. Some one inside must have drawn the bolt. Having succeeded in forcing the door, he inspects the flat, looking for confirmation of his suspicion. There is no one in his study, but he finds the drawers of his desk open and their contents scattered. There was, he knew, no money in the desk, so he does not pause to examine the drawers, but goes at once to the dining-room to inspect the silver. He finds that two silver cups have gone and also that the table silver has disappeared. These facts are ample confirmation of his belief that he has been robbed. But there is still the puzzling fact of the door bolted on the inside. As he walks down the passage he sees a light under the kitchen door. Perhaps the burglar is still in the flat. But the kitchen is empty. On the table are the remains of a meal. The window is wide open. He remembers the parcels lift and now feels that the situation is explained. Whatever the means of entry, the exit has been by

way of the parcels lift. The bolted front door was doubtless to give the burglar time to escape should the owner of the flat return too soon.[2]

Would the scientist treat this example in a different way? Essentially, no. Both the scientist and the common-sense thinker would attempt to collect and organize the facts in such a way as would provide an explanation.

The differences between common-sense thinking and the scientific approach become more obvious when a specific, easily observed, everyday phenomenon occurs and an explanation is demanded. Let us take as an example the apparent fact that memory for an event usually fades as time goes on. Chances are the layman has seldom thought about this ordinary happening. If his attention is directed to the phenomenon and he is asked to explain the reason for it, he might say, "It's just common sense that if you don't use the material you have learned, it disappears because of disuse." In his opinion he has cleverly answered your question and wonders why you could not have figured it out for yourself. But you, as a scientist, are not satisfied with this common-sense answer to what appears to him to be a simple, obvious answer to a commonplace question. So you decide to check and see if disuse alone can cause a fading of memory. Perhaps, as much of a surprise to both of you, you discover that it is not disuse alone that causes the memory fading, but rather it is mostly the so-called retroactive inhibition effect of learning during the interval between the original learning and the recall. A quick look in any good psychology-of-learning text would have told you the same thing. The experiment has not only shown that "common-sense" thinking can be wrong, but has demonstrated that the scientific approach can take a usual occurrence, find a verifiable answer for it, and, further, can suggest other hypotheses and solutions. Common-sense thinking alone seldom is able to do this.

The usual differences between the two ap-

2 Stebbing, L. S., *A Modern Introduction to Logic,* pp. 233–34, The Thomas Y. Crowell Company, New York, 1930. Reproduced here with the kind permission of the publishers.

proaches are these: the common-sense thinker is satisfied with an explanation that merely satisfies his immediate curiosity, while the scientist attempts to systematize the facts so that he may go beyond the obvious explanation. The layman feels the need for providing an explanation for only unusual happenings. The scientist feels the need of explaining any event, unusual or ordinary. Thus we see how the scientist differs from the common-sense thinker in both the way and degree to which he organizes the explanation and the type of events to which his curiosity extends. In addition, the scientist, because of his training in dealing with problems, introduces other elements when he deals with problem solution through the process of experimentation.

Woodworth (23) states:

An experimenter is said to control the conditions in which an event occurs. He has several advantages over an observer who simply follows the course of events without exercising control.

(*a*) The experimenter makes the event happen at a certain place and time and so is fully prepared to make an accurate observation.

(*b*) Controlled conditions become known conditions, the experimenter can set up his experiment a second time and repeat the observation. . . .

(*c*) The experimenter can systematically vary the conditions and note the concomitant variation in the results. . . .[3]

The layman is not expected to offer any more than common-sense answers. The scientist is. Much of the damage done to psychology as a profession, and to those who come seeking psychological help, is done by the self-styled "psychologist" who may be only a layman with a common-sense knowledge of psychology. The scientific psychologist should demand the best thinking possible from himself and colleagues and should make use of only those explanations arrived at by a sound scientific approach.

LOGIC AND SCIENCE

Two major overlapping logical systems have been set down for use as guiding rules for

[3] Woodworth, R. S., *Experimental Psychology*, p. 2, Henry Holt and Company, Inc., New York, 1938.

the scientist. These systems are known as (*a*) inductive and (*b*) deductive logic. See Bugelski (5, p. 46), Black (4, pp. 13, 291), and Andrews (1, p. 2).

Inductive logic assumes that the researcher begins his investigation by observing certain, separate instances of the occurrence of whatever phenomenon he is investigating. He observes, measures, and records these occurrences. Then, by examining the bundle of concrete data collected, he establishes some characteristic for these separate instances. As a result of his examination, he then makes a statement, or proposition, concerning the characteristic of the group from which the separate instances represented a sample. This is the inductive method.

Deductive logic has as its starting point a statement or proposition. From this premise an attempt is made to arrive at a specific, concrete truth by a process of reasoning. This concrete truth is called a deduction. A deduction is, thus, an inference that is believed to be valid and conclusive. Deductions are always preceded by "logical" reasons which appear to support the conclusion.

Inductive logic is often followed by deductive logic in the scientific process in that although inductive logic starts with the observation of phenomena, it ends with proof that the evidence justifies the conclusion. In this manner, inductive logic overlaps with deductive logic. The scientific methods of experimental inquiry are most heavily indebted to the inductive method. Validation of the results of experimentation owes its debt to deductive logic.

The following chart, TABLE 1, illustrates the relationship of the two systems of logic.

Cresswell (8) uses the following syllogism when attempting to represent logical inference symbolically.

Hypothesis: If *A* is *B*, then *C* is *D*.

Experimentation: Observation or experimentation shows that *C* is *D*.

Deduction: If there is no alternative explanation, *A* is probably *B*.

This syllogism could be applied to Torricelli's work leading to the invention of the barometer. If it were true that air has weight (*A* is *B*), then a column of mercury should

TABLE 1

The Relationship of Inductive and Deductive Logic

| INDUCTION | | DEDUCTION |
Concrete Data	Generalization	Conclusion
A certain percentage of the cerebral cortex was removed from a sample of monkeys. Their memory was significantly impaired.	Removal of a certain percentage of the cerebral cortex in monkeys is related to a significant decrement in memory function.	1. Removal of a certain percentage of the cerebral cortex in monkeys is related to a significant decrement in memory function. (Premise I) 2. Jo-Jo is a monkey not yet operated upon. (Premise II) 3. Therefore removal of a certain percentage of Jo-Jo's cerebral cortex will be related to a decrement in his memory function. (The Deduction)

be higher at sea level than on top of a mountain (C is D). It was demonstrated that a column of mercury stood higher at sea level (C is D), thus air probably has weight (A is B).

Many scientific psychologists refuse to accept the psychoanalytic theory because it makes use of, and, indeed, is built upon, certain nontestable hypotheses. The libido, id, ego, superego, etc., are postulates that have come into being in order to help explain human behavior. Because such concepts cannot be dealt with by rigid experimentation, they have been relegated, by some, to the area of nontestable hypotheses which we have labeled "mystical explanations."

Mystical explanations are so easy to invent and are so often logically self-consistent that it takes a firm believer in the scientific method approach to point out the fallacies. If the basic postulates are not capable of being proved or disproved, then any system of logical explanation built on them may be either right or wrong. If the premises are false, then all that follows is wrong, since the logical deductions would of necessity be consistent with a false premise. On the other hand, the basic premises assumed may be right, and in that case the system evolved would be a true system.

The psychoanalysts say that their basic postulates are sound because the system "works." What they mean by this is that their

deductions, when applied, work in the specific instances noted, and that the cures by psychoanalysis follow a logically expected sequence consistent with the system. That the system probably works is denied by few who have witnessed its application, but what worries the scientific psychologist is how it works, in that other explanations of the cures by psychoanalysis are possible wherein the postulates of psychoanalysis need not even be mentioned. Such are the difficulties of understanding a system built on nontestable hypotheses.

Most psychologists have chosen as their approach to the study of human behavior some system which is akin to behaviorism. This means studying the human being as an organism that has the capabilities of receiving stimuli, integrating these stimuli, and responding accordingly. In such a system of behavior explanation, one need not hypothesize forces other than those he can measure and manipulate. Such a system has its beginning in the observation of an organism's reactions to its environment and heredity. Such observations yield verifiable data from which premises may be made. The scientific psychologist may then deduce from these premises certain valid truths. An example of an explanation of the principles of behavior as deduced from behavioristic data is to be found in Hull's work (12).

The psychoanalytic theory may be as true

an explanation of human behavior as any other, but its system of explanation is more doubted by the scientific psychologist than systems that make less use of nontestable hypotheses.

SCIENTIFIC STEPS FROM
OBSERVATION TO GENERALIZATION

If we agree that the correct approach to the solution of a problem is by progressing through the inductive-deductive path, then our itinerary is well marked for us. Most researchers follow the four following steps in doing a piece of scientific research aimed at arriving at facts. Northrop (19, p. 34) presents a related discussion.

Observation. The researcher, during his contact with his field of study, is constantly alert through the process of observation for the detection of apparent relationships among factors. When such relationships are suspected, he prepares to go through the process necessary to account for these relationships. He will wish to connect any fact observed with a total situation so as to bring the isolated fact into a meaningful light.

Classification. A researcher does not jump into a research project without selecting some frame of reference from which to view his data. He may decide to discover the reason for a particular type of behavior in human beings but he still must further decide which frame of reference he will use. If he is a psychologist, he most likely will view his subjects, and thus classify his data, in a different fashion than would a physiologist, a biochemist, or an endocrinologist. During the classificatory stage, the scientist will guess at the cause of the relationships and make what is known as a hypothesis. A hypothesis is in itself a form of classification of the impression made as the result of observation.

A biologist may literally classify a number of specimens he has collected in terms of traits they possess in common with existing categories, and thus gain scientific knowledge of the specimens through this process of classification. See Northrop (19) and Cohen and Nagel (7, p. 223).

Verification. Having observed the problem and having made it meaningful in terms of a particular discipline, the researcher proceeds to design an experiment to test the validity of certain answers he has suggested. During the experimental stage leading to verification the researcher controls the conditions in which the phenomenon occurs. He varies only that factor or those factors whose influence he wishes to measure as related to other conditions. Data are thus gathered that will serve as the basis for derivation of propositions arrived at by the process of induction.

Generalization. On the basis of having established that certain factors are responsible for the phenomenon observed, the experimenter states certain general inferences, principles, theories, or laws. He then deduces from these propositions certain statements relating them to specific occurrences of the phenomenon.

These four steps are utilized by science and are the basic elements in the logical progression in man's attempts to establish an orderly and systematic knowledge of natural phenomena by scientific means. The most important step is verification. The most dangerously difficult step is generalization.

Thus psychology proceeds along a difficult road full of pitfalls and armed only with a method that will, if faithfully followed, safely and efficiently carry it through to the maximum amount of reliable knowledge in the area of scientific psychology.

PURE AND APPLIED SCIENCE

If a scientist is engaged in attempting to establish certain scientific laws as a result of the investigation of basic relationships between phenomena, then he may be said to be doing pure scientific research. A synonym for pure research is fundamental research. The reason for doing pure research is to gather facts for the simple reason that facts are worth gathering. Whether the facts are of immediate use in solving an existing problem or whether they may not be needed for a hundred years is of no concern to the pure researcher. He knows that all things in nature are related and that any new fact discovered will fit into the general scheme.

The "pure" researcher adds to our stock pile of information. He most often works on his own, unsupported, and follows his own inclination in the choice of research problems. Ebbinghaus was doing pure research in psychology when he gathered data on which to build his laws of learning. He was not meeting a current problem of his time, for his work assumed importance only after introspective psychology changed to applied psychology.

The "applied" scientist conducts experiments during which time he applies some basic law or laws of science to ascertain what will happen in a particular case of the law's application. He attempts to answer a problem which is at the time in need of an answer. Chapanis, Garner, and Morgan (17, p. 10) point out the two kinds of application of fundamental science, *applied research* and *design*. Applied research has to do with the techniques of science as they are used in gathering information in specific instances. The techniques of science in this case are used to answer a specific current problem. The use of applied science in design means the use of information gathered in the past (perhaps by the pure scientist) in the development or evaluation of new devices. The applied scientist most often is a member of an organization attempting to meet problems in a particular area, is supported by the organization, and may or may not have freedom in the choice of his research problems. Clinical psychologists at work today experimenting with and evaluating the shock therapies, military psychologists experimenting with propaganda techniques, and industrial psychologists testing new personnel selection batteries are examples of applied scientists working in the field of psychology.

PROBLEMS SPECIFIC TO
SCIENTIFIC PSYCHOLOGY

To do acceptable research in psychology places more demands on the experimenter than if he were experimenting in any of the other fields of science. If he is conducting an experiment in chemistry, he may walk about his laboratory and pick up or put down the materials with which he is working. He can hold in his hand the elements of carbon, magnesium, or copper. He can collect hydrogen in a bottle and watch it ignite when he brings a flame near it. He can be sure the concentration of his acids and purity of his salts are the same from bottle to bottle. The physicist can measure accurately the factors involved in his experiment. Heat, light, electricity, and mechanics all are capable of being highly controlled. The physicist can duplicate the conditions of his experiment just as accurately as can the chemist, for such variables as temperature and pressure, which might vary from experiment to experiment, or even during a single experiment, can be kept constant at any desired value. But not so for the psychological experimenter. He must deal with living organisms who have as their most common characteristic the accumulation of different experiences. No two individuals are alike, nor is any individual the same a moment after it has been established what he is like. The human being just will not stand still psychologically. Behavior is extremely variable.

The experimental psychologist does not deal with things such as chemicals or hot and cold metals; instead he deals most often with intangibles in the form of inferred "things," such as learning, personality, intelligence, and motivation. These intangibles are sometimes called *intervening variables*. An example will clarify this latter term.

A psychologist may decide to do a maze learning experiment wherein he will attempt to motivate his rats by depriving them of food for 24 hours. After 24 hours food deprivation the behavior of the rats is altered. They are now highly active and will race through the maze to get to food. Their food-seeking behavior has been observed and has been found to follow the removal of their normal food supply. Hunger as an intervening variable is, therefore, inferred from this situation, and the behavior of the animal is said to be due to hunger motivation. Actually no one could see hunger in rats, but only guess, quite logically, that hunger was the major factor motivating the animals. Hull's (12, p.

21) discussion of intervening variables should be consulted.

In this manner, the psychologist goes about experimenting with these unseen variables and treating them as if they were as obvious as the period at the end of this sentence. How can the psychologist deal with such intangibles? For instance, can he measure intelligence when neither he nor anyone else has ever seen it? The answer is simple. We seldom measure things as such in any of the sciences; we only measure their effects. Thus, is the problem of the physicist in measuring the effects of electricity much different from the problem of the psychologist in measuring the effects of intelligence? No one has ever seen electricity but most of us have noted its effects. Measuring instruments for electricity utilize the heating effect or the magnetic effect of electricity on metals or wire coils. These effects are then measured and the amount and kind of electricity present are inferred from these observations. The psychologist knows that the effects of intelligence are observed through the behavior of the individual. The individual who behaves in a way judged to be more intelligent is taken to be in possession of more of this inferred "thing" intelligence than is someone else who behaves "less intelligently." We can see, therefore, that psychology, while it most often deals with vague and intangible subject matter, can still gather its data and draw its inferences in a method used by the other sciences.

Although you may now believe that psychology is, and should be, recognized as a science and that the problems faced in psychology are also found in other sciences, I must stop you to point out that the latter is not entirely true. In the other sciences, a scientist observes and records the phenomena of nature about him. It is the picture of a human being, or a "mind" if you choose, observing nonmental or material events. But in the case of the psychologist, there is the picture of a human being or mind studying another human being or mind. Thus, the subject matter of psychology is made of the same stuff as the investigator.

Where does this strange situation leave us?

The main effect of a human being studying another human being is to introduce the probability for more errors to creep into the investigation. Less errors are probable when a human being studies, for example, a piece of iron. Why? First, the investigator in the latter situation will make some errors because he is human. Regardless of the true size, or weight, or composition of the piece of iron, the observer may never more than approximate a knowledge of its characteristics. He can read a scale just so accurately and no more. Second, the measuring instrument itself contains more or less error in measuring that which it says it measures. These are the main sources of error. But the psychologist observing, measuring, and recording the behavior of a human being makes not only the usual errors of measurement but also makes errors because his subject is changing more rapidly than is the piece of iron. The piece of iron does not get hungry, tired, angry, more pleasant, offended, ill, sleepy, bored, or a thousand other things which the human being may. Each of these factors named has some effect on the individual's behavior and thus introduces more chance for error to enter the observation.

There is a type of error in observation which results from the characteristics of the observer. When one human being observes the behavior of another, the attitudes of the observer in regard to bias, prejudice, projection, etc., may introduce errors into the observation.

Another large source of error in dealing with human beings is made when one neglects to equate them in terms of past experience. Since each individual has had a different series of experiences and since present behavior is altered in light of past and present experiences, the experimentalist in psychology may never make the assumption that two individuals can be as much alike as two pieces of iron. Both iron and human beings have past and present experiences, but because the human is so vastly complicated and is constantly reacting to a multiplicity of changing conditions, all nonliving, unconscious things appear relatively stable.

The psychological researcher who wishes

to operate from a scientific approach has chosen a rough row to hoe. He should look at himself as being a scientist, first, and a psychologist, second. Actually, he is a scientist who has simply chosen the behavior of organisms as his topic for research.

Causal Sequences and the Meaning of Explanation

THE untrained person is most naïve in his concept of what is meant by cause and effect. He speaks glibly of this being the cause of that. He assumes for the most part, and quite correctly, from a scientific point of view, that all events have a cause. But he is prone to assume that there is only one cause for an event. In addition, he sometimes jumps to conclusions. For example, many a man has been hanged for murder just because he was the only known person present when the victim died, and his accusers assumed that he caused the death. You push a light switch button and when the light goes on you make the assumption that you caused the light to glow. How can one be sure that anything causes any other thing to occur? This is an important question for everyday living, but it becomes the essential, vital question in experimentation.

DRAWING CAUSAL SEQUENCES

If one performs an action directed toward altering a situation and a change does take place in the situation, then the layman often assumes that the act of altering is the cause and the alteration of the situation is the effect. But the scientist is only too eager to point out that while you may have given an apparent demonstration of a cause-and-effect sequence, it has not been proved that what was done caused the effect. Science no longer speaks of cause and effect as such; instead, a different concept of cause and effect has arisen and is simply called *invariant relationship*. In the above instance, for example, the most the scientist could say is that there appeared to be a relationship between the act you just performed and the change in the situation. You must be careful in the use of the words *act* and *result,* or *antecedent* and *consequence* for, although they imply nothing, some persons infer cause and effect from the use of these words.

Now suppose you repeat the act again and the same change appears in the situation. Suppose you repeat the act a thousand times and always the same change appears. You would be more and more confident that you had caused the effect to appear. The relationship of the act and the result would appear to be an invariant relationship. Yet you would not have proved without a doubt that your act caused the effect. For example, suppose you had flicked a light switch on a thousand times and each time the bulb lit. You might be willing to wager that the light switch you had been flicking turned on the light. It might be both costly and embarrassing to you if the person with whom you had bet pointed out that he had been secretly turning the light on by means of a concealed switch each time you threw your switch on, and, furthermore, the switch you had been using was not even connected in the light circuit!

If one can be so easily fooled, and we all are fooled in a like manner many times each day in ordinary pursuits, it is obvious that those who would attempt to infer cause-and-effect relationships about complicated psychological processes must be sophisticated in the handling of inferences. The reader should see Cohen and Nagel (7, p. 245) for a further discussion of invariant relationships.

PRINCIPLE OF DETERMINISM

One who would seek for answers to the problems put forth by the universe must have a certain faith. He must believe in, or have faith in, two ideas. First, he must believe that all events have a cause. Second, he must believe that he is capable of finding these causes. All scientists performing research believe thus and act accordingly. A name has been given to the first belief mentioned above. It is called the *principle of determinism*. It is possible to believe in the principle of determinism without agreeing with the belief that man can know the causes of events. However, if one does not also believe that man can find the causes of events, then he cannot call himself a scientist. When one carries his belief in the principle of determinism into the field of psychology and makes the statement that all psychological events have a cause, he is affirming *psychic determinism*. Many persons will agree as to the cause of so-called material events but will pull up short when one states that the motives of an individual can be investigated by testing certain hypotheses. The nonscientific person would rather go to some outside force, nontestable, and attribute the desires of human beings to its influence. Or he might say desires are caused by something equally vague, such as human nature.

PRINCIPLE OF MULTIPLE CAUSATION

An event may have not one, but a number of causes. This is the *principle of multiple causation*. Somehow, we like to simplify things to a ridiculous extreme by constantly asking the question, "What was the one thing that caused this to happen?" Such a question can never be answered. A simple example should demonstrate this. Suppose an automobile slid on the wet pavement, going round a curve, and crashed into a tree, killing the driver. The newspaper account revealed that the driver had left his home immediately following a quarrel with his wife, had stopped at a tavern for a few drinks, and had driven rapidly away in his dilapidated car. What caused the death of the driver? A few possible causes are: emotion, alcohol, speed, poor traction due to wet pavement, faulty brakes, steering, etc., loss of blood, broken neck, deterioration of brain cells due to lack of oxygen, etc.

Take any event that you can think of and now tell without doubt what is the one cause of it. You cannot.

Referring again to the light switch example used previously and supposing the switch had been connected, tell what caused the light to glow. Was it the switch, or the electricity, or heat, or what?

Particularly do we run into difficulty in establishing cause-and-effect relationships when we attempt to deal with problems in the social sciences. When we think of the many causes of such things as divorce, crime, war, prejudice and suicide, to mention only a few, we must indeed be instilled with a faith in finding causes if we would venture into the business of determining relationships in these areas.

In the discussion of multiple causation two important related topics should be mentioned: *necessary* and *sufficient* conditions. Ruby (20, p. 381) defines a necessary condition as "an event or circumstance which must be present in order to get a certain result or effect, but which is not sufficient in itself to 'produce' the result." Suppose an automobile was parked on a steep hill and a child playing within the automobile released the emergency brake. The car coasted down the hill and crashed through a billboard. Did the release of the brake cause the accident? One might say that had the front wheels of the car been turned toward the curb the car would not have moved even if its brakes were released. The fact that the wheels were not turned toward the curb was a necessary condition for the accident to have taken place, but not a sufficient condition in itself for causing the accident. Ruby defines a sufficient condition as "one which can, by itself, produce the result, or effect, but which need not be present for the effect to occur." An example of a sufficient condition would be the following. A child is raised in a home where he is constantly prevented from and scolded for expressing himself. He grows into adulthood and demonstrates the characteristics of a repressed individual. This type of environment during childhood is perhaps a sufficient condition to produce a "repressed" adult, but the characteristics demonstrated by this adult could have been produced by other causes. Thus the sufficient cause might not have been the cause at all. To deal intelligently with cause and effect as relationships necessitates that whatever we say is the cause of an event must not only be a necessary but also a sufficient condition for causing the event. A quick glance through the chapter on causal analysis by Larrabee (15, p. 271) would supplement this discussion.

BASES FOR THE ASSUMPTION
OF CAUSAL SEQUENCE

It should be fairly obvious that the relationship of cause and effect is difficult if not impossible to prove. Several impressions arise when one subjects to close scrutiny that which he usually assumes cause and effect to be.

First, he usually assumes that the cause must precede the effect. However, many times effects appear to precede the causes and thus an important relationship may be missed. If a door starts to open before you push on it, you do not assume you opened the door. Yet you might have caused the door to open if you had unknowingly broken a light beam that interrupted a photoelectric circuit that released a spring that opened the door before you touched the door. In this case the effect would have appeared to have preceded the cause.

Second, one assumes a necessary connection between the cause and the effect. If a light comes on while you are not touching the switch, but merely rubbing your forehead, there is no apparent connection between the act and the light coming on. However, a friend, having seen you rub your forehead, assumed that your eyes were strained, and turned on the light. In that case the necessary connection was present but not apparent enough for you to draw a cause-and-effect relationship. As such, the cause of the event might easily have been overlooked.

Third, it soon becomes apparent under close observation that practically the only condition always present when you make a causal connection is *contiguity*. By this is meant two things occurring in a direct temporal sequence. If the effect occurs directly following your act, and this happens regularly, then you do not hesitate to call it cause and effect, because the occurrence now fits the definition of an invariant relationship.

These three bases for the assumption of a causal sequence are part of Hume's famous doctrine of cause and effect. Boring (3, p. 191) presents a short discussion of Hume's point of view on this topic.

Sometimes the apparent precipitating factor occurs and a delay follows after which the effect occurs. This is referred to as *delayed effects*. An example would be death following the consumption of a poison. We infer a series of physiological causes and effects finally terminating in the effect called death.

Because the taking of the poison and the effect called death occurred in a direct, though delayed, sequence, contiguity is assumed, although its strict definition is being strained.

We see, then, that contiguity is the most important condition we have that allows us to make inferences as to causal relationship. Although we know now how dangerous it is to make such inferences, it is the best we can do, and we must use it in the practical situation. We can and do in scientific work avoid the terms cause and effect wherever possible and substitute the word relationship instead. This allows the scientist to avoid the semantic difficulty involved. When he says relationship, he merely means that two events are related in their quantity and temporal appearance, but not necessarily part of a causal sequence. We shall later show how statistics will allow us to quantify the degree of relationship between two events and to make statements as to what level of confidence we have in the fact that they are related.

EXPLANATION BY LABELING

Some scientists in the past who have professed faith in the principle of determinism and thought they were dealing with testable hypotheses were only fooling themselves through a process of word magic. The meaning of fooling oneself by word magic is the practice of explaining the cause of an event by simply saying it is due to some unknown cause to which one has assigned a name.

The use of the term instinct is an outstanding example of this self-deception. Before scientists realized their error in the use of such a term, hundreds of causes of human and animal behaviorisms were attributed to the vague term instinct.

During the early 1900's it was a common and accepted practice to explain, particularly, social motives in terms of instincts. Just how was the word instinct used? Suppose you, as a student of behavior, asked the question, "What causes a particular phenomenon of behavior, A, to happen?" Any number of famous social psychologists would have answered, phenomenon A is caused by instinct A. They would have further said that instincts represent the original force that causes all activity in organisms and that without these instincts no behavior of organisms would take place. Some of these social psychologists would have said that there are 13 major instincts, some more important than others. McDougall (16) would have been typical of this group of social psychologists.

But actually, would you know any more about the cause of phenomenon A after someone said it was due to an instinct than you did before? No. Such explanations are dangerous, for they only cover up our ignorance by giving a name to it. When such a means of explaining events is carried far enough, one ends up with a knowledge of the causes of events that consists of only words that are in great need of explanation themselves. If one accepts as a cause of behavior the mere statement that an instinct causes it and goes away satisfied that he now knows the cause, he is indeed to be pitied for he knows nothing more now than he did when he asked the question.

Morgan and Stellar (17, p. 402) point out that "at the present time there is no real need for the term instinct, except as a conventional rubric for referring to certain kinds of complex motivated behavior." They further remind us that "instincts are under the combined control of stimuli in the external world and subtle changes in the internal environment."

Because the word instinct became a dangerous term to use, some psychologists began to substitute the words motive and drive. If the words motive and drive are used to explain behavior in the same manner as was the word instinct, then these words are no better than the word instinct and just as meaningless. However, if the user defines his concept and shows that the behavior is due to certain existing conditions that his word stands for, then he breaks away from the use of the magic of words to explain events. Klineberg (13, p. 56) has written an excellent chapter on instinct theories and could well be consulted at this point.

Such word magic is on its way out in psychology, but psychology must beware, for such bad actors often play return engagements under different stage names.

EXPLANATION BY STATING PURPOSE

There are many laymen and, according to some, too many scientists who believe in what is known as teleology. Teleology is a system for explaining the causes of events in which phenomena are not thought of as being determined exclusively by mechanical causes. In other words, the cause of an event is not defined in terms of precipitating mechanistic principles by teleologists, but rather events are thought to occur because they are directed to the final accomplishment of some unified whole. Thus, the reason an event occurs is because it must occur to fulfill some purpose or to further some superimposed scheme. While it is true that much of the behavior of man can be looked upon as occurring to fulfill some purpose and to enable him to reach some end, many careful scientists will not allow themselves to believe that they are explaining behavior by citing the pattern into which such behavior falls. Those who adopt this type of purposive explanation may, and often have, ended up by stating sweeping laws which they believe to be universal. Actually, they may have led themselves into believing in a nontestable hypothesis as the cause of behavior. A top spinning on the floor might have to spin or else it would fall over. But some scientists feel there are better ways to explain the reason the top is spinning than to attribute the cause to some purpose the top is fulfilling. If one answers the question, "Why does a chicken cross the road?" by saying, "To get to the other side," he is falling victim to teleological thinking.

EXPLANATION BY FAMILIARIZATION

One group feels that scientific explanation as well as any type of explanation is aimed at only one goal, that is, to make the unfamiliar more familiar. Thus, if one is attempting to explain the cause of any event, he must do so by beginning with those things already understood by the listener and proceed to the unknown. By associating the known with the unknown, the unfamiliar becomes familiar. Anything that is necessary to further the process of making the unfamiliar familiar is a necessary part of an explanation.

EXPLANATION BY STATING
THE INFERENTIAL PROCEDURE

Another approach would be to say that whenever one has by some logical procedure of inference, such as the inductive-deductive method, arrived at a truth concerning an event, the scientific explanation of the event would involve not only the thing dealt with but also the logical steps leading to the inference. Feigl (10) has elaborated on this topic and may be consulted for further information.

EXPLANATION BY DESCRIPTION

Some writers believe that there is no actual difference between description and explanation. They would further state that the only way events are explained at all is through a process of description. This may be so, for it does seem that science at present is at the descriptive level in its evolution. The scientist is called upon not only to tell what causes what but how it is accomplished. He is able to perform best when *describing* the events of nature.

To define an event in terms of an operation or a set of operations is perhaps the best description that can be given at the present time. If you are asked what effect morphine has on the human being, it might be that the best answer you could give would be to describe the changes that take place following the administration of the opiate. You could record what took place by describing not only your part in the process but also what happened to the subject. You might even advance your idea as to how the changes in the subject's physiological condition came about. But at the present time you could not go much further. You would probably have made many errors in just telling what happened and how it happened. Your description as to what happened would be no more valid or reliable than your most inaccurate and inconsistent tool of observation. Your theory as to how the effects came about would be based upon the *correct* and the *incorrect* observations of what effects occurred. In composing a theory of how the effects came about, you would be faced with the choice of a frame of reference from which you would draw your terminology. Would you choose to tell how the physiological effects occurred, the psychological effects, or draw upon some other frame of reference? If you chose only one point of view, you would not be revealing the entirety of the situation. It would be improbable that you could cover all of the facts pertaining to what occurred and even less probable that you would be able to tell how each and every effect came about since you would not have complete knowledge of all the factors present.

The best possible definition of a phenomenon would contain a description of all the relevant factors and their relationship to the phenomenon. However, seldom is this high level of explanation required. Instead, explanation starts with description of data and increases through a hierarchy of description until there is enough information revealed to account for the occurrence of the phenomenon to be explained. The following example may help in the understanding of this hierarchy of explanation.

You may think that some of your professors have completely explained a phenomenon for you, but it is probable that their explanations were far from complete. When faced with a question concerning the cause of a phenomenon, you attempt to relate to the questioner the events that immediately preceded the occurrence of the phenomenon and are apparently invariably related to the occurrence of the phenomenon. But the questioner might be insistent and push you farther with the question, "Yes, but why did the preceding events occur?" You then, in an attempt to further answer his question, relate the events that led up to the events that precipitated the event that became the subject of the question. You could go on this way *ad infinitum* and never find out just why the event in question occurred. However, in most explanations, it is seldom necessary to go much beyond a simple account of the facts that describe the setting in which the phenomenon occurred. If one wishes to go to higher levels of explanation then, according to Feigl (10), he may rise through the level of empirical laws where functional relationships are stated, or on to first-order theories where sets of assumptions using higher-order constructs as the result of abstraction and inference are involved, or on to second-order theories where still higher constructs are used.

Armchair Experimentation

[The following discussion] represents an attempt to defend the procedure of scientific experimentation against the practice of "armchair experimentation." By scientific experimentation is meant the actual work involved in directly dealing with the things about which one hypothesizes. Armchair experimentation refers to the habit of substituting reasoning alone for scientific experimentation in seeking the solution of a problem. It may seem that one is trying to knock down a "straw man" by arguing against armchair methods, but the beginning experimenter should know the reasons why he must "dirty his hands" to arrive at solutions to problems rather than by relying on his "gluteal omniscience" for solutions.

Armchair experimentation has been indulged in most heavily by philosophers whose knowledge of deduction has at times been outstanding. However, it is maintained here that deductive procedures without reference, for validation purposes, to the event under discussion is logic without logic.

Northrop (19, p. 19) points out that the philosopher makes no error when dealing with problems that merely involve deductions from true premises such as found in mathematics. For here the basic premises have been verified and preclude further verification. But the damage is done when the philosopher assumes certain premises to be true when they are not and then begins to build his card house on such false premises. There have been times when it would have been easy to check the basic premises but the philosopher either did not know how or did not want to take the time to verify his premises and deductions. It is to this laxity in some philosophers that the scientist objects.

The reasons armchair experimentation is dangerous are these. As indicated above, all deductive procedures begin with the acceptance of, usually, two premises as being true.

If these two premises are true, then deductions can be made and eventually validated. However, if only reasoning is used minus the personal contact of the reasoner with the material being reasoned about, then error may enter the process. Error may enter in at least three ways: (a) the reasoner assumes propositions or premises which may or may not hold with the facts of the case, (b) the deductive process consists of thinking as the medium of the manipulation of symbols and as such is susceptible to all the errors involved in thinking and in using symbols, and (c) the final answer or deduction cannot be validated until an appeal is made to the facts to see whether the deduction holds. Let us discuss these possible sources of error in some detail.

A person who decides to reason his way through to the solution of a problem must have several things at hand. First, he must have a problem that is capable of being answered. Second, he must have complete assurance that the information he will use as his basic premises is true in the particular context in which it is used. But can he assume such things unless he or someone else actually checks the basic assumptions in regard to their truthfulness? Certainly not.

Instead of appealing to facts, the reasoner often appeals to other quarters. He may use one or more of three diverse and unprofitable methods which, while they are recognized by scientists as merely stumbling blocks on the road to knowledge, do plague all who attempt to arrive at facts.

METHOD OF AUTHORITY

This method involves the statement that something is true because someone says it is true. The someone who says it is true is usually some well-known authority in his field and should know what is true. However, this appeal to authority only assumes but does not ensure that the authority has sufficient evidence to make the statement that something is true. The average person depends on the authorities for much of his knowledge. Thus if the authority is in error, so are those who cite him as an authority. The great thinkers of the past have often chosen to be blind to fact and to follow some authority instead.

Aristotle and Galen were considered to be irreproachable authorities for hundreds of years after their deaths. All that they had said was taken to be the absolute truth even when undeniable evidence was discovered that contradicted their views. In attempting to find fact, the method of authority must not be used blindly as a means of deciding the validity of suggested premises. The evidence back of the authority's statement must be *known* and *accepted* or the authority's statement should not be accepted at all.

METHOD OF TENACITY

This means believing something is true simply because one has always believed it. This method affects orderly thought because (*a*) continued belief in something does not make it true and (*b*) belief in one proposition for a long time may make one oblivious to any contradictory evidence. Anyone who would attempt to reason through to the solutions of problems would have to be free from the influence of this method or he would always be susceptible to the errors cited.

METHOD OF INTUITION

This method deals with the tendency of some thinkers to make statements which they feel to be true propositions simply because the statements are "self-evident." They feel that anyone who understands the proposition put forth must agree because the proposition is "undeniably and obviously true." At one time it was thought self-evident that man would never fly to the moon. It is considerably less self-evident today. Intuitions, therefore, are not necessarily true but must be tested as any hypotheses. To allow these self-evident truths to serve as basic premises in a deductive procedure is to court error. Northrop (19), Cohen and Nagel (7), and Ruby (20) give additional information relating to these practices.

PSEUDO SCIENCE

The assumption of certain propositions as true when it is possible to appeal to the facts is the unexcusable error made by armchair experimentation. As an example of pseudo science built upon false premises, let us look for a moment at phrenology and how it managed to thrive for a hundred years.

Gall (1758–1828) was an anatomist of some note. However, he allowed his early observations concerning bumps on the skull as related to mental characteristics in human beings to overcome any objectivity he might have possessed as a scientist. He based his thinking on three *untrue* premises. First, he assumed that the mind of an individual is not unitary but is broken up into a number of faculties, each possessing or controlling a particular function as demonstrated by the individual. Second, he assumed that the brain had various enlargements that influenced the conformation of the skull over the location of the enlargement. Third, he believed that the greater the possession of a trait, the greater the enlargement of the brain at the place where the particular trait was localized. Thus the logical conclusion would be that one could by studying the distribution and relative size of the protuberances on a person's head make a valid assessment of his mental traits. But we now know that the mind does not consist of units, nor does the outer surface of the skull conform to the shape of the outer surface of the brain, nor do particular faculties of the mind reside in different localized areas such that an enlargement of an area is correlated with a greater possession of a given trait. Had Gall, by actual experimentation, utilized the process of scientific investigation, he would have found no real basis for phrenology. Boring (3, p. 50) points out, after a similar discussion of phrenology, that today we would have been able to reject phrenology by the use of correlation techniques. Although the mathematics of correlation were not available to Gall, Boring indicates that physiologists at that time could have made personal observations and checks and safeguards but that such rigors depended upon the investigator rather than the sanctions of science. Thus observation plus verification before generalization could have taken Gall out of the armchair class of experimentation and into that of scientific experimentation. It is interesting to note that had Gall been more rigorous, there would have been no pseudo science of phrenology, and, consequently, Gall would probably not have been remembered.

LAWS OF THOUGHT

When one reasons, one thinks. The action of the thought processes involved may be described by several laws. Philosophers have for a long time denoted certain fundamental principles in reasoning and called them the *laws of thought*. Many philosophers in the past have held these laws to be logic itself and central to sound thinking. Whatever exceptions we can find to these laws we can offer as evidence against their use in the solution of problems by reasoning. If we can throw doubt on the validity of such "mental gymnastics" then we strengthen the position of experimental laboratory science as being a better approach to the discovery of facts. Let us take a look at these laws of thought.

The Principle of Identity. If something is X it is X. This means a cow is a cow. You may agree, but wait! The main objection to this principle is not in its statement but in its frequent misapplication. You, as X, for instance, may be well today but ill tomorrow. Thus, X today is not X tomorrow. A cow at this instant is not the same cow it was an hour ago, for not only has the cow changed physiologically during that time, your attitude toward it has also changed. This is the position taken by Korzybski (14) and Hayakawa (11) and some of the other members of a school of thought called general semantics. They would agree that since reasoning involves the assumption that there is a certain permanence of things, then the fact that all things are undergoing change at a faster or slower rate dilutes the validity of reasoning.

However, those who believe in the law of identity, and contrary to the general semanticists' attitude, point out that it is possible to communicate by words only because there is a certain identity in our meanings. Also they believe that even if there is a change, it must be in relation to something that is constant, and this constancy is the meaning with which we deal. They would say, then, that the

symbols used in reasoning are valid building blocks.

In order to make use of this law of thought properly, one must always give a time and place reference. An objection to this law then would be that too often such specific designations are omitted through a lack of knowledge, or carelessness, and thus may throw error into an otherwise logical progression of thought. If one reports that it is a clear day, he must be specific, for it may be raining only a hundred miles away. If one were to say it is a clear day in the city of Pittsburgh (unhappy choice) on April 1, 1952, at 12 noon, he would be specifying the time and place in such a way as would make his statement true for all time and place. In describing happenings, stating laws, or in any type of communication or reasoning, it becomes essential that a complete statement involving context is given so that the law of identity may apply.

The Principle of Contradiction. A thing cannot be both X and not X. For example, a man cannot be both tall and short at the same time. Those who object to this principle would do so by pointing out in the above example that a 5-foot man would be short in some tribes in Africa where the average height of males is considerably more, but the same 5-foot man would be considered tall by a band of pygmies. In a like manner, a certain table seen from directly above appears square (X) but when seen from one side appears rectangular (not X).

The objection to this law of thought is removed if the user again supplies a frame of reference involving time and place reference. Thus, the 5-foot man in a tribe where the average height is 5½ feet will always be considered short as long as he remains in that particular frame of reference. The only remaining objection is whether in a complicated problem composed of many variables, it is probable that all such designations could be handled accurately.

The Principle of Excluded Middle. Anything must be either X or not X. For example, this is either a book or not a book.

To many persons, this is the most objectionable of the three principles. These critics would say that nowhere in nature do you find that things are either one way or another with a gap in between. One simply finds no dichotomies or mutually exclusive classes in nature. There is always the area of overlap. You may think that black and white are completely different, but you cannot find that nature has drawn a line between black and white. Instead of a point of demarcation, one finds a shading of black into white through the middle area of gray. How can you draw a line separating the two? You may think coal is black, but it becomes gray by comparison when held against a piece of black velvet. For the thinker arbitrarily to put the continuous order of nature into pigeonholes by excluding the middle is to cast aside much of his contact with things as they really exist. Many of the great problems argued in philosophy have come about only because of the acceptance of this law of thought. Instead of a two-valued orientation consisting of either-or they would suggest a multivalued orientation.

Ruby (20, p. 258) points out that the error made by some in criticising this principle is based upon the confusion between contrariety and contradiction. The law says that a book is either red or not red, it does not say that it is either red or reddish brown.

These laws are tools we all must use in our thinking. However, fewer errors will be made in their application if certain precautions are taken: (*a*) always designate time and place reference, and (*b*) remember that man has in many cases imposed artificial categories on nature and as such has introduced an error in drawing lines where they do not actually exist. For a more complete treatment of the laws of thought, the reader should consult Ruby (20) and Cohen and Nagel (7).

ERRORS IN USING SYMBOLS

The most common source of error is made when the thinker assigns symbols to the elements of the problem with which he is dealing. Thus he begins to use, perhaps, the letters *A, B,* and *C* as designations for the variables or factors. These letters are now used by him in his thinking as though each is defined by the characteristics of the factor for which it stands. But this cannot be true, for he does not know all about the characteristics of *A*, or *B*, or *C*. If he did, it would not be necessary for him to go through his reasoning process, for there would be no problem. Thus if he continues to use the symbols in the absence of the things for which they stand and continues to build inference after inference on such a structure, he may, and most often does, get farther from reality and finds in the end that he has been dealing only with words and not things. If he would, at each step in his thinking, check his logical result by referring to the real situation again, then he might safely proceed. He would find that symbols are more static than the things they represent and that due to the stability of symbols and the variability of the things for which they stand, his result from reasoning might differ grossly from his results by experimentation.

An example might help here. I once saw a man design a circuit for a radio. He carefully calculated the exact value each condenser, resistor, and other parts should have. On paper, it was perfect. But when he constructed the radio from the diagram, the radio refused to play. The reason it would not function was that he had assumed the parts corresponded exactly to the symbols used in the diagram. Yet the radio parts were not perfect and only approximated the characteristics they were supposed to have. The combined errors of all these small differences added up to an error so large that the radio needed much adjustment before it finally operated efficiently.

Any word may have many meanings, one of which may be applicable to the particular thing for which it stands at a precise moment. But the thing denoted is constantly changing in its relationship to other things and thus may require a different word if we are to keep track of it a moment later. Treating words, then, as accurate substitutes for things is dangerous to sound thinking if one does not constantly keep in touch with the reality of the situation. The point is this, a symbol is only analogous to the thing for which it stands. For a more complete discussion of semantics, see Larrabee (5).

If one wishes to deal with facts, he must restrict himself to dealing with whatever experiences he may have as the result of observing facts directly. If he attempts to communicate these experiences to others, neither he nor they are dealing with facts—they are now dealing with *described* facts. And description, as has been pointed out, is full of error.

We see, therefore, the dangers involved in attempting to solve problems by the use of symbols rather than directly dealing with the elements of the problem. Real advances were never made in science until man left his armchair and entered the laboratory. Going into the laboratory does not mean the scientist leaves logic and reason behind. Scientific methods are based on logic. The reader should have the impression that logical progression of thought concerning a problem is useful only in that it may lead to testable hypotheses which can be accepted or rejected in light of experimental data. This is the safest way to build a sound science.

BIBLIOGRAPHY

1. ANDREWS, T. G.: *Methods of Psychology,* John Wiley & Sons, Inc., New York, 1948.
2. BARTLEY, S. HOWARD: *Beginning Experimental Psychology,* McGraw-Hill Book Company, Inc., New York, 1950.
3. BORING, E. G.: *A History of Experimental Psychology,* 2d ed., Appleton-Century-Crofts, Inc., New York, 1950.
4. BLACK, MAX: *Critical Thinking,* 2d ed., Prentice-Hall, Inc., New York, 1952.
5. BUGELSKI, B. R.: *A First Course in Experimental Psychology,* Henry Holt and Company, Inc., New York, 1951.
6. CHAPANIS, A., *et al.: Applied Experimental Psychology,* John Wiley & Sons, Inc., New York, 1949.
7. COHEN, M. R., and E. NAGEL: *An Introduction to Logic and Scientific Method,* Harcourt, Brace & World, Inc., New York, 1934.
8. CRESSWELL, J. R.: West Virginia University. Personal communication.
9. CRUZE, WENDELL W.: *General Psychology for College Students,* Prentice-Hall, Inc., New York, 1951.
10. FEIGL, HERBERT: Symposium on Operationism, *Psychol. Rev.,* Vol. 52, No. 5, September, 1945.
11. HAYAKAWA, S. I.: *Language in Action,* Harcourt, Brace & World, Inc., New York, 1941.
12. HULL, C. L.: *Principles of Behavior,* Appleton-Century-Crofts, Inc., New York, 1943.
13. KLINEBERG, OTTO: *Social Psychology,* Henry Holt and Company, Inc., New York, 1940.
14. KORZYBSKI, ALFRED: *Science and Sanity,* 2d ed., The Institute of General Semantics, Lakeville, Conn., 1941.
15. LARRABEE, HAROLD A.: *Reliable Knowledge,* Houghton Mifflin Company, Boston, 1945.
16. McDOUGALL, W.: *Introduction to Social Psychology,* 1st ed., 1908.
17. MORGAN, C. T., and E. STELLAR: *Physiological Psychology,* 2d ed., McGraw-Hill Book Company, Inc., New York, 1950.
18. MUNN, N. L.: *Psychology: The Fundamentals of Adjustment,* 2d ed., Houghton Mifflin Company, Boston, 1951.
19. NORTHROP, S. F. C.: *The Logic of the Sciences and the Humanities,* The Macmillan Company, New York, 1947.
20. RUBY, LIONEL: *Logic: An Introduction,* J. B. Lippincott Company, Philadelphia, 1950.
21. RUCH, FLOYD L.: *Psychology and Life,* 3d ed., Scott, Foresman & Company, Chicago, 1948.
22. STEBBING, L. S.: *A Modern Introduction to Logic,* The Thomas Y. Crowell Company, New York, 1930.
23. WOODWORTH, R. S.: *Experimental Psychology,* Henry Holt and Company, Inc., New York, 1938.
24. ZILBOORG, G., and G. H. HENRY: *A History of Medical Psychology,* W. W. Norton & Company, New York, 1941.

ARTHUR J. BACHRACH

2. *Psychological Research: An Introduction*

RESEARCH is *not* statistics. I am beginning this introduction to the study of psychological research with a negative statement because I feel that many students are scared away from the enjoyable pursuit of research because they equate it with tedium and involved statistical manipulations. This is not difficult to understand, for a student who picks up a book on research is likely to find that it is no more than a book on statistics in research design. This is not to disparage statistics in any way, but merely to indicate that statistics is a *tool* of research, a useful one to be sure, but no more than a technique for handling some (and not all) research data. I am going to deal with research from a different standpoint, briefly mentioning some of the basic features of research (such as control and experimental groups), but not making any attempt to introduce the student to statistical techniques. Rather, I want to concern myself with the origins of research, scientific method and practice, the meaning of data and theory, the ethical aspects of research with animal and human subjects, and, most important, with the curiosity of the scientist, his main attribute and his main source of pleasure. As the brilliant chemist Linus Pauling once observed, "Satisfaction of one's curiosity is one of the greatest sources of happiness in life."

Curiosity, Accident and Discovery

LET'S start with the curiosity of the scientist. Much research begins with accidental dis-

covery. A scientist is working diligently in his laboratory with a particular problem and a particular goal in view when something happens, perhaps something goes wrong. Sir Alexander Fleming had this happen when he was trying to culture some bacteria. You will recall that a little green mold was present in a dish in which he was culturing bacteria, and that the bacteria had been killed. This had probably happened to many scientists before him who might have sworn under their breaths about the ruined experiment, tossed the culture into the refuse and started again to culture the bacteria.

But this would have been contrary to scientific method in its ideal. As we will see later, after a problem has been selected, the scientific method consists fundamentally of two parts: (1) the collection of data and (2) the establishment of a functional relationship among these data. For Fleming, and those before him, there were two basic data: a bacteria culture was destroyed and a green mold was present in the dish. This is the fact: A and B coexisted. Now, was there a functional relationship between these two? Did A (the mold) have any effect on B (the bacteria)? This is the beginning of the research, to manipulate the conditions under which A and B coexisted so that an answer might be obtained. If they were functionally related (i.e., A had an effect on B) that would be one answer. If they were not and the coexistence was pure chance, that would also be an answer.

So Fleming started with an *observation*. To start his experiment he probably formulated some sort of *hypothesis* which might be stated roughly as follows: "The appearance of the green mold and the destruction of the colony of bacteria are related; the green mold was responsible for the destruction of the bacteria." From this point, he proceeded to an experiment to test his hypothesis. He might take the green mold and put a new colony of live bacteria in contact with it. The results of this experiment would either confirm or refute the hypothesis. If the second colony of bacteria also perished when in contact with the green mold, then the experimenter might feel more comfortable in assuming a causal relationship. There are other factors which might be taken into consideration, such as temperature changes, the presence or absence of sunlight. But for the moment, assuming that these variables have been controlled, the experiment would be to manipulate the green mold and the bacteria under various controlled conditions.

Of course, Fleming's research showed that the green mold was responsible for the bacterial destruction and penicillin emerged from his findings. I want to emphasize the most important aspect of this. Fleming discovered this green mold by *accident;* he was attempting to culture a particular colony of bacteria. A lesser man might have been irritated and annoyed at the death of the bacteria, would have ignored the mold, and washed the entire dish down the sink. The fact that Fleming did not do this illustrates one of the characteristics of a good scientist. He has his eyes open; he is never so bound up in a fixed path of experimentation that he is blinded to unusual events which may occur. Skinner (10) in one of his "unformalized principles of science" says, "When you run onto something interesting, drop everything else and study it." While this may not fit the image of science and the scientist that the student has conceived, it does illustrate the way much research originates and develops. To the person looking at science, it is often perceived as a logical, consistent, highly organized body of information revolving around a hard core of rigid pre-specified methodology. J. Z. Young in his treatise on science (11) had the following to say:

One of the characteristics of scientists and their work, curiously enough, is a confusion, almost a muddle. This may seem strange if you have come to think of science with a big S as being all clearness and light. There is indeed a most important sense in which science stands for law and certainty. Scientific laws are the basis of the staggering achievements of technology that have changed the Western world, making it, in spite of all its dangers, a more comfortable and a happier place. But if you talk to a scientist you may soon find that his ideas are not all well ordered. He loves discussion, but he does not think always with complete, consistent schemes, such as are used by philosophers, lawyers, or clergymen. Moreover, in his laboratory he does not spend much of his time thinking about scientific laws at all. He is busy with other things, trying to get some piece of apparatus to work, finding a way of measuring something more exactly, or making dissections that will show the parts of an animal or plant more clearly. You may feel that he hardly knows himself what law he is trying to prove. He is continually observing, but his work is a feeling out into the dark, as it were. When pressed to say what he is doing he may present a picture of uncertainty or doubt, even of actual confusion.

Although the methodology of the scientist may appear haphazard, there is an overall conception of the goals. Excursions into apparatus design, discussion and other enjoyable side paths nevertheless remain within the ultimate plan of knowledge and its discovery.

There are times when the curiosity of the scientist is piqued by the unusual and the unexplained in situations that do not lend themselves easily to experimentation, but which are potential stimuli to research. Let me give you an example of one such curious situation (9). Some time ago a famous world traveler gave the following description of the planet Mars and its satellites:

They have . . . discovered two lesser stars or satellites which revolve about Mars whereof the innermost is distant from the center of the primary planet exactly three of his diameters and the outermost five; the former revolves in the space of ten hours, and the latter in twenty-one and a half; so that the squares of their periodical times are very near in the same proportion with the cubes of their distance from the center of

Mars, which evidently shows them to be governed by the same law of gravitation that influences the other heavenly bodies.

This is an accurate picture of Mars. It does have two moons. The given revolutions are quite close to the actual periods. Phobos goes around Mars in the same direction that Mars rotates, but in about one-third the time. This makes it appear as though Phobos rises in the West and sets in the East. It has been noted that this is the only body in the universe that revolves around a central body faster than the latter rotates. Despite the fact that this is unique, it is in the traveler's description, and we find that it is a most accurate portrayal of Mars and the unusual nature of its satellites.

Why should this be so interesting? Because the famous world traveler who wrote this was Lemuel Gulliver in 1726 as represented by Jonathan Swift in *Gulliver's Travels*. While this was written in 1726, the two moons were not discovered until 1877, a century and a half after Gulliver's description. As a matter of fact, no telescope big enough to see the moons was built until about 1820.

This is one way research begins. How come? While this may be too colloquial for the scientific mind, it expresses the beginning of wonderment. How was Gulliver able to describe these moons so accurately 150 years before they were discovered? Is it coincidence? Is it possible that Jonathan Swift had some information which others did not have? Was it merely a good guess? We have no answer to this, but it does provide stimulation for possible investigation.

The Careful Casual

[Earlier] I suggested a fundamental law of research, rather an informal one, which states that "people don't usually do research the way people who write books about research say that people do research." This book, like so many others, primarily presents an ideal for research methodology or, perhaps, a general set of principles to guide but not to constrict a researcher.

Foremost among the qualities a good researcher needs is what Pasteur has called the prepared mind. It is clearly impossible for anyone engaged in research to predict all of the events that may occur. The researcher must begin with care in the planning and execution of his research, but he must not become so rigidly tied to the plan that he is rendered incapable of seeing accidental discoveries that may pop up, much in the way Fleming did in the example given above regarding the accidental discovery of penicillin. The researcher must be a little casual as well, for a relaxed but nevertheless alert view toward research may provide the occasion for unexpected discovery. This is what Pasteur means by the prepared mind, a combination of stored basic knowledge and a readiness to perceive the unusual.

Cannon, in his work on the way of an investigator (7), has referred to this type of accidental discovery as "serendipity." This is a term taken from Walpole's *Three Princes of Serendip,* a story of three princes who went around the world searching for something, did not find what they were seeking, but on their journeys discovered many things which they had not sought. Cannon indicates that serendipity, or accidental discovery, is a major quality of research and the prepared mind must be alert for it.

And so the researcher must be careful and casual. Another aspect of research is the way in which it is conceived and carried out. When an article appears in a professional scientific journal, it usually follows a predetermined and generally accepted format. Most articles will begin with an introduction, a review of the literature, a description of the experimental design, a presentation of the results obtained in the experiment, a discussion of those results and a summary, followed by a bibliography of relevant articles. Such scientific papers are usually astringent and formal and in no way truly reflect the very informal, enjoyable aspects of sitting around in a laboratory with one's colleagues and talking about the way research might be accomplished. The end product is a dehydrated form of the entire story.

Let me give you a personal example of such an event. In research some of my associates and I were doing on verbal behavior in human subjects, we were looking for some sort of reinforcer to use as a reward for speaking. Our subjects were equipped with individual microphones and we were studying the verbal patterns of individuals and of these same individuals in group interaction. They were paid by the hour for this. But it seemed to us, as we were sitting around talking about the experiment, that this was not an adequate reward for our purposes inasmuch as it did not matter how much or how loud the subject spoke during the session. He received the same amount no matter how much he talked. So we wondered what would happen if we tried to get him to speak louder or faster by rewarding him for such verbalization. Recognizing that money is a very good reward in our culture, we decided that it would be a fine idea to see what would happen if we paid the subject in money as he was speaking, so that each impulse spoken into the microphone would be rewarded. What would happen if we paid him by the spoken impulse? We thought that a coin dropping into a chute each time he spoke above a certain amplitude would be a good reinforcer to produce and maintain such behavior.

But then we started counting up the number of such impulses during an hour session and found that there would be several hundred. It would be financially impossible to use coins unless we were to use pennies. In the course of this informal discussion, it was decided that pennies are not really very good rewards in our culture because of an informal test which everyone has experienced. Even a $25,000-a-year executive is likely to stoop down and pick up a nickel if he sees it, but is likely to pass a penny by. There seems to be more than five times the rewarding value of a penny on a nickel. So the minimum successful financial reward in the form of a coin would probably be a nickel. This would become so expensive as a reward in such an experiment that if we did use the nickel the chances are the experimenters would try to change places with the subjects!

Someone suggested that we might try using poker chips which the subjects could exchange for money at the end of the session. In this way they would be working for a symbolic monetary reward, which is very strongly reinforced in our culture. We talked about the meaning of poker chips and the images that poker chips conjured up in the minds of various people in a group. Stacks of poker chips in front of a gambler in a smoke-filled room and the various dramatic associations of poker chips in the folklore of our culture were discussed. Of course there was a lot of joking about this and someone wanted to know if we would have to wear green eyeshades and roll up our sleeves and put garters on them, whether we would have to use a round table for the experiment with a green felt cloth over it and so on, invoking the humor of the gambling situation. We finally decided to use chips.

The above account is merely a capsule record of the many hours of discussion on an informal level which went on during this particular part of the experiment. When the paper was finally written up for publication in professional journals, it merely reported that "because of the generalized reinforcing nature of poker chips, they were used as a reinforcement for verbal behavior as a substitute for monetary reward (but symbolic of such secondary monetary reinforcement) and to be exchanged for money." Nothing about the green eyeshade, the green felt cloth, the sleeve-garters, the smoke-filled room—remarks which would be inappropriate for a scientific paper.

But I do think that it is somewhat unfortunate that the joking and informality of group research discussions are filtered out by the time they appear in a published form. Students who might otherwise consider research as an enjoyable career are given the idea that research is a tedious, astringent, rigid discipline. In short, the careful always appears in print but rarely the casual. Where the casual does appear is in the informal contacts among scientists, both in their own laboratories and in meetings, such as conventions. If there is one important function served by a convention of scientists (who get together perhaps once a year), it is not the presentation of papers but the informal contacts in bars and restaurants which provide the opportunity for the exchange of ideas and information.

A Case of Serendipity

IN a research report designed specifically to study examples of accidental discovery and the ways of an investigator, two sociologists, Barber and Fox (1), interviewed two well-qualified research scientists, both of whom had observed an event but only one of whom had followed through to an eventual discovery. Barber and Fox call this article "The Case of the Floppy Eared Rabbits: An Instance of Serendipity Gained and Serendipity Lost." Because this is one of the most valuable examples available of accidental discovery, I would like to discuss it in some detail.

Barber and Fox had heard of a discovery two researchers had made accidentally. One of these two scientists was Dr. Lewis Thomas, an eminent scientist who, at the time of the paper (1958), was head of the Department of Medicine at New York University's College of Medicine and formerly had been Professor and Chairman of the Department of Pathology. The other researcher was Dr. Aaron Kellner, associate professor in the Department of Pathology of Cornell University Medical College and director of its central laboratories.

Both of these scientists were well qualified, well respected and affiliated with excellent medical schools. In the course of their research in pathology, both men had had occasion to inject rabbits with an enzyme, papain, and both of them had observed that the ears of the rabbits collapsed following the injection. Despite the fact that both of them had observed the floppy ears following the intravenous injection of the rabbits, only one of them went on to discover the explanation for this unusual and funny event. The reasons for this present a fascinating picture of the conditions under which research usually occurs and what happens to researchers.

Barber and Fox quote from interviews with both Dr. Thomas and Dr. Kellner. Let us quote from Dr. Thomas, who first noticed the reversible collapse of the rabbits' ears when he was working on the effects of a class of enzymes, proteolytic enzymes.[1] Dr. Thomas said

I was trying to explore the notion that the cardiac and blood vessel lesions in certain hypersensitivity states may be due to release of proteolytic enzymes. It's an attractive idea on which there's little evidence. And it's been picked up at some time or another by almost everyone working on hypersensitivity. For this investigation I used trypsin, because it was the most available enzyme around the laboratory, and I got nothing. We also happened to have papain; I don't know where it had come from; but because it was there, I tried it. I also tried a third enzyme, ficin. It comes from figs, and it's commonly used. It has catholic tastes and so it's quite useful in the laboratory. So I had these three enzymes. The other two didn't produce lesions. Nor did papain. But what the papain did was always produce these bizarre cosmetic changes. . . . It was one of the most uniform reactions I'd ever seen in biology. It always happened. And it looked as if something important must have happened to cause this reaction. (2)

There are several particularly interesting phrases in this initial account of the discovery. For one thing he said, "For this investigation I used trypsin, because it was the *most available enzyme around the laboratory* . . ." (italics mine). He goes on "we also happened to have papain; I don't know where it had come from; but because it was there, I tried it." Here, indeed, is accident. "They happened to have" one enzyme and the other was "the most available" around the laboratory. Certainly there is none of the rigorous preconceived hypothesis-testing in the choice of these particular enzymes. It was mostly accident that they "happened" to be in the lab.

Being a good research scientist, Dr. Thomas did not let this unusual event go by. He goes on to describe his immediate search for an explanation:

I chased it like crazy. But I didn't do the right thing . . . I did the expected things. I had sections cut, and I had them stained by all the tech-

---

[1] Proteolytic enzymes are enzymes that by catalytic action accelerate the hydrolysis of proteins into simpler organic substances.

niques available at the time. And I studied what I believed to be the constituents of a rabbit's ear. I looked at all the sections, but I couldn't see anything the matter. The connective tissue was intact. There was no change in the amount of elastic tissue. There was no inflammation, no tissue damage. I expected to find a great deal, because I thought we had destroyed something. (3)

Here is another significant phrase appearing, "I did the expected things." He went on and cut the sections, and stained them by all the techniques available at the time of the experiment. He said that he "expected to find a great deal" because he thought that something had been destroyed. At that time he also indicated that he had studied the cartilage of the rabbit's ear and considered it normal. ". . . The cells were healthy-looking and there were nice nuclei. I decided there was no damage to the cartilage. And that was that . . ." He did say that his examination of the cartilage at that time was routine and fairly casual because he did not entertain the idea seriously that the collapse of the ears might be associated with cartilage change. "I hadn't thought of cartilage. You're not likely to, because it's not considered interesting . . . I know my own idea had always been that cartilage is a quiet, inactive tissue."

It is undoubtedly true that people do have preconceptions such as Dr. Thomas had. He thought that there must be some damage and found none. He assumed that the damage would be in the connective or elastic tissues of the ear and shared a conviction with others that cartilage is "inert and relatively uninteresting," so he didn't pay much attention to it. This made him unreceptive to the actual explanation for the floppy ears as changes in the cartilage. He discovered this explanation accidentally a number of years later.

Dr. Thomas was very anxious to get some explanation for this uniform biological event, but he finally was obliged to turn away from his floppy-eared rabbits because he was "terribly busy working on another problem at the time," a problem with which he was "making progress." And he also remarked that he had "already used up all the rabbits I could afford, so I was able to persuade

myself to abandon this other research." Here are two other impinging events which changed the course of the research. He was doing other research in which he was making progress (rewarding to him) and his budget could not provide for the large number of rabbits he felt he needed in order to pursue this adequately. So he was able to persuade himself to abandon this other research with the floppy-eared rabbits and temporarily accept the failure.

Barber and Fox note that it is usual not to report such negative experiments in the scientific literature for many reasons, not the least of which is the lack of available space for what might be interesting and perhaps valuable experiments but ones which are not worked out as relatively complete research projects. No one else, therefore, was formally told about Dr. Thomas' work with the floppy-eared rabbits. But he did not forget them and he kept the problem of the floppy ears alive through many informal contacts with colleagues who visited his labs and through other informal meetings. For example, he noted that twice he demonstrated this phenomenon for some of his unbelieving colleagues. As he said, "They didn't believe me when I told them what happened. They didn't really believe that you can get that much change and not a trace of anything having happened when you look in the microscope." In this way, the issue remained alive by informal exchanges among scientists.

A couple of years after this accidental discovery, Dr. Thomas was doing another type of experiment. He said

I was looking for a way . . . to reduce the level of fibrinogen in the blood of rabbits. I had been studying a form of fibrinoid which occurs inside blood vessels in the generalized Schwartzman reaction and which seems to be derived from fibrinogen. My working hypothesis was that if I depleted the fibrinogen and, as a result, fibrinoid did not occur, this would help. It had been reported that if you inject proteolytic enzymes, this will deplete fibrinogen. So I tried to inhibit the Schwartzman reaction by injecting papain intravenously into the rabbits. It didn't work with respect to fibrinogen . . . But the same damned thing happened again to the rabbits' ears!

This time, fortunately, Dr. Thomas was able to solve this puzzle of the floppy ears and to realize that it was an instance of accidental discovery. In his words this is what happened:

I was teaching second-year medical students in pathology. We have these small seminars with them: two-hour sessions in the morning, twice a week, with six to eight students. These are seminars devoted to experimental pathology and the theoretical aspects of the mechanism of disease. The students have a chance to see what we, the faculty, are up to in the laboratory. I happened to have a session with the students at the same time that this thing with the rabbits' ears happened again. I thought it would be an entertaining thing to show them . . . a spectacular thing. The students were very interested in it. I explained to them that we couldn't really explain what the hell was going on here. I did this experiment on purpose for them, to see what they would think . . . Besides which, I was in irons on my other experiments. There was not much doing on those. I was not being brilliant on these other problems . . . Well, this time I did what I didn't do before. I simultaneously cut sections of the ears of rabbits after I'd given them papain and sections of normal ears. This is the part of the story I'm most ashamed of. It still makes me writhe to think of it. There was no damage to the tissue in the sense of a lesion. But what had taken place was a quantitative change in the matrix of the cartilage. The only way you could make sense of this change was simultaneously to compare sections taken from the ears of rabbits which had been injected with papain with comparable sections from the ears of rabbits of the same age and size which had not received papain . . . Before this I had always been so struck by the enormity of the change that when I didn't see something obvious, I concluded there was nothing . . . Also, I didn't have a lot of rabbits to work with before. (4)

This is one of the major functions that students serve. They remind instructors of the way in which research should have been done originally. Because he was obliged to "do it right," in a sense, and carefully compare normal and papain-injected rabbits' ears as an example for the students, he went on to discover quantitative change in the carti-

lage which was the explanation for the floppy ears. Let me quote finally from Dr. Thomas' article (from the *Journal of Experimental Medicine*) in which he reported what had happened to the cartilage in the ears of the rabbits. It is quite technical but this is the final product of the years of informal contacts, puzzles, searching and accident. "The ear cartilage showed loss of a major portion of the intercellular matrix, and complete absence of basophilia from the small amount of remaining matrix. The cartilage cells appeared somewhat larger, and rounder than normal, and lay in close contact with each other. . . . (The contrast between the normal ear cartilage and tissue obtained 4 hours after injection is illustrated in Figs. 3A and 3B of [Dr. Thomas'] article.)" What a very formal way to report on the wonderfully human fun and bewilderment which had gone on for so many years in Dr. Thomas' laboratory!

One final interesting accidental discovery was made when Dr. Thomas was demonstrating to students.

I was so completely sold on the uniformity of this thing that I used the same rabbit (for each seminar). . . . The third time it didn't work. I was appalled by it. The students were there, and the rabbit's ears were still in place. . . . At first I thought that perhaps the technician had given him the wrong stuff. But then when I checked on that and gave the same stuff to the other rabbits and it *did* work I realized that the rabbit had become immune. This is a potentially hot finding. . . . (5)

This is the train of accident and discovery followed by Dr. Thomas. Dr. Kellner, an equally qualified scientist, saw the floppy-eared rabbits when he was working with injections of papain but did not go on to make the discovery, primarily because the train of discovery led him elsewhere. First of all, Dr. Kellner was interested in muscle tissue and cardiac research. When he observed the changes in the rabbits' ears during some research on heart muscle he said he was "a little curious about it at the time" and "followed it up to the extent of making sections of the rabbits' ears." Here his interest in muscle and his preconceived ideas about cartilage (the same as Dr. Thomas'—the inert quality) kept him from seeing further:

Since I was primarily interested in research questions having to do with the muscles of the heart, I was thinking in terms of muscle. That blinded me, so that changes in the cartilage didn't occur to me as a possibility. I was looking for muscles in the sections, and I never dreamed it was cartilage. (6)

One major influence on Dr. Kellner was the people associated with him in the laboratory, research colleagues who shared his interest in cardiac muscle and who reinforced his tendency to move away from the amusing puzzle of the floppy ears to other areas closer to everyone's interest. There were also some serendipitous discoveries attendant upon the floppy ears. Among other things, Dr. Kellner was able to discover a blood coagulation defect in papain-injected rabbits, a defect which resembled hemophilia in certain respects. So it is possible that serendipity here, while it did not lead to the cartilage explanation of the floppy ears, might lead to other eventual findings of critical importance.

Preconceived Ideas: Hypothesis Myopia

. . . It seems appropriate at this point to comment on *hypothesis myopia,* a common disease among researchers holding certain preconceived ideas that might get in the way of discovery. We have seen this illustrated in the case of two eminent scientists, Drs. Thomas and Kellner, both of whom were delayed in a discovery by a preconceived idea about the inert nature of cartilage. But these researchers missed a point only because they did not immediately go on to find some new facts. What I choose to call hypothesis myopia is a disorder of vision, a research nearsightedness in which the sufferer has the facts clearly in view and, because of preconceived notions, either refuses to accept them or attempts to explain them away. Let me give you two well-documented cases of hypothesis myopia, one reported during the time of Galileo and the other a more recent case.

Galileo, in looking through his newly in-vented telescope, discovered that there were spots on the sun. He presented these findings to his colleagues and one group, followers of an Aristotelian mode of thought, rejected his data. Their theory of the composition of celestial matter indicated to them that the sun could not possibly have spots, and so they refused to look through his telescope! Their argument in this was simple: the sun had no spots; if the telescope showed spots on the sun, then the telescope was distorting the perception. Inasmuch as they knew there were no spots, why should they bother to look through an obviously erroneous instrument?

There is some merit in one phase of that argument—the reliability of the instrument. A first step in such research would have to be a check of the reliability of the telescope and, in part, the Aristotelians were correct in questioning its accuracy. But they were myopic in refusing to make such a check (which could easily be done in a testable earth situation) and in refusing to allow any question of their "certain knowledge" of the lack of spots on the sun.

The second is a mild case of hypothesis myopia involving two physicists who performed a carefully devised experiment and obtained negative results.

In 1887 two physicists, Michelson and Morley, performed an experiment to measure the exact speed of light. They built a piece of apparatus to make this exact measurement, consisting of two lengths of pipe placed at right angles to one another. One pipe was pointed in the direction of the earth's movement around the sun, while the other was pointed across the direction of the earth's motion. They then placed a mirror at the end of each pipe and one at the point of intersection. They flashed a beam of light into each pipe at precisely the same moment; this beam struck the mirror at the point of intersection, reflected down the length of the pipes, struck the mirror at each end and reflected back to the central mirror. The prevailing theory at that time was that an invisible ether filled all space that wasn't occupied by solid objects. If this theory were correct, then one ray of light would have been going against the "current" of ether while the other would be going with the current, therefore faster. But this is not what happened. The two beams of light returned to the central mirror at exactly the same moment. The results of the experiment were considered negative, i.e., they failed to confirm the hypothesis that light would be slowed if the earth moved through ether. As Copeland and Bennett (8) observe, the experiment performed produced "a negative result [which] left a major problem of interpretation." Despite the evidence that light paths had wave characteristics, "previous examples of wave motion required a material medium" (as illustrated by sound in air) and it was difficult to find such a material medium for light. The conclusion of the experiment was necessarily that light was not propagated in a medium as sound is propagated in air.

Copeland and Bennett further note that Fitzgerald tried to explain the negative results in terms of contraction of one of the arms of the apparatus; i.e., the length of pipe pointed in the direction of the motion contracted just enough to compensate for the difference in interference. Other interpretations of the re-sults were also couched in terms of the prevailing theory of ether. While physicists accepted the data, they were unable to fit them into the existing hypotheses until Einstein, in 1905, provided a major reconstruction of the theory in his famous paper dealing with the Special Theory of Relativity. With regard to the "negative" results obtained by Michelson and Morley, he explained what had occurred. They had measured the speed of light accurately and the theory of the existence of ether was incorrect. He stated that light always travels at the same speed no matter what the conditions and that, moreover, the motion of the earth with regard to the sun has no effect on the speed of light. We might not expect Michelson and Morley to come up with the Special Theory of Relativity from their data, but we can expect that when results conflict with theory they question the theory. In a very real sense, there is no such thing as a negative result or a failure in an experiment. Every datum obtained provides information to the prepared mind which respects data and does not let hypotheses get in the way of research.

BIBLIOGRAPHY

1. BARBER, BERNARD and FOX, RENEE C., "The case of the floppy-eared rabbits: an instance of serendipity gained and serendipity lost," *American Journal of Sociology*, Vol. *54*, No. 2, September, 1958, pp. 128–136. Quoted by permission of The University of Chicago Press. Copyright 1958 by The University of Chicago.
2. *Ibid.*, p. 130.
3. *Ibid.*, p. 131.
4. *Ibid.*, p. 132.
5. *Ibid.*, p. 134.
6. *Ibid.*, p. 135.
7. CANNON, WALTER B., *The Way of An Investigator.* New York: W. W. Norton, 1945.
8. COPELAND, PAUL L. and BENNETT, WILLIAM E., *Elements of Modern Physics.* New York: Oxford University Press, 1961, p. 57.
9. GARDNER, MARTIN, *Fads and Fallacies in the Name of Science.* New York: Dover Publications, 1957, p. 30.
10. SKINNER, B. F., "A case history in scientific method," in *Cumulative Record,* New York: Macmillan, 1956, p. 81.
11. YOUNG, J. Z., *Doubt and Certainty in Science.* Oxford: Clarendon Press, 1951, pp. 1–2.

EDWIN G. BORING

3. *Psychological Factors in the Scientific Process*

T HE scientific process is partly observation and partly logic. You observe particular relations and then by induction you arrive at such a generalization as a fact, a function, a law, or a theory. Or, having formed a generalization by logic, insight, or hunch, you deduce from it a testable relationship and submit that to observation. There are other formulations that describe the scientific process, but my point here is nothing more than that science is a human activity and that you have, therefore, to take into account the properties of human beings when you are assessing facts and theories. This thought is not new. Errors of observation, both instrumental and human, have long been matters of scientific concern, and the discussion of how to treat them mathematically goes back to Daniel Bernoulli and Lagrange in the eighteenth century and, as almost everyone knows, to Laplace and Gauss in the nineteenth. It was in 1820 that the astronomers discovered, in the observation of the times of stellar transits, the personal equation, and this technical term has now come to be used for any individual bias that affects human judgment or action.

For all their antiquity, personal equations receive within science much less attention than their importance deserves. One exception to this general neglect has been the suggestion of C. W. Morris that we should recognize a field of study to be called *pragmatics,* a branch of the theory of signs that deals "with all the psychological, biological, and sociological phenomena which occur in the functioning of signs" (1). Much less esoteric than this

plan of Morris' is the program of Kubie for the study of certain problems that affect scientific careers, problems that arise from unrecognized neurotic forces and socio-economic forces (2). You do not have to go very far toward neurosis, however, to find the personal equation making trouble in science. You have to go only far enough to find egoism, which would seem to be no distance at all. What is it that creates scientific controversy? Ego-involvement. Ego-bias. Never do you find two scientists in bitter controversy because each believes the other is right and he himself wrong. I used to think that psychologists at least, knowing so much about emotion and ego-involvement, should be incapable of vanity in their professional controversies, but the record shows that I was wrong (3). When his own precious past achievement is involved, even the psychologist has pride.

Ego-involvement is not, however, the only or even the chief source of bias in the scientific process. A subtler and sometimes more sinister prejudicial force is to be found in the intellectual atmosphere that envelops the thinking of the scientist. It is commonplace to say that science depends on communication, that the invention of printing eventually advanced science enormously, that the publication of results is always essential, that the iron curtain and the secret classification of data are bad for science. All such obvious statements are concerned with whether or not the normal overt mechanisms of communications are working or blocked. On the other hand, there are covert influences that make up what has been called the climate of opin-

Reprinted by permission of The Society of the Sigma Xi and the author from *American Scientist,* 1954, vol. 42, pp. 639–45.

ion, and by Goethe the *Zeitgeist*—the conventions of thought and the unquestioned assumptions that are implicit in the culture in general and in science in particular. These forces act as *vires inertiae*. They constrain originality and reinforce tradition, as well as limiting the irresponsibility of the cranks who, excelling in originality, are deficient in critical wisdom. Conant has remarked that "a scientific discovery must fit the times. . . . A well-established concept may prove a barrier to the acceptance of a new one. If a conceptual scheme is highly satisfactory to those who use it, neither a few old facts which cannot be reconciled nor a few new ones will cause the concept to be abandoned. . . . Old concepts may be retained in spite of alleged facts to the contrary." The *horror vacui* that science cannot deny is the scientist's fear of being left without any theory at all. "It takes a new conceptual scheme to cause the abandonment of an old" (4).

It is obvious that there is a complementarity about the effects of both ego-involvement and the *Zeitgeist*. Each is both good and bad for progress. Out of egoism are derived the drive and enthusiasm that lead men to undertake research, to keep at it, to publish the results, to keep promoting the knowledge and use of these results. Also out of egoism is derived the emotional support for the cranks, for Velikovsky's collision of two worlds, for Hubbard's dyanetics, for every scientist who still holds on to a theory after the weight of evidence no longer justifies it (5). "New scientific truth does not triumph by convincing its opponents and making them see the light," said Max Planck, "but rather because its opponents eventually die" (6).

The complementarity of the *Zeitgeist* as intellectual inertia is equally clear. It makes progress slower but also surer, for it favors the caution and judiciousness that take time. That statement can be made of the climate of opinion as it pervades the culture of any period and of any geographically communicating region. It can also be applied to the intellectual atmosphere of any scientific in-group like a scientific school or the disciples of some leader. Their loyalty, enthusiasm, and egoism all promote research and en-courage effort and thoroughness, while also increasing inflexibility and narrowing the perspective. At the moment when new thought is being formed, these complementarities are genuine and inescapable; you cannot eat your cake and have it too. Nevertheless such psychological incompatibilities need not affect posterity who, free from past commitments, egoism, loyalties, and enthusiasm, see more clearly, remaining limited only by the unrecognized biases that always pervade the atmosphere of thinking (7).

The history of science shows how the explicit communication of fact and opinion influences research and promotes progress, and it may touch also upon the manner in which the inertia of accepted belief opposes the promotion of what is novel and original and upon the way in which presumably discarded beliefs keep returning to confuse and hamper later thinking. Seldom, however, does the history of science explain how the *Zeitgeist* works, how implicit views covertly distort thinking, without the thinker himself being aware of this influence or of its effect upon him. Nor may the psychologist conjure up the past and be certain that, even if Newton did discover the calculus independently of Leibnitz, he was not influenced by the lectures of his old teacher, Isaac Barrow at Trinity College, Cambridge; or that Johannes Müller conceived the idea of five specific nerve energies in ignorance of the fact that John Locke and Thomas Young and Charles Bell had each, although in very different ways, already made it clear that the properties of the sensory nerves are interposed between the mind and the objects that it perceives. What the psychologist does understand is how such influences can be effective without being "conscious"—in one of the two senses of that term. In a different sense, you are indeed aware of an idea if it influences you; its influence upon your thought is the sign of your awareness. But still you may not be at all aware of your awareness. You may be like an animal, perceiving an object without perceiving that he is perceiving. The greater part of consciousness in man, and presumably almost all of the consciousness in animals, must be of this unselfconscious kind.

Nor did it require Freud to make us believe in this kind of unconscious sensitivity, for the new conception was a gradual growth. Freud had scarcely had his new thought in Vienna before Külpe had a comparable inspiration in Würzburg, and I doubt if Külpe had heard of Freud in 1905. If he had, he would not have been impressed (8).

In fact, the argument for unconscious and semi-conscious effects of generally accepted views—of the *Zeitgeist*—upon thought arises from the many anticipations and synchronities noted in connection with scientific discoveries which have been recorded as original achievements. To discover anticipations of important theories—sometimes vague anticipations or early statements made on insufficient evidence—is a commonplace of the history of science. What is noteworthy is the way that such anticipations multiply as simultaneity is approached and how many discoveries, inventions, and new ideas occur so close together in time as practically to exclude direct cross-communication, thus making it appear that the coincidence is the consequence of some pre-established harmony that is maturing in the intellectual social climate, a *Zeitgeist* indeed.

In 1921, explicating this view, Ogburn and Thomas printed a list of one hundred forty-eight synchronous or nearly synchronous, seemingly independent discoveries and inventions (9). While this list contains some errors (for Helmholtz definitely based his color theory on Thomas Young's suggestion, and, besides, those two bits of originality were fifty-one years apart), the total effect of it is convincing. On the other hand, the investigator may not know the origin of his brilliant insight. That fact accords with a common maxim of psychology which, however, is not very often mentioned in the history of science. When men are sure of their own motives, as often as not they are apt to be clinging to rationalizations and are ignorant of the true reasons.

Since Freudian platitudes are apt to convince only those who have already accepted them, let me set down here what I can say about a recent case of two poets who were simultaneously inspired to write practically the same poem. Or were they? It is my conviction that on publication neither author believed he had borrowed from the other, but that one of them did actually borrow, having at one time known all about the other poem and having since forgotten it—perhaps because forgetting was convenient or perhaps not. The poets are Miss Victoria Sackville-West (VSW) and Mr. Clifford Dyment (CD), both of whom have generously given me permission to reprint their so nearly synchronous inspirations, in the interest of promoting further general knowledge of what sometimes makes inspiration happen. I shall use their initials because we are interested in a principle, not in persons, and note merely that this coincidence is already a matter of public record (10).

These two persons are poets of considerable importance, both with a distinguished list of publications to their credit. VSW, twenty-two years older than CD, belongs to a family distinguished for public service throughout three centuries of British history, and, being older, may be said at the moment to have achieved somewhat greater recognition as a writer. In 1949 CD published in a volume of his collected poems a poem called "Saint Augustine at 32." At almost the same time VSW published in *The Poetry Review* a poem which she called "The Novice to Her Lover." Here they are:

Saint Augustine at 32	*The Novice to Her Lover*
Girl, why do you follow me	Why must you follow me
When I come to the threshold of the holy place?	When I come to the threshold of this holy place?
My resolution falters: it seems a death to enter	My resolution falters and it seems death to enter
When, turning back, I look into your face.	When, turning back, I look upon your face.
I saw you when I lay alone	I could renounce you when I lay alone;
And ran from you as from a searching light	I ran from you as from a hungry light

Into the gentle, acquiescent
Obscurity of the night.

I crave communion that is not words
And life fulfilled in my cell alone—
And you, you come with your lips and your gold
  hair
And at your feet is a leaf that the wind has
  blown.

Into the gentle, the infinite, the healing
Clemency of the night.

I crave an eloquence that is not words,
I seek fulfillment in the kiss of stone—
But you, you come with your mouth and your
  dark hair
And at your feet a leaf that the wind has blown.

What happened? The two poems are almost identical, although each poet has given his own sex to the central figure in the poem. Does the *Zeitgeist* deal in ready-made poetry, or was there some unconscious communication that explains away this bit of pre-established harmony? What is true of poetry in this instance can also be true of scientific theory.

The editor of the magazine that first published the two poems in juxtaposition, having written to CD and VSW, printed their replies (10). CD said he had published his poem in a magazine in January 1943, then included it in a volume of his collected poems in 1944, and then again published it later in a larger collection of his poems that appeared in 1949. He was a gentleman; he made no suggestion as to the nature of VSW's inspiration. VSW said, in late 1949, that she had written the poem in 1942 or early in 1943, when she was writing about Ste. Thérèse of Lisieux, that she did not, however, publish it then, but copied it into a letter to a Catholic friend who was interested in Ste. Thérèse. The friend now says that she never copied the poem out of the letter nor showed it to anyone. VSW goes on to say that in 1949 she was asked by *The Poetry Review* for some unpublished poem to print in a special issue. She then hunted in her MSS book and found this one which she sent in to the magazine where it was published in the summer of 1949. When in November she read CD's poem in his 1949 volume, she recognized it at once as practically her own; so she wrote to CD about the matter, and he replied, reminding her that after he had published this poem in his 1944 volume, she had written him of her special admiration for it. Thus VSW, having by 1949 identified this particular poem with herself, forgot what had actually happened in 1944, and might in the same way have remembered what did not happen in 1942 or 1943.

It is not for us to say what really happened, but let us spin a plausible account which, if true, would surprise no psychologist. CD, we may suppose, did just exactly what he said he did: he published the poem early in 1943, and again in 1944 and 1949. In 1942 and early in 1943 VSW was writing about Ste. Thérèse and she published a book about her in 1943. Sometime in 1943 or 1944 she saw CD's poem and liked it. It is certain she saw it in the 1944 book, if not earlier, for at that time she wrote CD of her admiration for it. Presumably she had read CD's poem when she was still under the spell of enthusiasm for Ste. Thérèse, and the poem caught her fancy. She copied the poem, reversing the sexes to make it apply to Ste. Thérèse, made other small changes and improvements to suit both her taste and the reversal of the sexes, admired the result, and, wanting to preserve it, tucked the poem away in her MSS book. It does not matter whether she wrote to CD before or after she wrote out her own version. VSW would not have mentioned her parody, that was not yet near to becoming a plagiarism, to CD at that time. Then she forgot about what she had done, and, when she was asked five years later in 1949 to find some of her unpublished verse, she turned up this one among the odds and ends of her MSS. Her feeling about Ste. Thérèse and her liking for the poem revived, but there was no recall of the circumstances under which she had "written" the poem. Only a few months later VSW found CD's version in his 1949 book. She must have recognized the similarity at once but continued to suppress her memory of 1944 until CD reminded her of the letter she had written to him. It was a convenient suppression, for it saved VSW from embarrassment, and as such the phenomenon was not one to surprise a psychologist. That is the way this thing we call the mind works.

Others, commenting on this interesting case, have offered psychological explanations similar to mine (11), and one writer has noted that Hilaire Belloc had written a quatrain almost identical in thought and development with a quatrain of Voltaire's, although different in meter, rhyme-scheme, and language (English *vs.* French). When Belloc had this similarity pointed out to him, he replied that he had never heard this epigram of Voltaire's, but that he was not surprised; nor was he ever disturbed when accused of appropriation of "other people's ideas or even lines of verse," for that merely put him in company with Shakespeare, Marlowe, Catullus, and Homer (12).

Now let no reader misunderstand my meaning. I have no thought that most or even many of the synchronous discoveries and inventions that occur are unconscious plagiarisms, except as we all of us plagiarize the *Zeitgeist* again and again. When I was a ten-year-old I had a philosophy of life, picked up partly from my mother and partly from other vague sources, a philosophy that included items of thought from Descartes, Jeremy Bentham, and Herbert Spencer. I doubt if I had ever heard of any of these philosophers; certainly I had read about none of them at the age of ten. My point is that, if it is possible unconsciously to steal a specific poem, it is also possible unconsciously to appropriate thought from the common domain and from particular thinkers who cultivate some portion of that domain. The culture, the atmosphere of opinion, the *Zeitgeist* are the reservoirs from which the originator gets his materials and sometimes his elaborately prefabricated parts. He can perceive and select what he wants without perceiving his perceiving—like a bird building a nest.

These then are some of the ways in which personal equations enter into the content of science. Enthusiasm, loyalty, egoism—it is always some personal need that drives you to research and to publication, and perhaps beyond, so that you are impelled to advertise your results or to enter into controversy about them. The urge gets the work done, but it may also blind you to the defects and shortcomings of the work itself. Ultimately, instead of pushing progress on, the same need may lead to pushing it backwards, and the truth of objectivity may be left for others to perceive, or even reserved for posterity. You get your original ideas in part from your own insight, your skill, or good fortune in seeing novel relationships where no relations had been perceived before. You are helped to such insight when the new thought fits in with the current trend of thinking, and conversely you may be blocked from originality if the trend of the times is against the correct new thought that never became quite explicit enough to stick in your conscious mind.

Much of your dependence upon the thought of others is explicit, clear and overt, coming about by way of normal verbal communication in speech and print. A great deal of conventional thinking, on the other hand, is implicit, obscure and covert, being carried in the unexpressed assumptions and value-judgments of current common sense. You know all these common values and beliefs, but you do not assess them because you are apt not to be occupied with doing any knowing *about* your knowing. The habitual modes of thought that belong to a particular time and culture may help you to help these modes to advance further in the direction in which they already tend, but such modes of thought may also prevent you from having an insight that is inconsistent with the cultural background. Again and again scientific progress halts because the correct next step contravenes some firmly rooted theory or belief. The *Zeitgeist* may help or it may hinder, but always it is with us, and experiment and theory are inevitably formed under its influence.

REFERENCES

1. MORRIS, C. W. Foundations of the theory of signs. *Internat. Encycl. Unified Sci., 1,* no. 2, 29–42, 1938.

2. KUBIE, L. S. Some unsolved problems of the scientific career. *Amer. Sci., 41,* no. 4, 596–613, 1953; *ibid., 42,* 1, 104–112, 1954.

3. BORING, E. G. The psychology of controversy. *Psychol. Rev., 36,* 97–121, 1929.

4. CONANT, J. B. On Understanding Science. Yale University Press, New Haven, pp. 88–90 and 98–109, esp. 88, 103, 1947.

5. COHEN, I. B. Orthodoxy and scientific progress. *Prac. Amer. Philos. Soc., 96,* 505–512, 1952. BORING, E. G. The validation of scientific belief. *Ibid.,* 535–539.

6. PLANCK, MAX. Scientific Autobiography and Other Papers. Philos. Lib., New York, Eng. trans. 1949, 33*f.*

7. BORING, E. G. The dual role of the *Zeitgeist* in scientific creativity. *Scientific Monthly, 80,* 1955.

8. BORING, E. G. Great men and scientific progress. *Proc. Amer. Philos. Soc., 94,* 339–351, 1950.

9. OGBURN, W. F., and THOMAS, DOROTHY. Are inventions inevitable? A note on social evolution. *Polit. Sci. Quart., 37,* 83–93, 1922.

10. *Editor.* A question of inspiration. *New Statesman and Nation, 39,* 62, 1950.

11. *Various.* A question of inspiration. (Four letters commenting on this article and making suggestions not unlike the one in the text.) *New Statesman and Nation, 39,* 100, 1950.

12. HAMILTON, G. R. A question of inspiration. (A letter quoting Hilaire Belloc.) *New Statesman and Nation, 39,* 133, 1950.

JOSEPH R. ROYCE

4. *Psychology in Mid-twentieth Century*

IN THE fiscal year 1953–1954 over ten million dollars were spent for research in the field of psychology. While this is a small amount when compared with research expenditures in the physical sciences, it suggests that large numbers of psychologists are busily engaged in the business of finding out new things about the nature of human behavior. It is doubtful if any other science in history has had so much research money available to it at such a youthful age.

In 1945 the American Psychological Association had around 3000 members; in 1955 the membership of the APA was 13,475. The structure of the APA has changed from a single society to an assemblage of societies which takes the form of seventeen divisions reflecting the specialized interests of different groups of psychologists. The national meetings of our society used to be held annually at various universities throughout the United States. The attendance at these meetings is now so large that very few universities can adequately house the delegates; the APA convention is being held more and more often in large hotels in big cities. The digest of the psychological literature of the world, Psychological Abstracts, searches through close to 500 journals which contain contributions relevant to the advancement of psychological knowledge. The breadth of coverage which these journals provide is staggering. Psychologists have stepped outside their ivory towers into the market place, the hospital, the government offices, and the military base. There are now more psychologists employed in non-academic positions than in all academic posts combined. There is hardly a nook or cranny of life where their behavioral investigations

have not been conducted. Exactly what kinds of things are these psychologists doing? What kinds of questions are behavior scientists and practitioners trying to answer? To what extent is psychology a science? Our purpose is to shed some light on these and other questions concerning contemporary psychology.

Major Fields and Applications of Contemporary Psychology

IF we think of philosophy as the major tributary in the historical stream of knowledge, with modern specialization branching off from this central source, we find that psychology is the most recent scientific offshoot. From its simple beginnings in sensory psychophysiology in the 19th century to the present day, the field of psychology has proliferated and expanded in a manner typical of the older, more mature sciences. In addition to expanding the fundamental approaches (i.e., "pure" science) to scientific knowledge, psychology has also moved into many applied areas. This growth has been so extensive that it is difficult to encompass it. At least part of the reason for the diversity of modern psychology is due to the multiplicity of its origins. Medical men, biologists, neurologists, and physiologists, for example, have all had a hand in the early history of psychology. Psychiatry, a medical specialty, stressed the importance of studying the abnormal. And students of the brain could not help but wonder if their observations of what went on inside the skull had anything to do with their own behavior. Anthropologists stressed culture as the determining social matrix which shapes the personalities of men. And certain think-

Reprinted by permission of The Society of the Sigma Xi and the author from *American Scientist*, 1957, vol. 45, pp. 57–73.

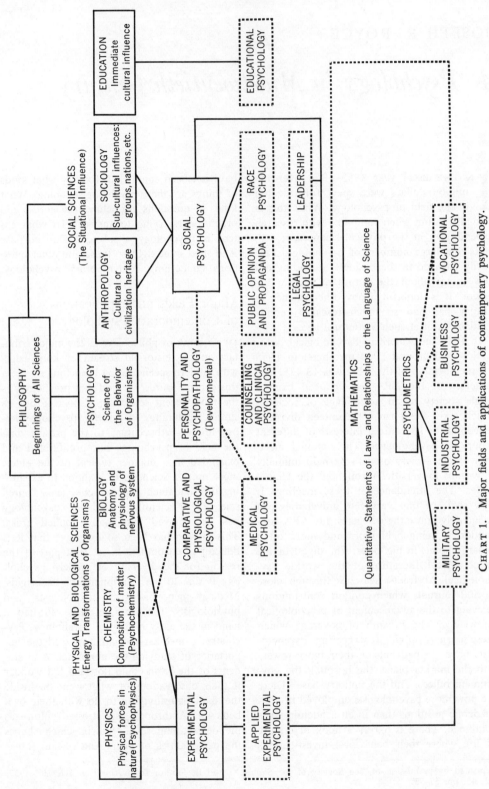

CHART 1. Major fields and applications of contemporary psychology.

ers with a mathematical orientation stressed the importance of measurement and of quantitative approaches in the study of behavior. Each of these points of view has found a fruitful outlet in psychology.

Another reason for the diversity of contemporary psychology is the demand which society has placed on the field for useful knowledge. The state mental institutions cry out for more fundamental knowledge concerning how their patients got that way. The psychobiology of feeble-mindedness remains a big unknown so that the state, again, must bear the burden of housing and caring for large numbers of incompetents. Industry is becoming increasingly concerned with how to select and assign the best man for the right job, and of course, all businessmen are concerned with psychological techniques which might tell them more about what people will buy. The military and government agencies are very much concerned with problems of morale, efficiency, leadership, psychological warfare, and maximum productivity. These various and sundry intellectual and practical forces have pushed and pulled psychology in a truly fantastic variety of directions. It leads one to the conclusion that wherever there are people, whatever they are doing, or feeling, or thinking, there is at least one psychologist lurking around making a study of these doings, feelings, or thoughts. How can we view this many-headed monster we call psychology? I propose that we view it piecemeal at first, and reserve our over-all view for later. We can facilitate this approach by referring to CHART 1.

The upper section of this chart shows the relationships between modern psychology and its most closely related fields. Thus, along an imaginary horizontal axis we note that the most closely related natural science is biology, anatomy and physiology in particular. Less closely related are the fields of physics and chemistry. Similarly, we note the importance of the fields of anthropology, sociology, and education. Along an imaginary vertical axis we note that psychology, like all other scientific fields, is continuously striving for greater and greater quantification. Thus, we have inserted a wide band denoting mathematics, indicating that mathematics underlies all fields of knowledge which strive to be scientific, whether pure or applied.

The major "pure" fields of psychology have been indicated in small, solid line rectangles. Most of these fields grew out of alliances with the natural and social sciences. The broken line rectangles represent the major fields of application which grew out of the subdivisions of psychology. The connecting solid lines show the major influences which were important in the development of a given field. The connecting broken lines denote secondary influences. The text which follows will be organized in terms of this chart. The applications which are primarily associated with a particular basic field will be discussed in the second portion of each section. The reader should coordinate the reading of the following sections with frequent glances at the relevant portion of CHART 1.

Experimental Psychology

THE contemporary field of psychology known as "experimental" is a misnomer. When the grandparents of this field started it somewhere around 1840–1870 it was known as psychophysics; they were concerned with relating psychological or subjective experiences to physical stimuli. The major goal in these early years of Weber, Fechner, and Wundt was to show that psychological problems could be attacked scientifically. After all, this had not been demonstrated before, and since the last word in being scientific was to be able to set up an experiment, it was important to these early men that they make their point, and make it repeatedly. Over the years, psychologists who identified themselves with this aspect of psychology literally became missionaries of science in spreading the gospel of experiment to a wide variety of behavioral phenomena. At first psychological experiments were conducted on the relatively simple phenomena of sensations and reaction time. Later Pavlov, Watson, and Ebbinghaus carried the banner to conditioning and learning. The Gestalt psychologists conducted brilliant qualitative experiments on perceptual phenomena in the 2nd and 3rd decades of the twentieth century, and today we find very few areas of psychology in which true experiments have not been carried out. Organisms have been rendered experimentally neurotic, hallucinations have been experimentally induced in monkeys and men, the effect of various group pressures on individual opinions and attitudes has been subjected to ingenious experimentation, and inroads have been made in setting up experiments on the processes of concept formation and thinking. In other words, all of psychology is experimental. There are, of course, many specific problems which are still refractory to experimentation. For example, although unconscious conditioning has been repeatedly demonstrated in the laboratory, nobody has devised an experimental approach to the study of dreams. And most of what Freud, Adler, Jung, and the other psychoanalysts write about is not based on experimental findings. Despite the misnomer, however, the field of experimental psychology is shedding its methodological connotations and has come to mean the psychology of conditioning and learning, the psychology of sensation and perception, and the psychology of motor phenomena. The experimental literature in each of these areas is vast. It represents little risk to prophesy that the term experimental psychology as a description of a basic field will be dropped from common usage by the end of the 20th century, and that each of the major segments of this broad area will become a specific area in its own right.

The field of applied experimental psychology is a post-World War II phenomenon. The need for applying what was known about a person's senses and perceptual-motor capacities grew primarily out of the highly technical demands of fighting a modern war. Much of what man does in carrying out an Atomic Age war is to manipulate mechanical and electronic gadgets of various kinds. This puts a very high premium on how well man's receptors and effectors can perform. It was found repeatedly that man could not keep up with the complexity of most of the World War II machines. Human factors all too frequently were found to be the weak link in the military chain of events. The cockpit of a modern bomber, for example, was constructed without regard to the limitations of the human operator. Panels of dials were set up with the zero points at different positions on the dial face. Important levers were pushed or pulled in various directions; sometimes they had to be manipulated without the pilot being able actually to see the lever before moving it. The military has come to realize the tremendous importance of understanding the operation of the man as well as the machine. And so the field of engineering psychology or applied experimental psychology has been created primarily out of the "pure" psychology of sensation and the "pure" psychology of perceptual-motor phenomena. Thus, the aviation psychologists at the Aero-Medical Laboratories in Dayton, Ohio, have been concerned about the various shapes and sizes of levers to be identified by touch sensitivity in the redesigning of the lever system of the modern bomber. The psychophysicists of the Navy, working with the engineers at the Navy Electronics Laboratory in San Diego, have worked on various visual problems which are involved in rapidly scanning a radarscope. And RAND Corporation, the private research and development arm of the Air Force, finds itself working on mammoth projects involving complicated "systems" of men, communications, and machines. As with psychological testing during and after World War I, the military again seems to be pointing the way for industry and government. With automatic factories and offices (i.e., automation) practically around the corner, the time is now for private enterprise to begin getting its feet wet in the business of coupling man's receptor and motor equipment to the already well-advanced electronic equipment.

Comparative and Physiological Psychology

THE field of comparative and physiological psychology has two major streams feeding into it. The comparative or animal psychology stream was started by the evolutionary theory of Darwin. It is similar to its sister areas, comparative anatomy and comparative physiology. A true comparative psychology is concerned with descriptions of the psychological processes of all animal forms from amoeba to man. Although a tremendous mass of factual data has been gathered and summarized by phyla (1), it is unfortunately true that recent developments in this area suggest that it would be more accurate to describe comparative psychology as rodent psychology. This trend is primarily due to the effects of neo-behaviorists to establish elementary laws of conditioning and learning in a relatively simple animal under relatively simple experimental conditions. The thinking is that the rat is a handy and relevant animal to use in carrying out such a program; that a behavior system which will predict rat behavior will eventually also help us understand human behavior. If we add the college sophomore as another favorite subject, we see what is behind the often heard statement that psychology is the science of the behavior of the rat and the college student.

Physiological psychology grew out of the early concern for the nervous system. The physiologically oriented psychologist is concerned with correlating what goes on under the skin with what goes on outside the skin. He believes there are internal mechanisms which are the major determinants of responses. In such a view the stimulus simply triggers a series of events which eventuate in a given, specifiable response. The physiological psychologist is still very much concerned with stimuli and responses, but he believes the physiological linkage between the two is the key to real understanding. And so he conducts brain damage studies in an attempt to localize intelligent behavior, administers vitamins and drugs in an attempt to make learning more efficient, or introduces electroshock in order to determine its effect on memory.

It becomes immediately apparent that while the physiological psychologist may use human subjects, most of his problems can be more adequately handled with animals. This is one of the major reasons that comparative and physiological psychologists fall rather naturally into a joint area of knowledge. It is important to note that the comparative-physiological psychologist does not pick his subjects at random or simply for the sake of convenience. A good knowledge of the special anatomical and physiological characteristics of a wide variety of animal species is extremely important in this area. Only this kind of information will lead the investigator to the most appropriate animal form for a given problem. For example, suppose we are interested in trying to determine the extent to which either a brain or a nervous system is required in order to elicit a conditioned response. Since it has only a very primitive brain, the earthworm would be an appropriate animal to include in testing for the first part of the question. And since the amoeba is essentially a glob of protoplasm, it would be relevant to the second part of the question. An answer to this question has, in fact, been put to the test on many animal forms. The answer seems to be that neither a brain nor a nervous system is necessary for conditioning. All that is necessary is some medium of conductivity. Single-celled animals have been conditioned after hundreds of training trials, and worms have been trained to make the proper choice in a simple T maze after 150 trials or even less. Since few psychologists or zoologists will be able to learn enough about the one million or so animal species, a certain degree of specialization is inevitable. Because of their obviously closer relevance to man, psychologists have stressed the importance of vertebrates, mammals in particular. When he was a young man Robert M. Yerkes had a dream about a laboratory devoted to the psychobiological study of sub-human primates. After a World War (1918), a decade or two of struggle, some luck, but mostly determination, he was able to establish the now famous Yerkes Laboratories of Primate Psychobiology at Orange Park, Florida. This laboratory, cooperatively administered by Harvard and Yale Universities, has been under the directorship of the great neuropsychologist Karl S. Lashley. The researches on monkeys, chimpanzees, gorillas, and other primates, which emerged from this laboratory are the most authoritative sources of information we have on the behavior of man's closest animal relative. Yerkes' early volumes on this subject are still regarded as the most comprehensive coverage of their social, mental, and emotional behavior.

A similar laboratory, devoted primarily to the study of conditioning and experimental neurosis, has been in existence for several decades at Ithaca, New York. It is called the Cornell Behavior Farm. It is administered by Cornell University and has been under the guidance of H. S. Liddell from the time of its founding. Scientific work of great importance to psychosomatic medicine and experimental psychopathology has been conducted at this laboratory.

The only experimental animal psychology laboratory in the world which exists independently of a university, hospital, or other type of "administrative" institution, is the recently established Hamilton Station, 8 miles outside of Bar Harbor, Maine. This converted farm, established as part of the Roscoe B. Jackson Memorial Laboratory (genetics and cancer) in 1945, was financed by the Rockefeller Foundation for the purpose of conducting long range research on the relationship between genetics and behavior. The major portion of the research program involves the use of various breeds of dogs. Since there are over one hundred different breeds, and since the dog is a complex enough animal to exhibit social, emotional, and intelligent behavior, the dog is a perfect animal form to use in studying the relationship between heredity and behavior. Most other comparative-physiological laboratories exist as a relatively small part of the larger American universities. There are very few animal psychology laboratories in other countries. In continental Europe most of the animal research is conducted by zoologists. In England, despite the influence of Darwin and other early British biologists, there has been surprisingly little interest in this area. While some interest in physiological psychology is world wide, the animal approach to physiological and other behavioral problems seems to be a typically American enterprise.

The applications of comparative and physiological psychology are difficult to place under a single heading. For example, the animal research on experimental neurosis is relevant to the field of clinical psychology

and the research on heredity and behavior is of importance to the field of education. However, many of the research findings in this area are not immediately of practical value. Of the various basic fields of psychology, this one is about as "pure" as they come. The findings which do have "immediate" practical implications are primarily in the area of medical psychology. The first experimental prefrontal lobotomies, for example, were conducted on monkeys by the psychologist Carlyle Jacobsen at the State University of Iowa in the nineteen-thirties. Psychosomatic medicine will look increasingly to comparative-physiological psychology, as well as to students of personality and social psychology, for greater understanding of psychogenic illnesses.

The various physiological approaches to problems of mental deficiency and mental illness show promising signs for the future. For example, there is some evidence that both carbon dioxide therapy and electroshock treatment improve certain types of mental disease. Perhaps the most dramatic psychiatric improvements, however, have been due to the effects of two drugs, chlorpromazine and reserpine. Their calming effect seems to be particularly effective in counteracting various manic psychotic states. There is also conflicting evidence concerning the ameliorative value of vitamins and glutamic acid when given to feebleminded children. At mid-twentieth century the promising correlation between the biological and the psychological has just begun.

Psychometrics

THE field of psychometrics grew directly out of practical demands placed on the authorities of the French school system. These educators were concerned with the problem of teaching very bright, average, and very dull children in the same classroom. They approached the famous psychologist Alfred Binet with this problem in 1900. This started a series of events which resulted in the development of one of the most widely used testing instruments in the history of psychology. Terman's 1937 revision of the Stanford-

Binet test grew directly out of the many earlier revisions of Binet's test of 1905. The inadequacies of testing for adult intelligence with the school-child oriented Binet test were soon felt by psychologists working in clinics and hospitals. And so the Wechsler Adult Intelligence Scale was developed and found to be much more suitable. It is interesting to note that Wechsler's Child Scale has been making strong inroads in replacing the Binet test in many school systems and child guidance clinics. This development is at least partially due to the relative ease of administering the Wechsler test in contrast to the cumbersome age-scale Binet test.

Following the tune of practicality, the test makers of World War I, faced with the problem of having to test thousands of recruits in one day, came up with the simple idea of developing standardized tests which could be administered in large groups. This simple maneuver freed the test makers from the limitations of time and expense which is so typical of individually administered tests. It also allowed them to take off in many directions, so that today we have hundreds of tests of intelligence, aptitudes, achievement, interest, and personality. With the duplication of group tests of intelligence, and every psychologist yelling "eureka!" every other year and proclaiming that he had developed the intelligence test to end all tests, the general public and fellow psychologists began to look with suspicion and with interest at what was going on. The suspicion expressed itself in the form of selecting and developing tests a little more carefully, especially with regard to such matters as reliability and validity. The interest expressed itself in the form of intercorrelating various combinations and batteries of tests.

After several decades of being led by the nose by practicality the test experts finally settled down to the more important and fundamental problems of measurement. If we look more carefully at the term psychometrics—almost literally psycho measurement—we cannot help but realize that the problems connected with measuring must be solved first before a full grown technology can be developed. For years Guilford's book,

Psychometric Methods, was the only reference work which contained a compilation of guiding principles for the psychometrician. Gradually a more mature mental test theory has begun to come on the scene (2). Psychologists are analytically describing several different types of test reliability and validity, they are minutely examining each item of a test and revising the item composition in terms of objective criteria, and they are asking searching questions about what it means to measure. Perhaps the most important of these recent theoretical developments has been the development of factor analysis.

The factorial approach can best be explained by an analogy. Many centuries ago early scientists described physical phenomena in terms of relatively gross units such as water and fire. Today the chemist does not speak of water, but rather of so much hydrogen and so much oxygen. In other words he has broken down a relatively complex phenomenon, water, into its component parts. Exactly the same step is taken in the factorial study of behavior. Let us take intelligence as an example. For the first few decades of modern psychology's existence the professional psychologist went along with the thinking of the man on the street concerning the nature of intelligence—namely, that if a person is smart, he is smart at everything. If he is stupid, he is stupid at everything. This general intelligence concept is essentially what is behind the Binet, the Wechsler, and most of the early group varieties of intelligence test. We come out with a single index of intelligence, the I.Q., which is supposed to tell us everything about a man's intelligence. Factor analysis has shown us that intelligence is not the unitary phenomenon most of us believed it to be, but rather, it is a complex, like water, which can be broken down into component parts. Some of the component parts of intelligence are Memory, Space, Reasoning, Perception, Number, Verbal Comprehension, and Verbal Fluency. Individuals differ in their particular profiles. Person A may be high in the Number, Space, and Reasoning components and relatively low in all the others, whereas person B may be just the reverse. In this connection it should be noted that these two individuals could even have exactly the same I.Q., but the distribution of their high and low points would differ. This point is brought out graphically by the two profiles depicted in CHART 2.

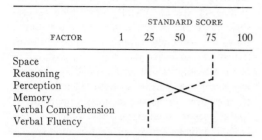

FACTOR	STANDARD SCORE				
	1	25	50	75	100
Space					
Reasoning					
Perception					
Memory					
Verbal Comprehension					
Verbal Fluency					

CHART 2. Showing two persons, A (solid line) and B (dotted line) with the same I.Q. but with opposite mental ability profiles.

If we average each of these two profiles, we get exactly the same value, namely 50. This would be equivalent to an I.Q. of 100. If the I.Q. was the only information available we would conclude that these two individuals are intellectually identical. It is obvious, however, that they are identical only in their performance on the perception factor. Otherwise, person A is essentially quantitative in his intellectual strength whereas person B is essentially verbal. The theoretical and practical implications of this relatively new analytical approach are truly revolutionary. Factor analysis provides the psychometrician with an analytical model which goes beyond intelligence to include the entire gamut of testing (and perhaps of behavior). In addition it provides a mathematical method, based on matrix algebra, which is elegantly precise and beautifully appropriate to the multiple variable field of psychology (3). And finally, it provides the educational and vocational guidance expert with the kind of useful information he would not want to do without. A vocational counselor can certainly offer more assistance to a counselee with the profile kind of information available in CHART 2 than he can with the information that the counselee has an I.Q. of 100.

The implications of psychological testing have not escaped the eyes of business and industry. Many of the larger companies of the United States use tests in one way or an-

other. The impetus to testing from World War II has been so great that a rash of industrial consulting firms broke out in New York, Chicago, and Los Angeles during the post-war years. While these industrial psychologists also consult on matters other than testing, the original stimulus for consulting work came from the demand for tests. The applications of personnel psychology have been considerable in schools and government, in addition to industry and the military. The federal and local civil service organizations frequently use commercially available tests in addition to their own home grown variety. The U.S. Civil Service Commission has a large staff of trained personnel psychologists in the various headquarters centers in Washington. Most universities make use of admission tests, diagnostic placement tests, and standardized achievement batteries in addition to the testing which goes on at a centralized examining board or a college counseling service. And many high school and elementary school systems are availing themselves of school psychometrists and school psychologists to integrate and administer their testing and vocational guidance programs. There can be little doubt of the tremendous need for and use of psychological tests.

Personality and Psychopathology

OUR view of the area of personality-psychopathology is broadly conceived. We shall mean it to include the study of the normal and abnormal personality from birth until death (i.e., developmental psychology). The study of the normal personality as an independent and legitimate area of investigation did not come about until the third decade of the twentieth century. Concern about the abnormal, on the other hand, was forced upon the intelligent consciousness of society centuries ago. It was not until the 19th century, however, that the medical treatment of the mentally ill began to make inroads on the earlier superstitious views of the "insane." The early organic approach to the alleviation of these behavior deviations soon turned out to be inadequate for most cases; this fact paved the way for the understanding of deviant behavior in terms of psychological processes. There was good reason for the neurologically trained psychiatrist Sigmund Freud to switch horses in midstream and turn to a functional rather than an organic orientation in the treatment of neuroses. His psychoanalytic procedures were more relevant to the problems at hand. While psychoanalysis is undeniably overrated as the panacea for the psychological ills of the world, particularly by the cocktail party set, there can be little doubt of the validity and the theoretically integrating value of much of Freud's thought. Freudian adjustment mechanism concepts such as rationalization, projection, sublimation, and repression represent the key to modern thinking about the integration of personality. The stress which Freud and other psychoanalysts put on sex, or inferiority, or compensatory drives, or mystical needs, are undoubtedly oversimplified versions of what motivates people. The important point is that Freud's thinking has moved beyond the dilettante set and is now being appraised by more critical eyes. Theoretical and experimental academicians are attempting to put many of the psychoanalytic concepts to experimental test. The experimental psychiatrist Masserman, for example, has successfully applied some of the therapeutic principles of psychoanalysis to organisms (cats) that had previously been rendered experimentally neurotic. Similarly, the psychologist J. M. Hunt has offered some experimental evidence for the important effect of early experiences on later behavior patterns. It must be candidly admitted at this point, however, that nobody knows how much of psychoanalysis will be able to withstand the test of rigorous observational data. In the meantime the psychoanalytic system and method provides the theoretical and practicing behavior specialist with a reasonable first approximation to an understanding of the motivations and desires of men.

In many ways the study of abnormal behavior has not been very fruitful. Our mental institutions continue to grow in number as well as number of inmates. It is estimated, for example, that in the U.S. there are about 680 mental hospitals and about 9,000,000 people suffering from mental illness and other personality disturbances. This represents about 6% of the present population, or about one in every sixteen people. On any one day in the year, there are about 650,000 patients in mental hospitals; the patients in mental hospitals make up about half of all the patients in all the hospitals in the United States. Furthermore, the intelligence of man does not have too much to say about just what should be done to alleviate the situation. While many neurotic and psychotic individuals have been "cured," little or no insight has been brought to the foreground to "explain" why. Success in therapy, to the extent that it exists at all, is essentially empirical. This is, of course, a proper expedient, but it is not very adequate science. Little, if anything, can be done for most individuals in chronic psychotic states. While physiological and verbal therapies have been helpful, even dramatically so at times, none of these procedures is sufficiently convincing. If they were, the inmates of mental institutions would be leaving in larger numbers. The psychoses have been particularly refractory to scientific investigation, and furthermore, the research money available for the solution of a task as monumental as this has been grossly inadequate.

While the availability of research funds has only improved slightly, with the recent establishment of the National Institute of Mental Health and other government support, the manpower future of clinical psychology looks more hopeful. The Veterans Administration, faced with the problem of having to care for many thousands of mentally disturbed patients, has been subsidizing a rather unusually complete clinical training program in order to meet the continuing shortage of properly educated personnel. Veterans Administration training stipends and supervised hospital internships are available to outstanding students of clinical psychology at many of the leading universities of the United States. The growth of clinical psychology due to this kind of support has been nothing short of spectacular.

It has been estimated that there are around 20,000 words in the English language which have been used to describe personality. This superficial fact, in itself, gives us some idea of the complexity and difficulty of studying the normal personality. Because of this complexity some psychologists have claimed that the area of personality study is simply too broad, that it is essentially identical with the entire field of psychology. After all, intelligence, aptitudes, reaction time, how one perceives, one's emotional make-up, are all aspects of one's unique personality. But these processes are also portions of other, diverse fields of psychology such as experimental and psychometrics. Perhaps the most reasonable basis for independent status lies in the global or gestalt view which the majority of personality specialists take in attempting to unravel the mysteries of their domain. Another basis for independence can be built around the importance placed on personality growth and differentiation. Child studies, such as those of Arnold Gesell, serve as a guide for modern young parents concerned about the normal psychological growth of their children. While adult and old age patterns of development have been studied relatively rarely, the recent interest which psychologists have shown in geriatrics may eventually complete the story which Gesell so ably started.

While the applications of the personality-psychopathology field are primarily clinical in nature, there are other outlets. For example, great interest in the closely allied field of counseling has been shown by both schools and industry. University counseling centers are rapidly becoming an expected service in the more progressive colleges and universities. These centers concern themselves with personal adjustment problems in addition to purely educational or vocational guidance problems. Setting up a service for the handling of "personality" problems has also received the careful consideration of top industrial management officers. Perhaps the most famous example of this was the introduction of a counseling center in the Hawthorne plant of Western Electric Co. about two decades ago. While an enlightened business management policy of this type is still relatively rare, inroads have been made, and there are definite signs that industrial counseling programs are on the increase. Clinical psychology itself has, of course, taken off in many directions.

While it is practiced most extensively in state mental hospitals and V.A. hospitals, many out-patient mental hygiene clinics and child guidance centers have been developed in recent years. Furthermore, the concern of the public schools for the mental as well as the physical health of the child has increased. This has resulted in the certification of school (clinical) psychologists in many states.

Social Psychology

THE basic unit of psychological study is the individual organism. The basic unit of sociological study is the group. Social psychology is a true interdisciplinary field which is concerned with the individual as a part of the group. The earliest investigations in this area were largely concerned with the behavior of relatively large groups. The psychology of masses, the why and wherefore of crowd behavior, and observations on conformity behavior were important empirical studies. It was not until two decades ago, however, that true laboratory experiments were carried out in this field. This was first demonstrated convincingly by Sherif, who used the traditional autokinetic phenomenon as a point of departure for making controlled observations on the effect of social pressure and prestige on personal judgments. The autokinetic effect involves observing a stationary pinpoint of light in a completely darkened room. Most people report some movement of the light source in spite of the fact that it does not actually move; hence the name, autokinetic, or self-movement phenomenon. Sherif extended this typical laboratory set-up by recording the difference in extent of movement reported by subjects under a variety of social conditions. For example, Sherif noted that subjects tended to report extent of movement in accordance with a group norm. If most of the group reported a lot of movement the remaining individuals also reported considerable movement. If most of the reports presented in the group session involved a relatively small amount of movement, so did the remaining reports. At other times Sherif introduced a prestige factor. Say ten subjects in a group had already established their individual and group norms concerning perceived movement and that the group norm was essentially that there was little movement. Sherif would now bring in a new subject of considerable local or national prestige, say the President of the college or the Governor of the state, and record the movement perceived by this new subject. If the "prestige" subject reported a great amount of movement, so did the ten individuals of the original group in subsequent reporting trials. In other words, Sherif has offered us clear-cut evidence for the importance of social norms in the determination of personal judgments.

The importance of group norms had been pointed out earlier by the cultural anthropologists. Franz Boas, Margaret Mead, and Ruth Benedict were struck by the importance of cultural and social factors in the determination of personality as a result of their extensive field studies on primitive societies. This anthropological type of study was undoubtedly stimulated by the extremist position which theorists such as McDougall and other social psychologists had taken in the early nineteen hundreds. McDougall claimed that social behavior was not learned. Long lists of "social instincts" were prepared by way of explanation for such things as aggressiveness, gregariousness, acquisitiveness, and self-assertion. The studies of the cultural anthropologists clearly showed that these social expressions were learned, and furthermore, that they were passed on to the individual by way of the culture and subcultures. In one cultural group perhaps aggressiveness would be played up as a desirable social norm; in another culture just the opposite would be the case. Ruth Benedict's book, *Patterns of Culture,* is a well-written account of the importance of these cultural differences in the determination of the personality of three very different peoples, the Pueblo Indians of New Mexico, the Kwakiutls of the Northwest, and the Dobuans of New Guinea. The Pueblos are described as being essentially self-effacing, the Kwakiutls as being concerned with glorification to the point of megolomania (definitely abnormal as viewed from our cultural standards), and the Dobuans as being a treacherous, and even murderous, lot.

The importance of cultural relativism to the understanding of human behavior cannot be overestimated. And, just as large groups, such as nations, or Western or Eastern civilizations, set the patterns by which people live, so do various subcultures serve as important determinants of behavior. This line of reasoning carries us right down to the small group kind of research which Sherif conducted in the laboratory. It also delineates a very important trend which was given considerable impetus by the late Kurt Lewin during the last two decades of his life. While he was at the State University of Iowa he conducted an important series of studies on what he called "social climate." He showed, for example, that greater productivity resulted from a boy's club which was led as a "democracy" as opposed to the productivity of the "laissez faire" or "autocratic" groups. This trend carries the name of group dynamics, and is currently one of the most active research areas in the entire field of social psychology. The Research Center for Group Dynamics, a large research institute first established at Massachusetts Institute of Technology by Lewin, and moved to the University of Michigan after his death, is the major source of research of this kind.

The practical implications of fundamental research on social psychology are potentially of greater significance than perhaps any of the other areas of psychology. Since all humans live in a social matrix from birth until death, the applications to everyday living are legion. Getting scientific answers to various psychological problems concerning racial differences, for example, would contribute considerably to international good will. More accurate knowledge of the social psychology of man could even contribute to the solution of man's most difficult world problem today—how to control the tendency toward war. Public opinion polling has obvious implications for the political life of the world as well as implications for business. The very same sampling, attitude scaling, and questionnaire techniques are used in both areas of application. The determination of attitudes by a team of social psychology experts was of considerable relevance to morale problems in the armed forces during World War II. As a matter of fact, an extensive attitude survey was actually used as the basis for establishing the discharge policy in the Army and the Air Force at the end of World War II. Similar polling procedures are used in enlightened business establishments. Many government and industrial organizations initiate their personnel overhauling procedures with an attitude survey. It provides an excellent method for identifying "problem" areas which need improving. Literature on the psychology of leadership was non-existent ten years ago. The crucial need for combat and administrative leadership in the mammoth expansive operation of World War II pointed up the complete void in our knowledge of this area. During the war studies on combat leadership were initiated and, in some cases, observations were made under actual combat conditions. The post-war series of studies which have been conducted at Ohio State University are an important contribution to the eventual solution of leadership problems. Psychologists have not been too vocal in the areas of penal and legal psychology. It is to be hoped that there will be sufficient advance in the fundamental knowledge of social psychology during the next few decades so as to provide the practicing social psychologist with sufficient ammunition to effect a change in many of the essentially archaic practices in the handling of criminals. Until psychology can prove itself more precisely in these matters, however, the legal profession cannot be ex-

pected to throw over the inherited practices of time for a new set of "questionable" procedures.

Concluding Remarks

WITHIN necessary limitations of space, we have tried to provide a panoramic view of psychology in mid-twentieth century. As has been seen, the area that psychology includes is vast. It covers the spectrum from the physical sciences, through biology, to the social sciences, and has amassed literally mountains of empirical data. If we look at the absolute number of incontrovertible facts and valid generalizations concerning behavior, or if we contemplate in what ways psychology has helped us to "understand" human nature thus far, we are not particularly impressed. On the other hand, if we contemplate what we knew about behavior in 1880 with what we know now, the extent of our progress is quite staggering. More important, perhaps, is the fact that we have firmly brought in the scientific method where it previously was not allowed. In about seventy-five years we have moved away from the habit of philosophizing about the nature of "mind" to a fairly healthy state of setting up observations and experiments when we want to put questions to human nature. It seems reasonable to predict that this stress on experimentation will continue to be the key activity of the psychologists of tomorrow.

REFERENCES

1. See MAIER, N. R. F., and SCHNEIRLA, T. C. Principles of Animal Psychology, New York: McGraw-Hill, 1935.
2. The most advanced work on this subject is the mathematical-theoretical treatment of GULLIKSEN, H. Theory of Mental Tests, New York: John Wiley & Sons, 1950.
3. For an elaboration of this point see ROYCE, J. R. A synthesis of experimental designs in program research. *J. Gen. Psychol.*, 1950, *43*, 295–303.

SECTION II

Physiology

THE *layman who is asked for a definition of psychology may reply, truthfully enough, that psychology is the study of the mind. He tends to forget, however, that the way psychologists study the mind is by observing the* behavior *of men and other animals. Because the observable responses an organism makes to its environment (its behavior) occur through the functioning of the organism's nervous system and sense organs, muscles, and glands, an understanding of how the body works is basic to psychological research.*

The scientist who attempts the difficult task of explicating the precise relationship between behavior and physiology has a choice of emphases. He may either begin with the observation of behavioral characteristics and then attempt to explain them by referring to physiology, or he may start with physiology and try to predict behavior from it. You will notice that many of the articles in this text, although their primary concern is behavior, also discuss psysiological functions. The articles in this section, however, focus primarily on physiological processes themselves.

Under normal living conditions, an organism receives a moderate amount of stimulation from the outside world. The body then enjoys a state of equilibrium, or homeostasis. However, in response to prolonged over- or under-stimulation the body is forced to depart from this state in ways which, though different, have one thing in common: all are harmful to the organism. A number of investigations of over-stimulation have been made in the laboratory of Dr. Hans Selye of the University of Montreal, and the first article reprinted here is by two of Dr. Selye's students, P. C. Constantinides and Niall Carey. In "The Alarm Reaction" they explain that unusual stress of any kind (chemical, muscular, etc.) provokes in an organism a "general adaptation syndrome" (GAS). This includes three phases: the body's initial "alarm reaction," a period of resistance, and finally, total exhaustion. What happens to an organism, on the other hand, when physical and mental stimulation are reduced almost to the vanishing point? In the second article, John C. Lilly reports that the results of the isolation experienced by, for example, lone sea voyagers, and the results of experimental isolation (the subject lies motionless in a dark, silent room) are similar: the mind tends to turn inward and then to project its own contents and processes outward in a distorted and hallucinatory fashion.

In "The Afferent Code for Sensory Quality," Carl Pfaffman says that the idea of "little pictures" transmitted via the sensory nerves to a sensorium located somewhere "inside the head" is out of date. His experiments concerning nerve impulses in the sensory fibers en route to the brain suggest a different and more complex interpretation of what happens in the body when one experiences the sensation of taste.

Man's most distinctively human behavior—learning and thinking, for example—is controlled by the cerebral cortex. Electrical stimulation of portions of the cortex will sometimes produce either experiential responses (the patient remembers some experience from his past in great detail) or interpretive responses (the patient changes his interpretation of his present experience—for example, he suddenly feels frightened). In "The Interpretive Cortex," Wilder Penfield describes the area of the cerebral cortex in which such reactions take place and suggests that this part of the brain may, under normal circumstances, contribute to one's comparison of present and past experiences and to one's perception or interpretation of the present.

A mature cerebral cortex, too, makes it possible for us to stay awake for about two-thirds of the day instead of waking only intermittently as a new-born baby does. Nathaniel Kleitman's well-known paper, "Sleep," discusses this voluntary wakefulness; it also describes the results of experimental sleep deprivation and the rhythms of temperature and temperament that lead one person to prefer night work while another is happy on a nine-to-five schedule.

In the last selection, "Mind, Drugs, and Behavior," Patrick L. McGeer provides a clear and thorough review of recent research in neurophysiology, neuropharmacology, and neurochemistry on the effects of drugs on behavior and experience. He suggests that what today may seem an abstract property of the mind, tomorrow (when we have learned more about the brain) may be explained physiologically; his paper illustrates the extent to which the various scientific disciplines overlap and enrich one another.

P. C. CONSTANTINIDES *and* NIALL CAREY

5. *The Alarm Reaction*

IN biology and medicine it is becoming increasingly difficult to see the forest for the trees. The specialization of modern research leads into ever-narrowing paths. One man spends an entire lifetime studying a single hormone, another an enzyme, another the circulation of the kidneys. Year by year the data pile up; yet in some respects this vast accumulation of facts is leading us no nearer to an understanding of the living organism as a whole. Biologists have pushed so far into their individual tunnels of exploration, and there are so many tunnels, that the relation of one finding to another may elude discovery for years. Obviously we have reached a point where it is highly desirable to widen the view, to conduct researches in breadth as well as in depth.

At the Institute of Experimental Medicine and Surgery, the University of Montreal, Dr. Hans Selye and his team of biologists have been pursuing such an investigation for more than a decade, with stimulating results. They have been studying the generalized reactions of a whole animal to the stresses produced by its environment. A living organism consists of salts, enzymes, hormones, energy and a host of other elements, each of which may react in a specific way to some assault from outside; but the response of the organism as a whole is more than the sum of all these reactions. Life, and even death, is a chain reaction, and it is this linked process that Selye's group has been examining.

The particular focus of the investigation is the adaptation of animals to various types of severe or prolonged injury that affect large sections of the body. From this work has come the discovery that the animal organism possesses a general defense mechanism which it automatically mobilizes against any damage, whatever the cause. The principal agent of the mechanism is the endocrine system. As the officers of the defense, the hormones call upon various organs of the body for extraordinary efforts. If the stress becomes too great, the animal is destroyed by its own defenses, for ultimately the strain is conveyed to the heart and the circulatory system. Thus the research leads directly to a study of high blood pressure, hardening of the arteries and heart failure—the principal causes of death among human beings today.

Selye started this work some 12 years ago as the result of certain unexpected findings during some experiments on rats. He was investigating their specific responses to various drugs, poisons and gland extracts. He injected heavy doses, sufficient to kill the rats in a day or two, and made a careful autopsy of every animal. He was surprised to find that every substance he injected produced exactly the same result in three of the animals' organs: 1) the adrenal glands swelled to twice their usual size and changed in color from yellow to brown; 2) the thymus withered away; and 3) the stomach lining was spotted with bleeding ulcers. The puzzling fact was that these reactions were caused by such widely diverse substances as atropine, strychnine, formalin, crude pituitary extracts—all entirely different in chemical structure and mechanism of action. The only factor that the many agents had in common was that all were injected in quantities dangerous to life. Selye reasoned that the responses he observed must represent a nonspecific reaction to general damage as such, regardless of the specific agent that caused the damage.

If this were true, other types of acute stress ought to provoke the same response. Selye tested this assumption by subjecting animals for some hours to cold, to excessive muscular exercise, to fasting, to emotional excitement and to numerous other kinds of injuries. Sure enough, all these nonchemical types of stress elicited in the animals the same unmistakable "alarm reaction" (AR), as he called it.

It was soon discovered that certain characteristic chemical changes in the tissues and body fluids always accompanied the AR. Among the first to be studied were the sugar and the chloride ions of the blood. During the first few hours of exposure to stress, it developed, both of these fall to subnormal concentrations. After a few more hours, they rise above normal values. The two periods are now known respectively as the "shock phase" and the "counter-shock phase" of the AR.

As a result of a great amount of work, done mostly in Canada and the U.S., we know considerably more about the AR today. Its anatomical and biochemical aspects have been studied in many other species besides the rat. There is no doubt that it represents a general defense reaction against sudden stress in many higher vertebrates, including man.

The most dramatic changes during the AR occur in the adrenal glands. The two adrenals of an average human adult weigh together not more than 10 grams—about one 7,000th of the total body weight. But they are extremely important organs; if they are destroyed, as in Addison's disease, death is inevitable. With the exception of the brain centers for breathing and vascular tonus, there is no other equally small part of the body whose destruction or removal results in so quick a death. You can remove both legs, two thirds of the liver or a whole kidney and life will not be endangered; but if you remove an animal's adrenals, it loses its resistance to the slightest damage and dies within a few days. Obviously, then, the adrenals hold a key position as regulators of vital functions.

The gland has a capsule, or cortex, enclosing a marrow, or medulla. It has been known since the beginning of the century that the medulla produces adrenalin, a hormone that constricts blood vessels, raises the blood pressure, and mobilizes sugar from the liver in emergency situations. The function of the cortex—the only portion that enlarges in the alarm reaction—is a more recent discovery. It is now known that the cortex produces hormones indispensable to life, storing them in fat droplets, or lipids, which give the cortex its yellow color. All of these hormones are steroids, that is, fat-soluble compounds with the same basic chemical structure as the sex hormones, the cancer-producing hydrocarbons, the active ingredient of digitalis and certain other substances. At least 20 adrenal cortex hormones are known.

These are the messengers that marshal the alarm reaction. During the first hours of the AR, the hormones in their lipid vehicles are rapidly discharged from the adrenal cortex into the bloodstream and race to the tissues of the body. There they perform their various functions, of which two are definitely known:

1. They keep the composition of the fluid cell environment constant, mainly by retaining salts, particularly sodium, in the solution between the cells. The most important salt-retaining hormone is desoxycorticosterone, more commonly known as DCA.

2. They promptly build up sugar, a ready energy donor, from other materials, particularly proteins.

How important these two functions are can easily be judged from the fact that animals whose adrenals are removed die with their blood almost drained of salt and sugar. On the other hand, the injection of salt-retaining and sugar-forming adrenal hormones can prolong the life of such animals considerably; it also raises their resistance to otherwise fatal stress.

Yet the adrenal itself does not act independently. It is merely an executive of higher coordinating centers, from which it receives orders as to when to act, how much to act and what hormones to discharge. The adrenal cortex, like almost all other endocrine glands, is under the direct command of the anterior part of the pituitary gland—the "leader of the endocrine orchestra." If the pituitary is removed, the adrenal cortex shrinks and becomes inactive. It can regain its normal size and function only if a new pituitary gland is transplanted into the animal or if pituitary extracts (*i.e.,* hormones) are injected.

Fundamentally, then, the AR is controlled by the pituitary. Remove this gland, and no AR can occur; when the animal is placed under stress there is no activation of the adrenals, no thymus destruction, none of the other typical AR changes. Yet the pituitary cannot act alone: an animal whose pituitary is left intact but whose adrenals are removed shows no AR in response to stress.

Thus a long series of experiments clearly outlined the AR mechanism. Acute stress acts on the anterior pituitary through some unknown pathway; the pituitary replies by mobilizing the adrenals, which discharge their hormones, which in turn destroy the thymus and effect most of the other changes. This process has been found to be set in train by hundreds of damaging agents. There are, however, a few interesting exceptions. Certain stress agents can destroy the thymus directly in animals whose adrenals have been removed. A significant fact is that all these "unusual" agents have something to do with cancer.

After the alarm reaction was established, the next major step in the experiments was an investigation of animals' long-range responses to stress. What would happen if the organism were exposed to continuous, prolonged stress of an intensity below the lethal level, a stress strong enough to strain the defenses almost to the limit, yet not sufficiently overwhelming to silence all defense at once?

Animals were subjected to sublethal daily stress with the same agents for several weeks instead of a few days. During the first few days, the organism responded with the usual AR. It showed the typical organic and chemical changes; growth and sex functions ceased, and all the signs of an intense tissue breakdown were present.

As the stress continued unabated, the animals that survived the AR began to recover.

The adrenals started to refill their empty stores with lipids and reverted to normal size; the thymus began to regain its mass, and such substances as sugar and chlorides in the blood rose to normal or even higher levels. At the height of that state the organism had in some way accomplished an adaptation to the continuing stress. Its organs and their functions were apparently returning to normal. In some instances it was difficult to distinguish such animals from control animals not under stress. This stage, lasting from a few weeks to a month or more, was called the "stage of resistance."

It should be noted, however, that resistance increased only against the one type of stress employed from the beginning. If, in the middle of this recovery period, the stress against which adaptation developed was replaced by a different one, the animals succumbed immediately. Quantitative experiments with graded amounts of stress showed that while the animal's specific resistance to the initial agent increased, its resistance to any other stress decreased.

The adaptation to the original stress was not permanent. As the strain continued after the recovery period, the animals became progressively weaker; the adrenals enlarged again and discharged their lipids; the thymus lost the mass it had recovered; sugar and chlorides fell to dangerous levels; after a few weeks all defenses collapsed and life ceased. This last "stage of exhaustion" was similar to the initial alarm reaction. The end was like the beginning.

Thus the struggle of life against stress was found to consist in three successive acts, all aiming at a balance which was not quite attained during the AR, was achieved during the stage of resistance but was lost again during the stage of exhaustion. Evidently the war of the organism against damage was waged at the expense of a finite capital of "adaptation energy." The whole battle was named the "general adaptation syndrome" (GAS).

The establishment of the GAS opened a number of fascinating fundamental problems. Life as a whole could be regarded as a GAS that ends when adaptation energy runs out.

More immediately, the phenomenon suggested some studies of great medical interest.

Some types of stress are so severe that an animal can develop resistance for only a very short period; others permit a prolonged adaptation before the animal becomes exhausted. Animals can adapt themselves to cold, for example, for periods as long as two or three months. And such animals presented quite unexpected changes. The arteries were enormously thickened and their bore was narrowed almost to obliteration in numerous districts of the body; the heart was abnormally large and filled with nodules very like those appearing in human rheumatic disease; the kidneys were largely destroyed through hardening and closing of their vessels—as in human nephrosclerosis—and the blood pressure rose more than 50 per cent. In other words, long-lasting stress had produced in these animals hypertension and cardiovascular disease.

This was a finding of the highest importance in experimental medicine. It suggested that these diseases might be caused by the pituitary-adrenal mechanism, perhaps by the excessive production of their hormones. If one could produce the changes found in these animals by loading the organism with large quantities of pituitary and adrenal hormones, then at least some forms of degenerative diseases would appear to be the consequences of "over-adaptation," i.e., the defense mechanism that an animal develops during the stage of prolonged resistance to stress.

The experiment was made. A number of animals were dosed with large amounts of these hormones. Extracts would not do for this purpose, for one can never be sure how much hormone they contain or that they include everything produced by the gland in the natural state. Fortunately the previously mentioned adrenal hormone desoxycorticosterone, or DCA, was available in pure, crystalline form. Because chemists have not succeeded in synthesizing any pituitary hormones, it was decided to use the whole anterior lobe of this gland, powdered and suspended in water. In laboratory terms the product, "lyophilized anterior pituitary," is referred to as LAP. Continuous injections of large amounts of DCA or LAP are equivalent to the prolonged and excessive secretion of hormones by the adrenal or the pituitary, respectively.

The results were remarkable. In three weeks the animals that were injected with DCA developed severe hypertension and hardening of the kidneys. Those treated with LAP showed a strikingly similar picture, though after a somewhat longer interval.

In medical research one can never lose sight of the ultimate objective, namely, the cure of patients. The investigator first devotes every effort to reproducing a disease in animals, and when he has succeeded he turns to the endeavor to destroy that disease. In searching for ways to combat the diseases produced by too much hormone production, one of the most obvious targets would be to try to neutralize the hormonal excess, in other words, to find a chemical antidote. Logical as it seems at first sight, this is too complicated a task at present. In the first place, we do not yet know the chemical mechanism of the hormones' action. Secondly, we must not forget that the organism needs those hormones, even if by overproducing them it poisons itself with its own defense substances.

A more practicable approach was suggested by experience in the treatment of other endocrine diseases. Some of these diseases can be alleviated by control of the diet. A case in point is diabetes, in which the basic trouble is a hormone deficiency. In moderate cases diabetes can be completely controlled by a diet low in sugar.

It was conceivable that the experimental hypertension produced in animals by overdoses of hormones or by stress might flourish on some diets and be suppressed by others. The animals were therefore subjected to a great variety of diets, a process which had to be pursued by trial and error because there was little indication as to what diets might be helpful.

From the many tests, two facts emerged clearly. One was that experimental hypertension produced by DCA was markedly affected by salt in the diet. A high salt intake increased both the frequency and the intensity of the pathological changes caused by that hormone. Contrariwise, when the animal was fed a salt-free diet, it was immune to hypertension, even when considerable amounts of DCA were injected. The second finding was that hypertension caused by stress or LAP was not affected by salt at all but was influenced by protein in the diet. A low-protein diet afforded considerable protection to the animals, while a high-protein intake aggravated the damage.

Thus sodium favored the adrenal hormones, and proteins favored stress or the pituitary hormones in their injurious effect on blood vessels and blood pressure. The why and wherefore of these results is still unknown. It may be that DCA cannot act without the simultaneous presence of sodium. Perhaps the pituitary manufactures adrenal-stimulating hormones from food proteins. Research on these questions is now going on. One of the present objectives is to find out whether it is the total quantity of proteins that counts or a protein constituent, *i.e.*, an amino acid.

In any event, these experiments tend to strengthen the case for the widely held belief that some forms of human cardiovascular disease are due to hormonal derangements. Medical experience has taught doctors that patients with high blood pressure fare best on a low-sodium, low-protein diet. This is exactly what the animals needed to withstand the destruction of their blood vessels by prolonged stress or by hormones.

The research of Selye's group yielded another key fact, namely, that in this whole general process the kidneys are somehow deeply involved. They are early victims of damage in the resistance phase of the GAS or during the inundation of the body with pituitary and adrenal hormones. But they also seem to be something more than passive targets. A great deal of work since the turn of the century has shown that the kidney itself can become the active cause of the most malignant hypertension. There is considerable evidence now that under certain abnormal conditions parts of the kidney tissue may stop their normal function, which consists in filtering the blood and producing urine, and

start producing hormones that raise blood pressure. In the rat, this was beautifully demonstrated by what is now known as the "endocrine kidney" of Selye. By a surgical operation that interferes with the blood supply of one kidney, the whole organ is transformed into an endocrine gland, and in a few days the blood pressure rises to fatal levels. It is a particular feature of the endocrine kidney technique that only one kidney is transformed into a gland while the other gets all the damage.

Correlation of the evidence derived from all the numerous experiments on the GAS has led Dr. Selye to formulate the following current hypothesis: Long-lasting stress provokes an excessive production of adrenal-stimulating hormone in the anterior pituitary; this forces the adrenal cortex to an intensive discharge of DCA-like hormones which, among other things, affect the kidney in such a way as to release hypertensive substances.

In a sense the research is only beginning. Its implications are tremendous. In the GAS we seem to see the merest outlines of a great biological chain reaction which can be set off by almost any stress and which may frequently lead to the suicide of the organism. Some of the links in this chain are still missing, but its essential structure has been amply confirmed. As a result, large-scale research in this field is now starting in many laboratories.

Should further research prove that chronic stress can produce the same disorders in man as in animals, it would appear that the most frequent and fatal diseases of today are due to the "wear and tear" of modern life. One might question whether stress is peculiarly characteristic of our sheltered civilization, with all its comforts and amenities. Yet these very protections—modern labor-saving devices, clothing, heating—have rendered us all the more vulnerable and sensitive to the slightest stress. What was a mild stress to our forebears now frequently represents a minor crisis. Moreover, the frustrations and repressions arising from emotional conflicts in the modern world, economic and political insecurity, the drudgery associated with many modern occupations—all these represent stresses as formidable as the most severe physical injury. We live under a constant strain; we are losing our ability to relax; we seek fresh forms of physical or mental stimulation.

Thus it would not be surprising to find that much of our organic disease derives from psychological trauma, with the general adaptation syndrome as the bridge that links one to the other. If this be true, medicine may eventually find a cure for the consequences of stress; but prevention of the basic causes will remain a task that lies beyond its reach.

JOHN C. LILLY

6. *Mental Effects of Reduction of Ordinary Levels of Physical Stimuli on Intact, Healthy Persons*

W E have been seeking answers to the question of what happens to a brain and its contained mind in the relative absence of physical stimulation. In neurophysiology, this is one form of the question: Freed of normal efferent and afferent activities, does the activity of the brain soon become that of coma or sleep, or is there some inherent mechanism which keeps it going, a pacemaker of the "awake" type of activity? In psychoanalysis, there is a similar, but not identical problem. If the healthy ego is freed of reality stimuli, does it maintain the secondary process, or does primary process take over? *i.e.,* Is the healthy ego independent of reality or dependent in some fashion, in some degree, on exchanges with the surroundings to maintain its structure?

In seeking answers, we have found pertinent autobiographical literature and reports of experiments by others, and have done experiments ourselves. The experiments are psychological ones on human subjects. Many psychological experiments in isolation have been done on animals, but are not recounted in detail here; parenthetically, the effect on very young animals can be an almost completely irreversible lack of development of whole systems, such as those necessary for the use of vision in accomplishing tasks put to the animal. No truly neurophysiological isolation experiments on either animals or man have yet been done.

Autobiographical Accounts

THE published autobiographical material has several drawbacks: In no case is there a sizeable reduction of all possibilities of stimulation and action; in most cases, other factors add complications' to the phenomena observed. We have collected 18 autobiographical cases from the polar and sea-faring literature (see References) which are more frank and revealing than most. We have interviewed two persons who have not published any of their material. In this account, we proceed from rather complicated situations to the more simple ones, *i.e.,* from a maximum number of factors to the most simple experimental situation.

From this literature we have found that isolation *per se* acts on most persons as a powerful stress. The effects observed are similar to those of any extreme stress, and other stressful factors add their effects to those of isolation to cause mental symptoms to appear more rapidly and more intensely. As is well known, stresses other than isolation can cause the same symptoms to appear in individuals in an isolated group.

Taking our last point first, we have the account by Walter Gibson given in his book, "The Boat." This is the case in which four persons out of an initial 135 survived in a lifeboat in the Indian Ocean in World War II. Gibson gives a vivid account of his ex-

Reprinted by permission of the American Psychiatric Association and the authors from *Psychiatric Research Reports*, March 9, 1956, pp. 1–9.

periences, and the symptoms resulting from loss of hope, dehydration, thirst, intense sunburn, and physical combat. Most of the group hallucinated rescue planes and drank salt water thinking it fresh; many despaired and committed suicide; others were murdered; and some were eaten by others. The whole structure of egos was shaken and recast in desperate efforts at survival. (It is interesting to note that many of those who committed suicide tried to sink the boat by removing the drain plugs before jumping overboard, i.e., sink the boat [and other persons] as well as the self; this dual destruction may be used by some of the non-surviving solitary sailors; see below.)

I cite this case because it gives a clue as to what to expect in those who do survive isolation in other conditions: Gibson survived— how? He says: (1) by previous out-of-doors training in the tropical sun for some years; (2) by having previously learned to be able to become completely passive (physically and mentally); (3) by having and maintaining the conviction that he would come through the experience; and, we add, (4) by having a woman, Doris Lim, beside him, who shared his passivity and convictions.

In all cases of survivors of isolation, at sea or in the polar night, it was the first exposure which caused the greatest fears and hence the greatest danger of giving way to symptoms; previous experience is a powerful aid in going ahead, despite the symptoms. Physical passivity is necessary during starvation, but, in some people, may be contra-indicated in social isolation in the absence of starvation. In all survivors, we run across the inner conviction that he or she will survive, or else there are definite reassurances from others that each will be rescued. In those cases of a man and a woman together, or even the probability of such a union within a few days, there is apparently not only a real assurance of survival, but a love of the situation can appear. (Such love can develop in a solitaire; see below.) Of course, such couples are the complete psychological antithesis of our major thesis of complete isolation; many symptoms can be avoided by healthy persons with such an arrangement.

Solitary sailors are in a more complex situation than the group of polar isolates. The sailing of a small boat across oceans requires a good deal of physical exertion, and the situation may be contaminated by a lack of sleep which can also cause symptoms. The solitary sailors, of which Joshua Slocum and Alain Bombard are outstanding examples, relate that the first days out of port are the dangerous ones; awe, humility, and fear in the face of the sea are most acute at this time. Bombard states that if the terror of the first week can be overcome, one can survive. Apparently, many do not survive this first period. Many single-handed boats have not arrived at their transoceanic destination. We have clues as to the causes from what sometimes happens with two persons on such crossings. There are several pairs of ocean-crossing sailors in which one of the couple became so terror-stricken, paranoid, and bent on murder and/or suicide, that he had to be tied to his bunk.

Once this first period is past, other symptoms develop, either from isolation itself or from isolation plus other stresses. In the South Atlantic, Joshua Slocum had a severe gastro-intestinal upset just before a gale hit his boat; he had reefed his sails, but should have taken them down. Under the circumstances, he was unable to move from the cabin. At this point he saw a man take over the tiller. At first he thought it was a pirate, but the man reassured him and said that he was the pilot of the Pinta and that he would take his boat safely through the storm. Slocum asked him to take down sail, but the man said, no, they must catch the Pinta ahead. The next morning Slocum recovered, and found his boat had covered 93 miles on true course, sailing itself. (His boat was quite capable of such a performance; he arranged it that way for long trips without his hand at the helm.) In a dream that night the pilot appeared and said he would come whenever Slocum needed him. During the next three years the helmsman appeared to Slocum several times, during gales.

This type of hallucination—delusion seems to be characteristic of the strong egos who survive: a "savior" type of hallucination rather than a "destroyer" type. Their inner conviction of survival is projected thoroughly.

Other symptoms that appear are: superstitiousness (Slocum thought a dangerous reef named M Reef was lucky because M is the 13th letter of the alphabet and 13 was his lucky number. He passed the reef without hitting it. Bombard thought the number of matches necessary to light a damp cigarette represented the number of days until the end of the voyage. He was wrong several times.); intense love of any living things (Slocum was revolted at the thought of killing food-animals, especially a goat given to him at one port. Ellam and Mudie became quite upset after catching and eating a fish that had followed the boat all day, and swore off further fish-eating.); conversations with inanimate objects (Bombard had bilateral conversations with a doll mascot.); and a feeling that when one lands, one had best be careful to listen before speaking to avoid being considered insane (Bernicot refused an invitation to dinner on another yacht after crossing the Atlantic alone, until he could recapture the proper things to talk about.). The inner life becomes so vivid and intense that it takes time to readjust to the life among other persons and to reestablish one's inner criteria of sanity (When placed with fellow prisoners, after 18 months in solitary confinement, Christopher Burney was afraid to speak for fear that he would show himself to be insane. After several days of listening he recaptured the usual criteria of sanity, and then could allow himself to speak.).

Life alone in the polar night, snowed-in, with the confining surroundings of a small hut is a more simple situation. However, there are other complicating factors: extreme cold, possibilities of carbon monoxide poisoning, collapse of the roof, etc. Richard Byrd, in his book "Alone," recounts in great detail his changes in mental functioning, and talks of a long period of CO poisoning resulting in a state close to catatonia. I refer you to his book for details. He experienced, as did Slocum and many others, an oceanic feeling, the being "of the universe," at one with it.

Christiane Ritter ("A Woman in the Polar Night") was exposed to isolation for periods up to 16 days at a time. She saw a monster, hallucinated her past as if in bright sunshine, became "at one" with the moon, and developed a monomania to go out over the snow. She was saved by an experienced Norwegian who put her to bed and fed her lavishly. She developed a love for the situation and found great difficulty in leaving Spitzbergen. For a thorough and sensitive account of symptoms, I recommend her book to you.

From these examples and several more (see References), we conclude the following:

1. Published autobiographies are of necessity incomplete. Social taboos, discretion to one's self, suppression and repression of painful or uncomfortable material, secondary elaboration, and rationalization severely limit the scope of the material available. (Interviews with two men, each of whom lived alone in the polar night, confirm this impression.)

2. Despite these limitations, we find that persons in isolation experience many, if not all, of the symptoms of the mentally ill.

3. In those who survive, the symptoms can be reversible. How easily reversible, we do not know. Most survivors report, after several weeks' exposure to isolation, a new inner security and a new integration of themselves on a deep and basic level.

4. The underlying mechanisms are obscure. It is obvious that inner factors in the mind tend to be projected outward, that some of the mind's activity which is usually reality-bound now becomes free to turn to phantasy and ultimately to hallucination and delusion. It is as if the laws of thought are projected into the realm of the laws of inanimate matter and of the universe. The primary process tends to absorb more and more of the time and energy usually taken by the secondary process. Such experiences either lead to improved mental functioning or to destruction. Why one person takes the healthy path and another person the sick one is not yet clear.

Experiments to clarify the necessary conditions for some of these effects have been done. One of the advantages of the experimental material is that simpler conditions can be set up and tested, and some of the additional stresses of natural life situations can be eliminated.

Experimental Isolation

THE longest exposure to isolation on the largest number of subjects has been carried out in Dr. Donald Hebb's Department of Psychology at McGill University by a group of graduate students. We started a similar project independently with different techniques at the National Institute of Mental Health. In the Canadian experiments, the aim is to reduce the *patterning* of stimuli to the lowest level; in ours, the objective is to reduce the *absolute intensity* of all physical stimuli to the lowest possible level.

In the McGill experiments, a subject is placed on a bed in an air-conditioned box with arms and hands restrained with cardboard sleeves, and eyes covered completely with translucent ski goggles. The subjects are college students motivated by payment of $20 per day for as long as they will stay in the box. An observer is present, watching through a window, and tests the subject in various ways verbally through a communication set.

In our experiments, the subject is suspended with the body and all but the top of the head immersed in a tank containing slowly flowing water at 34.5° C. (94.5° F.), wears a blacked-out mask (enclosing the whole head) for breathing, and wears nothing else. The water temperature is such that the subject feels neither hot nor cold. The experience is such that one tactually feels the supports and the mask, but not much else; a large fraction of the usual pressures on the body caused by gravity are lacking. The sound level is low; one hears only one's own breathing and some faint water sounds from the piping; the water-air interface does not transmit airborne sounds very efficiently. It is one of the most even and monotonous environments I have experienced. After the initial training period, no observer is present. Immediately after exposure, the subject writes personal notes on his experience.

At McGill, the subjects varied considerably in the details of their experiences. However,

a few general phenomena appeared. After several hours, each subject found that it was difficult to carry on organized, directed thinking for any sustained period. Suggestibility was very much increased. An extreme desire for stimuli and action developed. There were periods of thrashing around in the box in attempts to satisfy this need. The borderline between sleep and awakeness became diffuse and confused. At some time between 24 and 72 hours most subjects couldn't stand it any longer and left. Hallucinations and delusions of various sorts developed, mostly in those who could stay longer than two days.

The development of hallucinations in the visual sphere followed the stages seen with mescaline intoxication. When full-blown, the visual phenomena were complete projections maintaining the three dimensions of space in relation to the rest of the body and could be scanned by eye and head movements. The contents were surprising to the ego, and consisted of material like that of dreams, connected stories sharing past memories and recent real events. The subjects' reactions to these phenomena were generally amusement and a sense of relief from the pressing boredom. They could describe them vocally without abolishing the sequences. A small number of subjects experienced doubling of their body images. A few developed transient paranoid delusions, and one had a seizure-like episode after five days in the box with no positive EEG findings for epilepsy.

Our experiments have been more limited both in numbers of subjects and duration of exposures. There have been two subjects, and the longest exposure has been three hours. We have much preliminary data, and have gained enough experience to begin to guess at some of the mechanisms involved in the symptoms produced.

In these experiments, the subject always has a full night's rest before entering the tank. Instructions are to inhibit all movements as far as possible. An initial set of training exposures overcomes the fears of the situation itself.

In the tank, the following stages have been experienced:

1. For about the first three-quarters of an hour, the day's residues are predominant. One is aware of the surroundings, recent problems, etc.

2. Gradually, one begins to relax and more or less enjoy the experience. The feeling of being isolated in space and having nothing to do is restful and relaxing at this stage.

3. But slowly, during the next hour, a tension develops which can be called a "stimulus-action" hunger; hidden methods of self-stimulation develop: twitching muscles, slow swimming movements (which cause sensations as the water flows by the skin), stroking one finger with another, etc. If one can inhibit such maneuvers long enough, intense satisfaction is derived from later self-stimulations.

4. If inhibition can win out, the tension may ultimately develop to the point of forcing the subject to leave the tank.

5. Meanwhile, the attention is drawn powerfully to any residual stimulus: the mask, the suspension, each come in for their share of concentration. Such residual stimuli become the whole content of consciousness to an almost unbearable degree.

6. If this stage is passed without leaving the tank, one notices that one's thoughts have shifted from a directed type of thinking about problems to reveries and fantasies of a highly personal and emotionally charged nature. These are too personal to relate publicly, and probably vary greatly from subject to subject. The individual reactions to such fantasy material also probably varies considerably, from complete suppression to relaxing and enjoying them.

7. If the tension and the fantasies are withstood, one may experience the furthest stage which we have yet explored: projection of visual imagery. I have seen this once, after a two and one-half hour period. The black curtain in front of the eyes (such as one "sees" in a dark room with eyes closed) gradually opens out into a three-dimensional, dark, empty space in front of the body. This phenomenon captures one's interest immediately, and one waits to find out what comes next. Gradually forms of the type sometimes seen in hypnogogic states appear. In this case, they were small, strangely shaped objects with self-luminous borders. A tunnel whose inside "space" seemed to be emitting a blue light then appeared straight ahead. About this time, this experiment was terminated by a leakage of water into the mask through a faulty connector on the inspiratory tube.

It turns out that exposures to such conditions train one to be more tolerant of many internal activities. Fear lessens with experience, and personal integration can be speeded up. But, of course, there are pitfalls here to be avoided. The opposite effects may also be accelerated in certain cases. Fantasies about the experience (such as the illusion of "return to the womb," which is quite common) are dispelled; one realizes that at birth we start breathing air and hence cannot "return to the womb." One's breathing in the tank is extremely important: as a comforting, constant safeguard and a source of rhythmic stimulation.

In both the McGill experiments and in ours, certain aftereffects are noted: The McGill subjects had difficulty in orienting their perceptual mechanisms; various illusions persisted for several hours. In our experiments, we notice that after emersion the day apparently is started over. *i.e.,* The subject feels as if he has just arisen from bed afresh; this effect persists, and the subject finds he is out of step with the clock for the rest of that day. He also has to re-adjust to social intercourse in subtle ways. The night of the day of the exposure he finds that his bed exerts great pressure against his body. No bed is as comfortable as floating in water.

Experiments such as these demonstrate results similar to that given above for solitary polar living and sailing alone. If one is alone, long enough, and at levels of physical and human stimulation low enough, the mind turns inward and projects outward its own contents and processes; the brain not only stays active despite the lowered levels of input and output, but accumulates surplus energy to extreme degrees. In terms of libido theory, the total *amount* of libido increases with time of deprivation; body-libido reaches new high levels. If body-libido is not discharged somatically, discharge starts through fantasy; but apparently this is neither an adequate mode nor can it achieve an adequate rate of discharge in the presence of the rapidly rising level. At some point a new threshold appears for more definite phenomena of regression: hallucinations, delusions, oceanic bliss, etc. At this stage, given any opportunities for action or stimulation by external reality, the healthy ego seizes them and re-establishes more secondary process. Lacking such opportunities for a long enough interval of time, re-organization takes place, how reversibly and how permanently we do not yet know.

Apparently even healthy minds act this way in isolation. What this means to psychiatric research is obvious: We have yet to obtain a full, documented picture of the range available to the healthy human adult mind; some of the etiological factors in mental illness may be clarified and sharpened by such research. Of course, this is a limited region of investigation. We have not gone into details about loss of sleep, starvation, and other factors which have great power in changing healthy minds to sick ones. I think that you can see the parallels between these results and phenomena found in normal children and in psychotics. And, if we could give you a more detailed account, possible explanations of the role of isolation factors in involuntary indoctrination and its opposite, psychotherapy, would be more evident.

REFERENCES

1. SMALL, MAURICE H. April, 1900. On some psychical relations of society and solitude. *Pedagogical Seminary,* VII, No. 2.

Solitary Sailors

2. SLOCUM, CAPTAIN JOSHUA. 1948. *Sailing Alone Around the World.* Rupert Hart-Davis, London.
3. ELLAM, PATRICK AND COLIN MUDIE. 1953. *Sopranino.* W. W. Norton and Co., Inc., N.Y.
4. BOMBARD, DR. ALAIN. 1953. *The Voyage of the Hérétique.* Simon and Schuster, N.Y.
5. MERRIEN, JEAN. 1954. *Lonely Voyagers.* G. P. Putnam's Sons, N.Y.
6. MERRIEN, JEAN. 1954. *Les Navigateurs Solitaires.* Editiones Denoël.
7. BERNICOT, LOUIS. 1953. *The Voyage of Anahita—Single-Handed Round the World.* Rupert Hart-Davis, Soho Square, London.

Drastic Degrees of Stress

8. GIBSON, WALTER. 1953. *The Boat.* Houghton Mifflin Company (The Riverside Press), Boston, Mass.

Living in the Polar Night

9. SCOTT, J. M. 1953. *Portrait of an Ice Cap with Human Figures.* Chatto and Windus, London.
10. COURTAULD, A. July, 1932. Living alone under polar conditions. *The Polar Record,* No. 4. University Press, Cambridge.
11. BYRD, RICHARD E. 1938. *Alone.* G. P. Putnam's Sons, N.Y.
12. RITTER, CHRISTIANE. 1954. *A Woman in the Polar Night.* E. P. Dutton and Co., Inc., N.Y.

Forced Isolation and Confinement

13. BURNEY, CHRISTOPHER. 1952. *Solitary Confinement.* Coward-McCann, Inc., N.Y.
14. STYPULKOWSKI, Z. 1951. *Invitation to Moscow.* Thames and Hudson, London.

The Deaf and the Blind

15. COLLINGSWOOD, HERBERT W. 1923. *Adventures in Silence.* The Rural New Yorker, N.Y.
16. ORMOND, ARTHUR W., C.B.E., F.R.C.S. 1925. Visual hallucinations in sane people. *British Med. J.,* Vol. 2.
17. BARTLET, J. E. A. 1951. A case of organized visual hallucinations in an old man with cataract, and their relation to the phenomena of the phantom limb. *Brain,* Vol. 74, Part III, pp. 363–373.

Experimental Isolation

18. HERON, W., W. H. BEXTON, AND D. O. HEBB. August, 1953. Cognitive effects of a decreased variation to the sensory environment. *The Amer. Psychol.,* Vol. 8, No. 8, p. 366.

CARL PFAFFMANN

7. *The Afferent Code for Sensory Quality*

ONE of the basic problems in the psychology and physiology of sensation is that of the mechanism by which different sensory qualities are perceived. The classical dictum on this problem was propounded by Johannes Müeller in his doctrine of the Specific Energies of Nerves. Actually Charles Bell had enunciated (Carmichael, 1926) the principle somewhat earlier, but Müeller's version is better known. This doctrine made clear that "We are aware of the state of our nerves, not of the external stimulus itself." The eye, however stimulated, gives rise to sensations of light; the ear, to sensations of sound; and taste buds, to sensations of taste.

The further extension of the doctrine of Specific Nerve Energies to the different sensation qualities within a single modality was made by Helmholtz. According to his place theory of hearing, the perception of a particular pitch was attributed to the activity at a particular region of the basilar membrane of the inner ear, stimulation of individual nerve fibers at these specific locations gave rise to unique tonal qualities of pitch. *Pitch* depended upon *which* nerve fiber was activated (Boring, 1950). In the less complex modalities, like the cutaneous or gustatory senses, von Frey and his school propounded the view of "modalities within modalities." The cutaneous sense was said to consist of separate modalities: touch, pressure, warm, cold, and pain, each with their specific receptors. The history of research on cutaneous sensitivity is, in large measure, a history of the search for such receptors. In taste the "big four" are familiar to all; the qualities, salty, sour, bitter, and sweet, were each mediated by a specific receptor type.

Implicit in these formulations is an isomorphism between receptor structure and phenomenology. Pure sensation as a basic psychological entity was to be reduced to a physiological entity. Psychology (at least a part thereof) was to be "explained" by the underlying physiology, hence, "Physiological Psychology." This formulation, simple and direct, dominated the field of sensory psychology from the beginning with only an occasional and sporadic dissenting voice. The fact that the psychological entities were only postulated and the question of whether they were, in fact, valid were almost forgotten in the search for the "real thing."

Many of the more recent findings in sensory psychology and physiology derive from the application of electrophysiology to the study of sensory processes. The publication of E. D. Adrian's *The Basis of Sensation* in 1928 opened a new era. The invention of the electronic tube, appropriate amplifying circuits, and recording instruments made it possible to study directly the activity of the sense organs and their nerves. Since 1928, the advances in technique and instrumentation have been so dramatic that there is almost no part of the nervous system that cannot be probed by the inquisitive microelectrode. Psychologists have played a significant role in this development. One of their best-known early discoveries was that of Wever and Bray (1930), on the cochlea and VIIIth nerve.

This paper will review some experiments with this procedure on another sense, that of taste, and will discuss their general impli-

Presented as part of the Presidential Address to the Division of Experimental Psychology at the APA Annual Convention, September 3, 1957. Reprinted by permission of the American Psychological Association and the author from *The American Psychologist*, 1959, vol. 14, pp. 226–32.

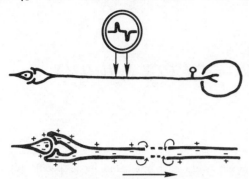

FIG. 1. Diagram of electrophysiological recording from a single sensory nerve fiber. Upper diagram shows a single fiber in contact with a single sense cell to the left. A diphasic response on the cathode ray tube is shown as an impulse passes the recording electrodes en route to the central nervous system schematized to the right. The lower figure shows in more detail the positive and negative charges around the cell membranes associated with the passage of the nerve impulse.

cations for the theory of afferent coding. It should be emphasized that sensation itself is not being studied. Rather the investigator "taps in" on the "basis of sensation" by recording and amplifying the nerve impulse traffic in the sensory fibers "en route" to the brain.

The sense of taste is particularly well suited to this problem because it consists of well defined differentiated structures, the taste buds, which are capable of mediating quite different sensory qualities, but the array of qualities and dimensions is not too complex for interpretation. The afferent message from receptor to brain can be studied directly in the afferent nerve fibers from the tongue, for the primary sensory nerve fibers from the receptive organs are relatively accessible with no synaptic complexities in the direct line from the receptors except for the junction between sense cell and sensory fiber.

The taste stimulus, like all stimuli, acts first upon a receptor cell. Changes in the receptor cell in turn activate or "trigger" impulses in the nerve fiber. Both the sense cell, as well as the nerve fiber, and in fact all living cells are like tiny batteries with a potential difference across the cell membrane. When stimulated, this membrane is depolarized, and it is this

depolarization that can be recorded. FIGURE 1 schematizes such recording from a single sensory nerve fiber shown in contact with a receptor cell to the left of the figure and entering the central nervous system (CNS) to the right. The recording electrodes on the fiber connect with an appropriate recording device such as a cathode ray oscillograph shown schematically. As the impulse passes the first electrode, there is an upward deflection; as it passes the second electrode, there is a downward deflection. By an appropriate arrangement, a single or monophasic deflection only may be obtained so that at each passage of an impulse there will be a "spike" on the oscillograph tracing. The lower figure shows schematically the electrical activity associated with the passage of a nerve impulse. The message delivered along any single nerve fiber therefore consists of a train of impulses, changes in excitation of the receptor are signaled by changes in the frequency of this train. Thus, changes in strength of solution bathing the tongue change the frequency of impulse discharge per second. In any one fiber, the size of the impulse is nearly constant. The sensory nerve message, therefore, is a digital process.

FIGURE 2 shows a typical series of oscillograph tracings obtained from a *single* nerve fiber when different concentrations of sodium chloride are applied to the tongue of the rat. The "spikes" signal the passage of each impulse past the recording electrode. With stronger stimuli there is a higher frequency of discharge. Threshold for this fiber lies at approximately 0.003 M. Other fibers will show similar behavior, but may possess higher thresholds for the tongue contains a population of taste receptors with thresholds of differing value.

This description applies to the impulse in the single sensory nerve fiber. Actually, the sensory nerve is a cable, made up of many different fibers each connected with one or more receptor cells. The single fiber recordings shown were obtained after the nerve cable had been dissected to a strand containing just one functional unit. Sometimes, the same effect is achieved by using microelectrodes.

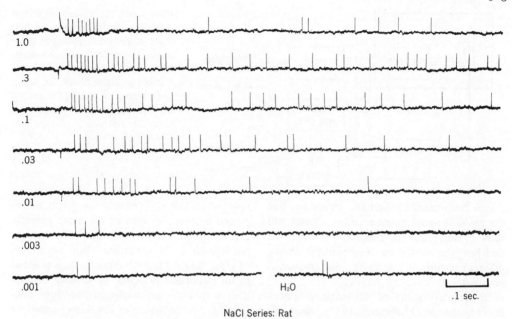

1.0

.3

.1

.03

.01

.003

.001   H₂O

.1 sec.

NaCl Series: Rat

FIG. 2. A series of oscillograph tracings obtained from a single taste nerve fiber when different concentrations of salt solution are placed on the tongue. Note that water as well as .001 M NaCl will elicit two impulses. A concentration of .003 M NaCl will elicit three impulses and may be considered as threshold. (Reproduced from the *Journal of Neurophysiology*.)

The nerve fibers subserving taste travel in three nerves from the mouth region: the lingual, glossopharyngeal, and vagus nerves which contain touch, temperature, pressure, and pain fibers as well as those concerned with taste. The taste fibers from the anterior tongue branch off from the lingual nerve to form the chorda tympani nerve where it is possible to record almost exclusively from taste nerve fibers. This nerve can be exposed by appropriate surgery in the anesthetized animal and placed on the electrodes leading to the recording apparatus.

A block diagram of the apparatus together with sample records is shown in FIGURE 3. The integrated record is readily adapted to quantitative treatment by measuring the magnitude of the deflection at each response and so provides a measure of the total activity of all the fibers in the nerve. An index of overall taste sensitivity can be obtained from such recordings. The curves in FIGURE 4 are such measures for the cat for quinine, hydrochloric acid, sodium chloride, potassium chlo-

ride, and sucrose solutions (Pfaffmann, 1955).

The basic taste stimuli can be arranged in order of thresholds from low to high as follows: quinine, hydrochloric acid, sodium chloride, potassium chloride, and sucrose. In this animal, as in man, quinine is effective in relatively low concentrations. Sugar at the other end of the scale requires relatively high concentrations, and the electrolytes are intermediate. Sugar produces a nerve response of small magnitude compared with that to other stimuli. Differences in response magnitudes are found from one species to another. In the hamster or guinea pig, for example, sugar will elicit a strong discharge, and other species differences with quinine and the salts have been observed (Beidler, Fishman, & Hardiman, 1955; Pfaffmann, 1953). Recently, Carpenter (1956) has correlated certain of these species differences with behavioral data using the preference method.

The representation in FIGURE 4 does not show that the animal can distinguish one sub-

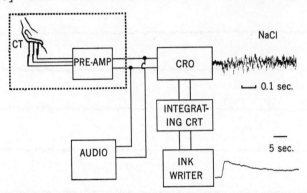

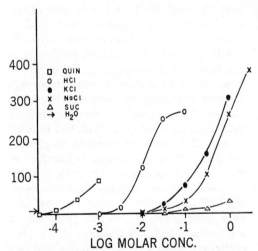

FIG. 3. A block diagram of the recording apparatus showing two types of record. The upper trace shows a typical asynchronous, multifiber discharge from a large number of active fibers; the lower trace shows the integrated record of such activity. (Reproduced from the *American Journal of Clinical Nutrition*.)

stance from another. Actually an animal like the rat will avoid quinine and acid, but will show a preference for NaCl and sucrose. To find how the animal can discriminate among different chemicals the single fiber analysis is required.

In the early study of the single gustatory fibers in the cat (Pfaffmann, 1941), three different kinds of fiber were found. One was responsive to sodium chloride and acid, another to quinine and acid, and a third to acid alone. Thus, acid stimulated all receptor-neural units found. This established not only that the gustatory endings were differentially sensitive to different chemicals but that the physiological receptor "types" *did not* correspond to the phenomenal categories as reported by man. In view of the more recently demonstrated species difference, this might not appear to be surprising. But, regardless of what the cat "tastes," these findings pointed to an important principle of sensory coding. This is that *the same afferent fiber may convey different information depending upon the amount of activity in another parallel fiber.* To illustrate, suppose A represents an acid-salt unit and C, an acid sensitive unit, then activity in A only would lead to salty; but activity in that same fiber, A, plus discharge in C would lead to sourness. Recent studies emphasize still another important point, namely, that some stimuli may decrease or inhibit the frequency of sensory discharge. Certain receptors, which can be stimulated by water (as well as other agents), may be inhibited by the application of dilute salt solutions (Liljestrand & Zotterman, 1954). Taste stimuli, therefore, may either increase or decrease, i.e., modulate, the amount of afferent nerve traffic. A diminution in activity may signal, not merely the withdrawal of a particular stimulus, but the application of a different one.

TABLE 1 taken from a recent paper from Zotterman's laboratory (Cohen, Hagiwara, & Zotterman, 1955) illustrates the afferent code or pattern which may be described for the cat based on a compilation of the "types" so far discovered for that species.

But the use of the term "fiber type" harks back to some of the errors of classical thinking. Types are defined only by the range of stimuli sampled, the wider the range, the more difficult will it be to define pure "types."

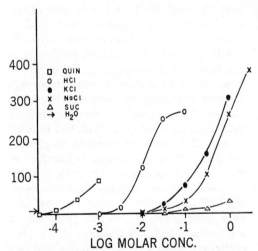

FIG. 4. Curves of taste response in the cat to four different taste stimuli as indicated by the integrated response method. (Reproduced from the *Journal of Neurophysiology*.)

TABLE 1 *

Fiber Type Response in the Cat

STIMULUS	"WATER" FIBER	"SALT" FIBER	"ACID" FIBER	"QUININE" FIBER	SENSATION EVOKED
H₂O (salt <0.03 M)	+	0	0	0	→ water
NaCl (0.05 M)	0	+	0	0	→ salt
HCl (pH 2.5)	+	+	+	0	→ sour
Quinine	+	0	0	+	→ bitter

* Cf., Cohen, Hagiwara, & Zotterman, 1955.

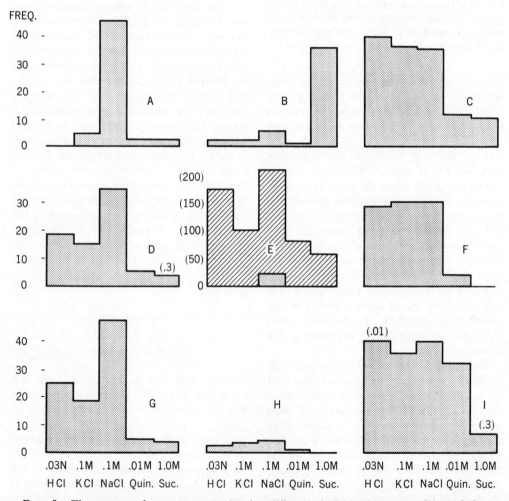

FIG. 5. The pattern of taste responses in nine different single sensory nerve fibers of the rat. The solid bar graphs give the frequency of response in impulses per second for different taste stimuli (indicated along the abscissa). The crosshatched bar graph shows the relative response of the total nerve (integrated response) to these same solutions. (Reproduced from the *Journal of Neurophysiology*.)

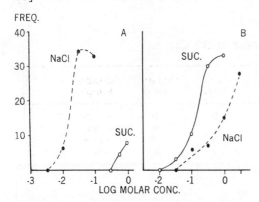

FIG. 6. The relation between frequency of discharge and concentration in two fibers both of which are sensitive to sugar and salt. (Reproduced from the *Journal of Neurophysiology*.)

"Taste types" may turn out to be as varied and individual as "personality types." FIGURE 5 shows the variety of response patterns of nine single fiber preparations to the following standard test solutions: .03 N HCl, .1 M KCl, .1 M NaCl, .01 M quinine hydrochloride, and 1.0 M sucrose (Pfaffmann, 1955).

The bar graph shows the magnitude of response in each of the single fiber preparations in impulses per second of discharge. The central crosshatched bar graph shows the relative magnitude of response to these same solutions in the integrated response of the whole nerve. It is apparent that the individual fibers do not all have the same pattern. The sum of activity of all fibers is shown by the crosshatched diagram. Furthermore, fiber types are not immediately apparent in this array.

The fact that the individual receptor cells possess combined sensitivity as salt plus acid, or salt plus sugar, cannot be dismissed as the result of multiple innervation of more than one receptor cell by a single fiber. Kimura (Beidler, 1957; Kimura & Beidler, 1956) has studied the sensitivity patterns of the individual taste cells by inserting micropipette electrodes directly into the sense cells themselves. The pattern of sensitivity found in the individual sensory cell is like that already described for the single afferent fiber. Thus, within the individual sense cell there must be different sites which are selectively

sensitive to different taste stimuli. These sites on the membrane may be determined by molecular configuration, the shape and size of pores in the membrane, or some such microcellular feature.

One additional principle must be introduced. This is that the relative rather than the absolute amount of activity in any one set of afferent fibers may determine the quality of sensation. FIGURE 6 shows frequency of discharge as a function of stimulus intensity for two units labelled A and B. Both are stimulated by both stimuli sugar and salt, but it is apparent that A is more sensitive to salt and B to sugar (Pfaffmann, 1955). Once each stimulus intensity exceeds the threshold for a particular receptor unit, the frequency of discharge increases with concentration. Thus the afferent pattern as the code for sensory quality must take account of the changing frequency of discharge with stimulus intensity. The pattern concept may be retained by recognizing that "pattern" is still apparent in the relative amount of activity of different fibers. In the two-fiber example shown in FIGURE 6, low concentrations of salt will discharge only A, higher concentrations will discharge both A and B, but activity in A will be greater than that in B. Low concentrations of sugar will activate only B, higher concentrations will activate both B and A, but B will be greater than A. Thus the sensory code might read:

FREQUENCY CODE

A > B = salty

B > A = sweet

where A or B may go to zero. It is not only the activity in parallel fibers that is important, it is the *relative amount* of such parallel activity.

Studies of the other senses indicate that these principles are not unique to taste. In the cutaneous senses there is a variety of different endings which overlap two or more of the classical skin modalities (Maruhashi, Mizuguchi, & Tasaki, 1952). For example, some pressure receptors in the cat's tongue are activated by cold (Hensel & Zotterman, 1951), and there are several different pressure, temperature, and nociceptor endings, some serving large or small areas, some adapting slowly, others rapidly to give a variety of temporal as well as spatial "discriminanda." These findings are reminiscent of Nafe's (1934) quantitative theory of feeling, and the recent anatomical studies of Weddell (1955) and his group are of similar import.

In audition, selective sensitivity among the individual primary afferent fibers is very broad. Those fibers arising from the basal turn of the cochlea respond to tones of any audible frequency; those arising in the upper part respond only to a band of low frequency tones (Tasaki, 1954). Further, it has been suggested (Wever, 1949) that the temporal patterning of the discharge, especially in the low frequencies, provides a basis for pitch discrimination. In vision, Granit (1955) has suggested that different impulse frequencies in the *same* third order neuron from the retina may signal different spectral events at the periphery.

These electrophysiological results should not have been surprising to us. That a particular sensory dimension is not isomorphic with a particular physical dimension is well known. Auditory loudness, functionally dependent upon sound pressure level, is not synonymous with physical intensity. Pitch is not the same as frequency, although the latter is its major determinant (Stevens & Davis, 1938). Visual brightness is not the same as physical luminance. It would, indeed, have been surprising if similar nonidentities had not been found at the physiological level.

And so in attacking Müeller's classic problem with modern techniques, we have found, at least, within the modalities, a solution different from that which was first anticipated. Differential sensitivity rather than specificity, patterned discharges rather than a mosaic of sensitivities is the form of our modern view. Müeller's principle did not answer a problem so much as it posed one. In the answers that I have attempted to suggest, we see, not only the details of the mechanism for which we have searched, but we can discern broader implications for the principles governing the relation between psychology and physiology. Psychology cannot rest content with a pseudophysiology based solely upon phenomenology. So long as the receptor surface was conceived to be a static mosaic where phenomenal qualities were reified (in some instances in the form of specific anatomical structures), sensory psychology and physiology were reduced to the study of how the "little pictures" were transmitted via the sensory nerves to the "sensorium" located presumably somewhere "inside the head." Such a view is not only out of date, but it diverts our attention from the proper study of the afferent influx, its dynamic properties and interactions and its relevance for all levels of neural integration and behavioral organization.

REFERENCES

ADRIAN, E. D. *The basis of sensation*. New York: Norton, 1928.

BEIDLER, L. M. Facts and theory on the mechanism of taste and odor perception. In *Chemistry of natural food flavors*. Quartermaster Res. and Eng. Center, 1957. Pp. 7–47.

BEIDLER, L. M., FISHMAN, I. Y., & HARDIMAN, C. W. Species differences in taste responses. *Amer. J. Physiol.*, 1955, 181, 235–239.

BORING, E. G. *A history of experimental psychology*. New York: Appleton-Century-Crofts, 1950.

CARMICHAEL, L. Sir Charles Bell: A contribution to the history of physiological psychology. *Psychol. Rev.*, 1926, 33, 188–217.

CARPENTER, J. A. Species differences in taste preferences. *J. comp. physiol. Psychol.*, 1956, 49, 139–144.

COHEN, M. J., HAGIWARA, S., & ZOTTERMAN, Y. The response spectrum of taste fibers in the cat: A single fiber analysis. *Acta physiol. Scand.*, 1955, 33, 316–332.

GRANIT, R. *Receptors and sensory perception*. New Haven: Yale Univer. Press, 1955.

HENSEL, H., & ZOTTERMAN, Y. The response of mechano-receptors to thermal stimulation. *J. Physiol.*, 1951, 115, 16–24.

KIMURA, K., & BEIDLER, L. M. Microelectrode study of taste bud of the rat. *Amer. J. Physiol.*, 1956, 187, 610.

LILJESTRAND, G., & ZOTTERMAN, Y. The water taste in mammals. *Acta physiol., Scand.,* 1954, 32, 291–303.

MARUHASHI, J., MIZUGUCHI, K., & TASAKI, I. Action currents in single afferent nerve fibers elicited by stimulation of the skin of the toad and the cat. *J. Physiol.,* 1952, 117, 129–151.

NAFE, J. P. The pressure, pain and temperature sense. In C. Murchusion (Ed.), *Handbook of general experimental psychology.* Worcester: Clark Univer. Press, 1934. Chap. 20.

PFAFFMANN, C. Gustatory afferent impulses. *J. cell. comp. Physiol.,* 1941, 17, 243–258.

PFAFFMANN, C. Species differences in taste sensitivity. *Science,* 1953, 117, 470.

PFAFFMANN, C. Gustatory nerve impulses in rat, cat, and rabbit. *J. Neurophysiol.,* 1955, 18, 429–440.

STEVENS, S. S., & DAVIS, H. *Hearing.* New York: Wiley, 1938.

TASAKI, I. Nerve impulses in individual auditory nerve fibers of guinea pigs. *J. Neurophysiol.,* 1954, 17, 97–122.

WEDDELL, G. Somesthesis and the chemical senses. *Ann. Rev. Psychol.,* 1955, 6, 119–136.

WEVER, E. G. *Theory of hearing.* New York: Wiley, 1949.

WEVER, E. G., & BRAY, C. W. Action currents in the auditory nerve in response to acoustical stimulation. *Proc. Nat. Acad. Sci.,* 1930, 16, 344–350.

WILDER PENFIELD

8. The Interpretive Cortex

THERE is an area of the surface of the human brain where local electrical stimulation can call back a sequence of past experience. An epileptic irritation in this area may do the same. It is as though a wire recorder, or a strip of cinematographic film with sound track, had been set in motion within the brain. The sights and sounds, and the thoughts, of a former day pass through the man's mind again.

The purpose of this article is to describe, for readers from various disciplines of science, the area of the cerebral cortex from which this neuron record of the past can be activated and to suggest what normal contribution it may make to cerebral function.

The human brain is the master organ of the human race. It differs from the brains of other mammals particularly in the greater extent of its cerebral cortex. The gray matter, or cortex, that covers the two cerebral hemispheres of the brain of man is so vast in nerve cell population that it could never have been contained within the human skull if it were not folded upon itself, and refolded, so as to form a very large number of fissures and convolutions (FIG. 1). The fissures are so deep and so devious that by far the greater

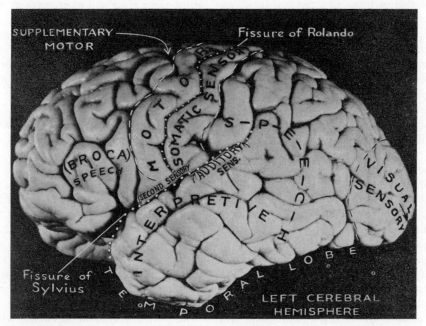

FIG. 1. Photograph of the left hemisphere of a human brain. The frontal lobe is on the left, the occipital lobe on the right. The major motor and sensory areas are indicated, as well as the speech areas and the interpretive area. [Penfield and Roberts (18)]

Reprinted by permission of the American Association for the Advancement of Science and the author from *Science*, 1959, vol. 129, pp. 1719–25.

portion of this ganglionic carpet (about 65 per cent) is hidden in them, below the surface (FIG. 2).

The portion that is labeled "interpretive" in FIGS. 1 and 3 covers a part of both temporal lobes. It is from these two homologous areas, and from nowhere else, that electrical stimulation has occasionally produced physical responses which may be divided into (i) experiential responses and (ii) interpretive responses.

Experiential Responses

OCCASIONALLY during the course of a neurosurgical operation under local anesthesia, gentle electrical stimulation in this temporal area, right or left, has caused the conscious patient to be aware of some previous experience (1). The experience seems to be picked out at random from his own past. But it comes back to him in great detail. He is suddenly aware again of those things to which he paid attention in that distant interval of time. This recollection of an experiential sequence stops suddenly when the electrical current is switched off or when the electrode is removed from contact with the cortex. This phenomenon we have chosen to call an experiential response to stimulation.

CASE EXAMPLES (2)

The patient S. Be. observed, when the electrode touched the temporal lobe (right superior temporal convolution), "There was a piano over there and someone playing. I could hear the song you know." When the cortex was stimulated again without warning, at approximately the same point, the patient had a different experience. He said: "Someone speaking to another, and he mentioned a name but I could not understand it . . . It was like a dream." Again the point was restimulated without his knowledge. He said quietly: "Yes, 'Oh Marie, Oh Marie'! Someone is singing it." When the point was stimulated a fourth time he heard the same song again and said it was the "theme song of a radio program."

The electrode was then applied to a point 4 centimeters farther forward on the first temporal convolution. While the electrode was still in place, S. Be. said: "Something brings back a memory. I can see Seven-Up Bottling Company—Harrison Bakery." He was evidently seeing two of Montreal's large illuminated advertisements.

The surgeon then warned him that he was about to apply the electrode again. Then, after a pause, the surgeon said "Now," but he did not stimulate. (The patient has no means of knowing when the electrode is applied, unless he is told, since the cortex itself is without sensation.) The patient replied promptly, "Nothing."

A woman (D.F.) (3) heard an orchestra playing an air while the electrode was held in place. The music stopped when the electrode was removed. It came again when the electrode was reapplied. On request, she hummed the tune, while the electrode was held in place, accompanying the orchestra. It was a popular song. Over and over again, restimulation at the same spot produced the same song. The music seemed always to begin at the same place and to progress at the normally expected tempo. All efforts to mislead her failed. She believed that a gramophone was being turned on in the operating room on each occasion, and she asserted her belief stoutly in a conversation some days after the operation.

A boy (R.W.) heard his mother talking to someone on the telephone when an electrode was applied to his right temporal cortex. When the stimulus was repeated without warning, he heard his mother again in the same conversation. When the stimulus was repeated after a lapse of time, he said, "My mother is telling my brother he has got his coat on backwards. I can just hear them."

The surgeon then asked the boy whether he remembered this happening. "Oh yes," he said, "just before I came here." Asked again whether this seemed like a dream, he replied: "No, it is like I go into a daze."

J.T. cried out in astonishment when the electrode was applied to the temporal cortex; "Yes doctor, yes doctor. Now I hear people laughing—my friends in South Africa!"

When asked about this, he explained the reason for his surprise. He seemed to be

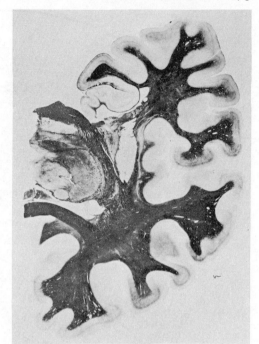

FIG. 2. At right is a photograph of a cross section of the left cerebral hemisphere [Jelgersma (19)]. The white matter is stained black and the gray matter is unstained. The major convolutions of the cerebral cortex and the subcortical masses of gray matter can be identified by reference to the diagram below. Below is a drawing of the cross section with additions. The surfaces and convolutions of the temporal lobe are identified, and the relationship of one hemisphere to the other and the relationship of the hemispheres to the brain stem and cerebellum are shown.

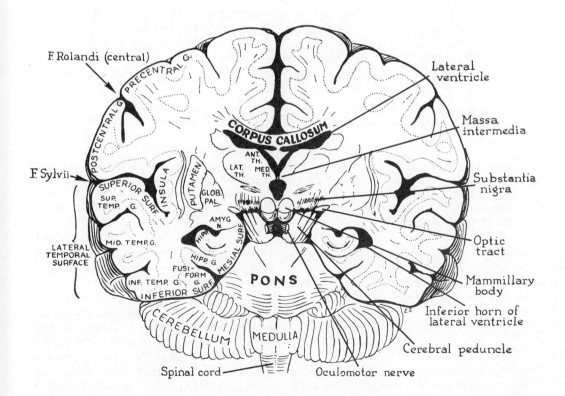

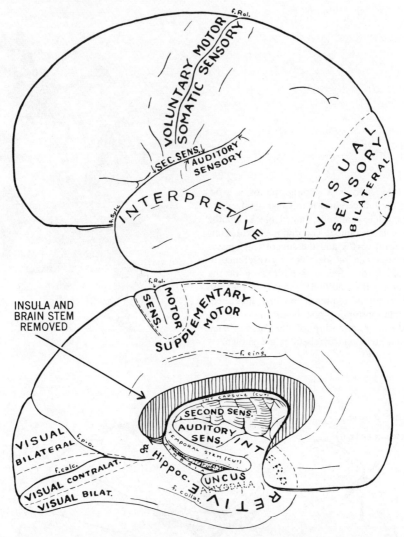

FIG. 3. The left cerebral hemisphere; the lateral surface is shown above and the mesial surface below. In the lower drawing the brain stem with the island of Reil has been removed to show the inner banks of the fissure of Sylvius and the superior surface of the temporal lobe. The interpretive cortex extends from the lateral to the superior surface of the temporal lobe. [Penfield and Roberts (18)]

laughing with his cousins, Bessie and Ann Wheliow, whom he had left behind him on a farm in South Africa, although he knew he was now on the operating table in Montreal.

Interpretive Responses

ON the other hand, similar stimulation in this same general area may produce quite a different response. The patient discovers, on stimulation, that he has somehow changed his own interpretation of what he is seeing at the moment, or hearing or thinking. For example, he may exclaim that his present experience seems familiar, as though he had seen it or heard it or thought it before. He realizes that this must be a false interpretation. Or, on the contrary, these things may seem suddenly strange, absurd. Sights or

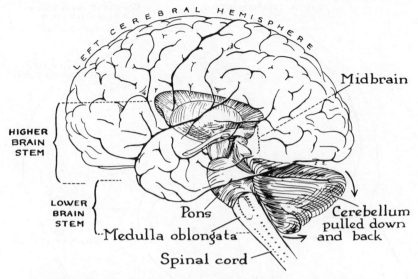

FIG. 4. Drawing of the left cerebral hemisphere, showing the higher brain stem, including the thalamus, within and the lower brain stem and spinal cord emerging below. The cerebellum is shown, attached to the lower brain stem. [Penfield and Roberts (18)]

sounds may seem distant and small, or they may come unexpectedly close and seem loud or large. He may feel suddenly afraid, as though his environment were threatening him, and he is possessed by a nameless dread or panic. Another patient may say he feels lonely or aloof, or as though he were observing himself at a distance.

Under normal circumstances anyone may make such interpretations of the present, and these interpretations serve him as guides to action or reaction. If the interpretations are accurate guides, they must be based upon previous comparable experience. It is conceivable, therefore, that the recall mechanism which is activated by the electrode during an experiental response and the mechanism activated in an interpretive response may be parts of a common inclusive mechanism of reflex recognition or interpretation.

No special function had been previously assigned by neurologists to the area in each temporal lobe that is marked "interpretive" in FIGs. 1 and 3, though some clinicians have suggested it might have to do with the recall of music. The term *interpretive cortex,* therefore, is no more than slang to be employed for the purposes of discussion. The terms *motor cortex, sensory cortex,* and *speech cortex* began as slang phrases and have served such a purpose. But such phrases must not be understood to signify independence of action of separated units in the case of any of these areas. Localization of function in the cerebral cortex means no more than specialization of function as compared with other cortical regions, not separation from the integrated action of the brain.

Before considering the interpretive cortex further, we may turn briefly to the motor and sensory areas and the speech areas of the cortex. After considering the effects of electrical stimulation there, we should be better able to understand the results of stimulation in the temporal lobes.

Specialization of Function in the Cortex

EVIDENCE for some degree of localization within the brain was recognized early in the 19th century by Flourens. He concluded from experiment that functional subdivision of "the organ of the mind" was possible. The forebrain (4), he said [cerebral hemispheres and higher brain stem (FIG. 4)] had to do with

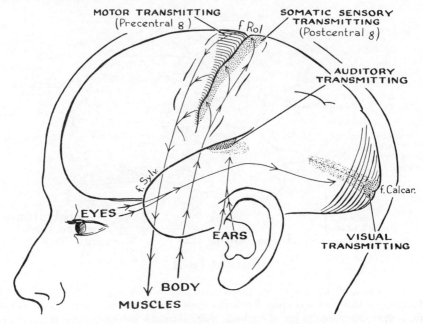

FIG. 5. Sensory and motor projection areas. The sensory areas are stippled, and the afferent pathways to them from eyes, ears, and body are indicated by entering arrows. The motor cortex is indicated by parallel lines, and the efferent corticospinal tract is indicated by emerging arrows. [Penfield and Roberts (18)]

thought and will power, while the cerebellum was involved in the coordination of movement.

In 1861, Paul Broca showed that a man with a relatively small area of destruction in a certain part of the left hemisphere alone might lose only the power of speech. It was soon realized that this was the speech area of man's dominant (left) hemisphere. In 1870, Fritsch and Hitzig applied an electric current to the exposed cortex of one hemisphere of a lightly anesthetized dog and caused the legs of the opposite side to move. Thus, an area of cortex called motor was discovered.

After that, localization of function became a research target for many clinicians and experimentalists. It was soon evident that in the case of man, the precentral gyrus (FIG. 5) in each hemisphere was related to voluntary control of the contralateral limbs and that there was an analogous area of motor cortex in the frontal lobes of animals. It appeared also that other separate areas of cortex (FIGS. 1 and 5) in each hemisphere were dedicated

to sensation (one for visual sensation, others for auditory, olfactory, and discriminative somatic sensation, respectively).

It was demonstrated, too, that from the "motor cortex" there was an efferent bundle of nerve fibers (the pyramidal tract) that ran down through the lower brain stem and the spinal cord to be relayed on out to the muscles. Through this efferent pathway, voluntary control of these muscles was actually carried out. It was evident, too, that there were separate sensory tracts carrying nerve impulses in the other direction, from the principal organs of special sense (eye, ear, nose, and skin and muscle) into separate sensory areas of the cortex.

These areas, motor and sensory, have been called "projection areas." They play a role in the projection of nerve currents to the cortex from the periphery of the body, and from the cortex to the periphery. This makes possible (sensory) awareness of environment and provides the individual with a means of outward (motor) expression. The motor cortex has a specialized use during voluntary action, and each of the several sensory areas has a specialized use, when the individual is seeing, hearing, smelling, or feeling.

Traveling Potentials

THE action of the living brain depends upon the movement, within it, of "transient electrical potentials traveling the fibers of the nervous system." This was Sherrington's phrase. Within the vast circuits of this master organ, potentials travel, here and there and yonder, like meteors that streak across the sky at night and line the firmament with trails of light. When the meteors pass, the paths of luminescence still glow a little while, then fade and are gone. The changing patterns of these paths of passing energy make possible the changing content of the mind. The patterns are never quite the same, and so it is with the content of the mind.

Specialized areas in the cortex are at times active and again relatively quiet. But, when a man is awake, there is always some central integration and coordination of the traveling potentials. There must be activity within the brain stem and some areas of the cortex. This is centrencephalic integration (5).

Sensory, Motor, and Psychical Responses to Cortical Stimulation

MY purpose in writing this article is to discuss in simple words (free of technical terms) the meaning of the "psychical" responses which appear only on stimulation of the so-called interpretive cortex. But before considering these responses let us consider the motor and sensory activity of the cortex for a moment.

When the streams of electrical potentials that pass normally through the various areas of sensory cortex are examined electrically, they do not seem to differ from each other except in pattern and timing. The essential difference is to be found in the fact that the visual stream passes to the visual cortex and then to one subcortical target and the auditory stream passes through the auditory cortex and then on to another subcortical target.

When the surgeon stimulates the intact

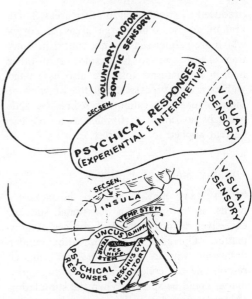

FIG. 6. The left cerebral hemisphere is shown with the temporal lobe cut across and turned down. The areas of cortex from which psychical responses have been elicited are indicated. [Penfield (1)]

sensory cortex he must be sending a current along the next "piece of road" to a subcortical destination. This electrode (delivering, for example, 60 "waves" per second of 2-millisecond duration and 1-volt intensity) produces no more than elementary sight when applied to visual cortex. The patient reports colors, lights, and shadows that move and take on crude outlines. The same electrode, applied to auditory cortex, causes him to hear a ringing or hissing or thumping sound. When applied to postcentral gyrus it produces tingling or a false sense of movement.

Thus, sensation is produced by the passage inward of electrical potentials. And when the electrode is applied to the motor cortex, movement is produced by passage of potentials outward to the muscles. In each case positive response is produced by conduction in the direction of normal physiological flow —that is, by dromic conduction (6).

Responses to electrical stimulation that may may be called "psychical," as distinguished from sensory or motor, have been elicited from certain areas of the human cortex (FIG. 6). But they have never been produced by stimulation in other areas. There are, of course, other large areas of cortex which are neither sensory nor motor in function. They seem to be employed in other neuron mechanisms that are also associated with psychical processes. But the function of these other areas cannot, it seems, be activated by so simple a stimulus as an electric current applied to the cortex.

Dreamy States of Epilepsy

"EPILEPSY" may be defined, in Jackson's words, as "the name for occasional, sudden, excessive, rapid and local discharges of grey matter." Our aim in the operations under discussion was to remove the gray matter responsible for epileptic attacks if that gray matter could be spared. When the stimulating electrode reproduced the psychical phenomenon that initiated the fit, it provided the guidance sought (7).

During the 19th century clinicians had recognized these phenomena as epileptic. They applied the term *intellectual aura* to such attacks. Jackson substituted the expression *dreamy states* (see 8). These were, he said, "psychical states during the onset of certain epileptic seizures, states which are much more elaborate than crude sensations." And again, he wrote, "These are all voluminous mental states and yet of different kinds; no doubt they ought to be classified, but for my present purpose they may be considered together."

"The state," he said, "is often like that occasionally experienced by healthy people as a feeling of 'reminiscence.' " Or the patient has "dreamy feelings," "dreams mixing up with present thoughts," "double consciousness," a "feeling of being somewhere else," a feeling "as if I went back to all that occurred in my childhood," "silly thoughts."

Jackson never did classify these states, but he did something more important. He localized the area of cortex from which epileptic discharge would produce dreamy states. His localization was in the anterior and deep portions of the temporal lobes, the same area that is labeled "interpretative" cortex in FIG. 3.

CASE EXAMPLE

Brief reference may be made to a specific case. The patient had seizures, and stimulation produced responses which were first recognized as psychical.

In 1936, a girl of 16 (J.V.) was admitted to the Montreal Neurological Institute complaining of epileptic attacks, each of which was ushered in by the same hallucination. It was a little dream, she said, in which an experience from early childhood was re-enacted, always the same train of events. She would then cry out with fear and run to her mother. Occasionally this was followed immediately by a major convulsive seizure.

At operation, under local anesthesia, we tried to set off the dream by a gentle electrical stimulus in the right temporal lobe. The attempt was successful. The dream was produced by the electrode. Stimulation at other points on the temporal cortex produced sudden fear without the dream. At still other points, stimulation caused her to say that she saw "someone coming toward me." At another point, stimulation caused her to say she heard the voices of her mother and her brothers (9).

This suggested a new order of cortical response to electrical stimulation. When the neighboring visual sensory area of the cortex is stimulated, any patient may report seeing stars of light or moving colors or black outlines but never "someone coming toward me." Stimulation of the auditory sensory cortex may cause any patient to report that he hears ringing, buzzing, blowing, or thumping sounds, perhaps, but never voices that speak. Stimulation in the areas of sensory cortex can call forth nothing more than the elements of visual or auditory or tactile sensation, never happenings that might have been previously experienced.

During the 23 years that have followed, although practically all areas of the cerebral cortex have been stimulated and studied in more than 1000 craniotomies, performed under local anesthesia, psychical responses of the experiential or interpretive variety have been produced only from the temporal cortex in the general areas that are marked "psychical responses" in FIG. 3 (10, 11).

Classification

IT seems reasonable to subdivide psychical responses and psychical seizures (epileptic dreamy states) in the same way, classifying them as "interpretive" or "experiential." Interpretive psychical responses are those involving interpretations of the present experience, or emotions related to it; experiential psychical responses are reenactments of past experiences. Interpretive seizures are those accompanied by auras and illusions; experiential seizures are those accompanied by auras and hallucinations.

The interpretive responses and seizures may be divided into groups (11) of which the commonest are as follows: (i) recognition, the illusion that things seen and heard and thought are familiar (*déjà vu* phenomenon); (ii) visual illusion, the illusion that things seen are changing—for example, coming nearer, growing larger (macropsia); (iii) auditory illusion, the illusion that things heard are changing—for example, coming near, going away, changing tempo; (iv) illusional emotion, the emotion of fear or, less often, loneliness, sorrow, or disgust.

Experiential phenomena (hallucinations) are an awareness of experiences from the past that come into the mind without complete loss of awareness of the present.

Discussion

WHAT, then, is the function of the interpretive cortex? This is a physiological question that follows the foregoing observations naturally.

An electrode, delivering, for example, 60 electrical pulses per second to the surface of the motor cortex, causes a man to make crude movements. When applied to the various sensory areas of the cortex, it causes him to have crude sensations of sight or sound or body feeling. This indicates only that these areas have something to do with the complicated mechanism of voluntary action or conscious sensation. It does not reveal what contribution the cortex may make, or in what way it may contribute to skill in making voluntary movement or qualify the incoming sensory streams.

In the case of the interpretive cortex, the observations are similar. We may say that the interpretive cortex has something to do with a mechanism that can reactivate the vivid record of the past. It has also something to do with a mechanism that can present to consciousness a reflex interpretation of the present. To conclude that here is the mechanism of memory would be an unjustified assumption. It would be too simple.

What a man remembers when he makes a voluntary effort is apt to be a generalization. If this were not so, he might be hopelessly lost in detail. On the other hand, the experiential responses described above are detailed reenactments of a single experience. Such experiences soon slip beyond the range of voluntary recall. A man may summon to mind a song at will. He hears it then in his mind, not all at once but advancing phrase by phrase. He may sing it or play it too, and one would call this memory.

But if a patient hears music in response to the electrode, he hears it in one particular strip of time. That time runs forward again at the original tempo, and he hears the orchestration, or he sees the player at a piano "over there." These are details he would have thought forgotten.

A vast amount of work remains to be done before the mechanism of memory, and how and where the recording takes place, are understood. This record is not laid down in the interpretive cortex, but it is kept in a part of the brain that is intimately connected with it.

Removal of large areas of interpretive cortex, even when carried out on both sides, may result in mild complaints of memory defect, but it does not abolish the capacity to remember recent events. On the other hand, surgical removals that result in bilateral interference with the underlying hippocampal zone do make the recording of recent events impossible, while distant memory is still preserved (12, 13).

The importance of the hippocampal area for memory was pointed out long ago in a forgotten publication by the Russian neurologist Bechterew (14). The year before publication Bechterew had demonstrated the case before the St. Petersburg Clinic for Nervous and Mental Diseases. The man on whom Bechterew reported had "extraordinary weakness of memory, falsifications of memory and great apathy." These defects were shown at autopsy to be secondary to lesions of the mesial surface of the cortex of both temporal lobes. The English neurologists Glees and Griffith (15) reported similar defects, a half century later, in a patient who had symmetrical lesions of the hippocampus and of hippocampal and fusiform gyri on both sides.

The way in which the interpretive cortex seems to be used may be suggested by an example: After years of absence you meet, by chance, a man whose very existence you had forgotten. On seeing him, you may be struck by a sudden sense of familiarity, even before you have time to "think." A signal seems to flash up in consciousness to tell you that you've seen that man before. You watch him as he smiles and moves and speaks. The sense of familiarity grows stronger. Then you remember him. You may even recall that his name was Jones. The sight and the sound of the man has given you an instant access, through some reflex, to the records of the past in which this man has played some part. The opening of this forgotten file was subconscious. It was not a voluntary act. You would have known him even against your will. Although Jones was a forgotten man a moment before, now you can summon the record in such detail that you remark at once the slowness of his gait or a new line about the mouth.

If Jones had been a source of danger to you, you might have felt fear as well as familiarity before you had time to consider the man. Thus, the signal of fear as well as the signal of familiarity may come to one as the result of subconscious comparison of present with similar past experience.

One more example may be given from common experience. A sudden increase in the size of objects seen and in sounds heard may mean the rapid approach of something that calls for instant avoidance action. These are signals that, because of previous experience, we sometimes act upon with little consideration.

Summary

THE interpretive cortex has in it a mechanism for instant reactivation of the detailed record of the past. It has a mechanism also for the production of interpretive signals. Such signals could only be significant if past records are scanned and relevant experiences are selected for comparison with present experience. This is a subconscious process. But it may well be that this scanning of past experience and selection from it also renders the relevant past available for conscious consideration as well. Thus, the individual may refer to the record as he employs other circuits of the brain.

Access to the record of the past seems to be as readily available from the temporal cortex of one side as from that of the other. Auditory illusions (or interpretations of the distance, loudness, or tempo of sounds) have been produced by stimulation of the temporal cortex of either side. The same is true of illusional emotions, such as fear and disgust.

But, on the contrary, visual illusions (interpretations of the distance, dimension, erectness, and tempo of things seen) are only produced by stimulation of the temporal cortex on the nondominant (normally, right) side of the brain. Illusions of recognition, such as familiarity or strangeness, were also elicited only from the nondominant side, except in one case.

Conclusion

"CONSCIOUSNESS," to quote William James (16), "is never quite the same in successive moments of time. It is a stream forever flowing, forever changing." The stream of changing states of mind that James described so well does flow through each man's waking hours until the time when he falls asleep to wake no more. But the stream, unlike a river, leaves a record in the living brain.

Transient electrical potentials move with it

through the circuits of the nervous system, leaving a path that can be followed again. The pattern of this pathway, from neuron to neuron along each nerve-cell body and fiber and junction, is the recorded pattern of each man's past. That complicated record is held there in temporal sequence through the principle of durable facilitation of conduction and connection.

A steady stream of electrical pulses applied through an electrode to some point in the interpretive cortex causes a stream of excitation to flow from the cortex to the place where past experience is recorded. This stream of excitation acts as a key to the past. It can enter the pathway of recorded consciousness at any random point, from childhood on through adult life. But having entered, the experience moves forward without interference from other experiences. And when the electrode is withdrawn there is a likelihood, which lasts for seconds or minutes, that the stream of excitation will enter the pathway again at the same moment of past time, even if the electrode is reapplied at neighboring points (17).

Finally, an electric current applied to the surface of what may be called the interpretive cortex of a conscious man (i) may cause the stream of former consciousness to flow again or (ii) may give him an interpretation of the present that is unexpected and involuntary. Therefore, it is concluded that, under normal circumstances, this area of cortex must make some functional contribution to reflex comparison of the present with related past experience. It contributes to reflex interpretation or perception of the present.

The combination and comparison of present experience with similar past experience must call for remarkable scanning of the past and classification of similarities. What contribution this area of the temporal cortex may make to the whole process is not clear. The term *interpretive cortex* will serve for identification until students of human physiology can shed more light on these fascinating findings.

REFERENCES AND NOTES

1. W. PENFIELD, *J. Mental Sci.* 101, 451 (1955).
2. These patients, designated by the same initials, have been described in previous publications in much greater detail. An index of patients (designated by initials) may be found in any of my books.
3. This case is reported in detail in W. Penfield and H. Jasper, *Epilepsy and the Functional Anatomy of the Human Brain* (Little, Brown, Boston, 1954) [published in abridged form in Russian (translation by N. P. Graschenkov and G. Smirnov) by the Soviet Academy of Sciences, 1958].
4. The forebrain, or prosencephalon, properly includes the diencephalon and the telencephalon, or higher brain stem, and hemispheres. Flourens probably had cerebral hemispheres in mind as distinguished from cerebellum.
5. "Within the brain, a central transactional core has been identified between the strictly sensory or motor systems of classical neurology. This central reticular mechanism has been found capable of grading the activity of most other parts of the brain"—H. Magoun, *The Waking Brain* (Thomas, Springfield, Ill., 1958).
6. W. PENFIELD, *The Excitable Cortex in Conscious Man* (Thomas, Springfield, Ill., 1958).
7. It did more than this; it produced illusions or hallucinations that had never been experienced by the patient during a seizure.
8. J. TAYLOR, Ed., *Selected Writings of John Hughlings Jackson* (Hodder and Stoughton, London, 1931), vol. 1, *On Epilepsy and Epileptiform Convulsions*.
9. Twenty-one years later this young woman, who is the daughter of a physician, was present at a meeting of the National Academy of Sciences in New York while her case was discussed. She could still recall the operation and the nature of the "dreams" that had preceded her seizures [W. Penfield, *Proc. Natl. Acad. Sci. U.S.* 44, 51 (1958)].
10. In a recent review of the series my associate, Dr. Phanor Perot, has found and summarized 35 out of 384 temporal lobe cases in which stimulation produced experiential responses. All such responses were elicited in the temporal cortex. In a study of 214 consecutive operations for temporal lobe epilepsy, my associate Sean Mullan found

70 cases in which interpretive illusion occurred in the minor seizures before operation, or in which an interpretive response was produced by stimulation during operation. In most cases it occurred both before and during operation.

11. S. MULLAN and W. PENFIELD, *A.M.A. Arch. Neurol. Psychiat.* 81, 269 (1959).

12. This area is marked "Hipp" and "Hipp. G" in FIG. 2 (bottom) and "g. Hippoc." and "amygdala" in FIG. 3.

13. W. PENFIELD and B. MILNER, *A.M.A. Arch. Neurol. Psychiat.* 79, 475 (1958).

14. W. V. BECHTEREW, "Demonstration eines Gehirns mit Zerstörung der vorderen und inneren Theile der Hirnrinde beider Schläfenlappen," *Neurol. Zentralbl. Leipzig* 19, 990 (1900). My attention was called to this case recently by Dr. Peter Gloor of Montreal.

15. P. GLEES and H. B. GRIFFITH, *Monatsschr. Psychiat. Neurol.* 123, 193 (1952).

16. W. JAMES, *The Principles of Psychology* (Holt, New York, 1910).

17. Thus, it is apparent that the beam of excitation that emanates from the interpretive cortex and seems to scan the record of the past is subject to the principles of transient facilitation already demonstrated for the anthropoid motor cortex [A. S. F. Grünbaum and C. Sherrington, *Proc. Roy. Soc.* (London) 72B, 152 (1901); T. Graham Brown and C. S. Sherrington, *ibid.* 85B, 250 (1912)]. Similarly subject to the principles of facilitation are the motor and the sensory cortex of man [W. Penfield and K. Welch, *J. Physiol.* (London) 109, 358 (1949)]. The patient D.F. heard the same orchestra playing the same music in the operating room more than 20 times when the electrode was reapplied to the superior surface of the temporal lobe. Each time the music began in the verse of a popular song. It proceeded to the chorus, if the electrode was kept in place.

18. W. PENFIELD and L. ROBERTS, *Speech and Brain Mechanisms* (Princeton Univ. Press, Princeton, N.J., 1959).

19. G. JELGERSMA, *Atlas anatomicum cerebri humani* (Scheltema and Holkema, Amsterdam).

NATHANIEL KLEITMAN

9. Sleep

WHY sleep? Must we waste one third of our life in sleep? What makes us sleep? Will a pill some day enable us to do without it? Such questions evidence a fundamental misconception of the nature of the alternation of sleep and wakefulness that characterizes our existence. They put the emphasis in the wrong place, for it is doubtful that we shall ever find a specific physiological mechanism that puts us to sleep; much more to the point is to find out what it is that keeps us awake.

If we turn the usual question around and ask, "Why wake up?" anyone can give a ready, and essentially correct, answer: to go to school or to work, to eat or drink, to take care of one's natural wants—in short, to do the many things that even kings and millionaires must do for themselves. But it is not the whole answer. In modern civilized society these necessary chores do not take more than seven or eight hours per day, and yet we remain awake twice that long —to play, read, attend shows, listen to the radio or watch television, visit with family and friends, contemplate the wonders of nature, meditate and ask questions.

This supplementary wakefulness of choice is the result of anatomical development and physiological maturation of the highest organ of our nervous system—the cerebral cortex. A newborn infant—for practical purposes an animal without a cortex—remains awake only for short periods, adding up altogether to about eight hours out of each 24. But the influences to which it is subjected—largely social—soon condition it to a daily rhythm which Arnold Gesell, the famed investigator of child development, has called accultura-

tion. The baby tends to consolidate the short periods of sleep into one continuous sleep phase during the quiet night hours (but with all too frequent departures, alas, from this ideal!). Daytime sleep is reduced to two naps after a few months and to one afternoon nap by the end of the first year. The nap is usually given up at kindergarten age or a little later. The wakefulness phase is gradually lengthened, and by the time one becomes an adult, he spends twice as much time awake as asleep, instead of the other way around.

We can see the connection between the cerebral cortex and sleep in a laboratory animal such as the dog, which has a sleep-wakefulness pattern similar to our own. When an adult dog is surgically deprived of its cerebral cortex, it reverts to its puppyhood state. It loses its regular daily pattern of sleep and awakens only from time to time when it is hungry. Almost immediately after it is fed, it stops activity and soon falls asleep. A decorticated dog is blind to specific objects, has forgotten everything it knew and is practically unable to learn or profit from experience. Except while it is being fed (the food must be put into its mouth), its emotional expressions are those of displeasure.

In nature's own laboratory human infants occasionally are born without a cerebral cortex and survive for a year or two. Like decorticated dogs, such infants awake from time to time and they can nurse, but they do not develop a diurnal sleep-wakefulness pattern. They fail to learn to recognize those who take care of them, and their emotional expressions resemble those of decorticated dogs.

Thus it is clear that the cerebral cortex is needed for wakefulness of choice and for adaptation of the sleep-wakefulness pattern to the cycle of night and day. On the other hand, the primitive, unlearned wakefulness of necessity depends on lower parts of the nervous system. If we remove an animal's entire cerebrum, we get a "preparation" which never wakes up. The animal, however, cannot be said to be asleep, for sleep as we know it is a *temporary* suspension of the waking state and clearly involves reversibility, or the capacity to be awakened. A decerebrated cat or dog can never be roused, though it may be kept alive for several days by keeping it warm and ministering to other needs. Again, an injury to the hypothalamus (a region in the brain stem), whether by disease or artificial destruction, produces "sleeping sickness"— another case of permanent inability to maintain the waking state.

What is the physiological mechanism for waking up—the "alarm clock" of the organism? Certainly it does not lie in the cerebral cortex alone. The Belgian neurophysiologist Frédéric Bremer showed this by investigating the activity of "decatted" brains (instead of debrained cats). He found that brain waves (electroencephalograms) from a cat's cerebral cortex showed patterns characteristic both of sleep and of wakefulness as long as the cortex was connected with the subcortical regions of the nervous system, but when these connections were cut, the only pattern from the cortex was that of sleep.

The inescapable conclusion is that sustained wakefulness of any kind is impossible without the active participation of a subcortical center. This "wakefulness center" not only radiates impulses upward to the cerebral cortex and downward to the rest of the central nervous system but is itself capable of being aroused and kept active by excitations from either or both of those directions. Conduction of nerve impulses is not one-way but recurrent over feed-back circuits. Sleep is a peaceful resting state, although the body's "household activities," such as circulation, respiration, digestion, metabolism, excretion and so on, go on unabated. When a stimulus is strong enough to irritate the wakefulness center, it disrupts the vegetative state of the organism and ushers in animalistic activities required to cope with the situation. In the absence of a cerebral cortex this primitive wakefulness of necessity is sustained only long enough to satisfy the internal needs or remove the external annoyances. As already mentioned, in a young animal or infant the interruption of sleep leads to expressions of displeasure. The peaceful state has been disturbed and must be restored as promptly as possible.

The cerebral cortex can prolong the waking state, but not beyond certain limits. Sixteen hours of wakefulness in 24 is probably near the physiological limit of tolerance over the long run for most of us. But the proportion, not the duration, of sleeping time is what counts. Our pattern of 16 hours of wakefulness followed by eight hours of sleep is dictated by the earth's 24-hour period of rotation rather than by physiological needs; a person can adjust himself to a routine of staying up 18 hours and sleeping nine, or being awake 12 hours and sleeping six.

Many sleep theorists, it seems, disregard this obvious explanation of our sleep pattern. They figure that we must sleep eight hours because it takes that long to restore some depleted substance in the body or to get rid of some accumulated poison. If this body-chemistry theory were correct, we should expect people to be most alert and efficient on waking up in the morning, but in fact their scores on mental and physical tests are no higher, and sometimes even slightly lower, in the morning than just before going to bed. This does not mean that no benefits accrue from sleep, as one can quickly discover by going without sleep for any length of time.

Experimental sleep deprivation has been a favorite method of attacking the sleep problem. When an individual is kept awake for 60 to 90 hours—four to six times the usual daily span of wakefulness—the most prominent effect is extreme muscular fatigue and lassitude. The subject of the experiment wants nothing more than to lie down and close his eyes. Yet that is exactly what the watcher must not permit him to do. Keeping a person awake involves making him move about, keep his eyes open and use some of his muscles at all times, even if no more than to talk or sing. As soon as he relaxes his muscles, he promptly falls asleep. Among the effects of prolonged wakefulness are irritability and mental disorganization, leading to daydreaming and automatic behavior, occasionally bordering on temporary insanity.

One striking aspect of the effects is that they fluctuate in a daily cycle; the subject reaches his lowest ebb during the early hours of the morning, roughly from 2 to 6 a.m. Quite by accident we discovered that the daily ups and downs in the ability to remain awake ran parallel to fluctuations in the body temperature.

Temperature affects life processes in many ways. Most protoplasmic activities, being chemical in nature, are speeded up by a rise in temperature and slowed down by its fall. Our bodies have a thermostatic mechanism which keeps the internal temperature fairly constant, but it can and does fluctuate normally within a range of one or two degrees; the neat and precise marking of 98.6 degrees Fahrenheit as the "normal" temperature on the ordinary clinical thermometer is rather meaningless. Our temperature regularly goes up and down each day on a fairly smooth, wave-like curve, with a peak or plateau in the middle of the waking period and a minimum at night during sleep. This diurnal temperature variation is not present at birth. It is acquired by each of us in the process of acculturation during the first year of life and thereafter is reinforced by our daily cycle of activities.

Our body temperature is about the same just before we go to bed at night as when we rise in the morning, which explains why there is no difference in efficiency of performance. During prolonged deprivation of sleep, a subject's alertness in each 24 hours waxes and wanes with the rise and fall of the temperature curve, his greatest sleepiness coinciding with the temperature trough in the wee morning hours.

To use a crude analogy, water in its liquid state may be likened to wakefulness, and, when frozen, to sleep. These two states of water can be distinguished from each other by direct inspection, as can frank sleep from wakefulness. But by feeling the water or ice with the hand, or, still better, by using a thermometer to determine its temperature, one can detect considerable gradations of cold in ice and of warmth in water. The freezing point and thawing point are identical and correspond to the drowsiness level of body temperature. The greater the agitation of the molecules, the higher the temperature of the water, which now represents increasing alertness with a rise of body temperature. The boiling of water at a certain temperature may be compared to the hyperactivity of a maniac. Quite a number of everyday expressions pertaining to human behavior are couched in temperature terms: cold reception, warm greeting, feverish activity, boiling mad and so on.

Indeed, the temperamental make-up of the individual (note that temperature and temperament have a common etymological derivation) seems to influence his ability to adjust himself to the community pattern of living. The social anthropologist W. H. Sheldon, who has exhaustively studied the relation of temperament to physical constitution, reported that the athletic, or "somatotonic," type is a "voluntary early riser." "Somatotonics feel good in the morning. They love to jump out of bed, take a shower, make a lot of noise and greet the sun." Sheldon also found that for "cerebrotonics," or thin people, "the process of getting up in the morning is often an extremely painful business." They "often become most alert and do their best work in the evening of the day. They are usually wide awake at bedtime, and they are often worthless in the early part of the morning."

Without passing on the validity of Sheldon's classification of temperaments, we can say that what distinguishes these two extremes of personality is the degree of ability or willingness to conform to the social pattern of living, which is, simply stated: first work, then leisure. By convention the usual hours of work are roughly between 9 a.m. and 5 p.m. and the evening hours are free. Thus the time of arising in the morning is in most cases community-fixed, whereas retiring for the night is a matter of personal choice. Going to bed early permits one to get enough rest —hence the dictum "early to bed, early to rise, etc." Late to bed and late to rise would be just as satisfactory physiologically, but is harder to manage in practice. The conformists who adjust themselves most easily to the group routine are the early birds who *spontaneously* wake up rather early in the morning and get sleepy at a fixed early hour in the evening. These individuals do their best creative work in the morning, and they characteristically reach their body temperature peak shortly before or after noon. The "night owls"—Sheldon's cerebrotonics—seldom get enough sleep and depend upon alarm clocks or other artificial promptings to wake them in the morning. They do not reach their temperature maximum until late in the afternoon or evening, and that is the part of their waking period when they are most alert. Night-owl types sometimes deliberately choose occupations that involve night work and permit them to sleep late in the morning. Naturally there are many gradations between these extreme types. The majority of the population apparently approaches the up-bright-and-early conformist type.

Can one, by changing his routine of living, switch from a morning to an evening alertness? Yes, under duress, but usually the shift is temporary. An evening-type housewife may conform as long as her children are little and have to be seen off to school early in the morning, but after her children are grown she will revert to the evening type. Of course it is relatively easy to shift the peak of body temperature and alertness to conform with a change in sunrise. Ship travelers crossing the Atlantic eastward find themselves getting up later and going to bed later from day to day as they pass to new time zones. When a traveler crosses the Atlantic by plane overnight, adjustment to the sudden five-hour shift in time is harder, but it takes only a day or two for his diurnal body-temperature curve to swing to the new time schedule.

What is the mechanism by which this rhythm is established and maintained? It cannot lie solely in the nervous system, for the fluctuations of body temperature are far too small to influence markedly the rate at which the nervous system performs. The fluctuations arise mainly from variations in muscular activity. The body muscles and the cerebral cortex act as a mutual feed-back circuit, for the muscles are not only doers but feelers. Muscle sense, truly a sixth sense, signals to the brain information about the position and activity of the body. Messages concerning the tonus of the muscles, which are under tension even when they merely maintain the body's posture, heighten the brain's level of activity and lead to a greater discharge from the cortex to the muscles. This in turn stimulates the muscles further. As muscle tonus rises, so does body temperature. Sooner or later, however, muscular fatigue stops this *crescendo*. The muscles begin to relax, and the cycle turns downward, bringing a *diminuendo* in cortical activity, alertness and body temperature. In fact, at any time of the day muscular relaxation, intentional or accidental, will cause a fall in body temperature and make it hard to stay awake.

In going to bed at night we lie down on a soft couch to relax our muscles, but this does not necessarily shut off stimulation. Any sort of emotional excitement, worry, anxiety or just thinking serves to keep the muscles tense. Under these conditions "trying" to go to sleep only makes matters worse. To fall asleep we must relax the muscles by laying aside disturbing thoughts. For this there are many familiar and tested devices: taking a hot bath, prolonged grooming (by women), reading indifferent material, reciting familiar prayers, counting imaginary sheep and (for children) the reassurance of being tucked in and kissed goodnight by a kindly parent or nurse.

What makes the conformist wake up every morning at precisely the same time and become sleepy at his customary bedtime? To put it another way: What regulates his diurnal rhythm of muscle tonus? It is tempting to suspect the pituitary gland, which is conveniently located close to the hypothalamus and is known to control several other daily rhythms in vertebrates. For example, the University of Wyoming zoologists H. Rahn and F. Rosendale found that removal of this gland from the *Anolis* lizard, which is usually bright green at night and dark brown in the daytime, makes the animal permanently green. The pituitary, often called the master gland of the body, influences the activity of nearly all the other endocrine glands, among them the adrenal cortex. There is some evidence of a diurnal variation in the functioning of the adrenal cortex. Our rhythm of wakefulness and sleep is started by conditioning of the nervous system, but it may end up as an endocrine rhythm, which both fortifies and is fortified by the nervous rhythm.

It is interesting to note that the seasonal disappearance of the cycle of darkness and light in the Arctic has little or no effect upon this rhythm. In civilized communities of northern Norway, where for weeks the sun does not set in summer nor rise in winter, the sleep-wakefulness pattern of the population remains unchanged. The only variation is that people tend to go to bed an hour later in summer than in winter and manage to get through the day on an hour's less sleep.

The round-the-clock needs of society of course require that many people follow an unconventional routine, working in the hours when most of us sleep. The number of night workers is not small: it includes myriads of people in transportation, communications, police and fire protection, hospitals, public utilities, industry and the military services. Some individuals prefer to work at night, but for most people this separation from the community pattern of living is unacceptable as a regular thing. As a result, it has become common practice to rotate workers between day and night shifts. Such a scheme will work well, however, only if a worker changes shifts no oftener than every four or six weeks, as it sometimes takes a week or so to swing into a new diurnal rhythm. It is essential to give him time to adjust to the new routine, for not only will he be more alert on the job, but the reversal of his body temperature rhythm will make it easier for him to sleep during the daytime.

PATRICK L. MC GEER

10. Mind, Drugs, and Behavior

THE manner in which the brain gives rise to phenomena associated with the mind is a problem which has fascinated scientists down through the ages. This mind-brain conundrum presents different aspects to different people. Most would now agree that the brain is the substrate organ of the mind, and that all of the functions associated with the mind must, in some way, be mediated through the several billion nerve cells of the brain. The evidence in favor of this point of view is too overwhelming to merit discussion. But, from this fundament, opinions diverge sharply. The physiologically oriented hold that when the brain is better understood most functions associated with the mind will be easily explained in terms of an operating electrochemical machine; the philosophically oriented hold that such a point of view is untenable inasmuch as mind is abstract whereas brain is physical. To most philosophers, even the most detailed understanding of the electrophysiological events of the brain would not permit insight into the mind: mind is of a different, non-physical construct, and physiological measurements of any kind are inappropriate in establishing relationships between brain and mind. This philosophic point of view was well expressed in 1951 by Lord Samuel:

Watch a chess player cogitating for half an hour whether to move his queen here or his pawn there; at last, stretching out his hand and doing the one or the other. The physiologist may describe the nervous and muscular mechanism which operates the movement, but not the process which has decided the choice. The chess player is evidently of a different order from the chessboard and pieces; in him there is activity going on which is not material; in them there is not. Intellectual creativity, the power of choice, are of a different order from chemical and electrical reactions (1).

It was the briefest time after this was written that computing machines were programmed to play a tolerable game of chess. Moreover, such machines were being taught to play checkers so that they improved with practice. They learned not to repeat errors and eventually were able to beat their human opponent. Newell has recently shown that computers can be programmed to solve problems in a manner similar to that used by students (2).

To press the obvious analogy between the programming of the mind as a human learns to play chess or checkers, and the programming of a computing machine, would be unjustified. One essential difference is that the human is motivated—he wants to play the game, and, usually, he wants to win. His drive comes from within. Computers to date have not been equipped with drives. They endlessly go through predetermined motions.

Motivations, both desirable and undesirable, are a property of mind and thus may share common parentage with emotional feelings, creative thought, and decision making. The fact that these properties, and others which we associate with mind, are abstract, does not necessarily mean that they cannot be associated with particular cells in the brain. It may be too soon to accept the philosopher's anti-somatic view of mind, just as it may be too pragmatic to accept the physiologist's corporeal one. Too little is at present known of the brain to justify a strong position in regard to this mind-brain problem. Newton did

Reprinted by permission of The Society of the Sigma Xi and the author from the *American Scientist,* 1962, vol. 50, pp. 322–38.

not derive equations to explain the interrelated motion of the planets before others had identified some of the planets and studied their relative courses. Mind-brain scientists are still groping in the confusion of a pre-Copernican sky.

The exciting discoveries made in the last decade, however, encourage the belief that, as greater knowledge accumulates, what now may seem an abstract property of mind may take on a distinctly physical connotation as far as brain is concerned. The discoveries lie in the fields of neurophysiology, neuropharmacology, and neurochemistry, and, although they may give little insight into how creative thinking and decision making occur in the brain, they do give an inkling of how the motivations for such things are provided, and how they may be modified.

Neurophysiological Investigations

CLASSICAL neurophysiology was largely concerned with investigating functions associated with the cerebral cortex, partly, no doubt, because the cortex is what confronts one first upon opening the skull. Any doubts regarding its top priority for investigation were dispelled by the knowledge that this is the part of the brain best developed in humans.

It became clear from studying the cerebral cortex that definite functions could be correlated with particular groups of cells. Thus, cells were found that controlled movement and speech; others that subserved sight and hearing, and so on. The significance of these largely mechanical functions was easy to grasp. Cells on the cortical surface were not located, at first, which could be associated with properties of mind, although there were large numbers of cells in the frontal lobes which were thought to be "silent."

The advent of stereotaxic equipment opened the door to investigating the functions of deeper, subcortical cells. Subcortical cells were long suspected of harboring "primitive functions" including emotion and motivational drives.

A spectacular breakthrough came in 1953. Olds and Milner were investigating subcor-

tical centers in rats in the hope of finding areas which, upon stimulation, would provoke the rat to perform some act to avoid the stimulus. To their surprise, they found that, in certain brain areas, the rats seemed to enjoy the stimulation. To confirm this impression, they placed a rat in a box with a pedal which the rat could press each time he wished to deliver a brief pulse of current to his brain. With this arrangement, and with electrodes placed in appropriate areas, the rat would stay at the pedal continuously for hours, stimulating his brain thousands of times. As Olds describes a typical rat he had prepared:

He begins to search and pursue eagerly after his very first stimulation. . . . Sometimes while the animal is self-stimulating, the circuit is cut off by the experimenter, so that stepping on the pedal will not produce any brain shock; in this case an animal that is self-stimulating will give a series of forceful ("frustrated-looking") responses and turn away finally from the pedal to groom himself for sleep; but he will go back from time to time and press the pedal (as though to make sure he is not missing anything).

The term "reward center" was devised to describe those areas of the brain where such self-stimulation could be elicited.

The avoidance effect, which had been originally sought, was also eventually found. In such brain areas, termed "punishment centers," the rat would never self-stimulate but would work to avoid getting stimulated.

With his simple experimental arrangement, Olds was able to map the rat brain for reward and punishment centers and to establish a hierarchy among the reward areas, based on how seriously the animal would seek such stimulation. He concluded that about 35% of the cells of the rat brain lay in reward centers, about 5% in punishment centers, and approximately 60% were neutral. Neocortical areas, i.e., the "newest" part of the brain developmentally, made up the majority of the neutral areas. The paleocortex, or ancient cortex, showed rates of approximately 200 stimulations per hour. This was increased up to 3000 per hour in certain subcortical nuclei, and, in "lower" regions yet, even higher rates were found. Thus, rats would self-stimulate up to 5000 times per hour in the hypothalamus and up to 7000 times per hour in certain areas of the brain stem. The sensory inflow to the brain and motor outflow from the brain pass through the relatively narrow brain stem, and, as one proceeds "lower" from the cortex toward the brain stem, there is usually a concentration of an effect. This principle seems to apply with regard to "pleasure" and "punishment."

Neither self-stimulation, nor avoidance of stimulation by itself, gives insight into the nature of the sensation being experienced by the animal. Different experiments were devised to provide such information. Rats were taught to run a maze for the privilege of self-stimulation. At times they would run faster for electrical stimulation than for food. Furthermore, with electrodes in certain hypothalamic areas, the rats would run faster for an electrical stimulus even when they were starved. Given the choice between food or electrical stimulation at the end of the maze, the rats would choose electrical stimulation.

In other experiments, a rat was obliged to run across a grid which gave him successively more unpleasant shocks in order to reach the pedal for stimulation. The shock delivered by the grid could be raised to the point where the rat would forego the pleasure of brain stimulation and no longer cross the box. But the animal would accept roughly twice as powerful electrical shocks for self-stimulation as he would for food even if he had been starved (3). The implication, then, is that electrical stimulation in these areas satisfied the equivalent of hunger centers in the brain, and that the electrical stimulation was more pleasant than the sensation which the brain received following food intake.

Rats in another series were castrated after they had been taught to self-stimulate. In animals with electrodes correctly placed, the rate of stimulation dropped after castration, but increased when sex hormone was given to the rat. In these areas, which are distinct from the "hunger centers," it seemed as though the stimulation was providing sexual satisfaction.

To determine if stimulation of some cells always produced pleasure and other cells always punishment, Olds placed electrodes in each rat of another series both in a presumed pleasure center and a presumed punishment center. Each rat was given various opportunities to self-stimulate; sometimes in the pleasure area, sometimes in the punishment area. The rat was also subjected to brain stimulation gratis on other occasions; sometimes to the pleasure area, sometimes to the punishment area. The rat always had the opportunity of terminating the free stimulation by pressing a pedal. In areas of powerful reward, rats would always self-stimulate but would never interrupt a free stimulation. In areas of strong punishment, the rat would never self-stimulate but would always interrupt a free stimulation. Some equivocal areas were found where both self-stimulation and interruption of free stimulation occurred. Stimulation of specific cells in these areas might be pleasant or unpleasant according to the circumstances, or it might be that the stimulation excited a pool of cells some of which exclusively represented reward and others exclusively represented punishment (4).

A further innovation was introduced by Dr. Larry Stein (5). He arranged that rats could stimulate their brains in reward centers, but each successive stimulation produced a smaller shock until, finally, the shock was worthless for reward. However, the rat could push another lever to reset the stimulation strength to its initial value. With such an arrangement, a given rat would always self-stimulate until the strength of the stimulation diminished to a fixed point; then he would leave the self-stimulation pedal to push the reset pedal. Such consistency made it possible to test the effects of various drugs upon the strength of stimulation required for reward.

Following Olds' discovery of self-stimulation centers in the brain of rats, it was not long before comparable studies were being undertaken in animals with more advanced brains. Cats, monkeys, dolphins and humans were all studied. The dolphin might seem a curious choice, but it has a large brain, with particularly well-developed cortical convolutions. Some scientists feel that the brain of the dolphin may hold as great potentialities as does the human brain (6).

Much of the early work in monkeys was done by Dr. John Lilly. The same general principles, established by Olds and other workers for animals with simpler brains, were found to apply. With the monkey, many electrodes could be implanted in the brain at once. This made it possible to give the monkey a choice between stimulation of different areas, and thereby to establish, in another way from that done in rats, the relative desirability of stimulating any given brain area. The hierarchy established was similar to that found in the rat, with the most powerful zones being found in the brain stem, and progressively less powerful ones being found as "higher" centers were approached. Once brain stimulation was started, it proved difficult to divert the monkey's attention to anything else. Lilly introduced the term "capture" to describe this attitude.

Stimulation of punishment zones produced obvious fright, dilated pupils, pilo-erection, shaking of the body, violent escape attempts, biting and tearing of objects placed in the vicinity even to the extent of breaking teeth out of the jaw. The monkey could be "captured" in such a punishment zone so that his attention was entirely concentrated on performing whatever operation was necessary to avoid the stimulation. According to Lilly, if the monkey is "captured" in a punishment zone for about three hours, there are deleterious effects which may persist for as long as two days afterwards. He becomes irritable, eats poorly and develops a gray and pallid expression. This whole picture can be reversed by stimulating him in a reward center. If this is done promptly, the animal revives in a few minutes.

Are humans different from lower animals? Opportunities for making observations in conscious humans during subcortical electrical stimulation have occurred with patients suffering from epilepsy, brain tumors, and mental illness. The pattern previously described for animals has so far been generally corroborated. Reward centers have been found in the human associated with intense, but non-specific feelings of well-being, with pleasant sensations ascribed to distinct parts of the body, and with sexual arousal. Punishment areas have also been found, the stimulation of which can elicit terror, anger or pain (7).

Reactions observed in humans are, however, far more complex than in lower animals. There is always an engendered association between the sensation produced by electrical stimulation and the people surrounding the patient at that time. Interpretation of the sensation is also colored by the particular person's past events and future expectations. Such alloyage presumably reflects the more complicated cerebral cortex of humans which permits far richer feedback to subcortical areas. The contrast between the human brain and that of lower animals thus may lie not so much in the nature of the sensation experienced in these pleasure and punishment centers, as it does in the complicated associations permitted by the cortex.

In every species studied, the specific areas of the brain involved in pleasure and punishment seem to be the same. They include certain areas of the paleocortex, basal ganglia, diencephalon, and upper brain stem.

The implication of all of these studies is that much learning and decision making, which presumably take place chiefly in the cortex, are directed toward stimulating pleasure centers, and away from stimulating punishment centers. In other words, the cells which are "neutral" for reward or punishment are marshalled to direct the animals' behavior in such a way as to provide a sensory input which is "just right" for pleasure and punishment cells. That many of the functions associated with pleasure and punishment should have survival value for self and species is, no doubt, of more than casual consequence to our own presence.

There are at least two further recent advances in neurophysiology which add significantly to our growing concepts of mind-brain relationships. The first of these is the discovery by Magoun and co-workers of the reticular activating system. The reticular activating system of neurons spreads through the upper part of the brain stem and lies, therefore, just below the most powerful reward and punishment centers. This system seems to have an influence on almost all sensory inflow to the brain as well as on the motor outflow from the brain. In particular, the activity of these cells seems to govern the level of consciousness. Irreversible damage to the reticular activating system results in a state of permanent coma. The brain waves in this circumstance constantly show a pattern of sleep. Such human "vegetables" are an occasional consequence of head and neck injuries in motor accidents.

Although an adequately functioning reticular activating system is necessary for consciousness, it does not seem to be responsible for focusing attention. A more rostrally located system in the diencephalon, termed the "diffuse thalamic system," has been generally regarded as responsible for selecting portions of the sensory inflow on which the brain concentrates; we are thus most conscious of what this system chooses. We are less conscious of more extraneous input and, of course, much is diverted into that reservoir for the psychoanalysts, the subconscious. Thus, normal function of both the "reticular activating" and the "diffuse thalamic" systems would be necessary for the pleasure and punishment centers to assert their influence (8).

Prior to these developments, W. R. Hess had largely completed his Nobel prize-winning series of investigations on the diencephalon. He conceived this region of the brain as integrating two opposing systems: the ergotropic system and the trophotropic system. As the name implies, the ergotropic system prepares the body for action, increasing muscular tone and activating the psychological state. Such activity, of course, requires the participation of both the reticular activating and diffuse thalamic systems and, as the studies of Olds and others clearly indicate, may easily involve seeking pleasure or avoiding punishment. The trophotropic system integrates recuperative functions, culminating in satisfaction of various sorts, including drowsiness and sleep. Thus, the ergotropic and trophotropic systems are visualized as coordinating visceral, somatic, and psychological activity, with over-all integration taking place in the diencephalon (9). The pattern of behavior reflects, in part, the balance between these two systems.

Most of the brain mass is taken up by the cerebral cortex (TABLE 1) and much of this is comprised of "silent" areas. Creative thinking is presumed to go on here, and analogies have been drawn between the way the human brain tackles a deductive problem and the way a computing machine does. But analogies so far do not exist between a computing machine and the subcortical neurophysiological systems we have discussed. These systems occupy a much smaller area of brain, and, as we have seen, account for such activities as the focusing of attention, the drives to undertake a task and the pleasures or displeasures associated with various situations. (As one of my colleagues tells his students, one finds represented here the patterns of activity which are daily reported in the "society pages" of the press, namely, feeding, mating, and migration.)

Mental problems, in the psychiatric sense, are almost entirely associated with emotional aspects of mind. Mental patients, who occupy one half of all our hospital beds, include the brilliant as well as the stupid, and difficulties in handling problems in creative thinking are seldom listed in the usual tedious roll of supposed "causes" of mental illness. Symptoms shown by mental patients fit more closely with upsets in the subcortical systems; thus, new concepts such as reward and punishment centers, ergotropic and trophotropic zones, and reticular activating and diffuse thalamic systems have greatly interested psychologists and psychiatrists. They wish to know if the activity of these systems can be adjusted or modified in any way, and if practical benefits might accrue from such control. For this we will probably have to look to brain chemistry.

In the final analysis, the brain, like other organs of the body, is a chemical machine. It is a very special chemical machine, of course, because each unit does not duplicate the function of every other unit as in the alveoli of the lung or the glomeruli of the kidney. The difference between the cells of the brain, and those of many other organs of the body might be likened to that between the individual tubes of a television set and the individual floodlights in a bank at a football stadium. If one of the floodlights at the stadium ceased to function, a relatively minor loss would ensue; but if one of the tubes in the television set ceased to function, a whole series of deficits might follow depending on the exact location and connections of that particular tube. Although this would be expected to happen even if all the tubes in the television set were identical, there are typically many different types of tubes in a television set, each basically similar but with distinct characteristics depending on the specialized job it is expected to perform.

So it may be with cells of the brain. We know that all the neurons of the brain have basic similarities just as do the tubes in a television set. The same energy-producing metabolic cycles exist in all brain cells, and these differ little from the chemical cycles in cells of pigeon breast or any other mammalian tissue. But, as with tubes in a typical television set, important differences in detail may be present. Such differences are essential if cells of one functional system are to be affected in preference to cells of another.

Is there any positive evidence that such differences exist? Evidence is available in the selective action of many drugs with powerful effects on the central nervous system. Let us briefly consider some drugs which are thought to act primarily on the systems we have been discussing and which produce pronounced alterations in mental functioning.

Neuropharmacological Studies

Two broad classes of drugs have linked the study of mind with pharmacology: Those drugs which disturb the mental functioning of normal people and those drugs which improve the mental functioning of abnormal people. The hallucinogens make up the former class, and were so named, in a provocative paper by Hoffer and co-workers in 1954 (10), because of their pronounced tendency to induce various types of hallucinations. The tranquilizing agents and the psychic energizers constitute the majority of the second class. Tranquilizing agents have quite different effects from psychic energizers; which

type of drug is used by the physician depends upon the symptoms he desires to alleviate.

Hallucinogenic drugs have been in use from time immemorial but, until recently, they were in the province of witch doctors and shamans rather than that of their more modern scientific counterparts. The accidental discovery of the hallucinogenic properties of a synthetic chemical, lysergic acid diethylamide (LSD), by Hofman in 1943 focused scientific attention on such agents. Many hallucinogens have since been discovered, some being synthetic and others natural products, but all having in common the ability to disturb mental processes and thereby to mimic, to a degree, certain aspects of mental illness.

As the name implies, the most striking disturbance is the production of hallucinations, usually visual. Particularly noteworthy in this respect is mescaline, the active principle of the cactus peyote used by North American Indians. Aldous Huxley has written much of the "other-worldly" experiences produced by hallucinogenic seeds, mushrooms, roots, and plants, and has vividly described the striking color patterns which are often seen after mescaline ingestion; these give rise to some of the pleasant sensations associated with its use.

In addition to visual hallucinations, disorders of time are often experienced under the influence of hallucinogens. It is as though an individual's innate time clock had its regulator readjusted, usually radically toward the slow side. Such an effect may be due to the "impedance" to trans-synaptic transmission which has been shown to be an effect of hallucinogens. Fabing has compared the emotional effect on the individual involved with that which would be aroused in baseball fans if a double play ball were lobbed indifferently from base to base instead of being thrown with maximum speed and precision. Even more unpleasant sensations may be excited by hallucinogens. Feelings of depersonalization, anxiety and even terror are characteristic of high doses of LSD. Many individuals, nonetheless, enjoy the milder sensations associated with ingestion of low doses.

The fact that pharmacological agents can produce aberrations in mental activity with only minor effects on other systems has added strength to theories that mental illness might have a simple chemical or physiological basis. But no one has yet found the physiological or chemical keys to this Pandora's box of troubles.

Simpler questions remain without definitive answers. Which brain cells are affected by hallucinogens and what chemical mechanisms are concerned? Extensive studies have been made on the distribution of various of these hallucinogens after administration. These studies indicate that the hallucinogens are taken up by all the tissues of the body with only a very small proportion reaching the brain. Again, in brain itself, the distribution is widespread so that the manner in which the hallucinogens assert their effects cannot be determined from a knowledge of their geographical spread. There must be something particular about certain cells in the brain which makes them susceptible to these agents, i.e., these cells must have something distinctive about them chemically. Neurophysiologists tell us that their evidence indicates that the hallucinogens act in the lower regions of the brain, i.e., those regions which loom so importantly in the already described work of Olds, *et al.,* Magoun and Hess. It remains for the neurochemists to learn the chemical peculiarities of cells in this area which render them sensitive to hallucinogenic agents. Some limited progress has been made.

The aromatic structures of LSD, mescaline, and many other hallucinogens suggested that aromatic constituents of the brain should be given particular consideration. The identification, in 1951, of one such material, serotonin, by Erspamer and, independently, by Rapport and his co-workers, was the culmination of several years of effort to isolate a principle with powerful activity against smooth muscle in such tissues as the uterus, gut, and vascular tree. Shortly thereafter, Twarog and Page discovered that serotonin was present in brain, being concentrated in the paleocortex, diencephalon, and brain stem. It remained for Woolley and Shaw to propose that LSD exerted its mental effects by interfering with serotonin and that schizophrenia could be due to abnormal serotonin metabolism (11). This ingenious and heuristic idea is yet to be proved or disproved despite eight years of research effort.

LSD is indeed a very powerful inhibitor of serotonin on some systems but so, too, is 2-bromo-LSD which also penetrates the brain but has little or no hallucinogenic activity. Intensive research effort has led to the accumulation of a mass of confusing and often conflicting data on the interactions of LSD and other hallucinogenic agents, not only with serotonin, but also with norepinephrine and other catecholamines, and with acetylcholine and histamine; all these amines occur in the central nervous system and have been proposed, at one time or another, as chemical transmitter substances. Some hallucinogens, at least, have been shown to modify carbohydrate metabolism and phosphorylation in brain slices, to increase phosphorus uptake by brain, to alter membrane permeability to sodium and potassium ions, and to affect various other metabolic systems. Which, if any, of these actions is important to the hallucinogenic effect? Although no one has yet found an Ariadnian thread to lead us out of this maze, the apparently selective action of the hallucinogens on certain areas of the brain seems most consistent with a mode of action involving one or more of the brain amines since these are concentrated in the appropriate areas. Further support for this position has been derived from a study of the interaction of these same brain amines and a number of newly discovered psychopharmacological agents.

Within the past decade, three families of potent psychopharmacological agents have been introduced into clinical medicine. These have had an inestimable effect on the treatment of the mentally ill. By 1957, their wide usage in North America had resulted, for the first time in recorded history, in a decrease in mental hospital populations. These new drugs have generally lessened the time required for hospital treatment and have even allowed the return to society of some cases previously judged as "hopeless." They have, moreover, changed the whole atmosphere of mental hospitals, have converted the all-too-frequently understaffed back ward from a dangerous bedlam to a place fit for human beings, and even conducive to recovery of their sanity. In addition, these drugs have permitted the alleviation of non-pathological anxiety and tension in many persons under temporary stress. Their discovery must be rated one of the most beneficial strokes of serendipity in medical history.

The progenitors of the three important families—phenothiazines, rauwolfia alkaloids, and monoamine oxidase inhibitors—were tried initially for pharmacological purposes other than psychiatric ones, and their mental effects were a completely unexpected dividend. The phenothiazines and rauwolfia alkaloids soon became known as "tranquilizers" and the monoamine oxidase inhibitors as "psychic energizers." These terms, used to describe the clinical effects, have become part of almost everyone's basic English vocabulary.

Reserpine, the first tranquilizer to be widely used, is an alkaloid derived from the plant *Rauwolfia Serpentina,* the powdered roots of which have been used for centuries in India for various ills. It was introduced in 1953 as an antihypertensive agent. Its tranquilizing properties were considered a nuisance until its introduction into psychiatric medicine. For a time, not even a reasonable hypothesis was available as to how it produced its tranquilizing and hypotensive effects. However, in 1955, Pletscher and others showed that reserpine depletes serotonin from its storage depots in the body (12), whether these be in the gut, blood platelets, brain, or other tissues. It does this by affecting the binding sites for serotonin in intracellular granules. For a short subsequent period, the actions of reserpine were thought to reflect simply a deficiency of serotonin. It was soon shown, however, that reserpine also depletes catecholamines from their storage sites in all parts of the body including sympathetic nerves and brain. The action of reserpine is now thought to reflect a depletion of one or more central amines but, despite numerous ingenious experiments, it is not known whether a deficiency in serotonin or in catecholamines plays the greater role.

Chlorpromazine, the first of the phenothiazines to be introduced clinically, was initially tried out as a basal anesthetic and an antinauseant. It was introduced into clinical psychiatry at about the same time as reserpine and met with instant success. Again, the mechanism of action was completely unknown even after chlorpromazine had come into wide clinical use. It was soon learned that chlorpromazine, like reserpine, acts on subcortical brain centers but only later was it determined that the phenothiazines were powerful blockers of some of the actions of catecholamines and serotonin. Many different phenothiazines have now been introduced clinically: some of these, such as chlorpromazine, have a blocking action against another central amine, histamine; others do not. Those phenothiazines with little or no antihistaminic action have a greater tendency to produce Parkinsonian-like reactions and a lesser tendency to produce sedative reactions than those with strong antihistaminic action. Thus, not only do the phenothiazines provide another link between central amines and tranquilization, but they suggest new approaches to the enigma of Parkinsonism.

The psychic energizers were introduced in 1957. Iproniazid, the prototype of the series, proved to be unsatisfactory as an anti-tubercular agent, but the euphoria it produced soon suggested its value for depressed mental patients. Zeller had already shown that iproniazid had the ability to inhibit the enzyme monoamine oxidase and, shortly after, Kline and co-workers (13) proposed this as the reason for its effect on mental patients. Monoamine oxidase is an important enzyme for destroying the catecholamines and serotonin, and it was reasoned that inhibitors of this enzyme might delay the destruction of these amines and thus lead to increases in their brain concentrations. This has been shown to be the case. Thus, we have three important new classes of psychopharmacological agents whose advent has been a tremendous value in treating the mentally ill. These agents, like the hallucinogens, affect many metabolic systems and it has so far proved impossible to determine the exact chemical mechanism of action. They all appear to act, however, at subcortical levels and the hypotheses most consistent with present knowledge link their psychopharmacological actions with their effects on the central amines, particularly the catecholamines and serotonin, possibly at synaptic sites. In general, blockade or depletion of these amines is accompanied by tranquilization, reduction of fear or anxiety, and a diminution of disturbed thought processes. Conversely, an increase in the effective level of these amines is accompanied by an enhanced psychic state and an elevation of mood.

Neurochemical Investigations

As, in the 1950's, electrophysiological investigations provided fascinating new insight into the function of subcortical areas which might be construed as being involved in mental illness, so did the introduction of new classes of psychotropic drugs provide evidence suggesting that these agents also might be acting on these same areas of the brain. Independently of the neuropharmacological and neurophysiological studies, neurochemical researches were being conducted on the location and physiological actions of certain central amines. Some, such as acetylcholine and norepinephrine, had been well studied in peripheral tissue where they had a well-defined role as neurotransmitter substances. The others, dopamine, serotonin, and histamine, were also familiar as peripheral humoral agents but with a much more vaguely defined role. For years, interest in discovering chemical neurotransmitter agents in brain has been running high, but unequivocal data are difficult to obtain.

The neurophysiologist has delicate electrical techniques with which to explore the function of small groups of cells in the brain. The neuropharmacologist has an ever-increasing armamentarium of centrally acting drugs with which to modify brain function and can use neurophysiological techniques to study their effects. But what weapons can the neurochemist bring to their common battle front? Unfortunately, he is still fighting with a bow and arrow in an atomic age. It can be said, as a general principle of neurochemistry, that, whenever the chemistry of the brain is perturbed, mental symptoms are an early and prominent result. This is seen, for example, in the anoxia of flyers, the hypoglycemia of the diabetic heading for insulin shock, or the early stages of anesthesia. In each case, mental symptoms are only a phase on the way to unconsciousness; if unconsciousness represents a mountainous perturbation in the chemistry of the brain, then mental symptoms represent the insignificant foothills. Minor perturbations in the chemistry of the brain are therefore probably all that would occur in mental disturbances. Furthermore, mental illness of all types is characterized primarily by emotional disturbances, except in the case of schizophrenia where emotional disturbance is overshadowed by a peculiar disorder of rational thinking often described as a "loosening of association." In most mental illness, therefore, one may expect the minor perturbations in brain chemistry to be limited to those subcortical areas shown by the neurophysiologist to be important for emotional response, and by the neuropharmacologist to be the primary site of action of psychopharmacological agents. The neurochemist, then, must look for minor changes in the chemistry of small, discrete brain areas with techniques which are barely capable of measuring accurately the concentration of many substances in the total brain.

It is small wonder that the only good correlations so far made between mental state and biochemistry involve constituents of the urine, where concentration mechanisms yield much larger amounts of material for analysis. In one study, Elmadjian (14) measured the epinephrine and norepinephrine excretion in the urine of the members of the Boston Bruins hockey team before and after their games. After a hard-played game, most players showed approximately a six-fold increase in norepinephrine excretion. Two injured players, who were unable to play and were concerned about their future with the team, excreted increased amounts of epinephrine instead, and one player who was ejected from a game for fighting, excreted increased amounts of both epinephrine and norepinephrine. The coach was variable in his excretion of epinephrine and norepinephrine depending on the performance of the team. The general finding that epinephrine tends to be excreted in anxiety-producing situations and norepinephrine in anger or action-producing situations has been well corroborated in other studies. Years ago, the great physiologist, Walter Cannon, had produced a view of the sympathetic nervous system, with its hormone "sympathin," as preparing the body for "fight or flight." It now appears that norepinephrine is the component of "sympathin" more closely associated with fight, whereas epinephrine is more closely associated with flight.

Is there an analogous correlation between specific mental states and the release of certain chemicals or groups of chemicals in the brain? None has been well demonstrated to date, but the technical difficulties are great. One cannot have the brain and measure it too, nor is it technically feasible to measure the chemical output, in the blood, of circumscribed brain areas. Nonetheless, some highly suggestive evidence is available, as to correlations between brain chemistry and behavior, again involving the central amines.

The central amines receiving most active attention are shown in TABLE 1, along with an approximate indication of their localization. The over-all concentration of each of these amines in whole brain is approximately $\frac{1}{1000}$ the concentration of energy-producing intermediates associated with glucose and oxygen metabolism. The enzymes for manufacturing and destroying these amines are also present in brain tissue. Furthermore, amines manufactured in other parts of the body do not seem to gain access to the brain except, possibly, in minute concentrations. The blood/brain barrier apparently assures that the brain uses only its own supply of amines. Their exact role so far has defied

definition, although it is clearly unrelated to energy metabolism.

To go back to the analogy of the television set, where the tubes all worked on the same basic principle but had slightly different operating characteristics, the cells of the brain all work on the same basic principle in that they derive their energy from glucose and oxygen consumption. But they may differ in their operating characteristics by using different chemicals to modulate their excitability and to relay messages across cell junctions or synapses. The central amines are eminently suited to such roles, both by their distinctive localization and by their known peripheral actions. This suitability has inspired presumptive descriptions of the amines as neurotransmitters, neurohormones, or neurohumoral agents, but only indirect evidence exists to support such a role.

One important line of evidence comes from the ability of the amines to modify the electroencephalogram (EEG) (15). Each of the amines has been shown capable of exciting the resting EEG pattern when injected in minute concentrations into the arterial circulation of the brain. Although the effect noted on the EEG is the same in each case, the individual amines need not be affecting the same cells. The EEG is recorded from the cortex and exciting any neurons in a chain passing through successive subcortical levels might produce such an effect. Evidence from lesions placed in the brain stem strongly suggests that the catecholamines exert their greatest influence on the EEG at this point, whereas acetylcholine acts considerably more rostrally. Exactly where histamine and serotonin exert their greatest effect remains to be determined.

TABLE 1

APPROX. WT. HUMANS	NEOCORTEX, 1150 g.	PALEOCORTEX, 60 g.	BASAL GANGLIA, 50 g.	DIENCEPHALON, 30 g.	BRAIN STEM, 20 g.
Dopamine	Trace	Trace	++++	++	++
Norepinephrine	Trace	Trace	+	+++	++
Serotonin	Trace	+	+	+++	++
Acetylcholine	++	++	+++	++	++
Histamine	+	+	+	+++	+
Pleasure or Punishment	0	+	++	+++	++++

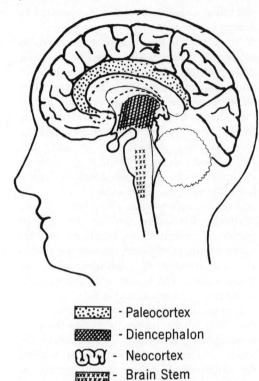

:::::: - Paleocortex
▓▓▓▓ - Diencephalon
ₘₘ - Neocortex
▒▒▒▒▒ - Brain Stem
‑ ‑ ‑ ‑ ‑ - Basal Ganglia

FIG. 1. Sagittal view of the human brain.

The EEG gives no indication of the behavioral effects of these amines; a better indication has been given in the discussion of the effects of drugs which influence them. TABLE 2 gives a summary of some drug-amine interactions. As can be seen from the table, the spectrum of action of the drugs is too broad to permit any strong correlations. Some additional information may, however, be added by experiments in which precursor amino acids of certain amines are combined with drugs.

Dihydroxyphenylalanine, the precursor amino acid of the catecholamines, when administered alone will enhance the ability of an animal to avoid an electric shock, but will not encourage his efforts to obtain a food reward. The precursor amino acid of serotonin, 5-hydroxytryptophan, when given alone will cause both a deterioration in an animal's ability to avoid shock, and his desire to work for food (16). Large doses of dihydroxyphenylalanine in animals will cause obvious signs of excitation along with marked heightening of response to any stimulus. Large doses of 5-hydroxytryptophan will cause gross tremors, irritability, and an inattention to the environment. Dihydroxyphenylalanine is quite effective at counteracting reserpine-induced sedation while 5-hydroxytryptophan is not. The effect of a monoamine oxidase inhibitor in combination with either of these two amino acids is to enhance the physiological result of the amino acid administration. Thus, it would appear as if the catecholamines are primarily responsible for changes in the degree of alertness of the animals, while serotonin is correlated with sensations of moods which are much less obvious. Similar experiments using histidine, the precursor amino acid of histamine, have not been tried, while acetylcholine, not having an amino acid precursor, does not lend itself to a comparable type of experiment.

It is evident that insufficient information is at present available to make strong correlations between subcortical neurophysiological systems important to the mental state, neuropharmacological agents, and the chemistry of

TABLE 2

	ACETYLCHOLINE	HISTAMINE	DOPAMINE	NOREPINEPHRINE	SEROTONIN	ACTION
Phenothiazines	0	0 or blocks	Blocks	Blocks	Blocks	Tranquilizer
Reserpine	0	0	Depletes	Depletes	Depletes	Tranquilizer
Monoamine oxidase inhibitors	0	?	Enhances	Enhances	Enhances	Psychic energizer
Lysergic acid diethylamide	Weak block	?	?	Weakly mimics	Strong block	Psychotomimetic
Mescaline	0	?	?	Weakly mimics	?	Psychotomimetic

the central amines. Postulates, however, have been made. Brodie and Shore (17), for example, suggested that serotonin may be the neurotransmitter for the trophotropic system of Hess, while norepinephrine may be the neurotransmitter substance for the ergotropic system. We have proposed that, at least as far as the extrapyramidal motor system is concerned, histamine and acetylcholine may be components of one modulating system while the catecholamines and possibly serotonin are components of another (18). More recent experiments suggest to us that histamine may be of importance to pain or punishment centers in the brain. Unfortunately, none of these ideas can be well tested because sufficiently delicate chemical analytical methods are not yet available.

As more refined methods of analysis are forthcoming, further efforts will certainly be made to draw correlations between mental state and brain biochemistry. Particular attention is bound to be paid to the central amines but, at the same time, chemists will be alert to spot other chemical features which may distinguish the subcortical cells concerned with behavior from other cells in brain. We may be sure, at least, that the struggle to understand brain and mind will continue.

REFERENCES

1. SAMUEL, VISCOUNT. *Essay in Physics,* Oxford University Press, 1951, p. 133.
2. NEWELL, A., SHAW, J. C., and SIMON, H. A. *IBM J. Res. Develop., 2,* 320 (1958). NEWELL, A., and SIMON, H. A. *Science, 134,* 3495 (1961).
3. OLDS, J. In: *Electrical Studies in the Unanesthetized Brain,* ed. E. R. Ramey and D. S. O'Doherty. Paul B. Hoeber, Inc., New York, 1960, pp. 17–52.
4. OLDS, J. *Am. J. Physiol., 199,* 965 (1960).
5. STEIN, L., and RAY, O. S., *Science, 130,* 570 (1959).
6. LILLY, J. *Man and Dolphin,* Doubleday and Co., Garden City, New York, 1961.
7. LILLY, J. *J. Amer. Psychoanal. Ass., 8,* 659 (1960).
8. MAGOUN, H. W. *The Waking Brain,* Charles C Thomas, Springfield, Illinois, 1958.
9. HESS, W. R. *Diencephalon, Autonomic and Extrapyramidal Functions,* Monogr. Biol. Med., *3,* Grune and Stratton, New York, 1954.
10. HOFFER, A., OSMOND, H., SMYTHIES, J., *J. Ment. Sci., 100,* 29 (1954).
11. WOOLLEY, D. W., and SHAW, E., *Brit. Med. J., 2,* 122 (1954).
12. PLETSCHER, A., SHORE, P. A., BRODIE, B. B., *Science, 122,* 374 (1955).
13. KLINE, N. S., Meeting, Amer. Psych. Ass., April, 1957. BAILEY, S. de'A., *et al. Ann. N. Y. Acad. Sci., 80,* 652 (1959).
14. ELMADJIAN, F., *Pharmacol. Rev., 11,* 409 (1959).
15. ROTHBALLER, A. B., *Pharmacol. Rev., 11,* 494 (1959). LING, G. M., *J. Neuropsychiat.,* in press.
16. WADA, J. A., *J. Neuropsychiat.,* in press.
17. BRODIE, B. B., SPECTOR, S., and SHORE, P. A., *Pharmacol. Rev., 11,* 548 (1959).
18. MCGEER, P. L., *et al. J.A.M.A., 177,* 665 (1961).

SECTION III

Heredity and Development

ARMCHAIR *psychologists have for years been interested in deciding which is responsible for a given characteristic: heredity or environment. Professional psychologists are also concerned with the roles heredity and environment play in development, but in a different way. Whereas the layman often assumes that either heredity or environment is responsible for a certain trait, the psychologist has found that in almost all cases heredity and environment interact; and while the layman depends primarily on common sense, the psychologist tries to test the relative importance of the two factors by scientific means.*

In the first article, Anne Anastasi suggests that psychologists ask not only whether heredity or environment influences a given trait more and how much influence each exerts, but that they try to find out as well just how heredity and environment influence development. She traces several current lines of research that offer promising techniques for analyzing in "Heredity, Environment, and the Question 'How?'"

Jerry Hirsch and James Boudreau, in "Studies in Experimental Behavior Genetics," show that it is possible to breed fruit flies for a given trait—reaction to light (phototaxis)—to produce, in other words, two strains of fruit flies with different sensitivities to light through genetic inheritance and without training. It is easy, however, to mistake an environmental variable for a genetic one, especially if one is not aware that environment affects even an unborn organism. David Spelt's study of conditioned response in the human fetus illustrates the influence environment can exercise on an organism even before birth.

In the final article, "The Discovery and Encouragement of Exceptional Talent," Lewis Terman points out that if superior innate intelligence is to lead to superior achievement it must be detected early and nurtured carefully. He discusses the tests used to determine a person's achievement potential and the studies, carried out over a period of years on persons of high innate ability, that tell us what factors may maximize the gifted person's chances for achievement.

ANNE ANASTASI

11. Heredity, Environment, and the Question "How?"

Two or three decades ago, the so-called heredity-environment question was the center of lively controversy. Today, on the other hand, many psychologists look upon it as a dead issue. It is now generally conceded that both hereditary and environmental factors enter into all behavior. The reacting organism is a product of its genes and its past environment, while present environment provides the immediate stimulus for current behavior. To be sure, it can be argued that, although a given trait may result from the combined influence of hereditary and environmental factors, a specific difference in this trait between individuals or between groups may be traceable to either hereditary or environmental factors alone. The design of most traditional investigations undertaken to identify such factors, however, has been such as to yield inconclusive answers. The same set of data has frequently led to opposite conclusions in the hands of psychologists with different orientations.

Nor have efforts to determine the proportional contribution of hereditary and environmental factors to observed individual differences in given traits met with any greater success. Apart from difficulties in controlling conditions, such investigations have usually been based upon the implicit assumption that hereditary and environmental factors combine in an additive fashion. Both geneticists and psychologists have repeatedly demonstrated, however, that a more tenable hypothesis is that of interaction (15, 22, 28, 40). In other words, the nature and extent of the influence of each type of factor depend upon the contribution of the other. Thus the proportional contribution of heredity to the variance of a given trait, rather than being a constant, will vary under different environmental conditions. Similarly, under different hereditary conditions, the relative contribution of environment will differ. Studies designed to estimate the proportional contribution of heredity and environment, however, have rarely included measures of such interaction. The only possible conclusion from such research would thus seem to be that both heredity and environment contribute to all behavior traits and that the extent of their respective contributions cannot be specified for any trait. Small wonder that some psychologists regard the heredity-environment question as unworthy of further consideration!

But is this really all we can find out about the operation of heredity and environment in the etiology of behavior? Perhaps we have simply been asking the wrong questions. The traditional questions about heredity and environment may be intrinsically unanswerable. Psychologists began by asking *which* type of factor, hereditary or environmental, is responsible for individual differences in a given trait. Later, they tried to discover *how much* of the variance was attributable to heredity and how much to environment. It is the primary contention of this paper that a more fruitful approach is to be found in the question *"How?"* There is still much to be learned about the specific *modus operandi* of hereditary and environmental factors in the de-

Address of the President, Division of General Psychology, American Psychological Association, September 4, 1957. Reprinted by permission of the American Psychological Association and the author from the *Psychological Review*, 1958, vol. 65, pp. 197–208.

velopment of behavioral differences. And there are several current lines of research which offer promising techniques for answering the question "How?"

Variety of Interaction Mechanisms

HEREDITARY FACTORS

IF we examine some of the specific ways in which hereditary factors may influence behavior, we cannot fail but be impressed by their wide diversity. At one extreme, we find such conditions as phenylpyruvic amentia and amaurotic idiocy. In these cases, certain essential physical prerequisites for normal intellectual development are lacking as a result of hereditary metabolic disorders. In our present state of knowledge, there is no environmental factor which can completely counteract this hereditary deficit. The individual will be mentally defective, regardless of the type of environmental conditions under which he is reared.

A somewhat different situation is illustrated by hereditary deafness, which may lead to intellectual retardation through interference with normal social interaction, language development, and schooling. In such a case, however, the hereditary handicap can be offset by appropriate adaptations of training procedures. It has been said, in fact, that the degree of intellectual backwardness of the deaf is an index of the state of development of special instructional facilities. As the latter improve, the intellectual retardation associated with deafness is correspondingly reduced.

A third example is provided by inherited susceptibility to certain physical diseases, with consequent protracted ill health. If environmental conditions are such that illness does in fact develop, a number of different behavioral effects may follow. Intellectually, the individual may be handicapped by his inability to attend school regularly. On the other hand, depending upon age of onset, home conditions, parental status, and similar factors, poor health may have the effect of concentrating the individual's energies upon intellectual pursuits. The curtailment of participation in athletics and social functions may serve to strengthen interest in reading and other sedentary activities. Concomitant circumstances would also determine the influence of such illness upon personality development. And it is well known that the latter effects could run the gamut from a deepening of human sympathy to psychiatric breakdown.

Finally, heredity may influence behavior through the mechanism of social stereotypes. A wide variety of inherited physical characteristics have served as the visible cues for identifying such stereotypes. These cues thus lead to behavioral restrictions or opportunities and—at a more subtle level—to social attitudes and expectancies. The individual's own self concept tends gradually to reflect such expectancies. All of these influences eventually leave their mark upon his abilities and inabilities, his emotional reactions, goals, ambitions, and outlook on life.

The geneticist Dobzhansky illustrates this type of mechanism by means of a dramatic hypothetical situation. He points out that, if there were a culture in which the carriers of blood group AB were considered aristocrats and those of blood group O laborers, then the blood-group genes would become important hereditary determiners of behavior (12, p. 147). Obviously the association between blood group and behavior would be specific to that culture. But such specificity is an essential property of the causal mechanism under consideration.

More realistic examples are not hard to find. The most familiar instances occur in connection with constitutional types, sex, and race. Sex and skin pigmentation obviously depend upon heredity. General body build is strongly influenced by hereditary components, although also susceptible to environmental modification. That all these physical characteristics may exert a pronounced effect upon behavior within a given culture is well known. It is equally apparent, of course, that in different cultures the behavioral correlates of such hereditary physical traits may be quite unlike. A specific physical cue may be completely unrelated to individual differences in psychological traits in one culture, while closely correlated with them in another. Or it may be associated with totally dissimilar behavior characteristics in two different cultures.

It might be objected that some of the illustrations which have been cited do not properly exemplify the operation of hereditary mechanisms in behavior development, since hereditary factors enter only indirectly into the behavior in question. Closer examination, however, shows this distinction to be untenable. First it may be noted that the influence of heredity upon behavior is always indirect. No psychological trait is ever inherited as such. All we can ever say directly from behavioral observations is that a given trait shows evidence of being influenced by certain "inheritable unknowns." This merely defines a problem for genetic research; it does not provide a causal explanation. Unlike the blood groups, which are close to the level of primary gene products, psychological traits are related to genes by highly indirect and devious routes. Even the mental deficiency associated with phenylketonuria is several steps removed from the chemically defective genes that represent its hereditary basis. Moreover, hereditary influences cannot be dichotomized into the more direct and the less direct. Rather do they represent a whole "continuum of indirectness," along which are found all degrees of remoteness of causal links. The examples already cited illustrate a few of the points on this continuum.

It should be noted that as we proceed along the continuum of indirectness, the range of variation of possible outcomes of hereditary factors expands rapidly. At each step in the causal chain, there is fresh opportunity for interaction with other hereditary factors as well as with environmental factors. And since each interaction in turn determines the direction of subsequent interactions, there is an ever-widening network of possible outcomes. If we visualize a simple sequential grid with only two alternatives at each point, it is obvious that there are two possible outcomes in the one-stage situation, four outcomes at the second stage, eight at the third, and so on in geometric progression. The actual situation is undoubtedly much more complex, since there will usually be more than two alternatives at any one point.

In the case of the blood groups, the relation to specific genes is so close that no other concomitant hereditary or environmental conditions can alter the outcome. If the organism survives at all, it will have the blood group determined by its genes. Among psychological traits, on the other hand, some variation in outcome is always possible as a result of concurrent circumstances. Even in cases of phenylketonuria, intellectual development will exhibit some relationship with the type of care and training available to the individual. That behavioral outcomes show progressive diversification as we proceed along the continuum of indirectness is brought out by the other examples which were cited. Chronic illness *can* lead to scholarly renown or to intellectual immaturity; a mesomorphic physique *can* be a contributing factor in juvenile delinquency or in the attainment of a college presidency! Published data on Sheldon somatotypes provide some support for both of the latter outcomes.

Parenthetically, it may be noted that geneticists have sometimes used the term "norm of reaction" to designate the range of variation of possible outcomes of gene properties (cf. 13, p. 161). Thus heredity sets the "norm" or limits within which environmental differences determine the eventual outcome. In the case of some traits, such as blood groups or eye color, this norm is much narrower than in the case of other traits. Owing to the rather different psychological connotations of both the words "norm" and "reaction," however, it seems less confusing to speak of the "range of variation" in this context.

A large portion of the continuum of hereditary influences which we have described coincides with the domain of somatopsychological relations, as defined by Barker et al. (6). Under this heading, Barker includes "variations in physique that affect the psychological situation of a person by influencing the effectiveness of his body as a tool for actions or by serving as a stimulus to himself or others" (6, p. 1). Relatively direct neurological influences on behavior, which have been the traditional concern of physiological psychology, are excluded from this definition, Barker being primarily concerned with what he calls the "social psychology of physique." Of the examples cited in the present paper, deafness, severe illness, and the physical characteristics associated with social stereotypes would meet the specifications of somatopsychological factors.

The somatic factors to which Barker refers, however, are not limited to those of hereditary origin. Bodily conditions attributable to environmental causes operate in the same sorts of somatopsychological relations as those traceable to heredity. In fact, heredity-environment distinctions play a minor part in Barker's approach.

ENVIRONMENTAL FACTORS: ORGANIC

Turning now to an analysis of the role of environmental factors in behavior, we find the same etiological mechanisms which were observed in the case of hereditary factors. First, however, we must differentiate between two classes of environmental influences: (a) those producing organic effects which may in turn influence behavior and (b) those serving as direct stimuli for psychological reactions. The former may be illustrated by food intake or by exposure to bacterial infection; the latter, by tribal initiation ceremonies or by a course in algebra. There are no completely satisfactory names by which to designate these two classes of influences. In an earlier paper by Anastasi and Foley (4), the terms "structural" and "functional" were employed. However, "organic" and "behavioral" have the advantage of greater familiarity in this context and may be less open to misinterpretation. Accordingly, these terms will be used in the present paper.

Like hereditary factors, environmental influences of an organic nature can also be ordered along a continuum of indirectness with regard to their relation to behavior. This continuum closely parallels that of hereditary factors. One end is typified by such conditions as mental deficiency resulting from cerebral birth injury or from prenatal nutritional inadequacies. A more indirect etiological mechanism is illustrated by severe motor disorder— as in certain cases of cerebral palsy—*without*

accompanying injury to higher neurological centers. In such instances, intellectual retardation may occur as an indirect result of the motor handicap, through the curtailment of educational and social activities. Obviously this causal mechanism corresponds closely to that of hereditary deafness cited earlier in the paper.

Finally, we may consider an environmental parallel to the previously discussed social stereotypes which were mediated by hereditary physical cues. Let us suppose that a young woman with mousy brown hair becomes transformed into a dazzling golden blonde through environmental techniques currently available in our culture. It is highly probable that this metamorphosis will alter, not only the reactions of her associates toward her, but also her own self concept and subsequent behavior. The effects could range all the way from a rise in social poise to a drop in clerical accuracy!

Among the examples of environmentally determined organic influences which have been described, all but the first two fit Barker's definition of somatopsychological factors. With the exception of birth injuries and nutritional deficiencies, all fall within the social psychology of physique. Nevertheless, the individual factors exhibit wide diversity in their specific *modus operandi*—a diversity which has important practical as well as theoretical implications.

ENVIRONMENTAL FACTORS: BEHAVIORAL

The second major class of environmental factors—the behavioral as contrasted to the organic—are by definition direct influences. The immediate effect of such environmental factors is always a behavioral change. To be sure, some of the initial behavioral effects may themselves indirectly affect the individual's later behavior. But this relationship can perhaps be best conceptualized in terms of breadth and permanence of effects. Thus it could be said that we are now dealing, not with a continuum of indirectness, as in the case of hereditary and organic-environmental factors, but rather with a continuum of breadth.

Social class membership may serve as an

illustration of a relatively broad, pervasive, and enduring environmental factor. Its influence upon behavior development may operate through many channels. Thus social level may determine the range and nature of intellectual stimulation provided by home and community through books, music, art, play activities, and the like. Even more far-reaching may be the effects upon interests and motivation, as illustrated by the desire to perform abstract intellectual tasks, to surpass others in competitive situations, to succeed in school, or to gain social approval. Emotional and social traits may likewise be influenced by the nature of interpersonal relations characterizing homes at different socioeconomic levels. Somewhat more restricted in scope than social class, although still exerting a relatively broad influence, is amount of formal schooling which the individual is able to obtain.

A factor which may be wide or narrow in its effects, depending upon concomitant circumstances, is language handicap. Thus the bilingualism of an adult who moves to a foreign country with inadequate mastery of the new language represents a relatively limited handicap which can be readily overcome in most cases. At most, the difficulty is one of communication. On the other hand, some kinds of bilingualism in childhood may exert a retarding influence upon intellectual development and may under certain conditions affect personality development adversely (2, 5, 10). A common pattern in the homes of immigrants is that the child speaks one language at home and another in school, so that his knowledge of each language is limited to certain types of situations. Inadequate facility with the language of the school interferes with the acquisition of basic concepts, intellectual skills, and information. The frustration engendered by scholastic difficulties may in turn lead to discouragement and general dislike of school. Such reactions can be found, for example, among a number of Puerto Rican children in New York City schools (3). In the case of certain groups, moreover, the child's foreign language background may be perceived by himself and his associates as a symbol of minority group status and may thereby augment any emotional maladjustment arising from such status (34).

A highly restricted environmental influence is to be found in the opportunity to acquire specific items of information occurring in a particular intelligence test. The fact that such opportunities may vary with culture, social class, or individual experiential background is at the basis of the test user's concern with the problem of coaching and with "culture-free" or "culture-fair" tests (cf. 1, 2). If the advantage or disadvantage which such experiential differences confer upon certain individuals is strictly confined to performance on the given test, it will obviously reduce the validity of the test and should be eliminated.

In this connection, however, it is essential to know the breadth of the environmental influence in question. A fallacy inherent in many attempts to develop culture-fair tests is that the breadth of cultural differentials is not taken into account. Failure to consider breadth of effect likewise characterizes certain discussions of coaching. If, in coaching a student for a college admission test, we can improve his knowledge of verbal concepts and his reading comprehension, he will be better equipped to succeed in college courses. His performance level will thus be raised, not only on the test, but also on the criterion which the test is intended to predict. To try to devise a test which is not susceptible to such coaching would merely reduce the effectiveness of the test. Similarly, efforts to rule out cultural differentials from test items so as to make them equally "fair" to subjects in different social classes or in different cultures may merely limit the usefulness of the test, since the same cultural differentials may operate within the broader area of behavior which the test is designed to sample.

Methodological Approaches

THE examples considered so far should suffice to highlight the wide variety of ways in which hereditary and environmental factors may interact in the course of behavior development. There is clearly a need for identifying explicitly the etiological mechanism whereby any given hereditary or environmental condition ultimately leads to a behavioral characteristic—in other words, the "how" of heredity and environment. Accordingly, we may now take a quick look at some promising methodological approaches to the question "how."

Within the past decade, an increasing number of studies have been designed to trace the connection between specific factors in the hereditary backgrounds or in the reactional biographies of individuals and their observed behavioral characteristics. There has been a definite shift away from the predominantly descriptive and correlational approach of the earlier decades toward more deliberate attempts to verify explanatory hypotheses. Similarly, the cataloguing of group differences in psychological traits has been giving way gradually to research on *changes* in group characteristics following altered conditions.

Among recent methodological developments, we have chosen seven as being particularly relevant to the analysis of etiological mechanisms. The first represents an extension of selective breeding investigations to permit the identification of specific hereditary conditions underlying the observed behavioral differences. When early selective breeding investigations such as those of Tryon (36) on rats indicated that "maze learning ability" was inherited, we were still a long way from knowing what was actually being transmitted by the genes. It was obviously not "maze learning ability" as such. Twenty—or even ten—years ago, some psychologists would have suggested that it was probably general intelligence. And a few might even have drawn a parallel with the inheritance of human intelligence.

But today investigators have been asking: Just what makes one group of rats learn mazes more quickly than the other? Is it differences in motivation, emotionality, speed of running, general activity level? If so, are these behavioral characteristics in turn dependent upon group differences in glandular development, body weight, brain size, biochemical factors, or some other organic conditions? A number of recent and ongoing investigations indicate that attempts are being made to trace, at least part of the way, the steps whereby certain chemical properties of the genes may ultimately lead to specified behavior characteristics.

An example of such a study is provided by Searle's (31) follow-up of Tryon's research. Working with the strains of maze-bright and maze-dull rats developed by Tryon, Searle demonstrated that the two strains differed in a number of emotional and motivational factors, rather than in ability. Thus the strain differences were traced one step further, although many links still remain to be found between maze learning and genes. A promising methodological development within the same general area is to be found in the recent research of Hirsch and Tryon (18). Utilizing a specially devised technique for measuring individual differences in behavior among lower organisms, these investigators launched a series of studies on selective breeding for behavioral characteristics in the fruit fly, *Drosophila*. Such research can capitalize on the mass of available genetic knowledge regarding the morphology of *Drosophila*, as well as on other advantages of using such an organism in genetic studies.

Further evidence of current interest in the specific hereditary factors which influence behavior is to be found in an extensive research program in progress at the Jackson Memorial Laboratory, under the direction of Scott and Fuller (30). In general, the project is concerned with the behavioral characteristics of various breeds and cross-breeds of dogs. Analyses of some of the data gathered to date again suggest that "differences in performance are produced by differences in emotional, motivational, and peripheral processes, and that genetically caused differences in central processes may be either slight or nonexistent" (29, p. 225). In other parts of the same project, breed differences in physiological characteristics, which may in turn be related to behavioral differences, have been established.

A second line of attack is the exploration of possible relationships between behavioral characteristics and physiological variables which may in turn be traceable to hereditary factors. Research on EEG, autonomic balance, metabolic processes, and biochemical factors illustrates this approach. A lucid demonstration of the process of tracing a psychological condition to genetic factors is provided by the identification and subsequent investigation of phenylpyruvic amentia. In this case, the causal chain from defective gene, through metabolic disorder and consequent cerebral malfunctioning, to feeblemindedness and other overt symptoms can be described step by step (cf. 32; 33, pp. 389–391). Also relevant are the recent researches on neurological and biochemical correlates of schizophrenia (9). Owing to inadequate methodological controls, however, most of the findings of the latter studies must be regarded as tentative (19).

Prenatal environmental factors provide a third avenue of fruitful investigation. Especially noteworthy is the recent work of Pasamanick and his associates (27), which demonstrated a tie-up between socioeconomic level, complications of pregnancy and parturition, and psychological disorders of the offspring. In a series of studies on large samples of whites and Negroes in Baltimore, these investigators showed that various prenatal and paranatal disorders are significantly related to the occurrence of mental defect and psychiatric disorders in the child. An important source of such irregularities in the process of childbearing and birth is to be found in deficiencies of maternal diet and in other conditions associated with low socioeconomic status. An analysis of the data did in fact reveal a much higher frequency of all such medical complications in lower than in higher socioeconomic levels, and a higher frequency among Negroes than among whites.

Direct evidence of the influence of prenatal nutritional factors upon subsequent intellectual development is to be found in a recent, well-controlled experiment by Harrell et al. (16). The subjects were pregnant women in low-income groups, whose normal diets were generally quite deficient. A dietary supplement was administered to some of these women during pregnancy and lactation, while an equated control group received placebos. When tested at the ages of three and four years, the offspring of the experimental group obtained a significantly higher mean IQ than did the offspring of the controls.

Mention should also be made of animal experiments on the effects of such factors as prenatal radiation and neonatal asphyxia upon cerebral anomalies as well as upon subsequent behavior development. These experimental studies merge imperceptibly into the fourth approach to be considered, namely, the investigation of the influence of early experience upon the eventual behavioral characteristics of animals. Research in this area has been accumulating at a rapid rate. In 1954, Beach and Jaynes (8) surveyed this literature for the *Psychological Bulletin,* listing over 130 references. Several new studies have appeared since that date (e.g., 14, 21, 24, 25, 35). The variety of factors covered ranges from the type and quantity of available food to the extent of contact with human culture. A large number of experiments have been concerned with various forms of sensory deprivation and with diminished opportunities for motor exercise. Effects have been observed in many kinds of animals and in almost all aspects of behavior, including perceptual responses, motor activity, learning, emotionality, and social reactions.

In their review, Beach and Jaynes pointed out that research in this area has been stimulated by at least four distinct theoretical interests. Some studies were motivated by the traditional concern with the relative contribution of maturation and learning to behavior development. Others were designed in an effort to test certain psychoanalytic theories regarding infantile experiences, as illustrated by studies which limited the feeding responses of young animals. A third relevant influence is to be found in the work of the European biologist Lorenz (23) on early social stimulation of birds, and in particular on the special type of learning for which the term "imprinting" has been coined. A relatively large number of recent studies have centered around Hebb's (17) theory regarding the importance of early perceptual experiences upon subsequent performance in learning situations. All this research represents a rapidly growing and promising attack on the *modus operandi* of specific environmental factors.

The human counterpart of these animal studies may be found in the comparative investigation of child-rearing practices in different cultures and subcultures. This represents the fifth approach in our list. An outstanding example of such a study is that by Whiting and Child (38), published in 1953. Utilizing data on 75 primitive societies from the Cross-Cultural Files of the Yale Institute of Human Relations, these investigators set out to test a number of hypotheses regarding the relationships between child-rearing practices and personality development. This analysis was followed up by field observations in five cultures, the results of which have not yet been reported (cf. 37).

Within our own culture, similar surveys have been concerned with the diverse psychological environments provided by different social classes (11). Of particular interest are the study by Williams and Scott (39) on the association between socioeconomic level, permissiveness, and motor development among Negro children, and the exploratory research by Milner (26) on the relationship between reading readiness in first-grade children and patterns of parent-child interaction. Milner found that upon school entrance the lower-class child seems to lack chiefly two advantages enjoyed by the middle-class child. The first is described as "a warm positive family atmosphere or adult-relationship pattern which is more and more being recognized as a motivational prerequisite of any kind of adult-controlled learning." The lower-class children in Milner's study perceived adults as predominantly hostile. The second advantage is an extensive opportunity to interact verbally with adults in the family. The latter point is illustrated by parental attitudes toward mealtime conversation, lower-class parents tending to inhibit and discourage such conversation, while middle-class parents encourage it.

Most traditional studies on child-rearing practices have been designed in terms of a psychoanalytic orientation. There is need for more data pertaining to other types of hypotheses. Findings such as those of Milner on opportunities for verbalization and the resulting effects upon reading readiness represent a step in this direction. Another possible source of future data is the application of the intensive observational techniques of psychological ecology developed by Barker and Wright (7) to widely diverse socioeconomic groups.

A sixth major approach involves research on the previously cited somatopsychological relationships (6). To date, little direct information is available on the precise operation of this class of factors in psychological development. The multiplicity of ways in which physical traits—whether hereditary or environmental in origin—may influence behavior thus offers a relatively unexplored field for future study.

The seventh and final approach to be considered represents an adaptation of traditional twin studies. From the standpoint of the question "How?" there is need for closer coordination between the usual data on twin resemblance and observations of the family interactions of twins. Available data already suggest, for example, that closeness of contact and extent of environmental similarity are greater in the case of monozygotic than in the case of dizygotic twins (cf. 2). Information on the social reactions of twins toward each other and the specialization of roles is likewise of interest (2). Especially useful would be longitudinal studies of twins, beginning in early infancy and following the subjects through school age. The operation of differential environmental pressures, the development of specialized roles, and other environmental influences could thus be more clearly identified and correlated with intellectual and personality changes in the growing twins.

Parenthetically, I should like to add a remark about the traditional applications of the twin method, in which persons in different degrees of hereditary and environmental relationships to each other are simply compared for behavioral similarity. In these studies, attention has been focused principally upon the amount of resemblance of monozygotic as contrasted to dizygotic twins. Yet such a comparison is particularly difficult to interpret because of the many subtle differences in the environmental situations of the two types of twins. A more fruitful comparison would seem to be that between dizygotic twins and siblings, for whom the hereditary similarity is known to be the same. In Kallmann's monumental research on psychiatric disorders among twins (20), for example, one of the most convincing bits of evidence for the operation of hereditary factors in schizophrenia is the fact that the degrees of concordance for dizygotic twins and for siblings were practically identical. In contrast, it will be recalled that in intelligence test scores dizygotic twins resemble each other much more closely than do siblings—a finding which reveals the influence of environmental factors in intellectual development.

Summary

THE heredity-environment problem is still very much alive. Its viability is assured by the gradual replacement of the questions, "Which one?" and "How much?" by the more basic and appropriate question, "How?" Hereditary influences—as well as environmental factors of an organic nature—vary along a "continuum of indirectness." The more indirect their connection with behavior, the wider will be the range of variation of possible outcomes. One extreme of the continuum of indirectness may be illustrated by brain damage leading to mental deficiency; the other extreme, by physical characteristics associated with social stereotypes. Examples of factors falling at intermediate points include deafness, physical diseases, and motor disorders. Those environmental factors which act directly upon behavior can be ordered along a continuum of breadth or permanence of effect, as exemplified by social class membership, amount of formal schooling, language handicap, and familiarity with specific test items.

Several current lines of research offer promising techniques for exploring the *modus operandi* of hereditary and environmental factors. Outstanding among them are investigations of: (*a*) hereditary conditions which underlie behavioral differences between selectively bred groups of animals; (*b*) relations between physiological variables and individual differences in behavior, especially in the case of pathological deviations; (*c*) role of prenatal physiological factors in behavior development; (*d*) influence of early experience upon eventual behavioral characteristics; (*e*) cultural differences in child-rearing practices in relation to intellectual and emotional development; (*f*) mechanisms of somatopsychological relationships; and (*g*) psychological development of twins from infancy to maturity, together with observations of their social environment. Such approaches are extremely varied with regard to subjects employed, nature of psychological functions studied, and specific experimental procedures followed. But it is just such heterogeneity of methodology that is demanded by the wide diversity of ways in which hereditary and environmental factors interact in behavior development.

REFERENCES

1. ANASTASI, ANNE. *Psychological testing.* New York: Macmillan, 1954.

2. ANASTASI, ANNE. *Differential psychology.* (3rd ed.) New York: Macmillan, 1958.

3. ANASTASI, ANNE, & CORDOVA, F. A. Some effects of bilingualism upon the intelligence test performance of Puerto Rican children in New York City. *J. educ. Psychol.,* 1953, 44, 1–19.

4. ANASTASI, ANNE, & FOLEY, J. P., JR. A proposed reorientation in the heredity-environment controversy. *Psychol. Rev.,* 1948, 55, 239–249.

5. ARSENIAN, S. Bilingualism in the post-war world. *Psychol. Bull.,* 1945, 42, 65–86.

6. BARKER, R. G., WRIGHT, BEATRICE A., MYERSON, L., & GONICK, MOLLIE R. Adjustment to physical handicap and illness: A survey of the social psychology of physique and disability. *Soc. Sci. Res. Coun. Bull.,* 1953, No. 55 (Rev.).

7. BARKER, R. G., & WRIGHT, H. F. *Midwest*

and its children: The psychological ecology of an American town. Evanston, Ill.: Row, Peterson, 1955.

8. BEACH, F. A., & JAYNES, J. Effects of early experience upon the behavior of animals. *Psychol. Bull.*, 1954, 51, 239–263.

9. BRACKBILL, G. A. Studies of brain dysfunction in schizophrenia. *Psychol. Bull.*, 1956, 53, 210–226.

10. DARCY, NATALIE T. A review of the literature on the effects of bilingualism upon the measurement of intelligence. *J. genet. Psychol.*, 1953, 82, 21–57.

11. DAVIS, A., & HAVIGHURST, R. J. Social class and color differences in child rearing. *Amer. sociol. Rev.*, 1946, 11, 698–710.

12. DOBZHANSKY, T. The genetic nature of differences among men. In S. Persons (Ed.), *Evolutionary thought in America.* New Haven: Yale Univer. Press, 1950. Pp. 86–155.

13. DOBZHANSKY, T. Heredity, environment, and evolution. *Science,* 1950, 111, 161–166.

14. FORGUS, R. H. The effect of early perceptual learning on the behavioral organization of adult rats. *J. comp. physiol. Psychol.*, 1954, 47, 331–336.

15. HALDANE, J. B. S. *Heredity and politics.* New York: Norton, 1938.

16. HARRELL, RUTH F., WOODYARD, ELLA, & GATES, A. I. *The effect of mothers' diets on the intelligence of the offspring.* New York: Bur. Publ., Teach. Coll., Columbia Univer., 1955.

17. HEBB, D. O. *The organization of behavior.* New York: Wiley, 1949.

18. HIRSCH, J., & TRYON, R. C. Mass screening and reliable individual measurement in the experimental behavior genetics of lower organisms. *Psychol. Bull.*, 1956, 53, 402–410.

19. HORWITT, M. K. Fact and artifact in the biology of schizophrenia. *Science,* 1956, 124, 429–430.

20. KALLMANN, F. J. *Heredity in health and mental disorder; Principles of psychiatric genetics in the light of comparative twin studies.* New York: Norton, 1953.

21. KING, J. A., & GURNEY, NANCY L. Effect of early social experience on adult aggressive behavior in C57BL10 mice. *J. comp. physiol. Psychol.*, 1954, 47, 326–330.

22. LOEVINGER, JANE. On the proportional contributions of differences in nature and in nurture to differences in intel-

ligence. *Psychol. Bull.*, 1943, 40, 725–756.

23. LORENZ, K. Der Kumpan in der Umwelt des Vogels. Der Artgenosse als auslösendes Moment sozialer Verhaltungsweisen. *J. Orn., Lpz.*, 1935, 83, 137–213; 289–413.

24. LUCHINS, A. S., & FORGUS, R. H. The effect of differential postweaning environment on the rigidity of an animal's behavior. *J. genet. Psychol.*, 1955, 86, 51–58.

25. MELZACK, R. The genesis of emotional behavior: An experimental study of the dog. *J. comp. physiol. Psychol.*, 1954, 47, 166–168.

26. MILNER, ESTHER A. A study of the relationships between reading readiness in grade one school children and patterns of parent-child interaction. *Child Develpm.*, 1951, 22, 95–112.

21. PASAMANICK, B., KNOBLOCH, HILDA, & LILIENFELD, A. M. Socioeconomic status and some precursors of neuropsychiatric disorder. *Amer. J. Orthopsychiat.*, 1956, 26, 594–601.

28. SCHWESINGER, GLADYS C. *Heredity and environment.* New York: Macmillan, 1933.

29. SCOTT, J. P., & CHARLES, MARGARET S. Some problems of heredity and social behavior. *J. gen. Psychol.*, 1953, 48, 209–230.

30. SCOTT, J. P., & FULLER, J. L. Research on genetics and social behavior at the Roscoe B. Jackson Memorial Laboratory, 1946–1951—A progress report. *J. Hered.*, 1951, 42, 191–197.

31. SEARLE, L. V. The organization of hereditary maze-brightness and maze-dullness. *Genet. Psychol. Monogr.*, 1949, 39, 279–325.

32. SNYDER, L. H. The genetic approach to human individuality. *Sci. Mon., N. Y.*, 1949, 68, 165–171.

33. SNYDER, L. H., & DAVID, P. R. *The principles of heredity.* (5th ed.) Boston: Heath, 1957.

34. SPOERL, DOROTHY T. Bilinguality and emotional adjustment. *J. abnorm. soc. Psychol.*, 1943, 38, 37–57.

35. THOMPSON, W. R., & MELZACK, R. Early environment. *Sci Amer.*, 1956, 194 (1), 38–42.

36. TRYON, R. C. Genetic differences in maze-learning ability in rats. *Yearb. nat. Soc. Stud. Educ.*, 1940, 39, Part I, 111–119.

37. WHITING, J. W. M., et al. *Field guide for a study of socialization in five societies.* Cambridge, Mass.: Harvard Univer., 1954 (mimeo.).

38. WHITING, J. W. M., & CHILD, I. L. *Child*

training and personality: A cross-cultural study. New Haven: Yale Univer. Press, 1953.

39. WILLIAMS, JUDITH R., & SCOTT, R. G. Growth and development of Negro infants: IV. Motor development and its relationship to child rearing practices in two groups of Negro infants. *Child Develpm.,* 1953, 24, 103–121.

40. WOODWORTH, R. S. Heredity and environment: A critical survey of recently published material on twins and foster children. *Soc. Sci. Res. Coun. Bull.,* 1941, No. 47.

JERRY HIRSCH *and* JAMES C. BOUDREAU

12. *The Heritability of Phototaxis in a Population of* Drosophila Melanogaster

IT has been frequently observed that individual differences (IDs) in behavior can be inherited; e.g., Tryon (11) has reported on the inheritance of maze-learning ability, and Kallmann and Baroff (5) on the inheritance of behavior pathologies. The present paper extends the study of the inheritance of IDs in behavior to a part of the phylogenetic series at which experimental behavior genetic (BG) analysis is feasible, viz., the genus *Drosophila*. The behavior chosen for BG analysis is the reaction to light, phototaxis—an apparently innate or unconditioned response. Taxes have the advantage of representing relatively constant S-R relationships: the repeated presentation of a single stimulus value appears to elicit, depending on the method of measurement, either a characteristic response or a characteristic probability of response. Both the characteristics of the response and the probability of the response have been shown to vary as a function of two parameters, the value of the stimulus presented and the strain of organisms stimulated (1, 8).

Brown and Hall have measured strain differences in phototaxis. The immediate purpose of the present study is to measure IDs in, and to estimate the heritability of, phototaxis within a single strain. (Roughly, "heritability," h^2, refers to that portion of the total variance due to additive genetic causes [6, p. 111].) This is one of several studies of *Drosophila* behavior in which an experimental attack is being made on the long unresolved question of whether abilities are under the control of one general factor (9) or many specific factors (10).

At present three *Drosophila* behaviors are under study: phototaxis, geotaxis (3), and eating rate (2).

Method

EXPERIMENTAL DESIGN

INDIVIDUAL differences in phototaxis were measured in a Y maze by the method of mass screening (4). The measurements consisted of ten mass-screening trials, which in the foundation population had the reliability, $r_{tt} = 0.673$ (4, Formula 6).

Selection pressure was applied, and a system of assortative mating was used, i.e., the highest-scoring animals within the high strain and the lowest-scoring animals within the low strain were bred together, respectively.

BEHAVIORAL ANALYSIS

Apparatus. Individual differences in the approach to light were studied in the Y maze shown in FIGURE 1. The maze consisted of three 5-in. lengths of acrylic tubing, *f, e, d,* having ½-in. inside diameter. These tubes were attached to a Y joint, *a,* having ½-in. outside diameter and ⅜-in. inside diameter. Tubes *d* and *e,* which served as the starting path and the lighted arm of the Y, respectively, were attached to the center unit, *a,* by plastic sleeves, *b* and *c.* Both sleeves were fitted with sliding plastic "doors" 0.02-in. thick to prevent premature approach to the choice point and retracing after a choice.

Reprinted by permission of the American Psychological Association and the authors from the *Journal of Comparative and Physiological Psychology*, 1958, vol. 51, pp. 647–51.

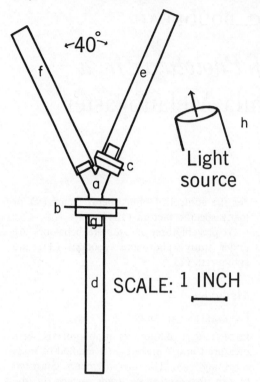

FIG. 1. Apparatus for measuring the reaction of *Drosophila* to light.

All parts of the maze were painted black on the outside with the exception of the starting tube, *d*, and the lighted tube, *e*. To eliminate reflections, the cotton plunger in the starting tube was dyed black. The attrahent was light reflected from cotton at the end of Arm *e*. Although the same tube (Arm *e*) was always illuminated, the illuminated side was varied after each block of two trials (tests have shown that the tubes themselves do not act as stimuli). This was accomplished by rotating the entire front section of the maze 180° on the Y joint and shifting the light to the other side. A microscope light was placed at *h* and focused on the cotton at the end of *e*. The distance from the light source to the cotton was 6 in. The illumination at this distance is 100 ft-c., as measured by a Weston illumination meter, Model 756. Thus, the stimulating source of light was indirect. This was necessary because in preliminary studies using a direct source, i.e., a light shining through *e* to *d*, it was evident that secondary reflections were being set up in the starting arm, *d*, and that these constituted competing attrahents with the result that many flies never left the starting tube.

Procedure. The sexes were run separately on successive days. Each generation the males were run one day after hatching and the females two days after hatching. The role of heredity in determining IDs in behavior was assessed by the response of the population to selection. Virgin females are necessary for selective breeding. Since *melanogaster* females remain virgin for only the first 7 to 8 hr. after hatching, the cultures were cleared of all flies the day before an experiment, and only those flies that hatched in the following 7 hr. were tested. Occasionally, to obtain larger samples, flies were collected over two consecutive 7-hr. periods. Hence, the maximum age difference among the animals never exceeded 14 hr.

The behavior experiment consisted of introducing a group of flies into the starting tube of the Y maze and inserting a plug of black cotton behind them to seal the tube. The cotton was immediately pushed forward to within 0.5-in. of the door to the choice point so that all flies would be in the vicinity of the choice point at the start of a trial.

A trial lasted 30 sec. Both doors were opened at the beginning of a trial, and 30 sec. later the door to the illuminated arm of the Y was closed. In this way, on each trial the flies that approached the light were separated from the others. That is, on Trial 1 the initial group of flies was separated into two pass-fail subgroups. On Trial 2 both the pass group and the fail group from Trial 1 were tested and were in turn subdivided into pass-fail subgroups. In the method of mass screening, the subgroups obtained on one trial are retested separately on the next trial and further subdivided. A complete account of the method is given elsewhere (4). In this experiment ten mass-screening trials were used; therefore, the distribution of final scores ranges from 0 through 10.

Dyes were added to the medium on which the flies were raised. Bismark brown was used for the low strain and Nile blue for the high strain (tests have shown that reversing the colors does not affect the behavior). The colors were ingested along with the food. Since the females of the high and low strains could be distinguished by the colors they had absorbed, they were run in the apparatus together. It was necessary, however, to run the males in separate groups, since they did not show the colors clearly.

GENETIC ANALYSIS

Subjects. The Ss were 3,424 fruit flies, *Drosophila melanogaster,* Formosa wild type. The initial sample of animals was obtained from regular stocks in the genetics laboratory of the zoology department of the University of California, Berkeley. The flies were raised on standard *Drosophila* medium (to which color had been added) in ½ pt. culture bottles at 25° C.

Mating system. Selection pressure of variable intensity was applied under a system of restricted assortative mating. Animals were mated on the basis of phenotypic merit without regard to family relationship. In the foundation population animals with similar extreme phototactic scores were mated. In all filial generations the same selection criteria were applied with the further restriction that matings were always within and never between the two strains established by selection from the foundation population. Thus, the high and low strains were reproductively isolated, and inbreeding undoubtedly increased down through the generations.

If a sufficient number of animals received extreme scores, i.e., 0 or 10, only members of these classes were chosen for breeding. If not, individuals in adjacent classes were also used for breeding. The intensity of selection pressure increased because the percentage of animals receiving extreme scores increased as selection progressed. Selection was carried on over 29 generations with the exception of Generations 10, 11, 12, and 13, when mass mating was permitted (within the separate strains) and no behavior tests were made.[1]

1 As the medium on which to establish the basic principles of BG, *Drosophila* is thus an animal quite

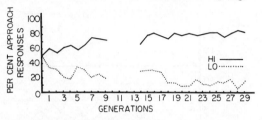

FIG. 2. Percentage of trials on which light was approached per generation.

Results

MALE and female data have been combined except for Generations 7, 8, and 9, for which female data alone are presented. In these generations the males were given only enough test trials to identify the extreme scorers for breeding. Data are not available for Generations 10 through 13 or for Generation 16, when the apparatus broke.

FIGURE 2 presents the percentage of trials on which the light was approached by the high and low strains over 29 generations of selection. Clearly, there is an early response to selection, and despite fluctuations the expected values of the selected strains show progressive divergence from the foundation population value of 51.6% to asymptotic values of approximately 80.0% for the high strain and 15.0% for the low strain.

FIGURE 3 presents the distribution of phototactic scores for the foundation population and for filial Generations 1, 2, 7, and 29. Inspection of the figure reveals that selection effects marked changes in dispersion as well as in central tendency. The changes in dispersion are shown in FIGURE 4, where the ratio of the variance of each selected generation to that of the foundation population is plotted.

It has been predicted that the limits of selective breeding would depend upon the reliability of the ID measurements in the foundation population (4, p. 410), i.e., when the variance in the selected lines decreases to the size of the variance error of measurement in the foundation population, further

superior to the laboratory mammals such as mice, rats, or guinea pigs. Compare the present results, obtained in about a year, with the Tryon study (11), which required over 15 years.

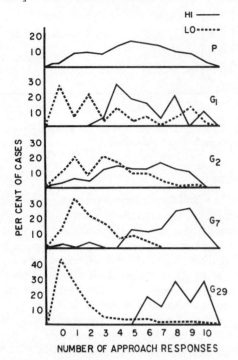

FIG. 3. Distribution of light-approach scores for Generations 0, 1, 2, 7, and 29.

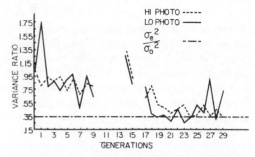

FIG. 4. The ratio of the variance of each selected generation to the variance of the foundation population, σ_i^2/σ_0^2, for the "high" and "low" phototactic strains. σ_e^2/σ_0^2 is the asymptote predicted from the reliability of the foundation population scores (see text).

selection should be ineffective, since at that point the method of observation is no longer discriminating among individuals. In the present study the foundation population measurements have a reliability $r_{tt} = 0.673$, a variance $\sigma_0^2 = 6.38$, and a variance error of measurement $\sigma_e^2 = \sigma_0^2 (1 - r_{tt}) = 6.38 (1 - 0.673) = 2.09$ (4, Formula 8). Hence the ratio of the variance of the selected strains to that of the foundation population should approach the asymptote:

$$\frac{\sigma_e^2}{\sigma_0^2} = 2.09/6.38 = 0.327$$

In FIGURE 4 it can be seen that the variance ratio for the high photo strain appears to be settling down near the line 0.327. The variance ratio for the low strain, however, has not stabilized enough yet to determine whether it is approaching the predicted asymptote.

Next, let us examine the extent to which IDs in phototaxis are genetically determined. If it is assumed that the average of the vari-

ances of the two selected strains over Generations 28 and 29 represents an upper limit to the variability to be expected in an isogenic line, then we have available a conservative estimate of the heritability, h^2, of phototaxis in the foundation population under the present experimental conditions.

All methods of estimating heritability rest on measuring how much more closely animals with similar genotypes resemble each other than less closely related animals do. . . . Variation within isogenic lines is wholly environmental. Comparing this with the variation in an otherwise similar random breeding population may give an estimate of heritability (7, p. 92).

For the high strain $\sigma_{28}^2 = 2.88$ and $\sigma_{29}^2 = 2.08$, for the low strain $\sigma_{28}^2 = 1.63$ and $\sigma_{29}^2 = 4.51$. The average of these four variances is $\overline{\sigma^2} = 2.77$. Hence: $h^2 = (\sigma_0^2 - \overline{\sigma^2})/\sigma_0^2 = (6.38 - 2.77)/6.38 = 0.566$, i.e., at least 57% of the phenotypic variance is genetic variance. This is a conservative estimate because the value of the reliability coefficient sets an upper limit to the values an estimate may take (as calculated, h^2 is 84% of the reliable phenotypic variance). Furthermore, h^2 contains only the additive portions of the genetic variance; it does not include variance due to dominance or to epistasis (i.e., dominance of nonallelic genes).

No estimate can be made of the heredity-environment interaction because only a single stimulus condition has been employed.

Discussion

THE aim of the present experiment has been both exploratory and descriptive. Its purpose has been to examine the possibility of studying IDs in behavior and their genetic bases in a species on which detailed genetic analysis can be performed.

The results which have been reported indicate that the study of *Drosophila* behavior is quite feasible, that IDs in performance can be measured in groups both reliably and efficiently by the method of mass screening, and that the IDs' variance contains a large genetic component to which the techniques of experimental genetics may now be applied.

Since the present data have been obtained with a laboratory stock considered to be rather inbred [2] and therefore not very heterogeneous genetically, it is to be expected that a larger genetic variance would be found in a less inbred natural population. These findings have implications for psychological theory.

Theory testing in psychology is usually done on human *S*s or on laboratory strains of animals which, it is reasonable to assume, are genetically much less alike than our *Drosoph-*

2 Personal communication from Th. Dobzhansky.

ila. (The Formosa stock has been maintained in the laboratory in small cultures for more than 20 years. Inbreeding has, therefore, had over 700 generations in which to exercise its homogenizing influence. Within the same period of time laboratory strains of rats would have completed about 70 generations. Furthermore, *Drosophila melanogaster* have only 4 independently assorting pairs of chromosomes whereas rats have 21 and human beings at least 23.) If large genetic differences do exist in the populations now being studied by psychologists, it should be of interest to determine in what ways stimulus control of behavior depends upon the genotype under stimulation.

Summary

BEHAVIOR genetic analysis of the unconditioned response, phototaxis, has been carried through several steps: Individual differences in phototaxis have been measured reliably and efficiently in a *Drosophila* population by the method of mass screening. The genetic determination of individual differences in behavior has been demonstrated by the response to selection, and the heritability has been estimated to be more than one-half the phenotypic variance.

REFERENCES

1. BROWN, F. A., & HALL, V. A. The directive influence of light upon *Drosophila melanogaster* Meig and some of its eye mutants. *J. exp. Zool.,* 1936, 74, 205–220.

2. DURKIN, R. D. Eating behavior of *Drosophila melanogaster.* Unpublished honors study, Psychology Department, Columbia Univer., 1957.

3. HIRSCH, J. Behavior genetic studies of individual differences in *Drosophila melanogaster. Amer. Psychologist,* 1956, 11, 450–451. (Abstract)

4. HIRSCH, J., & TRYON, R. C. Mass screening and reliable individual measurement in the experimental behavior genetics of lower organisms. *Psychol. Bull.,* 1956, 53, 402–410.

5. KALLMANN, F. J., & BAROFF, G. S. Abnormal psychology. *Ann. Rev. Psychol.,* 1956, 6, 297–326.

6. LERNER, I. M. *Population genetics and animal improvement.* Cambridge: Cambridge Univer. Press, 1950.

7. LUSH, J. L. *Animal breeding plans.* Ames, Iowa: Collegiate Press, 1945.

8. SCOTT, J. P. Effects of single genes on the behavior of *Drosophila. Amer. Naturalist,* 1943, 77, 184–190.

9. SPEARMAN, C. *The abilities of man.* New York: Macmillan, 1927.

10. TRYON, R. C. A theory of psychological components—an alternative to "mathematical factors." *Psychol. Rev.,* 1935, 42, 425–454.

11. TRYON, R. C. Genetic differences in maze-learning ability in rats. In *Yearb. nat. Soc. Stud. Educ.,* 1940, 39(I), 111–119.

DAVID K. SPELT

13. The Conditioning of the Human Fetus in Utero

IT is commonly recognized that environmental factors influence the organism from the moment of fertilization, but experimental studies of their effects on the behavior of mammalian fetuses have usually disturbed the fetal environment severely. The possibility that conditioned response technique provides a method which would eliminate resort to surgery has long been seen. Successful conditioning of young infants (2, 3, 6, 7, 8, 10) and of sub-human mammals in which neural structures had been damaged (1, 11, 12, 13) indicated that lack of cortical development in the fetus presented no problem. Ray (15) made the first attempt, using the previously reported fetal response to loud sound (4, 14) which he sought to condition to a vibrotactile stimulation applied to the maternal abdomen. Although results on his single case were inconclusive, his use of individual receiving tambours, taped to the maternal abdomen over the fetus, eliminated much distortion of records by maternal breathing. This study was suggested by Ray's work and resembles his in general procedure.

Apparatus

THE source of noise (US) was a box 29¾ in. square, 10⅝ in. deep, made of ½ in. pine stock. It stood on one side, surmounted by a metal framework which carried an oak clapper five in. wide, 22½ in. long, and one in. thick. Pivoted one in. from the top, the clapper had a narrow steel handle nine in. long. A steel spring ran from each edge of this handle to the supporting framework, so that a pull of some eight pounds was necessary to raise the clapper, through an arc of 85°, to the stop which limited its excursion. When released the clapper struck the face of the box sharply, closing a circuit through a dry cell and signal marker. On top of the box were mounted all the controls for E's use.

Vibrotactile stimulation (CS) was provided by an ordinary doorbell, with the gong removed, the striker bent outward at an angle of 90° to its original position, and the interrupter soldered shut. The striker vibrated strongly but almost silently in response to four volts of 60-cycle A.C. This stimulator, fastened to a block of wood, was held in an adjustable metal clamp at the end of a movable support affixed to the side of the bed in which the Ss lay. Thus, the striker could be made to vibrate perpendicularly to the surface of any part of the abdomen. A dual key controlled the transformer-stimulator circuit and a dry cell-signal marker circuit.

Fetal movements were recorded by means of three pairs of 50-mm. receiving tambours taped to the maternal abdomen, each pair

This study was conducted, under the direction of Dr. J. F. Dashiell, in partial fulfillment of the requirements for the doctoral degree at the University of North Carolina. Reprinted by permission of the American Psychological Association and the author from the *Journal of Experimental Psychology*, 1948, vol. 38, pp. 338–46.

[This study has been criticized for possibly confusing the classical conditioning procedure, which produces learning, with the pseudoconditioning procedure, which produces a lower threshold of response to similar stimuli such as vibrations due to sound and touch. The necessary controlled experiment has not been done. However in either case the responsiveness of the human fetal infant to physical changes in the environment is demonstrated.—Ed.]

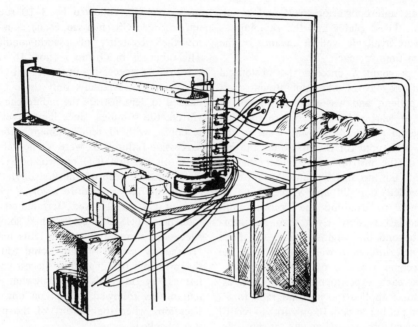

FIG. 1. Sketch of apparatus arrangement for fetal conditioning study.

connected to a one-inch recording tambour. The method of placing the tambours is described below. S operated a signal marker whenever she felt fetal movement by pressing a push button which she held in her hand. A Manning pneumograph (16) connected to a one-in. recording tambour supplied records of maternal breathing. An electric clock and signal marker provided a time line marked in intervals of five sec.

All recording devices were vertically moving ink-writers which bore upon an electrically driven long-paper kymograph. The kymograph, apparatus controls, and E were screened from S's view when she lay in bed, as indicated in FIG. 1.

Subjects and Procedure

EXCEPT for three non-pregnant control Ss and one of the pregnant Ss, all 16 Ss were selected from patients attending the obstetrical clinic of an urban hospital. All but two were past the seventh calendar month of gestation. Only patients whose histories were free from evidence of pathology during pregnancy were considered, and only

those willing to participate actually served as Ss. Not that Ss knew they were taking part in an experiment, for the word was scrupulously avoided by everyone who dealt with them. Ss were told that since confinement was approaching and since their progress thus far had been excellent, the staff wanted some 'special information' to be obtained from X-ray pictures and from records of fetal movements to be made twice daily for 10 days or two weeks. They were told that no cost was involved, and that they would be guaranteed free care in the hospital's obstetrical ward when they came to term. Since the hospital was sufficiently crowded to admit only a fraction of the group attending the clinic, certainty of admission was an important reward. It was made quite clear, however, that they were free to decline without jeopardizing the normal chance of admission, for no record was made of their decision on the clinic card. A few of those interviewed did so decline.

After appointments for subsequent admission to the hospital had been arranged, each S went to the radiological department, where two X-ray pictures of the abdomen were made: an anteroposterior view and a lateral view. These plates and the radiologist's report were available well in advance of the admission time for each S.

Each pregnant S entered the obstetrical ward on the day of her appointment as a regular patient, and was required to rest in bed for at least a half-day before the first experimental period. When she went to the experimental room for the first time, the operation of the instruments was superficially explained, but no insight into the problem was provided, nor did any S ever have an opportunity to examine the records until after her last session. Even then no information beyond the original statements made in the first interview was offered, lest the study become a matter of ward gossip.

Before each experimental period the assisting nurse applied the pneumograph to S's chest and put her to bed. In an effort to record fetal movements as adequately as possible, the data from X-rays, external manual examination, and fetal heart sounds were employed to determine the position of the fetus. One pair of receiving tambours was taped to the abdomen over the fetal head, another over the fetal arms, and the third over fetal legs.[1] It was never supposed, however, that selective records were thus obtained, or that movements recorded from one area had different significance from movements recorded elsewhere. Next, the vibrotactile stimulator was adjusted at some convenient spot on the abdomen, although its location varied for every S from time to time. Then S took the push button with which she indicated that she felt fetal movement. Finally, E connected the abdominal tambours and the pneumograph to the recording apparatus, and started the clock and kymograph.

Procedure during the first experimental periods varied slightly for different Ss. Most Ss had two sessions daily, lasting from 30 to 75 min. each, depending largely on S's comfort. Three Ss in the experimental group (Group I, nos. 10, 12, 15) received 8–16

[1] In 12 of 13 cases the fetus was in cephalic presentation at the time of X-ray; in 10 of 13 cases, the fetal back was to the left, with the head usually in the left occiput anterior position.

successive US, followed by 3–10 successive unreinforced CS (five sec. each) as a control for the possibility of pseudo-conditioning. The other Ss in Group I (nos. 16, 17) received 5–15 successive unreinforced CS without prior US. Actually, only three CS were needed to demonstrate the indifference of the vibrotactile stimulus, since it never elicited a response, without reinforcement, after three successive failures. Ss were warned about the noise on the first trial or two, but very few were startled, even on the first day.

Conditioning procedure involved presentation of CS for five sec., terminated by the loud noise (US). Since Ray had shown that successful stimulation of the fetus induces a "refractory period" lasting some four min., the principle of separating successive stimulations by intervals of somewhat greater length was followed, except on one or two occasions when the validity of the principle was checked.

Special control groups were treated somewhat differently. Thus, Group II consisted of six Ss (nos. 1, 3, 4, 8, 9, 14) with whom the CS alone was tested for indifference during the last two months of pregnancy. Group III included three non-pregnant Ss (nos. 19, 20, 21) each of whom served for two "conditioning" periods. In Group IV were two Ss (nos. 5, 18) with whom the effect of fetal age on the response to sound (US) alone was investigated by beginning presentation in the seventh month of gestation.

Results

GROUP I

Two Ss in this group had displayed indications that the conditioning procedure had been effective, when the experiment was interrupted by labor. S-10 during the first four sessions received 16 successive US followed by 10 successive CS. Although the fetus responded regularly to the noise, the vibrotactile stimulus was ineffective. By the eighth session three successive responses to CS alone appeared, but labor began the following day. Similarly, with S-17 three successive responses to CS alone appeared by the eighth session,

TABLE 1

Results from Subject 16

Trial numbers in italics indicate unreinforced presentations of the conditioned stimulus; all others are paired presentations. Letters in the Resp. column show which recording systems revealed the response: H—fetal head; A—fetal arms; L—fetal legs; M—maternal signal. This S had only one experimental period per day; the interval between successive days is indicated by the dashes.

TRIAL	RESP.	TRIAL	RESP.	TRIAL	RESP.	TRIAL	RESP.	TRIAL	RESP.
14	LM	32	HALM	50	HA M	67	H LM	84	
15	LM	33	HALM	-----	-----	68	H	85	
16	H LM	34	HALM	51	ALM	69	H M	86	H M
17	H LM	35	LM	52	H M	70	HALM	87	
18	LM	36	LM	53	LM	71	HALM	88	HALM
19	H LM	37	ALM	54	ALM	72	H	89	
20	ALM	-----	-----	55	HALM	73	HALM	90	
21	LM	38	H LM	56	M	74	ALM	91	H LM
22	M	39	H LM	57	LM	75	HALM	92	
23	H LM	40	H LM	58	ALM	76	HALM	93	
24	HALM	41	H LM	59	HALM	77	HALM	94	
-----	-----	42		60	ALM	78	HALM	95	
25	LM	43	ALM	61		79	HALM	-----	-----
26	A M	44	HA M	62	ALM	-----	-----	96	
27	ALM	45	H M	-----	-----	80	A M	97	
28	ALM	46	HALM	63	H M	81	H LM	98	
29	H LM	47	HALM	64	H M	82	HALM	99	HALM
30	HALM	48	A M	65	H LM	83	H M	100	
31		49		66	HALM				

but the onset of labor precluded further experimenting.

Results with the other three Ss in Group I will be presented in greater detail. Records of S-16 showed the first fetal response to CS alone after 21 paired stimulations, and others appeared at intervals until in the sixth session, after 59 reinforced presentations, a series of seven successive CRs occurred. At the beginning of the seventh session the next morning, and with no reinforcement, four more CRs were elicited, followed by irregularly spaced responses as experimental extinction developed. There was no indication of recovery of the response the following day, although US was still effective. These data are summarized in TABLE 1.

S-15 received 10 successive US followed by three successive CS during the first two sessions. As before, the noise was effective, the vibrotactile stimulus ineffective. The first response to CS alone occurred in the sixth session after 16 paired stimulations. Others occurred irregularly, but since this S was still in the eighth month of gestation, she was allowed to leave the hospital at her own request after the eleventh session. She returned two weeks later and the experiment was resumed. The CS alone was ineffective, but after 31 reinforcements six successive CRs appeared, followed by experimental extinction. With 12 more reinforcements the CR was reinstated at the end of the session. The data obtained after S's return are summarized in TABLE 2.

S-12 was perhaps the most interesting of the group, because of the extensive study of the CR which was possible. During her first two sessions, eight successive US were followed by four successive CS which were ineffective. The earliest response to CS alone came in the seventh session after 21 paired stimulations, when on two successive trials (TABLE 3, nos. 27–28) CRs occurred. Three more CRs were obtained at the beginning of the ninth (nos. 40–44). When four successive CS produced no direct record of fetal response (nos. 55–58), S was permitted a 24-hour rest period to see whether spontaneous recovery would develop. That such re-

TABLE 2

Results from Subject 15

Trial numbers in italics indicate unreinforced presentations of the conditioned stimulus; all others are paired presentations. Letters in the Resp. column show which recording systems revealed the response: H—fetal head; A—fetal arms; L—fetal legs; M—maternal signal. Intervals between sessions on a single day are shown by asterisks, between sessions on successive days by dashes.

TRIAL	RESP.	TRIAL	RESP.	TRIAL	RESP.	TRIAL	RESP.	TRIAL	RESP.
72		86	AL	98	A	111	ALM	124	LM
73	HALM	-----	-----	99	HA	112	HALM	* * * * *	* * * * *
74	L	87		100	A	113	HALM	125	
75		88	HAL	101		114	HALM	126	L
76		89	L	102	HALM	115	HALM	127	L
77	ALM	90		103	HALM	116	HALM	128	
78		91	HA	104	L	* * * * *	* * * * *	129	ALM
79		92	HA M	105	HALM	117	AL	130	LM
* * * * *	* * * * *	93	HALM	-----	-----	118	L	131	ALM
80		94	HALM	106	LM	119		132	ALM
81		95	HA M	107	AL	120		133	
82	ALM	* * * * *	* * * * *	108		121		134	M
83	L	96	LM	109	L	122	L	135	
84	L	97	L	110	HA	123	HAL	136	LM
85	HALM								

TABLE 3

Results from Subject 12

Trial numbers in italics indicate unreinforced presentations of the conditioned stimulus alone; all others are paired presentations except no. 91, which was the sound alone. Letters in the Resp. column show which recording systems revealed the response: H—fetal head; A—fetal arms; L—fetal legs; M—maternal signal. Intervals between sessions on a single day are shown by asterisks, between intervals on successive days by dashes. Longer intervals are specifically stated.

TRIAL	RESP.	TRIAL	RESP.	TRIAL	RESP.	TRIAL	RESP.	TRIAL	RESP.
22	M	41	LM	58		77		95	
23	L	-----	-----	-----	-----	78		96	
24	A	42	LM	59	M	Three weeks'		97	ALM
25	LM	43	L	60	ALM	interval		98	LM
26	LM	44	LM	61		79		* * * * *	* * * * *
-----	-----	45		62	LM	80	AL	99	HAL
27	ALM	46		63		81	L	100	AL
28	A M	47		64	ALM	82	L	101	HAL
29	M	48		65	L	83		102	L
30	A M	* * * * *	* * * * *	66	M	84	ALM	103	
31	ALM	49		67	LM	85	LM	104	L
32	L	50	ALM	* * * * *	* * * * *	86	LM	105	
33	ALM	51	M	68	ALM	87	A	106	L
* * * * *	* * * * *	52	LM	69	ALM	88		107	
34	LM	53	ALM	70		89		13 days'	interval
35	LM	54	LM	71		90		108	
36	LM	-----	-----	72		91	LM	109	
37		55	M	73		-----	-----	110	
38	L	56		74		92		111	
39	LM	57		75	ALM	93	LM	112	HALM
40	ALM			76	LM	94		113	AL

covery occurred is evident. Eleven successive CS alone produced six clear reactions in the fetal records and on two other trials the maternal signal was pressed (cf. TABLE 3, trials 59–69). The response was then extinguished again, although the fetus still responded to the noise. S was then discharged, but returned to the hospital 18 days later as a result of false labor. Hence it was possible to resume experimental work exactly three weeks after the last previous session. In the next two periods, CS was presented alone 12 times in succession; seven of the first nine stimuli were effective, showing retention of the response over this interval, while the last three were ineffective. On the next day only two CRs were elicited in eight trials, and S was again discharged. She returned 13 days later, when X-rays showed that the fetus was probably past term, but it was possible to run one more experimental session before labor was medically induced. There was no response to CS alone although the two stimuli together were effective. These data appear in TABLE 3.

GROUP II

This group included six Ss, all in the late eighth or the ninth month of pregnancy, with whom the CS alone was tested to discover whether it became effective simply as a result of advancing fetal maturity. Although each S received 4–7 unreinforced vibrotactile stimuli, none of the 32 trials elicited a response.

GROUP III

In this group were three non-pregnant Ss, members of the hospital's staff, each of whom served for two standard experimental periods. Presentation of the two stimuli in varying combinations, for 16–23 trials per S during the two sessions, yielded no records remotely resembling those obtained with pregnant Ss.

GROUP IV

This group consisted of two Ss whose records indicated that the US used (noise) was ineffective before the eighth calendar month of gestation. S-5, in whom gestation had progressed to the latter part of the seventh month

was exposed to 39 successive US. On only one occasion did the records show what might have been a fetal response. On eight other trials the maternal signal appeared without evidence of movement in the fetal records.

S-18 was tested at intervals from the middle of the seventh month to the middle of the eighth. During the seventh month 60 US yielded no indication of movement, either in the fetal or the maternal records. During the eighth month the US was presented four times during the first week, with the maternal signal indicating fetal movement unsupported by the direct records. In the third week, seven stimuli produced three definite fetal reactions and one indicated by the maternal signal only.

Discussion

AT present no experimental procedure will permit one to test Holt's thesis (5, pp. 37–43) that intra-uterine conditioning accounts for certain of the behavioral characteristics of the human neonate. On the other hand, it is clear that the human fetus can be conditioned experimentally during the last two months of pregnancy. The records, of course, cannot be expected to yield data on comparative motility of fetal head, arms, and legs. The placement of the fetal body during the last weeks of gestation and the limitations imposed by recording only from the abdominal surface preclude such interpretation. Furthermore, it is impossible to derive precise quantitative values for latency, duration, or extent of response, for much the same reasons. Actually, examination of the records indicates that responses to paired stimuli have shorter latencies than do CRs, but the distributions overlap. In the same way, although both sharp, quick responses and slower, longer lasting movements appear, it has not been possible to attach any significance to the difference.

If these records do not permit analysis of the sort mentioned, they are, none the less, not greatly distorted by such factors as maternal breathing and gross bodily movement. When such distortion does occur, as the result of a deep sigh for example, it can be readily detected because all three fetal curves move in the same direction simultaneously, and the irregularity appears in the maternal breathing curve as well. This is never true of fetal responses, and the fact is obviously of importance in reading the curves.

The amount of agreement between the direct records and the maternal signal indicating perceived fetal movement is significant. As a measure of the degree of correspondence, a bi-serial r was computed, based upon the number of fetal curves (0–3) in which a given response appeared, and upon its presence or absence in the maternally made record. For 529 stimulations of the 13 pregnant Ss, $r_{bis} = .784$, $\sigma_r = .017$.

Obviously, further study of more Ss is to be desired. Analysis of the effective unconditioned stimuli which may be used, of the length of retention which may be obtained, and of the age at which sensitivity to auditory stimuli develops would be profitable. In this last connection, it may be significant that Langworthy (9) found fibers of the cochlear branch of the eighth cranial nerve much more lightly myelinated in a seven months fetus

than in the eighth months old specimen which he examined. It will be recalled that in our two Ss who served during the seventh month of pregnancy, the noise was almost completely ineffective as a stimulus to fetal movement. There are, then, enough problems still deserving investigation to justify further study of the fetal conditioned reaction.

Summary

UTILIZING a vibrotactile CS and a loud noise as US, it was possible to establish a CR in the human fetus in utero during the last two months of gestation. Some 15–20 paired stimulations were required to establish the response to the point at which one could anticipate three or four successive responses to CS alone, but additional practice made possible as many as 11 successive CRs. Experimental extinction, spontaneous recovery, and retention of the response over a three weeks' interval were demonstrated, as well as a significant degree of agreement between direct records of fetal movements and maternal report of perception of fetal movement.

REFERENCES

1. BROGDEN, W. J., & GANTT, W. H. Cerebellar conditioned reflexes. Amer. J. Physiol., 1937, 119, 277–278.

2. DENISOVA, M. P., & FIGURIN, N. L. [The problem of the first associated food reflexes in infants.] (Vopr. Genet. Refleks. Pedol. Mladen., 1929, 1, 81–88.) See: Arch. Psychol., 1933, 23, No. 148, 73–75.

3. FIGURIN, N. L., & DENISOVA, M. P. [The physiology of the differentiation of external stimuli. Based upon experimental data on the formation of differentiations in infants under one year.] (Vopr. Genet. Refleks. Pedol. Mladen., 1929, 1, 131–165.) See: Arch. Psychol., 1933, 23, No. 148, 75–76.

4. FORBES, H. S., & FORBES, H. B. Fetal sense reactions: hearing. J. comp. Psychol., 1927, 7, 353–355.

5. HOLT, E. B. Animal drive and the learning process. New York: Holt, 1931.

6. JONES, H. E. The retention of conditioned emotional reactions in infancy. J. genet. Psychol., 1930, 37, 485–498.

7. KANTROW, R. W. An investigation of conditioned feeding responses and concomitant adaptive behavior in young infants. Univ. Ia. Stud. Child Welf., 1937, 13, No. 3.

8. KASATKIN, N. I., & LEVIKOVA, A. M. On the development of early conditioned reflexes and differentiation of auditory stimuli in infants. J. exp. Psychol., 1935, 18, 1–19.

9. LANGWORTHY, O. R. Development of behavior patterns and myelinization of the nervous system in the human fetus and infant. Carnegie Instn. Publ. No. 443, 1–57.

10. LEVIKOVA, A. M., & NEVYMAKOVA, G. A. [The problem of the formation and differentiation of associated reflexes to auditory stimuli in infants.] (Vopr. Genet. Refleks. Pedol. Mladen., 1929, 1, 89–105.) See: Arch. Psychol., 1933, 23, No. 148, 77–78.

11. LIGHT, J. S., & GANTT, W. H. Essential part of reflex arc for establishment of conditioned reflex. Formation of conditioned reflex after exclusion of motor peripheral end. J. comp. Psychol., 1936, 21, 19–36.

12. MARQUIS, D. G., & HILGARD, E. R. Conditioned lid responses to light in dogs after removal of the visual cortex. *J. comp. Psychol.*, 1936, 22, 157–178.

13. MARQUIS, D. G., & HILGARD, E. R. Conditioned responses to light in monkeys after removal of the occipital lobes. *Brain*, 1937, 60, 1–12.

14. PEIPER, A. Sinnesempfindungen des Kindes vor seiner Geburt. *Mschr. Kinderheilk.*, 1925, 29, 236–241.

15. RAY, W. S. A preliminary study of fetal conditioning. *Child Develpm.*, 1932, 3, 173–177.

16. SPELT, D. K. The Manning pneumograph. *Amer. J. Psychol.*, 1939, 52, 116.

LEWIS M. TERMAN

14. The Discovery and Encouragement of Exceptional Talent

· · ·

I HAVE often been asked how I happened to become interested in mental tests and gifted children. My first introduction to the scientific problems posed by intellectual differences occurred well over a half-century ago when I was a senior in psychology at Indiana University and was asked to prepare two reports for a seminar, one on mental deficiency and one on genius. Up to that time, despite the fact that I had graduated from a normal college as a Bachelor of Pedagogy and had taught school for five years, I had never so much as heard of a mental test. The reading for those two reports opened up a new world to me, the world of Galton, Binet, and their contemporaries. The following year my MA thesis on leadership among children (10) was based in part on tests used by Binet in his studies of suggestibility.

Then I entered Clark University, where I spent considerable time during the first year in reading on mental tests and precocious children. Child prodigies, I soon learned, were at that time in bad repute because of the prevailing belief that they were usually psychotic or otherwise abnormal and almost sure to burn themselves out quickly or to develop postadolescent stupidity. "Early ripe, early rot" was a slogan frequently encountered. By the time I reached my last graduate year, I decided to find out for myself how precocious children differ from the mentally backward, and accordingly chose as my doctoral dissertation an experimental study of the intellectual processes of fourteen boys, seven

of them picked as the brightest and seven as the dullest in a large city school (11). These subjects I put through a great variety of intelligence tests, some of them borrowed from Binet and others, many of them new. The tests were given individually and required a total of 40 or 50 hours for each subject. The experiment contributed little or nothing to science, but it contributed a lot to my future thinking. Besides "selling" me completely on the value of mental tests as a research method, it offered an ideal escape from the kinds of laboratory work which I disliked and in which I was more than ordinarily inept. (Edward Thorndike confessed to me once that *his* lack of mechanical skill was partly responsible for turning *him* to mental tests and to the kinds of experiments on learning that required no apparatus.)

However, it was not until I got to Stanford in 1910 that I was able to pick up with mental tests where I had left off at Clark University. By that time Binet's 1905 and 1908 scales had been published, and the first thing I undertook at Stanford was a tentative revision of his 1908 scale. This, after further revisions, was published in 1916. The standardization of the scale was based on tests of a thousand children whose IQ's ranged from 60 to 145. The contrast in intellectual performance between the dullest and the brightest of a given age so intensified my earlier interest in the gifted that I decided to launch an ambitious study of such children at the earliest opportunity.

My dream was realized in the spring of

Address delivered at the University of California at Berkeley, March 25, 1954, as the first lecture in the Walter Van Dyke Bingham series. Reprinted by permission of the American Psychological Association and the author's estate from the *American Psychologist*, 1954, vol. 9, pp. 221–30.

1921 when I obtained a generous grant from the Commonwealth Fund of New York City for the purpose of locating a thousand subjects of IQ 140 or higher. More than that number were selected by Stanford-Binet tests from the kindergarten through the eighth grade, and a group mental test given in 95 high schools provided nearly 400 additional subjects. The latter, plus those I had located before 1921, brought the number close to 1,500. The average IQ was approximately 150, and 80 were 170 or higher (13).

The twofold purpose of the project was, first of all, to find what traits characterize children of high IQ, and secondly, to follow them for as many years as possible to see what kind of adults they might become. This meant that it was necessary to select a group representative of high-testing children in general. With the help of four field assistants, we canvassed a school population of nearly a quarter-million in the urban and semi-urban areas of California. Two careful checks on the methods used showed that not more than 10 or 12 per cent of the children who could have qualified for the group in the schools canvassed were missed. A sample of close to 90 per cent insured that whatever traits were typical of these children would be typical of high-testing children in any comparable school population.

Time does not permit me to describe the physical measurements, medical examinations, achievement tests, character and interest tests, or the trait ratings and other supplementary information obtained from parents and teachers. Nor can I here describe the comparative data we obtained for control groups of unselected children. The more important results, however, can be stated briefly: children of IQ 140 or higher are, in general, appreciably superior to unselected children in physique, health, and social adjustment; markedly superior in moral attitudes as measured either by character tests or by trait ratings; and vastly superior in their mastery of school subjects as shown by a three-hour battery of achievement tests. In fact, the typical child of the group had mastered the school subjects to a point about two grades beyond the one in which he was enrolled, some of

them three or four grades beyond. Moreover, his ability as evidenced by achievement in the different school subjects is so general as to refute completely the traditional belief that gifted children are usually one-sided. I take some pride in the fact that not one of the major conclusions we drew in the early 1920's regarding the traits that are typical of gifted children has been overthrown in the three decades since then.

Results of thirty years' follow-up of these subjects by field studies in 1927–28, 1939–40, and 1951–52, and by mail follow-up at other dates, show that the incidence of mortality, ill health, insanity, and alcoholism is in each case below that for the generality of corresponding age, that the great majority are still well adjusted socially, and that the delinquency rate is but a fraction of what it is in the general population. Two forms of our difficult Concept Mastery Test, devised especially to reach into the stratosphere of adult intelligence, have been administered to all members of the group who could be visited by the field assistants, including some 950 tested in 1939–40 and more than 1,000 in 1951–52. On both tests they scored on the average about as far above the generality of adults as they had scored above the generality of children when we selected them. Moreover, as Dr. Bayley and Mrs. Oden have shown, in the twelve-year interval between the two tests, 90 per cent increased their intellectual stature as measured by this test. "Early ripe, early rot" simply does not hold for these subjects. So far, no one has developed postadolescent stupidity!

As for schooling, close to 90 per cent entered college and 70 per cent graduated. Of those graduating, 30 per cent were awarded honors and about two-thirds remained for graduate work. The educational record would have been still better but for the fact that a majority reached college age during the great depression. In their undergraduate years 40 per cent of the men and 20 per cent of the women earned half or more of their college expenses, and the total of undergraduate and graduate expenses earned amounted to $670,-000, not counting stipends from scholarships and fellowships, which amounted to $350,000.

The cooperation of the subjects is indicated by the fact that we have been able to keep track of more than 98 per cent of the original group, thanks to the rapport fostered by the incomparable field and office assistants I have had from the beginning of the study to the present. I dislike to think how differently things could have gone with helpers even a little less competent.

The achievement of the group to midlife is best illustrated by the case histories of the 800 men, since only a minority of the women have gone out for professional careers (15). By 1950, when the men had an average age of 40 years, they had published 67 books (including 46 in the fields of science, arts, and the humanities, and 21 books of fiction). They had published more than 1,400 scientific, technical, and professional articles; over 200 short stories, novelettes, and plays; and 236 miscellaneous articles on a great variety of subjects. They had also authored more than 150 patents. The figures on publications do not include the hundreds of publications by journalists that classify as news stories, editorials, or newspaper columns; nor do they include the hundreds if not thousands of radio and TV scripts.

The 800 men include 78 who have taken a PhD degree or its equivalent, 48 with a medical degree, 85 with a law degree, 74 who are teaching or have taught in a four-year college or university, 51 who have done basic research in the physical sciences or engineering, and 104 who are engineers but have done only applied research or none. Of the scientists, 47 are listed in the 1949 edition of American Men of Science. Nearly all of these numbers are from 10 to 20 or 30 times as large as would be found for 800 men of corresponding age picked at random in the general population, and are sufficient answer to those who belittle the significance of IQ differences.

The follow-up of these gifted subjects has proved beyond question that tests of "general intelligence," given as early as six, eight, or ten years, tell a great deal about the ability to achieve either presently or 30 years hence. Such tests do not, however, enable us to predict what direction the achievement will take, and least of all do they tell us what personality factors or what accidents of fortune will affect the fruition of exceptional ability. Granting that both interest patterns and special aptitudes play important roles in the making of a gifted scientist, mathematician, mechanic, artist, poet, or musical composer, I am convinced that to achieve greatly in almost any field, the special talents have to be backed up by a lot of Spearman's g, by which is meant the kind of general intelligence that requires ability to form many sharply defined concepts, to manipulate them, and to perceive subtle relationships between them; in other words, the ability to engage in abstract thinking.

The study by Catharine Cox of the childhood traits of historical geniuses gives additional evidence regarding the role of general intelligence in exceptional achievement. That study was part of our original plan to investigate superior ability by two methods of approach: (a) by identifying and following living gifted subjects from childhood onward; and (b) by proceeding in the opposite direction and tracing the mature genius back to his childhood promise. With a second grant from the Commonwealth Fund, the latter approach got under way only a year later than the former and resulted in the magnum opus by Cox entitled The Early Mental Traits of Three Hundred Geniuses (1). Her subjects represented an unbiased selection from the top 510 in Cattell's objectively compiled list of the 1,000 most eminent men of history. Cox and two able assistants then scanned some 3,000 biographies in search of information that would throw light on the early mental development of these subjects. The information thus obtained filled more than 6,000 typed pages. Next, three psychologists familiar with mental age norms read the documentary evidence on all the subjects and estimated for each the IQ that presumably would be necessary to account for the intellectual behavior recorded for given chronological ages. Average of the three IQ estimates was used as the index of intelligence. In fact two IQ's were estimated for each subject, one based on the evidence to age 17, and the other on evidence to the mid-twenties. The recorded evidence on development to age 17 varied from very little to an amount that yielded about as valid an IQ as a good intelligence test would give. Examples of the latter are Goethe, John Stuart Mill, and Francis Galton. It was the documentary information on Galton, which I summarized and published in 1917 (12), that decided me to prepare plans for the kind of study that was carried out by Cox. The average of estimated IQ's for her 300 geniuses was 155, with many going as high as 175 and several as high as 200. Estimates below 120 occurred only when there was little biographical evidence about the early years.

It is easy to scoff at these post-mortem IQ's, but as one of the three psychologists who examined the evidence and made the IQ ratings, I think the author's main conclusion is fully warranted; namely, that "the genius who achieves highest eminence is one whom intelligence tests would have identified as gifted in childhood."

Special attention was given the geniuses who had sometime or other been labeled as backward in childhood, and in every one of these cases the facts clearly contradicted the legend. One of them was Oliver Goldsmith, of whom his childhood teacher is said to have said "Never was so dull a boy." The fact is that little Oliver was writing clever verse at 7 years and at 8 was reading Ovid and Horace. Another was Sir Walter Scott, who at 7 not only read widely in poetry but was using correctly in his written prose such words as "melancholy" and "exotic." Other alleged childhood dullards included a number who disliked the usual diet of Latin and Greek but had a natural talent for science. Among these were the celebrated German chemist Justus von Liebig, the great English anatomist John Hunter, and the naturalist Alexander von Humboldt, whose name is scattered so widely over the maps of the world.

In the cases just cited one notes a tendency for the direction of later achievement to be foreshadowed by the interests and preoccupations of childhood. I have tried to determine how frequently this was true of the 100 subjects in Cox's group whose childhood was best documented. Very marked foreshadowing was noted in the case of more

than half of the group, none at all in less than a fourth. Macaulay, for example, began his career as historian at the age of 6 with what he called a "Compendium of Universal History," filling a quire of paper before he lost interest in the project. Ben Franklin before the age of 17 had displayed nearly all the traits that characterized him in middle life: scientific curiosity, religious heterodoxy, wit and buffoonery, political and business shrewdness, and ability to write. At 11 Pascal was so interested in mathematics that his father thought it best to deprive him of books on this subject until he had first mastered Latin and Greek. Pascal secretly proceeded to construct a geometry of his own and covered the ground as far as the 32nd proposition of Euclid. His father then relented. At 14 Leibnitz was writing on logic and philosophy and composing what he called "An Alphabet of Human Thought." He relates that at this age he took a walk one afternoon to consider whether he should accept the "doctrine of substantial forms."

Similar foreshadowing is disclosed by the case histories of my gifted subjects. A recent study of the scientists and nonscientists among our 800 gifted men (15) showed many highly significant differences between the early interests and social attitudes of those who became physical scientists and those who majored in the social sciences, law, or the humanities. Those in medical or biological sciences usually rated on such variables somewhere between the physical scientists and the nonscientists.

What I especially want to emphasize, however, is that both the evidence on early mental development of historical geniuses and that obtained by follow-up of gifted subjects selected in childhood by mental tests point to the conclusion that capacity to achieve far beyond the average can be detected early in life by a well-constructed ability test that is heavily weighted with the g factor. It remains to be seen how much the prediction of future achievement can be made more specific as to field by getting, in addition, measures of ability factors that are largely independent of g. It would seem that a 20-year follow-up of the thousands of school children who have been given Thurstone's test of seven "primary mental abilities" would help to provide the answer. At present the factor analysts don't agree on how many "primary" mental abilities there are, nor exactly on what they are. The experts in this field are divided into two schools. The British school, represented by Thomson, Vernon, and Burt, usually stop with the identification of at most three or four group factors in addition to *g*, while some representing the American school feed the scores of 40 or 50 kinds of tests into a hopper and manage to extract from them what they believe to be a dozen or fifteen separate factors. Members of the British school are as a rule very skeptical about the realities underlying the minor group factors. There are also American psychologists, highly skilled in psychometrics, who share this skepticism. It is to be hoped that further research will give us more information than we now have about the predictive value of the group factors. Until such information is available, the scores on group factors can contribute little to vocational guidance beyond what a good test of general intelligence will provide.

I have always stressed the importance of *early* discovery of exceptional abilities. Its importance is now highlighted by the facts Harvey Lehman has disclosed in his monumental studies of the relation between age and creative achievement (8). The striking thing about his age curves is how early in life the period of maximum creativity is reached. In nearly all fields of science, the best work is done between ages 25 and 35, and rarely later than 40. The peak productivity for works of lesser merit is usually reached 5 to 10 years later; this is true in some twenty fields of science, in philosophy, in most kinds of musical composition, in art, and in literature of many varieties. The lesson for us from Lehman's statistics is that the youth of high achievement potential should be well trained for his life work before too many of his most creative years have been passed.

This raises the issue of educational acceleration for the gifted. It seems that the schools are more opposed to acceleration now than they were thirty years ago. The lockstep seems to have become more and more the fashion, notwithstanding the fact that practically everyone who has investigated the subject is against it. Of my gifted group, 29 per cent managed to graduate from high school before the age of 16½ years (62 of these before 15½), but I doubt if so many would be allowed to do so now. The other 71 per cent graduated between 16½ and 18½. We have compared the accelerated with the nonaccelerated on numerous case-history variables. The two groups differed very little in childhood IQ, their health records are equally good, and as adults they are equally well adjusted socially. More of the accelerates graduated from college, and on the average nearly a year and a half earlier than the nonaccelerates; they averaged higher in college grades and more often remained for graduate work. Moreover, the accelerates on the average married .7 of a year earlier, have a trifle lower divorce rate, and score just a little higher on a test of marital happiness (14). So far as college records of accelerates and nonaccelerates are concerned, our data closely parallel those obtained by the late Noel Keys (3) at the University of California and those by Pressey (9) and his associates at Ohio State University.

The Ford Fund for the Advancement of Education has awarded annually since 1951 some 400 college scholarships to gifted students who are not over 16½ years old, are a year or even two years short of high school graduation, but show good evidence of ability to do college work. Three quarters of them are between 15½ and 16½ at the time of college entrance. A dozen colleges and universities accept these students and are keeping close track of their success. A summary of their records for the first year shows that they not only get higher grades than their classmates, who average about two years older, but that they are also equally well adjusted socially and participate in as many extracurricular activities (17). The main problem the boys have is in finding girls to date who are not too old for them! Some of them have started a campaign to remedy the situation by urging that more of these scholarships be awarded to girls.

The facts I have given do not mean that all gifted children should be rushed through school just as rapidly as possible. If that were done, a majority with IQ of 140 could graduate from high school before the age of 15. I do believe, however, that such children should be promoted rapidly enough to permit college entrance by the age of 17 at latest, and that a majority would be better off to enter at 16. The exceptionally bright student who is kept with his age group finds little to challenge his intelligence and all too often develops habits of laziness that later wreck his college career. I could give you some choice examples of this in my gifted group. In the case of a college student who is preparing for a profession in science, medicine, law, or any field of advanced scholarship, graduation at 20 instead of the usual 22 means two years added to his professional career; or the two years saved could be used for additional training beyond the doctorate, if that were deemed preferable.

Learned and Wood (7) have shown by objective achievement tests in some 40 Pennsylvania colleges how little correlation there is between the student's knowledge and the number of months or years of his college attendance. They found some beginning sophomores who had acquired more knowledge than some seniors near their graduation. They found similarly low correlations between the number of course units a student had in a given field and the amount he knew in that field. Some with only one year of Latin had learned more than others with three years. And, believe it or not, they even found boys just graduating from high school who had more knowledge of science than some college seniors who had majored in science and were about to begin teaching science in high schools! The sensible thing to do, it seems, would be to quit crediting the individual high school or the individual college and begin crediting the individual student. That, essentially, is what the Ford Fund scholarships are intended to encourage.

Instruments that permit the identification of gifted subjects are available in great variety and at nearly all levels from the primary grades to the graduate schools in universities. My rough guess is that at the present time tests of achievement in the school subjects are being given in this country to children below high school at a rate of perhaps ten or twelve million a year, and to high school students another million or two. In addition, perhaps two million tests of intelligence are given annually in the elementary and high schools. The testing of college students began in a small way only 30 years ago; now almost every college in the country requires applicants for admission to take some kind of aptitude test. This is usually a test of general aptitude, but subject-matter tests and tests of special aptitudes are sometimes given to supplement the tests of general aptitude.

The testing movement has also spread rapidly in other countries, especially in Britain and the Commonwealth countries. Godfrey Thomson devised what is now called the Moray House test of intelligence in 1921 to aid in selecting the more gifted 11-year-olds in the primary schools for the privilege of free secondary education. This test has been revised and is given annually to about a half million scholarship candidates. The Moray House tests now include tests of English, arithmetic, and history. In 1932 the Scottish Council for Research in Education (18) arranged to give the Moray House test of intelligence (a group test) to all the 90,000 children in Scotland who were born in 1921, and actually tested some 87,000 of them. The Stanford-Binet tests have been translated and adapted for use in nearly all the countries of Europe and in several countries of Asia and Latin America. Behind the Iron Curtain, however, mental tests are now banned.

I have discussed only tests of intelligence and of school achievement. There is time to mention only a few of the many kinds of personality tests that have been developed during the last thirty-five years: personality inventories, projective techniques by the dozen, attitude scales by the hundred, interest tests, tests of psychotic and predelinquent tendencies, tests of leadership, marital aptitude, masculinity-femininity, et cetera. The current output of research on personality tests probably equals or exceeds that on intelligence and achievement tests, and is even more exciting.

Along with the increasing use of tests, and perhaps largely as a result of it, there is a growing interest, both here and abroad, in improving educational methods for the gifted. Acceleration of a year or two or three, however desirable, is but a fraction of what is needed to keep the gifted child or youth working at his intellectual best. The method most often advocated is curriculum enrichment for the gifted without segregating them from the ordinary class. Under ideal conditions enrichment can accomplish much, but in these days of crowded schools, when so many teachers are overworked, underpaid, and inadequately trained, curriculum enrichment for a few gifted in a large mixed class cannot begin to solve the problem. The best survey of thought and action in this field of education is the book entitled *The Gifted Child,* written by many authors and published in 1951 (16). In planning for and sponsoring this book, The American Association for Gifted Children has rendered a great service to education.

But however efficient our tests may be in discovering exceptional talents, and whatever the schools may do to foster those discovered, it is the prevailing *Zeitgeist* that will decide, by the rewards it gives or withholds, what talents will come to flower. In Western Europe of the Middle Ages, the favored talents were those that served the Church by providing its priests, the architects of its cathedrals, and the painters of religious themes. A few centuries later the same countries had a renaissance that included science and literature as well as the arts. Although presumably there are as many potential composers of great music as there ever were, and as many potentially great artists as in the days of Leonardo da Vinci and Michaelangelo, I am reliably informed that in this country today it is almost impossible for a composer of *serious* music to earn his living except by teaching, and that the situation is much the same, though somewhat less critical, with respect to artists.

The talents most favored by the current *Zeitgeist* are those that can contribute to science and technology. If intelligence and achievement tests don't discover the potential scientist, there is a good chance that the annual Science Talent Search will, though not until the high school years. Since Westinghouse inaugurated in 1942 this annual search for the high school seniors most likely to become creative scientists, nearly 4,000 boys and girls have been picked for honors by Science Service out of the many thousands who have competed. As a result, "Science Clubs of America" now number 15,000 with a third of a million members—a twentyfold increase in a dozen years (2). As our need for more and better scientists is real and urgent, one can rejoice at what the talent search and the science clubs are accomplishing. One may regret, however, that the spirit of the times is not equally favorable to the discovery and encouragement of potential poets, prose writers, artists, statesmen, and social leaders.

But in addition to the over-all climates that reflect the *Zeitgeist,* there are localized climates that favor or hinder the encouragement of given talents in particular colleges and universities. I have in mind especially two recent investigations of the differences among colleges in the later achievement of their graduates. One by Knapp and Goodrich (4) dealt with the undergraduate origin of 18,000 scientists who got the bachelor's degree between 1924 and 1934 and were listed in the 1944 edition of *American Men of Science.* The list of 18,000 was composed chiefly of men who had taken a PhD degree, but included a few without a PhD who were starred scientists. The IBM cards for these men were then sorted according to the college from which they obtained the bachelor's degree, and an index of productivity was computed for each college in terms of the proportion of its male graduates who were in the list of 18,000. Some of the results were surprising, not to say sensational. The institutions that were most productive of future scientists between 1924 and 1934 were not the great universities, but the small liberal arts colleges. Reed College topped the list with an index of 132 per thousand male graduates. The California Institute of Technology was second with an index of 70. Kalamazoo College was third with 66, Earlham fourth with 57, and Oberlin fifth with 56. Only a half-dozen of the great universities were in the top fifty with a productivity index of 25 or more.

The second study referred to was by Knapp and Greenbaum (5), who rated educational institutions according to the proportion of their graduates who received certain awards at the graduate level in the six-year period from 1946 to 1951. Three kinds of awards were considered: a PhD degree, a graduate scholarship or fellowship paying at least $400 a year, or a prize at the graduate level won in open competition. The roster of awardees they compiled included 7,000 students who had graduated from 377 colleges and universities. This study differs from the former in three respects: (a) it deals with recent graduates, who had not had time to become distinguished but who could be regarded as good bets for the future; (b) these good bets were classified according to whether the major field was science, social science, or the humanities; and (c) data were obtained for both sexes, though what I shall report here relates only to men. In this study the great universities make a better showing than in the other, but still only a dozen of them are in the top fifty institutions in the production of men who are good bets. In the top ten, the University of Chicago is third, Princeton is eighth, and Harvard is tenth; the other seven in order of rank are Swarthmore 1, Reed 2, Oberlin 4, Haverford 5, California Institute of Technology 6, Carleton 7, and Antioch 9. When the schools were listed separately for production of men who were good bets in science, social science, and the humanities, there were eight that rated in the top twenty on all three lists. These were Swarthmore, Reed, Chicago, Harvard, Oberlin, Antioch, Carleton, and Princeton.

The causes of these differences are not entirely clear. Scores on aptitude tests show that the intelligence of students in a given institution is by no means the sole factor, though it is an important one. Other important factors are the quality of the school's intellectual climate, the proportion of able and in-spiring teachers on its faculty, and the amount of conscious effort that is made not only to discover but also to motivate the most highly gifted. The influence of motivation can hardly be exaggerated.

In this address I have twice alluded to the fact that achievement in school is influenced by many things other than the sum total of intellectual abilities. The same is true of success in life. In closing I will tell you briefly about an attempt we made a dozen years ago to identify some of the nonintellectual factors that have influenced life success among the men in my gifted group. Three judges, working independently, examined the records (to 1940) of the 730 men who were then 25 years old or older, and rated each on life success. The criterion of "success" was the extent to which a subject had made use of his superior intellectual ability, little weight being given to earned income. The 150 men rated highest for success and the 150 rated lowest were then compared on some 200 items of information obtained from childhood onward (14). How did the two groups differ?

During the elementary school years, the A's and C's (as we call them) were almost equally successful. The average grades were about the same, and average scores on achievement tests were only a trifle higher for the A's. Early in high school the groups began to draw apart in scholarship, and by the end of high school the slump of the C's was quite marked. The slump could not be blamed on extracurricular activities, for these were almost twice as common among the A's. Nor was much of it due to difference in intelligence. Although the A's tested on the average a little higher than the C's both in 1922 and 1940, the average score made by the C's in 1940 was high enough to permit brilliant college work, in fact was equaled by only 15 per cent of our highly selected Stanford students. Of the A's, 97 per cent entered college and 90 per cent graduated; of the C's, 68 per cent entered but only 37 per cent graduated. Of those who graduated, 52 per cent of the A's but only 14 per cent of the C's graduated with honors. The A's were also more accelerated in school; on the average they were six months younger on completing the eighth grade, 10 months younger at high school graduation, and 15 months younger at graduation from college.

The differences between the educational histories of the A's and C's reflect to some degree the differences in their family backgrounds. Half of the A fathers but only 15 per cent of the C fathers were college graduates, and twice as many of A siblings as of C siblings graduated. The estimated number of books in the A homes was nearly 50 per cent greater than in the C homes. As of 1928, when the average age of the subjects was about 16 years, more than twice as many of the C parents as of A parents had been divorced.

Interesting differences between the groups were found in the childhood data on emotional stability, social adjustments, and various traits of personality. Of the 25 traits on which each child was rated by parent and teacher in 1922 (18 years before the A and C groups were made up), the only trait on which the C's averaged as high as the A's was general health. The superiority of the A's was especially marked in four volitional traits: prudence, self-confidence, perseverance, and desire to excel. The A's also rated significantly higher in 1922 on leadership, popularity, and sensitiveness to approval or disapproval. By 1940 the difference between the groups in social adjustment and all-round mental stability had greatly increased and showed itself in many ways. By that time four-fifths of the A's had married, but only two-thirds of the C's, and the divorce rate for those who had married was twice as high for the C's as for the A's. Moreover, the A's made better marriages; their wives on the average came from better homes, were better educated, and scored higher on intelligence tests.

But the most spectacular differences between the two groups came from three sets of ratings, made in 1940, on a dozen personality traits. Each man rated himself on all the traits, was rated on them by his wife if he had a wife, and by a parent if a parent was still living. Although the three sets of ratings were made independently, they agreed unanimously on the four traits in which the A and C groups differed most widely. These were "persistence in the accomplishment of ends," "integration toward goals, as contrasted with drifting," "self-confidence," and "freedom from inferiority feelings." For each trait three critical ratios were computed showing, respectively, the reliability of the A–C differences in average of self-ratings, ratings by wives, and ratings by parents. The average of the three critical ratios was 5.5 for perseverance, 5.6 for integration toward goals, 3.7 for self-confidence, and 3.1 for freedom from inferiority feelings. These closely parallel the traits that Cox found to be especially characteristic of the 100 leading geniuses in her group whom she rated on many aspects of personality; their three outstanding traits she defined as "persistence of motive and effort," "confidence in their abilities," and "strength or force of character."

There was one trait on which only the parents of our A and C men were asked to rate them; that trait was designated "common sense." As judged by parents, the A's are again reliably superior, the A–C difference in average rating having a critical ratio of 3.9. We are still wondering what self-ratings by the subjects and ratings of them by their wives on common sense would have shown if we had been impudent enough to ask for them!

Everything considered, there is nothing in which our A and C groups present a greater contrast than in drive to achieve and in all-round mental and social adjustment. Our data do not support the theory of Lange-Eichbaum (6) that great achievement usually stems from emotional tensions that border on the abnormal. In our gifted group, success is associated with stability rather than instability, with absence rather than with presence of disturbing conflicts—in short with well-balanced temperament and with freedom from excessive frustrations. The Lange-Eichbaum theory may explain a Hitler, but hardly a Churchill; the junior senator from Wisconsin, possibly, but not a Jefferson or a Washington.

At any rate, we have seen that intellect and achievement are far from perfectly correlated. To identify the internal and external factors that help or hinder the fruition of exceptional talent, and to measure the extent of their influences, are surely among the major problems of our time. These problems are not new; their existence has been recognized by countless men from Plato to Francis Galton. What is new is the general awareness of them caused by the manpower shortage of scientists, engineers, moral leaders, statesmen, scholars, and teachers that the country must have if it is to survive in a threatened world. These problems are now being investigated on a scale never before approached, and by a new generation of workers in several related fields. Within a couple of decades vastly more should be known than we know today about our resources of potential genius, the environmental circumstances that favor its expression, the emotional compulsions that give it dynamic quality, and the personality distortions that can make it dangerous.

REFERENCES

1. Cox, Catharine C. *The early mental traits of three hundred geniuses.* Vol. II of *Genetic studies of genius,* Terman, L. M. (Ed.) Stanford: Stanford Univer. Press, 1926.
2. Davis, W. Communicating science. *J. atomic Scientists,* 1953, 337–340.
3. Keys, N. The underage student in high school and college. *Univer. Calif. Publ. Educ.,* 1938, 7, 145–272.
4. Knapp, R. H., & Goodrich, H. B. *Origins of American scientists.* Chicago: Univer. of Chicago Press, 1952.
5. Knapp, R. H., & Greenbaum, J. J. *The younger American scholar: his collegiate origins.* Chicago: Univer. of Chicago Press, 1953.
6. Lange-Eichbaum, W. *The problem of genius.* New York: Macmillan, 1932.
7. Learned, W. S., & Wood, B. D. The student and his knowledge. *Carnegie Found. Adv. Teaching Bull.,* 1938, No. 29.
8. Lehman, H. C. *Age and achievement.* Princeton, N.J.: Princeton Univer. Press, 1953.
9. Pressey, S. L. *Educational acceleration: appraisals and basic problems.* Columbus: Ohio State Univer. Press, 1949.
10. Terman, L. M. A preliminary study in the psychology and pedagogy of leadership. *Pedag. Sem.,* 1904, 11, 413–451.
11. Terman, L. M. Genius and stupidity: a study of some of the intellectual processes of seven "bright" and seven "dull" boys. *Pedag. Sem.,* 1906, 13, 307–373.
12. Terman, L. M. The intelligence quotient of Francis Galton in childhood. *Amer. J. Psychol.,* 1917, 28, 209–215.
13. Terman, L. M. (Ed.), *et al. Mental and physical traits of a thousand gifted children.* Vol. I of *Genetic studies of genius,* Terman, L. M. (Ed.) Stanford: Stanford Univer. Press, 1925.
14. Terman, L. M., & Oden, M. H. *The gifted child grows up.* Vol. IV of *Genetic studies of genius,* Terman, L. M. (Ed.) Stanford: Stanford Univer. Press, 1947.
15. Terman, L. M. Scientists and nonscientists in a group of 800 gifted men. *Psychol. Monogr.,* 1954, 68, in press.
16. Witty, P. (Ed.) *The gifted child.* Boston: Heath, 1951.
17. *Bridging the gap between school and college.* New York: The Fund for the Advancement of Education, 1953.
18. *The intelligence of Scottish children.* Scottish Council for Research in Education. London: Univer. of London Press, 1933.

SECTION IV

Perception

THERE *must be almost as many ways to study perception as there are things to perceive. In selecting articles for this section we have been able to sample only a few of the many questions about perception that psychologists try to answer: Is the ability to perceive innate or learned? How do need, set (or suggestion), and prior experience influence perception? Is perception always conscious?*

Austin H. Riesen sets out in "Arrested Vision" to discover how much of the capacity to see is innate or acquired through natural maturation of the eyes during the early years, and how much is the result of learning. The results show that, although prolonged lack of use can prevent the normal development of vision, innate visual ability is nonetheless developed during the first few months of an infant's life by growth factors that are entirely independent of practice. In the second article, "Experiments with Goggles," Ivo Kohler shows how the sense organs can adapt to changing conditions. His experiments indicate that the eye has a remarkable ability to learn to discount or adapt to highly complex distortions of both space and color.

The next three articles in this section concern the effects of need, set, and prior experience on perception. "The Projective Expression of Needs" concerns an experiment in which a group of Navy men, deprived of food for different amounts of time, were asked to report their impressions of ambiguous visual stimuli. David C. McClelland and John W. Atkinson have tabulated the results to see how many "food responses" were obtained and to compare the subjects' size and number estimates of food-related and neutral objects. In "A Lecture Experiment in Hallucinations," E. E. Slosson uses a classroom demonstration to show the influence of set. When he uncapped a test tube of pure water and told the class they would perceive a powerful odor, the set was so strong that some students were overcome by the "odor" and had to leave the room. Leo Postman et al., in "Personal Values as Selective Factors in Perception," tested the hypothesis that personal values are demonstrable determinants of what the individual selects perceptually from his environment. They asked their subjects to identify what for them were low- and high-value words, flashed briefly on a screen, in order to see how the value of the word for the subjects influenced their perception of it.

If one is not aware that one perceives a thing, then how can one react to it? Through subception, the name Richard S. Lazarus and Robert A. McCleary have given to the process by which some kind of discrimination is made when the subject is unable to make correct conscious discriminations. "Autonomic Discrimination Without Awareness" discusses the conditions under which subception can be tested and some of the implications these subception tests have for perceptual and clinical theory.

AUSTIN H. RIESEN

15. Arrested Vision

MANY primitive organisms show immediate and highly uniform reactions to light from the moment of birth. In man vision is a much more complex skill that develops gradually through the years of infancy and childhood. How much of this capacity is innate and how much is acquired by learning or through the natural maturation of the eyes during the child's early years? What are the factors that determine visual perception? If we knew the answers to these questions we could do a great deal more than we can now to improve defective vision.

The task of separating the hereditary factors from the effects of experience in human vision obviously is not easy. For example, a newborn infant at first shows no clear indication of any response to a bright disk presented before its eyes. Only after several weeks does the growing infant begin to look at the disk. Is this the result of growth, of experience or of both? Does the change in response come about through practice in the use of the eyes, or through a natural maturation that occurs, quite independently of use, in the retina of the eye, in the eye or neck muscles, in fiber tracts of the central nervous system or in several of these parts combined?

Scientific studies of the growth of behavior have shown that certain abilities do develop without use as animals mature. Thus tadpoles raised under anesthesia to prevent swimming movements nevertheless improve in swimming ability. Chicks and rats kept in darkness for a time show some progress in vision-controlled behavior. Children also demonstrate a basic rate of maturation in some capacities: there is a limit to the degree of retardation or acceleration of these abilities that can be effected by restricting or expanding their training.

But some of these studies have revealed curious contradictions. Wendell Cruze at North Carolina State College found that after newly hatched chicks had been kept in darkness for five days, they were generally able to peck at and hit 24 of the first 25 grains presented to them; this score was 12 per cent better than the average of hits by chicks immediately after hatching. On the other hand, S. G. Padilla at the University of Michigan showed that if the period of darkness was extended to 14 days, the pecking response failed to appear, presumably because the instinct to peck at spots on the ground died out through disuse. The chicks began to starve in the midst of plenty. So it appears that lack of practice, at least if sufficiently prolonged, can interfere with the development of behavior which is basically instinctive or reflex in nature.

In human beings the most nearly pertinent evidence on this problem has come from studies of patients operated upon at advanced ages for congenital cataracts. These patients, who have passed all their lives in near-blindness, ranging from the bare ability to tell day from night to some ability to distinguish colors and localize light, invariably report an immediate awareness of a change after a successful operation. They begin at once to distinguish differences in the parts of the visual field, although they cannot identify an object or describe its shape. After a few days' practice they can name colors. From this point on progress is slow, often highly discouraging, and some patients never get beyond the ability to distinguish brightness and color. Others, over a period of months and even years, develop the ability to identify simple geometric figures, read letters and numbers and, in rare cases, to identify complex patterns such as words, outline drawings and faces. During their efforts to improve their visual skill the patients go through a long period of picking out elements in an object and inferring the nature of the object from these elements—often erroneously. For example, a child of 12, some months after her operation, is reported by her doctor to have pointed to a picture and called it "a camel, because it has a hump." What she identified as a hump was the dorsal fin of a fish.

But such cases of congenital cataract do not give us very satisfactory evidence on the elementary problem of how disuse affects the development of visual behavior. There are too many other variables; we must take into account (1) the degree of the patient's previous blindness, since he was not in total darkness, (2) the limit that is imposed on his potentialities for improvement by the fact that the eye operated on lacks a lens, and (3) the circumstance that in all these cases there appears to be another visual handicap —jerky movements of the eyeballs known as spontaneous nystagmus. The effects of these combined difficulties are not readily calculable. For a more meaningful study it is highly desirable to eliminate these variables by setting up a controlled experiment that will determine the effects of disuse on normal eyes. Obviously such an experiment cannot be risked in human beings; no one would wish to impose permanent reading difficulties on any person having to adjust himself to a civilized society. The most logical subject for the experiment is another higher primate. The chimpanzee was chosen, because its behavior, like man's, is dominated by vision, and because it is intelligent and tractable.

In 1942 at the Yerkes Laboratories of Primate Biology in Orange Park, Fla., an infant male chimpanzee was separated from its mother on the day of birth and blindfolded with a gauze bandage and adhesive tape. This animal defeated the experimenters by loosening the tape at the side of his left nostril and habitually peeking down his nose with his left eye. By the age of 16 weeks he gained full freedom from facial bandages. Although he did not recognize his feeding bottle at this

time, nor show fixation of persons or objects, he developed fairly adequate visual behavior within a few weeks.

In 1945 the experimenters tried again. This time two newborn chimpanzee infants, a male and a female respectively named Snark and Alfalfa, were housed in a completely darkened room. During the first 16 months the only light these infants experienced was an electric lamp turned on for intervals of 45 seconds several times daily for their routine care and feeding. When they were first tested for visual perception at the age of 16 months, both chimpanzees showed extreme incompetence. Their reflex responses indicated that their eyes were sensitive to light—the pupils constricted; sudden changes of illumination startled the animals; they responded to a slowly waving flashlight with jerky pursuit movements of the eyes and side to side following motions of the head. But both chimpanzees failed to show any visual responses to complex patterns of light until after they had spent many hours in illuminated surroundings. They did not respond to play objects or their feeding bottles unless these touched some part of the body. They did not blink at a threatening motion toward the face. When an object was advanced slowly toward the face, there was no reaction until the object actually touched the face, and then the animal gave a startled jump.

After the 16-month period of darkness, Alfalfa was placed on a limited light schedule until the age of 21 months and Snark until 33 months. When Alfalfa was later moved into a normal daylight environment, in the course of many months she developed normal recognition of objects, began to blink in response to threats and ceased to be startled by a touch. Snark was much more retarded. Between the ages of 20 and 27 months, while he was still on rationed light, he learned after many hundreds of trials to tell the difference between contrasting signs, differing in color or pattern, which indicated either food or a mild electric shock. His visual acuity, as measured by ability to discriminate between horizontal and vertical lines, was well below that of normally raised animals. At the end of 33 months he began to live in the normally lighted chimpanzee nursery and later out of doors with chimpanzees of his own age. It was expected that he would rapidly acquire normal visual behavior. He did improve slightly at first, but after this small initial improvement he actually lost ground in visual responsiveness, until even reflex activity began to die away.

What is the explanation of this deterioration? Had the development of his eyes been permanently arrested by the absence of light? There had been no previous evidence that stimulation by light is essential for the normal growth of the primate retina or optic nerve. It was a surprise to find that, while the eyes of these chimpanzees remained sensitive to light after 16 months in darkness, the retina and optic disk in both animals did not reflect as much light as normal chimpanzee eyes do. Snark later developed a marked pallor of the optic disk in both eyes. There is other evidence suggesting that fish and amphibians, at least, need light-stimulation for normal eye development. So the physiological effects of the lack of light may be part of the explanation for Snark's loss of visual function. But it is not the whole explanation for all the visual abnormalities in these two chimpanzees, nor does it explain the visual difficulties of the cataract patients. These patients have excellent color discrimination, and, incidentally, do not show pallor of the optic disk. Moreover, we now have clear evidence from further experiments with chimpanzees that not merely light itself but stimulation by visual patterns is essential to normal visual development.

In these experiments three other newborn chimpanzees, two females and a male, were put into the darkroom. Debi was raised for seven months in complete darkness, even during her feedings and other care. Kora was raised for the same period on a ration of an average of one and a half hours of light daily, but the light, admitted through a white Plexiglas mask, was diffuse and unpatterned. Lad was given one and a half hours of patterned light daily: he could observe the edges of his crib, the variations in pattern introduced by movements of his own body and appendages, and all the accompaniments of bottle-feed-

ing, including the moving about of persons in the moderately lighted room.

At seven months, when the three subjects were removed to normal daylight surroundings, Lad's visual performance was indistinguishable from that of chimpanzees raised normally. Kora and Debi, however, showed the same kinds of retardation as had Snark and Alfalfa, with some minor exceptions. Kora did not develop the blink response to a moving object until six days after her removal from darkness, and Debi not until 15 days. It took Kora 13 days and Debi 30 days to acquire the ability to pursue a moving person with the eyes, and they did this by a series of refixations instead of following smoothly as normal animals of comparable age do; it took Kora 20 days and Debi 16 days to pursue visually a moving feeding bottle; Kora 13 days and Debi 30 days to fixate the image of a stationary person.

These differences between Debi and Kora may lie within the range of variation that would occur in a group of animals treated exactly the same as either Debi or Kora. This question could be checked only by repeating the experiment many times.

Between seven and 10 months of age Debi and Kora both showed a moderate and intermittent outward (wall-eyed) deviation of the eyes. This gradually was overcome. Both infants also showed an initial spontaneous nystagmus, i.e., jerky eye movements. It appeared only sporadically, and was more pronounced under general excitement than when the animals were well relaxed.

Normal animals of seven months learn to avoid a large yellow and black striped disk after receiving one or two mild electric shocks from it. Debi and Kora, however, were shocked by the disk twice a day for six and nine days, respectively, before they so much as whimpered when it was shown. Only after 13 days in Kora's case and 15 days in Debi's did they consistently indicate by some sort of avoidance response that they saw the disk within five seconds of the time that it was raised in front of their eyes.

In still another study an infant chimpanzee named Kandy was put in the darkroom for only the first three months of life. After she was removed to daylight surroundings, her progress on the same tests was approximately parallel to that of Debi and Kora. There were three interesting differences: 1) Kandy showed a convergent squint (cross-eyes), which cleared up in a little less than two months; 2) she did not have spontaneous nystagmus; 3) she required 24 days, as compared with 13 or 15, to develop consistent avoidance of the black and yellow shock-disk. The last difference suggests that Kandy learned more slowly because of her younger age; in other words, that the development of visual discrimination was a matter of maturity as well as learning. This conclusion was strongly supported by the finding that an infant chimpanzee started through the same training at the age of two days failed to show avoidance in a month's time.

All these observations demonstrate that vision must be put to use if it is to develop normally, but they also indicate that during the first few months of an infant's life visual development is advanced by growth factors which are entirely independent of practice. Normally reared animals, for example, do not blink in response to the movement of objects across the visual field until they have reached the age of two months; the older darkroom animals, despite previous lack of experience, began to show this response within about two weeks after they were transferred to daylight surroundings.

The development and maintenance of normal visual functions in higher primates depends on a whole complex of interrelated factors, hereditary and environmental, and it can readily be disturbed at any stage of the individual's growth. This was shown in an experiment with a chimpanzee named Faik. Faik was raised in the normal light of the laboratory's nursery until the age of seven months. At that time the standard series of tests described above showed that he had excellent use of vision. Then from the age of eight to 24 months he was kept in the darkroom. He lived an active life filled with tactile, auditory, olfactory, gustatory and kinesthetic stimulation. He invited rough-house play from his caretakers at feeding times, and his general state of health remained entirely satisfactory.

When Faik was returned to daylight living quarters at 24 months, he had lost all ability to utilize vision in his interplay with the environment. He no longer recognized the feeding bottle, and failed to look at objects or persons, either stationary or moving. More than this, he possessed a strong spontaneous nystagmus and was even unable to follow a moving light in a darkroom until the fifth day after he was put back into a lighted environment. His first visual following movements, like those of all the darkroom-raised subjects, were not smooth but a series of jerky refixations, made even more jerky by the pronounced spontaneous nystagmus.

Even in direct sunlight Faik failed to grimace or close his eyelids; he gave no indication of the slightest discomfort when the sun shone in his eyes. (The chimpanzees raised in the darkroom from birth did close their lids in intense light.) Faik showed pallor similar to that of Snark and Alfalfa in his optic disks. His recovery of vision has been slow and is still only partial. Explanation of his case, and that of Snark, remains a challenge to further research.

These chimpanzee studies have established several fundamental points. They show that newborn animals, and older infants that have been kept in darkness for a time, exhibit visual reflexes when they are first subjected to light. Some responses that bear a close resemblance to reflex behavior, such as blinking at something rapidly approaching the face, become automatic only after considerable practice. Visual pursuit of moving objects, the coordination of the two eyes and convergent fixation, and the first recognition of objects come only after many hours or weeks of experience in use of the eyes. It takes the chimpanzee hundreds of hours of active utilization of the eyes to develop its vision to the stage where it can adequately guide locomotion and complex manipulations. The findings in the cases of two subjects that were kept in darkness for long periods indicate that the postponement of light exposure for too long can result in making the development of normal visual mechanisms extremely difficult if not impossible.

IVO KOHLER

16. *Experiments with Goggles*

O F all the senses the one most intensively studied is undoubtedly vision. Much has been learned about the physical and physiological basis of visual perception, but understanding of the process remains primitive. Vision is perhaps the most complex of the senses; nonetheless it offers the investigator a tantalizing opportunity to learn how the brain processes sensory data and constructs an effective image of the outside world. Presumably this image is the result of an unconscious learning process; the image is "better" than it should be, considering the known defects in the visual system. For example, the lens of the eye is not corrected for spherical aberration; hence straight lines should look slightly curved. By the same token, lines of a certain curvature should appear straight. It is also well known that the eye is not corrected for color; as a result different wavelengths of light—originating at a common point—do not come to a common focus on the retina. One would expect this defect, called chromatic aberration, to have a noticeable effect on vision, but it does not, except under special conditions.

One way to explore the unconscious learning process that goes on in normal vision is to investigate how the visual system responds to images that are systematically distorted by specially constructed goggles. In this article I shall describe some of our studies, conducted at the University of Innsbruck in Austria, which show that the eye has a remarkable ability to discount or adapt to highly complex distortions involving both spatial geometry and color. But we have been surprised to discover that the eye does not adapt to certain other distortions that seem, superficially at least, less severe than those to which the eye does adapt. Some of these findings appear to be incompatible with traditional theories of vision in general and of color vision in particular.

In addition to contributing to the understanding of vision, experiments with goggles have immediate practical importance for ophthalmologists. If the ophthalmologist knows the extent to which the visual system can adapt to "wrongly" constructed experimental glasses, he will be less reluctant to prescribe strong glasses for his patients. The stronger a glass, meaning the higher its refractive power, the greater its capacity to distort images and produce a fringe of color around them. The ophthalmologist can tell a patient in need of strong glasses that the initially disagreeable distortions and rainbow fringes will disappear if he wears the glasses faithfully for several weeks. Or, to give another example, an operation to repair a detached retina sometimes leaves a fold in the retina that causes a bulge in the patient's visual world. On the basis of goggle experiments, the physician can assure the patient that the bulge will become less noticeable with time and will probably disappear altogether. The fold in the retina will remain, but the patient's vision will gradually adapt to discount its presence. What this implies, of course, is that an individual born with a fold or similar imperfection in his retina may never be aware of it.

We conclude, therefore, that sense organs are not rigid machines but living and variable systems, the functioning of which is itself subject to variation. If a sensory system is exposed to a new and prolonged stimulus situation that departs from the one normally experienced, the system can be expected to undergo a fundamental change in its normal mode of operation.

The use of distorting goggles seems to be the simplest way of producing novel and prolonged visual-stimulus situations. The volunteer subject can be said to be wearing the laboratory on his nose; he cannot leave the laboratory unless he closes his eyes or removes the goggles. The entire visual system, including the manifold projection regions in the brain of which we still know so little, is subjected in a certain way to a completely novel and disturbing situation. Finally it "breaks down"; established habits are abandoned and the visual system begins to respond in a new manner.

When we make the system break down and learn a new way of functioning, we do not believe we are forcing the system to function artificially or abnormally. We assume, rather, that a single mechanism is at work at all times. The mechanism that removes or minimizes an artificially created disturbance is the same one that brings about a normal functioning of the sensory system under normal conditions. If this assumption is correct, the development of the normal visual system—in so far as its development depends on the environment—can be explored by the goggle method.

The application of distorting goggles to the study of visual adaptation dates back to the work of G. M. Stratton of the University of California, who used himself as a subject. Primarily because of the difficulty of finding subjects willing to wear goggles for days, weeks or even months, the method was little employed until about 1928. Then, independently and simultaneously, goggle experiments were undertaken by Theodor Erismann at the University of Innsbruck and by James J. Gibson at Smith College. Gibson's subjects wore goggles that placed a glass wedge, or prism, in front of each eye. Erismann experimented not only with prism goggles but also with more elaborate devices that transposed the visual field from right to left or from top to bottom. Another device allowed the subject to see only directly to the rear, as if he had eyes in the back of his head. After several weeks of wearing goggles that transposed right and left, one of Erismann's subjects became so at home in his reversed world that he was able to drive a motorcycle through Innsbruck while wearing the goggles.

Although Gibson's subjects wore goggles for only a few days at a time, they were the first to discover adaptation to the color fringes and line curvature that a prism produces. Depending on the extent to which the front and rear faces of a prism depart from the parallel, light rays passing through the glass are bent to a greater or lesser degree. This property is called the deviation of the prism. The deviation angle is approximately half the angle between the two faces. Deviations between five and 15 degrees are most useful for goggle experiments. Color fringes arise because light of short wavelength, such as blue light, is bent more than light of longer wavelength. As a result the line marking the edge of an object is spread out into a small spectrum, which becomes more noticeable the greater the contrast between the brightness of the object and that of its background.

The curvature of lines is part of a more general prism effect that produces a variable change in the curvature, angle and distance of observed objects. The effect arises because the angle of deviation varies with the direction of the light reaching the front face of the prism. Rays entering at an oblique angle are bent more than rays entering at a right angle. Consequently straight lines appear curved, right angles seem to be acute or obtuse and distances seem to be expanded or foreshortened.

To a subject wearing prism goggles these assorted distortions produce a visual world whose appearance changes drastically as he turns his head. One of our subjects reported that it is "as if the world were made of rubber." When the head is turned to right or left, objects become broader or narrower, producing a "concertina" effect. When the head is moved up or down, objects seem to slant first one way, then the other. We have called this the rocking-chair effect.

Although the distortions arising from prism movement are severe, they might present the eye with a straightforward adaptation problem if the prism were held in rigid alignment with the central axis of the eye. In this case the rays reaching any particular area of the retina would always be deflected by the same amount and would therefore maintain a fixed angular relationship to rays striking adjacent retinal areas. Such a rigid relationship between prism and eye could be achieved if the prism could be worn as a contact lens resting directly on the cornea.

In the Erismann and Gibson experiments, however, as well as in our more recent ones, there is a small distance between the eye and the prism. As a result the eye can, and frequently does, move with respect to the glasses. Two kinds of relative motion arise. In one case the eye can be fixed on a given object while the head and goggles move. In the second case the head and goggles remain fixed while the eye moves. If one analyzes the geometry of the rays striking the retina, one finds that the adaptation problem is much more severe than if the prism and the eye could be held in rigid relationship. Let us consider a single retinal area, for example the important small region called the fovea, near the center of the retina, where the eye has its maximum acuity. The images reaching the fovea will be distorted more when the eye is looking obliquely through the prism than they will be when it is looking straight ahead. In fact, the distortion changes with every change in the angle that the axis of the eye makes in relation to the prism.

In the accounts of his experiments Gibson neglected the free mobility of the eyes with respect to the glasses. Since his experiments were of short duration it is not clear how much adaptation took place among his subjects. He refers specifically only to adaptation to color fringes and to the curvature of lines. The latter is often called the Gibson effect.

In our much longer experiments, which extended the investigations begun by Erismann, a finely differentiated adaptation can be observed. Like Gibson's subjects, ours adapt rather quickly to color fringes and line curvature. We refer to these as constant distortions because they are essentially independent of head and eye movement. After wearing prism goggles for several weeks, however, our subjects also adapt to the more complex variable distortions, which are generated partly by movement of the head and goggles and partly by movement of the eyes behind the goggles.

I should like to stress the distinction between constant and variable distortions. Adaptation to the latter category apparently involves a process more complex than all previously known processes of visual adaptation. Let us suppose that the subject is provided with goggles that have prisms whose bases point to the right. When, at the start of the experiment, the subject turns his head to the left and glances to the right, he sees an image that contracts in its horizontal dimensions. Conversely, when he turns his head to the right and glances to the left, he sees an expanding image. After several weeks, however, an adaptation occurs that counteracts both of these forms of distortion. This process of double adaptation tends ultimately to eliminate the concertina effect. What seems so remarkable is that this takes place in spite of the fact that the fovea and other retinal areas have been exposed to a random mixture of these variable images. Somehow the visual system has learned a general rule: a contracted image must be expanded and an expanded image must be contracted, depending on the respective position of head and eyes.

If, after weeks or months, the subject is allowed to remove his goggles, the adaptation continues to operate when he views the normal world. The result is an apparent squeezing of images when he glances one way and an expansion when he glances the other. It is as if he were looking for the first time through prisms that have an orientation exactly opposite to those he has been wearing for so long. Moreover, all the other distortions, such as the rocking-chair effect, to which his eyes have slowly become adapted now appear in reverse when the goggles are removed. These aftereffects in their turn diminish in strength over a period of days, and the subject finally sees the stable world he used to know.

Both adaptation and aftereffects are vividly reported by our subjects. But in addition we have built devices that provide an objective measurement of the phenomena. These devices, for example, present the subject with a variety of horizontal and vertical lines that he can adjust in orientation and curvature until they look "right." Another device allows the subject to look through prisms and select the one with the strength appropriate to cancel the aftereffects induced by wearing prism goggles.

Let us now consider the adaptation to the color fringes a prism produces. If a prism with base to the right is placed before the eye and one looks at a white card on a black background, one sees a blue border along the left vertical edge of the card and a yellow-orange border along the right edge. The explanation is that the various colors of light reflected from the card and carrying its image no longer overlap precisely after passing through the prism. The result is a whole series of slightly offset colored images: yellow to left of red, green to left of yellow and blue to left of green. Across most of the area of the white card the multiplicity of colored images is not apparent because the various colors recombine to form white light. But at the left edge, where the card meets the black background, the blue image, which is shifted farthest to the left, can be seen as a blue border. Similarly, the red image appears along the right edge. (When the prism is weak, the right border looks yellow or orange rather than red because red and yellow lie so close together in the spectrum.)

If one views the world through goggles with their prism bases fixed in the same direction, the rainbow fringes diminish rather quickly in intensity and within a few days virtually disappear. Here again, as a result of adaptation, a complementary aftereffect appears when the glasses are removed. The adaptation that has canceled the blue fringe on objects produces a yellowish fringe and vice versa. This complementary aftereffect, which we call the rainbow phantom, can appear after goggles have been worn for less than a day.

At first consideration the rainbow phantom may not seem surprising. Everyone is familiar with the complementary afterimage that can be induced by staring for about 20 seconds at a brightly colored pattern. Evidently the retinal elements that have been intensively exposed to a given color change in some manner, so that when they are subsequently stimulated by a neutral light, they produce a different signal from adjacent elements that are still fresh. In accordance with the work of the German psychologist Ewald Hering, we ascribe such phenomena to a process of self-regulation. The sensory response becomes shifted in such a way as to make a persisting color stimulus appear more and more neutral. As a result a second color stimulus that had previously seemed neutral now appears shifted along the spectrum; for example, toward the blue-green if the first stimulus was red.

The puzzling aspect of the rainbow phantom is that blue and yellow are themselves complementary colors. Moreover, the small foveal area, which provides most of the eye's sensitivity to color, is randomly exposed to both yellow and blue stimuli during prism-goggle experiments. Consequently the response of the fovea should become equally modified to both colors, and since each is the complement of the other their aftereffects should cancel.

Nevertheless, the rainbow adaptation and its aftereffect, the rainbow phantom, do take place. How can they be explained? As in the case of adaptation to variable distortions of geometry, we must evidently assume a similar kind of multiple (at least double) adaptation for color vision also. The two aspects are the distortion itself and the context or situation in which the distortion occurs. I have already indicated that adaptation to the concertina effect requires the visual system to learn that images contract when one looks in one direction and expand when one looks in the other. In the case of color fringing the distortion is related to a brightness gradient. The subject looking at the world through prisms that have their bases facing to the right unconsciously learns a new rule: The boundary between a dark field on the left and a light field on the right always has a fringe of blue; when the dark field lies to the right of the light field, the fringe is always yellow. We must assume that the total adaptation process requires simultaneous adjustment to these two conditions. The rainbow phantom, which appears when the goggles are removed, can then be explained as a direct consequence of the complex adaptation process.

Once we had arrived at this explanatory concept, we undertook a further exploration of "situational color adaptation." For this purpose we designed goggles in which each lens was made up of two differently colored half-segments. For example, each lens might be half blue and half yellow. Wearing such goggles, a subject sees a blue-tinted world when he looks to the left and a yellow-tinted world when he looks to the right. If the two colors are complementary, the situation is somewhat analogous to the rainbow effect of prism goggles. The difference is that the colors are related not to a brightness gradient but to specific positions of the head and eyes; in other words, to a "kinesthetic" gradient.

The experimental results were in accord with those obtained with prism goggles. As before, we found that the visual system adapts to complementary color stimuli so long as the colors are invariably associated with a particular situation—in this case, particular head-and-eye positions. The illustrations [not reproduced here] show the results of measuring color adaptation on the first day and on the 60th day of an experiment with blue-yellow glasses. The measurements are obtained through the use of an illuminated window whose color can be varied by turning a dial. The subject first looks at the window through the yellow half of his glasses and turns the dial until the window appears white or neutral in color. To achieve this condition the window must actually be made somewhat blue. The amount of blue light required is automatically recorded. The subject then readjusts the color of the window while looking through the blue half of his glasses. Finally he views the window without glasses, with his eyes turned first to the right and then to the left.

When the subject eventually removes his two-color goggles after wearing them continuously for 60 days, there is no doubt that his visual world is tinged distinctly yellow when he looks in the direction that his goggles had been blue and blue in the direction that his goggles had been yellow. The movement of the eyes, either to right or left, seems to act as a signal for the foveal area to switch over in its color response, compensating for a yellow image in one case and a blue image in the other.

At this point in our investigations everything seemed reasonably clear, but suddenly a new and mystifying phenomenon appeared, the implications of which have not yet been fully explored. During our prism experiments we had also constructed glasses in which the prisms in front of each eye were mounted with their bases pointed in opposite directions. Similar glasses are regularly prescribed by ophthalmologists to correct strabismus, also known as squinting. People with strabismus are unable to focus both eyes on the same object because the eyes turn either inward or outward; crossed eyes are an example. Ophthalmologists are often reluctant to prescribe corrective prism glasses for strabismus because of their concern that the patient may be disturbed by the distortions and color fringes that such glasses produce.

It was partly this prejudice that prompted our experiments. Because our subjects did not have strabismus they found the wearing of "squint glasses" difficult until they learned to squint; that is, to turn their eyes either inward or outward, depending on the orientation of the prisms. We found, nevertheless, that adaptation is possible and that it occurs just as rapidly as it does with our usual prismatic goggles.

Our interest, however, was soon drawn to some special effects produced by squint glasses. Because the prism bases face in opposite directions, the glasses create novel stereoscopic effects in addition to those normally seen in binocular vision. The stereoscopic effects involve geometric figures and, more important, colors. If one looks at a vertical rod with prism glasses of the type described earlier, the rod will seem to bend either to the left or to the right, depending on which way the prism bases face. If the same rod is viewed with squint glasses equipped with prism bases facing outward, the rod will appear to be bent away from the observer. Similarly, plane surfaces will look concave.

But it was the stereoscopic effects involving color that took us most by surprise. On September 10, 1952, the first day of an extended experiment with squint glasses, one of our subjects described his discovery as follows.

"In the course of a trip through town, I made the following peculiar observations: multicolored posters, traffic signs, people wearing multicolored clothes, and so on, did not appear as before to lie in one plane, but blue seemed to protrude far beyond the object plane, whereas red seemed to recede, depending on whether the background was bright or dark. A woman carrying a red bag slung over her back seemed to be transparent, and the bag to be inside her, somewhere near her stomach. . . . Most peculiar was a woman wearing a red blouse. She had no upper body, and the red blouse seemed to be following her about a pace behind, moving its empty sleeves in rhythm with the movement of her arms."

After explaining to ourselves this "color-stereo" effect, we were impatient to learn whether or not the subject's eyes would ultimately adapt and restore colored objects to their proper place. The explanation is not difficult. Each prism deflects colors differentially according to wavelength but in opposite directions since the prism bases are in opposition. When the bases face outward, the blues are deflected outward more than other colors and the eyes must actually converge more to bring blue images into focus then to focus red images, which are deflected less by the two prisms. As a result, blue images seem closer to the observer than red images, and images in other colors seem to lie somewhere between the two, according to wavelength.

Again we were surprised by the outcome of the experiment. We have discovered that there is not the slightest adaptation to the color-stereo effect. This was true even in our longest test, in which a subject wore squint glasses for 52 days.

. . . Although the [color-stereo] effect is more vivid with two prisms, or even one, it can be observed by making use of the chromatic aberration present in the normal eye. The procedure was described almost a century ago by the German physicist Hermann von Helmholtz. One covers the outer half of each pupil, using two fingers or two pieces of paper. With the outer half of each lens covered, light passes only through the inner halves, which act as if they were prisms with bases facing outward. If the inner halves of the two lenses are covered, a reverse stereo effect takes place and red objects look closer than blue ones. (The reverse effect is difficult to obtain with prisms because it is hard to force the eyes to diverge enough when the bases of the prisms face inward.)

In a small percentage of people the prismatic defects of the eye are large enough so that they can obtain a color-stereo effect even without prisms or the use of Helmholtz' procedure. A sensitive check for such defects can be made with the help of [a] green-red figure, . . . viewed with each eye separately. To a normal eye the green and red halves of the figure meet cleanly, without any noticeable peculiarity. A defective eye, however, will see either a thin black line or a thin white line where the two colors meet. A black line indicates that the green area is being displaced slightly farther to the left than the red, as it would be by a prism having its base to the right. A white line indicates that the green is being deflected to the right as by a prism with base to the left. When the green shifts to the right, it overlaps the red image, and the combination of green and red reflected light creates a white boundary. People with prismatic defects of the eye have a certain advantage over people with normal eyes, for they can differentiate colors not only by hue but also by the color-stereo effect.

Although it may not be immediately obvious, the color-stereo effect does not depend on the ability of the eye to see color. Like a prism, the lens of the eye bends light according to wavelength regardless of the hue we have come to associate with any particular wavelength. . . . It follows from this that one could enable a color-blind person to discriminate colors by providing him with prism glasses. He could be taught, for example, that the green in a traffic light will look closer to him than yellow and that yellow will look closer than red.

The color-stereo effect may also have general implications for biology. It has always seemed strange that in the eyes of most animals, including man, the fovea lies to one side of the optical axis of the lens system. This lack of alignment may combine with the eye's chromatic aberration to produce prismatic effects that are opposite for the left and right eyes, thereby producing a weak color-stereo effect. When we consider that these defects—off-center fovea and chromatic aberration—have persisted through millions of generations of animals without being "corrected" by evolution, we cannot refrain from speculating that the defects may have functional utility. Perhaps in the development of the vertebrate eye the color-stereo effect provided the first form of color discrimination, the colors being associated not with hue but with subtle differences in the depth of images. As a matter of fact, cats, mice and other animals, which are known to be color-blind, sometimes puzzle psychologists by their apparent ability to distinguish a few strong colors in visual tests. Although this color sensitivity is likely to be demonstrated by only a few animals in any experimental group, the ability cannot be ignored, and the explanation may well be that the unusual animals possess a heightened sensitivity to the color-stereo effect.

My colleague Anton Hajos can be credited with showing, by rigorous measurement, that not the slightest adaptation to the color-stereo effect occurs among subjects wearing squint glasses. He also conceived the idea of intensifying the stereo effect to see if it heightened the sensation of color. To test this idea we were fortunate to find in Innsbruck a man who had lost his color vision as the result of an accident. When he put on a pair of our squint glasses, he reported that he was instantly able to see all the colors he had not seen for years. When he removed the glasses, the colors disappeared again. We are carrying on a further investigation of this and related cases.

What shall we make of the finding that the eye adapts rather readily to various intense distortions of geometry and color but fails totally to adapt to the type of distortion embodied in the color-stereo effect? One possible explanation is that in all cases where adaptation occurs the eye is provided with certain systematic clues as to the nature of the distortion. Straight lines always curve in the same direction; blue or yellow color fringes occur in fixed relation to light-dark boundaries; blue and yellow glasses present the eye with color fields that remain consistently either on the right or on the left; even the rubber world is rubbery in a consistent way. The color-stereo effect, however, presents the visual mechanism with a random and nearly unpredictable assortment of displaced images. As the focus of the eye shifts from one point to another, it is just as likely to encounter one color as another, and, depending on wavelength, brightness and background, the stereoscopic position of the colored image is shifted forward or back. Although the eye might conceivably learn to correlate color and displacement and thereby use the former as a basis for correcting the latter, the task is evidently beyond the power of the eye's adaptation mechanism. There is, however, an alternative possibility: the color-stereo effect may represent a primitive way of identifying colors. The failure of the visual system to adapt to this effect, when presented in exaggerated form by squint glasses, may be evidence that spatial displacement of colors indeed played such an evolutionary role.

DAVID C. MCCLELLAND *and* JOHN W. ATKINSON

17. The Effect of Different Intensities of the Hunger Drive on Perception

IN the field of clinical psychology projective techniques or tests (such as play analysis, dream analysis, the Rorschach test, and the Thematic Apperception Test) are widely used and are generally regarded as the most promising method of obtaining information on personality. Yet very little information is available on exactly what a person projects or perceives under different conditions. In a review of experimental work on projection up to 1944, Sears states that though the assumption is widely held that perception is in part a function of motivation, "the details of the relation between motive and percept have been little considered" (11, p. 324).

The usual method of validation of what a perceptual or imaginative response signifies is first, to infer from the subject's projection [1] what psychological process or need must have produced the response, and second, to check by other means (case history, consistency of several tests, etc.) to see whether the process or need actually existed. In many instances only the first step in this procedure is followed. For example, Murray, who was re-

sponsible for much of the interest in projective techniques, discusses at some length (7, pp. 243–256) the problems involved in trying to estimate from a projection what needs are operating and how strong they are. He argues for greater use of trained "critical emotional participation" rather than mechanical aids and then gives a list of some 23 indices of need strength which can be of use to the observer in trying to make his decisions as to what needs are present and in what strength. Actually, of course, no one decision by a single observer was accepted by Murray's group as evidence until it had been checked by other observers and by other judgments under different conditions. Unfortunately in clinical practice such care is seldom taken.

The present series of experiments was undertaken with the purpose of attacking the problem in a radically different way. They have begun with creating a specific motivational tension or need of more or less known strength and then proceeded to measure its effects on perception and projection rather than proceeding in the usual way to infer from the percept the need which must have produced it. The hope of this new approach is that certain principles can be established of the ways in which needs of different strengths affect projection so that there will be real experimental support for inferences from projections to needs. In other words these experiments will try to collect evidence in support (or contradiction) of the clues

---

[1] The hope that this word will be used in the defensive sense originally meant by Freud seems faint. Although the authors recognize that they may be departing in the usage from what Freud and other psychoanalysts meant by the word, so many psychologists use the word to mean anything which the subject may perceive or imagine which is primarily determined subjectively rather than objectively that it will be used in that sense in these papers. Perhaps the phrase defensive projection can be reserved for the more technical meaning.

Reprinted by permission of the Journal Press and the authors from the *Journal of Psychology*, 1948, vol. 25, pp. 205–22.

which Murray suggests should be used in diagnosing the existence of needs from projections.

The first experiment in the series begins at what appeared to be the simplest level— namely, the effect on perception of different strengths of a known physiological need. Hunger was chosen as this need, because its strength can presumably be fairly easily controlled by different lengths of food deprivation and because more is known about its effects on imaginal processes (5, 9, 10). A secondary purpose of this first exploratory experiment was to try to discover, under the simplest conditions, what techniques for eliciting responses were most successful in producing percepts which accurately reflected the known state of hunger in the subjects.

Procedure

THE subjects were 108 Navy men, modal age 18 years, tested at the U.S. Naval Submarine Base at New London, Conn., through the assistance of the Medical Research Laboratory. They were usually tested during their first 10 days at the base while they were waiting for admission to the submarine training school which they had requested. Motivation was usually high. The men coöperated in anything they were asked to do because it might have something to do with their admission to the school. Some judgment had to be used, however, in throwing out papers of men who obviously were not coöperating, who had obviously misunderstood instructions, or who had taken the test before. The practical criterion for eliminating papers was set at no responses on one-half or more of the test items. The 108 men used represent 70 per cent of a larger group.

Forty of the men were tested in the morning between 10:00 and 11:00 A.M. after having been deprived of food since supper at 5:30–6:00 P.M. the night before. To make certain that there were no infringements of the prohibition against eating the men were put under guard and spent the night in a special medical barracks until the time they were to be tested. Informal questioning by the examiner did not reveal that this angered

or frustrated them particularly. So far as they were concerned it was following another routine order which meant they could sleep late in the morning, etc. This group will be referred to as the 16-hour deprivation group, although the actual hours deprivation varied between 16 and 18.

Twenty-four men were tested at the same time in the morning having eaten breakfast about four hours earlier between 6:00 and 6:30 A.M. They will be referred to as the 4-hour deprivation group. The remaining 44 men were tested approximately 1–2 hours after lunch from 1:30–3:00 P.M. (a few after breakfast at 9:00 A.M.) and will be referred to as the 1-hour deprivation group. The men were tested in small groups of 10–15 at a time over a period extending from March to July, 1947.

In designing a test of perception under the influence of hunger, it was decided to pick a situation which was as ambiguous as possible, that is, in which the actual realistic sensory cues were minimal. It was therefore decided to use a procedure somewhat similar to Perky's (8) and Miller's (6) and disguise the experiment as one in subliminal visual perception. The subjects were seated in front of a screen with a projector behind them and were given in substance the following explanation:

This is an experiment in visual perception. It has been demonstrated that persons are able to respond to visual stimulation at very low intensities. That is, they have an impression that they see something although they are not actually aware that they see anything. If asked to tell what their impression was, they would feel that they were just guessing. Experiments have shown that the number of right guesses is greater than what can be attributed to pure chance. The persons were not guessing even though they thought they were. Actually they were reporting impressions of a very slight visual stimulus that were accurate in many cases. Of course, all persons are not of equal ability in responding to very low illumination. I do not have to emphasize the importance of sensitive vision in submarine work. At present we are testing this kind of perception under different physiological conditions. Please do your best on this test. Clear your minds and relax.

The procedure followed hereafter is best indicated by the remaining instructions given the subjects:

On the desk before each of you is a little booklet and a pencil with which to record your impressions of pictures that will be focussed on the screen before you. The pictures will be projected at very low illumination. *You must write down something for every projection.* (Repeat) Remember that your strongest impression is not just a guess. Focus your eyes on the screen when I say "ready now" . . . then concentrate on the screen. Do not write anything until I say "write." My assistant will pull up a shade to allow light for writing. There is one page in the little booklet for each response. After writing down as completely as possible your strongest impression for one picture . . . fold back the page for the next picture just like a book. I may give you some hints as to what is in the picture and ask a question. On the basis of your impressions you will answer the question.

For several of the pictures your scoring sheet will have a choice of answers. After I show the picture I will tell you the possible answers (I will project the three possible answers on the screen). There will be three possible answers *A, B,* or *C* . . . and there are three possibilities on your answer sheet *A, B,* and *C.* Put a check along the line next to each possible answer to show how strong your impression is for each possible answer. Put a check on each line anywhere from strongest impression to weakest impression to give us an idea of how strong your impression was for each possibility. Suppose I show this picture (show car). Now look at the cover of your answer booklet. . . . (Put in three choices in projector.) This is how you would answer if your strongest impression was a car . . . weakest impression that it was a house . . . but some impression that it was a box. Does everyone understand? . . . You put a mark on the line from the strongest impression to the weakest impression to show your own feelings about each possibility.

Let me run through the procedure. . . .

1. I will say "ready now" and you will concentrate on the screen.
2. The pictures will be projected on the screen for 20 seconds. At the end of five seconds I will give you a hint.
3. At the end of 20 seconds I will say "write" at which point you will record your answer. The assistant will shift a shade in the rear of the

room to provide enough light. I will remind you of the page number. Thirty seconds is allowed for writing.

4. I will say "all right," the assistant will pull down the shade. When the room is dark, you will turn to the next page in booklet.

Please follow these instructions. . . .

Do not talk at all during the test or make any verbal exclamations.

Write down something for every picture. You are not guessing even though you think you are. When you are certain you don't see anything then your guess is the impression we want. Don't expect to be certain on these.

Don't expect to see much at all—it may look like a shadow—it may have no shadows at all. Concentrate on the screen and write down the impression that comes to your mind. I'll show you one or two of the pictures after the test so you will get an idea of how accurate you were. Are there any questions?

After the experiment was over the subjects were asked to check their subjective feeling of hunger on a 5-step scale with 1 representing very hungry and 5 not very hungry.

There were 12 "pictures" theoretically thrown on the screen. Actually all of these were blanks although the examiner went through the motions of putting a picture in the projector. In order to convince the subjects that something was being shown, a car was projected, as described in the instructions, and the illumination gradually diminished by means of a Variac in series with the projector until the car was only faintly visible. These 12 were selected out of 20 used in some preliminary experimentation. In an effort to collect data on the accuracy of different types of perceptions in reflecting hunger, the items were selected from several different groups as follows: Three called for object-naming responses. For example, when the fourth slide was "presented" the experimenter said: *"Three objects on a table. What are they?"* Two called for activity or instrumental act responses (Example: *"All the people in this picture are enjoying themselves. What are they doing?"*). Two called for subjective feeling responses (Example: *"A face. Describe his feeling"*). Two called for places possibly related to food or eating (Example: *"A room. Describe it"*). And three were projected with the comment, *"No hints on this one."* This use of different kinds of items was adopted to see whether hunger affected some kinds of perceptual responses more than others.

Two additional methodological changes were introduced. In the first place, as described in the instructions, some of the items called for the choice among three possible responses given in the record booklet. There were two such well-structured items. In addition there were the three completely unstructured items on which no hints were given, and the seven remaining "loosely structured" items when a hint was given but no alternatives were stated. Hence it was possible to compare the effect of hunger on three degrees of structurization of responses called for to see which was most effective in differentiating between hungry and non-hungry subjects.

In the second place, 15 additional subjects in the 16-hour and seven in the 4-hour deprivation groups were run when smudges or shadows were projected on the screen instead of the usual blanks. This was done to follow up a suggestion from Levine, Chein, and Murphy's study (5) that the degree of structurization of the *stimulus* made a difference in the number of food responses.

The experimental design so far calls for a differentiation of hungry and non-hungry groups primarily in terms of *frequency* of food-related responses. If the theoretical position of Brunswik (cf. 1), Ansbacher (1), Bruner and Goodman (3) is correct, the need should also influence perceptions of *size* and *number*. To test this possibility 17 subjects from the 16-hour group, 20 subjects from the 4-hour group and 18 from the 1-hour group were run in an additional experiment, the instructions for which follow:

On the last test we were testing your ability to make out objects. On this next test we want to see how good you are at estimating size and number. Pictures will be projected at very low intensity and you will be asked to give your impression of the number of objects or the size of some object in the picture. Don't make the mistake of thinking that because an automobile is larger than a book in real life it will be larger

in the picture for there may be a small picture of a big object and a large picture of a small object, like this one. Does everyone understand?

Please record the first impression that comes to your mind after I ask the question. We will go a little faster on this test.

The size items called for a comparison in size of a food-related and a non-food-related object. (Example: *"An ash-tray and a hamburger—which is larger?"* *"A plate and a picture—which is larger?"*) The number items called for an estimate of the actual number of food-related and non-food-related objects (Examples: *"Some pencils—how many? Some forks—how many?"*). There were 15 such items, five of which called for size comparisons, and remaining 10 of which permitted estimates of numbers of food-related and non-food-related items.

In scoring the results obtained in the frequency part of the experiment and in making up the items in the size and number part, the problem naturally arose as to what should be considered a food-related response. Sanford (9, 10) and Levine, Chein and Murphy (5) had decided in favor of counting only those responses which were names of food objects or verbs signifying eating. Since the scope of this experiment was broader and particularly was designed to get the number of different kinds of food-related responses, the interpretation of what constituted a food response was more liberal. The general principle followed was to count any imagery unmistakably related to the goal response (eating), the goal object (food) or objects instrumental to eating (knife, fork, plate, dining room table, etc.). Doubtful responses such as hunting, fishing, etc., were not counted.

Results

TABLE 1 presents the main results in terms of the mean number of food-related responses per subject for the different degrees of drive strength. The steady increase of the average frequency of food responses as hours of deprivation increase is in line with several previous investigations (5, 9, 10). The difference between the 1-hour and 16-hour groups is

TABLE 1

Mean Number of Food-Related Responses per Subject Out of Possible 14 * for Three Degrees of Strength of the Hunger Drive

HOURS FOOD DEPRIVATION	N	AV. RATED DRIVE STR.	σm	STRENGTH OF DRIVE	MEAN FOOD RELATED R'S	σm	$P_{diff.}$ OCCURRING BY CHANCE WITH	
							4-hr.	16-hr.
1	44	3.30	.17	weak	2.14	.24	<.10	<.002
4	24	2.02	.17	medium	2.88	.36		<.42
16	40	1.90	.14	strong	3.22	.23		

* Counting three possible responses for the item which asked for three objects, any or all of which could be food-related.

highly reliable. The interesting fact is that while there is a significant increase in subjective drive strength between one and four hours' deprivation, there is not a correspondingly reliable increase in number of food-related R's produced. However, in general the rated hunger state seems to increase with negative acceleration just as does the number of food-related R's.[2]

Was there a greater percentage of food responses to some types of items rather than others? TABLE 2 gives the answer. Some items do elicit more food responses (particularly the object items) but in general no type of item reflects more sensitively the degree of hunger—i.e., no type of item can conclusively be said to yield a more valid index of the amount of food deprivation. The same conclusion must be reached from TABLE 3 which presents the data on the proportion of food responses obtained when there was structuring to different degrees of the responses the subject could make. That is, there were far

[2] A more extended discussion of the relation of subjective state to drive strength is reserved for a separate paper.

more food choices when the subject was told to pick a response out of three possible responses, one of which was a food response (the well-structured items), than when he was left completely free to write anything that came into his head. But there was no significantly greater differential in the percentage of food responses for any of the types of responses for different degrees of hunger. Various attempts were made to break down the food responses actually given into various categories to see whether hours deprivation had any differential effects. For the most part the frequencies were too small to establish any reliable trends. But there was an exception. The largest number of food responses was given to Item 3 (*"Three objects on a table. What are they?"*). These were broken down into "instrumental" food-related responses (e.g., dish, spoon, knife, plate, salt, etc.) and "goal object" food-related responses (e.g., milk, bread, apple, orange, candy, etc.). The same breakdown was then made for several other items which permitted it. The results presented in TABLE 4 show that there was a reliable increase in the number of "instru-

TABLE 2

Percentage of the Subjects Giving Food-Related Responses to Various Kinds of Items

HOURS DEP- RIVATION	N	ITEM NO.: 1	OBJECTS 2	3	ACTS 4	5	FEELINGS 6	7	PLACES 8	9	UNSTRUCTURED 10	11	12
1	44	30	46	9	14	61	0	0	5	0	0	0	5
4	24	33	54	13	17	67	0	0	4	0	4	0	0
16	40	35	73	13	10	83	5	8	5	3	3	3	5

TABLE 3

Percentage of Food Responses to Various Degrees of Structurization Out of the Total Possible Food Responses (No. *S*'s × No. Items)

HOURS DEPRIVATION	UNSTRUCTURED ITEMS (3)	LOOSELY STRUC- TURED ITEMS (7)	WELL-STRUC- TURED ITEMS (2)
1	1.5%	10.4%	45.5%
4	1.4	12.5	50.0
16	3.3	16.4	58.8

mental" food responses as hours of deprivation increased while the number of "goal object" responses stayed practically the same. Another way of stating it is that the hungry group saw more ($P < .06$) objects related to getting food than they did actual food objects, whereas the non-hungry group saw an equal number of each.

An analysis was also made of the number of rejections to check the finding obtained by Levine, Chein, and Murphy (5) that the number increased with the increase in hunger. There were 43 rejections for the 1-hour group or an average of .98 per subject, 20 for the 4-hour group or an average of .83 per subject, and 34 for the 16-hour group or .85 per subject. These differences are very small and unreliable and do not confirm those obtained by Levine, Chein, and Murphy. A further check on the number of *S*'s voided in each of the three groups for failure to respond showed no differences.

Introduction of some hazy shadows or smudges on the screen cut down the average number of food responses. Fifteen subjects in the 16-hour group averaged only 2.33 food responses ($\sigma m = .41$) as compared with 3.22 for the blank screen group. The critical ratio of the difference is 1.89, $P < .06$. Seven subjects after four hours without food also averaged less—only 1.57 ($\sigma m = .42$) as compared with 2.88 for the regular group. The difference approaches significance ($CR = 2.34$, $P < .04$). Despite the fact that there was approximately the same increase in food responses from the 4- to 16-hour group as was obtained with the blank screen, the number of responses was so much smaller it was decided to discontinue experimentation with the "smudged" screen.

SIZE AND NUMBER

Hunger increases the apparent size of food objects. At least TABLE 5 shows that in comparisons of food objects with neutral objects judged equally large normally, the 16-hour deprivation group judged the food objects to be larger 75 per cent of the time—despite the fact, of course, that neither object could be seen or was there to be seen. The difference between the 1- and 16-hour groups is highly significant with the 4-hour group falling in between as usual. The data permitted a breakdown into "instrumental" and "goal" objects as in previous comparisons,

TABLE 4

Mean Number of Instrumental and Goal Object Responses

HOURS DEPRIVATION	N	INSTRUMENTAL OBJECTS	σm	$P_{diff.}$ OCCURRING BY CHANCE WITH 4-hr.	16-hr.	GOAL OBJECTS	σm
1	44	.55	.15	<.08	<.03	.50	.15
4	24	1.08	.25		<.50	.58	.22
16	40	1.10	.19			.68	.15

TABLE 5

Number of Times the Food Object Is Seen as Larger Than a Comparison Neutral
Object as a Percentage of the Total Possible Number
of Comparisons (S's $\times$ Items)

HOURS FOOD DEPRIVATION	NO. S's	TOTAL COM- PARISONS	FOOD LARGER	PER CENT	CHI-SQUARE WITH 4-hr.	16-hr.
1	18	72	36	50	1.95	9.29
4	20	80	49	61		3.17
16	17	68	51	75		

but the results were nearly identical [3] for the two categories which have been combined in TABLE 5. This indicates that the hungry person not only sees food objects which can be eaten as larger but also instrumental food objects like plates and spoons. However, when he was forced to choose between an instrumental object and a goal object (*"A bowl and a cake, which is larger?"*), he said the cake was larger 80 per cent of the time after four hours' deprivation and 77 per cent of the time after 16 hours' deprivation as compared with 50 per cent of the time after one hour deprivation. The chi-square of the difference between the 1- and 4-hour groups is 3.8 ($P < .05$).

3 The values are for the 1-hour, 4-hour and 16-hour deprivation groups respectively: 50, 60, and 74 per cent for the instrumental objects and 50, 63 and 77 per cent for the goal objects. The χ^2 of the difference between the 1-hour and 16-hour groups is 4.09 ($P < .05$) for the instrumental objects and 5.25 ($P < .05$) for the goal objects.

Similar but for the most part unreliable trends show up in TABLE 6 which summarizes the results for the estimation of absolute numbers of objects projected. The increases for food-related responses in both the instrumental and goal object columns are in the direction expected but unfortunately the subjects occasionally made very large number estimates which increased variabilities considerably and lowered the reliability of the differences, none of which is significant beyond the .10 level. On the other hand there was a quite unexpected and highly reliable increase (Critical ratio = 2.96, $P < .01$) in the estimates of neutral instrumental objects from the 1-hour to the 16-hour deprivation group. This difference does not appear in the neutral goal objects but is naturally reflected in the combined score for both categories. The two instrumental neutral items concerned asked for estimates of numbers of books and pencils as compared with the neu-

TABLE 6

Mean Estimated Numbers of Food-Related and Neutral Objects for Both
Instrumental and Goal Objects (Items Combined)

FOOD DEPRIVATION	NO. S's	FOOD-RELATED OBJECTS Instrumental (3 items)	Goal (3 items)	TOTAL	NEUTRAL OBJECTS Instrumental (2 items)	Goal (2 items)	TOTAL
1-hr.	18	3.19	4.10	3.60	3.09	4.33	3.72
σm		.27	.29	.23	.33	.92	.23
4-hr.	20	3.60	4.48	4.01	4.63	4.70	4.66
σm		.30	.44	.30	.52	.73	.45
16-hr.	17	4.41	4.84	4.51	5.49	4.75	5.12
σm		.62	.47	.50	.74	.64	.49

tral goal objects of cigarettes and golf balls. Books and pencils were considered as instrumental to some such need as need achievement or need mastery. It is difficult to see how this need could have been stimulated by food deprivation or to explain in any way for that matter this peculiar result.

Discussion

THE HUNGER DRIVE

MANY questions could be raised about the wisdom of choosing hunger as the physiological drive with which to do the exploratory work in this field. For instance, it is certainly not typical of psychogenic needs in that there is no ego-involvement. The subjects know they are going to be fed. More than this it is known to be cyclical in its effect and any experimentation is likely to be influenced by the position in the cycle at which it is performed. Nevertheless hunger was chosen for three main reasons: (a) there seemed to be no other physiological drive to which there was not equally or more serious objections; (b) more is known about the effects of hunger on psychic processes than any other drive; and (c) it is easier to control than any other drive.

To what extent was it controlled successfully in the present experimental set up? It was possible to control rigorously the amount of food intake during the hours of deprivation, but unfortunately little was known about the degree of satiation at the beginning of the "fast." It is a fact that subjects in the 16-hour deprivation group rated themselves in every step on the hunger rating scale except the last one (Step 5), whereas subjects who had recently finished lunch rated themselves in every step except the first (Step 1). The modal step rating was different, of course, for the three deprivation groups, but the question remains as to whether hours of deprivation is a good way to control the strength of the hunger drive. Would it not be better simply to use subjective ratings regardless of hours of deprivation?

There would seem to be some logic to this since the number of food responses followed the subjective ratings very closely. Perhaps the subjective state should have been considered the main determinant of the food responses and used rather than hours deprivation to differentiate the three hunger groups throughout the rest of the experiment. But the situation is not so simple as this. It is also possible to argue that the subjective state of hunger is a response to a physiological condition just as the number of food responses is. Both are negatively accelerated functions of the amount of deprivation. From this viewpoint subjective state would be considered coordinate with (and highly correlated with) food responses rather than as their chief determinant. Although the problem warrants a much more thorough treatment than this, it was on the basis of this kind of reasoning that it was decided to use hours deprivation rather than subjective hunger rating as the basis for isolating three degrees of the hunger drive.

THE TECHNIQUES EMPLOYED

One of the purposes of this preliminary experiment was to try and find methods of presentation which would provide responses which were more sensitive to the degree of hunger. Most of the results were negative. The introduction of blots which provided some visual material on which to build responses only decreased the number of food responses —apparently indicating that the fewer the objective determinants, the greater the influence of the subjective or behavioral (2) determinants of perception. This would suggest that stimulus situations even less structured than the Rorschach or the *TAT*, if they could be made practical, would yield more sensitive measures of personality characteristics. Of course, the less "realistic" the situation is the harder it becomes for the subject, and the number of rejections and subject's failures increases. There was no evidence, however, that the number of rejections or failures increased with the strength of the hunger drive as Levine, Chein, and Murphy found (5). Perhaps this experimental situation was already so unrealistic that it could not become more so as hunger increased.

Opportunity was given for hunger to express itself more fully in perceptions of different parts of a behavior sequence involving food-getting-feelings, acts, associated places, and goal and instrumental objects. It was expected that a need might reflect itself more in perceptions of feelings, for instance, than in perceptions of places associated with eating. The results were disappointing in this respect. They show that no particular kind of percept (with one exception discussed below) is more influenced by the need than any other. True, perceptions of objects (at least objects on a table) are more often food-related than are perceptions of places (for example), but this is true of the satiated group as well, and the differential between the 1-hour and 16-hour group for objects is not reliably greater than for other kinds of items. That different techniques may raise or lower the overall frequency of food-related responses was also demonstrated by the fact that the frequency was greatly raised by providing alternatives for the subject to pick, one of which was a food response. Once again, however, the gradient of increase as hunger increased was the same for the items yielding frequent food responses as for the items yielding infrequent food responses. Although it is certainly not safe to generalize from this situation to the standard projective technique situations, this result suggests that norms would be very important for the latter. For example, in the *TAT* it would be possible to pick a picture which would either yield very few aggressive responses which, if they appeared, would almost certainly indicate aggressiveness, or very many, which would indicate aggression only in comparison to some normative number (cf. 2). By analogy with the present results, either picture would be all right as an indicator of a need (though the more productive one would be more practical) provided the experimenter knew its characteristics—i.e., how many responses it "normally" gave rise to. The same could be said of the multiple choice Rorschach. It should yield more "false positives" just as the multiple choice items did here, but if norms could be set up as to how many responses to expect just from the suggestion of the situation rather than from determinants within the individual, there is no reason why it shouldn't be as effective a

tool in discriminating between those who have certain characteristics and those who don't. Practically, of course, in clinical situations, it has proven necessary to compromise and choose items which give enough responses to be sensitive but not so many as to be meaningless. Ideally, norms should be established by experimental means similar to those used here.

THE INCREASE IN FOOD-RELATED RESPONSES

The general finding that the frequency of food-related responses and estimates of the size and number of food objects increase as hunger increases is in line with other similar experimental results and their theoretical formulations. In Brunswik's and Ansbacher's (1) terms this is a situation in which the conscious pole of intention (the "real" number of food objects, etc.) is non-existent and the percept or judgment is wholly determined by the latent pole of intent or latent attitudes, one of which is hunger. Or in Bruner and Goodman's terms (3) there are no autochthonous determinants of the percept here. They are wholly behavioral. Since their three principles (3, pp. 36–37) do not take account of this limiting case and are stated in terms of the extent to which behavioral determinants win out over the autochthonous ones, it is necessary to extend the formulation of their second hypothesis so that it reads: *The greater the individual need for a valued object, the more vivid will its perception be, vividness being understood to include greater apparent size, number, and frequency as well as clarity and brightness.*

But stating the general principle leaves much to be explained. Why does it hold true? Are there limits to its application? Or more specifically, why was there no decrease like Levine, Chein, and Murphy's (5) in the number of food responses as the drive continued to increase? Why should the number of objects which could be eaten show no increase in frequency (though they did in size!) while the number of objects which could be used to eat with show an increase?

In general there seem to be two somewhat different interpretations of the results obtained. The first one starts with the null hypothesis that there should be no effect on perception of an increase in drive strength. It would discard the results on estimates of number (particularly the increase in estimated numbers of neutral instrumental objects) as due to some extraneous influence. It would accept the failure of goal objects to increase in frequency as to be expected and would be left with the necessity of explaining only the increased frequency of "instrumental" food-related objects and the increase in apparent size of "instrumental" and "goal" food-related objects. It could explain the increased "vividness" of instrumental objects by application of a general principle arrived at from Knapp's study of rumor (4) to the effect that as wish or need increases in intensity, there is a "Drang nach Realität." That is, as a need gets more intense a person's phantasy and perception begins to concern itself more and more with realistic means of satisfying the need. For example, a relatively satiated person may dream of food but a hungry person begins to dream of ways of getting food—of walking out of the room, for example. This is by no means the whole of Knapp's theoretical formulation, but this much of it could be applied here if it can be assumed that spoons, plates, and dishes can be subsumed under the heading of getting food in the same general way as covert, imagined *acts* of food-getting can be. The extension of the principle from imagined instrumental acts to instrumental objects is logical, though it is not quite as easy to see the biological utility of imagining the objects.

This leaves unexplained only the increase in apparent size of goal objects which would have to be considered one of the perversities of nature or explained by reference to some *ad hoc* principle drawn from the second interpretation.

This second interpretation would start with a quite different assumption—namely that as a need such as hunger increases it mobilizes the perceiving responses of the organism just as it mobilizes the motor responses. This hypothesis would lead one to expect an increase in the frequency of all food-related responses

and in the size and number of food-related objects. The energizing function might even spread to include the problematical over-estimation of the numbers of neutral instrumental objects.[4] The fact which then needs explaining is the failure of food goal objects to increase in frequency. This could be handled by reference to an active suppressing tendency such as Sanford (10) found it necessary to assume. He was surprised at the relatively slight increase in food responses between his control and 24-hour deprivation groups. This is not so surprising in the light of the present results, since he recorded only what would be considered here "goal object" responses. With these responses he found it "necessary to conceive of at least one process which tended to inhibit the giving of food responses." This process he considered was probably the attempt "to reduce the displeasure of frustration by suppressing thoughts of the goal" (10, p. 158). Its operation seems to be confirmed by Levine, Chein, and Murphy's finding (5) that there is an actual decrease of food responses (again counting goal responses only) from six to nine hours' deprivation.

If this principle does explain the failure of the goal responses to appear more frequently with increased hunger, it somehow does not operate to prevent the increase in the size of food objects once the subject is told they are there. This is not so contradictory a finding as it appears to be. The suppressing tendency may operate only to keep food goal objects from mind. Once they are presented, however, the damage is done so to speak, and the general tendency to overesti-

4 This finding defies adequate interpretation. There seems no reason to assume that books and pencils are more associated with the time of day (10–11 A.M.) when the hungry groups took the test. The possibility that hunger generally increases perceptual productivity, an effect which would appear only here because only food responses were recorded elsewhere was checked by counting the average word output on a given item (*"An outdoor scene. Describe it."*) for the 1-hour and 16-hour deprivation groups. The average output was 5.8 and 5.6 words respectively. Anyway any such tendency should also affect neutral goal objects but it doesn't. There remains the remote possibility that increase in the hunger drive increases other drives such as need achievement for which objects like pencils and books could be considered instrumental.

mate food-related objects asserts itself. A hungry person may prefer not to think of a beefsteak at all but if he sees one it may appear larger and juicier than normal.

Whichever of these explanations is adopted (and there are others which combine elements of both) the facts, if confirmed at a more complex level, suggest some important implications for interpreting projective records such as the *TAT*. First, they do not support the logical assumption, made by Murray (7), that the stronger a need is the greater will be the terminal or goal response activity projected. Second, they do indicate that as a need increases, goal objects which satisfy it *if presented* will appear more vivid (larger and more numerous). Third, they support the general principle formulated by Knapp that as a need increases, there is an increase in the projection of activities (here objects) instrumental to satisfying the need. Fourth, they indicate that the increase in strength of one need may have important side effects so that it may even increase the frequency of objects related to other needs.

Summary

ONE hundred thirty men, candidates for submarine training school at the New London, Conn., U.S. Navy Submarine Base, acted as subjects in an experiment purporting to measure the ability to see faint or subliminal visual cues. For 22 of the S's faint blots were projected, but for the remaining 108 nothing was shown although various hints were given for many of the slides to maintain the impression that it was a test of visual acuity. Of the 108 S's 44 took the test 1–2 hours after eating, 24 4–5 hours after eating, and 40 16–18 hours after eating. Their reactions were analyzed into frequency of food-related responses, and comparative size and number estimates of food-related and neutral objects. Analysis was also made of the differential effect of hunger on various types of perceptual responses. The following conclusions appear justified:

1. Introduction of blots decreases the number of food-related responses over the blank screen condition.

2. The frequency of food-related responses increases reliably as hours of food deprivation (or subjective hunger) increases.

3. The increase in food-related responses as a function of degree of food deprivation occurs for instrumental (e.g., knives) but not for goal objects (e.g., apples).

4. Both instrumental and goal object food-related responses are judged larger in comparison with neutral objects by hungry S's and not by satiated S's.

5. The same trend as in Conclusion 4 appeared though not reliably for estimates of numbers of neutral and food-related objects, but was complicated by a reliable increase in the estimated numbers of neutral instrumental objects for the hungry S's.

6. The greater the structuring of the response called for (i.e., the stronger the hint), the greater the frequency of food-related responses, but there was no change in the differential effect of hunger for the different degrees of structuring. That is, the increase in frequency of food-related responses as a function of degree of structuring occurred proportionally for the non-hungry and hungry groups.

7. Items calling for object responses in general produced larger numbers of food-related responses than did items calling for feelings, places, or acts, but again no type of item was more sensitive to differences in degree of hunger.

The bearing of these results on projective techniques is discussed. They represent the first step in an attempt to measure the effects on perception and apperception of known intensities of need strength. They suggest some modifications in the interpretation of projective records, the most important of which is, if confirmed, that the amount of instrumental activity appearing is a more valid index of the strength of a need than is the amount of goal response activity.

REFERENCES

1. ANSBACHER, H. Perception of number as affected by the monetary value of the objects. *Arch. of Psychol.*, 1937, No. 215.

2. BELLAK, L. The concept of projection. *Psychiatry*, 1944, 7, 353–370.

3. BRUNER, J. S., & GOODMAN, C. C. Value and need as organizing factors in perception. *J. Abn. & Soc. Psychol.*, 1947, 42, 33–44.

4. KNAPP, R. H. Experiments in serial reproduction and related aspects of the psychology of rumor. Unpublished Ph.D. thesis, Harvard University, 1948.

5. LEVINE, R., CHEIN, I., & MURPHY, G. The relation of the intensity of a need to the amount of perceptual distortion: a preliminary report. *J. of Psychol.*, 1942, 13, 283–293.

6. MILLER, J. G. Discrimination without awareness. *Amer. J. Psychol.*, 1939, 52, 562–578.

7. MURRAY, H. A., *et al.* Explorations in Personality. New York: Oxford Univ. Press, 1938.

8. PERKY, C. W. An experimental study of imagination. *Amer. J. Psychol.*, 1910, 21, 422–452.

9. SANFORD, R. N. The effect of abstinence from food upon imaginal processes: a preliminary experiment. *J. of Psychol.*, 1936, 2, 129–136.

10. ———. The effect of abstinence from food upon imaginal processes: a further experiment. *J. of Psychol.*, 1937, 3, 145–159.

11. SEARS, R. R. Experimental analysis of psychoanalytic phenomena. Chapter 9 in Hunt, J. McV. (*Ed.*) *Personality and the Behavior Disorders.* New York: Ronald Press, 1944.

E. E. SLOSSON

18. A Lecture Experiment in Hallucinations

An experiment to illustrate a popular lecture must be striking, quick and sure to work. As it is not always easy to tell beforehand whether an experiment will answer these requirements, the following scheme for the production of a hallucination of smell may be worth recording. I had prepared a bottle filled with distilled water carefully wrapped in cotton and packed in a box. After some other experiments I stated that I wished to see how rapidly an odor would be diffused through the air, and requested that as soon as anyone perceived the odor he should raise his hand. I then unpacked the bottle in the front of the hall, poured the water over the cotton, holding my head away during the operation and started a stopwatch. While awaiting results I explained that I was quite sure that no one in the audience had ever smelled the chemical compound which I had poured out, and expressed the hope that, while they might find the odor strong and peculiar, it would not be too disagreeable to anyone. In fifteen seconds most of those in the front row had raised their hands, and in forty seconds the "odor" had spread to the back of the hall, keeping a pretty regular "wave front" as it passed on. About three-fourths of the audience claimed to perceive the smell, the obstinate minority including more men than the average of the whole. More would probably have succumbed to the suggestion, but at the end of a minute I was obliged to stop the experiment, for some on the front seats were being unpleasantly affected and were about to leave the room. No one in the audience seemed offended when it was explained that the real object of the experiment was the production of a hallucination.

Hallucinations of temperature or pain are easily induced by suggestion in susceptible individuals by the use of magnets, though the experiment is not suitable for lecture purposes. It is, of course, necessary that the subject should have hazy ideas about magnetism, but it is unfortunately only too easy to find such persons. The "magnet" need not be magnetized, but should have plainly marked poles and the suggestion be conveyed by suitable "patter," to use a conjurer's phrase. Sensations of heat may be produced by the north pole of the magnet, and cold by the south, or one pole may be made to give a tingling or smarting pain in the right hand and side of the body, and the south pole on the left, or any other such scheme not too complicated. The illustrated magazine articles of the effects produced on hypnotized subjects by Luys, with magnets and sealed tubes of chemicals, are useful to reinforce the suggestions. Of course, the deception should be thoroughly explained after the experiment, not only because otherwise the subject sometimes complains of pain in the hand worked upon, but also in order that the experiment may serve as a lesson to the subject no less than to the spectators.

Slight hallucinations of sound are easily induced; but I have never succeeded in getting unhypnotized subjects to see red and blue flames on the poles of a magnet, or in obtaining any similar hallucinations of sight. Simple experiments in suggestion on persons in a normal state are generally better for demonstration than the more striking results obtained in hypnosis.

From the *Psychological Review*, 1899, vol. 6, pp. 407–08.

LEO POSTMAN, JEROME S. BRUNER, *and*
ELLIOTT MC GINNIES

19. *Personal Values as Selective Factors in Perception*

WHAT one sees, what one observes, is inevitably what one selects from a near infinitude of potential percepts. Perceptual selection depends not only upon the "primary determinants of attention" but is also a servant of one's interests, needs, and values.

Can one lean on the slender reed of "the limited span of attention" and its primary determinants to explain the selectivity of perception? That there is a limited span can hardly be denied. But to invoke it in explanation of itself leaves unexplained the differences in the perceptions of individuals faced with the same stimuli and all hampered by a "limited span of attention" and governed by common primary determinants.

The properties of the stimulus field as they affect the range and fluctuation of attention have been amply investigated: "intensity, quality, repetition, suddenness, movement, novelty, congruity with the present contents of consciousness are one and all [primary] determinants of attention" (13, p. 270). Yet, however far one pushes such research, half of the question remains unanswered: what does the individual contribute to perceptual selection over and above a healthy pair of eyes and the appropriate response mechanisms? The concepts of secondary and derived primary attention are merely restatements of the problem, affirming that the organism can and does attend to things in spite of the absence of primary determinants (13). To say that there are "individual differences"

in perceptual behavior is merely another way to restate the problem and to dismiss one of the most fruitful sources of psychological research.

Psychologists have in recent years been increasingly concerned with what may be called organismic or adjustive determinants in perception. Professor E. G. Boring has, for example, pointed out that "the purpose of perception is economy of thinking. It picks out and establishes what is permanent and therefore important to the organism for its survival and welfare" (2). In general, however, "survival and welfare" have been treated as synonymous with the "primary biological needs" of the organism. The supposed utility of perceptual constancies described in terms of "regression to the real object" illustrates well this generalized organismic approach to the problem.

But survival and welfare obviously encompass more than purely biological needs. There remains the evanescent residual category of "personality," at once too broad to be operationally useful to the student of perception and too ubiquitous to be neglected. What is required are dimensions of variation in personality which are both measurable and intrinsically important, and which can be related to individual differences in perception.

One such dimension of variation in personality is personal interest or value. It is with this dimension of personality in its relation to perceptual selectivity that the present study is concerned. Our hypothesis, briefly, is that

Reprinted by permission of the American Psychological Association and the authors from the *Journal of Abnormal and Social Psychology*, 1948, vol. 43, pp. 142–53.

personal values are demonstrable determinants of what the individual selects perceptually from his environment.

The Experiment

PERCEPTUAL selectivity may be investigated in different ways. A subject may be faced with a complex field from which he selects this or that item or configuration. This type of selection may be called *spatial selection*. Or, a subject may be presented with a series of items one at a time, each well within his span of attention, and the *speed* with which the various items are correctly recognized may be compared. This type of selection may be called *temporal selection*. These two forms of selectivity are alike in that they both reflect differential tuning of the individual to stimulus objects in the environment. In the experiment here reported temporal selection was studied.

Twenty-five subjects, students at Harvard and Radcliffe, were shown 36 words, one at a time, in a modified Dodge tachistoscope. The words, typed in capital letters, were chosen to represent the six values measured by the Allport-Vernon Study of Values—theoretical, economic, aesthetic, social, political, and religious. These words were unanimously chosen by three independent judges familiar with the Spranger value classification from a preliminary list of 96 words equally distributed among the six values. The final list, comprising six words for each value, was balanced for length of words by using an equal number of six- and seven-letter words for each value. Insofar as possible, an attempt was made to choose words of equal

familiarity. The stimulus words are listed by value category in TABLE 1.[1]

The 36 words were shown to the subject in random order. Each word was exposed three times for .01 second. If the subject failed to recognize the word, three exposures were then given at .02, .03 second, etc., at exposure times increasing in even steps of .01 second until recognition occurred. A full record was kept of all the subject's pre-recognition responses. Subjects were instructed simply to report everything that they saw or thought they saw.

To obtain an independent measure of personal value orientation, the Allport-Vernon Study of Values (1) was administered individually to each subject. The test was given either some weeks in advance of the perceptual experiment or after the experiment.

In summary, then, the following records were obtained for each subject:

1. Time of recognition for 36 words representing the six Spranger values.

2. Attempted solutions preceding recognition of the actual words.

[1] A word should be said in explanation of the Spranger values. In some cases, titles of value categories do not fully correspond to common usage. *Theoretical* refers to a dominant interest in the discovery of truth. *Economic* value is focused on usefulness and practicality. The *aesthetic* value emphasizes form and harmony. Love of people and sympathy characterize those high in *social* value. Interest in power is the defining property of *political* value which transcends interest in the narrow field of politics as ordinarily understood. Finally, *religious* value denotes an urge for unity, a desire to identify with some larger and more comprehensive totality. Here again the definition of religious value goes beyond the narrower meaning of religious practice. A full discussion of these values may be found in Spranger (12), and Vernon and Allport (14).

TABLE 1

Stimulus Words Representing the Six Spranger Value Categories

THEORETICAL	ECONOMIC	AESTHETIC	SOCIAL	POLITICAL	RELIGIOUS
theory	income	beauty	loving	govern	prayer
verify	useful	artist	kindly	famous	sacred
science	wealthy	poetry	devoted	compete	worship
logical	finance	elegant	helpful	citizen	blessed
research	economic	literary	friendly	politics	religion
analysis	commerce	graceful	sociable	dominate	reverent

3. Score profiles on the Allport-Vernon test, which could be evaluated against population norms.

Results of the Experiment

ANALYSIS OF RECOGNITION THRESHOLDS

Is time of recognition significantly influenced by the value which a given stimulus word represents? Each subject's value profile was compared with his "time-of-recognition profile." The value profile is a type of psychograph on which the subject's scores in the six Spranger values as measured by the Allport-Vernon Study are plotted. The average times of recognition for the sets of six words representing each of the value areas constitute the time-of-recognition profile. The two profiles for each of the 25 subjects are presented in FIGURE 1.

Along the baseline the value-areas are indicated. Allport-Vernon scores are plotted against the left-hand ordinate and average times of recognition against the right-hand ordinate.[2] Inspection of these profiles at once reveals considerable variability but also a marked tendency for high-value words to be recognized at shorter time exposures than low-value ones. In a few cases there is virtually one-to-one correspondence between the two profiles (e.g., the profiles of RB and IV). Such striking relationships are not, of course, the rule. One isolated case (JC) shows what appears to be a reversal, high-value words requiring, on the whole, a longer exposure time than less-valued words. Certainly visual inspection indicates that, for the sample as a whole, time of recognition varies as a function of value.

Statistical analysis confirms this impression. The value scores of each subject were classified as falling above or below the population mean (30) for the Allport-Vernon test.

His time-of-recognition scores were similarly divided into those falling below or above *his own* mean time of recognition. Combining the results for all subjects into a two-by-two contingency table (TABLE 2), a chi-square test of independence was performed. The obtained chi-square value of 11.87 indicates, at a high level of confidence, that the association between value orientation and time of recognition is not random.[3]

An analysis in terms of a two-by-two table, though useful, can do little more than indicate that a general relationship does exist. For purposes of more detailed analysis, each subject's value scores were, therefore, ranked from highest (Rank 1) to lowest (Rank 6). For the group as a whole, the average time of recognition was computed for each of the six ranks. Note that the analysis here is in terms of *rank of value* rather than in terms of *specific* value areas. That is to say, Rank 1 could be any one of the six values for a given subject, and so on down for the remaining ranks. The mean times of recognition for the six value ranks are presented numerically in TABLE 3 and graphically in FIGURE 2.

The significance of the difference between the mean times of recognition of stimulus words was tested for all possible combinations of value ranks. As TABLE 4 shows, the words symbolizing the subjects' highest ranking value are recognized at exposure times significantly shorter than those required for words symbolizing their lowest ranking value. A comparison of the highest ranking and second lowest value (Ranks 1 and 5) yields a similar result. All other differences fail to reach statistical significance although they are predominantly in the expected direction.

The great majority of subjects, then, conform to a general pattern. *The higher the value represented by a word, the more rapidly it is likely to be recognized.*

---

2 Since according to our hypothesis a high-value word should be recognized more quickly than a low-value one, time values on the ordinate of the time-of-recognition profile are plotted in descending rather than in ascending order. This arrangement makes value profiles and time-of-recognition profiles directly comparable.

3 Our findings are congruent with the results of earlier research carried out by A. G. Woolbert as reported by Cantril and Allport (6). Woolbert found that subjects perceived preferentially those items in a dummy newspaper which were most closely related to their dominant values as measured by the Allport-Vernon Study of Values.

TABLE 2

Chi-Square Test of Significance of Association between Value Preference and Time of Recognition

Theoretical frequencies are in italics.

	VALUE SCORES		
	Above Mean	Below Mean	
TIME OF RECOGNITION — Above Mean	156 *181.40*	216 *190.55*	372
Below Mean	283 *257.56*	245 *270.45*	528
	439	461	

$$\chi^2 = 11.87 \qquad P = <.01$$

ANALYSIS OF ATTEMPTED SOLUTIONS

Statistical analysis shows that value acts as a *sensitizer*, lowers the perceptual threshold. But value orientation does more than that. It is an active, selective disposition which in many subtle ways affects the hypotheses and attempts at solution which precede the actual recognition of a stimulus word. Much can be

TABLE 3

Mean Times of Recognition as a Function of Individual Value Ranks Represented by the Stimulus Words

VALUE RANK	MEAN TIME OF RECOGNITION IN SECONDS
1	.075
2	.082
3	.082
4	.089
5	.098
6	.097

learned about the role of value as an organizing factor in perception from an analysis of pre-solution behavior.

Each subject's perceptual behavior forms an individualized pattern and our preceding analysis of group data inevitably sacrifices a great deal of highly suggestive information about individual "styles" of perceiving. As a first approximation to a more intensive investigation of perceptual behavior, we have examined carefully and sought to classify individual pre-solution responses. Our effort has been to find categories of classification which might throw into relief the directive influence of value orientation on perception.

The following categories for the analysis of pre-solution responses or hypotheses have emerged:

Covaluant responses. This category comprises responses which can be unambiguously classified as representing the same value area as the stimulus word. The subject who saw

FIG. 1. Value profiles and time-of-recognition profiles of the individual subjects. The values tested by the Allport-Vernon Study are indicated along the abscissa. Value scores are plotted against the left-hand ordinate. Average recognition times for the words representing these values are plotted against the right-hand ordinate. Solid lines represent value scores, dotted lines represent times of recognition.

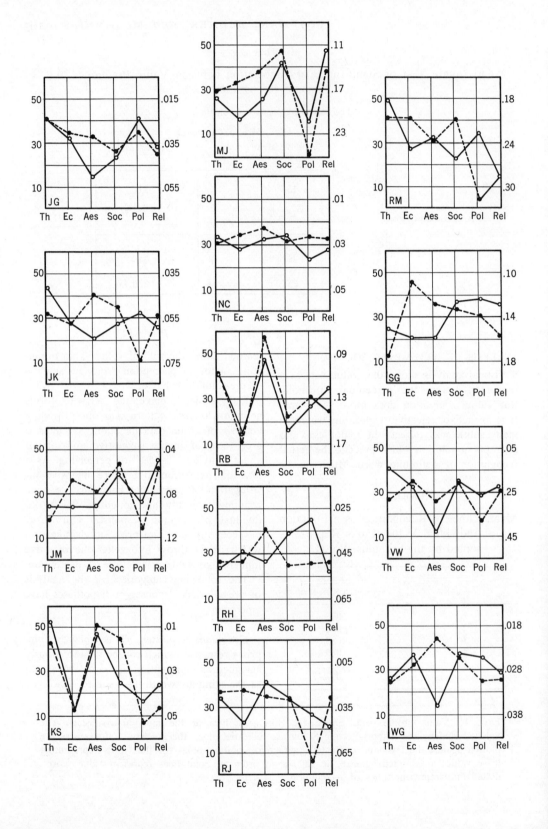

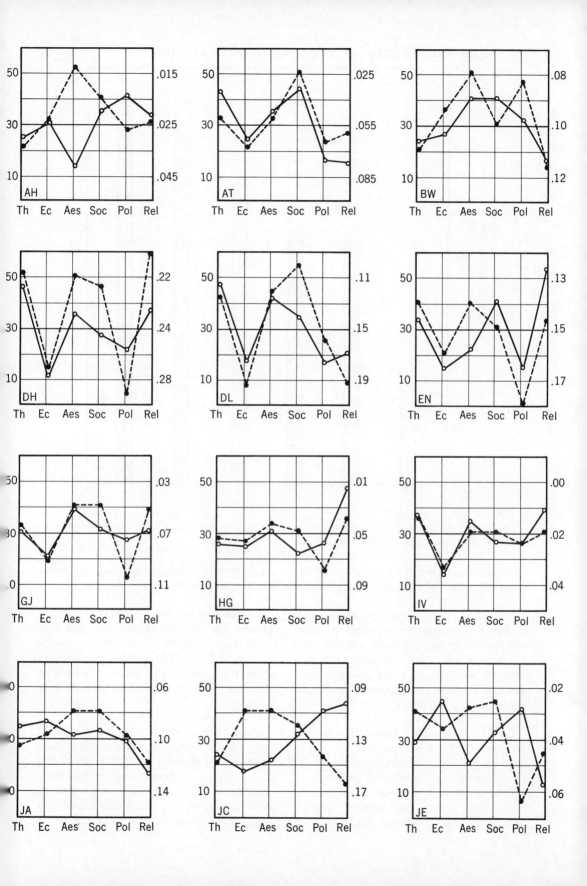

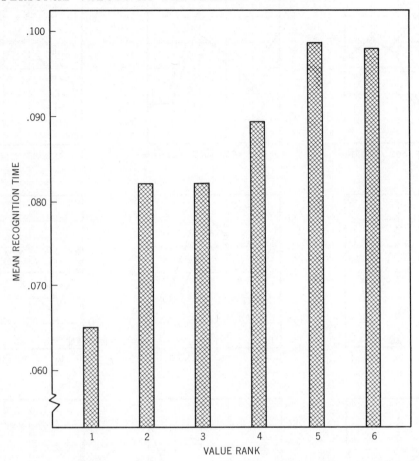

FIG. 2. Average times of recognition for the words representing the six values of the Allport-Vernon Study arranged in rank order.

the word *Easter* when the stimulus word was *sacred* illustrates the covaluant category.

Contravaluant responses. In some cases, the words reported in the pre-solution period were opposite in meaning to the stimulus word or served to derogate it. An instance is provided by a subject who saw *scornful* upon presentation of the stimulus word *helpful.* Or *revenge* instead of *blessed.*

Structural responses. Under this heading fall the very frequent incorrect hypotheses based on the structural characteristics of the stimulus word. An illustrative sequence of hypotheses given by one subject in response to the word *loving* was: *movies, mowing, moving, lowing,* and finally *loving.* A fre-

quent stimulus-bound, structural hypothesis was the response *turkey* for *theory.*

Nonsense responses. Two types of responses are included here: (*a*) nonsense words, such as *linone* for *income,* or *weelby* for *wealthy;* and (*b*) partial responses in which the subject's hypothesis consisted of an enumeration of parts of a word or individual letters.

Unrelated responses. This is our residual category. All responses which could not be related to the stimulus word in terms of any of the above categories were provisionally classified as unrelated. Responses such as *upper* and *carol* to a word like *useful* may serve as an illustration. We do not for a

TABLE 4

Significance of Differences between Mean Recognition Times for All Combinations of Value Ranks

Entries in the table represent values of *t*, and *P* (in italics)

	1	2	3	4	5	6
1						
2	.83 *.40*					
3	.80 *>.40*	.07 *>.90*				
4	1.64 *.10*	.76 *>.40*	.87 *.40*			
5	2.32 *.02*	1.52 *>.10*	1.62 *.10*	.84 *.40*		
6	2.42 *<.02*	1.54 *>.10*	1.67 *.10*	.80 *>.40*	.09 *>.90*	

moment believe that they are haphazard responses. The fact that this category turned out to be the most numerous is a commentary on the inadequacy of existing analytic categories in the study of pre-solution behavior in perception.

TABLE 5 represents the mean frequency with which each of these kinds of pre-solution hypotheses occurred per stimulus word in the subjects' high-value (Ranks 1, 2, and 3) and low-value (Ranks 4, 5, and 6) areas. TABLE 5 also shows the significance of the differences in the mean frequency of the various response categories when high- and low-value areas are compared.

We are ready to grant at the outset that the categories of classification used in the analysis of pre-solution hypotheses are ten-

tative. Their reliability has not as yet been demonstrated. The categories, moreover, are not always mutually exclusive. Without claiming any high degree of precision in our measurements, we nonetheless present the results of our classification as the simplest and most convenient description of general trends.

That several of our categories did discriminate between pre-solution responses to high- and low-value words may be taken as a presumptive demonstration of their validity. Covaluant hypotheses occur with significantly higher frequency in response to high-value words than they do in response to low-value words. A complementary finding is that both contravaluant and nonsense hypotheses appear more prominently among responses to low-value words. There is a similar tend-

TABLE 5

Mean Frequency per Word of Different Pre-solution Hypotheses for High-Value and Low-Value Words

TYPE OF HYPOTHESIS	ALL WORDS	HIGH-VALUE WORDS	LOW-VALUE WORDS	SIGNIFICANCE OF DIFFERENCES *
Covaluant	.13	.16	.10	2.04 (<.05)
Contravaluant	.03	.02	.05	2.0 (<.05)
Structural	.44	.49	.40	1.35 (>.10)
Nonsense	.13	.09	.16	2.05 (<.05)
Unrelated	.56	.56	.57	.10 (.92)

* Entries represent values of t, entries in parentheses are values of P.

ency for structural hypotheses to be associated more frequently with high-value words, though the difference falls short of statistical significance. Our residual category, unrelated hypotheses, favors neither high- nor low-value stimulus words, nor is there any particular reason why it should.

The Role of Value Orientation in Perceptual Selection

SELECTION is one of the three basic adaptive processes that operate in perception. In-

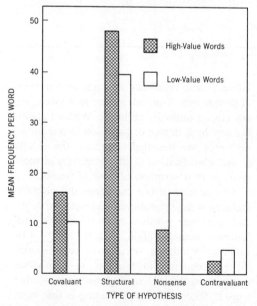

FIG. 3. Mean frequency with which various types of pre-recognition hypotheses were given in response to high-value and low-value words.

extricably linked with selection are accentuation and fixation. Once selected, a percept may be accentuated, i.e., certain of its features may be emphasized (3, 4, 5). Fixation denotes the persistence and preferential retention of certain selected percepts. Any perceptual behavior exhibits the three processes. The experiments reported here focus upon one aspect of this tripartite process which as a whole constitutes perception: the mechanisms through which value orientation becomes a determinant of selection.

Our results lead us to propose three complementary selective mechanisms. Value orientation acts as a sensitizer, lowering thresholds for acceptable stimulus objects. Let us call this mechanism *selective sensitization*. Value orientation may, on the other hand, raise thresholds for unacceptable stimulus objects. We shall refer to this mechanism as *perceptual defense*. Finally, the perceiver, whatever the nature of the stimulus, favors the pre-solution hypotheses which reflect his value orientation. He will, therefore, perceive more readily stimulus objects which lie within the same value area as his preferred pre-solution hypotheses. This third mechanism we shall term *value resonance*.

SELECTIVE SENSITIZATION

The primary evidence supporting this concept is provided, as we have indicated, by the significantly lower thresholds of recognition for high-value words. Selective sensitization may well be a specific case of a more general phenomenon. Lashley has proposed, for example, that one of the mechanisms through which "instinctive" or "drive" behavior operates is perceptual sensitization (9). The organism's threshold is lowered for objects which may serve to reduce drive. We should like to emphasize here that such a process of perceptual sensitization is not limited to the types of behavior commonly regarded as instinctive. Value orientation too, the result of a long process of socialization, may serve as a sensitizer in much the same way.

That value orientation significantly affects the threshold time for the recognition of words leads to a reconsideration of the parameters which must be taken into account in the measurement of any threshold. It is not always sufficient to state the stimulus conditions and instructions to the subject under which threshold measurements are made. The words representing the six value areas were all equated as far as possible in terms of such physical properties as length, size, degree of illumination, and all responses were given under the same general instruction. Yet widely different thresholds are obtained when the subjects' "set" or orientation toward the stimulus materials is taken into account. Had we failed to consider the subjects' *predisposition* to respond to some values more readily than to others, we should probably have ascribed these individual differences merely to "chance fluctuations in the measurement of the span of attention"! If the concepts of threshold and sensitivity are to be extended to types of perceptual phenomena more complex than sheer sensory acuity, the crucial role played by such attitudinal factors as value and need must be recognized.[4]

PERCEPTUAL DEFENSE

Value orientation not only contributes to the selection and accentuation of certain percepts in preference to others, it also erects barriers against percepts and hypotheses incongruent with or threatening to the individual's values. We suggest that a defense mechanism similar to repression operates in perceptual behavior.

4 As our experiments indicate, the utility of the *threshold* concept far transcends the measurement of sensory acuity where, it is true, such factors as value orientation are expressly minimized by the investigator.

The high thresholds for low-value words may result in part from such perceptual barriers. Not only do low-value words fail to benefit from selective sensitization, their recognition is also blocked by perceptual defense mechanisms. The clearest evidence for the operation of such perceptual defenses comes from the analysis of pre-solution responses.

Pre-solution responses to low-value words appear to take the form of avoidance of meaning. As indicated in TABLE 5, subjects have a pronounced tendency to see nonsense words when low-value stimulus words are presented for recognition. Such nonsense hypotheses take either the form of meaningless words or incomplete segments of words. Avoidance of meaning manifests itself even more accurately in the greater incidence of contravaluant hypotheses preceding the recognition of low-value words. Consider some examples. A subject, with little interest in religious values, when confronted with the word *sacred* gives the following sequence of hypotheses: *sucked, sacked, shocked, sacred.* Another, lacking in aesthetic values, sees *hypocrisy* for *elegant.*

Still another manifestation of perceptual defense is a frequent failure to use such available cues as word structure in forming hypotheses. Fewer pre-solution responses based on letter structure were given to low-value words than to high-value. Reluctance to use structural hypotheses fits well into perceptual defense behavior. Formation of an hypothesis based on structure too easily leads to recognition of the word being avoided. One may inquire at this point, "How does the subject 'know' that a word should be avoided? In order to 'repress' he must first recognize it for what it is." We have no answer to propose. What mediates the phenomena of hysterical or hypnotically induced blindness (8, 10)? Of only one thing we can be fairly sure: reactions do occur without conscious awareness of what one is reacting to. Psychological defense in perception is but one instance of such "unconscious" reaction.

VALUE RESONANCE

The nature of pre-solution hypotheses, no less than recognition itself, reflects value orientation. "Guesses" are not haphazard. As frequently as possible and as long as possible perceptual guesses are made in congruence with prevailing value orientation. This congruence between "guesses" and dominant values accounts, we believe, for the significantly greater number of covaluant responses to high-value words.

When stimulus words reflecting the same values as the subject's preferred hypotheses are presented to him, they are recognized more rapidly since they conform to, or are resonant with, his general set to respond in terms of his major values. That a generalized set lowers the recognition threshold for specific stimuli within its compass, has, of course, been known since the early work of the Würzburg School (7, 11). Thus, covaluant responses and sensitization work, as it were, hand in glove. Covaluant responses, reflecting the person's major values, help to prepare him for recognition of stimuli symbolizing these same major values. Consider, for example, the responses of a religious subject to a religious stimulus word, *reverence*, at the low exposure time of .01 second; *divinity, sentiment, reverence*. The first two responses, structurally unrelated to the stimulus, are clearly covaluent responses. That the subject recognized the correct word on the third exposure at .01 second illustrates the sensitizing action of a generalized set.

If the subject's typically preferred hypotheses reflect a value different from that symbolized by the stimulus word before him, his generalized set may serve to slow down recognition. His hypotheses, in such cases, may appear to the investigator as candidates for our "unrelated" category. An instance is provided by a subject of strongly theoretical bent who also scores high in aesthetic and social values but who is low in economic interest. Confronted with the word *income*, he gave these responses prior to recognition at .11 second: *learning, tomorrow, learning, knowledge, literature, learning, loving, income.* The exposure of .11 second required for recognition of this low-value word compares poorly indeed with his overall mean recognition time of .03 second.

Our aim in these pages has been to point to the relation of value orientation and perceptual selectivity. The experimental evidence leads us to the formulation of three mechanisms to account for the interrelationship of these phenomena in perceptual behavior. Value orientation makes for *perceptual sensitization* to valued stimuli, leads to *perceptual defense* against inimical stimuli, and gives rise to a process of *value resonance* which keeps the person responding in terms of objects valuable to him even when such objects are absent from his immediate environment. These processes of selectivity must be considered in any perceptual theory which lays claim to comprehensiveness.

REFERENCES

1. ALLPORT, G. W., & VERNON, P. E. *A study of values.* Boston: Houghton Mifflin, 1931.
2. BORING, E. G. The perception of objects. *Amer. J. Physics,* 1946, 14, 99–107.
3. BRUNER, J. S., & GOODMAN, C. C. Need and value as organizing factors in perception. *J. abnorm. and soc. Psychol.,* 1947, 42, 33–44.
4. BRUNER, J. S., & POSTMAN, L. Symbolic value as an organizing factor in perception. *J. soc. Psychol.* (in press).
5. BRUNER, J. S., & POSTMAN, L. Tension and tension-release as organizing factors in perception. *J. Personality,* 1947, 15, 300–308.
6. CANTRIL, H., & ALLPORT, G. W. Recent applications of the Study of Values. *J. abnorm and soc. Psychol.,* 1933, 28, 259–273.
7. GIBSON, J. J. A critical review of the concept of set in contemporary experimental psychology. *Psychol. Bull.,* 1941, 38, 781–817.
8. JANET, P. *The mental state of hystericals.* New York: Putnam, 1901.
9. LASHLEY, K. S. Experimental analysis of instinctive behavior. *Psychol. Rev.,* 1938, 45, 445–471.

10. PATTIE, F. A., JR. A report of attempts to produce uniocular blindness by hypnotic suggestion. *Brit. J. med. Psychol.,* 1935, 15, 230–241.

11. REES, H. J., & ISRAEL, H. E. An investigation of the establishment and operation of mental sets. *Psychol. Monogr.,* 1935, 46, No. 210, 1–26.

12. SPRANGER, E. *Types of men.* (Trans. from 5th German ed.) New York: Steckert, 1928.

13. Titchener, E. B. *A textbook of psychology.* New York: Macmillan, 1910.

14. VERNON, P. E., & ALLPORT, G. W. A test for personal values. *J. abnorm. and soc. Psychol.,* 1931, 26, 231–248.

RICHARD S. LAZARUS *and* ROBERT A. MCCLEARY

20. *Autonomic Discrimination without Awareness: A Study of Subception*

Introduction

THIS paper is a report of an experiment which extends and supports findings which we have previously described in an interim report (13). The results indicate that at tachistoscopic exposure speeds too rapid for correct recognition, subjects are able to give discriminatory responses as measured by their galvanic skin response (GSR). This perceptual process was called by the authors *subception*. The data also suggest that it is important to control for the verbal response preferences of the subjects when evaluating their perceptual accuracy.

A number of considerations prompted the coining of the new term, subception. Despite the inadvisability of recklessly increasing the "deadwood" in the psychological vocabulary, we know of no other term that precisely defines a *process by which some kind of discrimination is made when the subject is unable to make a correct conscious discrimination*. We rejected "subconscious perception" (the only standard terminology that occurred to us) for several reasons. In the first place, the word "subconscious" or "un-

conscious" is replete with controversial implications, none of which are pertinent to the present case. We particularly wished to avoid the psychoanalytic notions concerning the subconscious, and the alternate notion that the subconscious is one level of awareness— on the inattentive fringe of consciousness, so to speak. Secondly, although there is less quarrel with the word perception, it too often implies awareness on the part of the perceiving organism. In fact, three of the four definitions of perception in Warren's dictionary use the term "awareness." Even if one believes that awareness is not necessary for perception and thus regards subception as simply a special case of perception, we feel that it is a sufficiently unique case to require a unique term. There is, of course, some intrinsic value in using a single word rather than a more cumbersome phrase to identify this perceptual process.

The original impetus for this study came from the recent interest in the role of needs in perceptual behavior. It has been reported frequently that stimuli of different need significance may have different recognition thresholds (1, 6, 10, 12, 14, 19, 20, 24).

Reprinted by permission of the American Psychological Association and the authors from the *Psychological Review*, 1951, vol. 58, pp. 113–22.

This study precipitated a series of subsequent efforts to challenge the interpretation offered here of a "subception" process ". . . by which some kind of discrimination is made when the *S* is unable to make a conscious discrimination." Focusing on the adequacy of the measure of conscious discrimination, critics succeeded in showing that recognition scores equal to those given by the galvanic skin response could be obtained if *S*s were forced to guess or choose among stimuli, thus raising the question of which process the term "subception" should denote. Lazarus (1956) suggests that *S*s do not usually try to go beyond the normal restrictions of language (as they do in guessing) and that it is not necessary to assert that the GSR is more sensitive than verbal processes. Students interested in the discussion should see Charles W. Eriksen, "Subception: Fact or Artifact?" *Psychological Review*, 1956, vol. 63, pp. 74–80; and Don E. Dulany and Charles W. Eriksen, "Accuracy of Brightness Discrimination as Measured by Concurrent Verbal Responses and GSRs," *Journal of Abnormal and Social Psychology*, 1959, vol. 59, pp. 418–23.

Although theorizing in this field has lacked precision and completeness, it is possible to find two general frames of reference which have been used to interpret the "need in perception" observations. The first might be identified as the "response availability" approach. The second could be termed the "dynamic" point of view. Both views are by no means incompatible.

Writers who have preferred to use the concept of response availability have pointed out that, for different individuals, some words have greater frequency of occurrence than others (2, 7). Differences in this response availability could act in two ways to produce differential recognition thresholds, depending in part upon the degree of ambiguity of the stimulus material. On the one hand, the subject is more likely to make use of minimal cues from words which are more readily at his disposal than from those which are not. This aspect of the concept appears to be very much like the old notion of attention or set. On the other hand, if the cues are so minimal that the subject appears to be guessing, the presence of certain words in his response repertoire will increase the statistical probability of these words being correctly identified.

Other workers, notably the clinically oriented writers, have implied the unconscious participation of the individual in actively selecting and rejecting the presented material in accordance with his needs (6, 8, 10, 14, 15). For example, McGinnies (14), summarizing some of the work in this area, states, "it seems well established, then, that the perceptual 'filtering' of visual stimuli serves, in many instances, to protect the observer as long as possible from an awareness of objects which have unpleasant emotional significance for him." In elaborating this type of approach, Eriksen (6) and Lazarus *et al.* (10) have talked about such variables as type of ego defense and the acceptability of the need—factors which, they believe, can influence the degree to which the subject is able to verbalize and recognize the stimulus material.

Whatever the merits of these two points of view may be, the latter approach, which we have loosely called "dynamic," places its proponents in the difficult position of having to postulate some process of discrimination occurring prior to the ability of the subject to report correct recognition. More specifically, if the observation that a subject can recognize the word "sacred" at faster exposure speeds than the word "income," is attributed to their differential need value, it would be necessary to assume that the subject is somehow identifying the significance of the two words before he is able to report recognition of them. The purpose of the present experiment was to attempt to test this assumption. We have asked the question, "Can subjects make discriminatory responses even when they are not able to report the stimulus correctly?"

There have been other attempts to get at the problem of "discrimination without awareness." Miller (16), in a paper reporting an experiment of his own, reviewed investigations of this problem over a period extending from 1863 to 1938. Miller's experiment, and all the studies he mentioned, differ from the present research in some important ways. For example, Miller showed that accuracy of discrimination was better than chance below the subjects' "limen of awareness." His criterion of discrimination was the correctness of the subject's verbal statement. In the present experiment we are asking whether a discrimination can be made when recognition, as defined by a correct verbal report, is impossible. The problems are therefore not the same. A second major difference in the Miller experiment lies in the fact that whether or not a subject was actually performing below his "threshold" was entirely a subjective and statistical matter. The subjects' limens were obtained by the method of limits. In the present experiment, as you will see, a subject is judged to be operating below his "threshold" when his verbal report is wrong. The danger in Miller's approach is emphasized by the earlier findings of Perky (18), who showed that subjects could not tell the difference between real images which were slightly supraliminal and impressions which were imaginary.

There are several other experiments which

are relevant here because of their use of conditioning procedures or the galvanic skin response. A novel approach has been used by Redlich (21) and Levine (11). By the use of hypnotically induced anesthesia, or patients with hysterical anesthesias, these investigators showed that subjects gave psychogalvanic responses to stimuli applied to an anesthetic area. Scott (22) conditioned a finger-withdrawal response during a trance state and tested for the persistence of the conditioned response during the post-trance amnestic period. Presenting mean scores for the eight subjects, he concluded that there was some residual conditioning in the post-trance period, even though the subjects remembered nothing of the conditioning trials and consequently were not "aware" of the significance of the conditioned stimulus.

A different line of attack has been the attempt to condition responses to stimuli which, by various criteria, are below the subject's psychophysical threshold. Silverman and Baker (23) used subliminal alternating current as the conditioned stimulus and paired it with several kinds of emitted responses in human subjects. Although the authors saw some evidence of eye-wink conditioning in three out of ten subjects, the results do not warrant positive conclusions on a statistical basis. Newhall and Sears (17) conditioned finger-withdrawal to a supraliminal light stimulus and tested for conditioned responses at and below the psychophysically determined limen. They reported obtaining conditioned responses with stimuli which were below the limen, and "in several instances visual stimuli that were individually reported unperceived, had evoked the conditioned response." This latter observation was incidental to the main interest of the experiment, and Newhall and Sears stated that they believed the problem of whether a conditioned response could occur without consciousness of the stimulus was still open to question.

In this vein it might be possible to have the conditioned stimulus well above the subject's sensory threshold but, by proper training procedures, have the subject unaware of the fact that the stimulus was a conditioned one. This was the idea behind the work of Diven (5). He used the GSR for his response and masked the conditioned nature of the stimulus by applying the unconditioned stimulus after a 12-second delay. During the delay the subjects free associated to the conditioned stimulus. Most of the subjects reported no awareness of the relationship between the conditioned and unconditioned stimulus, and yet showed conditioned GSR's. Since the confounding effect of stimulus generalization in this experiment cannot be evaluated, Diven's results, showing conditioning without awareness, remain inclusive.

A more recent study which attempted to demonstrate discrimination prior to correct recognition was reported by McGinnies (14). Using tachistoscopic presentation and employing a method which was in some respects similar to the present study, he found that subjects gave GSR's which were greater for emotional words than for neutral words, before the words had been consciously recognized. A crucial shortcoming of the experimental design was that the subjects could have been motivated to withhold their report of the socially taboo words (such as *whore, bitch, raped,* etc.) even after some suspicion of their meaning was present. In other words, the GSR during the pre-recognition trials could very well have been an emotional response to recognized words which were not yet reported.

This matter of withholding of reports was treated at some length by Howes and Solomon (7), who also attempted an interpretation of McGinnies' findings based on their notions of word-frequency as a determiner of perceptual accuracy. We have briefly discussed this kind of theoretical orientation under the heading of "response availability." McGinnies (15), in a reply to the note of Howes and Solomon, handled the specific word-frequency criticisms adequately but was unable to explain away the possibility that the subjects were motivated to withhold their report of the taboo words. McGinnies wrote, "It must be admitted that this possibility does, in fact, constitute one of the knottier problems in this kind of research." The experimental design in our experiment was planned to unravel this knot, because the present authors are in agreement with Howes and Solomon that the danger of withholding responses is indeed crucial to McGinnies' conclusion.

Considering the approaches used and the data reported, the authors believe that previous research has not satisfactorily demonstrated that a process of discrimination can operate prior to conscious recognition and in the absence of the possibility of the correct verbal report.

Procedure

IN the present experiment, we recorded the subject's GSR by means of an AC bridge apparatus.[1] Dry silver recording electrodes, ¼" square, were attached to the right forefinger and right middle finger tip of the subject. GSR's were read directly as peak deflections on a Ballantine Electronic Voltmeter. These readings were converted into actual impedance changes by substituting a variable resistance box in the circuit in place of the subject, and matching the Voltmeter readings obtained when the subject was in the circuit, with the phase angle of the bridge set at zero. We could read pure impedance change because the AC bridge was designed so that the subject's apparent capacitance change could be balanced out during the experiment by operating a dial that kept a Lissajous figure closed when the phase angle of the subject and the bridge were exactly equated. This impedance change (ohms) was then transformed into admittance change (mhos) in keeping with physiological (4) and statistical (9) suggestions as to the most meaningful unit of measure for the GSR.

We presented the stimulus words on a beaded screen seven feet from the subject by means of a projection tachistoscope. This arrangement allowed for a variation of exposure speeds from 1/150 second to one second. The illumination and range of exposure speeds varied from subject to subject depending upon his perceptual performance and, once established, were held constant for each subject. Five different exposure speeds were se-

1 The authors are indebted to Thomas G. Arnold, at present in the Department of Medicine, The Johns Hopkins Hospital, for the design and development of the GSR apparatus used in this research.

lected for each subject such that the slowest speed resulted in near 100 per cent accuracy of recognition of the syllables. In all cases, the fastest exposure speed resulted in accuracy of recognition which did not differ significantly from chance.

Five-letter nonsense syllables were used as the stimuli to minimize as far as possible differences in familiarity. Moreover, the use of nonsense syllables precluded the possibility that subjects would have any motivation to withhold their report. This was, you will recall, a crucial inadequacy in the experiment by McGinnies (14). Ten syllables were presented: YILIM, ZIFIL, GAHIW, GEXAX, JEJIC, JIVID, YUVUF, ZEWUH, VAVUK, VECYD.

The procedure for each subject can be divided into three parts.

EQUATION PERIOD

After practice at recognition we presented each subject with the ten nonsense syllables tachistoscopically. The syllables were randomized for both order of presentation and exposure speed. Even at speeds where accurate recognition was impossible, each subject was required to make a choice verbally from the ten syllables which he knew made up the stimulus material being presented to him. To aid in this choice each subject used, in succession, ten different lists of the syllables. Each list was in a different order to preclude list-order preference on the part of the subject. After 100 presentations (each of the ten syllables having been flashed twice at each of the five exposure speeds), we divided the ten syllables into two groups of five each, equated for both the number of times the subject used the syllables in the entire 100 responses and the number of times they were correctly recognized. In all cases it was possible to make this two-group division with a high degree of equality. Also, in this phase of the experiment, we noted the exposure speed at which near 100 per cent accuracy of recognition occurred, and used it as the slowest speed in the final test period.

CONDITIONING PERIOD

In this part of the experiment we employed a one-second exposure speed for all syllable presentations. The GSR was conditioned to the five experimental syllables using electric shock as the unconditioned stimulus. Partial reinforcement was employed, with one-third of all presentations of the five experimental syllables being shocked in random order. During this conditioning period each of the ten syllables was presented an equal number of times to prevent unequal familiarity. This procedure was continued until consistent conditioned responses to the five experimental syllables were established. We instructed subjects not to report during the conditioning trials but merely to identify to themselves the syllables presented to them. This was done to avoid associating the shock with the subject's verbal report and thus influencing his response preference during the final test period. We instructed the subjects at the beginning of the conditioning trials that when they were shocked it would be two or three seconds following presentation of the experimental syllables. This allowed us to read the GSR before the shock was applied. They were further instructed that they would never be shocked after any presentation of the five control syllables.

FINAL TEST PERIOD

The procedure of random presentation of the syllables used during the Equation Period was repeated here. The exposure speeds were set so that the subject had near 100 per cent recognition at the slowest of the five exposure speeds. This time, however, GSR's were recorded during the time between the tachistoscopic flash and the subject's verbal report. We told the subject to delay his report until signalled, which was about five seconds after the tachistoscopic flash. This delay was used to prevent the verbal report from contaminating the GSR, and the signal was not given until the GSR was recorded for each syllable presentation.

During this final period no shock was paired with any of the syllables. Because of the rapid exposure speeds used in this period, we had feared that reinforcement at this point would result in extinction of the clear-cut GSR discrimination acquired during the Conditioning Period. This inability to use rein-

forcement in the final phase, however, created no special difficulties. As a result of the instructions and the prior experience with partial reinforcement, the subject's expectancy of being shocked—and consequently the "conditioned GSR"—was maintained throughout the syllable presentations without further use of shock. We had found with preliminary subjects that in the absence of this continuing expectancy of shock, the GSR promptly disappeared. This is in keeping with the findings of Cook and Harris (3).

The following raw data were recorded during the Final Test Period:

1. The syllable flashed.
2. The exposure speed of the syllable.
3. The subject's verbal choice from the ten possible syllables (whether or not he was correct and whether he reported a "shock" or whether he reported a "non-shock" syllable).
4. The subject's GSR for each syllable presentation.

Results

THE results of this experiment can be discussed under three main headings: (1) The galvanic skin responses during the Final Test Period; (2) the relations between response frequency and the accuracy of report for various syllables; and (3) the effect of electric shock on the perceptual thresholds.

GSR DATA

By far the most striking finding to be reported here concerns the autonomic activity of the subjects in the Final Test Period. These GSR data are shown in the bar graphs in the figure. The average GSR's are put in various columns on the basis of certain criteria. The first main division is dependent upon whether or not the syllable flashed had been associated with shock during the Conditioning Period; this is the Stimulus Category ("shock" vs. "non-shock"). The other breakdown is based on the nature of the subject's verbal report; this is the Response Category. There are three kinds of responses in each of the two stimulus categories: "WS" means that the report was wrong and a "shock" syllable was given by the subject; "WN" indicates that the report was wrong and a "non-shock" syllable was given; "RS" and "RN" signify responses of the appropriate stimulus category which were right. "Response N" refers to the number of separate GSR's contributing to the mean for each column.

The two "MW" (mean wrong) bars are the important GSR measures to note. These represent the average GSR of the "WS" and "WN" categories for each of the two types of stimuli. Therefore these "MW" columns give the average GSR (equated for both "shock" and "non-shock" responses) when the subject was not able to perceive (*i.e.,* report) the flashed syllable. It was necessary to average the GSR's associated with wrong responses because the verbal report itself had an effect on the GSR. You will notice that this "response effect" can be seen in the bar graphs as larger GSR's when the subject used a "shock" syllable as his report. By averaging "WS" and "WN" categories, this "response effect" was effectively controlled.

In every subject the "MW" column is larger when the stimulus presented was a "shock" syllable, and you will recall that in this "MW" category the subject was not able to perceive the syllable correctly. This is the *subception effect.* It is summarized [in FIG. 1] in the bar graph entitled "Mean of All Subjects." Student's "t" for this difference is 7.45, which is significant far below the one per cent level of confidence for eight degrees of freedom. The subception effect was found at all five tachistoscopic exposure speeds when wrong responses were made. It was smallest at the speeds which resulted in either very low or very high accuracy. The systematic increase in the effect as a function of decreasing exposure speed which was suggested in the interim report was not substantiated with further data. *There seems to be little doubt that subjects can make autonomic discriminations when they are unable to report conscious recognition.*

RESPONSE FREQUENCY

Since this experiment provided a limited multiple-choice response situation for the sub-jects, it was possible to obtain some information about the importance of response frequency in relation to perceptual accuracy. A product moment correlation was obtained between the number of times each syllable was used and the number of times it was correctly reported. This was done separately for both the Equation Period and Final Test Period data. Statistical independence of the arrays was achieved by subtracting the number of times each syllable was right from the number of times it was given as a response. These correlations were +.61 and +.67 respectively. With ten syllables, neither of the relationships is significant. They do suggest, however, that in this kind of situation perceptual accuracy may bear some close relation to frequency of usage. This finding gives some added substance to the arguments to consider statistical response preference as an important variable in some perceptual recognition experiments. These data are relevant to the concept of "response availability" discussed earlier in this paper.

PERCEPTUAL ACCURACY

There is one final observation to be made from our results. Although the major purpose of this experiment was not to study the effect of a need variable on perceptual accuracy, it was possible to analyze our data for such an effect. Since the experimental and control lists of syllables were equated for accuracy and frequency of use during the Equation Period and one of the lists was associated with electric shock, it was possible to see whether the shock had any effect on final perceptual performance. The data were analyzed in two ways to get at this problem. The accuracy for shock and non-shock syllables was compared both with and without a statistical correction [2] for response preference.

2 We are indebted to Dr. Alphonse Chapanis for assisting us in formulating this statement of our correction procedure:

$$A_C = R_A - R_{A_G}, \qquad (1)$$

where

A_C = corrected accuracy score
R_A = number of correct responses to syllable A
R_{A_G} = number of correct responses to syllable A in which the subject was guessing

In both cases no significant differences were found between "shock" and "non-shock" syllables. However, it might be noted that when no correction for response frequency was made, seven out of nine subjects showed a greater accuracy for the "shock" syllables and a higher frequency of usage for the "non-shock" group. On the other hand, when the correction was made, there was (for one subject) a reversal from higher accuracy for "shock" syllables to higher accuracy for the "non-shock" syllables. Correcting for this preference actually reversed the apparent accuracy picture for this subject. Although the other subjects did not show such a marked change when response frequency was taken into account there were in most cases some changes in the relative accuracy of the two lists of syllables. This result further supports the correlations found between response frequency and perceptual accuracy. We believe that this is an important methodological point.

$$R_{AG} = G_A p_A, \qquad (2)$$

where

G_A = number of responses to syllable A in which the subject was guessing

p_A = probability of the subject using syllable p when he is guessing

Equation (2), however, involves two unknowns, R_{AG} and G_A, and cannot be solved. But note that

$$W_A = G_A q_A, \qquad (3)$$

where

W_A = number of wrong responses to syllable A

q_A = $(1 - p_A)$ = probability of the subject not using syllable A when he is guessing, and here we have two known quantities, W_A and q_A. Thus

$$G_A = W_A/q_A. \qquad (4)$$

Substituting this value of G_A in (2) gives

$$R_{AG} = [W_A/q_A]p_A = W_A[p_A/q_A]. \qquad (5)$$

This value of R_{AG} may be substituted in (1) to give the final equation

$$A_C = R_A - W_A[p_A/q_A]. \qquad (6)$$

As you will probably notice, this is the precise form of the correction used in "true and false" and "multiple-choice" examinations. In these cases, however, a theoretical value of p is used. For example, in a series of "multiple-choice" questions having four items, $p_A = \frac{1}{4}$, and

$$A_C = R_A - W_A[\tfrac{1}{4}/\tfrac{3}{4}] = R_A - W_A/3.$$

In the present study, we used an empirical value of p_A such that

$$p_A = \frac{A_W}{W},$$

where

A_W = the total number of times that A was used as a wrong response

W = the total number of wrong responses

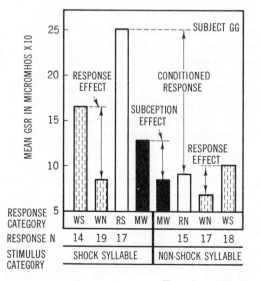

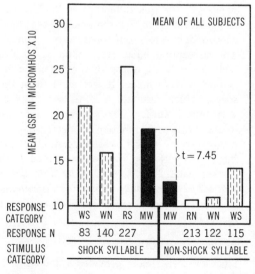

FIG. 1.   GSR data from final test period.

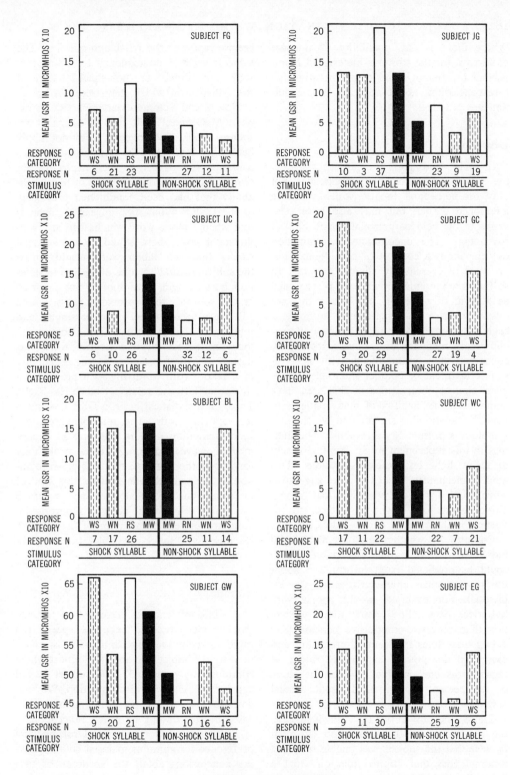

GSR data from final test period.

Where there is any possibility of unequal preference for the stimulus material, it is important to attempt some such correction before conclusions about accuracy of recognition are practical.

Discussion

THE major finding of the present research, the subception effect, has implications not only for perceptual theory, which we have mentioned earlier, but may also have relevance in the field of personality and clinical psychology. The unconscious determination of behavior is a concept of considerable importance in present-day clinical thinking. In so far as autonomic activity can be regarded as a form of behavior, we believe that we may have here an experimental instance of such an unconscious process. The field of psychosomatic medicine is, of course, specifically concerned with autonomic activity as a response to threat or conflict situations. Moreover, clinical observations in this area have emphasized the inability of many patients to identify the stimulus situation to which their symptom is presumably a response. The findings in this experiment might eventually help to throw light on these observations. This kind of mechanism is all the more suggestive when coupled with the possibility that "recognition thresholds" might be subject to influence by the "needs" of the individual.

One may ask whether there are meaningful individual differences in "subception" which could be predicted from information about the psychological characteristics of the individual. For example, would people with hysterical personalities show more subception than obsessive-compulsive personalities? Along these lines the kind of procedure employed in the present experiment might be regarded as one possible tool for the study of the perceptual side of different clinical conditions.

There is nothing in our data which suggests the mechanism of the subception effect. It is clear that the subject was unable to detect minimal cues that "tipped him off" that a "shock" syllable was being presented even though the cues were not sufficient to permit precise report of the syllable in question. The subjects showed no tendency to report correctly the "shock" or "non-shock" nature of the syllables on which they were wrong.

Howes and Solomon's attempt (7) to explain McGinnies' GSR data in terms of response probability concepts does not apply here. They say, "Only the most probable word could be reported after each exposure, but GSR's could occur to any word of high probability that had been conditioned previously to the GSR." What they appear to mean is that when a taboo word was flashed at a subthreshold level, there would be a finite possibility that this taboo word would "cross the subject's mind" as one of his pre-recognition guesses, and, even though not reported as the subject's most probable guess, would still have been present as a possibility and thus be able to produce a GSR. Conversely, they argue that when a neutral word was flashed at a subthreshold level, the probability of a taboo word occurring as a pre-recognition possibility was relatively much less likely. Thus, on a statistical basis, a GSR was much less apt to occur. The multiple-choice response situation used in this present experiment, however, encourages equal probability for any of the words to occur as pre-recognition guesses and thus invalidates this kind of interpretation. As a matter of fact, it turned out that when the subject was reporting incorrectly, there were many more "non-shock" responses to "shock" syllables than the reverse.

Summary

1. GSR evidence is presented to indicate that at tachistoscopic exposure speeds too rapid for conscious discrimination (as measured by the subject's inability to report which stimulus was presented), the subject is still capable of making a discrimination. We suggest that the level of perceptual activity indicated by this finding be called *subception*.

2. It is important to control for unequal preference for stimulus material before drawing conclusions about the accuracy of perceptual recognition.

3. Pairing some of the stimuli with electric

shock does not result in a change in the frequency with which they are accurately identified at various exposure speeds.

4. Some of the implications of this experiment for perceptual and clinical theory are discussed.

REFERENCES

1. BRUNER, J., & POSTMAN, L. Emotional selectivity in perception and reaction. *J. Personality*, 1947, 16, 69–77.

2. COFER, C. Personal communication.

3. COOK, S. W., & HARRIS, R. E. The verbal conditioning of the galvanic skin reflex. *J. exp. Psychol.*, 1937, 21, 202–210.

4. DARROW, C. W. The significance of the galvanic skin reflex in the light of its relation to quantitative measurements of perspiration. *Psychol. Bull.*, 1934, 31, 697–698.

5. DIVEN, K. Certain determinants in the conditioning of anxiety reactions. *J. Psychol.*, 1937, 3, 291–308.

6. ERIKSEN, C. W. Perceptual defense: The elevation of perceptual recognition thresholds as a function of unacceptable needs. Unpublished Ph.D. dissertation, Stanford University, 1950.

7. HOWES, D. H., & SOLOMON, R. L. A note on McGinnies' "Emotionality and perceptual defense." *Psychol. Rev.*, 1950, 57, 229–234.

8. KLEIN, G. S., & SCHLESINGER, H. Where is the perceiver in perceptual theory? *J. Personality*, 1949, 18, 32–47.

9. LACEY, O. L. *et al.* An analysis of the unit of measurement of the galvanic skin response. *J. exp. Psychol.*, 1949, 39, 122–127.

10. LAZARUS, R. S., SHAFFER, G. W., FONDA, C. P., & HEISTAD, G. T. Clinical dynamics and auditory perception. Paper given at APA meetings, September, 1950.

11. LEVINE, M. Psychogalvanic reflex to painful stimuli in hypnotic and hysterical anesthesia. *Johns Hopk. Hosp. Bull.*, 1930, 46, 331–339.

12. MCCLELLAND, D. C., & LIBERMAN, A. M. The effect of need for achievement on recognition of need-related words. *J. Personality*, 1949, 18, 236–251.

13. MCCLEARY, R. A., & LAZARUS, R. S. Autonomic discrimination without awareness: An interim report. *J. Personality*, 1949, 18, 171–179.

14. MCGINNIES, E. Emotionality and perceptual defense. *Psychol. Rev.*, 1949, 56, 244–251.

15. ———. Discussion of Howes and Solomon's note on "Emotionality and perceptual defense." *Psychol. Rev.*, 1950, 57, 235–240.

16. MILLER, J. G. Discrimination without awareness. *Amer. J. Psychol.*, 1939, 52, 562–578.

17. NEWHALL, L. M., & SEARS, R. R. Conditioned finger retraction to visual stimuli near the absolute threshold. *Comp. Psychol. Monogr.*, 1933, 9, No. 43.

18. PERKY, C. W. An experimental study of imagination. *Amer. J. Psychol.*, 1910, 21, 422–452.

19. POSTMAN, L., BRUNER, J., & MCGINNIES, E. Personal values as selective factors in perception. *J. abnorm. soc. Psychol.*, 1948, 43, 142–154.

20. ———, & SOLOMON, R. L. Perceptual sensitivity to completed and incompleted tasks. *J. Personality*, 1950, 18, 347–357.

21. REDLICH, F. C. Organic and hysterical anesthesia. *Amer. J. Psychol.*, 1945, 102, 318–324.

22. SCOTT, H. D. Hypnosis and the conditioned reflex. *J. gen. Psychol.*, 1930, 4, 113–130.

23. SILVERMAN, A., & BAKER, L. E. An attempt to condition various responses to subliminal electrical stimulation. *J. exp. Psychol.*, 1935, 18, 246–254.

24. VANDERPLAS, J. M., & BLAKE, R. R. Selective sensitization in auditory perception. *J. Personality*, 1949, 18, 252–266.

SECTION V

Learning

THE vast amount of research on learning engaged in by contemporary psychologists is based on many different approaches, methods, and theories. The major introductory texts cite an excellent range of literature on learning. In the limited amount of space available here, however, we could not represent all points of view. Instead we have selected a few theoretical articles that describe some of the important positions still held today. They will, we hope, give the student a sense of the diversity of the theories behind current research on learning as well as a specific knowledge of some of these theories.

The early treatment of Pavlov by Robert M. Yerkes and Sergius Morgulis, which anticipates Pavlov's tremendous influence on psychology, describes the technique and results of the experiments that have become the model of classical conditioning: Pavlov's experiments with the salivary reflex in dogs.

Clark Hull, in "Simple Trial-and-Error Learning," analyzes the type of learning in which each trial act is reinforced if successful but unreinforced if unsuccessful to illustrate the deductive explanation of learning he proposes. Edwin R. Guthrie, on the other hand, resists the formal analysis Hull proposes and makes an appealing case for simplification of theory. He suggests that the more important and established facts of learning (for instance, that an organism learns through practice and responds to patterns as such) may all be instances of simple conditioning. Pavlov, the Gestalt psychologists, and others have, he feels, neglected the proprioceptive sense organs in favor of the "highly speculative characteristics of the cerebral cortex."

"Cognitive Maps in Rats and Men" reflects both a reaction against Hullian formalism and a rejection of the stimulus-response theory of learning. Edward C. Tolman maintains that, in the course of learning, sets are built up in the nervous system of an organism which function like cognitive maps, and that these maps vary from narrow strips to broader, comprehensive fields. Human disorders such as regression and fixation may, Tolman suggests, be explained as a narrowing of these cognitive maps.

Finally, B. F. Skinner advocates working toward the elimination of theory—which he defines as any explanation of an observed fact that appeals to events taking place at other levels of observation, described in different terms, and measured, if at all, in different dimensions—through the examination of known functions and relationships between an organism and its environment.

ROBERT M. YERKES *and* SERGIUS MORGULIS

21. The Method of Pawlow in Animal Psychology

ABOUT eight years ago Professor J. P. Pawlow, Director of the physiological department of the Institute of Experimental Medicine in St. Petersburg, devised and introduced into his great research laboratory an ingenious and valuable new method of investigating the physiology of the nervous system in its relations to the so-called psychic reactions of organisms. This method —now widely known as the Pawlow salivary reflex method—has been extensively employed by Pawlow and his students in St. Petersburg. Recently it has been introduced into the Physiological Institute of Berlin by Nicolai, a former student of Pawlow. It consists in the quantitative study of those modifications of the salivary reflex which are conditioned by complex receptive and elaborative processes (psychic reactions) in the central nervous system.

Inasmuch as practically all of the results of the method have been published in Russia, it has seemed to us important that a general description of the technique of the method,

together with a statement of certain of the important results which it has yielded, should be published at this time in English. Our purposes in preparing this article were two: first, to present a body of facts which is of great importance to both physiologists and animal psychologists; and second, to familiarize American investigators with the salivary reflex method and hasten the time when it shall be as advantageously used in this country as it now is in Russia.

The materials for this discussion we have obtained chiefly from six papers.[1] Of these the first four are, in the main, general accounts of the method and its results from the strikingly different points of view and interests of Pawlow and Nicolai. The papers of Selionyi and Orbeli are admirable reports of facts. At the end of this article we present a complete bibliography of the subject to 1909. We are indebted to Professor Pawlow for a number of the titles included in this list and also for a thorough revision and correction of the bibliography.

---

1 (1) Pawlow, J. P., "Sur la sécrétion psychique des glandes salivaires (Phénomènes nerveux complexes dans le travail des glandes salivaires)." *Arch. intern. de physiol.*, T. 1, pp. 119–135, 1904.

(2) Pawlow, J. P., "The scientific investigation of the psychical faculties or processes in the higher animals" (The Huxley lecture, 1906). *Lancet*, 1906, pp. 911–915. The lecture is reported in part in *British Med. Jour.*, 1906, pp. 871–873, and in *Science*, N. S., Vol. 24, pp. 613–619, 1906. In justice to Professor Pawlow, it should be stated that *Lancet* alone gives the reader an adequate knowledge of the structure and materials of the address. It is deplorable that neither the *British Medical Journal* nor *Science* states that the lecture is published in condensed form.

(3) Nicolai, G. F., "Die physiologische Methodik zur Erforschung der Tierpsyche, ihre Möglichkeit und ihre Anwendung." *Jour. f. Psychol. und Neurol.*, Bd. 10, S. 1–27, 1907.

(4) Nicolai, G. F., "Das Lernen der Tiere (auf Grund von Versuchen mit Pawlowscher Speichelfistel)." *Centralblatt f. Physiol.*, Bd. 22, S. 362–364, 1908.

(5) Selionyi, G. P., "Contribution to the study of the reactions of the dog to auditory stimuli." Dissertation, St. Petersburg, 1907. Pp. 125 (in Russian).

(6) Orbeli, L. A., "Conditioned reflexes resulting from optical stimulation of the dog." Dissertation, St. Petersburg, 1908. Pp. 111 (in Russian).

Reprinted with abridgment by permission of the American Psychological Association from the *Psychological Bulletin*, 1909, vol. 6, pp. 257–62 and 269–73.

Our discussion naturally falls into four parts: (1) A general description of the method of its application, from the standpoints of Pawlow, Nicolai, and Selionyi; (2) an expository summary of the study of the auditory reactions of the dog as reported by Selionyi; (3) a similar summary of Orbeli's study of the visual reactions of the dog; and (4) a general summary of the results of the method. [Parts 2 and 3 are not reproduced here.] To give a complete account of the investigations of the St. Petersburg laboratory—for already more than forty papers have been published—would be possible only if each paper were dismissed with a sentence or two. We have preferred to consider two representative papers in some detail instead of mentioning several casually.

Description of
the Salivary Reflex Method

THE salivary reflex (secretion of saliva) occurs under two strikingly different conditions: (*a*) when the mouth is stimulated by certain chemical processes (the specific stimuli for secretion); and (*b*) when the animal is stimulated by sights, sounds, odors, temperatures, touches which have been present previously in connection with stimuli of the first class. The environment of the dog [2] may be said to consist of two sets of properties, the essential and non-essential. Essential, for a given reaction, are those stimulating properties of an object which regularly and definitely determine that reaction of the organism; non-essential, for the reaction in point, are those properties of an object which only in a highly variable and inconstant manner condition the reaction. The chemical property of food, whereby it acts upon the receptors of the mouth of the dog, is an "essential" property, for it invariably causes a salivary reflex. The appearance of the same food—its lightness, color, etc.—is a "non-essential," for it may or may not cause the reflex. Pawlow has termed

reflexes in response to "essential" properties "unconditioned," and those in response to "non-essential" properties "conditioned." [3]

It was Pawlow's idea that the perfectly constant and dependable "unconditioned" salivary reflex might be used to advantage as a basis for the investigation of those complex nervous processes one of whose expressions is a "conditioned" reflex of the same glands. Since many, if not all, changes in the nervous system gain expression in one way or another, through the salivary reflex, why not, Pawlow asks, investigate these processes by observing their relation to this particular reflex? That there was nothing novel in this idea is evident when we recollect that numerous reflexes have been used, by other investigators, for the study of psychic reactions. Respiration, heartbeat, and certain secretory changes have been studied, in this connection, with varying success. But what Pawlow may claim, apparently, is the discovery of that particular reflex which seems to be best adapted for the investigation of complex nervous processes.

. . . . .

The experimental procedure is as follows. A normally active and healthy dog of vigorous salivary reaction having been selected, the duct of one of the salivary glands—the parotid for example—is exposed on the outer surface of the cheek and a salivary fistula is formed. The wound heals completely within a few days and the dog exhibits no signs of discomfort or inconvenience. Those who have used the method insist, indeed, that their animals are perfectly normal in all respects. In further preparation for the study of the salivary reflex a small glass funnel is fastened over the opening to the duct with Mendelejeff cement. To this funnel is attached a tube which conducts the saliva to a graduate. Three methods of measuring the quantity

2 Throughout this discussion we shall deal only with the dog, in as much as it has been used for all of the Russian investigations. According to Nicolai a mixed race of hunting dogs has been used in most instances.

3 Conditioned and unconditioned are the terms used in the only discussion of this subject by Pawlow which has appeared in English. The Russian terms, however, have as their English equivalents conditional and unconditional. But as it seems highly probable that Professor Pawlow sanctioned the terms conditioned and unconditioned, which appear in the Huxley Lecture (*Lancet*, 1906), we shall use them.

of saliva secreted are in use. (1) As the secretion flows from the tube into a graduate the drops are counted, and if the experimenter so desires, an additional measurement may subsequently be obtained by readings from the scale of the graduate. (2) The saliva is permitted . . . to flow through a short tube into a graduate bottle and the amount of the secretion is then determined by reading the scale on the bottle. This method necessitates the replacing of the partially filled bottle by a clean one and the careful cleaning of the funnel between experiments. (3) A small metal canula, inserted in the duct of the gland, is connected by a heavy walled rubber tube with a small glass tube. The saliva drops from this tube upon the lever of a Marey tambour. . . . As it falls drop by drop upon this lever a record is made upon a smoked drum. From this record the experimenter may read the quantity of the secretion in drops and the rate of flow, i.e., how many drops fell in a given interval. This graphic method of recording the salivary reaction is Nicolai's improvement on the Pawlow method as used in Russia. In addition to enabling the experimenter to obtain more detailed and accurate data concerning the reaction, it has the important advantage of permitting him to withdraw from the experiment room during the experiments. This is desirable because his presence is likely to influence the dog in unexpected and undesirable ways.

The Pawlow method lends itself readily to the investigation of many psychic reactions. In order to get clearly in mind the remaining essential points of experimental procedure we may consider its application to the study of visual discrimination of colors. A dog, which has been selected for observation and in which a salivary fistula has been created, is subjected to a course of training to establish a "conditioned" reflex on the basis of visual stimulation. This is accomplished by showing the animal a particular color—say green—at intervals and at the same time giving it food. After numerous repetitions of this procedure the visual stimulus becomes the sign of food and induces the salivary reflex in the absence of the food. An animal so trained is ready for experiments on the discrimination of colors. If it appears that no color except green produces the "conditioned" reflex, there is reason to believe that the dog perceives green as distinct from the other colors.

Pawlow devised and employs this method not for the study of psychic phenomena, as Nicolai proposes to do, but simply as a means of approach to the physiology of the nervous system. Of his insistence upon the objective point of view the following quotation from his Huxley lecture is excellent proof. "Up to the present time the physiology of the eye, the ear, and other superficial organs which are of importance as recipients of impressions has been regarded almost exclusively in its subjective aspect; this presented some advantages, but at the same time, of course, limited the range of inquiry. In the investigation of the conditioned stimuli in the higher animals, this limitation is got rid of and a number of important questions in this field of research can be at once examined with the aid of all the immense resources which experiments on animals place in the hands of the physiologist. . . . The investigation of the conditioned reflexes is of very great importance for the physiology of the higher parts of the central nervous system. Hitherto this department of physiology has throughout most of its extent availed itself of ideas not its own, ideas borrowed from psychology, but now there is a possibility of its being liberated from such evil influences. The conditioned reflexes lead us to the consideration of the position of animals in nature: this is a subject of immense extent and one that must be treated objectively." [4]

Although psychology—or rather psychologists—deserves all of the criticisms which the physiologists have made, students of animal behavior and comparative psychology should not allow Pawlow's attitude to discourage them. Nor should they be slow to appreciate the immediate importance, and promise for the advancement of their science, of the Pawlow method and its results. That it can be

4 *Lancet*, 1906, p. 915.

used to advantage by animal psychologists, as well as by those physiologists for whom the psychic phenomenon is merely an unescapable nuisance, is obvious.

Already Nicholai has ably discussed the relations of the method to psychological problems. He contends, with reason, that the salivary reflex method possesses the four essential characteristics of a scientific method in psychology: (*a*) it is general, in its applicability to the study of psychic processes; (*b*) it is constant; (*c*) it permits accurate measurement; and (*d*) it is specific.

Undoubtedly the method may be applied to the study of various aspects of sensation and the mutual relations of sensations, to memory and ideation, to the formation of judgments and will acts. Its obvious limitation appears in the number of organisms with which it may be employed. Evidently it can not be used for the study of animals which lack salivary glands, and even among those animals which do possess these glands there are many which surely would not lend themselves satisfactorily to the method. It seems, therefore, as if Pawlow's method were especially important in animal psychology as a means to the intensive study of the mental life of a limited number of mammals. The dog evidently is especially well suited to the experiments.

. . . . .

LAWS OF CONDITIONED REFLEXES AND CONCLUSIONS CONCERNING THE RELATIVE IMPORTANCE OF THE SENSES OF THE DOG

The work in Pawlow's laboratory has rendered it possible to formulate a number of laws concerning the conditioned reflex. We shall mention only three of the most important of these, as examples.

Law I. A conditioned reflex can be worn out or destroyed by repetition of its conditioning stimulus or stimulus complex. Whereas at first a particular sound, sight, or odor which is indicative of food causes the secretion of several drops of saliva, after a few repetitions at short intervals and without the presentation of food to the dog it causes no secretion. This wearing out of the conditioned reflex serves to distinguish it from the unconditioned reflex.

Law II. The destruction of a conditioned reflex by repetition does not influence other conditioned reflexes. For example, the wearing out of the conditioned reflex to the sight of a particular kind of food leaves unmodified the reflex to the odor of the food.

Law III. Irrelevant stimuli (a sudden noise, a new object in the environment, etc.), produce a depressing effect upon conditioned reflexes. In regard to the nature of their influence, they may be conveniently classed in two groups: (1) those that temporarily diminish or even suspend the activity of the conditioned reflex, but lose this retarding effect after a few repetitions; (2) those which at first tend to reduce the intensity of the reflex and finally inhibit it completely.

Many other laws of importance for investigators who wish to make use of the salivary reflex as a means of studying animal behavior are to be found in the various papers mentioned in the bibliography at the end of this article.

Nicolai, in summing up the results of the investigations concerning the senses of the dog, mentions the following interesting points:

1. Cold, which when applied to a particular spot on the skin in the dog calls forth a conditioned reflex, has a like effect when applied to another region of the skin. Localization apparently is not precise.

2. Mechanical stimuli, which when applied to a particular region of the body cause conditioned reflexes, do not have this effect when applied to other regions. In this case localization is fairly precise.

3. Warmth stimuli are distinguished by the dog from cold stimuli and both of these are distinguished from mechanical stimuli, such as tickling, scratching, rubbing.

4. The dog's hearing seems to be very well developed. To markedly different tones or

noises specific salivary reflexes are given, after training. But when a sound differs only slightly, in pitch for example, from the "familiar" tone it may cause merely a quantitative change in the reaction. If to a particular "familiar" tone a dog reacts by the secretion of ten drops of saliva, to one a quarter of a tone higher it may respond with only eight drops, to one a half tone higher with four drops, to one a full tone higher with only one drop, while greater differences may cause no visible reaction.

5. Nicolai, like Orbeli, has failed to obtain evidences of color vision in the dog. Of the difficulties and dangers of error in the investigation of this subject the following observation is a significant indication. Nicolai discovered that a dog which was apparently able to distinguish green from red was in fact depending for its means of discrimination upon a slight difference in the action of the two different keys which were used to give the stimuli. Color had nothing to do with the reactions. For the human observer the stimuli which served to control the behavior of the dog were practically imperceptible. Evidently, visual stimuli which affect us very differently are the same for the dog; whereas certain other forms of stimulation which are for us insignificant are readily distinguished by the dog.

6. We obtain no quantitative expression of the value of the brightness, size, form, or movement perception from the papers on the visual reactions of the dog, but the presence of these several kinds of visual ability is demonstrated.

7. Two stimuli may be compared as to intensity (stimulating value) by comparison of the amounts of saliva which they cause to be secreted.

8. Comparison of stimuli of different sense modes indicates that the following is the order of diminishing importance for the dog: Smell, hearing, cutaneous sense (mechanical stimuli), vision, temperature senses. The dog is preëminently a nose-animal. Indeed, so acute is the sense of smell that it has thus far proved impossible to study it to advantage. Our color vision may enable us to teach the dog to distinguish colors, but he is in a position to give us instruction in smelling!

Finally we may be permitted to quote from Nicolai his conclusions concerning the relation of the Pawlow method to animal psychology.

"The Pawlow salivary reflex is a relatively complicated process which is connected only indirectly with the exciting stimulus and for the occurrence of which the idea of eating is always necessary."

"Pawlow's salivary reflex method gives us a better explanation of the manner in which a dog learns spontaneously [than do most other methods], but it remains to be shown how far the learning can be carried. In the solving of related questions, the method does not seem to be superior to Kalischer's training method, and the latter is much the more convenient."

"One can show experimentally that a dog learns by subsuming certain new ideas under general ideas which he has already acquired in the course of the experiment."[5]

5 *Centralb. f. Physiol.*, Bd. 22, S. 364, 1908.

BIBLIOGRAPHY TO 1909

ALJASSON, M. E. On the problem of the restoration of the conditioned reflex. *Trans. Soc. Russ. Physicians, St. Petersburg,* 1907. (Russian.)

ALJASSON, M. E. A study of the auditory capacity of the dog under normal conditions and after partial extirpation of the auditory cortex. Dissertation. St. Petersburg, 1908. (Russian.)

BABKINE, B. P. An experimental contribution to the systematic study of complex nervous phenomena in the dog. Diss. St.P., 1904. (Russian.)

BELITZKY, J. On the influence of the centre of the cortex for salivary secretion upon the salivary reflexes. (From Bechtereff's Laboratory.) *Review of Psychiat., Neurol., and Exp. Psychol.,* 1906. (Russian.)

BOLDIREFF, V. H. The artificial production of conditioned reflexes and their characteristics. *Trans. Soc. Russ. Physicians, St. Petersburg.*

First communication, 1905; Second communication, 1906. (Russian.)

BOLDIREFF, V. H. Conditioned reflexes and the possibility of reinforcing and inhibiting them. *Kharkov Medical Journal,* 1907. (Russian.)

FOLBORT, G. V. Contribution to the physiology of conditioned reflexes. *Trans. Soc. Russ. Physicians, St. Petersburg,* 1907–08. (Russian.)

HEIMAN. On the influence of stimulation of the mouth cavity upon the activity of the salivary glands. Diss. St. Petersburg, 1904. (Russian.)

KASHERININOVA, N. A. A new artificial conditioned reflex in the salivary glands. *Trans. Soc. Russ. Physicians, St. Petersburg,* 1906. (Russian.)

KASHERININOVA, N. A. On mechanical irritation of the skin as a means of stimulating the salivary glands. *Trans. Soc. Russ. Physicians, St. Petersburg,* 1906. (Russian.)

KASHERININOVA, N. A. Conditioned reflexes of the salivary glands resulting from mechanical stimulation of the skin. Diss. St.P., 1908. (Russ.)

KHAZEP, S. B. On the correlation of the intensities of unconditioned and conditioned salivary reflexes. Dissertation. St. Petersburg, 1908. (Russian.)

KRASNOGORSKY. Conditioned reflexes in children. (From Rauchfus' Clinic.) *Trans. Soc. Russ. Physicians, St. Petersburg,* 1907–08. (Russian.)

MAKOVSKY, I. S. Auditory reflexes after the removal of the temporal regions of the cerebral hemispheres in the dog. Diss. St.P., 1907. (Russ.)

MISHTOVT, G. V. Acquired inhibition of an artificially induced conditioned reflex of the salivary glands. Dissertation. St. Petersburg, 1907. (Russian.)

NEITZ, E. A. The interaction of conditioned reflexes. *Trans. Soc. Russ. Physicians, St. Petersburg,* 1908. (Russian.)

NICOLAI, G. F. Die physiologische Methodik zur Erforschung der Tierpsyche. *Jour. f. Psychol. und Neurol.,* Bd. 10, S. 1–27. 1907.

NICOLAI, G. F. (und DR. BAUDOUIN). Das Lernen der Tiere (auf Grund von Versuchen mit Pawlowscher Speichelfistel). *Centralblatt f. Physiol.,* Bd. 22, S. 362–364, 1908.

ORBELI, L. A. Concerning the problem of the localization of conditioned reflexes in the central nervous system. *Trans. Soc. Russ. Physicians, St. Petersburg,* 1907. (Russian.)

ORBELI, L. A. Conditioned reflexes resulting from optical stimulation of the dog. Dissertation. St. Petersburg, 1908. (Russian.)

PALLADIN, A. The artificial formation of conditioned reflexes by summation of combined stimuli. *Trans. Soc. Russ. Physicians, St.P.,* 1906. (Russ.)

PARFENOFF, N. P. A peculiar case in the functioning of the salivary glands of the dog. *Trans. Soc. Russ. Physicians, St. Petersburg,* 1905–6. (Russian.)

PAWLOW, J. P. Experimental psychology and the psycho-pathology of animals. *Bull. of the Imperial Medical Acad.,* Vol. 7, 1903. (Russian.)

PAWLOW, J. P. Sur la sécrétion psychique des glandes salivaires. *Arch. intern. de Physiol.,* T. 1, 1904.

PAWLOW, J. P. Festschrift: "To M. Jean Pawlow on the occasion of the twenty-fifth anniversary of his scientific career this work is dedicated by his colleagues, students, and admirers." *Arch. des sciences biologiques, publiées par l'institut imperial de med. exp. à St. Petersburg,* Vol. 11, Supplement, 1904. (Russian and French. Gives list of Pawlow's publications.)

PAWLOW, J. P. The scientific investigation of the psychical faculties or processes in the higher animals. Huxley Lecture for 1906. *Lancet,* 1906, pp. 911–915 (published in full); also *British Medical Journal,* 1906, pp. 871–873 (in part); also *Science* N. S., Vol. 24, pp. 613–619, 1906 (in part).

PAWLOW, J. P. Conditioned reflexes after destruction of various portions of the cerebral hemispheres. *Trans. Soc. Russ. Physicians, St.P.,* 1908. (Russ.)

PERELTZVEIG, I. P. Contribution to the study of conditioned reflexes. Dissertation. St. Petersburg, 1907. (Russian.)

PIMENOFF, P. P. Study of a special group of conditioned reflexes. Dissertation. St. Petersburg, 1907. (Russian.)

SELIONYI, G. P. The orientation of the dog to sounds. *Trans. Soc. Russ. Physicians, St. Petersburg,* 1905–06. (Russian.)

SELIONYI, G. P. Contribution to the study of the reactions of the dog to auditory stimuli. Dissertation. St. Petersburg, 1907. (Russian.)

SELIONYI, G. P. A new conditioned reflex (caused by the cessation of sound). *Kharkov Medical Journ.,* 1908. (Russian.)

SNARSKY, A. T. Analysis of the normal conditions of functioning of the salivary glands in the dog. Dissertation. St. Petersburg, 1902. (Russian.)

TIKHOMIROFF, N. P. Experiments in strictly objective studies of the functions of the cerebral hemispheres of the dog. Diss. St.P., 1906. (Russ.)

TOLOTCHINOFF, J. Contribution à l'étude de la physiologie des glandes salivaires. *C. r. du congrès d. natural. et méd. du Nord à Helsingfors,* 1902.

TOROPOFF, N. K. Conditioned reflexes produced by optical stimulation of the dog after extirpation of the cortical region of the cerebral hemispheres. Dissertation. St. Petersburg, 1908. (Russian.)

VASILIEF, P. H. The influence of an irrelevant stimulus on an established conditioned reflex. *Trans. Soc. Russ. Physicians, St.P.,* 1906. (Russ.)

VOSKOBOINIKOVA-GRANSTREM, E. E. A temperature of 50° C. as a new artificial conditioned stimulus for the salivary reflex. *Trans. Soc.* *Russ. Physicians, St. Petersburg,* 1906. (Russian.)

WULFESON, S. G. The function of the salivary glands. Dissertation. St. Petersburg, 1899. (Russian.)

ZAVADSKY, J. V. Inhibition and reawakening of conditioned reflexes. Dissertation. St. Petersburg, 1908. (Russian.)

ZAVADSKY, J. V. An attempt at the application of the conditioned reflex method to pharmacology. *Trans. Soc. Russ. Physicians, St. Petersburg,* 1908. (Russian.)

ZELHEIM, A. P. The function of the salivary glands before and after the cutting of the glosso-pharyngeal and lingual nerves. Dissertation. St. Petersburg, 1906. (Russian.)

CLARK L. HULL

22. Simple Trial-and-Error Learning: A Study in Psychological Theory

I

SCIENCE proceeds by a double movement. For the most part, scientific discoveries are accomplished by means of observation and experiment. Occasionally, however, it happens that a discovery is made by means of a more or less complex logical process or "gedanken experiment." Einstein's mathematical deduction and prediction of what may be observed in the behavior of light when it passes near the sun is perhaps as good an example of this as any.

Frequently, after the existence and characteristics of natural phenomena have been discovered empirically, it is seen that these things might very well have been deduced from facts and principles already known. When the deduction is thus performed, as a kind of afterthought, the process is more properly termed explanation. Actual prediction is more dramatic than explanation, but the two processes are logically very similar. A true deductive explanation possesses a quality of logical necessity closely akin to prediction regardless of when the empirical observation takes place. It is of the mass of such interlocking deductive explanations that scientific systems are made. In general, that science is most perfectly systematized which can show the greatest proportion of its phenomena as logically deducible from recognized principles and other known phenomena. Moreover it seems reasonable that rival systems within a science may also be evaluated on the basis of this same criterion.

It is evident that much of what passes for explanation fails of this true deductive quality. It avails little merely to subsume a known phenomenon under some more or less general principle. It is true enough to say of any actual event that it is a case of conservation of energy, or of cause and effect. But such bare general principles of themselves alone can hardly enable one to deduce the existence and characteristics of natural phenomena. In a similar manner, the typical undergraduate behaviorist's glib explanation of the more complex forms of habit phenomena by saying of each that it is a case of stimulus and response, utterly fails of the true deductive quality. The same may be said of the fairly common, but equally futile, invocation of complexes, equilibrium, *Gestalten*, closures, *Einsicht* and the like for a similar purpose.

For an explanation to form the substance of a true system, the deduction must eventuate in some kind of genuine novelty as compared with what is contained in the original premises. This element of novelty is what was referred to above as a predictive quality in real explanation. The deductive process is a true generative activity. The known principles give rise to new knowledge as the result of a causal sequence in a high-class redintegrative organism. According to one plausible hypothesis, principles are symbolic habits which, as a result of their functional interaction within the organism possessing them, give rise to new and distinct habits. These latter constitute the new knowledge.

Reprinted by permission of the American Psychological Association from the *Psychological Review*, 1930, vol. 37, pp. 241–56.

Thus the new knowledge, while derived from the original principles, is not the principles, but something newly come into existence. By the accumulation of these bits of deductive explanation, scientific systems become enlarged very much as have systems of mathematics.

Perhaps no theorists have been more naïve in their attempts at system construction than those who seek in the principles of stimulus-response the main explanation of those forms of behavior usually called mental. It may even be that, thus far, none have failed much worse in evolving the solid substance of genuine explanation. Even so, the author has considerable confidence in the possibilities of this point of view. As a concrete example in miniature of what is believed to be a desirable direction for this movement toward systematization to take, there is given the following account of a *simple* type of trial-and-error learning. This may be taken as a relatively uninvolved example of what has been spoken of above as a deductive explanation.

II

THERE appear to be a number of fairly distinct types of trial-and-error learning. The particular principles necessary to employ in their explanation, as well as the mode of combining the principles, differ somewhat according to the type of learning to be explained. Of the true trial-and-error learning, we have the relatively complex type exemplified by maze learning, where the *obvious* reinforcement of the conditioning process (or the lack of reinforcement) for the most part comes only at the end of a series or particular combination of trial acts. A strict deductive explanation of this type of learning presents special difficulties and very probably will turn out to involve some principles not needed for the explanation of the less complex types. A second and relatively simple type of trial-and-error learning is seen where each act or trial is definitely and immediately reinforced positively, if successful, or is followed by punishment (negative reinforcement) if unsuccessful. A still differ-

ent, and perhaps simpler, type is where each trial act is reinforced, if successful, but is followed by no special stimulus (is merely unreinforced) if unsuccessful. It is this last type of learning *only* which we shall consider in the following paragraphs.

Numerous phenomena characteristic of this third type of learning call for explanation. These problems can perhaps best be formulated as a series of questions:

1. Why does the organism persist in its trials or attempts even after repeated failure?

2. Why, in case success does not result from its first attempts, does the organism vary its reactions, often over a very wide range?

3. What principle or mechanism limits the range of the variation of the reactions which an organism will make to any problem situation?

4. Why do organisms of the same general type sometimes differ so widely from each other in their reactions to the same (external) problem situation?

5. What principle determines the order of appearance of the several trial acts of a trial-and-error sequence?

6. Why, in the series of trial acts preceding the first success, does the organism often stupidly commit the same erroneous reaction repeatedly?

7. What constitutes success itself?

8. Why should the trial sequence come to an end as soon as success has been attained? Why should it not continue exactly as before?

9. Why, even after the successful reaction cycle has been performed one or more times, do reactions, repeatedly found to be unsuccessful, quite illogically continue sometimes to be made?

10. Why, in general, do these erroneous reactions become less and less frequent with each successful solution, and why do they at length cease altogether?

11. Why, for a particular organism, are certain trial-and-error problems so much more readily solved than are others? Why, for certain organisms, is the same problem so much more difficult of solution than for

other organisms, presumably of equally good natural endowment?

12. Why, on the whole, are the trial reactions in "blind" trial-and-error learning so much more likely to prove successful than would be a mere random sampling from the entire repertory of the organism's possible movements? Why is the organism so much more likely to try a successful act early in the trial-and-error sequence than pure random sampling might be expected to bring about?

III

LET it be assumed, at the outset, that there exist a number of unconditioned stimuli, S_x, S_y, and S_z; and that these stimuli evoke in a certain organism the responses R_x, R_y, and R_z, respectively. It is assumed, further, that these responses involve the same "final common path" so that no two of them can take place simultaneously. Let S_1 represent a very mild neutral stimulus evoking at the outset no observable response whatever.

Now if S_1 should accompany S_x in the same stimulus complex a number of times there will be set up the conditioned reaction tendency

$$S_1 \longrightarrow R_x.$$

In a similar manner, if S_1 accompanies S_y in another stimulus complex a number of times there will be set up the conditioned reaction tendency

$$S_1 \longrightarrow R_y.$$

Similarly, there may also be set up the conditioned reaction tendency

$$S_1 \longrightarrow R_z.$$

Thus S_1 may come to possess a number of distinct and mutually incompatible excitatory tendencies or "bonds." Presumably each of these tendencies to action will have a strength or potency different from that of the others. For the sake of definiteness and simplicity of the logical consequences, we may let the strength of these excitatory tendencies stand, at this stage, in the ratio respectively of 3, 2, and 1. Lastly let it be assumed that reaction

R_z is the one and only response which is biologically successful, i.e., the one which is followed by reinforcement and which terminates the stimulus S_1.

Under the conditions as assumed, what might logically be expected to result in case the organism should be stimulated by S_1, either alone or in conjunction with certain other approximately neutral stimuli? It is obvious at once that there will arise a kind of competition or rivalry among the three mutually incompatible excitatory tendencies. This competition may conveniently be represented thus:

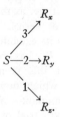

Since the excitatory tendency flowing from S_1 to R_x is strongest, this reaction will be the first trial act. By hypothesis this reaction will not be reinforced. According to the principle of experimental extinction this failure of reinforcement will weaken the tendency of S_1 to evoke R_x, leaving it, let us say, with a value of 2.1.[1] But since this excitatory tendency, even after its weakening, is stronger than either of the other two, it will still be dominant. By hypothesis, S_1 continues without interruption. Accordingly, after the brief refractory phase following the R_x response, this same reaction will be repeated as the second trial act. A second experimental extinction at once reduces the tendency to R_x to a strength of 1.2. This leaves the tendency to R_y dominant at the beginning of the

[1] See TABLE 1 for a systematic and detailed summary of the characteristic incidents of this hypothetical learning episode. No special significance should be attached to the quantitative values employed. Presumably the several types of loss and gain in strength of excitatory processes in all cases should become progressively less as the maximum effect is approached, instead of being constant as shown. The simpler constant values have been chosen with a view to simplifying the exposition. For the same reason forgetting tendencies have been neglected as well as complications involved in the acquisition of the three conditioned reactions.

third trial. S_1 continues to act. Accordingly R_y is evoked as the third trial. Here, for the first time, we note the phenomenon of variability in the trial acts.

But since R_y will not be reinforced, this excitatory tendency also will suffer extinction, reducing it to 1.1. Meanwhile, R_x has spontaneously recovered to a strength of 1.5. By hypothesis, S_1 still persists. As a result, R_x is evoked as the fourth trial of the series. Failure of reinforcement at once reduces it to the value of .6. During this time R_y has recovered to 1.4, which gives it a position of dominance. S_1 accordingly evokes this reaction for a second time, as the fifth trial act of the trial-and-error series. Failure of reinforcement reduces its excitatory potentiality to .5. Meanwhile, R_x has recovered to a strength of .9, but this is not enough to equal that of R_z, which now for the first time becomes dominant. S_1 accordingly evokes R_z as the sixth trial of the series. By hypothesis this reaction is a success and is followed by reinforcement. Since this act also terminates S_1, R_z is the last trial of the first trial-and-error sequence or behavior cycle.

The second time the organism encounters the stimulus S_1 (the beginning of the second behavior cycle) the values of all the excitatory tendencies have increased over those existent at the conclusion of the previous behavior cycle. The tendency to R_x is dominant, and this reaction follows at once. The trial is unsuccessful, extinction follows, and stimulus S_1 persists. Thereupon R_y becomes dominant, and therefore becomes the second trial act. This also is an error. Meanwhile, R_x once more has recovered to a state of dominance, and it accordingly becomes the third trial. R_x is weakened again by failure of reinforcement, which leaves dominant the correct reaction R_z. This reaction brings the second problem cycle to a successful conclusion and R_z is reinforced a second time.

The third time the stimulus S_1 is encountered it finds the three excitatory tendencies in still a different combination of strengths. R_x is dominant and becomes the first trial, an error. Its consequent weakening leaves R_z dominant. S_1 accordingly evokes R_z as the

second trial. This success, as before, is followed by reinforcement.

On the fourth occasion that the organism encounters the stimulus S_1, for the first time it finds R_z dominant at the outset. Accordingly the first trial act is a success. At this point the process of trial-and-error learning may be considered as functionally complete.

IV

WE may now summarize the results of our deduction by answering the questions formulated above.

1. The organism persists in its attempts because the stimulus which evokes the attempts itself persists.

2. The organism varies its reaction, when one reaction fails, because the consequent weakening of the primarily dominant excitatory tendency leaves dominant a second and distinct excitatory tendency conditioned to the same stimulus situation.

3. The range or variety of reactions which may be evoked by a given problem situation is limited to the reactions which have become conditioned during the life of the organism to one or another stimulus component of that situation.

4. Organisms superficially quite similar in general constitution may differ very widely in the nature of their trial attempts at problem solution, because their previous life history has resulted in both qualitative and quantitative differences in their stock of excitatory tendencies evocable by the several stimulus components of the problem situation.

5. The principle which determines which of the possible trial acts shall be evoked first, second, third, etc., in the trial-and-error series is: That trial act is evoked at any given stage of the trial-and-error process which at that time is dominant, i.e., strongest.

6. The reason that the organism frequently, and apparently quite stupidly, tries an unsuccessful act over and over during the first problem cycle, despite failure of reinforcement, is quite simply that the several processes which are continually varying the strengths of the different excitatory tendencies may on more than one occasion leave

any particular excitatory tendency dominant. This may even result in the same erroneous act taking place two or more times in immediate succession, as in Trials 1 and 2 of Behavior Cycle I. (See TABLE 1.)

7. Not enough is yet known concerning the psychology of learning to give a completely general definition of success in objective biological terms. In the case of hunger, success consists in the eating of food. Ordinarily the successful act results in a cessation of the persisting stimulus S_1. In the case of hunger, S_1 is generally considered to be the cramping of the walls of the upper digestive tract.

8. The trials cease after success has been attained simply because success terminates the stimulus (S_1) which evokes the trials.

9. Erroneous acts continue to be made even after the correct solution has been "discovered" one or more times by successful trials because the reinforcement, by success, of a weak excitatory tendency is not always great enough to make it equal in strength to excitatory tendencies which were originally more potent and which have had time to recover greatly from the effects of experimental extinction suffered just previous to the successful reaction.

10. The erroneous reactions become less and less frequent as the trial-and-error process continues, because the basic superiority in the strength of the excitatory tendencies leading to erroneous responses becomes less and less dominant. This in turn is owing (a) to the

TABLE 1

Table showing the progressive changes that would take place in a simple case of trial-and-error learning if the influence of experimental extinction each time should be to diminish an unreinforced excitatory tendency .9 points,[2] the influence of spontaneous recovery should be to restore the loss from experimental extinction .3 points for each interval between successive trials (say one hour) and for the interval between problem cycles (say 24 hours) to restore two-thirds of the maximum diminution resulting from the experimental extinction of the preceding cycle.[3] Each successful reaction reinforces its excitatory tendency by .3 points,[4] this reinforcement being assumed to take place immediately.

TRIAL NO.	BEHAVIOR CYCLE I Status of Excitatory Tendencies Preceding Reaction	Resulting Reaction	BEHAVIOR CYCLE II Status of Excitatory Tendencies Preceding Reaction	Resulting Reaction	BEHAVIOR CYCLE III Status of Excitatory Tendencies Preceding Reaction	Resulting Reaction	BEHAVIOR CYCLE IV Status of Excitatory Tendencies Preceding Reaction	Resulting Reaction
1	$x = 3.0$ $y = 2.0$ $z = 1.0$	R_x	$x = 2.2$ $y = 1.5$ $z = 1.3$	R_x	$x = 1.7$ $y = 1.2$ $z = 1.6$	R_x	$x = 1.4$ $y = 1.2$ $z = 1.9$	R_z
2	$x = 2.1$ $y = 2.0$ $z = 1.0$	R_x	$x = 1.3$ $y = 1.5$ $z = 1.3$	R_y	$x = .8$ $y = 1.2$ $z = 1.6$	R_z		
3	$x = 1.2$ $y = 2.0$ $z = 1.0$	R_y	$x = 1.6$ $y = .6$ $z = 1.3$	R_x				
4	$x = 1.5$ $y = 1.1$ $z = 1.0$	R_x	$x = .7$ $y = .9$ $z = 1.3$	R_z				
5	$x = .6$ $y = 1.4$ $z = 1.1$	R_y						
6	$x = .9$ $y = .5$ $z = 1.0$	R_z						

2 I. P. Pavlov, Conditioned reflexes, pp. 48 ff.   3 Idem, *op. cit.*, p. 58.   4 Idem, *op. cit.*, p. 40.

action of experimental extinction which continually weakens such erroneous reactions as chance to become functionally dominant, and (b) to the action of reinforcement which strengthens the excitatory tendency which, when dominant, evokes successful responses. Ultimately this process must lead to a state in which the successful excitatory tendency will be dominant at the very outset of a behavior cycle.

If this first case of success on the initial trial of a behavior cycle should chance to take place under circumstances such that the spontaneous recovery from extinction by the unsuccessful tendencies had not had time to take place (as might have happened if Cycle II had begun very soon after the conclusion of Cycle I), then we should expect to find errors made repeatedly after one or several perfect initial performances had occurred.

11. One problem is more readily solved than another for a given organism because in its particular stock of reaction tendencies the one tending to the successful reaction chances to be relatively stronger than in the other problem situation. In case the excitatory tendency evoking the successful reaction chances to be dominant at the outset, the correct reaction will be made at the first trial and no errors whatever will occur. On the other hand, the same problem may be more difficult for one organism than another, both of which can ultimately master it, because the previous history of the two organisms has so conditioned them that the successful tendency is relatively more dominant in one than in the other. Such relative similarity in the difficulty of problems for different specimens of a given type of organism as actually exists presumably depends upon the relative similarity in the stimulating situations encountered in their lives. This is usually considerable.

12. From the foregoing, it is obvious that trial-and-error learning, while "blind" in the sense that it is not assumed that there is available for its guidance and control any disembodied soul or spirit, is *not* blind in the sense that it does not operate according to recognized principles. In the first place, the trials are not made from the total repertory of the organism, but from only those movements which have by previous stimulation become conditioned to one or another stimulus component of the problem situation. This fact at once automatically limits enormously the number of trial reactions from which selection must be made, and thus largely accounts for such efficiency as it displays. In the second place, of those acts which may be evoked by the stimulus situation, it seems reasonable to expect that in the long run the stronger excitatory tendencies will be more likely to evoke successful reactions than the weaker, and the weaker ones than those reactions within the repertoire of the organism, which have not become conditioned at all to any component of the problem stimulus complex.[5] Since the trial acts are evoked in the order of their strength, this factor will also greatly favor an early success over a mere random sampling from the possible reactions of the organism. It is true that such a system would not always succeed early, and might fail completely of the solution of a problem. Unfortunately this also agrees with the facts of life. Problems are often solved only after much delay, and not infrequently they are not solved at all.

V

FROM the point of view of the longevity of hypotheses, it is extremely dangerous for them to become thoroughly definite and specific. The very definiteness of an hypothesis makes it possible to determine with relative ease whether its implications agree with the known phenomena which it proposes to explain. In case of failure to conform, the unambiguous nature of the comparison is peculiarly fatal. Worse yet, an unambiguous hypothesis is likely to permit the deductive forecast of what should be observed under various experimental conditions which may as yet be untried. A single well-planned experiment may at any moment yield results quite different from the deductive forecast,

5 Space is inadequate to elaborate this point. It is touched on briefly, however, in "A functional interpretation of the conditioned reflex," *Psychological Review*, 1929, 36, p. 498.

and thus topple the entire hypothetical structure. This, of course, is all quite as it should be. The healthy development of a science demands that the implications of its hypotheses be deduced as promptly and unambiguously as possible. This will make it possible for them, if verified by experiment, to be incorporated into the structure or system of the science; or, if found to disagree with experimental findings, the hypotheses may be recast or simply discarded as errors in the long trial-and-error process of system construction. At the least, such hypotheses may be credited with the virtue of having stimulated experimental research. But if an hypothesis be so vague and indefinite, or so lacking in relevancy to the phenomena which it seeks to explain that the results neither of previous experiments nor those of experiments subsequently to be performed may be deduced from it, it will be difficult indeed to prove it false. And if, in addition, the hypothesis should appeal in some subtle fashion to the predilections of a culture in which it gains currency, it should enjoy a long and honored existence. Unfortunately, because of its very sterility and barrenness in the above deductive sense, such an hypothesis should have no status whatever in science. It savors more of metaphysics, religion, or theology.

Substantially the only significant criticism of the stimulus-response, or mechanistic movement in psychology, has been made by members of the Wertheimer branch of the *Gestalt* school, notably by W. Köhler and K. Koffka, particularly the latter. This painstaking criticism of theoretical stimulus-response constructs has been a distinct service to science. Better still, they have put forward a quite different set of principles to explain the same phenomena, which are proposed as alternative, because assumed to be superior, concepts. The issue has thus been joined in a manner quite frank and deliberate. Best of all the contest, instead of taking place in a field of pure speculation where a decision can rarely be reached, is to be conducted in the laboratory where the decision must ultimately be submitted to the impartial arbitration of the facts. That hypothesis, or set of hypotheses, which can show the highest achievement in the things which are recognized by scientists as the functions or virtues of hypotheses must in the end be judged the superior.

As a beginning in this direction there may be considered the above theoretical construct concerning one extremely limited type of trial-and-error learning. Here the question at once arises: Are the concepts or principles, by which the *Gestalt* psychologists would explain the kind of behavior under consideration, of such a nature that answers to the above questions can also be deduced from them? The present writer is frank to confess that such concepts as closure, *Pragnanz, Einsicht* and the like appear to him either too vague or too general to permit any significant deductions whatever to be drawn. He is quite free to admit, however, that this may be due merely to his failure to grasp the true significance and virtue of these concepts. The real test is whether the *Gestalt* psychologists themselves can do so. It is entirely possible, of course, that they may repudiate in whole or in part the very existence of conditions implied in the questions propounded. In that event it would seem fair to expect an exhibition of the deductive explanation of parallel phenomena as they conceive them to exist.

VI

IT is admitted on all hands that one of the very best tests of an hypothesis or explanatory system is to deduce correctly the result of experimental observations not yet made, particularly when the latter are made by observers disinterested in the outcome. This is a severe test, but it is a fair one, and no system should shrink from it. A number of such possibilities lie sufficiently near to the range of the very simple conditions assumed above for first-approximation forecasts of the outcome of certain experimental procedures to be ventured. Space is lacking for the presentation of but one of these. We shall make our own deduction from the same set of principles already employed. A friendly invitation is extended to the *Gestalt* psychologists, and to such other schools as put forward distinctive theories of learning, to exhibit in similar detail a similar deduction from their own principles. If no such deductive forecast can be derived, there will be an indication of immaturity, possibly of inadequacy. If a deduction is evolved in which recognized stimulus-response principles are employed, the indication will be that the psychology in question is not so distinct as might otherwise have been supposed. If a rigorous deduction from genuinely distinct principles should appear, but one in which the same outcome is arrived at as by the stimulus-response principles here employed, an extremely interesting situation of parallelism would be presented, which might very well be mutually illuminating to all parties to the discussion. Finally, if any two deductions should arrive at quite distinct forecasts as to the outcome of the experimental procedures, the laboratory may be evoked as the final court of appeal. Indeed, the laboratory must pass the final verdict even if there were no difference of opinion whatever.

FORECAST

In cases of relatively simple trial-and-error learning by mammalian organisms below the anthropoids where, as above, but a single act is required for success; where the several trial acts are relatively distinct and uniform; and where the first one-fourth of the behavior cycles required for complete learning have been both fairly protracted and in fairly close succession: it is predicted that there will be a tendency for the proportion of erroneous acts (R_x and R_y) to successful acts (R_z) to be greater at the first trial act of new cycles when the new cycle begins a relatively long time after the conclusion of the preceding one than when it begins relatively soon after.

DEDUCTION

From TABLE 1 it is quite obvious that if Behavior Cycle II should begin at once after the conclusion of Cycle I, R_z will be dominant since the status of the excitatory tendencies will be:

$$x = .9$$
$$y = .5$$
$$z = 1.3$$

But if, instead, an hour intervenes, the relative strength of the tendencies will be:

$$x = 1.2$$
$$y = .8$$
$$z = 1.3$$

At this point R_z and R_x are about equally likely to take place. Or if, as a third alternative, still more time elapses between the close of Cycle I and the beginning of the next cycle, R_x and R_y will both become progressively more dominant over R_z until at length we shall have the condition obtaining at the first trial act of Cycle II as shown in TABLE 1.

It must be especially emphasized that the type of learning here considered is not only very simple, but very special in its simplicity. Its nature is perhaps best indicated in the early parts of Sections II and III. It naturally will require some ingenuity fully to satisfy these conditions in an experiment. In particular it may be difficult to set up an experimental situation where all the components of the stimulus complex, except a single dynamic core (S_1), will remain practically neutral throughout the reaction sequence.[6] However, ingenious experimentalists will be able to approach those conditions closely enough to make possible significant comparisons of results.

VII

IN conclusion it may be observed that the behavior deduced above, particularly the persistence of effort at solution by means of varied response, is one of the most commonly remarked differences between behavior, usu-

6 In this connection it may be asked why the implications of such a simplified situation should be studied. The answer is found in the history of mathematical procedures. It is often possible to understand the implications of simple situations when, at the outset, the understanding of more complex situations would be impossible. The previous solution of simple situations should make the later solution of progressively more complex situations possible. There is reason to hope that this shall prove to be the case in the present instance.

ally called psychic or mental, and that of ordinary automatic machines. Indeed it is common, by way of contrast, to call such behavior "intelligent" and "purposive." It is the belief of the present author that these latter terms represent extremely important aspects of mammalian behavior, but that instead of being ultimate entities, all may be derived from certain combinations of more basic principles. It is believed, for example, that the account sketched above in Section III deduces a type of behavior which, if observed in an animal, would be called purposive by most psychologists though it does not show the type of purpose involving plan.[7]

Moreover, if the type of explanation put forward above be really a sound deduction, it should be a matter of no great difficulty to construct parallel inanimate mechanisms, even from inorganic materials, which will genuinely manifest the qualities of intelligence, insight, and purpose, and which, in

so far, will be truly psychic. Such a mechanism would represent a radically new order of automaticity, one not yet dreamed of by the ordinary designer of automatic machinery. That such mechanisms have not been constructed before is doubtless due to the paralyzing influence of metaphysical idealism. The appearance of such "psychic" mechanisms in the not very remote future may be anticipated with considerable confidence. Dr. H. D. Baernstein, in collaboration with the present author, has already succeeded in constructing an electro-chemical mechanism which shows the more important of the phenomena of the simple conditioned reflex.[8] There has also been constructed a model which manifests the phenomenon of simple rote learning. It is not inconceivable that "psychic" machines may ultimately play an appreciable rôle in the life of industrialized communities. On the side of psychology it is possible that these mechanisms may dissolve the age-old problem of the opposition of mind to matter by practically demonstrating the characteristic mechanisms by means of which matter manifests the forms of behavior called psychic.

---

7 It is a plausible hypothesis that the type of purpose involving plan and fore-sight (or foreknowledge) requires, in addition to a persisting dynamic core in the stimulus complex, as in the case elaborated above, a flexible symbolic habit system. The implications of such an accessory habit system for trial-and-error learning, as well as further implications of the persisting-stimulus principle, are reserved for later examination.

8 C. L. Hull and H. D. Baernstein, A mechanical parallel to the conditioned reflex, *Science,* 1929, 70, pp. 14–15.

EDWIN R. GUTHRIE

23. *Conditioning as a Principle of Learning*

A THEORY of learning, to be effective, must account for the facts which have been established. The significance of the facts themselves is, unfortunately, not at present clear. Most experimental investigations have necessarily measured learning in terms of certain end results, however these were accomplished, leaving undetermined whether the subject has learned to do one thing in one way or one thing in many different ways. And most experimental investigations have concerned such intricate special activities that their results cannot be generalized. Theories of learning can attempt to systematize only the facts of the more elementary forms of learning.

Most of the facts of learning are derived from common knowledge. The elementary facts of learning were fairly well understood by the associationists. The role of experiment in this field is as a rule illustrative. Pavlov's "conditioned reflex" is accepted because it fits into a body of common knowledge about human and animal nature. That burned children dread fires is accepted before hearing of Pavlov. If Pavlov's results had contradicted this body of common knowledge they would have been met with sceptical analysis. Even though they seem to corroborate common knowledge they deserve thorough examination.

I

THE following paragraphs will serve to call to mind the more important and established facts of learning. The summary is necessarily incomplete because it will be restricted to such facts as are recognized by common consent.

CONDITIONING

Stimuli which accompany a response tend, on their recurrence, to evoke that response. Sometimes called "association by contiguity in time" or "redintegration" or "associative memory." This generalization has long been recognized.

INHIBITORY CONDITIONING

Stimuli which tend to call out a response may lose that tendency, or, if they occur without the response, go further and acquire inhibiting effects. "Negative adaptation" is the term proposed by Stevenson Smith and the writer a number of years ago for this characteristic of learning. The term "conditioned inhibition" has also been used. "Inhibitory conditioning" is perhaps better than either.

REMOTE CONDITIONING

So little attention has been given to the precise time factors in conditioning that conditioning has generally been taken to include those cases in which the conditioning stimulus does not immediately precede its response, but may, an interval intervening, precede it or even follow it. According to Pavlov the interval in delayed and trace conditioning may be as great as thirty minutes. Pavlov would deny that the conditioning stimulus may follow its response, but studies in backward association would indicate that something

Reprinted by permission of the American Psychological Association and the estate of the author from the *Psychological Review*, 1930, vol. 37, pp. 412–28.

resembling conditioning may occur in man when we have the time order, first response, then stimulus.

EFFECTS OF PRACTICE

Practice sometimes makes perfect. Repetition of a sequence of stimulus and response seems to establish the certainty of the sequence more firmly. "Laws" of frequency or exercise are included in most theories of learning.

FORGETTING

The effects of learning seem to disappear at a somewhat predictable rate. The "curve of forgetting" discovered by Ebbinghaus for nonsense material applies with variations to many forms of learning, characterized by rapid disappearance at the interval just following the last practice and a more gradual disappearance as time goes on. There are some odd exceptions to this general form of the curve, however. It is reported that the disappearance of learning is affected by intervening activity. After a period of sleep retention is better than after a period of waking. After a period occupied in a quite different activity, retention is better than after a period in which the situation is like (but not too like) the situation during learning.

TEMPORARY EXTINCTION

In direct contradiction to the preceding generalization, Dunlap and Pavlov have pointed out cases in which the repetition of a habit sequence serves to disrupt the habit. Dunlap reports the successful use of practice to break up annoying habits. Pavlov reports (and his report is well verified by common human experience) that conditioning will disappear if a conditioning stimulus is repeatedly given at short intervals without the support of the unconditioned stimulus. After an interval the habit will be found somewhat restored.

EMOTIONAL REINFORCEMENT

The familiar fact that learning is facilitated by states of general excitement has been illustrated by recent experiment showing that nonsense material is better learned by subjects under slight muscular strain than by relaxed subjects. We may associate this characteristic of learning with what has been called dynamogenesis, the facilitation of learning by adventitious stimuli which might well be expected to diminish learning.

IRRADIATION

Lacking a better term we may use the one offered by the translator of Pavlov for a phenomenon which he describes and which is easily demonstrated for human behavior as well as for animal behavior. After a stimulus has been established as a conditioner of a response it may be found that other stimuli to the same class of receptors or, in some cases, to different receptors, are able to elicit the response, though they lacked this connection before the experiment. With a touch on the flank used in connection with acid as a stimulus for salivary secretion, touches on other parts of the body prove less effective as their distance from the flank is increased. With practice of the original combination this conditioning power of neighboring stimuli tends to disappear.

PATTERNS

Having learned to read, we find that reading appears to be more or less independent of the actual distance of the print from our eyes, and this means that similar patterns of stimuli are effective without reference to the particular receptor elements stimulated. The Gestalt psychologists assert that this response to patterns as such occurs without learning. It is here included as a characteristic of learning because the writer believes that it is dependent on learning. Reasons for this belief will be offered later.

INSIGHT

As in the case of reaction to patterns as such the Gestalt psychologists have pointed out that the higher animals and man occasionally meet a new situation with an adequate and new response. The process of trial and error made so much of in recent behavioristic accounts of learning seems to be omitted in many acts, which are characterized by the Gestalt psychologists as cases of insight. This fact is here listed among the characteristics of learning because it is also the author's belief that insight is dependent on learning. Reasons for this belief will be cited later.

The experimental literature suggests many more characteristics of learning. Most of these, however, are either debatable or are complicated with factors other than learning which make their significance for a theory of learning slight. The experiments on distribution of practice are complicated by fatigue. The results in whole and part learning are ambiguous and depend on the nature of the material. So-called "reminiscence," in which children prove to be able to reproduce more material after an interval than at the end of practice, has not so far been rid of the suspicion of continued unrecorded practice. A theory of learning which undertakes to explain all the suggested facts is apt to be caught predicting results which do not occur.

Is there a single formula which can be made to include all or most of the established generalizations concerning the nature of learning? If there is such a formula it will in all probability be some form of the ancient principle of association by contiguity in time, which has been a part of all theories of memory and learning since before Aristotle, and has retained its essential character in spite of a variety of names, such as "conditioning," "associative memory," "redintegration." The remainder of this paper will consider the possibility that the facts of learning may possibly all be cited as instances of simple conditioning.

In order to examine its possibilities, the principle of conditioning may be stated in a simple form: *Stimuli acting at a given instant tend to acquire some effectiveness toward the eliciting of concurrent responses, and this effectiveness tends to last indefinitely.*

The phrase "tend to acquire" is used instead of "acquire" because we have no assurance that this acquisition always occurs. It is the contention of this paper that this acquisition, when it does occur, is the fundamental mode of learning. The presumptive changes which make this re-routing of impulses lasting are the physiological basis of learning.

The principle is deliberately formulated to apply only to the momentary event. It is assumed that the phenomenon occurs during that small fraction of a second occupied by the conduction of an impulse through a center.

One more remark needs to be made concerning the language of the principle. The word "stimuli" need not be taken in the sense of elementary stimuli to the individual receptor cells. It seems quite probable that patterns of such elementary stimuli may act as functional units and be subject to conditioning as units, that the elementary stimulus group $ABCD$ may as a group excite a group of pathways P, while another stimulus group, $AEFG$, excites pathway Q. Conditioning redirection at remote association areas would affect these stimulus groups as functional units and not as elements. The stimulus A would be a conditioner of one response element through P and a conditioner of another, possibly an antagonistic element through the pathway Q.

The notion that such stimulus patterns might act as functional units *is not to be confused with the suggestion of the Gestalt psychologists that the patterns might act as functional units without reference to the receptors excited.* That is a very different matter.

We may now undertake an examination of the facts of learning in the light of this formulation of the ancient principle of association or conditioning. This amounts to an attempt to describe all of the forms of learning mentioned in the beginning as instances of the first, namely, simple, simultaneous conditioning. *This does not at all mean that learning is described in terms of conditioned reflexes.* This phrase assumes a fixed unit of behavior which is organized in stereotyped form. It tends to obscure the fact that the behavior of an intelligent organism at any instant is a resultant of the total stimulus situation including internal stimuli. Reflexes and responses are never twice alike, because the total stimulus situation is never repeated. We may, at the outset, distinguish a theory of learning in terms of *conditioning* from a theory of learning in terms of *conditioned reflexes.* We have made no assumptions concerning the elementary acts which comprise behavior.

II

THE characteristics of learning mentioned at the beginning of the paper were: (1) Conditioning; (2) Inhibitory conditioning; (3) Remote conditioning; (4) Improvement by practice; (5) Forgetting; (6) Temporary extinction; (7) Emotional reinforcement; (8) Irradiation; (9) Response to pattern as such; (10) Insight. We may attack these in order.

CONDITIONING

This is, of course, the principle itself, and hence needs no reduction. Our inquiry concerns the possibility of reducing the other facts of learning to instances of this. We may then begin with the second.

INHIBITORY CONDITIONING

The circumstances under which a stimulus combination which has previously elicited a response will lose the power to evoke that response may be briefly stated. If the stimulus combination occurs, and the response is prevented by any means, the stimulus combination loses its power to elicit the response and, if the situation is repeated, will acquire a positive inhibiting effect on its former response. The response may have been prevented by inhibition from incompatible responses which prevail because the conditioning combination is weakened. Inhibitory conditioning is essentially the conditioning of inhibiting responses, and behaves like other conditioning in that it shows the effects of practice, is subject to forgetting, and so on.

REMOTE CONDITIONING

In Pavlov's experiments a new stimulus is presented several seconds or minutes before an unconditioned stimulus, and then acquires the power to elicit the response unsupported, with a latent period corresponding to the interval used in the experiment. Pavlov's explanation attributes this delay to mysterious latencies in the nervous system. He supposes the impulse to be somehow "held up" in the cortex. This assumption is quite unnecessary.

Like Bechterev, Pavlov tends to forget that his experimental animals have sense organs which are stimulated by their own movements. When the bell rings the dog responds by "listening," which is a series of movements, postural changes, turning of the head, pricking of the ears, and the like. When the salivary glands begin to secrete, the accompanying stimuli are not furnished by the bell but by these responses to the bell. The direct response to the bell is probably over in a small fraction of a second. After that the dog is responding to his first response to the bell. Just as when we answer the telephone we are, strictly speaking, answering the telephone only for an instant. After that we are answering ourselves, answering our start to answer the bell.

Such an explanation would account for a number of features of the "delayed" and the "trace" reflex. These are subject to inhibition or sudden release by new stimuli. What these new stimuli probably do is to alter the regular series of movements which comprise listening and the gradual recovery from listening. Delayed and trace reflexes are probably not direct conditioning at all. The true conditioning of saliva flow is on a stimulus pattern which follows the bell and is a consequence of the bell.

The apparent separation in time of a conditioning stimulus and its response is then quite possibly an illusion, and the assumption that responses to stimuli are either immediate or else do not occur at all is quite in accord with Pavlov's facts.

In delayed and trace reflexes the conditioning stimulus precedes the unconditioned. Pavlov states that no conditioning occurs if the stimulus to be made a conditioner follows the unconditioned stimulus. In a University of Washington experiment soon to be published something strongly resembling such "backward" conditioning was found with human subjects. The results of experiments on backward association suggest this also. This form of remote conditioning may also be in reality based upon simultaneous conditioning. No acts are instantaneous. Contracted muscles, through their own sense organs, tend to maintain their contraction. A new stimulus which follows the stimulus for a particular act may easily be simultaneous with the proprioceptive stimulation involved in the act itself, and hence become a conditioner of the act.

THE EFFECTS OF PRACTICE

Improvement as the result of practice is a familiar fact. The increased certainty of successful performance which results on repeated practice has led numerous psychologists to the notion that the attachment of a conditioning stimulus to its response is somehow increased by repetition of the sequence, which is a very different matter. Improvement demands more *detachment* of stimuli *from* responses than *attachment* of stimuli *to* responses. In order to improve in a performance the awkward, embarrassing, misdirected movements must be eliminated and replaced by movements which lead to a successful outcome. At the end of training the individual must be doing something quite different from what he was doing at the beginning of training.

The assumption that a stimulus-response sequence is made more certain by repetition has been embodied in a number of "laws of exercise" or "laws of frequency." It is quite possible, however, that the assumption is a mistaken one.

Pavlov's results in experiments in conditioning seem at first glance to indicate unambiguously that a conditioning stimulus is "established" by its repetition with a stimulus combination which elicits salivary flow, and to indicate that the "strength" or certainty and lasting quality of its establishment is a function of the number of occasions on which the two stimuli have been paired.

These experiments may be given a quite different interpretation. Conditioning, so far as elementary conditioning stimuli are concerned, may be an all-or-nothing affair, analogous to the setting of a switch, and not analogous to the wearing of a path, which has been a favorite simile. The increased certainty of response following on a given stimulus situation may involve an increase in the number of conditioners, rather than an increased "strength" of individual condition-

ers. In Pavlov's experiment, for instance, the bell signals results in extensive movements of orientation and postural adjustment, each movement causing appropriate stimulation to proprioceptors and exteroceptors. These movements are not identical each time the bell is struck because they depend in part on initial posture as well as on the bell. Repetition of the bell may enlist an increasing number of postural and other reflexes as conditioners of saliva flow, and hence gradually increase the certainty that salivary secretion will follow the bell.

It is entirely possible that if Pavlov could have controlled all stimuli instead of a very few, conditioning would be definitely established with one trial instead of fifty or more. The writer suggests that it is quite plausible that the more nearly such a complete control is established, the more nearly certain will be the result of the bell as a conditioner. Pavlov's whole method and experience suggest this.

The "strengthening" of a stimulus-response connection with repetition may very possibly be the result of the enlistment of increasing numbers of stimuli as conditioners, and not the result of the "strengthening" of individual connections.

FORGETTING

The conception of forgetting presented in the text-books has been that the effects of learning tend to be dissipated by some sort of physiological change at synapses which is a function of time. The form of the forgetting curve, though it differs for different sorts of material, indicates that forgetting is comparatively rapid when practice is discontinued and that the rate regularly diminishes.

There are some signs of a shift of opinion toward an explanation of forgetting in terms of conditioning. Hunter, in his article on learning in the recent volume of "The fundamentals of experimental psychology," quotes with approval the statement of Jenkins and Dallenbach in an article on "Obliviscence during sleep and waking" that "the results of our study as a whole indicate that forgetting is not so much a matter of decay of old impressions and associations as it is a matter of interference, inhibition, or obliteration of the old by the new."

The evidence that forgetting is to be explained in terms of new conditioning is of several kinds. Forgetting is radically affected by intervening activities. If the intervening situations are materially different from the practice situations forgetting is less evident than when a certain amount of similarity holds of the situations. Probably the stimuli which are repeated while new responses prevail lose their conditioning effect on their previous responses and become conditioners of the new responses, and consequently inhibitors of the original ones. Furthermore, forgetting during a period of sleep is less than forgetting during a period of waking activity. This seems to be readily explained in the same terms. The stimuli which had become conditioners of certain responses are not repeated during sleep, and have no chance to be alienated from their attachment to these responses. During a period of waking, multitudes of stimuli from postural adjustments, movements, or from exteroceptive sources, which had been made conditioners of the activities in question are components of new situations and become conditioners of new responses. If we accept evidence from outside the laboratory we may quote those instances of vivid and detailed memories conserved for many years, which would, incidentally, have depended on one conditioning occasion rather than a practice series. The occasion for the restoration of such memories is probably an unusually complete restoration of situation, usually aided by such an absence of present distraction and inhibition as is found when we are on the border of sleep. Marcel Proust has described a common experience in which a memory evoked while lying in bed with closed eyes has persisted until a change in posture dissipated it completely. Association *may* occur after one connection, and *may* last indefinitely.

If forgetting is to be explained as new conditioning which replaces the old, how is the form of the curve of forgetting to be explained? Is it not entirely possible that the increased uncertainty of a conditioned response to a stimulus situation is due to the progressive alienation of conditioners from their response, an alienation explained by their acquisition of new allegiances? The curves of forgetting may owe their shapes to the cumulative effect of this alienation. Since the bulk of the conditioners are probably proprioceptive, the result of the organism's own movements, the activities following on a given case of conditioning would alienate whole regiments of conditioners at the start and a decreasing number as time elapsed, because there would be a decreasing number to eliminate.

This statistical decrease in conditioners with time which is described by the forgetting curve would resemble, to use a frivolous illustration, the decreased expenditures of a certain artist whose method of protecting himself from starvation was to change the proceeds of his rare sales into dimes and broadcast these about his large and disordered studio. The following day dimes were retrieved easily in numbers. As time went on more and more search was required, though he seldom reached such a pass that an afternoon's search would not yield a dime.

These last faithful dimes resemble the last faithful conditioners which are indicated by the failure of forgetting curves to reach the zero point. The fact that some forgetting occurs during sleep may be due to the fact that some activity occurs during sleep, and hence some chance for the alienation of stimuli.

This conception of forgetting explains forgetting entirely in terms of new conditioning. It is, of course, not denied that there may be physiological changes like those in senility which do result in the deterioration of memory, but the normal occasion of forgetting is the alienation of cues following the occurrence of these cues at times when their conditioned responses are excluded by the general situation.

TEMPORARY EXTINCTION

Pavlov's temporary extinction and Dunlap's Beta law are also conceivable as instances of the general principle of conditioning. They might be described as forced forgetting.

When an established conditioner is repeated without the unconditioned stimulus, why should it quickly lose its conditioning power? Pavlov connects this loss with the brevity of the interval between applications. On his own showing this is not the determining factor. It is rather the *number of times the unsupported stimulus is repeated* that determines the extinction. Pavlov conceals this from himself by recording the results in terms of elapsed time from the start of the experiment. With short intervals, less elapsed time is required to extinguish, but in the case of both long and short intervals the number of applications is approximately the same.

If temporary extinction depends upon the number of times the conditioner is applied without support from the unconditioned stimulus, it is possible to explain temporary extinction in terms of the general principle of conditioning.

It should be noted, in the first place, that this temporary extinction or tendency to disappear with repetition is not an absolute generalization as it stands. It represents an exception to the rule of frequency. Sometimes one of these effects occurs, and sometimes the other. Obviously, in those cases in which temporary extinction prevails a special condition must have held. This special condition is probably what Pavlov asserts, the withdrawal of the unconditioned stimulus. It is the unconditioned stimulus that represents the most powerful determiner of the response. With the unconditioned stimulus withdrawn only occasional combinations of conditioners elicit the response, for it should be remembered that the animal is, in spite of sound-proof room and uniform lighting, in constant motion and subject to a continuously changing pattern of stimulation. At times there are more conditioners present, and at other times fewer. When the response fails, or is diminished because relatively few conditioners are present, these and other stimuli present become inhibitors, or, what is the same thing, conditioners of other responses.

There remains to be explained the reëstablishment of the conditioned response after a lapse of time. We have a hint toward this explanation in the fact that a sudden extraneous and unusual stimulus may cause the conditioned response to recover its original strength and certainty. It is possible that the inhibiting stimuli in this case include the somewhat specific details of posture and environment which hold during the process of extinction. A sudden interruption disorganizes posture and orientation, removes many recently conditioned inhibitors, and allows the original posture and conditioners to prevail again. The reflex is restored much as a baulky horse is startled out of his baulking, or a man who has built up an obstinate attitude may be shaken out of it by a sudden change in situation.

EMOTIONAL REINFORCEMENT AND DYNAMOGENESIS

Explanation of the facilitating effect of exciting emotion on learning cannot be complete until a satisfactory physiology of the emotions has appeared. In the meantime attention may be called to the fact that exciting emotion involves general muscular tonus, and may possibly consist very largely in such increase in general tension. The physiologists have described many types of muscle-to-muscle reflexes which are excited by muscular contraction, the stretching of a muscle, or resistance to the contraction of a muscle. Intense stimulation of one receptor field resulting in the contraction of a limited number of muscles results in the contraction of other muscle groups through such muscle-to-muscle reflexes. States of general tension may be built up by the "reverberation" of impulses in this fashion.

The origin of such states of general tension probably lies in intense stimulation of some receptor field, or in obstacles to free movement. In such states of general tension the acts which "go through" are more energetic and complete. They involve the stimulation of many proprioceptor systems which would be undisturbed by action not so energetic.

The increased stimulation would give opportunity for increased conditioners, especially since the excitement itself is subject to conditioned revival.

In what has been called "dynamogenesis" we have possibly two ways in which the irrelevant stimuli may facilitate learning. The new stimuli may serve to increase general tonus through the "reverberation" which has been described above and so serve to make action more vigorous and complete; and they may also, through the tendency to deflection which constitutes conditioning, serve to reinforce directly the prevailing responses.

IRRADIATION

What Pavlov describes as irradiation, namely, the acquisition of conditioning effect by neighboring receptors which were not stimulated in training, may well be the result of simple conditioning, instead of the result of a direct spread of an entirely speculative condition with an inexplicable delay to neighboring portions of the projection areas of the cortex. It has already been suggested that the bell signal is not the direct conditioner in any of Pavlov's experiments, especially when it is learned that by "simultaneous" presentation he usually means sounding the bell some two seconds before the food is presented. In two seconds many things may have happened. In direct response to the bell the dog "listens." The act of listening may be much the same whether the signal is a bell or a whistle of another pitch. Since the real conditioners of the salivary flow are the movements of listening, and not the bell, the whistle may result in salivary flow.

To a touch on the flank the dog responds by shifting his posture. This shift furnishes the conditioners of the glandular response. To a touch on a nearby point the response is a shift in posture involving much the same muscle groups as in the first case. To a touch on a more distant point the response will be different. The decreasing effect of stimulation of more remote areas may be the consequence of the decreasing likeness of the postural adjustment.

If we accept this much, Pavlov's experiments suggest the reason why "irradiation" decreases with practice, since it is explained that with practice there is an increasing tendency for listening movements or defensive postural adjustments to disappear and give place to the eating movements and the eating posture.

One feature of these experiments as reported in "Conditioned reflexes" remains unexplained. This is the statement that corresponding points on the two sides of the dog have exactly equal effect. Being unable to explain this, the writer may be forgiven for expressing some scepticism concerning the facts, which seem to have no analogue in human behavior.

PATTERNS

That we do respond to patterns as such is not open to question. And this would seem to involve the complete breakdown of any theory of conditioning such as is being presented, for at varying distances the actual receptors and afferent paths activated by a visual pattern must be quite distinct. The fact, indeed, cannot be questioned, though it should be noted that it is not a general or uniform occurrence. The child who has learned to read the raised letters on his blocks will not ordinarily recognize the letters when he sits on them. The effectiveness of patterns applies only within very limited fields.

Is it not entirely possible that the method by which we come to recognize a face at different distances as that of one and the same person is essentially the same method by which we come to recognize the rear aspect of this same person as his own back? In this case of recognition there is no question of similar patterns, for the back of his head resembles his face less than his face resembles the faces of others. If we maintain an attitude, or repeat a response to an object while that object is the occasion of shifting stimulation and of new stimulus patterns the maintained response may be conditioned on the new stimuli. Our response to a person at different distances is the same, with differences appropriate to the distance. Why may we not attribute this sameness and this difference to the samenesses and the differences originally present in the stimuli furnished by our original behavior in his presence?

If we accept conditioning as an explanation for responding appropriately to a person on hearing his footstep, which offers a stimulation pattern quite different from the visual pattern to which we previously responded, why should we consider it mysterious that the appropriate response could be called out by the stimulation of a quite different group of visual receptors? The fact that they have the same pattern is irrelevant.

The Gestalt psychologists assert not only that we respond in similar ways to similar patterns, which we undoubtedly do, but also that we do this *without any opportunity for conditioning,* which the writer does not at all believe. In the case of the hen which performed its trick using the eye which had been blindfolded during learning it is entirely possible that the cues for the proper movement were not primarily visual, but were furnished by movements connected with vision before the experiment was begun. Animals and man both have movements of skeletal muscles congenitally associated with vision. These movements may be in part identical for stimulation of either retina. If the act is conditioned on these movements, it might be elicited from either eye, without regard to which eye entered into practice.

INSIGHT

Concerning insight as described by the Gestalt psychologists the writer has much the same opinion as concerning response to patterns. The facts which are reported are not to be questioned and are typical of the behavior of the higher animals. An important part of the report has, however, been omitted. If the behavior described as insight is asserted to occur without previous learning, the essential part of the experiment would be the control of previous learning, and in the experiments the histories of insight are conspicuously lacking. No new category of facts concerning learning has been shown to be offered by the behavior described as insight.

In the writer's experience, insight in animals and in man is the result of accumulated habit. It was not a strange coincidence that the most ingenious person ever at work in the local laboratory has been a practical engineer for many years. When this member of the staff solved with little hesitation problems which had baffled the writer, there was a choice of explanations. It could be said that one man had insight and the other none, which seemed the poorer explanation; or it could be pointed out that one man had had previous training and the other none, an explanation much more charitable.

Summary and Comments

THIS paper has attempted to show that the main characteristics of learning, to wit, conditioning, inhibitory conditioning, remote conditioning, the effects of practice, forgetting, temporary extinction, emotional reinforcement, irradiation, response to patterns as such, and insight, may all be understood as instances of a very simple and very familiar principle, the ancient principle of association by contiguity in time. If the paper were not already too long many minor details which are readily described as instances of conditioning might be added. In their explanations of learning, Pavlov, the Gestalt psychologists, and many others have not examined sufficiently the possibilities of our proprioceptive sense organs in the role of determiners of behavior, and have tended to place the whole burden of explanation on highly speculative characteristics of the cerebral cortex.

This paper should be followed by some consideration of Lashley's work which appears to be at first sight a challenge to a general theory of conditioning. In the writer's opinion this work offers no objection whatever to the concept of conditioning. It does suggest that the simplest acts involve the stimulation of multitudes of receptors, the neglected proprioceptors among others, and the activation of multitudes of cortical pathways. As a single example it might be suggested that what appears to be a visual discrimination may actually be conditioned upon movements which are reflex responses to visual stimulation through subcortical paths. But a proper consideration of Lashley's work would require many pages.

EDWARD C. TOLMAN

24. *Cognitive Maps in Rats and Men*

I SHALL devote the body of this paper to a description of experiments with rats. But I shall also attempt in a few words at the close to indicate the significance of these findings on rats for the clinical behavior of men. Most of the rat investigations, which I shall report, were carried out in the Berkeley laboratory. But I shall also include, occasionally, accounts of the behavior of non-Berkeley rats who obviously have misspent their lives in out-of-State laboratories. Furthermore, in reporting our Berkeley experiments I shall have to omit a very great many. The ones I *shall* talk about were carried out by graduate students (or underpaid research assistants) who, supposedly, got some of their ideas from me. And a few, though a very few, were even carried out by me myself.

. . . In the typical experiment a hungry rat is put at the entrance of [a] maze (alley or elevated), and wanders about through the various true path segments and blind alleys until he finally comes to the food box and eats. This is repeated (again in the typical experiment) one trial every 24 hours and the animal tends to make fewer and fewer errors (that is, blind-alley entrances) and to take less and less time between start and goal-box until finally he is entering no blinds at all and running in a very few seconds from start to goal. The results are usually presented in the form of average curves of blind-entrances, or of seconds from start to finish, for groups of rats.

All students agree as to the facts. They disagree, however, on theory and explanation.

1. First, there is a school of animal psychologists which believes that the maze be-havior of rats is a matter of mere simple stimulus-response connections. Learning, according to them, consists in the strengthening of some of these connections and in the weakening of others. According to this "stimulus-response" school the rat in progressing down the maze is helplessly responding to a succession of external stimuli—sights, sounds, smells, pressures, etc. impinging upon his external sense organs—plus internal stimuli coming from the viscera and from the skeletal muscles. These external and internal stimuli call out the walkings, runnings, turnings, retracings, smellings, rearings, and the like which appear. The rat's central nervous system, according to this view, may be likened to a complicated telephone switchboard. There are the incoming calls from sense-organs and there are the outgoing messages to muscles. Before the learning of a specific maze, the connecting switches (synapses according to the physiologist) are closed in one set of ways and produce the primarily exploratory responses which appear in the early trials. *Learning,* according to this view, consists in the respective strengthening and weakening of various of these connections; those connections which result in the animal's going down the true path become relatively more open to the passage of nervous impulses, whereas those which lead him into the blinds become relatively less open.

It must be noted in addition, however, that this stimulus-response school divides further into two subgroups.

a. There is a subgroup which holds that the mere mechanics involved in the running of a maze is such that the crucial stimuli from

34th Annual Faculty Research Lecture, delivered at the University of California, Berkeley, March 17, 1947. Reprinted by permission of the American Psychological Association and the author's estate from the *Psychological Review*, 1948, vol. 55, pp. 189–208.

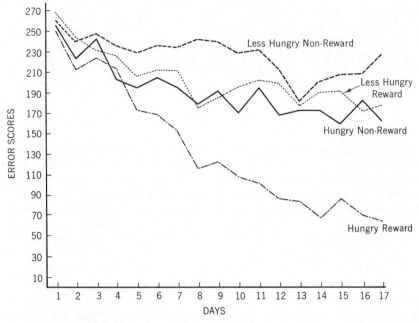

FIG. 1. Error curves for four groups, 36 rats. (From E. C. Tolman and C. H. Honzik, Degrees of hunger, reward and non-reward, and maze learning in rats. *Univ. Calif. Publ. Psychol.*, 1930, 4, No. 16, p. 246. [An] alley maze . . . was used.)

the maze get presented simultaneously with the correct responses more frequently than they do with any of the incorrect responses. Hence, just on a basis of this greater frequency, the neural connections between the crucial stimuli and the correct responses will tend, it is said, to get strengthened at the expense of the incorrect connections.

b. There is a second subgroup in this stimulus-response school which holds that the reason the appropriate connections get strengthened relatively to the inappropriate ones is, rather, the fact that the responses resulting from the correct connections are followed more closely in time by need-reductions. Thus a hungry rat in a maze tends to get to food and have his hunger reduced *sooner* as a result of the true path responses than as a result of the blind-alley responses. And such immediately following need-reductions or, to use another term, such "positive reinforcements" tend somehow, it is said, to strengthen the connections which have most closely preceded them. Thus it is as if—although this is certainly not the way this sub-

group would themselves state it—the satisfaction-receiving part of the rat telephoned back to Central and said to the girl: "Hold that connection; it was good; and see to it that you blankety-blank well use it again the next time these same stimuli come in." These theorists also assume (at least some of them do some of the time) that, if bad results— "annoyances," "negative reinforcements"— follow, then this same satisfaction-and-annoyance-receiving part of the rat will telephone back and say, "Break that connection and don't you dare use it next time either."

So much for a brief summary of the two subvarieties of the "stimulus-response," or telephone switchboard school.

2. Let us turn now to the second main school. This group (and I belong to them) may be called the field theorists. We believe that in the course of learning something like a field map of the environment gets established in the rat's brain. We agree with the other school that the rat in running a maze is exposed to stimuli and is finally led as a

result of these stimuli to the responses which actually occur. We feel, however, that the intervening brain processes are more complicated, more patterned and often, pragmatically speaking, more autonomous than do the stimulus-response psychologists. Although we admit that the rat is bombarded by stimuli, we hold that his nervous system is surprisingly selective as to which of these stimuli it will let in at any given time.

Secondly, we assert that the central office itself is far more like a map control room than it is like an old-fashioned telephone exchange. The stimuli, which are allowed in, are not connected by just simple one-to-one switches to the outgoing responses. Rather, the incoming impulses are usually worked over and elaborated in the central control room into a tentative, cognitive-like map of the environment. And it is this tentative map, indicating routes and paths and environmental relationships, which finally determines what responses, if any, the animal will finally release.

Finally, I, personally, would hold further that it is also important to discover in how far these maps are relatively narrow and strip-like or relatively broad and comprehensive. Both strip maps and comprehensive maps may be either correct or incorrect in the sense that they may (or may not), when acted upon, lead successfully to the animal's goal. The differences between such strip maps and such comprehensive maps will appear only when the rat is later presented with some change within the given environment. Then, the narrower and more strip-like the original map, the less will it carry over successfully to the new problem; whereas, the wider and the more comprehensive it was, the more adequately it will serve in the new set-up. In a strip-map the given position of the animal is connected by only a relatively simple and single path to the position of the goal. In a comprehensive-map a wider arc of the environment is represented, so that, if the starting position of the animal be changed or variations in the specific routes be introduced, this wider map will allow the animal still to behave relatively correctly and to choose the appropriate new route.

But let us turn, now, to the actual experiments. The ones, out of many, which I have selected to report are simply ones which seem especially important in reinforcing the theoretical position I have been presenting. This position, I repeat, contains two assumptions: First, that learning consists not in stimulus-response connections but in the building up in the nervous system of sets which function like cognitive maps, and second, that such cognitive maps may be usefully characterized as varying from a narrow strip variety to a broader comprehensive variety.

The experiments fall under five heads: (1) "latent learning," (2) "vicarious trial and error" or "VTE," (3) "searching for the stimulus," (4) "hypotheses" and (5) "spatial orientation."

"LATENT LEARNING" EXPERIMENTS

The first of the latent learning experiments was performed at Berkeley by Blodgett. It was published in 1929. Blodgett not only performed the experiments, he also originated the concept. He ran three groups of rats through a six-unit alley maze. . . . He had a control group and two experimental groups. The error curves for these groups appear in FIG. 2. The solid line shows the error curve for Group I, the control group. These animals were run in orthodox fashion. That is, they were run one trial a day and found food in the goal-box at the end of each trial. Groups II and III were the experimental groups. The animals of Group II, the dash line, were not fed in the maze for the first six days but only in their home cages some two hours later. On the seventh day (indicated by the small cross) the rats found food at the end of the maze for the first time and continued to find it on subsequent days. The animals of Group III were treated similarly except that they first found food at the end of the maze on the third day and continued to find it there on subsequent days. It will be observed that the experimental groups as long as they were not finding food did not appear to learn much. (Their error curves did not drop.) But on the days immediately succeeding their first finding of the food their error curves did drop astoundingly. It appeared, in short, that dur-

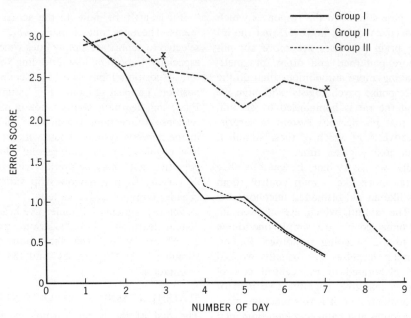

FIG. 2. (From H. C. Blodgett, The effect of the introduction of reward upon the maze performance of rats. *Univ. Calif. Publ. Psychol.,* 1929, 4, No. 8, p. 120.)

ing the non-rewarded trials these animals had been learning much more than they had exhibited. This learning, which did not manifest itself until after the food had been introduced, Blodgett called "latent learning." Interpreting these results anthropomorphically, we would say that as long as the animals were not getting any food at the end of the maze they continued to take their time in going through it—they continued to enter many blinds. Once, however, they knew they were to get food, they demonstrated that during these preceding non-rewarded trials they had learned where many of the blinds were. They had been building up a "map," and could utilize the latter as soon as they were motivated to do so.

Honzik and myself repeated the experiments (or rather he did and I got some of the credit) with . . . 14-unit T-mazes . . . , and with larger groups of animals, and got similar results. The resulting curves are shown in FIG. 3. We used two control groups—one that never found food in the maze (HNR) and one that found it throughout (HR). The experimental group (HNR–R) found food at the end of the maze from the 11th day on and showed the same sort of a sudden drop.

But probably the best experiment demonstrating latent learning was, unfortunately, done not in Berkeley but at the University of Iowa, by Spence and Lippitt. Only an abstract of this experiment has as yet been published. However, Spence has sent a preliminary manuscript from which the following account is summarized. A simple Y-maze . . . with two goal-boxes was used. Water was at the end of the right arm of the Y and food at the end of the left arm. During the training period the rats were run neither hungry nor thirsty. They were satiated for both food and water before each day's trials. However, they were willing to run because after each run they were taken out of whichever end box they had got to and put into a living cage, with other animals in it. They were given four trials a day in this fashion for seven days, two trials to the right and two to the left.

In the crucial test the animals were divided into two subgroups one made solely hungry and one solely thirsty. It was then found that on the first trial the hungry group went at once to the left, where the food had been, statistically more frequently than to the right;

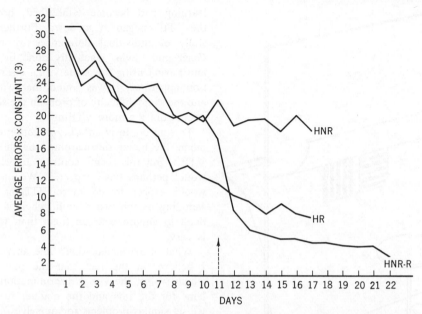

FIG. 3.   Error curves for HR, HNR, and HNR–R. (From E. C. Tolman and C. H. Honzik, Introduction and removal of reward, and maze performance in rats. *Univ. Calif. Publ. Psychol.*, 1930, 4, No. 19, p. 267.)

and the thirsty group went to the right, where the water had been, statistically more frequently than to the left. These results indicated that under the previous non-differential and very mild rewarding conditions of merely being returned to the home cages the animals had nevertheless been learning where the water was and where the food was. In short, they had acquired a cognitive map to the effect that food was to the left and water to the right, although during the acquisition of this map they had not exhibited any stimulus-response propensities to go more to the side which became later the side of the appropriate goal.

There have been numerous other latent learning experiments done in the Berkeley laboratory and elsewhere. In general, they have for the most part all confirmed the above sort of findings.

Let us turn now to the second group of experiments.

"VICARIOUS TRIAL AND ERROR"
OR "VTE"

The term Vicarious Trial and Error (abbreviated as VTE) was invented by Prof. Muenz-

inger at Colorado [1] to designate the hesitating, looking-back-and-forth, sort of behavior which rats can often be observed to indulge in at a choice-point before actually going one way or the other.

Quite a number of experiments upon VTE-ing have been carried out in our laboratory. I shall report only a few. In most of them what is called a discrimination set-up has been used. In one characteristic type of visual discrimination apparatus designed by Lashley (shown in FIG. 4) the animal is put on a jumping stand and faced with two doors which differ in some visual property say, as here shown, vertical stripes vs. horizontal stripes.

One of each such pair of visual stimuli is made always correct and the other wrong; and the two are interchanged from side to side in random fashion. The animal is required to learn, say, that the vertically striped door is always the correct one. If he jumps to it, the door falls open and he gets to food

1 *Vide:* K. F. Muenzinger, Vicarious trial and error at a point of choice: I. A general survey of its relation to learning efficiency. *J. genet. Psychol.*, 1938, 53, 75–86.

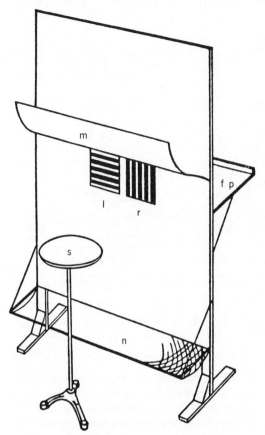

FIG. 4. Apparatus used for testing discrimination of visual patterns. (From K. S. Lashley, The mechanism of vision. I. A method for rapid analyses of pattern-vision in the rat. *J. genet. Psychol.*, 1930, 37, p. 454.)

on a platform behind. If, on the other hand, he jumps incorrectly, he finds the door locked and falls into a net some two feet below from which he is picked up and started over again.

Using a similar set-up . . . , but with landing platforms in front of the doors so that if the rat chose incorrectly he could jump back again and start over, I found that when the choice was an easy one, say between a white door and a black door, the animals not only learned sooner but also did more VTEing than when the choice was difficult, say between a white door and a gray door (see FIG. 5). It appeared further (see FIG. 6) that the VTEing began to appear just as (or just before) the rats began to learn. After the

learning had become established, however, the VTE's began to go down. Further, in a study of individual differences by myself, Geier and Levin [2] (actually done by Geier and Levin) using this same visual discrimination apparatus, it was found that with one and the same difficulty of problem the smarter animal did the more VTEing.

To sum up, in *visual discrimination* experiments the better the learning, the more the VTE's. But this seems contrary to what we would perhaps have expected. We ourselves would expect to do more VTEing, more sampling of the two stimuli, when it is difficult to choose between them than when it is easy.

What is the explanation? The answer lies, I believe, in the fact that the manner in which we set the visual discrimination problems for the rats and the manner in which we set similar problems for ourselves are different. *We* already have our "instructions." We know beforehand what it is we are to do. We are told, or we tell ourselves, that it is the lighter of the two grays, the heavier of the two weights, or the like, which is to be chosen. In such a setting we do more sampling, more VTEing, when the stimulus-difference is small. But for the rats the usual problem in a discrimination apparatus is quite different. They do not know what is wanted of them. The major part of their learning in most such experiments seems to consist in their discovering the instructions. The rats have to discover that it is the differences in visual brightness, not the differences between left and right, which they are to pay attention to. Their VTEing appears when they begin to "catch on." The greater the difference between the two stimuli the more the animals are attracted by this difference. Hence the sooner they catch on, and during this catching on, the more they VTE.

That this is a reasonable interpretation appeared further, from an experiment by myself and Minium (the actual work done, of course, by Minium) in which a group of six rats was

2 F. M. Geier, M. Levin & E. C. Tolman, Individual differences in emotionality, hypothesis formation, vicarious trial and error and visual discrimination learning in rats. *Compar. Psychol. Monogr.*, 1941, 17, No. 3.

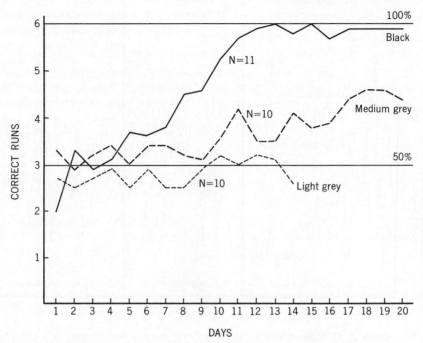

FIG. 5. Learning curves: average number of correct runs per day. (From E. C. Tolman, Prediction of vicarious trial and error by means of the schematic sowbug. *Psychol. Rev.,* 1939, 46, p. 319.)

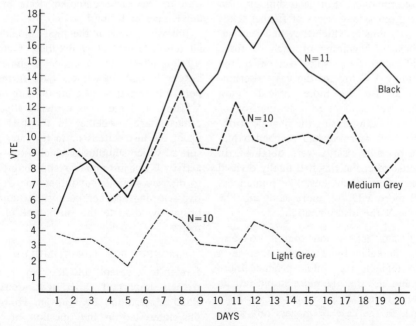

FIG. 6. Average number of VTE's per day. (From E. C. Tolman, Prediction of vicarious trial and error by means of the schematic sowbug. *Psychol. Rev.,* 1939, 46, p. 320.)

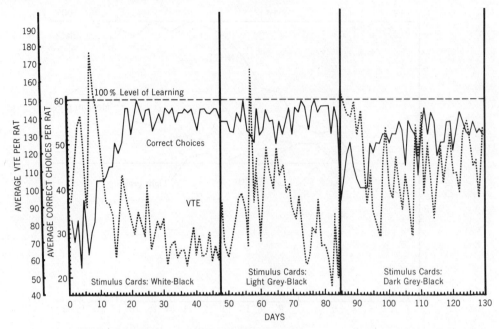

FIG. 7. (From E. C. Tolman and E. Minium, VTE in rats: overlearning and difficulty of discrimination. *J. comp. Psychol.*, 1942, 34, p. 303.)

first taught a white vs. black discrimination, then two successively more difficult gray vs. black discriminations. For each difficulty the rats were given a long series of further trials beyond the points at which they had learned. Comparing the beginning of each of these three difficulties the results were that the rats did more VTEing for the easy discriminations than for the more difficult ones. When, however, it came to a comparison of amounts of VTEing during the final performance after each learning had reached a plateau, the opposite results were obtained. In other words, after the rats had finally divined their instructions, then they, like human beings, did more VTEing, more sampling, the more difficult the discrimination.

Finally, now let us note that it was also found at Berkeley by Jackson [3] that in a maze the difficult maze units produce more VTEing and also that the more stupid rats do the more VTEing. The explanation, as I see it, is that, in the case of mazes, rats know

[3] L. L. Jackson, V. T. E. on an elevated maze. *J. comp. Psychol.*, 1943, 36, 99–107.

their instructions. For them it is natural to expect that the same spatial path will always lead to the same outcome. Rats in mazes don't have to be told.

But what, now, is the final significance of all this VTEing? How do these facts about VTEing affect our theoretical argument? My answer is that these facts lend further support to the doctrine of a building up of maps. VTEing, as I see it, is evidence that in the critical stages—whether in the first picking up of the instructions or in the later making sure of which stimulus is which—the animal's activity is not just one of responding passively to discrete stimuli, but rather one of the active selecting and comparing of stimuli. This brings me then to the third type of experiment.

"SEARCHING FOR THE STIMULUS"

I refer to a recent, and it seems to me extremely important experiment, done for a Ph.D. dissertation by Hudson. Hudson was first interested in the question of whether or not rats could learn an avoidance reaction in one trial. His animals were tested one at

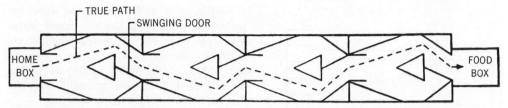

TRUE PATH
SWINGING DOOR
HOME BOX
FOOD BOX

FIG. 8. (From I. Krechevsky [now D. Krech], The genesis of "hypotheses" in rats. *Univ. Calif. Publ. Psychol.*, 1932, 6, No. 4, p. 46.)

a time in a living cage . . . with a small striped visual pattern at the end, on which was mounted a food cup. The hungry rat approached this food cup and ate. An electrical arrangement was provided so that when the rat touched the cup he could be given an electric shock. And one such shock did appear to be enough. For when the rat was replaced in this same cage days or even weeks afterwards, he usually demonstrated immediately strong avoidance reactions to the visual pattern. The animal withdrew from that end of the cage, or piled up sawdust and covered the pattern, or showed various other amusing responses all of which were in the nature of withdrawing from the pattern or making it disappear.

But the particular finding which I am interested in now appeared as a result of a modification of this standard procedure. Hudson noticed that the animals, anthropomorphically speaking, often seemed to look around *after* the shock to see what it was that had hit them. Hence it occurred to him that, if the pattern were made to disappear the instant the shock occurred, the rats might not establish the association. And this indeed is what happened in the case of many individuals. Hudson added further electrical connections so that when the shock was received during the eating, the lights went out, the pattern and the food cup dropped out of sight, and the lights came on again all within the matter of a second. When such animals were again put in the cage 24 hours later, a large percentage showed no avoidance of the pattern. Or to quote Hudson's own words:

Learning what object to avoid . . . may occur exclusively during the period *after* the shock. For if the object from which the shock was ac-

tually received is removed at the moment of the shock, a significant number of animals fail to learn to avoid it, some selecting other features in the environment for avoidance, and others avoiding nothing.

In other words, I feel that this experiment reinforces the notion of the largely active selective character in the rat's building up of his cognitive map. He often has to look actively for the significant stimuli in order to form his map and does not merely passively receive and react to all the stimuli which are physically present.

Turn now to the fourth type of experiment.

THE "HYPOTHESIS" EXPERIMENTS

Both the notion of hypotheses in rats and the design of the experiments to demonstrate such hypotheses are to be credited to Krech. Krech used a four-compartment discrimination-box. In such a four-choice box the correct door at each choice-point may be determined by the experimenter in terms of its being lighted or dark, left or right, or various combinations of these. If all possibilities are randomized for the 40 choices made in 10 runs of each day's test, the problem could be made insoluble.

When this was done, Krech found that the individual rat went through a succession of systematic choices. That is, the individual animal might perhaps begin by choosing practically all right-hand doors, then he might give this up for choosing practically all left-hand doors, and then, for choosing all dark doors, and so on. These relatively persistent, and well-above-chance systematic types of choice Krech called "hypotheses." In using this term he obviously did not mean to imply verbal processes in the rat but merely referred to what I have been calling cogni-

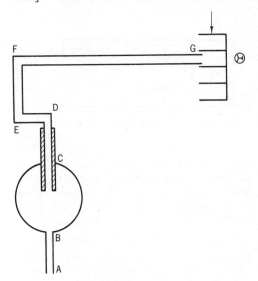

FIG. 9. Apparatus used in preliminary training. (From E. C. Tolman, B. F. Ritchie and D. Kalish, Studies in spatial learning. I. Orientation and the short-cut. *J. exp. Psychol.*, 1946, 36, p. 16.)

tive maps which, it appears from his experiments, get set up in a tentative fashion to be tried out first one and then another until, if possible, one is found which works.

Finally, it is to be noted that these hypothesis experiments, like the latent learning, VTE, and "looking for the stimulus" experiments, do not, as such, throw light upon the widths of the maps which are picked up but do indicate the generally map-like and self-initiated character of learning.

For the beginning of an attack upon the problem of the width of the maps let me turn to the last group of experiments.

"SPATIAL ORIENTATION" EXPERIMENTS

As early as 1929, Lashley reported incidentally the case of a couple of his rats who, after having learned an alley maze, pushed back the cover near the starting box, climbed out and ran directly across the top to the goal-box where they climbed down in again and ate. Other investigators have reported related findings. All such observations suggest that rats really develop wider spatial maps which include more than the mere trained-on specific paths. In the experiments now to be reported this possibility has been subjected to further examination.

In the first experiment, Tolman, Ritchie and Kalish (actually Ritchie and Kalish) used the set-up shown in FIG. 9.

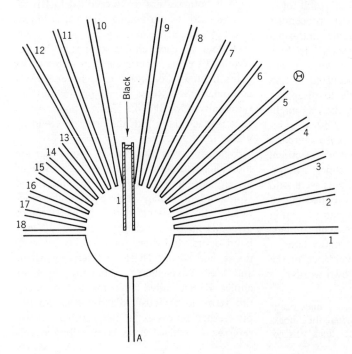

FIG. 10. Apparatus used in the test trial. (From E. C. Tolman, B. F. Ritchie and D. Kalish, Studies in spatial learning. I. Orientation and short-cut. *J. exp. Psychol.*, 1946, 36, p. 17.)

This was an elevated maze. The animals ran from A across the open circular table through CD (which had alley walls) and finally to G, the food box. H was a light which shone directly down the path from G to F. After four nights, three trials per night, in which the rats learned to run directly and without hesitation from A to G, the apparatus was changed to the sun-burst shown in FIG. 10. The starting path and the table remained the same but a series of radiating paths was added.

The animals were again started at A and ran across the circular table into the alley and found themselves blocked. They then returned onto the table and began exploring practically all the radiating paths. After going out a few inches only on any one path, each rat finally chose to run all the way out on one. The percentages of rats finally choosing each of the long paths from 1 to 12 are shown in FIG. 11. It appears that there was a preponderant tendency to choose path No. 6 which ran to a point some four inches in front of where the entrance to the food-box had been. The only other path chosen with any appreciable frequency was No. 1—that is, the path which pointed perpendicularly to the food-side of the room.

These results seem to indicate that the rats in this experiment had learned not only to run rapidly down the original roundabout route but also, when this was blocked and radiating paths presented, to select one pointing rather directly towards the point where the food had been or else at least to select a path running perpendicularly to the food-side of the room.

As a result of their original training, the rats had, it would seem, acquired not merely a strip-map to the effect that the original specifically trained-on path led to food but, rather, a wider comprehensive map to the effect that food was located in such and such a direction in the room.

Consider now a further experiment done by Ritchie alone. This experiment tested still further the breadth of the spatial map which is acquired. In this further experiment the rats were again run across the table—this time to the arms of a simple T. (See FIG. 12.)

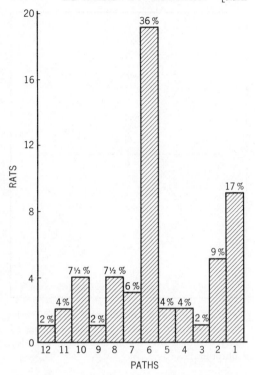

FIG. 11. Numbers of rats which chose each of the paths. (From E. C. Tolman, B. F. Ritchie and D. Kalish, Studies in spatial learning. I. Orientation and the short-cut. *J. exp. Psychol.*, 1946, 36, p. 19.)

Twenty-five animals were trained for seven days, 20 trials in all, to find food at F_1; and twenty-five animals were trained to find it at F_2. The L's in the diagram indicate lights. On the eighth day the starting path and table top were rotated through 180 degrees so that they were now in the position shown in FIG. 13. The dotted lines represent the old position. And a series of radiating paths was added. What happened? Again the rats ran across the table into the central alley. When, however, they found themselves blocked, they turned back onto the table and this time also spent many seconds touching and trying out for only a few steps practically all the paths. Finally, however, within seven minutes, 42 of the 50 rats chose one path and ran all the way out on it. The paths finally chosen by the 19 of these animals that had been fed at F_1 and by the 23 that had been fed at F_2 are shown in FIG. 14.

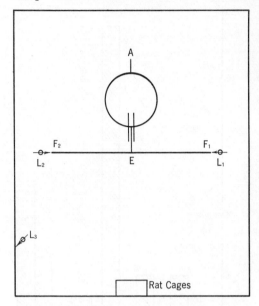

FIG. 12. (From B. F. Ritchie. Ph.D. Thesis: "Spatial learning in rats." On deposit in the Library of the University of California, Berkeley, California.)

FIG. 13. (From B. F. Ritchie. Ph.D. Thesis: "Spatial learning in rats." On deposit in the Library of the University of California, Berkeley, California.)

This time the rats tended to choose, not the paths which pointed directly to the spots where the food had been, but rather paths which ran perpendicularly to the corresponding sides of the room. The spatial maps of these rats, when the animals were started from the opposite side of the room, were thus not completely adequate to the precise goal positions but were adequate as to the correct sides of the room. The maps of these animals were, in short, not altogether strip-like and narrow.

This completes my report of experiments. There were the *latent learning experiments,* the *VTE experiments,* the *searching for the stimulus experiment,* the *hypothesis experiments,* and these last *spatial orientation experiments.*

And now, at last, I come to the humanly significant and exciting problem: namely, what are the conditions which favor narrow strip-maps and what are those which tend to favor broad comprehensive maps not only in rats but also in men?

There is considerable evidence scattered throughout the literature bearing on this question both for rats and for men. Some of this evidence was obtained in Berkeley and some of it elsewhere. I have not time to present it in any detail. I can merely summarize it by saying that narrow strip maps rather than broad comprehensive maps seem to be induced: (1) by a damaged brain, (2) by an inadequate array of environmentally presented cues, (3) by an overdose of repetitions on the original trained-on path and (4) by the presence of too strongly motivational or of too strongly frustrating conditions.

It is this fourth factor which I wish to elaborate upon briefly in my concluding remarks. For it is going to be my contention that some, at least, of the so-called "psychological mechanisms" which the clinical psychologists and the other students of personality have uncovered as the devils underlying many of our individual and social maladjustments can be interpreted as narrowings of our cognitive maps due to too strong motivations or to too intense frustration.

My argument will be brief, cavalier, and dogmatic. For I am not myself a clinician or

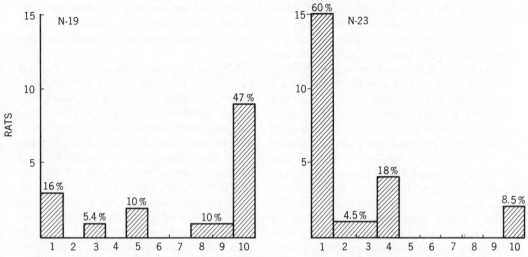

FIG. 14. Paths chosen by rats in the F_1 (left) and F_2 (right) groups. (From B. F. Ritchie. Ph.D. Thesis: "Spatial learning in rats." On deposit in the Library of the University of California, Berkeley, California.)

a social psychologist. What I am going to say must be considered, therefore, simply as in the nature of a *rat* psychologist's *rat*iocinations offered free.

By way of illustration, let me suggest that at least the three dynamisms called, respectively, "regression," "fixation," and "displacement of aggression onto outgroups" are expressions of cognitive maps which are too narrow and which get built up in us as a result of too violent motivation or of too intense frustration.

(a) Consider *regression*. This is the term used for those cases in which an individual, in the face of too difficult a problem, returns to earlier more childish ways of behaving. Thus, to take an example, the overprotected middle-aged woman (reported a couple of years ago in *Time Magazine*) who, after losing her husband, regressed (much to the distress of her growing daughters) into dressing in too youthful a fashion and into competing for her beaux and then finally into behaving like a child requiring continuous care, would be an illustration of regression. I would not wish you to put too much confidence in the reportorial accuracy of *Time,* but such an extreme case is not too different from many actually to be found in our mental hospitals or even sometimes in ourselves. In all

such instances my argument would be (1) that such regression results from too strong a present emotional situation and (2) that it consists in going back to too narrow an earlier map, itself due to too much frustration or motivation in early childhood. *Time's* middle-aged woman was presented by too frustrating an emotional situation at her husband's death and she regressed, I would wager, to too narrow adolescent and childhood maps since these latter had been originally excessively impressed because of overstressful experiences at the time she was growing up.

(b) Consider *fixation*. Regression and fixation tend to go hand in hand. For another way of stating the fact of the undue persistence of early maps is to say that they were fixated. This has even been demonstrated in rats. If rats are too strongly motivated in their original learning, they find it very difficult to relearn when the original path is no longer correct. Also after they have relearned, if they are given an electric shock they, like *Time's* woman, tend to regress back again to choosing the earlier path.

(c) Finally, consider the *"displacement of aggressions onto outgroups."* Adherence to one's own group is an ever-present tendency among primates. It is found in chimpanzees and monkeys as strongly as in men. We primates operate in groups. And each individual in such a group tends to identify with his whole group in the sense that the group's goals become his goals, the group's life and immortality, his life and immortality. Furthermore, each individual soon learns that, when as an individual he is frustrated, he must not take out his aggressions on the other members of his own group. He learns instead to displace his aggressions onto outgroups. Such a displacement of aggression I would claim is also a narrowing of the cognitive map. The individual comes no longer to distinguish the true locus of the cause of his frustration. The poor Southern whites, who take it out on the Negroes, are displacing their aggressions from the landlords, the southern economic system, the northern capitalists, or wherever the true cause of their frustration may lie, onto a mere convenient outgroup. The physicists on the Faculty who criticize the humanities, or we psychologists who criticize all the other departments, or the University as a whole which criticizes the Secondary School system or, vice versa, the Secondary School system which criticizes the University—or, on a still larger and far more dangerous scene—we Americans who criticize the Russians and the Russians who criticize us, are also engaging, at least in part, in nothing more than such irrational displacements of our aggressions onto outgroups.

I do not mean to imply that there may not be some true interferences by the one group with the goals of the other and hence that the aggressions of the members of the one group against the members of the other are necessarily *wholly* and *merely* displaced aggressions. But I do assert that often and in large part they are such mere displacements.

Over and over again men are blinded by too violent motivations and too intense frustrations into blind and unintelligent and in the end desperately dangerous hates of outsiders. And the expression of these their displaced hates ranges all the way from discrimination against minorities to world conflagrations.

What in the name of Heaven and Psychology can we do about it? My only answer is to preach again the virtues of reason—of, that is, broad cognitive maps. And to suggest that the child-trainers and the world-planners of the future can only, if at all, bring about the presence of the required rationality (*i.e.*, comprehensive maps) if they see to it that nobody's children are too over-motivated or too frustrated. Only then can these children learn to look before and after, learn to see that there are often round-about and safer paths to their quite proper goals—learn, that is, to realize that the well-beings of White and of Negro, of Catholic and of Protestant, of Christian and of Jew, of American and of Russian (and even of males and females) are mutually interdependent.

We dare not let ourselves or others become so over-emotional, so hungry, so ill-clad, so over-motivated that only narrow strip-maps will be developed. All of us in Europe as well as in America, in the Orient as well as in the Occident, must be made calm enough and well-fed enough to be able to develop truly comprehensive maps, or, as Freud would have put it, to be able to learn to live according to the Reality Principle rather than according to the too narrow and too immediate Pleasure Principle.

We must, in short, subject our children and ourselves (as the kindly experimenter would his rats) to the optimal conditions of moderate motivation and of an absence of unnecessary frustrations, whenever we put them and ourselves before that great God-given maze which is our human world. I cannot predict whether or not we will be able, or be allowed, to do this; but I *can* say that, only insofar as we *are* able and *are* allowed, have we cause for hope.

B. F. SKINNER

25. *Are Theories of Learning Necessary?*

ERTAIN basic assumptions, essential to any scientific activity, are sometimes called theories. That nature is orderly rather than capricious is an example. Certain statements are also theories simply to the extent that they are not yet facts. A scientist may guess at the result of an experiment before the experiment is carried out. The prediction and the later statement of result may be composed of the same terms in the same syntactic arrangement, the difference being in the degree of confidence. No empirical statement is wholly nontheoretical in this sense, because evidence is never complete, nor is any prediction probably ever made wholly without evidence. The term "theory" will not refer here to statements of these sorts but rather to any explanation of an observed fact which appeals to events taking place somewhere else, at some other level of observation, described in different terms, and measured, if at all, in different dimensions.

Three types of theory in the field of learning satisfy this definition. The most characteristic is to be found in the field of physiological psychology. We are all familiar with the changes that are supposed to take place in the nervous system when an organism learns. Synaptic connections are made or broken, electrical fields are disrupted or reorganized, concentrations of ions are built up or allowed to diffuse away, and so on. In the science of neurophysiology statements of this sort are not necessarily theories in the present sense. But in a science of behavior, where we are concerned with whether or not an organism secretes saliva when a bell rings, or jumps toward a gray triangle, or says *bik* when a card reads *tuz*, or loves someone who resembles his mother, all statements about the nervous system are theories in the sense that they are not expressed in the same terms and could not be confirmed with the same methods of observation as the facts for which they are said to account.

A second type of learning theory is in practice not far from the physiological, although there is less agreement about the method of direct observation. Theories of this type have always dominated the field of human behavior. They consist of references to "mental" events, as in saying that an organism learns to behave in a certain way because it "finds something pleasant" or because it "expects something to happen." To the mentalistic psychologist these explanatory events are no more theoretical than synaptic connections to the neurophysiologist, but in a science of behavior they are theories because the methods and terms appropriate to the events to be explained differ from the methods and terms appropriate to the explaining events.

In a third type of learning theory the explanatory events are not directly observed. The writer's suggestion that the letters CNS be regarded as representing, not the Central Nervous System, but the Conceptual Nervous System (2, p. 421), seems to have been taken seriously. Many theorists point out that they are not talking about the nervous system as an actual structure undergoing physiological or bio-chemical changes but only as a system with a certain dynamic output. Theories of this sort are multiplying fast, and so are par-

Address of the president, Midwestern Psychological Association, Chicago, Illinois, May, 1949. Reprinted by permission of the American Psychological Association and the author from the *Psychological Review*, 1950, vol. 57, pp. 193–216.

allel operational versions of mental events. A purely behavioral definition of expectancy has the advantage that the problem of mental observation is avoided and with it the problem of how a mental event can cause a physical one. But such theories do not go so far as to assert that the explanatory events are identical with the behavioral facts which they purport to explain. A statement about behavior may support such a theory but will never resemble it in terms or syntax. Postulates are good examples. True postulates cannot become facts. Theorems may be deduced from them which, as tentative statements about behavior, may or may not be confirmed, but theorems are not theories in the present sense. Postulates remain theories until the end.

It is not the purpose of this paper to show that any of these theories cannot be put in good scientific order, or that the events to which they refer may not actually occur or be studied by appropriate sciences. It would be foolhardy to deny the achievements of theories of this sort in the history of science. The question of whether they are necessary, however, has other implications and is worth asking. If the answer is no, then it may be possible to argue effectively against theory in the field of learning. A science of behavior must eventually deal with behavior in its relation to certain manipulable variables. Theories—whether neural, mental, or conceptual—talk about intervening steps in these relationships. But instead of prompting us to search for and explore relevant variables, they frequently have quite the opposite effect. When we attribute behavior to a neural or mental event, real or conceptual, we are likely to forget that we still have the task of accounting for the neural or mental event. When we assert that an animal acts in a given way because it expects to receive food, then what began as the task of accounting for learned behavior becomes the task of accounting for expectancy. The problem is at least equally complex and probably more difficult. We are likely to close our eyes to it and to use the theory to give us answers in place of the answers we might find through further study.

It might be argued that the principal function of learning theory to date has been, not to suggest appropriate research, but to create a false sense of security, an unwarranted satisfaction with the *status quo*.

Research designed with respect to theory is also likely to be wasteful. That a theory generates research does not prove its value unless the research is valuable. Much useless experimentation results from theories, and much energy and skill are absorbed by them. Most theories are eventually overthrown, and the greater part of the associated research is discarded. This could be justified if it were true that productive research requires a theory, as is, of course, often claimed. It is argued that research would be aimless and disorganized without a theory to guide it. The view is supported by psychological texts that take their cue from the logicians rather than empirical science and describe thinking as necessarily involving stages of hypothesis, deduction, experimental test, and confirmation. But this is not the way most scientists actually work. It is possible to design significant experiments for other reasons and the possibility to be examined is that such research will lead more directly to the kind of information that a science usually accumulates.

The alternatives are at least worth considering. How much can be done without theory? What other sorts of scientific activity are possible? And what light do alternative practices throw upon our present preoccupation with theory?

It would be inconsistent to try to answer these questions at a theoretical level. Let us therefore turn to some experimental material in three areas in which theories of learning now flourish and raise the question of the function of theory in a more concrete fashion.[1]

---

1 Some of the material that follows was obtained in 1941–42 in a cooperative study on the behavior of the pigeon in which Keller Breland, Norman Guttman, and W. K. Estes collaborated. Some of it is selected from subsequent, as yet unpublished, work on the pigeon conducted by the author at Indiana University and Harvard University. Limitations of space make it impossible to report full details here.

The Basic Datum in Learning

WHAT actually happens when an organism learns is not an easy question. Those who are interested in a science of behavior will insist that learning is a change in behavior, but they tend to avoid explicit references to responses or acts as such. "Learning is adjustment, or adaptation to a situation." But of what stuff are adjustments and adaptations made? Are they data, or inferences from data? "Learning is improvement." But improvement in what? And from whose point of view? "Learning is restoration of equilibrium." But what is in equilibrium and how is it put there? "Learning is problem solving." But what are the physical dimensions of a problem—or of a solution? Definitions of this sort show an unwillingness to take what appears before the eyes in a learning experiment as a basic datum. Particular observations seem too trivial. An error score falls; but we are not ready to say that this is learning rather than merely the result of learning. An organism meets a criterion of ten successful trials; but an arbitrary criterion is at variance with our conception of the generality of the learning process.

This is where theory steps in. If it is not the time required to get out of a puzzle box that changes in learning, but rather the strength of a bond, or the conductivity of a neural pathway, or the excitatory potential of a habit, then problems seem to vanish. Getting out of a box faster and faster is not learning; it is merely performance. The learning goes on somewhere else, in a different dimensional system. And although the time required depends upon arbitrary conditions, often varies discontinuously, and is subject to reversals of magnitude, we feel sure that the learning process itself is continuous, orderly, and beyond the accidents of measurement. Nothing could better illustrate the use of theory as a refuge from the data.

But we must eventually get back to an observable datum. If learning is the process we suppose it to be, then it must appear so in the situations in which we study it. Even if the basic process belongs to some other

dimensional system, our measures must have relevant and comparable properties. But productive experimental situations are hard to find, particularly if we accept certain plausible restrictions. To show an orderly change in the behavior of the *average* rat or ape or child is not enough, since learning is a process in the behavior of the individual. To record the beginning and end of learning or a few discrete steps will not suffice, since a series of cross-sections will not give complete coverage of a continuous process. The dimensions of the change must spring from the behavior itself; they must not be imposed by an external judgment of success or failure or an external criterion of completeness. But when we review the literature with these requirements in mind, we find little justification for the theoretical process in which we take so much comfort.

The energy level or work-output of behavior, for example, does not change in appropriate ways. In the sort of behavior adapted to the Pavlovian experiment (respondent behavior) there may be a progressive increase in the magnitude of response during learning. But we do not shout our responses louder and louder as we learn verbal material, nor does a rat press a lever harder and harder as conditioning proceeds. In operant behavior the energy or magnitude of response changes significantly only when some arbitrary value is differentially reinforced—when such a change is what is learned.

The emergence of a right response in competition with wrong responses is another datum frequently used in the study of learning. The maze and the discrimination box yield results which may be reduced to these terms. But a behavior-ratio of right *vs.* wrong cannot yield a continuously changing measure in a single experiment on a single organism. The point at which one response takes precedence over another cannot give us the whole history of the change in either response. Averaging curves for groups of trials or organisms will not solve this problem.

Increasing attention has recently been given to latency, the relevance of which, like that

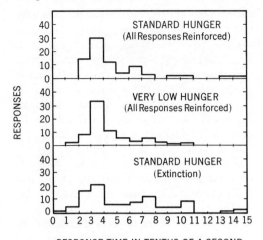

FIG. 1

ing behavior. The rat eventually stays near and facing the door. The resulting shorter starting-time is not due to a reduction in the latency of a response, but to the conditioning of favorable preliminary behavior.

Latencies in a single organism do not follow a simple learning process. Relevant data on this point were obtained as part of an extensive study of reaction time. A pigeon, enclosed in a box, is conditioned to peck at a recessed disc in one wall. Food is presented as reinforcement by exposing a hopper through a hole below the disc. If responses are reinforced only after a stimulus has been presented, responses at other times disappear. Very short reaction times are obtained by differentially reinforcing responses which occur very soon after the stimulus (4). But responses also come to be made very quickly without differential reinforcement. Inspection shows that this is due to the development of effective waiting. The bird comes to stand before the disc with its head in good striking position. Under optimal conditions, without differential reinforcement, the mean time between stimulus and response will be of the order of ⅓ sec. This is not a true reflex latency, since the stimulus is discriminative rather than eliciting, but it is a fair example of the latency used in the study of learning. The point is that this measure does not vary continuously or in an orderly fashion. By giving the bird more food, for example, we induce a condition in which it does not always respond. But the responses that occur show approximately the same temporal relation to the stimulus (FIG. 1, middle curve). In extinction, of special interest here, there is a scattering of latencies because lack of reinforcement generates an emotional condition. Some responses occur sooner and others are delayed, but the commonest value remains unchanged (bottom curve in FIG. 1). The longer latencies are easily explained by inspection. Emotional behavior, of which examples will be mentioned later, is likely to be in progress when the ready-signal is presented. It is often not discontinued before the "go" signal is presented, and the result is a long starting-time. Cases also begin to appear in which the bird simply does not re-

of energy level, is suggested by the properties of conditioned and unconditioned reflexes. But in operant behavior the relation to a stimulus is different. A measure of latency involves other considerations, as inspection of any case will show. Most operant responses may be emitted in the absence of what is regarded as a relevant stimulus. In such a case the response is likely to appear before the stimulus is presented. It is no solution to escape this embarrassment by locking a lever so that an organism cannot press it until the stimulus is presented, since we can scarcely be content with temporal relations that have been forced into compliance with our expectations. Runway latencies are subject to this objection. In a typical experiment the door of a starting box is opened and the time that elapses before a rat leaves the box is measured. Opening the door is not only a stimulus, it is a change in the situation that makes the response possible for the first time. The time measured is by no means as simple as a latency and requires another formulation. A great deal depends upon what the rat is doing at the moment the stimulus is presented. Some experimenters wait until the rat is facing the door, but to do so is to tamper with the measurement being taken. If, on the other hand, the door is opened without reference to what the rat is doing, the first major effect is the conditioning of favorable wait-

spond at all during a specified time. If we average a large number of readings, either from one bird or many, we may create what looks like a progressive lengthening of latency. But the data for an individual organism do not show a continuous process.

Another datum to be examined is the rate at which a response is emitted. Fortunately the story here is different. We study this rate by designing a situation in which a response may be freely repeated, choosing a response (for example, touching or pressing a small lever or key) that may be easily observed and counted. The responses may be recorded on a polygraph, but a more convenient form is a cumulative curve from which rate of responding is immediately read as slope. The rate at which a response is emitted in such a situation comes close to our preconception of the learning process. As the organism learns, the rate rises. As it unlearns (for example, in extinction) the rate falls. Various sorts of discriminative stimuli may be brought into control of the response with corresponding modifications of the rate. Motivational changes alter the rate in a sensitive way. So do those events which we speak of as generating emotion. The range through which the rate varies significantly may be as great as of the order of 1000:1. Changes in rate are satisfactorily smooth in the individual case, so that it is not necessary to average cases. A given value is often quite stable: in the pigeon a rate of four or five thousand responses per hour may be maintained without interruption for as long as fifteen hours.

Rate of responding appears to be the only datum that varies significantly and in the expected direction under conditions which are relevant to the "learning process." We may, therefore, be tempted to accept it as our long-sought-for measure of strength of bond, excitatory potential, etc. Once in possession of an effective datum, however, we may feel little need for any theoretical construct of this sort. Progress in a scientific field usually waits upon the discovery of a satisfactory dependent variable. Until such a variable has been discovered, we resort to theory. The entities which have figured so prominently in learning theory have served mainly as sub-

stitutes for a directly observable and productive datum. They have little reason to survive when such a datum has been found.

It is no accident that rate of responding is successful as a datum, because it is particularly appropriate to the fundamental task of a science of behavior. If we are to predict behavior (and possibly to control it), we must deal with *probability of response*. The business of a science of behavior is to evaluate this probability and explore the conditions that determine it. Strength of bond, expectancy, excitatory potential, and so on, carry the notion of probability in an easily imagined form, but the additional properties suggested by these terms have hindered the search for suitable measures. Rate of responding is not a "measure" of probability but it is the only appropriate datum in a formulation in these terms.

As other scientific disciplines can attest, probabilities are not easy to handle. We wish to make statements about the likelihood of occurrence of a single future response, but our data are in the form of frequencies of responses that have already occurred. These responses were presumably similar to each other and to the response to be predicted. But this raises the troublesome problem of response-instance *vs.* response-class. Precisely what responses are we to take into account in predicting a future instance? Certainly not the responses made by a population of different organisms, for such a statistical datum raises more problems than it solves. To consider the frequency of repeated responses in an individual demands something like the experimental situation just described.

This solution of the problem of a basic datum is based upon the view that operant behavior is essentially an emissive phenomenon. Latency and magnitude of response fail as measures because they do not take this into account. They are concepts appropriate to the field of the reflex, where the all but invariable control exercised by the eliciting stimulus makes the notion of probability of response trivial. Consider, for example, the case of latency. Because of our acquaintance with simple reflexes we infer that a response that is more likely to be emitted will be emitted more quickly. But is this true? What can the word "quickly" mean? Probability of response, as well as prediction of response, is concerned with the moment of emission. This is a point in time, but it does not have the temporal dimension of a latency. The execution may take time after the response has been initiated, but the moment of occurrence has no duration.[2] In recognizing the emissive character of operant behavior and the central position of probability of response as a datum, latency is seen to be irrelevant to our present task.

Various objections have been made to the use of rate of responding as a basic datum. For example, such a program may seem to bar us from dealing with many events which are unique occurrences in the life of the individual. A man does not decide upon a career, get married, make a million dollars, or get killed in an accident often enough to make a rate of response meaningful. But these activities are not responses. They are not simple unitary events lending themselves to prediction as such. If we are to predict marriage, success, accidents, and so on, in anything more than statistical terms, we must deal with the smaller units of behavior which lead to and compose these unitary episodes. If the units appear in repeatable form, the present analysis may be applied. In the field of learn-

ing a similar objection takes the form of asking how the present analysis may be extended to experimental situations in which it is impossible to observe frequencies. It does not follow that learning is not taking place in such situations. The notion of probability is usually extrapolated to cases in which a frequency analysis cannot be carried out. In the field of behavior we arrange a situation in which frequencies are available as data, but we use the notion of probability in analyzing and formulating instances or even types of behavior which are not susceptible to this analysis.

Another common objection is that a rate of response is just a set of latencies and hence not a new datum at all. This is easily shown to be wrong. When we measure the time elapsing between two responses, we are in no doubt as to what the organism was doing when we started our clock. We know that it was just executing a response. This is a natural zero—quite unlike the arbitrary point from which latencies are measured. The free repetition of a response yields a rhythmic or periodic datum very different from latency. Many periodic physical processes suggest parallels.

We do not choose rate of responding as a basic datum merely from an analysis of the fundamental task of a science of behavior. The ultimate appeal is to its success in an experimental science. The material which follows is offered as a sample of what can be done. It is not intended as a complete demonstration, but it should confirm the fact that when we are in possession of a datum which varies in a significant fashion, we are less likely to resort to theoretical entities carrying the notion of probability of response.

Why Learning Occurs

WE may define learning as a change in probability of response but we must also specify the conditions under which it comes about. To do this we must survey some of the independent variables of which probability of response is a function. Here we meet another kind of learning theory.

---

2 It cannot, in fact, be shortened or lengthened. Where a latency appears to be forced toward a minimal value by differential reinforcement, another interpretation is called for. Although we may differentially reinforce more energetic behavior or the faster execution of behavior after it begins, it is meaningless to speak of differentially reinforcing responses with short or long latencies. What we actually reinforce differentially are (a) favorable waiting behavior and (b) more vigorous responses. When we ask a subject to respond "as soon as possible" in the human reaction-time experiment, we essentially ask him (a) to carry out as much of the response as possible without actually reaching the criterion of emission, (b) to do as little else as possible, and (c) to respond energetically after the stimulus has been given. This may yield a minimal measurable time between stimulus and response, but this time is not necessarily a basic datum nor have our instructions altered it as such. A parallel interpretation of the differential reinforcement of long "latencies" is required. This is easily established by inspection. In the experiments with pigeons previously cited, preliminary behavior is conditioned that postpones the response to the key until the proper time. Behavior that "marks time" is usually conspicuous.

An effective class-room demonstration of the Law of Effect may be arranged in the following way. A pigeon, reduced to 80 per cent of its *ad lib* weight, is habituated to a small, semi-circular amphitheatre and is fed there for several days from a food hopper, which the experimenter presents by closing a hand switch. The demonstration consists of establishing a selected response by suitable reinforcement with food. For example, by sighting across the amphitheatre at a scale on the opposite wall, it is possible to present the hopper whenever the top of the pigeon's head rises above a given mark. Higher and higher marks are chosen until, within a few minutes, the pigeon is walking about the cage with its head held as high as possible. In another demonstration the bird is conditioned to strike a marble placed on the floor of the amphitheatre. This may be done in a few minutes by reinforcing successive steps. Food is presented first when the bird is merely moving near the marble, later when it looks down in the direction of the marble, later still when it moves its head toward the marble, and finally when it pecks it. Anyone who has seen such a demonstration knows that the Law of Effect is no theory. It simply specifies a procedure for altering the probability of a chosen response.

But when we try to say *why* reinforcement has this effect, theories arise. Learning is said to take place because the reinforcement is pleasant, satisfying, tension reducing, and so on. The converse process of extinction is explained with comparable theories. If the rate of responding is first raised to a high point by reinforcement and reinforcement then withheld, the response is observed to occur less and less frequently thereafter. One common theory explains this by asserting that a state is built up which suppresses the behavior. This "experimental inhibition" or "reaction inhibition" must be assigned to a different dimensional system, since nothing at the level of behavior corresponds to opposed processes of excitation and inhibition. Rate of responding is simply increased by one operation and decreased by another. Certain effects commonly interpreted as showing release from a suppressing force may be interpreted in other ways. Disinhibition, for example, is not necessarily the uncovering of suppressed strength; it may be a sign of supplementary strength from an extraneous variable. The process of spontaneous recovery, often cited to support the notion of suppression, has an alternative explanation, to be noted in a moment.

Let us evaluate the question of why learning takes place by turning again to some data. Since conditioning is usually too rapid to be easily followed, the process of extinction will provide us with a more useful case. A number of different types of curves have been consistently obtained from rats and pigeons using various schedules of prior reinforcement. By considering some of the relevant conditions we may see what room is left for theoretical processes.

The mere passage of time between conditioning and extinction is a variable that has surprisingly little effect. The rat is too short-lived to make an extended experiment feasible, but the pigeon, which may live ten or fifteen years, is an ideal subject. More than five years ago, twenty pigeons were conditioned to strike a large translucent key upon which a complex visual pattern was projected. Reinforcement was contingent upon the maintenance of a high and steady rate of responding and upon striking a particular feature of the visual pattern. These birds were set aside in order to study retention. They were transferred to the usual living quarters, where they served as breeders. Small groups were tested for extinction at the end of six months, one year, two years, and four years. Before the test each bird was transferred to a separate living cage. A controlled feeding schedule was used to reduce the weight to approximately 80 per cent of the *ad lib* weight. The bird was then fed in the dimly lighted experimental apparatus in the absence of the key for several days, during which emotional responses to the apparatus disappeared. On the day of the test the bird was placed in the darkened box. The translucent key was present but not lighted. No responses were made. When the pattern was projected upon the key, all four birds responded quickly and extensively. FIG. 2

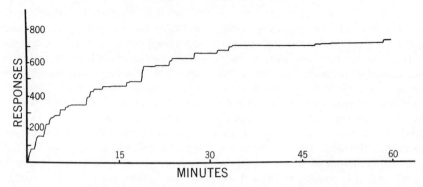

FIG. 2. Extinction four years after conditioning.

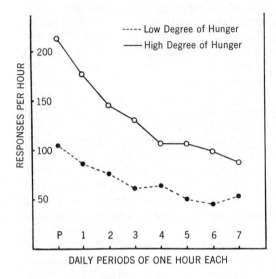

DAILY PERIODS OF ONE HOUR EACH

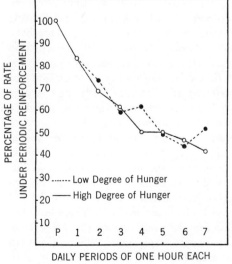

DAILY PERIODS OF ONE HOUR EACH

FIG. 3

shows the largest curve obtained. This bird struck the key within two seconds after presentation of a visual pattern that it had not seen for four years, and at the precise spot upon which differential reinforcement had previously been based. It continued to respond for the next hour, emitting about 700 responses. This is of the order of one-half to one-quarter of the responses it would have emitted if extinction had not been delayed four years, but otherwise, the curve is fairly typical.

Level of motivation is another variable to be taken into account. An example of the effect of hunger has been reported elsewhere (3). The response of pressing a lever was established in eight rats with a schedule of periodic reinforcement. They were fed the main part of their ration on alternate days so that the rates of responding on successive days were alternately high and low. Two subgroups of four rats each were matched on the basis of the rate maintained under periodic reinforcement under these conditions. The response was then extinguished—in one group on alternate days when the hunger was high, in the other group on alternate days when the hunger was low. (The same amount of food was eaten on the nonexperimental days as before.) The result is shown in Fig. 3. The upper graph gives the raw data. The levels of hunger are indicated by the points at P on the abscissa, the rates prevailing under periodic reinforcement. The subsequent points show the decline in extinction. If we multiply the lower curve through by a factor chosen to superimpose the points at P, the curves are reasonably closely superimposed, as shown in the lower graph. Several other experiments on both rats and pigeons have confirmed this general principle. If a given ratio of responding prevails under periodic reinforcement, the slopes of later extinction curves show the same ratio. Level of hunger determines the slope of the extinction curve but not its curvature.

Another variable, difficulty of response, is especially relevant because it has been used to test the theory of reaction inhibition (1), on the assumption that a response requiring considerable energy will build up more reaction inhibition than an easy response and lead, therefore, to faster extinction. The theory requires that the curvature of the extinction curve be altered, not merely its slope. Yet there is evidence that difficulty of response acts like level of hunger simply to alter the slope. Some data have been reported .but not published (5). A pigeon is suspended in a jacket which confines its wings and legs but leaves its head and neck free to respond to a key and a food magazine. Its behavior in this situation is quantitatively much like that of a bird moving freely in an experimental box. But the use of the jacket has the advantage that the response to the key may be made easy or difficult by changing the distance the bird must reach. In one experiment these distances were expressed in seven equal but arbitrary units. At distance 7 the bird could barely reach the key, at 3 it could strike without appreciably extending its neck. Periodic reinforcement gave a straight base-line upon which it was possible to observe the effect of difficulty by quickly changing position during the experimental period. Each of the five records in FIG. 4 covers a fifteen minute experimental period under periodic reinforcement. Distances of the bird from the key are indicated by numerals above the records. It will be observed that the rate of responding at distance 7 is generally quite low while that at distance 3 is high. Intermediate distances produce intermediate slopes. It should also be noted that the change from one position to another is felt immediately. If repeated responding in a difficult position were to build a considerable

amount of reaction inhibition, we should expect the rate to be low for some little time after returning to an easy response. Contrariwise, if an easy response were to build little reaction inhibition, we should expect a fairly high rate of responding for some time after a difficult position is assumed. Nothing like this occurs. The "more rapid extinction" of a difficult response is an ambiguous expression. The slope constant is affected and with it the number of responses in extinction to a criterion, but there may be no effect upon curvature.

One way of considering the question of why extinction curves are curved is to regard extinction as a process of exhaustion comparable to the loss of heat from source to sink or the fall in the level of a reservoir when an outlet is opened. Conditioning builds up a predisposition to respond—a "reserve"—which extinction exhausts. This is perhaps a defensible description at the level of behavior. The reserve is not necessarily a theory in the present sense, since it is not assigned to a different dimensional system. It could be operationally defined as a predicted extinction curve, even though, linguistically, it makes a statement about the momentary condition of a response. But it is not a particularly useful concept, nor does the view that extinction is a process of exhaustion add much to the observed fact that extinction curves are curved in a certain way.

There are, however, two variables that affect the rate, both of which operate during extinction to alter the curvature. One of these falls within the field of emotion. When we fail to reinforce a response that has previously been reinforced, we not only initiate a process of extinction, we set up an emotional response—perhaps what is often meant by frustration. The pigeon coos in an identifiable pattern, moves rapidly about the cage, defecates, or flaps its wings rapidly in a squatting position that suggests treading (mating) behavior. This competes with the response of striking a key and is perhaps enough to account for the decline in rate in early extinction. It is also possible that the probability of a response based upon food deprivation is directly reduced as part of such an emo-

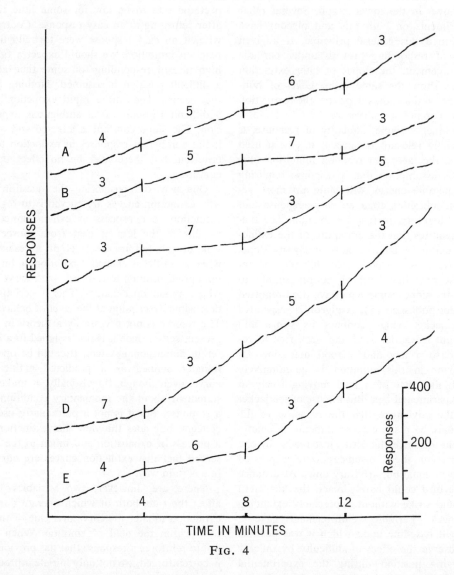

TIME IN MINUTES

FIG. 4

tional reaction. Whatever its nature, the effect of this variable is eliminated through adaptation. Repeated extinction curves become smoother, and in some of the schedules to be described shortly there is little or no evidence of an emotional modification of rate.

A second variable has a much more serious effect. Maximal responding during extinction is obtained only when the conditions under which the response was reinforced are precisely reproduced. A rat conditioned in the presence of a light will not extinguish fully in the absence of the light. It will begin to respond more rapidly when the light is again introduced. This is true for other kinds of stimuli, as the following class-room experiment illustrates. Nine pigeons were conditioned to strike a yellow triangle under intermittent reinforcement. In the session represented by Fig. 5 the birds were first reinforced on this schedule for 30 minutes. The combined cumulative curve is essentially a straight line, showing more than 1100 responses per bird during this period. A red triangle was then substituted for the yellow and no responses were reinforced thereafter. The effect was a sharp drop in responding, with only a slight recovery during the next fifteen minutes. When the yellow triangle was replaced, rapid responding began immediately and the usual extinction curve followed. Similar experiments have shown that the pitch of an incidental tone, the shape of a pattern being struck, or the size of a pattern, if present during conditioning, will to some extent control the rate of responding during extinction. Some properties are more effective than others, and a quantitative evaluation is possible. By changing to several values of a stimulus in random order repeatedly during the extinction process, the gradient for stimulus generalization may be read directly in the rates of responding under each value.

Something very much like this must go on during extinction. Let us suppose that all responses to a key have been reinforced and that each has been followed by a short period of eating. When we extinguish the behavior, we create a situation in which responses are not reinforced, in which no eating takes place, and in which there are probably new emotional responses. The situation could easily be as novel as a red triangle after a yellow. If so, it could explain the decline in rate during extinction. We might have obtained a smooth curve, *shaped like an extinction curve,* between the vertical lines in Fig. 5 by *gradually* changing the color of the triangle from yellow to red. This might have happened even though no other sort of extinction were taking place. The very conditions of extinction seem to presuppose a growing novelty in the experimental situation. Is this why the extinction curve is curved?

Some evidence comes from the data of "spontaneous recovery." Even after prolonged extinction an organism will often respond at a higher rate for at least a few moments at the beginning of another session. One theory contends that this shows spontaneous recovery from some sort of inhibition, but another explanation is possible. No matter how carefully an animal is handled, the stimulation coincident with the beginning of an experiment must be extensive and unlike anything

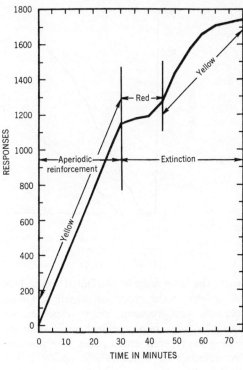

FIG. 5

occurring in the later part of an experimental period. Responses have been reinforced in the presence of, or shortly following, this stimulation. In extinction it is present for only a few moments. When the organism is again placed in the experimental situation, the stimulation is restored; further responses are emitted as in the case of the yellow triangle. The only way to achieve full extinction in the presence of the stimulation of starting an experiment is to start the experiment repeatedly.

Other evidence of the effect of novelty comes from the study of periodic reinforcement. The fact that intermittent reinforcement produces bigger extinction curves than continuous reinforcement is a troublesome difficulty for those who expect a simple relation between number of reinforcements and number of responses in extinction. But this relation is actually quite complex. One result of periodic reinforcement is that emotional changes adapt out. This may be responsible for the smoothness of subsequent extinction curves but probably not for their greater ex-

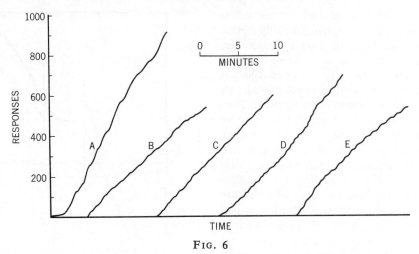

FIG. 6

tent. The latter may be attributed to the lack of novelty in the extinction situation. Under periodic reinforcement many responses are made without reinforcement and when no eating has recently taken place. The situation in extinction is therefore not wholly novel.

Periodic reinforcement is not, however, a simple solution. If we reinforce on a regular schedule—say, every minute—the organism soon forms a discrimination. Little or no responding occurs just after reinforcement, since stimulation from eating is correlated with absence of subsequent reinforcement. How rapidly the discrimination may develop is shown in FIG. 6, which reproduces the first five curves obtained from a pigeon under periodic reinforcement in experimental periods of fifteen minutes each. In the fifth period (or after about one hour of periodic reinforcement) the discrimination yields a pause after each reinforcement, resulting in a markedly stepwise curve. As a result of this discrimination the bird is almost always responding rapidly when reinforced. This is the basis for another discrimination. Rapid responding becomes a favorable stimulating condition.

A good example of the effect upon the subsequent extinction curve is shown in FIG. 7. This pigeon had been reinforced once every minute during daily experimental periods of fifteen minutes each for several weeks. In the extinction curve shown, the bird begins to respond at the rate prevailing under the preceding schedule. A quick positive acceleration at the start is lost in the reduction of the record. The pigeon quickly reaches and sustains a rate that is higher than the overall-rate during periodic reinforcement. During this period the pigeon creates a stimulating condition previously optimally correlated with reinforcement. Eventually, as some sort of exhaustion intervenes, the rate falls off rapidly to a much lower but fairly stable value and then to practically zero. A condition then prevails under which a response is not normally reinforced. The bird is therefore not likely to begin to respond again. When it does respond, however, the situation is slightly improved and, if it continues to respond, the conditions rapidly become similar to those under which reinforcement has been received. Under this "autocatalysis" a high rate is quickly reached, and more than 500 responses are emitted in a second burst. The rate then declines quickly and fairly smoothly, again to nearly zero. This curve is not by any means disorderly. Most of the curvature is smooth. But the burst of responding at forty-five minutes shows a considerable residual strength which, if extinction were merely exhaustion, should have appeared earlier in the curve. The curve may be reasonably accounted for by assuming that the bird is largely controlled by the preceding spurious correlation between reinforcement and rapid responding.

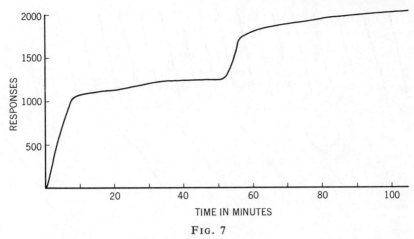

RESPONSES

TIME IN MINUTES

FIG. 7

This assumption may be checked by constructing a schedule of reinforcement in which a differential contingency between rate of responding and reinforcement is impossible. In one such schedule of what may be called "aperiodic reinforcement" one interval between successive reinforced responses is so short that no unreinforced responses intervene while the longest interval is about two minutes. Other intervals are distributed arithmetically between these values, the average remaining one minute. The intervals are roughly randomized to compose a program of reinforcement. Under this program the probability of reinforcement does not change with respect to previous reinforcements, and the curves never acquire the step-wise character of curve E in FIG. 6. (FIG. 9 shows curves from a similar program.) As a result

no correlation between different rates of responding and different probabilities of reinforcement can develop.

An extinction curve following a brief exposure to aperiodic reinforcement is shown in FIG. 8.

It begins characteristically at the rate prevailing under aperiodic reinforcement and, unlike the curve following regular periodic reinforcement, does not accelerate to a higher overall rate. There is no evidence of the "autocatalytic" production of an optimal stimulating condition. Also characteristically, there are no significant discontinuities or sudden changes in rate in either direction. The curve extends over a period of eight hours, as against not quite two hours in FIG. 7, and seems to represent a single orderly process. The total number of responses is higher, per-

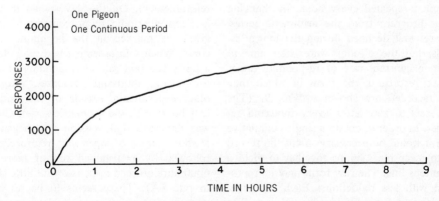

One Pigeon
One Continuous Period

RESPONSES

TIME IN HOURS

FIG. 8. Extinction after aperiodic reinforcement, arithmetic series. Mean: one reinforcement per minute.

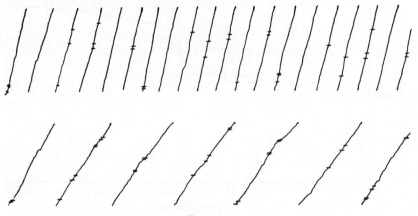

FIG. 9

haps because of the greater time allowed for emission. All of this can be explained by the single fact that we have made it impossible for the pigeon to form a pair of discriminations based, first, upon stimulation from eating and, second, upon stimulation from rapid responding.

Since the longest interval between reinforcement was only two minutes, a certain novelty must still have been introduced as time passed. Whether this explains the curvature in FIG. 8 may be tested to some extent with other programs of reinforcement containing much longer intervals. A geometric progression was constructed by beginning with 10 seconds as the shortest interval and repeatedly multiplying through by a ratio of 1.54. This yielded a set of intervals averaging 5 minutes, the longest of which was more than 21 minutes. Such a set was randomized in a program of reinforcement repeated every hour. In changing to this program from the arithmetic series, the rates first declined during the longer intervals, but the pigeons were soon able to sustain a constant rate of responding under it. Two records in the form in which they were recorded are shown in FIG. 9. (The pen resets to zero after every thousand responses. In order to obtain a single cumulative curve it would be necessary to cut the record and to piece the sections together to yield a continuous line. The raw form may be reproduced with less reduction.) Each reinforcement is represented by a horizontal dash. The time covered is about 3 hours. Records are shown for two pigeons that maintained different overall rates under this program of reinforcement.

Under such a schedule a constant rate of responding is sustained for at least 21 minutes without reinforcement, after which a reinforcement is received. Less novelty should therefore develop during succeeding extinction. In Curve 1 of FIG. 10 the pigeon had been exposed to several sessions of several hours each with this geometric set of intervals. The number of responses emitted in extinction is about twice that of the curve in FIG. 8 after the arithmetic set of intervals averaging one minute, but the curves are otherwise much alike. Further exposure to the geometric schedule builds up longer runs during which the rate does not change significantly. Curve 2 followed Curve 1 after two and one-half hours of further aperiodic reinforcement. On the day shown in Curve 2 a few aperiodic reinforcements were first given, as marked at the beginning of the curve. When reinforcement was discontinued, a fairly constant rate of responding prevailed for several thousand responses. After another experimental session of two and one-half hours with the geometric series, Curve 3 was recorded. This session also began with a short series of aperiodic reinforcements, followed by a sustained run of more than 6000 unreinforced responses with little change in rate (A). There seems to be no reason why other series averaging perhaps more than five minutes per interval and containing much

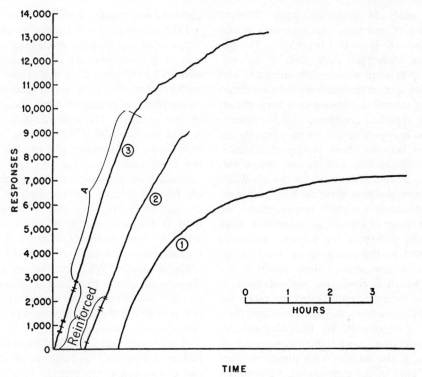

FIG. 10. Extinction after continued aperiodic reinforcement, geometric series.

longer exceptional intervals would not carry such a straight line much further.

In this attack upon the problem of extinction we create a schedule of reinforcement which is so much like the conditions that will prevail during extinction that no decline in rate takes place for a long time. In other words we generate extinction with no curvature. Eventually some kind of exhaustion sets in, but it is not approached gradually. The last part of Curve 3 (unfortunately much reduced in the figure) may possibly suggest exhaustion in the slight overall curvature, but it is a small part of the whole process. The record is composed mainly of runs of a few hundred responses each, most of them at approximately the same rate as that maintained under periodic reinforcement. The pigeon stops abruptly; when it starts to respond again, it quickly reaches the rate of responding under which it was reinforced. This recalls the spurious correlation between rapid responding and reinforcement under regular reinforcement. We have not, of course, entirely eliminated this correlation. Even though there is no longer a differential reinforcement of high against low rates, practically all reinforcements have occurred under a constant rate of responding.

Further study of reinforcing schedules may or may not answer the question of whether the novelty appearing in the extinction situation is entirely responsible for the curvature. It would appear to be necessary to make the conditions prevailing during extinction identical with the conditions prevailing during conditioning. This may be impossible, but in that case the question is academic. The hypothesis, meanwhile, is not a theory in the present sense, since it makes no statements about a parallel process in any other universe of discourse.[3]

3 It is true that it appeals to stimulation generated in part by the pigeon's own behavior. This may be difficult to specify or manipulate, but it is not theoretical in the present sense. So long as we are willing to assume a one-to-one correspondence between action and stimulation, a physical specification is possible.

The study of extinction after different schedules of aperiodic reinforcement is not addressed wholly to this hypothesis. The object is an economical description of the conditions prevailing during reinforcement and extinction and of the relations between them. In using rate of responding as a basic datum we may appeal to conditions that are observable and manipulable and we may express the relations between them in objective terms. To the extent that our datum makes this possible, it reduces the need for theory. When we observe a pigeon emitting 7000 responses at a constant rate without reinforcement, we are not likely to explain an extinction curve containing perhaps a few hundred responses by appeal to the piling up of reaction inhibition or any other fatigue product. Research which is conducted without commitment to theory is more likely to carry the study of extinction into new areas and new orders of magnitude. By hastening the accumulation of data, we speed the departure of theories. If the theories have played no part in the design of our experiments, we need not be sorry to see them go.

Complex Learning

A THIRD type of learning theory is illustrated by terms like *preferring, choosing, discriminating,* and *matching.* An effort may be made to define these solely in terms of behavior, but in traditional practice they refer to processes in another dimensional system. A response to one of two available stimuli may be called choice, but it is commoner to say that it is the result of choice, meaning by the latter a theoretical pre-behavioral activity. The higher mental processes are the best examples of theories of this sort; neurological parallels have not been well worked out. The appeal to theory is encouraged by the fact that choosing (like discriminating, matching, and so on) is not a particular piece of behavior. It is not a response or an act with specified topography. The term characterizes a larger segment of behavior in relation to other variables or events. Can we formulate and study the behavior to which these terms would usually be applied without recourse to the theories which generally accompany them?

Discrimination is a relatively simple case. Suppose we find that the probability of emission of a given response is not significantly affected by changing from one of two stimuli to the other. We then make reinforcement of the response contingent upon the presence of one of them. The well-established result is that the probability of response remains high under this stimulus and reaches a very low point under the other. We say that the organism now discriminates between the stimuli. But discrimination is not itself an action, or necessarily even a unique process. Problems in the field of discrimination may be stated in other terms. How much induction obtains between stimuli of different magnitudes or classes? What are the smallest differences in stimuli that yield a difference in control? And so on. Questions of this sort do not presuppose theoretical activities in other dimensional systems.

A somewhat larger segment must be specified in dealing with the behavior of choosing one of two concurrent stimuli. This has been studied in the pigeon by examining responses to two keys differing in position (right or left) or in some property like color randomized with respect to position. By occasionally reinforcing a response on one key or the other without favoring either key, we obtain equal rates of responding on the two keys. The behavior approaches a simple alternation from one key to the other. This follows the rule that tendencies to respond eventually correspond to the probabilities of reinforcement. Given a system in which one key or the other is occasionally connected with the magazine by an external clock, then if the right key has just been struck, the probability of reinforcement *via* the left key is higher than that *via* the right since a greater interval of time has elapsed during which the clock may have closed the circuit to the left key. But the bird's behavior does not correspond to this probability merely out of respect for mathematics. The specific result of such a contingency of reinforcement is that changing-to-the-other-key-and-striking is more often reinforced than striking-the-same-key-a-second-time. We are no longer dealing with just two responses. In order to analyze "choice" we must consider a single final response, striking, without respect to the position or color of the key, and in addition the responses of changing from one key or color to the other.

Quantitative results are compatible with this analysis. If we periodically reinforce responses to the right key only, the rate of responding on the right will rise while that on the left will fall. The response of changing-from-right-to-left is never reinforced while the response of changing-from-left-to-right is occasionally so. When the bird is striking on the right, there is no great tendency to change keys; when it is striking on the left, there is a strong tendency to change. Many more responses come to be made to the right key. The need for considering the behavior of changing over is clearly shown if we now reverse these conditions and reinforce responses to the left key only. The ultimate result is a high rate of responding on the left key and a low rate on the right. By reversing the conditions again the high rate can be shifted back to the right key. In FIG. 11 a group of eight curves have been averaged to follow this change during six experimental periods of 45 minutes each. Beginning on the second day in the graph responses to the right key (R^R) decline in extinction while responses to the left key (R^L) increase through periodic reinforcement. The mean rate shows no significant variation, since periodic reinforcement is continued on the same schedule. The mean rate shows the condition of strength of the response of striking a key regardless of position. The distribution of responses between right and left depends upon the relative strength of the responses of changing over. If this were simply a case of the extinction of one response and the concurrent reconditioning of another, the mean curve would not remain approximately horizontal since reconditioning occurs much more rapidly than extinction.[4]

The rate with which the bird changes from

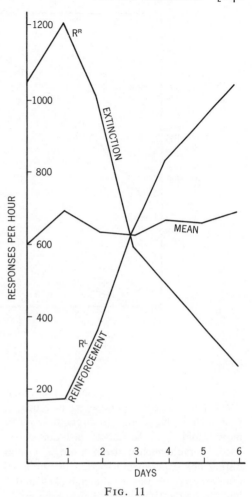

FIG. 11

one key to the other depends upon the distance between the keys. This distance is a rough measure of the stimulus-difference between the two keys. It also determines the scope of the response of changing-over, with an implied difference in sensory feed-back. It also modifies the spread of reinforcement to responses supposedly not reinforced, since if the keys are close together, a response reinforced on one side may occur sooner after a preceding response on the other side. In FIG. 11 the two keys were about one inch apart. They were therefore fairly similar with respect to position in the experimental box. Changing from one to the other involved a minimum of sensory feed-back, and reinforcement of a response to one key could follow

[4] Two topographically independent responses, capable of emission at the same time and hence not requiring change-over, show separate processes of reconditioning and extinction, and the combined rate of responding varies.

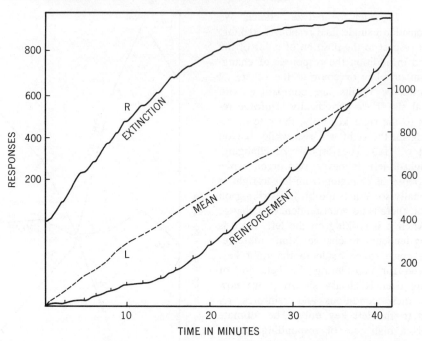

FIG. 12

very shortly upon a response to the other. When the keys are separated by as much as four inches, the change in strength is much more rapid. FIG. 12 shows two curves recorded simultaneously from a single pigeon during one experimental period of about 40 minutes. A high rate to the right key and a low rate to the left had previously been established. In the figure no responses to the right were reinforced, but those to the left were reinforced every minute as indicated by the vertical dashes above curve L. The slope of R declines in a fairly smooth fashion while that of L increases, also fairly smoothly, to a value comparable to the initial value of R. The bird has conformed to the changed contingency within a single experimental period. The mean rate of responding is shown by a dotted line, which again shows no significant curvature.

What is called "preference" enters into this formulation. At any stage of the process shown in FIG. 12 preference might be expressed in terms of the relative rates of responding to the two keys. This preference, however, is not in striking a key but in chang-

ing from one key to the other. The probability that the bird will strike a key regardless of its identifying properties behaves independently of the preferential response of changing from one key to the other. Several experiments have revealed an additional fact. A preference remains fixed if reinforcement is withheld. FIG. 13 is an example. It shows simultaneous extinction curves from two keys during seven daily experimental periods of one hour each. Prior to extinction the relative strength of the responses of changing-to-R and changing-to-L yielded a "preference" of about 3 to 1 for R. The constancy of the rate throughout the process of extinction has been shown in the figure by multiplying L through by a suitable constant and entering the points as small circles on R. If extinction altered the preference, the two curves could not be superimposed in this way.

These formulations of discrimination and choosing enable us to deal with what is generally regarded as a much more complex process—matching to sample. Suppose we arrange three translucent keys, each of which may be illuminated with red or green light.

The middle key functions as the sample and we color it either red or green in random order. We color the two side keys one red and one green, also in random order. The "problem" is to strike the side key which corresponds in color to the middle key. There are only four three-key patterns in such a case, and it is possible that a pigeon could learn to make an appropriate response to each pattern. This does not happen, at least within the temporal span of the experiments to date. If we simply present a series of settings of the three colors and reinforce successful responses, the pigeon will strike the side keys without respect to color or pattern and be reinforced 50 per cent of the time. This is, in effect, a schedule of "fixed ratio" reinforcement which is adequate to maintain a high rate of responding.

Nevertheless it is possible to get a pigeon to match to sample by reinforcing the discriminative responses of striking-red-after-being-stimulated-by-red and striking-green-after-being-stimulated-by-green while extinguishing the other two possibilities. The difficulty is in arranging the proper stimulation at the time of the response. The sample might be made conspicuous—for example, by having the sample color in the general illumination of the experimental box. In such a case the pigeon would learn to strike red keys in a red light and green keys in a green light (assuming a neutral illumination of the background of the keys). But a procedure which holds more closely to the notion of matching is to induce the pigeon to "look at the sample" by means of a separate reinforcement. We may do this by presenting the color on the middle key first, leaving the side keys uncolored. A response to the middle key is then reinforced (secondarily) by illuminating the side keys. The pigeon learns to make two responses in quick succession—to the middle key and then to one side key. The response to the side key follows quickly upon the visual stimulation from the middle key, which is the requisite condition for a discrimination. Successful matching was readily established in all ten pigeons tested with this technique. Choosing the opposite is also easily set up. The discriminative response of striking-red-

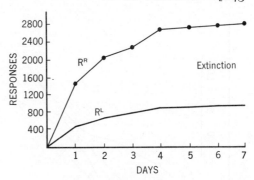

FIG. 13. Extinction.

after-being-stimulated-by-red is apparently no easier to establish than striking-red-after-being-stimulated-by-green. When the response is to a key of the same color, however, generalization may make it possible for the bird to match a new color. This is an extension of the notion of matching that has not yet been studied with this method.

Even when matching behavior has been well established, the bird will not respond correctly if all three keys are now presented at the same time. The bird does not possess strong behavior of looking at the sample. The experimenter must maintain a separate reinforcement to keep this behavior in strength. In monkeys, apes, and human subjects the ultimate success in choosing is apparently sufficient to reinforce and maintain the behavior of looking at the sample. It is possible that this species difference is simply a difference in the temporal relations required for reinforcement.

The behavior of matching survives unchanged when all reinforcement is withheld. An intermediate case has been established in which the correct matching response is only periodically reinforced. In one experiment one color appeared on the middle key for one minute; it was then changed or not changed, at random, to the other color. A response to this key illuminated the side keys, one red and one green, in random order. A response to a side key cut off the illumination to both side keys, until the middle key had again been struck. The apparatus recorded all matching responses on one graph and all nonmatching on another. Pigeons which have

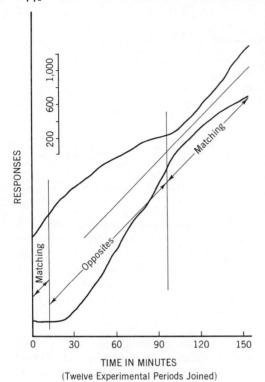

RESPONSES

1,000
600
200

Matching

Opposites

Matching

0   30   60   90   120   150

TIME IN MINUTES
(Twelve Experimental Periods Joined)

FIG. 14

acquired matching behavior under continuous reinforcement have maintained this behavior when reinforced no oftener than once per minute on the average. They may make thousands of matching responses per hour while being reinforced for no more than sixty of them. This schedule will not necessarily develop matching behavior in a naive bird, for the problem can be solved in three ways. The bird will receive practically as many reinforcements if it responds to (1) only one key or (2) only one color, since the programming of the experiment makes any persistent response eventually the correct one.

A sample of the data obtained in a complex experiment of this sort is given in FIG. 14. Although this pigeon had learned to match color under continuous reinforcement, it changed to the spurious solution of a color preference under periodic reinforcement. Whenever the sample was red, it struck both the sample and the red side key and received

all reinforcements. When the sample was green, it did not respond and the side keys were not illuminated. The result shown at the beginning of the graph in FIG. 14 is a high rate of responding on the upper graph, which records matching responses. (The record is actually step-wise, following the presence or absence of the red sample, but this is lost in the reduction in the figure.) A color preference, however, is not a solution to the problem of opposites. By changing to this problem, it was possible to change the bird's behavior as shown between the two vertical lines in the figure. The upper curve between these lines shows the decline in matching responses which had resulted from the color preference. The lower curve between the same lines shows the development of responding to and matching the opposite color. At the second vertical line the reinforcement was again made contingent upon matching. The upper curve shows the reestablishment of matching behavior while the lower curve shows a decline in striking the opposite color. The result was a true solution: the pigeon struck the sample, no matter what its color, and then the corresponding side key. The lighter line connects the means of a series of points on the two curves. It seems to follow the same rule as in the case of choosing: changes in the distribution of responses between two keys do not involve the over-all rate of responding to a key. This mean rate will not remain constant under the spurious solution achieved with a color preference, as at the beginning of this figure.

These experiments on a few higher processes have necessarily been very briefly described. They are not offered as proving that theories of learning are not necessary, but they may suggest an alternative program in this difficult area. The data in the field of the higher mental processes transcend single responses or single stimulus-response relationships. But they appear to be susceptible to formulation in terms of the differentiation of concurrent responses, the discrimination of stimuli, the establishment of various sequences of responses, and so on. There seems to be no a priori reason why a complete account is not possible without appeal to theoretical processes in other dimensional systems.

Conclusion

PERHAPS to do without theories altogether is a *tour de force* that is too much to expect as a general practice. Theories are fun. But it is possible that the most rapid progress toward an understanding of learning may be made by research that is not designed to test theories. An adequate impetus is supplied by the inclination to obtain data showing orderly changes characteristic of the learning process. An acceptable scientific program is to collect data of this sort and to relate them to manipulable variables, selected for study through a common sense exploration of the field.

This does not exclude the possibility of theory in another sense. Beyond the collection of uniform relationships lies the need for a formal representation of the data reduced to a minimal number of terms. A theoretical construction may yield greater generality than any assemblage of facts. But such a construction will not refer to another dimensional system and will not, therefore, fall within our present definition. It will not stand in the way of our search for functional relations because it will arise only after relevant variables have been found and studied. Though it may be difficult to understand, it will not be easily misunderstood, and it will have none of the objectionable effects of the theories here considered.

We do not seem to be ready for theory in this sense. At the moment we make little effective use of empirical, let alone rational, equations. A few of the present curves could have been fairly closely fitted. But the most elementary preliminary research shows that there are many relevant variables, and until their importance has been experimentally determined, an equation that allows for them will have so many arbitrary constants that a good fit will be a matter of course and a cause for very little satisfaction.

REFERENCES

1. MOWRER, O. H., & JONES, H. M. Extinction and behavior variability as functions of effortfulness of task. *J. exp. Psychol.*, 1943, 33, 369–386.
2. SKINNER, B. F. *The behavior of organisms.* New York: D. Appleton-Century Co., 1938.
3. ———. The nature of the operant reserve. *Psychol. Bull.*, 1940, 37, 423 (abstract).
4. ———. Differential reinforcement with respect to time. *Amer. Psychol.*, 1946, 1, 274–275 (abstract).
5. ———. The effect of the difficulty of a response upon its rate of emission. *Amer. Psychol.*, 1946, 1, 462 (abstract).

SECTION VI

Language and Thinking

MAN *is distinguished from the lower animals in part by his ability to think (to formulate ideas by means of representational or symbolic processes) and his ability to use language (a set of verbalized symbols) to express his thoughts. There is obviously a close relationship between language and thinking: much that is said arises from the speaker's desire to communicate his thoughts, and is received as an indication of what he thinks; thinking occurs with a sense of words and sentences, even though they are unspoken. However, speech can occur without the intention to communicate, as it does in infants, and occasionally, when our thoughts take an unexpected turn or encounter a block, we realize that part of the thinking process is wordless or unconscious.*

How is language learned and used? How does thought vary with the language of the speaker? How is the thinking process required for problem-solving influenced by previous habits of language and thought? What is the relationship between possessing the knowledge required to solve a problem and being able to reach the solution? These are some of the questions investigated in the articles that follow.

In "Speech Development in the Young Child," O. H. Mowrer suggests that an infant's first efforts to speak have an autistic purpose: the infant is pleased when his chance sounds approximate his mother's voice because such sounds give him a sense of well-being, and he strives to perfect this reproduction. Thus the infant's pleasure is his "reward" for correct "responses," and learning to speak becomes, to a large extent, a matter of self-instruction.

Roger W. Brown and Eric Lenneberg compared the ease with which subjects could name and recognize colors in order to explore the relationship between one's language and one's view of the world. They report, in "A Study in Language and Cognition," that lexical differences do indicate cognitive differences, suggesting that there may be general laws relating codability to the cognitive process.

An established viewpoint can, however, make it hard for an individual to solve a problem, for what he knows about an object may inhibit his ability to use it in a new situation. Robert E. Adamson found that subjects without "functional fixedness" were able to solve problems requiring the use of familiar objects in unfamiliar ways more often and more quickly than subjects in whom "functional fixedness" had been established.

L. Székely asked students to solve problems involving Archimedes' principle so that he could study the ways in which they used their naïve empirical knowledge ("wood floats, metal sinks") and their knowledge of the specific principle con-

cerned. He found that knowledge must be restructured in response to the specific stimuli of a problem before it can operate functionally. Furthermore, how effectively a person can accomplish this restructuring depends more on the degree to which he understands the piece of knowledge when he learns it, even if he "forgets" it later, than on his ability to reproduce the knowledge verbally.

O. H. MOWRER

26. The Autism Theory of Speech Development and Some Clinical Applications

RECENTLY there has emerged, as a deduction from modern learning theory and psychoanalysis, an hypothesis concerning normal speech acquisition which promises to have interesting applications in the field of speech pathology.

More particularly this hypothesis comes from an investigation which the author started some five years ago in an attempt to see what could be learned about language and its development in human beings from a study of the so-called talking birds. From an analysis of such anecdotal literature as is available and our own observations with a small number of birds (including two parrots, a Mynah bird, two common crows, two Western magpies, and a number of Australian parakeets), it is apparent that birds learn to talk when and only when the human teacher becomes a *love object* for them. This interpretation is consistent with expectations generated by the principle of secondary reinforcement (learning theory) and the principle of identification (psychoanalysis).

Operationally, the first step in teaching a bird to talk is to make a "pet" of it, which is to say, tame, care for, and "baby" it in such a way as to deflect the interests and emotional attachments of the bird away from members of its own species to another species, namely *homo sapiens*. This is commonly done by isolating the bird from its own kind and making it dependent for food, water, and social attention and diversion upon its human caretakers.

But there is another step involved which only a few species of birds—and apparently no mammal save man—can make. As one cares for and plays with these creatures, one makes certain characteristic noises. These may or may not be parts of conventional speech: any kind of a noise will do—be it a word or phrase, a whistled or sung fragment of a tune, a nonsense vocalization, or even a mechanical sound like the creaking of a door or the opening of a food box—anything so long as it is intimately and consistently associated with the trainer and his care-taking activities. As a result of the association of these sounds with basic satisfactions for the bird, they become positively conditioned, i.e., they become *good sounds;* and in the course of its own, at first largely random vocalizations, the bird will eventually make somewhat *similar* sounds. By the principle of generalization, some of the derived satisfaction or pleasure which has become attached to the trainer's sounds will now be experienced when the bird itself makes and hears like sounds; and when this begins to happen the stage is set for the bird's learning to "talk."

In terms of learning theory, what has happened is that initially neutral sounds, by virtue of their occurrence in temporal contiguity with primary reinforcements, have ac-

Reprinted by permission of the American Speech and Hearing Association and the author from the *Journal of Speech and Hearing Disorders*, 1952, vol. 17, pp. 263–68. A fuller elaboration and documentation of the ideas here expressed is given in Mowrer (4).

quired secondary reinforcing properties. When the bird itself happens to make somewhat similar sounds, it is now secondarily rewarded for having done so and tries to perfect these sounds so as to make them match as exactly as possible the original sounds, and thus derive from them the maximum of pleasure and comfort.

In terms of psychoanalytic theory, the bird, as a result of developing "positive cathexis" (love) for its human trainer, or "foster parent," identifies with and tries to *be like* that person. Birds cannot do much by way of making themselves *look like* human beings, and even if they could they would not ordinarily be able to see themselves and enjoy this resemblance; but they can make themselves *sound like* human beings, and this they do, under the conditions indicated, with evident satisfaction.

Once words, phrases, whistles, snatches of song, or other distinctively human sounds have been perfected on the autistic or self-satisfaction basis just described, these same responses can, of course, be employed socially or communicatively. Birds that have learned human sounds on an autistic basis can later use these sounds instrumentally, as a means of indicating some desire or need or perhaps just as a device for assembling and holding an admiring and reassuring audience. But the essential first step in this developmental sequence, in the author's belief, is one in which the reproduction and perfection of human sounds occurs, not because of their objective utility, but because of the *subjective* comfort and satisfaction they provide.

So far as can be determined at present, essentially the same account holds, at least up to a point, for acquisition of speech by human infants. Words or other human sounds are first made by infants, it seems, because the sounds have been associated with relief and other satisfactions and, as a result, have themselves come to sound good. Human infants, like birds, are vocally versatile creatures and in the course of random activities in this area will eventually make sounds somewhat similar to those which have already acquired pleasant connotations and will, for reasons already indicated, have a special incentive for

trying to repeat and refine these sounds.[1]

Soon, however, the infant discovers that the making of these sounds can be used not only to comfort, reassure, and satisfy himself directly but also to interest, satisfy, and control mother, father, and others.[2] Up to this point the speech learning of birds and babies seems to be virtually identical; but before long, somewhere around 18 months or two years of age, human infants begin to do something of which birds, even the most talented of them, are incapable. It is always a big event for the rest of the family (and probably for the baby, too!) when a baby begins to "put words together," i.e., to make original, functional sentences. Birds may learn to repeat, "parrot fashion," phrases, sentences, or even longer sequences of human speech; but the indications are that these are never understood and used by birds with their full import and meaning. As De Laguna (1) has remarked, *predication* is the thing that gives language at the human level its most distinctive quality, and it seems that this is never achieved by infrahuman organisms.

An entirely different example of the same type of psychological mechanism is the trick of teaching a dog to "shake hands." The pro-

1 It is remarkable that those organisms which are structurally most similar to man in most respects, namely the anthropoid apes, have so little flair for speech. The work of Hayes and Hayes (2) with an infant chimpanzee has recently confirmed what was already suggested by earlier studies, namely that voluntary control of the vocal cords is so poorly developed in these creatures (probably because of specific cortical deficiencies) as to incapacitate them for even so rudimentary a type of speech development as can be obtained in the talking birds. With an amount of attention and effort equal to—and in respect to speech training a good deal greater than —that which a human infant ordinarily receives, Hayes and Hayes have succeeded in teaching their baby chimpanzee, now three years old, to say only three words—mama, papa, and cup—and even these words are merely whispered instead of being fully voiced.

2 One may thus say that words are first reproduced by infants as a means of recapturing some of the pleasures which parents have provided when parents are not immediately available. By the second use of words, just described, the infant actually recovers the parents, literally "gets them back," and in so doing reduces the necessity for relying upon the autistic, self-supplied satisfactions. It is well known that small children who have "responsive" and "attentive" parents do not rely upon fantasy (also a form of autistic satisfaction) so extensively and protractedly as do neglected children.

cedure commonly used consists of *passively* moving the dog's leg in the desired manner and then giving a reward of some sort, such as a morsel of food. Like the buzzer in Pavlov's famous salivary conditioning experiments, the proprioceptive stimuli associated with the passive leg movement come to signify that something agreeable will shortly occur and therefore acquire secondary reinforcing properties. But there is this difference: under ordinary circumstances, Pavlov's dogs could not themselves make the food-promising buzzer sound; they had to *wait* for it to occur. In the present example, however, there is a stimulus pattern which the dog itself *can* produce, merely by performing *actively,* or "voluntarily," the same movement that has previously been performed passively by the trainer, in a manner analogous to the way in which a bird or a baby reproduces auditory stimulation which was originally produced by another.

The discovery that lifting the foreleg which has been involved in the passive hand-shaking training *feels good* (is comforting, reassuring, "promising") may be made by the dog when alone; and the satisfaction thus experienced will tend to insure, on a purely autistic basis, the repetition of the response, and eventually the response will probably be made in the master's presence. The response will then almost certainly be powerfully rewarded externally, just as the first words of a bird or baby which are heard by others are rewarded.[3]

In all the examples given, then, there is a procedure for short-cutting the delay which would be involved if one waited for a given response which one wished to teach to a baby, a bird, or a dog to occur spontaneously. By the procedures indicated, the response is, so to speak, *baited* in advance with secondary reinforcement so that whenever it or a closely related response occurs, a satisfying experience is assured, without our necessarily being present to provide a reward. The autistic satisfaction thus experienced is, of course, likely to be relatively weak and ephemeral,

3 Konorski (3) has independently made a similar analysis of the mechanism involved in a dog's learning to "shake hands."

but it is often strong enough to carry the desired response along until it can occur in the presence of another organism and thus elicit a more powerful, external reinforcement. Then its stability can be assured.

Perhaps this psychological mechanism can be given further substance by contrasting it with *punishment*. In the latter case, a painful stimulus is used to get *fear* attached to some other, formerly neutral stimulus. This stimulus or "danger signal" may be an external event such as a buzzer or a blinking light, or it may be the particular pattern of internal stimuli associated with the execution of a particular movement. Where punishment has followed a movement, in the future this movement is less likely to be made, because it will produce stimuli which in turn will arouse fear. What is here suggested as the mechanism involved in speech acquisition is, in a sense, the reverse of punishment. In punishment an internal mechanism is set up which tends to *discourage* the occurrence of a particular response, whereas in preparing an infant or a bird for speech an internal mechanism is set up which will tend to *encourage* the occurrence of a particular response, so as to increase the probability of its occurrence, over and beyond what it would be on the basis of chance alone. When one considers how unlikely it is that a baby or a bird would ever, in the course of purely random behavior, produce word-like noises which could then be specifically rewarded, it becomes apparent how necessary is some mechanism of the kind just described.

Implications for Speech Pathology

Two years ago a young woman reported that tests had recently confirmed what she and her husband had suspected for some time, namely that their two-year-old daughter was very hard of hearing and that as a result her language development was being seriously retarded. In fact, the child had no real words, and she showed no interest in and refused to wear a hearing aid. The mother was convinced that the little girl had some hearing, as evidenced by the fact that if she were engaged in some forbidden activity and the mother shouted "No," the child, even though her back was turned to the mother, would respond.

It was apparent from these meager facts that the only sounds that were getting through to this child were "bad" sounds, and one could conjecture that the less often she heard them the better it suited her. There was, in short, no "appetite" for the vocalizations of others and consequently no desire to make similar sounds herself.

When the situation was interpreted to the mother in these terms, she quickly consented to a regime in which vocalizations would not be used for disciplinary purposes at all but would instead be associated as often and as deliberately as possible with *agreeable* experiences. Ordinarily one announces pleasant events in a soft tone of voice, reserving the raised voice for warnings and condemnations. The prescribed plan thus called for a reversal of the usual situation. The mother was able to carry through, however, and very quickly the child became *interested* in words, was soon willing to tolerate a hearing aid so that she would be more clearly aware of them, and within six months was herself effectively making and using quite a number of words.

More recent follow-up data are not available on this case, nor has there been opportunity to test this type of thinking systematically, with a statistically meaningful number of cases. One case can serve as well as many, however, to illustrate a remedial procedure and the rationale behind it. Other investigators, with more numerous cases of a similar kind at their disposal, may be able to validate the procedure. Even though the theory be entirely correct, one cannot, of course, expect success in all instances. The method's effectiveness presupposes, above all else, parents—and in particular a *mother*— who can and will make the indicated changes in vocal habits. Not all parents have the requisite degree of flexibility and motivation to accomplish this end, but it seems likely that the demands which the method places upon parents will usually be acceptable and in such cases the method, given other favorable circumstances, should work as well as in the case described.

Sanger, in an unpublished study directed by the author, observed the relationships of a number of mothers and their infants over a period of many months, with special reference to the role of vocalization by mother and by infant. One of the first things discovered was that most mothers—and particularly those who, by other criteria, seemed to be the *good* mothers—kept their infants "bathed in sound" most of their waking hours. While caring for their infants or just spending leisure time with them, these mothers vocalized almost continuously; and even when other duties took them to adjoining rooms, they would commonly sing or call to the baby intermittently.

This pattern of behavior is well calculated to make the mother's voice a welcome and reassuring sound, and it seems probable that much of the motivation for the babbling and cooing that infants normally engage in stems from the fact that the human voice, by virtue of the circumstances just described, has taken on pleasurable (secondary reinforcing) properties. Although baby's voice does not sound exactly like mother's voice, the similarity will usually be sufficient to cause a carry-over of some of the pleasurable qualities of one to the other; and we may surmise that the production of mother-like sounds, in the form of babbling, is a first and highly useful step in the child's progression toward fully articulate speech.[4]

The fact that congenitally deaf babies babble very little, if any, and do not, without highly specialized instruction, learn to talk at all indicates how crucial is the capacity to hear and inwardly enjoy first the pleasant, reassuring voices of others and then one's own somewhat similar sounds. Although congenitally deaf children usually have completely normal voice organs and although their parents would only too gladly reward them for using these organs to make word-like noises, the fact that such responses, because

4 Because a woman's voice is closer to that of an infant or small child than is a man's voice, it is probably more efficient for women to have primary responsibility for the verbal development of children than it would be for men to have this responsibility.

of the deafness, are not autistically satisfying to the child is a crucial handicap.

It is usually only after a normal infant has had many months of experience with the mother's voice as a good sound that he begins to hear it, on occasion, with implications of warning and threat. That this is an unwelcome development is dramatically indicated by the fact that when parents are scolding or admonishing them, small children will sometimes be seen to put their fingers in their ears, thus shutting out the now distinctly unwelcome human voice. But ordinarily, by the time that parents begin to discipline their offspring by means of speech, the speech-learning process will have already gained sufficient momentum to be able to withstand the shock of this negative use of voice; and the impact of this discipline, however else it may be reflected, almost never has a permanently harmful effect upon language functions.

When, however, the gentle, loving sounds which good mothers make to their infants have been missed, due to hearing defects, and when the first human sounds to get through to the child are shouts of displeasure and proscription, it is almost axiomatic that the child thus handicapped will not *want* to hear, will not *want* to use even that small portion of his hearing equipment which may still be functional. When this abnormal course of events has occurred, the theory here explored would dictate the corrective procedure already described; and with reasonably favorable attending circumstances, one should expect results comparable to those obtained in the case reported.

REFERENCES

1. DE LAGUNA, G. *Speech: Its Function and Development.* New Haven, Conn.: Yale Univ. Press, 1927.
2. HAYES, K. J. and HAYES, C. The intellectual development of a home-raised chimpanzee. *Proc. Amer. phil. Soc.,* 95, 1951, 105–109.
3. KONORSKI, J. Mechanisms of learning. *Physiological Mechanism in Animal Behavior* (Danielli and Brown, eds.). New York: Academic Press, 1951.
4. MOWRER, O. H. *Learning Theory and Personality Dynamics.* New York: Ronald Press, 1950.

ROGER W. BROWN *and* ERIC H. LENNEBERG

27. *A Study in Language and Cognition*

IT is popularly believed that reality is present in much the same form to all men of sound mind. There are objects like a house or a cat and qualities like red or wet and events like eating or singing and relationships like near to or between. Languages are itemized inventories of this reality. They differ, of course, in the sounds they employ, but the inventory is always the same. The esthetic predilections of the Italian lead him to prefer euphonious vowels, while the German is addicted to harsh consonant groupings, but the things and events named are the same in both tongues. We are confirmed in this view by our linguistic education, which requires us to memorize lists of French or German or Latin words and their exact English equivalents.

There are, of course, poetic persons who claim to find in each language some special genius that peculiarly fits it for the expression of certain ideas. But the majority of us are at a loss to understand how this can be, since there is apparently a relationship of mutual translatability among the languages we learn. To be sure, we can see that one language might contain a few items more than another. If the Germans were to invent a new kind of automobile and we had not yet thought of such a machine, their dictionary would have one entry more than ours until we heard of the discovery and named it for ourselves. But these inequalities are in the lexical fringe. They do not disturb the great core of common inventory.

The Whorf Thesis

THIS linguistic ethnocentrism will be seriously disturbed by the study of languages that lie outside the Indo-European group. It has not prepared us for finding that there is a language in which noun and verb categories apparently do not exist, or that there is another in which the colors gray and brown are called by the same name. Such data from the study of American Indian tongues led Whorf (18) to reject the usual view of the relationship between language and thought. He suggested that each language embodies and perpetuates a particular world view. The speakers of a language are partners to an agreement to see and think of the world in a certain way —not the only possible way. The world can be structured in many ways, and the language we learn as children directs the formation of our particular structure. Language is not a cloak following the contours of thought. Languages are molds into which infant minds are poured. Whorf thus departs from the common sense view in (*a*) holding that the world is differently experienced and conceived in different linguistic communities and (*b*) suggesting that language is causally related to these psychological differences.[1]

Other authors have believed that the relationship between language and thought is somewhat as proposed by Whorf. Cassirer (2), the distinguished philosopher, maintained that language is the direct manifestation of knowledge; he explicitly denied a form-content relationship between words or language structure and isolates of knowledge. In this he was in agreement with such other German writers as Wundt (19) and Bühler (1). Orwell (15) in his novel *Nineteen eighty-four* describes a totalitarian England of the

1 While this seems a fair statement of Whorf's usual views, he occasionally took a somewhat more conservative position.

Reprinted by permission of the American Psychological Association and the authors from the *Journal of Abnormal and Social Psychology*, 1954, vol. 49, pp. 454–62.

future. The really efficient dictatorship of that day invents a language—Newspeak—in which it is impossible not only to express, but even to think, a rebellious thought. An equally great faith in the causal efficacy of language lies behind the General Semantics movement. Korzybski (8), for instance, holds that clear thinking and social progress are to be attained through the reform of language.

COGNITIVE DIFFERENCES BETWEEN LINGUISTIC COMMUNITIES

The first tenet of the Whorf thesis is that the world is differently experienced and conceived in different linguistic communities. The evidence presented in support of this claim is entirely linguistic. It will be helpful to distinguish between the conclusions based on lexical features of two languages and those based on structural features.

Lexical features. In the Eskimo lexicon there are three words to distinguish three varieties of snow. There are no single-word equivalents for these in English. The word "snow" would be used to describe all three. What psychological conclusions can be drawn from these data? Does the Eskimo see differences and similarities that we are unable to see?

Psychologists ordinarily infer perceptual discrimination when a subject is consistently able to respond differently to distinctive stimulus situations. The subject may be rat, dog, or man. The response may be running, salivation, or speech. Words are used meaningfully when they are selectively employed with reference to some kind of environment —whether physical, social, or linguistic. The linguist in the field may discover the referent of a term by noting the pattern of its usage. The Eskimo's three "snows" are sufficient evidence from which to infer that he discriminates three varieties of snow. These selective verbal responses satisfy the conditions for inferring perceptual discrimination.

What can be said of the English speaker's ability to distinguish the same three kinds of snow? When different stimuli do not elicit differential responses, the stimuli may or may not be discriminated. A subject may be perfectly able to distinguish two situations and still not care to do anything about it. Consequently the fact that English speakers do not have different names for several kinds of snow cannot be taken to mean that they are *unable* to see the differences. It would seem, then, that all such comparisons are psychologically inconclusive. The Eskimo and American may or may not see the world differently.

There is, however, other evidence to indicate that the speaker of English can classify snows as the Eskimo does. If we listen to the talk of small boys, it is clear that they perceive at least two kinds of snow—good-packing snow and bad-packing snow. This is a distinction of the greatest importance to anyone interested in making snowballs. This discrimination is evidenced by differential response—not distinct lexical items but combinations of items—"good-packing snow" and "bad-packing snow." Whorf himself must have been able to see snow as the Eskimos did since his article describes and pictures the referents for the words. Since both Eskimo and American are able to make differential responses to snows, we must conclude that both are able to see differences. This seems to lead us to the conclusion that the Eskimo and American world views do not differ in this regard.

Although the three kinds of snow are namable in both Eskimo and English, each of them requires a phrase in ordinary English, whereas single words will do it for the Eskimo. Zipf (20) has shown that there exists a tendency in Peiping Chinese, Plautine Latin, and American and British English for the length of a word to be negatively correlated with its frequency of usage. This is true whether word length is measured in phonemes or syllables. It is not difficult to find examples of this relationship in English. New inventions are usually given long names of Greek or Latin derivation, but as the products become widely known and frequently used in conversation the linguistic community finds shorter tags for them. Thus the "automobile" becomes the "car" and "television" shrinks first to "video" and eventually to "TV." Three-dimensional movies are predictably described as "3-D."

Doob (3) has suggested that this principle bears on Whorf's thesis. Suppose we generalize the findings even beyond Zipf's formulation and propose that the length of a verbal expression provides an index of its frequency in speech and that this, in turn, is an index of the frequency with which the relevant perceptual judgments of difference and equivalence are made. If this is true, it would follow that the Eskimo distinguishes his three kinds of snow more often than Americans do. It would mean—to cite another example—that the Hopi is less often called upon to distinguish airplanes, aviators, and butterflies than is the American, since the Hopi has but a single name for all three of these. Such conclusions are, of course, supported by extralinguistic cultural analysis, which reveals the importance of snow in the Eskimo's life and the comparative indifference of the Hopi to airplanes and aviators.

We will go further and propose that increased frequency of a perceptual categorization will mean a generally greater "availability" of that category. In the experimental study of memory we are accustomed to think of the methods of recall, recognition, and relearning as increasingly sensitive indices of retention. In the experimental study of categorizing behavior there are two principal methods: (a) Goldstein's (6) technique of presenting a subject with an array of objects and asking him to group them, and (b) Hull's (7) discrimination learning technique. Hull's method seems to be the more sensitive of the two. We should guess that when the Eskimo steps from his igloo in the morning and is confronted by a snowy world, these snows will fall into named categories for him in a way that they will not for the American. If, however, the American were subjected to a discrimination learning experiment, or if the perceptual structure were otherwise made worth his while, he could see snow as does the Eskimo. We think, really, that more namable categories are nearer the top of the cognitive "deck."

Structural features. Members of structural categories have no phonetic common denominator. They are grouped together because they have the same structural relations with other forms in the language. In English, nouns constitute a structural category; its members can appear with definite and indefinite articles, can form plurals in certain ways, etc. In French all nouns of the feminine gender belong to one structural category since they all require the feminine articles and suffixes.

Whorf generally assumes that structural categories are also symbolic categories. When he finds structural differences in languages he concludes that there are parallel cognitive differences. There are in Hopi two structural categories showing some similarity to our verb and noun categories, with the difference that one of the Hopi classes includes only the names for such short-term events as lightning, flame, and spasm, while the other includes only such long-term events as man, house, and lifetime. Whorf concludes that the Hopi organizes his world on a dimension we usually overlook. When the structural class has such obvious semantic properties, Whorf's conclusions have a kind of plausibility.

However, very few structural classes have such clear and consistent meanings. In the languages we know best, those of the Indo-European family, there are many structural categories with no discernible meaning. In French, for instance, it is not clear that the gender of a form signifies anything to a speaker. Certainly it is difficult to find any common attributes in the references for French nouns of feminine gender. Not even the majority of them manifest feminine sexuality—even in the extended sense of Freud. The French speak of *"le* balcon" in spite of their saying, "Elle a du balcon." The linguist Charles Fries (5) has shown how difficult it is to describe a semantic for the English "parts of speeech." If the noun can be defined as "the name of a person, place, or thing," this is only because "thing" is left unexplicated. It serves handily to designate whatever is nominalized and yet neither person nor place.

Even where the ethnolinguist can discover consistent structural meanings, it does not follow that these meanings are present to the native speakers of a language. Suppose that a subject in the laboratory were required to signal his recognition of each of ten different musical chords by raising that one of his ten fingers which has been designated for each chord. If all extraneous sensory information were excluded, his ability to pattern correctly the movements of his fingers would be evidence of his ability to identify the chords. The experimenter might introduce a potential structural meaning by ruling that the fingers of the right hand would always be raised for chords in the major mode and the fingers of the left hand for minor chords. The subject's responses might follow this pattern and yet he need never have detected the major and minor modes. Similarly, even if there were some semantic to French gender, one could speak the language without detecting it. "La fille" and "la femme" could be learned without noticing that both are in the feminine mode. No safe inferences about cognition can be made on the basis of the simple existence of the structural classes described by Whorf. The structural evidence is extremely difficult to interpret, and it seems clear that psychological data are needed to supplement those of the linguist.

LANGUAGE IN
CAUSAL RELATION TO COGNITION

The second major tenet of Whorf's thesis is that language causes a particular cognitive structure. In what way can this occur? There seem to be two possibilities. Suppose that the colors red and green are not "given" categories but must be learned. A father who has formed these categories may play a game with his child that will teach the categories. The green blocks are to be used for building a house and the red ones for a barn. The child cannot properly pattern the blocks without learning to make the visual distinctions involved. Notice that the barn and house are not essential here. A father could ask his child to tell him whether each block is red or green. In learning this game, too, the child necessarily would learn to perceive the colors. Because words have symbolic properties, because their usage is patterned with reference to the total environment, language can cause a cognitive structure. To the degree that chil-

dren are motivated to speak a language as it is spoken in their community they are motivated to share the world view of that community. To be sure, linguistic training is not the only means of procuring cognitive socialization; the house-barn game demonstrates that. The word game has the tremendous advantage that it can be played constantly and concurrently with many other activities. The child and his adult tutor can chatter together whether they are walking or riding, playing or working. In this chatter more is taught than a simple motor skill involving the muscles of articulation. A total culture is internalized.

There is a second, more dubious, avenue for the influence of language on thought. If life is a river, speech is a babbling brook whose course parallels that of the river. The brook is smaller and simpler than the river. A child can learn the phonemic structure of his language fairly easily. He will also realize that as the phonemic patterns he hears spoken change there are important changes in the nonlinguistic world. There is, for instance, an important difference that goes with the shift of speech from "father" to "mother." When, on the other hand, combinations of phonemes are repeated, two situations are equivalent in some important way. Consider the "strike" and the "ball" in baseball. These are rather difficult categories. The differences between them are subtle and complex. A naive observer of a baseball game would have a difficult time learning these categories by simply observing the game. It makes a great difference that the umpire calls out "strike!" each time a member of that category occurs and "ball!" to identify an instance of the other category. The umpire's shout directs us to look here and now to discover something of importance. The word spotlights a moment of consciousness and puts it in connection with other events similarly spotlighted. The various "strikes" are equivalent in some way and distinct as a category from the events labelled "ball." The babbling brook can, then, be a guide to the structure of the more complex but also more interesting river.

All of our reasoning cannot be said to prove the validity of any set of psychological conclusions. It does, however, point the direction for such a proof and suggests empirical steps that will advance our knowledge of this problem. We have made a small beginning in this work.

Our findings bear on only one of the claims made by Whorf—that there are cognitive differences correlated with lexical differences. We have developed lexical differences into the variable of "codability" and attempted to spell out the relationship between this variable and a single cognitive performance—recognition.

The Experiment

SENSORY psychologists have described the world of color with a solid using three psychological dimensions: hue, brightness, and saturation. The color solid is divisible into millions of just noticeable differences; *Science of Color* (14) estimates 7,500,000. The largest collection (4, 11) of English color names runs to less than 4,000 entries, and of these only about 8 occur very commonly (17). Evidently there is considerable categorization of colors. It seems likely to us that all human beings with normal vision will be able to make approximately the same set of discriminations. This ability appears to depend on the visual system, which is standard equipment for the species. Whatever individual differences do exist are probably not related to culture, linguistic or extralinguistic. It does not follow that people everywhere either see or think of the color world in the same way. Cultural differences probably operate on the level of categorization rather than controlled laboratory discrimination.

Our explorations in the Yale Cross-Cultural Index turned up many reports of differences on this level. Seroshevskii (16), for instance, has reported that in the Iakuti language there is a single word for both green and blue. This is the kind of language difference discussed in the first section of this paper. A region of experience is lexically differentiated in one culture but undifferentiated in another. Color categories differ from such categories as snows in that they have boundaries that can be plotted on known dimensions. Color categories, furthermore, are continuous with one another, sharing their boundaries. Consider for a moment the single dimension of hue taken at a high level of saturation and brightness. Native speakers of English could be shown various shades and asked to give the usual color name for each stimulus presented. For each common color name there would be some shades invariably called by that name. There would be other shades sometimes associated with one name, sometimes with another. When the responses are divided about equally between two or more names, we should have boundaries between categories. If a native speaker of Iakuti were asked to provide the usual color names for the various shades, we should anticipate a somewhat different pattern. English speakers would have trouble naming the hues in the boundary region between green and blue. Probably they would hesitate, disagree among themselves, and sometimes use phrases or such combination names as "greenish blue." For the Iakuti, on the other hand, this region is right in the center of a category and would be named with great ease.

Of course, our example is greatly simplified over the actual case since we have dealt with the single dimension of hue whereas the color lexicon is actually patterned with respect to all of the three dimensions of visual experience. When these are considered, the range of applicability of a color term is a space within the color solid rather than a distance along a line. The simplification was for expository purposes and does not alter the logic of the argument.

This example of a cultural difference serves to introduce the variable *codability*. Certain colors are differentially codable in the Iakuti and English languages. So long as the data collected are of the usual linguistic variety, this difference of codability will be manifest in only one way—environmental distinctions expressed lexically in one language are expressed with word combinations in another language. Our reasoning led us to expect differential availability of reference categories in such a case. We undertook experimental work to discover additional behavioral indices of codability, and hoped to find one more sensitive than that which can be teased out of linguistic data. If we found such an index, we would go on to explore the behavioral consequences of differential availability of cognitive categories.

There are differences of codability within English itself. Some shades fall safely within the province of a given name while others lie within boundary regions. Here it is a matter of comparing the English codability of one region of visual experience with another region, whereas the ethnolinguist has usually compared the codability of one region of experience in several languages. If we explore the codability variable in English, it seems likely that our discoveries will apply to the cultural differences with which the inquiry began. If a general law can be found relating codability to availability, individual cultures may conform to the law though they differ among themselves in the values these variables assume in particular regions of experience.

MEASUREMENT OF CODABILITY

The entire series of Munsell colors for the highest level of saturation ("chroma" as Munsell calls it) was mounted on cards in systematic fashion. Five judges were asked to pick out the best red, orange, yellow, green, blue, purple, pink, and brown from these 240 colors. These names are the most frequently appearing color terms in English (17). For each name the color chip most often selected was added to our test list. Agreement among judges was high, and it is quite clear, therefore, that there is in this series one particular color chip with the best claim to each color name. The number of colors was then raised to 24 by adding chips that would, in combination with the first 8, provide as even a coverage of the color space as practicable. These colors are specified in TABLE 1. One set of the 24 chips was mounted on white 3 × 5 cards, one chip to a card. Another set was arranged randomly on a single large card.

To expose the single small cards a drop shutter was mounted in a 3 × 2-foot gray (Munsell neutral value 6, reflectance 30 per cent) board. The board was about three feet from the subject's (S's) eyes and was illu-

minated from above and behind by a General Electric standard daylight fluorescent lamp.

The Ss were 24 Harvard and Radcliffe students who spoke English as a native language and had no particular training in distinguishing colors. They were screened for color blindness with the standard Pseudo-Isochromatic Plates.

The Ss were first shown the 24-color random chart for about five minutes. After the chart was removed, they were told that each of the colors on the chart would appear individually in the tachistoscope and that S's task was to give the name of each as it appeared. "Name" was defined as the word or words one would ordinarily use to describe the color to a friend. The Ss were urged to be both quick and accurate.

The 24 colors were presented in a predetermined random order for each S. No order was repeated. Each color was exposed until S had named it. In our trial procedure we used a voice key and chronoscope to measure the reaction time. The scope was activated by the opening shutter of the tachistoscope and stopped by S's first vocalization. This method proved to be unsuitable since Ss would frequently burst out with something other than a color name, which, of course, stopped the undiscriminating chronoscope. Consequently, we abandoned this technique and used the stop watch. The watch was started as the experimenter (E) dropped the shutter and stopped at first mention of a color name.

The variable of codability was measured in five ways. (a) The average length of naming response to each color was obtained by counting syllables. (b) The average length was also obtained by counting words. (c) The average reaction time for each color was obtained by ranking all of the reaction times of an individual S and taking the mean rank across Ss for every color. (d) The degree to which Ss agreed with one another in naming a color was assessed as follows: We counted the total number of different responses to a color (DR) and also the number of Ss who agreed on whatever response was most often given to a particular color (CR). The first value was subtracted from the second and a constant of 20 added to keep the results positive (CR −

TABLE 1

The Munsell Notation and Scores for Discriminability, Codability, and Recognition
for the 24 Test Colors

MUNSELL NOTATION *	DISCRIMI- NABILITY		CODABILITY		RECOGNITION (GROUP C TABLE 3)	
	Score	Rank	Score	Rank	Score	Rank
2.5R 7/8	38	2	18	9.5	.875	8
2.5R 5/10	27.5	6	7	18.5	.694	11
5R 4/14	23	10.5	19	7.5	1.020	5
7.5R 8/4	18	15	7	18.5	.236	18
2.5YR 6/14	38	2	29	1.5	1.499	2
5YR 3/4	24	9	26	3	.972	7
7.5YR 5/8	26	7.5	8	16	.736	9
2.5Y 7/10	12	19	3	24	.486	13
5Y 8/12	37	4	25	4	2.450	1
7.5Y 6/8	13	17	4	23	.250	17
3GY 7.5/11.2	23	10.5	14	12	1.222	4
7.5GY 3/4	9.5	23	14	12	0.000	23.5
2.5G 5/8	18.5	14	23	6	.986	6
7.5G 8/4	17.5	16	19	7.5	.167	19
5BG 3/6	4.5	24	12	15	.111	22
10BG 6/6	21	12	7	18.5	.458	14
8.5B 3/6.8	38	2	13	14	0.000	23.5
2.5PB 7/6	19	13	18	9.5	.436	16
5PB 4/10	10.5	21	29	1.5	.695	10
10PB 5/10	12	19	7	18.5	.125	20.5
5P 8/4	12	19	14	12	.547	12
10P 3/10	10	22	24	5	.444	15
5RP 6/10	26	7.5	6	21.5	.125	20.5
3RP 3.4/12.1	31	5	6	21.5	1.464	3

* For conversion to C.I.E. Tristimulus values and Source C, C.I.E. chromaticity coordinates
see Nickerson, Tomaszewski, and Boyd (13).

DR + 20). Color 18, for example, was given the following eight different names: gray-blue, blue, light gray-blue, light blue, very pale blue, light blue-gray, pale blue, and powder blue. Of these, the single-word response "blue" occurred most often—six times. Color 18, then, scored 6 − 8 + 20, or 18. (e) The degree to which Ss agreed with themselves from one time to another in naming a color was calculated as follows: Five Ss were recalled after a period of one month and subjected to a repetition of the naming procedure. When an S gave identical responses to a color on the two occasions, we counted one agreement. We determined the number of agreements for each S and considered that to be unity. Each individual agreement was then given the appropriate fractional value. Suppose an S had eight agreements. If he agreed

in his name for Color 11, he would add ⅛ to the score for that color. The agreement score is, then, the sum of the individual performances weighted for each individual's over-all tendency to agreement.

In TABLE 2 the intercorrelations of scores on these five measures appear. All correlations are in the predicted direction and most of them are significant, with .355 the smallest. With a single iteration this matrix yielded a general factor which we call codability. No correlations over .113 remain after the extraction of this single factor. Our fourth index, the degree of agreement between Ss, has by far the largest factor loading. It was selected as the measure of codability for the second phase of the experiment. The obtained codability values for the 24 colors are listed in TABLE 1.

TABLE 2

Correlation Matrix for Five Indices of Codability

MEASURE	1	2	3	4	5
Number of syllables					
Number of words	.425 *				
Reaction time	.387	.368			
Interpersonal agreement	.630 *	.486 *	.864 *		
Intrapersonal agreement	.355	.537 *	.649 *	.773 *	
k from second factoring	.589	.587	.787	.976	.795
Communality from first factoring	.403	.378	.671	.873	.653

$* p \leqq .05.$

CODABILITY AND RECOGNITION

Once the codability variable suggested by Whorf's ethnolinguistic observations had been operationalized, it remained to relate this variable to some nonlinguistic behavior which might be considered an index of availability. We selected the recognition of colors.

From the 240 Munsell chips taken at highest saturation we selected out alternate chips, taking care to include the 24 colors for which codability data had been collected. The resultant collection of 120 colors was systematically mounted on a white card. Hue varied along the vertical dimension of the card and brightness on the horizontal dimension. Since there were 20 steps of hue and only 6 of brightness, we divided the total colors in half and mounted one half above the other so as to make a more manipulable display.

New *S*s were screened, as before, for color blindness and language background. The basic procedure was to expose simultaneously 4 of the 24 colors, remove them, and ask *S*s to point to the colors just seen, on the large chart of 120. Neither *E* nor *S* mentioned any color name during the session. The recognition score for a color was computed as follows: We determined the number of correct identifications made by each *S* and considered this number to be unity. Each individual correct identification was given the appropriate fractional value. Suppose for instance, that an *S* who correctly identified a total of six colors recognized Color 24. This recognition would have counted as ⅙ on the total recognition score for that color. Another *S* for whom Color 24 was one of eight correctly identified colors would have contributed ⅛ to the score for Color 24. In other words, the recognition score for a color is the sum of the individual performances weighted for each *S*'s over-all ability to recognize colors. The scores for the 24 colors appear in TABLE 1.

In trial runs, *S*s were asked how they managed to retain the four colors in memory after they were removed from sight. Most *S*s reported that they named the colors when they were exposed and "stored" the names. It seemed likely, therefore, that those colors that are quite unequivocally coded would be most likely to be recognized. When a color elicits a considerable range of names, the chances of recovering the color from the name would be reduced. This expectation was fulfilled by a rank-order correlation of .415 between codability and recognition scores.

There is, however, another variable that influenced recognition. The 120 colors used are not perceptually perfectly equidistant. The manufacture of equidistant color chips is technically difficult and expensive and, indeed, above a certain level of saturation, impossible. Since we were unable to control experimentally the variable "discriminability," we must ask whether or not our findings were due to a positive correlation between codability and discriminability. Could it be that our codable colors were so distant, perceptually, from their nearest neighbors that their superior recognizability was actually due to these better discrimination conditions? To obtain an answer to this question we determined the true perceptual distance between each of the colors used from the Newhall, Nickerson, and Judd (12) charts. These charts convert every Munsell book notation into a renotation which is the specification of a true perceptual locus of each color within the Munsell coordinate system. The difference between two renotations expresses quantitatively the perceptual distance between the colors.

For each of the 24 test colors we computed a discriminability score which describes its distinctiveness from the colors surrounding it. The difference between two renotations yields three numbers, one for each dimension. To make these numbers perceptually commensurable (i.e., to reduce them to a common denominator), the Optical Society of America Subcommittee on the Spacing of the Munsell Colors suggests the values 3, 2, and 1 for hue, chroma, and value, respectively. Since every color has two neighbors on each of the three dimensions, a total of six numbers will express, in a rough way, the discriminability of that color. The sum of these yields the unadjusted discriminability score. Adjustments of this score are necessary (a) because if a color appears on the margin of our chart it has a lower chance of being recognized correctly and (b) because a color that has a very close neighbor on one side and distant neighbors on three others might come out with a good discriminability score although the close contiguity on one side would hinder correct recognition considerably. Consequently, colors appearing on the margin of our chart had the constant 3 subtracted from their unadjusted discriminability score, and colors with a close neighbor had the constant 6 subtracted.

Our scoring method is to a certain degree arbitrary, to be sure, but since the equation of perceptual distances on different visual dimensions is an unsolved problem, there seems to be no more objective method available. In addition, of course, all decisions were made without knowledge of recognition scores.

Since we were unable to control discriminability experimentally, we controlled it statistically. The partial correlation between codability and recognition, with discriminability constant, is .438. Furthermore, the correlation between codability and discriminability is .074, which is not significant. Evidently the relation between codability and recognition is not a consequence of variations in discriminability.

Since the reports of our early Ss indicated that colors were stored in linguistic code, it seemed likely that color codability would increase in importance as the storage factor was maximized in the recognition situation. Discriminability, on the other hand, should remain at the same level of importance or possibly decline somewhat. If, for example, a single color were exposed, removed, and then identified with minimal delay, Ss might retain some direct memory of the color, perhaps as a visual image. In this situation discriminability would be a determinant of recognition but codability would not be. However, when the number of colors is increased and the interval prolonged and filled with activity, the importance of linguistic coding should increase. TABLE 3 describes the experimental variations we used. Groups A, B, C, and D are arranged in what we believed to be an order of increasingly difficult storage of colors. Group C is our major group, for which results have already been described. The tasks which filled the interval for Group D were simple but absorbing—the kind of thing often used in experiments on the Zeigarnik phenomenon.

It can be seen from the data in TABLE 4 that

TABLE 3

Recognition Procedures

GROUP	N	NUMBER OF COLORS ORIGINALLY EXPOSED	LENGTH OF INTERVAL	CONTENT OF INTERVAL
A	9	1	7 seconds	
B	9	4	7 seconds	
C	16	4	30 seconds	
D	9	4	3 minutes	Tasks

Note: Exposure time for all groups was 3 seconds.

TABLE 4

Correlations Involving Scores on Codability (C), Discriminability (D), and Recognition (R) with Four Experimental Conditions for Recognition

GROUP	C WITH R	D WITH R	C WITH R, D CONSTANT
A	.248	.540 *	.248
B	.411	.460 *	.426 *
C	.415	.503 *	.438 *
D	.487 *	.505 *	.523 *

$* p \leqq .05$.

the correlation between recognition and codability scores does increase as the importance of storage in the recognition task increases.[2] The particular order obtained would occur by chance only once in 24 times.

TABLE 4 also shows that discriminability is most closely related to recognition in Group A, for which the possibility of some direct memory of the color is maximized. The importance of discriminability declines slightly but not significantly as the recognition is made more difficult. Our expectations with regard to both codability and discriminability are generally confirmed.

In the first section of this paper we concluded our discussion of lexical differences between languages with the prediction that a given set of cognitive categories will be more available to the speakers of a language that lexically codes these categories than to the speakers of a language in which the categories are not represented in the lexicon. Lexical differences have been expanded into the variable of codability, and category availability has been operationalized as a recognition score. We found that differences in the English codability of colors are related to differences in the recognition of these colors. We expected these results to apply to the cross-cultural case, and some confirmation of this expectation is available in the results of a study by Lenneberg and Roberts (10).

2 Kurtz and Hovland (9) have shown that verbalization during observation of stimulus objects facilitates recognition under certain circumstances.

This study of Zuni Indians used a field adaptation of our methods and apparatus. The Zuni color lexicon codes the colors we call orange and yellow with a single term. Monolingual Zuni Ss in their recognition task frequently confused the orange and yellow colors in our stimulus set. Our English-speaking Ss never made this error. It is a distinction which is highly codable in English and highly uncodable in Zuni. Interestingly, bilingual Zunis who knew English fell between the monolingual Zuni and the native speaker of English in the frequency with which they made these errors.

The Whorf thesis claims more than a simple relationship between language and cognition; language is held to be causally related to cognitive structure. Our correlational evidence does not, of course, establish the direction of causality. If we may be permitted a guess it is that in the history of a culture the peculiar features of the language and thought of a people probably develop together.

In the history of an individual born into a linguistic community the story is quite different. The patterned responses are all about him. They exist before he has the cognitive structure that will enable him to pattern his behavior in the approved fashion. Simple exposure to speech will not shape anyone's mind. To the degree that the unacculturated individual is motivated to learn the language of a community, to the degree that he uses its structure as a guide to reality, language can assume a formative role.

Summary

THE Whorf thesis on the relationship between language and thought is found to involve the following two propositions: (a) Different linguistic communities perceive and conceive reality in different ways. (b) The language spoken in a community helps to shape the cognitive structure of the individuals speaking that language. The evidence for the first proposition derives from a comparison of the lexical and structural characteristics of various languages. The linguistic comparisons alone do not establish the proposition. They need to be complemented with psychological data. The second proposition is not directly supported by any data. However, it is clear that language can be described as a molder of thought since speech is a patterned response that is learned only when the governing cognitive patterns have been grasped. It is also possible that the lexical structure of the speech he hears guides the infant in categorizing his environment. These matters require empirical exploration.

An experiment is described which investigates a part of proposition *a*—the idea that lexical differences are indicative of cognitive differences. Whorf reports many cases in which a given range of experience is lexically differentiated in one language whereas the same discriminations can only be described with phrases in another language. Rather than compare members of different linguistic communities, we chose to work with native speakers of English and to compare their linguistic coding of two regions of experience. Within the realm of color vision there are colors that can be named with a single word and others

that require a phrase. This kind of linguistic difference in the length of name (measured by words or syllables) was found to be correlated with the latency of the naming response and the reliability of the response from person to person within the linguistic community and from time to time in one person. A factor analysis of these measures yielded a single general factor—codability. The measure carrying the largest factor loading was the reliability of naming response between individuals who speak the same language. This variable—the codability of a color—proved to be related to Ss' ability to recognize colors. Codability accounted for more variance in the recognition task as the task was delayed and complicated to increase the importance of the storage factor. Data obtained from the Zuni Indians show a similar relationship between codability and recognition. It is suggested that there may be general laws relating codability to cognitive processes. All cultures could conform to these laws although they differ among themselves in the values the variables assume in particular regions of experience.

REFERENCES

1. BÜHLER, K. *Sprachtheorie.* Jena: G. Fischer, 1934.
2. CASSIRER, E. *The philosophy of symbolic forms.* Vol. 1. *Language.* New Haven: Yale Univer. Press, 1953.
3. DOOB, L. W. *Social psychology.* New York: Holt, 1952.
4. EVANS, R. M. *An introduction to color.* New York: Wiley, 1948.
5. FRIES, C. C. *The structure of English.* New York: Harcourt, Brace, 1952.
6. GOLDSTEIN, K. *Language and language disturbances.* New York: Grune & Stratton, 1948.
7. HULL, C. L. Quantitative aspects of the evolution of concepts. *Psychol. Monogr.,* 1920, 28, No. 1 (Whole No. 123).
8. KORZYBSKI, A. The role of language in the perceptual processes. In R. R. Blake & G. V. Ramsey (Eds.), *Perception; an approach to personality.* New York: Ronald, 1951. Pp. 170–205.

9. KURTZ, K. H., & HOVLAND, C. I. The effect of verbalization during observation of stimulus objects upon accuracy of recognition and recall. *J. exp. Psychol.,* 1953, 45, 157–164.
10. LENNEBERG, E. H., & ROBERTS, J. M. The denotata of color terms. Paper read at Linguistic Society of America, Bloomington, Indiana, August, 1953.
11. MAERZ, A., & PAUL, M. R. *A dictionary of color.* New York: McGraw-Hill, 1930.
12. NEWHALL, S. M., NICKERSON, D., & JUDD, D. B. Final report of the OSA subcommittee on the spacing of the Munsell colors. *J. opt. Soc. Amer.,* 1943, 33, 385–418.
13. NICKERSON, D., TOMASZEWSKI, J. J., & BOYD, T. F. Colorimetric specifications of Munsell repaints. *J. opt. Soc. Amer.,* 1953, 43, 163–171.
14. OPTICAL SOCIETY OF AMERICA, COMMITTEE ON COLORIMETRY. *The science of color.* New York: Crowell, 1953.

15. ORWELL, G. *Nineteen eighty-four.* New York: Harcourt, Brace, 1949.
16. SEROSHEVSKII, V. R. *Iakuti.* St. Petersburg: Royal Geographical Society, 1896.
17. THORNDIKE, E. L., & LORGE, I. *The teacher's word book of 30,000 words.* New York: Teachers Coll., Columbia Univer., 1944.
18. WHORF, B. L. *Four articles on metalinguistics.* Washington: Foreign Service Institute, 1950.
19. WUNDT, W. *Völkerpsychologie.* Vol. 1. *Die Sprache,* Leipzig: Engelmann, 1900.
20. ZIPF, G. K. *The psycho-biology of language.* Boston: Houghton Mifflin, 1935.

ROBERT E. ADAMSON

28. *Functional Fixedness as Related to Problem Solving: A Repetition of Three Experiments*

THE study of problem solving and think-ing has been retarded by the lack of agreed-upon theoretical concepts sup-ported by adequate data from experiments. As a part of a larger program concerned with these matters, some of the more promising hypotheses have been assembled, and pre-liminary experiments undertaken to repeat the demonstrations upon which these hypotheses rest.

One inviting hypothesis is that problem solving may in some instances be delayed through the "functional fixedness" of solution objects. That is, owing to his previous use of the object in a function dissimilar to that de-manded by the present problem, S is inhibited in discovering the appropriate new use of the object. This hypothesis was proposed by Duncker (3), who designed ingenious ex-periments to support it, but carried the ex-periments through with but 14 Ss and under poorly specified experimental conditions. It seemed wise, therefore, to repeat some of his experiments both to substantiate his results, if possible, and to ascertain the efficacy of the problems for use in further investigations. The success of Birch and Rabinowitz (1) in demonstrating functional fixedness in a re-lated experiment encouraged us to hope for positive results.

Procedure

SUBJECTS

ALL Ss taking part in this study were college students from elementary psychology classes.

There were 57 Ss, of whom 35 were men, 22 women. Twenty-nine Ss were assigned to the experimental group, 28 to the control group. All Ss were of proximate ages and had been exposed to little experimentation.

PROBLEMS

Duncker's "box," "gimlet," and "paperclip" problems were presented to each S in the order named. In the first of these, the box problem, S's task is to mount three candles vertically on a screen, at a height of about 5 ft., using to accomplish this task any of a large number of objects which are lying be-fore S on a table. Among these objects are three pasteboard boxes of varying sizes, five matches, and five thumbtacks, the crucial ob-jects for solution of the problem. The solu-tion is to mount one candle on each box by melting wax on the box and sticking the candle to it, then to tack the boxes to the screen.

The gimlet problem involves suspending three cords from a board attached to an over-head beam. Among the variety of objects available are two screw-hooks and the gimlet itself, the objects from which the cords may be hung.

The paperclip problem consists of first at-taching four small black cardboard squares to a large white square, then hanging the large square from an eyelet screwed into the afore-mentioned beam. Included among the objects lying before S on the table are a number of paperclips. These may be used to attach the

Reprinted by permission of the American Psychological Association and the author from the *Journal of Experimental Psychology*, 1952, vol. 44, pp. 288–91.

small squares to the large one, and one of them, when bent to form a hook, will serve to hang the large square from the eyelet.

DESIGN

The experimental and control groups were given the same problems to solve. For the experimental group, however, at least one of the solution objects was "burdened" with a prior function in each problem. Thus, the candles, matches, and tacks for the box problem were placed in the three boxes before they were given to S. Hence, the boxes had for their initial function that of containing, whereas in their solution function they had to be used as supports or platforms. Similarly the gimlet initially had to be used to start holes for the screw-hooks, and in the paper-clip problem, the four black squares had to be attached to the white one with paperclips. Duncker referred to the experimental group as the "after pre-utilization" group.

The control group was given the problems without any pre-utilization. In the case of the box problem, the empty boxes were placed on the table at varying distances from the other crucial solution objects. Holes into which the screw-hooks and the gimlet could be screwed were already drilled into the beam in the case of the gimlet problem; the four black squares were stapled to the white one in the paper-clip problem. Thus, none of the crucial objects was used with a function prior to its use as a solution object.

Solution scores were taken as one possible measure of functional fixedness, and time-to-solution constituted another measure. A maximum time of 20 min. was allowed for solution of each of the problems.

Results

BOX PROBLEM

THE results of the box problem, presented in TABLE 1, confirm Duncker's finding that functional fixedness results from pre-utilization. The performance of the experimental group was markedly inferior to that of the control with respect both to the number of solutions obtained and the time required to reach solution. Prior usage of the boxes as containers inhibited their being used as platforms.

The chi-square value comparing the two groups on the time score was obtained by using as a cutting point the median time-to-solution of the combined groups. All cases for which there was no solution were assigned to the above-median category. With 1 df, each of the chi squares was highly significant. Since the direction of the difference was predicted, a one-tail test of significance was employed for both this and the following two problems.

GIMLET PROBLEM

Since only three Ss failed to solve this problem, all from the experimental group, the solution score could not demonstrate a difference between the experimental and control groups. Accordingly, only the results from the time measure are given in TABLE 2. The three Ss failing to reach solution were not considered in the analysis of the data, thus reducing the total n to 54 for this experiment.

Since, as shown in TABLE 2, the variances for the two groups are not homogeneous, the use of t as a test of significance was inappropriate. Instead, t' was employed.[1] The

[1] This technique was suggested by Dr. Quinn McNemar. Instead of utilizing one estimate of the

TABLE 1

Box Problem

GROUP	n	NUMBER SOLVING	TIME-TO-SOLUTION *
Exper.	29	12 (41%)	7 (24%)
Control	28	24 (86%)	22 (78%)
		$\chi^2 = 12.0 \ p = .001$	$\chi^2 = 14.8 \ p = .001$

* Number below median of combined group.

TABLE 2

Gimlet and Paperclip Problems

PROBLEM AND GROUP	n	MEAN TIME-TO-SOLUTION (SEC.)	SD	t'	p*
Gimlet					
Exper.	26	246.6	124.7	3.71	.001
Control	28	144.0	67.7		
Paperclip					
Exper.	29	107.9	96.0	2.38	.01
Control	28	63.0	31.5		

* Single-tail test.

highly significant difference obtained shows clearly the presence of functional fixedness.

PAPERCLIP PROBLEM

The results from the paperclip problem are also shown in TABLE 2. Since all Ss were able to solve this problem, only time scores are given. As in the first two problems, pre-utilization of the solution objects with a function different from that demanded by the problem resulted in significantly poorer performance by the experimental group.

RELIABILITY OF INDIVIDUAL PERFORMANCE

An analysis was made of the performance of the experimental group to determine whether individual achievement on one of the three problems was significantly related to achievement on either of the other two. Chi square was used to test whether individuals scoring below the median in time-to-solution for one of two problems also showed a significant tendency to score below the median for the other. (Since only 12 of 29 Ss solved the box problem, a median time-to-solution could not be obtained; instead, the distribution was dichotomized in terms of solution or no-solution.) A relation significant at the .05 level was found between the box problem and the paperclip problem. Neither of the other chi

population variance, t' incorporates the estimated variances from two populations (2). It is, in consequence, useful in such a situation as the present one, replacing t which assumes homogeneity of variance.

squares was significant. Clearly, achievement on a single problem involving pre-utilization is not a reliable measure of individual susceptibility to functional fixedness.

Discussion

DUNCKER's study (3), involving these three experiments, used two measures of performance: number of presolutions, and number of solutions. In the present study, the number of presolutions was discarded as a measure, because it was found to be overly dependent upon the subjective judgment of E. Number of solutions proved to be a satisfactory measure for only the box problem. Since all Ss solved the paperclip problem, and all but three solved the gimlet problem, no difference between the experimental and the control groups could be revealed by this measure. It would appear that the Ss in the present study were more able than those employed by Duncker.

Although the measures previously used by Duncker failed to show functional fixedness in two of the three present experiments, a new measure, time-to-solution, gave positive results in all three experiments. Essentially, then, the present results confirm those obtained by Duncker.

The results of Duncker, of Birch and Rabinowitz, and those obtained in this study afford convincing proof of the existence of functional fixedness. The reality of this phenomenon having been established, two lines of investigation are of immediate interest: (a) determination of those conditions which influence the occurrence of functional fixedness, and (b) exploration of its relation to other kinds of set in problem solving. A study now nearing completion involves both of these lines of experimentation.

Summary

1. Three of Duncker's experiments on functional fixedness were repeated in this study. Fifty-seven Ss were used, 29 serving as the experimental and 28 as the control group. Both groups were given the "box," "gimlet,"

and "paperclip" problems in that order. Experimental Ss were given each problem after first having used the solution objects for that problem in a function dissimilar to that demanded for solution. Control Ss were given the problems without such preutilization.

2. Two measures of performance were used: number of solutions, and time-to-solution. The former measure discriminated between the experimental and control groups on only the box problem; the latter measure gave highly significant differences in the expected direction for all three problems.

3. Functional fixedness was shown to result from the pre-utilization of solution objects. Duncker's results were confirmed in a study using a larger n and having more carefully specified experimental conditions.

REFERENCES

1. BIRCH, H. G., & RABINOWITZ, H. S. The negative effect of previous experience on productive thinking. *J. exp. Psychol.,* 1951, 41, 121–125.

2. COCHRAN, W. G., & COX, G. M. *Experimental design.* New York: John Wiley & Sons, 1950.

3. DUNCKER, K. On problem-solving. *Psychol. Monogr.,* 1945, 58, No. 5 (Whole No. 270).

L. SZÉKELY

29. *Knowledge and Thinking*

"The ability to foresee and to plan ahead, that is the ability to use past experiences in order to establish future conditions corresponding to the needs, desires and the aspirations of man, is the first essential prerequisite of freedom."

—B. Malinowski, "Freedom and civilisation."

A N examination question may serve as the best introduction to the problem of our investigation.

At the juridical faculty of B. University the candidates are tested with respect to their knowledge of the Penal Code. Under discussion is a rule of law stating that "Whoever damages or destroys for revenge another person's property is guilty of a crime . . . ," whereupon punitive measures are stated.

The examiner then asks the first candidate: "Suppose you were the judge and had to give a decision on the following practical case. Somebody has been accused of having wilfully, for revenge, thrown someone else's ring into a river. . . . " The candidate: "I would find him guilty." Examiner: "But the ring was not damaged or destroyed. If a diver brings it to the surface, it will be exactly as it was before. What about you, candidate B?" "I would acquit him." "Why?" "Because the ring is undamaged." "Well, in that case any person could take revenge by throwing other people's property into a river. Should he get away with that?"

Six or seven other candidates are unable to find their way out of this legal dilemma. Finally someone says: "I would find the defendant guilty." "Why?" "It is true that the ring as a physical object is undamaged. But the ring has also a value. It is a valuable that one can pawn, sell, etc. Lying at the bottom of the river, however, the ring has no value. It regains its value only after the diver

has brought it back to the surface. That means that its value was restored through human labor. Labor for its part, has its specific price. In the end, the cost of this labor was equivalent to the actual damage." This answer was accepted.

In what way is the solution of the problem attained? The ring is considered from a new point of view. It is not just a physical object, it is also an object of value. The criminalistic fact of the damage or destruction is shifted from the physical aspect of the object to the aspect of its value. The "concept" ring is restructured, reorganized.

Is it really such an unusual idea that the ring represents an object of value? Not at all. On the contrary, that aspect of a ring which usually presents itself foremost to our mind is that of its value. To the question of what they would give for a ring lying at the bottom of a river, all candidates undoubtedly would have replied, "Nothing. There it has no value." What is then, in fact, so original, new and unusual about the idea that led to the solution of the problem?

In the process of thinking normally those qualities of the object impress us which are characteristic of its common use (R. Katz 6). We approach a ring with tendencies like "have," "acquire," "sell," etc., and these tendencies usually provoke the question, "What is its value?" Our juridical examination case, however, refers to destructive activities. Here the crucial aspect under consideration is the destruction or damaging of the physical na-

Reprinted by permission of North-Holland Publishing Company and the author from *Acta Psychologica*, 1950, pp. 1–24. Translated by Dr. R. Palm.

ture of the object, and the candidates constantly view the problem from this angle.

Can we assume that the difference in the reaction of the candidates, their success or failure in solving the problem, stems from individual differences in their knowledge? Very unlikely. They all were equally familiar with the wording of the law and the fact that the ring has value was no secret to any of them. The difference is to be explained by the fact that in the mind of the one candidate a certain quality which was not brought out by the situation as such became "thematic," while in the mind of the others only the habitual aspects of this situation were functionally operative.

Our examination case is typical for those situations in which we are confronted with the problem of the relation between knowledge and thinking. To solve a problem, a certain knowledge is required. But out of a group of persons with the same and, for the particular problem, sufficient knowledge only relatively few are able to use their knowledge effectively and productively.

Experiences of every-day life often have affected the handling of scientific problems. Experiences of this kind led to certain, not very clearly defined, theories about the temporal localization of productive processes. According to these theories, all the mental processes involved in productive thinking would take place only during the act of problem solving itself. Whether or not a solution of the problem is attained would depend exclusively on the present solution process and would be independent from the characteristics of all the previous processes through which the present knowledge and experience was acquired.

It is the aim of the following investigation to examine the correctness of this assumption.

Relation between Knowledge and Thinking

THE functional relation between learning (acquiring of experience), knowing and thinking can be approached from three different angles.

Knowledge is first of all the end-result of learning, of experiencing or, in rarer cases, of independent thinking and reflecting.

Secondly, knowledge can be the starting point for the absorption and the understanding of something new, or for thought continuation (thought progress). Our attitude towards a present event, f.i., is dependent on our past experiences. It depends on our past experiences whether we put the present one as self-evident "ad acta," or whether we are surprised about it, try to find an explanation for it, are stimulated to further thinking, etc. (Székely 13).

Thirdly, our stock of knowledge serves as the matter and as the aid which one applies in the thought process, in the solving of a present problem and in coming to terms with a new situation.

One can therefore investigate knowledge in its function of (1) end-result, (2) starting point, and (3) medium of learning and thinking.

In the field of memory psychology a great deal of attention has been given to the problem of knowledge as the end-result of learning and experiencing. Also knowledge as the end-result of thinking has been studied by a number of authors. In this connection the studies about theory-formation in children by R. Katz (6), Piaget (9), Huang (3), E. Becker (2), C. Raspe (10) should be mentioned. As is known, all these studies have been conducted mainly by the method of questioning.

Knowledge as [the] starting point of independent thinking has not as yet been investigated experimentally. The studies of Székely (11, 13, 16) represent the first beginning in this direction. Knowledge as [the] starting point of independent thinking might be investigated through certain experiments in which the subject has to forethink what might happen in a certain never-before-experienced situation. In that way it is possible to observe whether and how the subject applies a certain piece of knowledge accessible to his memory; also whether and how a certain piece of knowledge which is no longer accessible to the "representative" memory (that is, "forgotten" knowledge) can nevertheless be used.

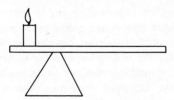

FIG. 1.   Equilibrium task.

For the investigation of knowledge as [the] medium ("vehicle") of thinking, certain problem-solving tasks are instrumental.

In order to examine the methodological value of these different possibilities and especially in order to clarify the theoretical situation, we have—in a few preliminary experiments—presented the same thought problem from all three angles. In the first experiment the subject is confronted with a phenomenon which is new to him, in order to obtain (post factum) his explanation of what happened. In the second experiment the same phenomenon has to be forethought before it manifests itself (ante factum). In a third experiment the same phenomenon has to be experimented upon freely by the subject in order to find the solution. Of course, different subjects have to be used for each of the three experiments.

Preliminary Experiments

TO EXPLAIN A NEW PHENOMENON AFTER OBSERVING IT (POST FACTUM)

A CANDLE is placed on one end of a quadrangular lever, about forty centimeters long, and the lever is balanced on the beveled edge of a triangular prism (FIG. 1). Then the candle is lighted. After a few minutes the lever tips over. The subject now has to explain why the lever fell down.

TO THINK OUT AN EVENT IN ADVANCE (ANTE FACTUM)

The same arrangement, but without lighting the candle. The subject is asked: "What would happen if the candle were lighted?"

Experiments showed that it is more difficult to foresee an event than to explain it after it has happened. Small children cannot an-

ticipate the tipping-over of the lever, but are able to give an explanation post factum. The ability to foresee, to forethink, is generally the more important social function. Anybody in everyday life may find himself in situations where he has to make a decision in favor of one or the other way of acting and his choice will depend on his ability to forethink.

TO FIND A SOLUTION THROUGH FREE EXPERIMENTATION

A lever, a prism and a number of small objects, among them a candle and a box of matches, are placed on the table in front of the subject (Székely 11). The subject is supposed to balance the lever, after burdening it on one end with an appropriate object, on the edge of the prism, but in such a way that it tips over automatically, i.e., without being touched, after a few minutes.

In this form the problem is the most difficult and its solution requires, in the vast majority of cases, several minutes and considerable mental effort.

Discussion of the Results

WE confine ourselves to a qualitative evaluation of the results. The essential piece of knowledge, the application of which leads to the solution of this problem in all three situations, is the fact that through burning the candle loses in weight. This fact is, it would seem, common knowledge. Why then is it so difficult for a considerable number of the subjects to dispose of this knowledge? What exactly makes this problem such a difficult one? How does the idea arise: "Light the candle, place it on the lever, and balance the latter?" These are the questions which interest us. The introspection of the subject, however, fails us entirely.

It is the investigators and not the subject's task to describe the process involved. He has to form a hypothesis and then test it through appropriate variation of the experimental conditions. It is our hypothesis that in the common notion of the average present-day adult solid physical bodies, amongst them the candle, have a constant weight. Weight, however, is by no means a relevant or characteristic quality of the candle. Loss in weight through burning is not an essential part of the conceptual structure "candle." We rarely observe this quality of the candle in its everyday use, as we hardly ever have to react to it. It is, in psychological terms, a latent quality of the thought object. The solution of the problem is attained through the discovery of this latent quality, i.e., through restructuration of the concept "candle." This hypothesis cannot be verified or disproved through introspection of the subject, but only through control experiments.

The problem task is now being altered in such a way that, among the various objects offered for choice, there is a small bottle with the inscription "ether" or "benzine." Ether and benzine are volatile substances. Their volatility is not a latent but a manifest quality, highly relevant for their practical use, a quality to which we are accustomed to react. While in the case of the candle the difficulty consisted in the fact that a latent quality had to be discovered, i.e., a piece of knowledge had to be reorganized, this difficulty does not exist in the case of ether or benzine.

This was confirmed by our experiments. In the latter form the problem task is so easy that even malaria-treated paralytics, who otherwise came to be entirely incapable of productive thinking, were able to solve the problem promptly. When they, however, were told that there was still another way of solving the problem whereby not the phial but another object had to be used, the patient failed (Székely 11). We now have gained our first insight into the functional relation between knowledge and thinking:

1. There is what one might call an "initial knowledge" (f.i., that "solid bodies have a constant weight") which phenomenologically does not reveal itself in the process of thinking, but which is nevertheless functionally operative. The different propositions for the problem solution are dependent on the initial knowledge—and for that reason may or may not lead to the goal. The substance of this initial knowledge and its functional operation

are disclosed through appropriate variation of the experimental conditions. The introspection of the subject does not render any information about it.

2. In the process of productive thinking a piece of knowledge is reorganized.

3. The reorganization of the initial knowledge takes place on a thought object (f.i., the candle) in which the initial knowledge is so to speak "embodied." The problem solution is dependent on the outcome of this reorganization.

4. The vicissitudes of this initial knowledge, its transformation, its reorganization in the process of productive thinking, all this does not reveal itself phenomenologically. Only the result of this reorganization emerges as "idea" or as "aha-experience." Explanation about the fate of knowledge in the course of the thought process can thus be found only by way of systematic experiments and not through introspection.

There is, in principle, no difference whether the subject searches for a post-factum explanation, forethinks or devises means to reach the goal. The subject starts out with an initial knowledge that is being reorganized in the process of thinking; he starts out from a thought object that is being enriched with new qualities, and in the end he leaves the problem situation with a modified knowledge. The three situations differ from each other in the degree of difficulty with which the restructuration is achieved. This leads our attention to the fact that the restructuration of a piece of knowledge not only depends on this knowledge by itself but also on the total situation (Székely 12, 15). In the present study, however, we shall not go any further into this problem.

The preliminary experiments have to some extent clarified the relation between knowledge and thinking. The next step will be to investigate the *functional relation between learning, knowledge and thinking*. For this purpose we have chosen a problem task that requires an initial knowledge which itself is a result (or residue) of previous learning.

The knowledge of the Hydrostatic Principle (Archimedes' Theorem) proved suitable for experimental purposes. The subjects were given a thought problem, the solution of which presupposed their familiarity with this physical law.

Experimental Series I

INCLINED PLANE TASK (SZÉKELY 13)

IN the middle of an inclined plane stands a small carriage, attached to a string. This string leads around a pulley which is fastened at the upper end of the plane. On the opposite end of the string a metal weight is attached. Under this weight is a glass container, half filled with water, in which the weight is partially immersed. Carriage and weight are balanced, the carriage thus being at rest. Besides this, there is in the table another half-filled water container and a glass pipette (FIG. 2).

EXPERIMENTAL PROCEDURE

The subject is asked the following question: "How can you, by means of the pipette, set the carriage in motion and make it move upwards for about 1–2 centimeters? You are not permitted to push it or touch it in any way. Think how you could solve this problem."

After this problem is solved—or after the subject has failed—the metal weight is replaced by a piece of wood. The latter also partially sinks into the water and thus the carriage is brought to a balance again so that it stays at rest in its initial position. At this point the subject is again asked the same question.

This experiment is followed by a series of other thought problems, which equally imply familiarity with the Hydrostatic Principle as initial knowledge. These experiments will be discussed in the following. At the end the

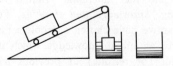

FIG. 2. Inclined plane task.

subjects were tested orally in respect to their knowledge of the Hydrostatic Principle.

Thirty-eight subjects, graduate and undergraduate students of Stockholm University, submitted to the experiments.

RESULTS

First a few typical protocols.

Protocol 1. Subject deliberates silently . . . ". . . I am not at all trained in physics . . . would nevertheless think it possible . . . (long, silent deliberation) . . . that . . . one . . . has to take out some water . . . (hesitating) . . . (Experimenter: Why?) . . . Should the carriage move upwards? . . . (Experimenter: Yes.) . . . Aha! . . . I imagine the weight should then sink down . . . no, just a moment . . . but this is not possible . . . if there were no water . . . one has to add more water . . . (Experimenter: Why?) . . . Because, in my opinion more water would exert heavier pressure on the metal weight and thereby make it sink deeper." (Subject is uncertain, has no clear picture of what would happen.)

Experiment with the wooden weight:
Subject: "This weight is of wood . . . Aha! Now it is clear to me! Take water out. If water were added, the weight would rise, would float upwards . . . so one has to take water out." (Subject is entirely certain.)

Protocol 2. "When a body is immersed in water, its loss in weight equals the weight of the displaced quantity of water . . . but in this case I am very uncertain . . . the weight hangs on the string . . . I don't know which is the decisive factor, the weight on the string or the loss in weight per gram of water? . . . well, being in water one is lighter than after one comes out of it . . . Here is a case of analogy. To make the load heavier, the factor of water, which causes the corresponding loss of weight, has to be eliminated."

Experiment with the wooden weight:
"Here the principle is the same, even though the wood is lighter." After this the subject remarks: "Now the reasoning is much easier."

Protocol 3. "Take water out. Every body loses weight in water. So if there is no water, or less water, then it will sink." "And in the case of the wooden weight?" "The same way."

Many of the subjects were puzzled by the metal weight arrangement. "Could adding or taking out of water cause the weight to move?" "It would have to get heavier, but does it get heavier by adding or removing water?" "The weight hangs on the string; what can the water have to do with it?" "The weight does not change, even if one adds more water," etc.

With the wooden weight all subjects understood immediately that the water level had to be lowered in order to make the weight sink and to pull the carriage upwards. In the case of the metal weight arrangement, however, it was to some of the subjects not at all, or at least not immediately, clear what had to be done and how these changes were causally connected. Some of them succeeded in solving the first task (metal) only after the second experiment (wood). It suddenly struck them that the water level had "naturally" to be lowered and that there was no fundamental difference between wood and metal. Others, however, were of the opinion that with the metal weight arrangement one had to proceed in a way opposite to the one with the wooden weight, because "metal sinks, wood floats."

To many of the subjects the arrangement with the wooden weight was "more clearly understandable" than the one with the metal weight. When the metal was replaced by the wood, the sudden change in the intelligibility, the perspicuity of the situation was obvious. Why, in fact, is one situation so much easier to understand than the other?

As long as the metal weight hangs on the string and is partially immersed in the water, there is—in the mind of the subjects—no connection between the spatial position of the weight and the height of the water level. A little bit more or less of water does not alter the position of the weight. For that reason the subjects actually have no idea as to what to do about the water. But as soon as they deal with the wooden weight, they are at once

aware that its position is definitely determined by the water level. Wood floats. Metal does not float, but sinks in water; and if, as in our case, it does not sink, then only because all its weight is carried by the string to which it is attached. In the case of the metal weight, the water level is—in the opinion of the subjects—an element of the experimental arrangement which can be changed at will, without at the same time affecting the other elements (position of the metal weight and of the carriage). With the wooden weight, however, any change of the water level brings about a change in the other elements (position of the wooden weight and of the carriage).

From the way they approach these two tasks one can draw conclusions in regard to the "initial knowledge" functionally operative in the mind of the subjects. They approach the solution of the problem with the naive empirical knowledge of everyday life. According to this conception—"wood floats, metal sinks"—floating and sinking are qualities of the objects and opposite ones at that. Those subjects to whom the metal weight arrangement was clear from the beginning approached the solution with a different initial knowledge: with the knowledge of the Hydrostatic Principle acquired through the study of physics. According to this principle floating and sinking are not qualities of the bodies but functions of gravity. Whether a body floats or sinks depends on the ratio between its weight and the weight of the displaced quantity of water. Floating and sinking are not opposites; both are governed by the same principle. There were finally a few subjects who only after longer deliberations, in some cases only after finding the solution of the wood arrangement, began to understand the arrangement with the metal weight. With these subjects the initial knowledge changed in the process of problem solving.

All subjects had at one time learned the Hydrostatic Principle. So it may safely be assumed that those subjects in whom this knowledge was inoperative (i.e., did not function as initial knowledge) had forgotten what they had learned. The examination of the memorized knowledge showed that eighteen subjects could recall the Hydrostatic Principle,

TABLE 1

Initial Knowledge Functionally Operative in the Solution of:
The Inclined Plane Task (Metal Weight)

	KNOWLEDGE OF THE HYDROSTATIC PRINCIPLE	NAIVE EMPIRICAL KNOWLEDGE	HESITANCY
S. with adequate memorized knowledge N : 18	17	1	0
S. without adequate memorized knowledge N : 20	8	9	3

$r_B = 0,57 \; \epsilon_r = 0 = 0,16$

that is, could adequately reproduce its essence. Twenty subjects were not able to recall it or to reproduce its essential meaning. The first category of subjects we will call "subjects with adequate memorized knowledge," the second one "subjects without adequate memorized knowledge." TABLE 1 indicates the solution frequency with the metal weight arrangement for the two groups.

This table shows that all subjects with adequate memorized knowledge could solve the Inclined Plane Task with the metal weight. Some of them, however, were hesitant and arrived at a clear understanding only after having solved the task with the wooden weight. Yet in earlier experiments with the

same task (Székely 13, 15) we found a number of subjects who, notwithstanding their adequate memorized knowledge, were not able to solve the metal weight task. On the other hand eight of the subjects without adequate memorized knowledge nevertheless solved the metal weight task right away. Thus a piece of knowledge that was no more accessible to their representative memory was— strangely enough— functionally operative and could in a problem situation perform the function of the initial knowledge. How is this to be explained?

In earlier studies (Székely 13, 15) the following hypothesis about "understanding" was formulated: When the subjects were taught

TABLE 2

Initial Knowledge Functionally Operative in the Solution of:

Hydrost. Lever Task II   Hydrost. Lever Task III
(Metal Weight)   (Unsymmetrical)

	KNOWL. OF HYDROST. PRINCIPLE	NAIVE EMPIR. KNOWL.	HESIT.	KNOWL. OF HYDROST. PRINCIPLE	NAIVE EMPIR. KNOWL.	HESIT.
S. with adequate memorized knowledge N : 32	17	13	2	4	15	18
S. without adequate memorized knowledge N : 18	9	8	1	1	16	1

the Hydrostatic Principle, they had already some idea about hydrostatics. They knew, f.i., that "wood floats, metal sinks," etc., but they did not know the law behind it. Their knowledge, before having learned the Hydrostatic Principle, is equivalent with what we previously defined as "naive empirical knowledge." With the intake of the new learning material this naive empirical knowledge functions as initial knowledge. The vicissitudes of this initial knowledge in the course of the thought process—whether it is transformed or remains unchanged—is essential for the psychological assimilation ("understanding") of the new learning material.

The "naive empirical knowledge" seems to be incompatible with the knowledge of the Hydrostatic Principle. According to the first, the physical bodies would fall into two groups with opposite qualities: those which swim and those which sink in water. After understanding the Hydrostatic Principle a person gains a different conception of the physical world. Swimming and sinking bodies now do not constitute two groups with opposite qualities, but are subject to the same physical law. Thus the "naive empirical knowledge" is transformed, reorganized. The "understanding," "comprehending" of the learning material and this process of reorganization are correlated.

Where this process evolves, meaningful learning takes place. Thus the knowledge of the Hydrostatic Principle may in a later problem situation (like, f.i., the Inclined Plane Task) assume the function of the initial knowledge. If, however, this reorganization process does not take place, the subject has not comprehended the learning material. When later on a thought problem has to be solved, then only the naive empirical knowledge, which remained unchanged, can be functionally operative.

In the course of years the verbal contents of the learning material may be forgotten: yet this would be of no consequence. No matter whether or not the verbal contents remain accessible to the representative memory, subsequent problem solving is determined by the previous assimilation of the learning material, which in turn made use of the already existent empirical knowledge.

This hypothesis of meaningful learning contains two theorems:

Theorem of the analogy or correlation between meaningful learning and productive thinking. There is in the beginning a certain initial knowledge present or functionally operative which in both processes is changed, reorganized. Thus both these processes result in the transformation of a piece of knowledge.

Theorem of the functional continuity between meaningful learning and productive thinking. It depends on the proper assimilation of the learning material whether or not it can be used later on in a problem-solving process. Only the knowledge (experience) that was really absorbed, assimilated effectively, can serve as material for a new productive process. The initial knowledge with which, in a certain problem situation, the solving process starts out is in its turn dependent on the characteristic elements of an earlier learning process.

Katona (4) proved already that "understanding" goes hand in hand with a certain organization of the absorbed learning material. Our first theorem, however, goes one step further. While Katona refers only to the organization of the newly absorbed learning material, our theorem maintains that in addition to the assimiliated new material also old learning material is included into and transformed in the process.

But our two theorems may perhaps not be necessary for the explanation of our findings gained through the Inclined Plane Task. One can make the opposite assumption, that the functionally operative initial knowledge is not dependent on the characteristic elements of a previous learning process, but on the structure of the present problem situation.

Let us now examine this assumption and to this end alter the problem task. The new thought problem consists, like the Inclined Plane Task, of two parts. One part can be solved only through knowledge of the Hydrostatic Principle, whereas the second part can

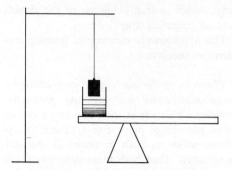

FIG. 3. Hydrostatic lever task II.

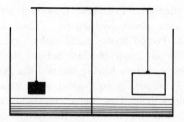

FIG. 4. Hydrostatic lever task III (symmetrical).

be solved on the basis [of] this knowledge as well as on the basis of the naive empirical knowledge.

Experimental Series II

THIS series of experiments consists of two problems: Hydrostatic Lever Tasks II and III. . . .

HYDROSTATIC LEVER TASK II

The arrangement consists of a long, narrow board (50 × 10 centimeters) which serves as a seesaw. In the presence of the subject this board is burdened on one end with a half-filled water container, and then balanced on the narrow beveled edge of a prism (FIG. 3). Over the container a metal weight is suspended, on a string which is fastened to a pole. The subject is asked the following question: "Imagine that this metal object were lowered until it is about halfway immersed in the water. The object does not touch the bottom of the container, nor does it anywhere touch its walls. Will something happen, and if so, what?" After the subject has expressed his ideas, doubts, etc. or has left the question undecided, the metal object is replaced by a wooden object of approximately the same size, and the question is repeated.

HYDROSTATIC LEVER TASK III

Symmetrical arrangement. The arrangement consists of a quadrangular lever, about 50 centimeters long, which can be balanced on the top of a pole. From each end of the lever a body is suspended: at the left a large wooden object, at the right a small metal one,

both of the same weight. Thus, when in balance, both arms of the lever are of equal length (FIG. 4). Underneath is a large container. The following question is put before the subject: "Suppose we filled the container with water. The rising water level would simultaneously touch the bottom of both objects. Now we let more water run in, until both objects are immersed by about 2 centimeters. What will happen?"

After this question has been discussed, we proceed to a new problem.

Unsymmetrical arrangement. The large wooden object is replaced by a small one which is of the same size and shape as the metal object (but of different weight). Then the lever is balanced again. The lever arm with the light wooden body is considerably longer than the arm with the metal body (FIG. 5). The subject is asked the same question as above.

All the thirty-eight subjects who participated in the Inclined Plane Task, were also asked to solve Hydrostatic Lever Task II. Only twenty-one subjects took part in the experiments with Hydrostatic Lever Task III.

Implications of the Solution

IN what consists the essential difference between the Inclined Plane Task and Hydrostatic Lever Task II?

In physics we learn that according to Archimedes' Principle all bodies, when immersed in water, appear to lose a certain part of their weight. However, it frequently does not become clear to us that the "lost weight" corresponds with an equal increase in the pressure of the water. Most people never become aware that there is a problem in connection with the "lost weight." In our experiment, however, this problem has to be considered.

It is of course very well possible, that a number of subjects who solved the Inclined Plane Task (metal) would be able to solve this new task by means of their naive empirical knowledge. For them the metal hangs on the string. When immersed in water its pull on the string is decreased; the weight of the water in the container, however, is not increased.

With the wooden body things are, in the opinion of the subjects, quite different. This body "partly hangs on the string, partly floats" (this conception is frequently expressed), and the floating part weighs on the water, the other part on the lever arm.

In all probability some subjects will immediately realize that the weight of the container will increase and the corresponding lever arm will move downwards.

Hydrostatic Lever Task III (Symmetrical) can be solved through the naive empirical knowledge as well as through the knowledge of the Hydrostatic Principle. The situation can be interpreted in the following way: "Wood floats, metal sinks," therefore the lever arm with the wood will move upwards. The other interpretation would be: "The wooden body is larger, has a greater displacement which causes a greater loss in weight. The lever arm on this side will therefore move upwards."

The most difficult to anticipate is what will happen in the case of the unsymmetric arrangement. When the water level starts rising, both bodies seem to lose an equal amount of their weight, as they displace an equal amount of water. The balance is nevertheless slightly disturbed, because the metal weight hangs on a shorter arm. The disturbance is, however, compensated through a slight change of position and the equilibrium remains undisturbed up to the moment when the wooden body begins to float, without submerging any deeper into the water, even though the water level keeps rising. Now the load on this side of the lever is zero and the metal body keeps—with the remainder of its weight

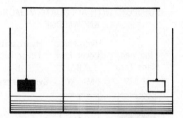

FIG. 5. Hydrostatic lever task III (unsymmetrical).

—the longer lever arm in balance. If the water level rises still higher, the metal weight rises too and the arm with the wooden body gives downward. (If the metal body would not rise, but would gradually submerge deeper, then it would lose more and more of its weight and could not hold the longer arm in balance.)

Results

THE outcome of the experiments was as expected. A considerable number of subjects (FIG. 6) who understood and solved the Inclined Plane Task through their knowledge of the Hydrostatic Principle were in the case of Hydrostatic Lever Task II not able to forethink that, through immersing of the metal weight, the water container becomes heavier. The knowledge of the Hydrostatic Principle was therefore not in both tasks functionally operative. On the other hand, it never happened that the knowledge of the Hydrostatic Principle was operative in Hydrostatic Lever Task II, but not in the Inclined Plane Task. With some subjects this knowledge was functionally operative in both tasks (FIG. 6). Furthermore, of those subjects who could adequately apply their knowledge of the Hydrostatic Principle in Hydrostatic Lever Task II, only a few were able to make adequate use of their knowledge in Task III. It was, however, never observed, that a subject who was unable to solve Task II, reacted correctly to Task III. In short, not in every task can knowledge, acquired through meaningful learning, be applied with equal effect. In this respect subjects with and without adequate memorized knowledge reacted in the same way (FIG. 6).

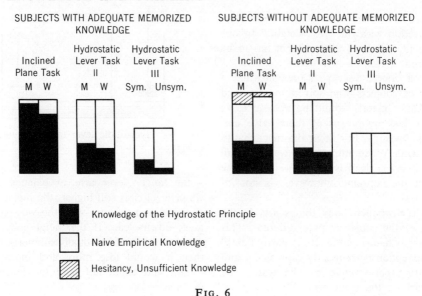

SUBJECTS WITH ADEQUATE MEMORIZED KNOWLEDGE

SUBJECTS WITHOUT ADEQUATE MEMORIZED KNOWLEDGE

Inclined Plane Task — Hydrostatic Lever Task II — Hydrostatic Lever Task III — M W — M W — Sym. Unsym.

Knowledge of the Hydrostatic Principle

Naive Empirical Knowledge

Hesitancy, Unsufficient Knowledge

FIG. 6

In accordance with Bartlett's (1) and Wolters' (17) findings we may therefore speak of a greater or smaller functional generalization of meaningful knowledge. The functional generalization is the largest with a subject who understands all three tasks, it is smaller with one who solves the first two tasks and the smallest with one who solves only the Inclined Plane Task.

DISCUSSION OF THE RESULTS

We previously raised the alternative question: Is the initial knowledge, from which in a certain problem situation the solution process takes its start, dependent on the prior assimilation of relevant learning material or on the present problem situation? Our experiments prove without any doubt that it is dependent on the problem situation. Matters which we have understood do not constitute permanent thought material that is always at our disposal in any problem situation in which it is needed. This, however, does not exclude the other alternative; this question cannot even be settled through our present experiments, because we only changed and checked the problem situations, but not the conditions of the learning process. Therefore the question remains open, whether or not the degree of the functional generalization of knowledge is dependent upon certain peculiarities of the learning process—in other words dependent upon the way in which the learning material was psychologically assimilated.

Summary

THE object of our inquiry is the functional relation between knowledge (previous experiences) and productive, creative thinking.

1. In the process of productive thinking, knowledge can have three different functions: the functions of (a) starting point, (b) medium, and (c) end-result.

2. At the beginning of every problem-solution process a certain "initial knowledge" is functionally operative. In the course of the solution process this initial knowledge is transformed, restructured. Latent qualities of the thought object are discovered, disconnections removed, new connections established, etc. Result of the thought process is (a) a modified, enriched knowledge and (b) a plan for action.

3. In two experimental sets we examined the function of acquired school knowledge by varying the problem situations. To this end we chose the Hydrostatic Principle (Archimedes' Theorem). In these three tasks

knowledge had a different function. In the Inclined Plane Task it functioned as means to reach the goal. In the two other tasks (Hydrostatic Lever Task II and III) it was possible to forethink, on the basis of the initial knowledge, what would happen.

4. Two different kinds of knowledge functioned as initial knowledge: (a) the naive empirical knowledge: "Wood floats, metal sinks" and (b) the knowledge of the Hydrostatic Principle: "In water all physical bodies appear to lose a certain part of their weight."

5. Not with all subjects who could recall it and reproduce it verbally was the knowledge of the Hydrostatic Principle functionally operative.

6. Knowledge of the Hydrostatic Principle was operative with many subjects who had "forgotten" their school knowledge and were not able to reproduce it verbally.

7. The degree in which the knowledge of the Hydrostatic Principle is functionally operative differs within the series of the three problem situations. With some of the subjects this knowledge was operative only in the Inclined Plane Task, with others in the Inclined Plane Task as well as in Hydrostatic Lever Task II and in very few of the subjects in all three tasks.

8. Where the functional operation of this knowledge ends, there usually the naive empirical knowledge assumes the function of the initial knowledge.

9. On the basis of these findings the following hypothesis is formulated: (a) In the process of meaningful learning the naive empirical knowledge is restructured. (b) Such restructuration or reorganization can comprise areas of varying extent. The extent of the restructured area and the functional generalization of the results of learning, that is the "depth of understanding," are correlated. (c) Meaningful learning and productive thinking have something in common. In both instances a piece of initial knowledge is restructured. (d) Meaningful learning and productive thinking are functionally related; it depends on certain particulars of the learning process whether, and to what extent, acquired knowledge can be utilized, that is, reorganized in the process of productive thinking.

10. The hypothesis formulated under 9 is not as yet empirically substantiated in all the details. Empirically proven was only that the productive processes are dependent on the structure of the actual problem situation.

11. The usefulness of the method of introspection for the solution of thought problems is a very limited one. Knowledge, though functionally operative, generally does not reveal itself phenomenologically. Its transformation, reorganization in the process of learning, of comprehension and of problem solving cannot be disclosed through introspection. Only the objective results gained through systematic, planful variation of the experimental conditions make it possible to reconstruct knowledge and its fate.

12. Memorized, verbally reproducible knowledge—to which the school attaches so much importance—is often not functionally operative; knowledge which is not accessible to the representative memory can be functionally operative in solving a thought problem or in comprehending something new. Essential for the effectiveness of knowledge is not how easily it can be reproduced, but how well it has been assimilated, that is, understood originally.

13. Terminology and classification of types of knowledge:

a. In regard to its manifestation:
   1. Knowledge that reveals itself phenomenologically, i.e., [that] is accessible to the representative memory.
   2. Knowledge that is functionally operative.
b. In regard to the way in which it was acquired:
   1. Naive empirical knowledge.
   2. Knowledge acquired through learning.
c. In regard to its function in the process of thinking:
   1. Initial knowledge.
   2. Medium of thinking.
   3. Result of thinking.

BIBLIOGRAPHY

1. BARTLETT, F. C., "Remembering," Cambridge, Cambr. Univ. Press, 1932.
2. BECKER, E., "Untersuchungen zur kindlichen Theoriebildung," Z. Psychol. 129, 1933.
3. HUANG, I., "Children's explanation of strange phenomena," Psychol. Forschg. 14, 1930.
4. KATONA, G., "Organizing and memorizing. Studies in the psychology of learning and teaching," New York, Columb. Univ. Press, 1940.
5. KATZ, D. and R., "Gespräche mit Kindern," Berlin, 1928.
6. KATZ, R., "Motorisk och psykisk omställning," In Barnpsykologiska studier. Stockholm, 1941.
7. KÖHLER, W., "Das Wesen der Intelligenz," In: A. Keller: Kind and Umwelt. 1930.
8. OLDFIELD, R. C. and ZANGWILL, O. L., "Heads concept of the schema and its application in contemporary British psychology. IV," Wolters theory of thinking. Brit. J. Psychol. 33, 1943.
9. PIAGET, I., "La causalité physique chez l'enfant," Paris, 1927.
10. RASPE, C., "Kindliche Selbstbeobachtung und Theoriebildung," Z. angew. Psychol. 23, 1924.
11. SZÉKELY, L., "Studien zur Psychologie des Denkens: Zur Topologie des Einfalls," Acta Psychol. 5, 1940.
12. ———, "Die Bedeutung der Situation für das Denken. Ansätze zu einer Feldtheorie des Denkens," Theoria, 9, 1943.
13. ———, "Tänkande och vetande, jämte ett bidrag till förståendets psykologi," Tidskrift f. psykol. och pedag. 1, 1943.
14. ———, "Dynamics in thought motivation," Amer. J. Psychol. 56, 1943.
15. ———, "Zur Psychologie des geistigen Schaffens," Schweizer Z. f. Psychol. 4, 1945.
16. ———, "Fortsatta försök rörande inlärning, vetande och tänkande," Tidskrift f. psykol. o. pedag. 3, 1946.
17. WOLTERS, A. W., "Some biological aspects of thinking," Brit. J. Psychol. 33, 1943.

SECTION VII

Motivation and Conflict

THE articles in this section are empirical studies of several complex motivational problems: How are the motives that establish behavior patterns acquired? How do motives, once acquired, help create new motives and behavior patterns? In what ways does an organism resolve conflicting motives?

The first three papers concern the acquisition of motives. The first two of these deal with fear, an emotion that, with tension and indecision, often results from a conflict between motives. In "On the Nature of Fear," D. O. Hebb describes the appearance of fear reactions in chimpanzees and suggests that these are not determined only by a sensory event such as the appearance of an inert, mutilated, or dismembered body. Autonomous central processes are also involved; therefore an adequate hypothesis concerning the nature of fear must take into account the facts of cerebral physiology. John B. Watson and Rosalie Rayner taught an infant to be afraid of a white rat by striking a steel bar at the same time the infant touched the rat. They found, in addition, that the infant later transferred his fear to similar objects, like a white rabbit. "Conditioned Emotional Reactions" is a classic study of the acquisition of fear through associative conditioning. In "Central Stimulation and Other New Approaches to Motivation and Reward," Neal E. Miller discusses the use of techniques like electrical stimulation (which can produce hunger and thirst, pain and fear), chemical stimulation, and electrical recording to discover how the mechanisms of motivation and reward produce their effects. This research on the physiological sites of complex drives emphasizes the importance of biology in the study of motivation.

Once a motive is acquired, it leads to new motives and behavior patterns. The experiments of Judson S. Brown and Alfred Jacobs indicate that fear can motivate or energize behavior, with fear-reduction acting as the reinforcing event in the learning of new responses. Leon Festinger and James M. Carlsmith (by paying students to report a rather boring experiment as interesting) tested whether, if a person is induced to do or say something contrary to his private opinion, he will tend to change his private opinion, bringing it into closer correspondence with what he has said or done. Their experiment shows how acting on one motive (the urge to attain a reward) can modify a conflicting motive (the urge to tell the truth) by effecting a change in cognition.

Conflicts between motives lead individuals to devise defense mechanisms that will reduce the strength of the conflicts. The next two selections show how such defense mechanisms can be studied experimentally. Neal Miller attempts to translate Freudian displacement theory (according to which, for example, a man will transfer aggressive feelings aroused by his boss to his wife and children) into the language of learning theory. He maintains that displacement can be described in stimulus-response terms as a transfer of training, or generalization. That is, a rat trained to strike another rat in order to escape an electric shock may strike a celluloid doll when another rat is not present because he is generalizing from what he learned originally, not because he is displacing his aggressions. Seymour Feshbach induced aggression by insulting groups of students and then gave them fantasy or non-fantasy activities and measured the remaining aggressive drive. The results confirm the hypothesis that the expression of a motive through fantasy reduces the strength of the motive by means of symbolic satisfaction.

In "The Effect of Dream Deprivation," William Dement reports that subjects whose dreams have been repeatedly interrupted will dream more than usual when allowed to sleep without interruption, and that during the time of dream deprivation the subjects suffered from anxiety, irritability, and difficulty in concentrating. His data suggest that dreams may be an indispensable way for human beings to ease tensions or conflicts.

D. O. HEBB

30. *On the Nature of Fear*

I N the course of an experiment dealing
with individual differences of behavior
among chimpanzees, observations of fear
were made which held an immediate interest.
Besides extending the information concerning
the causes of anthropoid fear which is provided by the work of Köhler (23), Jacobsen,
Jacobsen and Yoshioka (17), Yerkes and
Yerkes (42), Haslerud (10), McCulloch and
Haslerud (31) and Hebb and Riesen (14),
the new data brought up again the question of
mechanism. Analysis of the behavior leads,
in the present discussion, to a review of the
whole problem and an attempt to formulate
an hypothesis of the causes and nature of
fear.

Nature of the Data

VALIDITY AND RELIABILITY

T HE validity of naming fear in chimpanzees,
or recognizing something in animals which
can be identified with fear in man and the
reliability of naming have been discussed elsewhere (13). There it was shown that the recognition of emotion in an animal is possible
in the same way as in another human being.
Fear named in an animal means either that
there was actual avoidance of some object or
place, or that the observer inferred from incidental behavior ("associated signs") that
avoidance was imminent and likely to appear
with further stimulation. When such inferences are made with confidence by experienced observers, it appears that they are valid
and reliable, the criterion being the animal's
subsequent behavior.

DEFINITION OF FEAR BEHAVIOR

The symbol "W," for withdrawal, was recorded when the animal actually moved away
from a test object in such a way as to show
that he did not move by coincidence, but was
responding to the test situation. The evidence
was of several kinds: (1) when change of
position of the test object produced a corresponding movement of the animal, maintaining his distance from it; (2) when the
original movement was abrupt and coincided
exactly with the appearance of the test object;
(3) when there was coincident evidence of
unusual excitation, such as erection of hair,
screaming, threatening gestures directed at
the test object, or continued orientation of
gaze at the object while moving directly away
from it. On occasions one of these three
forms of evidence alone, if exceptionally clear,
might provide the basis for an entry of "W"
in the record; usually, at least two were present before the entry was made. In many instances the experimenter was certain that an
animal would be afraid to approach the test
object, but did not record his opinion since
the formal behavioral criteria were not met.

Experimental Method

T HE experimental procedures were part of a
study of individual differences of emotionality
and temperament, and not planned to meet
the problem of defining the adequate stimulus
to fear. Thus the range of test objects was
limited, and the order in which they were
presented does not permit an exact comparison of the excitatory value of each.

Reprinted by permission of the American Psychological Association and the author from the *Psychological
Review*, 1946, vol. 53, pp. 259–76.

TEST OBJECTS

The test objects were representations of animals, from reptile to man, varying considerably in completeness and verisimilitude. They fall in three classes: primate objects, pictures of primates, and nonprimate objects. It was not expected that the pictures would induce fear—they were used for another purpose—but they were presented in the same way as the other objects and consequently are useful as control material.

PRIMATE OBJECTS

There were 9 objects "representing" primates. The responses to these are the main interest of the study.

1. An adult chimpanzee head, three-fifths life size, made of papier-maché and painted to appear reasonably lifelike.

2. An unclothed doll representing a human infant, one-half life size.

3. An infant chimpanzee's head and shoulders, nearly life size, modelled in wax and painted—about as lifelike as the adult chimpanzee head.

4. The cadaver of a chimpanzee infant, newborn, fixed in formalin.

5. A lifelike full-sized human head from a window-display dummy.

6. The skull of a 5-year-old chimpanzee, with movable jaw controlled by a string.

7. The roughly mounted skin of a spider monkey, with head and shoulders movable by means of string.

8. An unpainted plaster of Paris cast of the visage of an adult chimpanzee without the ears or the rest of the head, made from a death mask.

9. The cured and flexible hide of a 5-year-old chimpanzee, somewhat denuded of hair; the proportions of the skin about the head and face were distorted out of recognition, but the hands and feet were recognizable.

The pictures are not described in detail, since they are important here only as 14 emotionally unexciting objects, presented in the same way as the others.

Nonprimate objects varied greatly in verisimilitude, from a careful replica of a snake to a "bug" which was a rectangular block of wood on coiled-spring legs.

1. A dog's head and forequarters, of cloth, slipped over the hand and manipulated from inside with the fingers; this common toy is surprisingly lifelike in its movements.

2. A model of an imaginary white "grub," 4 inches long, with long white legs.

3. A grub identical in proportions and color, one-third as large.

4. A rubber tube, ½ inch diameter, 24 inches long, with a roughly carved wooden snake's head at one end; so mounted, with string inside the tube, that it could be given a snakelike movement without apparent external agency.

5. A rectangular wooden "bug," 6 inches long. It was capable of an oscillating movement, since it was mounted on six coiled-wire legs, and had oscillating "antennae."

6. A "grasshopper," a mechanical toy with moving legs.

7. A similar "turtle."

8. A rubber dog, 3½ inches high.

9. A brightly colored cloth dog, 7 inches high.

10. A painted wax replica of a coiled 24-inch snake.

PROCEDURE

Test objects were presented to the animals while they were in their own living cages. The animal or pair of animals was first brought to the front of the cage by an offer of a small amount of food. The hinged top and front of the presentation box (which was wheeled from cage to cage) was then lifted, exposing one test object to the chimpanzee. At the end of 15 seconds the test object was set in motion, if it had movable parts; if not, it was moved forward about 6 inches nearer the animal. The presentation box was closed at the end of another 15 seconds; total exposure was thus 30 seconds. The box had three compartments, and three objects were shown in succession on each experimental period, once or twice a week. The objects were shown to all animals in the same order with the same time intervals.

Experimental Results

WITH a fixed order of presentation to all subjects, there is a probability that the serial position of a test object will affect the degree of response to it, either by negative adaptation or cumulative effect. There were marked indications that such effects occurred. Some animals apparently learned that the test objects, at first terrifying, would not move out of the presentation box; others began to show fear in the later trials before the box was opened at all.

The total number of animals making fear responses to any object, therefore, is not a wholly satisfactory index of its relative effectiveness in provoking fear. However, there is evidence that the amount of such error is limited. In each group of three objects one or more pictures were included. The number of avoidance responses was consistently low for these pictures, while remaining high for objects, such as dog or snake, known from the work of others (Yerkes, Haslerud) to be

fear provoking. This means that transfer or generalization effects were limited. Also there was no sign of a steady increase or decrease of fear responses as the experiment progressed. The animals' responses were highly selective. Preliminary observations, and tests made after the completion of the experiment, also make it clear that such objects as a head without the body attached are in themselves capable of eliciting panic, and that the number of fear responses to human or chimpanzee head, recorded experimentally, is not due to an association of these test objects with the others.

The table presents the number of fear responses to each test object, separating primate, pictorial and nonprimate objects. The table gives the order of presentation and also shows which three objects were grouped together for each test period. It is assumed, partly on the basis of evidence not presented here, that what particular pictures were used is irrelevant and that the number of animals avoiding the pictures is an index of the "spread" of

TABLE 1

Number of Animals (from a Total of 30) Making Fear Responses to "Primate" Test Objects, "Pictures," and "Nonprimate" Objects

(M) indicates that the object was put in motion during the presentation.

TEST	PRIMATE		PICTURE		NONPRIMATE	
I	Adult ape head:	7	picture:	0	dog head (M):	10
II	Doll:	4	picture:	1	large grub:	3
III	Infant ape head:	3	picture:	2	rubber tube (M):	3
IV	Infant:	1	picture:	1	wood-wire bug (M):	3
V			picture:	0	mechanical	
			picture:	1	grasshopper (M):	4
VI	Human head:	12	picture:	0	rubber dog:	5
VII	Skull (M):	24	picture:	4		
	Monkey (M):	16				
VIII			picture:	4	small grub:	2
					mechanical	
					turtle (M):	8
IX	Cast of ape visage:	14	picture:	0	cloth dog:	8
X	Ape hide:	5	picture:	0		
			picture:	0		
XI			picture:	0		
			picture:	0	cast of snake:	21
	Total = 86		Total = 13		Total = 67	
	Mean = 9.6		Mean = 0.9		Mean = 6.7	

fear from exciting to neutral objects. From a total of 30 animals the mean number making fear responses to each primate test object was 9.6; to pictures, 0.9; to nonprimate objects, 6.7. These scores, it must be remembered, are the number of actual overt withdrawals which met the criteria set up in advance for a definable fear response. They take no account of signs of fear which were peculiar to an individual animal. Also, they are the number of such responses made while animal and test object were separated by a stout wire mesh. Tests in other circumstances show a higher percentage of avoidance, and show also that the relative effectiveness of two objects as causes of fear may vary somewhat according to the mode of presentation. In the conditions of the experiment, the following are the most effective stimuli, in descending order: *skull* (with moving jaw); painted wax *snake; monkey* (with moving head); plaster cast of *chimpanzee visage;* and *human head.* Least exciting are, in ascending order, chimpanzee infant; small wax grub; infant chimpanzee head; large wax grub; moving rubber tube ("snake"); and moving wood-and-wire "bug."

Supplementary Observations

THE chimpanzee's fear of toy animals and snakes is of course well known (23, 42). The data which are new and which were the occasion of this report are those showing that the chimpanzee is excited by, and avoids, parts of chimpanzee or human bodies. It was evident that such a conclusion had important implications, and that further observations would be desirable as a control of the data. Control observations, accordingly, were made after the formal experiment was completed. Their purpose was to discover whether some peculiarity of the actual experimental objects, or some detail of procedure, might have been the true cause of fear; or whether the behavior falls into a more general class related to the common human avoidance of a mutilated face and of dead bodies.

Preliminary experiments had already shown that all the adult chimpanzees were excited at the first sight of a chimpanzee head modelled in clay and carried in the hand from cage to cage. A majority showed avoidance, which was outright panic in five or six of the thirty subjects. In the supplementary observations an unpainted plaster cast of the clay model, and also an actual head from a dead chimpanzee, produced definite avoidance.

With different presentations the results were essentially the same, although intensity of response varied, in part with adaptation to sight of so many similar objects. Avoidance was observed when a head was carried by hand; when it was exposed by removing a cloth or opening a box; and when the head was first put in the chimpanzee's cage and the animal admitted afterward. In another observation the head was placed behind a small ledge, so that the actual termination of the neck was not visible (although the chimpanzee "knew" from familiarity with the cage in which the test was made that there was no space large enough for a body beneath the head). The chimpanzee was then admitted from a detaining inner room from which none of the preparations could be seen. A marked fear response occurred immediately, before the lapse of enough time to make the unresponsiveness of the head abnormal. Thus lack of movement in the test object did not determine the fear, nor yet an actual perception of the termination of the neck.

A painted human eye and eyebrow (sawn from a plaster manikin's head) produced marked avoidance.

Finally, observations were made with anesthetized chimpanzees as stimulus objects. Four adults were shown an anesthetized infant, two years old, carried by two members of the staff. The infant was recovering from nembutal, and made some spontaneous movements of an arm and hand. Three of the four adults were very excited and one at least afraid, in spite of the fact that they had often seen young chimpanzees being carried by the staff. A more deeply anesthetized adult was taken on a low, flat, two-wheeled barrow up to the cages of nine of the adults. Definite fear was shown by six, aggression (possibly related to fear) by two others, and the remaining animal was almost certainly afraid but remained at a distance without showing definable avoidance.

The fear evoked by a detached face or head in the formal experiment, therefore, was not a product of some uncontrolled detail of procedure or of the construction of the test objects. Any of a number of related stimuli have the same effect, in a number of situations.

From the data it appears that *either* lack of responsiveness in a whole animal, *or* an evident lack of a body when the head or part of the head is seen, can determine the fear. The first conclusion depends on the observations with anesthetized animals as stimuli. The second follows from the fact that avoidance of an isolated head was immediate and certainly was not delayed long enough for an unusual unresponsiveness, as such, to have become apparent before fear occurred.

Spontaneity of the Fear

THE fears observed must also have been spontaneous,[1] and not conditioned by some association of the test objects with a more primitive source of fear such as pain. This is shown by the following considerations.

There are two ways in which fear of a detached head or an anesthetized animal could be due to learning. Fear might occur (1) because the subjects recognized part of a whole which they had learned to fear in the past, or (2) because of an earlier association of a class of objects (detached heads, abnormally unresponsive chimpanzees) with a more primitive cause of fear.

1. The first explanation can be ruled out. The dummy human head represented an ordinary young man whom the adults of the colony might have teased or injured, as they often tend to do with strangers whose general appearance is similar to that of members of the laboratory staff, but whom they would not have feared. The cast of a face was a faithful

1 The term "spontaneous" is used here to mean that the fear is not built up by association, as a learned response. The term is not synonymous with "innate" since there are definite factors of past experience involved, as will appear in the later discussion.

replica of the chimpanzee Lita's, made from a death mask. She had died not long before the experiment began, and certainly would not have been a source of fear to any of the other chimpanzees with cage wire intervening, as in the conditions of the experiment. The anesthetized infant in his normal state would not have been feared by an adult; and the anesthetized adult who was used as a stimulus object was Don, who is dominated by almost all of the other adults of the colony. The test object which aroused fear therefore did not do so because it was recognized as part of a whole which in its normal completeness would have caused the response.

2. The second possibility to be examined is that an association had been formed earlier between the class of stimulus objects and some event such as pain, loud noise, or a fall. For animals born in the bush and captured when their mothers were killed this is a real possibility. But nine of the adolescent and adult subjects of the experiment were born and reared in captivity and definitely had no opportunity to make such associations. None of these had seen a detached human or chimpanzee head; a few of them had seen a dead chimpanzee, but no more primitive cause of fear would be associated with the sight. The nine animals who are known not to have such associations showed on the average rather more frequent and stronger avoidance than the remaining twenty-one animals.

These facts require the conclusion that the fears discussed are spontaneous. Further support for the conclusion is found in the behavior of human beings.

Human Avoidance of Mutilated and Dead Bodies

HUMAN emotional responses to the dead and to such things as the sight of a major operation or of a badly mutilated face cannot reasonably be attributed to conditioning. The responses tend to be strongest on the first experience, which eliminates direct conditioning as an explanation and requires the supporting assumption of a preliminary verbal conditioning which forms the whole basis of the response. But if avoidance were so readily established, with no innate tendency toward fear of the conditioned stimulus itself, one could easily keep children from playing in dangerous places or train adults to drive automobiles carefully—by verbal instruction alone. This is the essence of Valentine's (39) brilliant criticism of Watsonian theory and my rejection of the explanation by conditioning rests upon his argument. What he did was to show how easy it is to condition fear of some things, how hard with others, and thus demonstrated the existence of emotional susceptibilities which are the basis of spontaneous and almost spontaneous fears.

Watson's (40) theory of fear has rightly had a profound effect upon psychological thought, and a radical departure from his ideas is not easily accepted. Yet the present situation is that the theory has been demolished, with no good substitute in sight. Jones and Jones' (22) experiment on the human fear of snakes constituted a strong and radical attack on Watson's theory. The evidence adduced by Valentine (39) reinforced the attack with evidence from a variety of fears. He has shown that there is a wide range of situations, not easily defined or classified, which have some tendency to evoke human fear. Finally, Hebb and Riesen (14) have shown the existence of a spontaneous fear of strangers in infant chimpanzees, where the customary appeal to the subject's unknown past experience is impossible and the explanation by conditioning ruled out.

Watson's work, consequently, provides no more than a starting point in determining the causes of fear and gives no reason to reject the conclusion that human fear of dead or mutilated bodies is spontaneous. The conclusion is also not affected by the fact that an almost complete adaptation to such stimuli is possible, nor by the fact that some persons may not have an emotional disturbance at their first sight of an operation, autopsy or dissection. It has sometimes been assumed that if a fear is not general it must have been learned by those who do have it: that an innate fear should be found in all persons. This argument of course is quite invalid, in view of the existence of individual genetic differences, and it has been seen that some of the chimpanzee fears discussed in this paper are not found in all animals and yet cannot be ascribed to learning.

The evidence therefore is that both in man and in chimpanzee there occur spontaneous fears of mutilated and unresponsive bodies. The chimpanzee knows nothing of anesthesia, has no abstract conception of death, and presumably may confuse a model of a head and the real thing. Considering the intellectual differences between the species and the extent to which man's behavior is influenced by speech, one must say that human and chimpanzee fear susceptibilities, with dismembered or inert bodies as stimulus objects, are remarkably similar. In this fact there is further support for the idea that such fears are spontaneous and not associative or conditioned.

So that this conclusion will be seen in the proper perspective, the reader is reminded that the importance of learning is not minimized. There are essential factors of past experience in the fears which have been discussed; and the hypothesis which is to be presented lays a good deal of emphasis on learning as an element in the development of any fear.

Central Versus Sensory Factors Determining Fear

THE first step in an analysis of fear is a better definition of the problem and of its relation to other psychological investigations.

It should be specified that the problem is not simply that of the subcortical motor integration of fear behavior. The earlier studies of Bard (2) had the effect of concentrating attention on the hypothalamus, but it is now evident that more must be taken into account. The analysis by Lashley (24) and Masserman (32) has limited the emotional functions of the diencephalon to a motor integration. More recently, Bard (3) has described rage in a cat lacking *only* the hypothalamic region which he formerly considered to be essential to emotional activity. In view also of the marked differences of the stimuli which are effective in each case, and the absence of "after-discharge" in the decorticate preparation, it is evident that the processes of normal and decorticate emotions cannot be equated. Fear behavior has been demonstrated by Bard in the decorticate cat, but only with auditory stimuli. An essential problem remains in understanding cortico-subcortical interaction and the important role of perception in the fear responses of the normal animal.

The evidence presented has shown that the chimpanzee's fear of a detached head is in some way related to the physical lack of an attached body or of movement, or both. But our real interest is not in the physical properties of the stimulus object but in the way they act on the organism. The first question to be asked concerns the existence of a sensory control of the response: can one find any property of the sensory excitation which in itself determines the occurrence and form of the response?

The answer seems to be no. In the first place, the physical lack in the stimulus object cannot be equated with a sensory lack by saying that the sight of a head without the normally associated sight of a body causes fear, for the statement would not be true. When a chimpanzee sees a man's head only, without movement and with the rest of the man's body out of sight behind a door, he is not afraid. There are certainly sensory cues which distinguish the two situations (*i.e.,* detached head *vs.* attached head with body hidden) but I have not been able to find any generalization that distinguishes the purely sensory [2] event which causes fear from the one which does not. In the second place, it has been shown that the fears are spontaneous. If they were also sensorily determined, it would follow that there are innate connections from the sensory cells excited in seeing any chimpanzee or human head to the motor centers determining avoidance; or in a more *Gestalt* formulation, that the dynamic properties of every such sensory excitation have an innately selective action on those particu-

2 "Sensory" in the present discussion is defined as referring to activity, in afferent structures, which is directly determined by environmental events; roughly, activity in the receptor organ and afferent tracts, up to and including the corresponding sensory projection area.

lar motor centers. It would follow further that this sensori-motor relationship is consistently inhibited and nonfunctional throughout the animal's lifetime, no matter how many times he sees a human or chimpanzee head, unless by chance the head has been cut off from its owner. The improbability of such ideas is evident. They seem to be a product of the assumption (quite reasonable in itself) that the form of a response is fully determined by the sensory event that precipitates it: since a physical lack in the stimulus object cannot excite receptor cells, the assumption means that the part of the stimulus object which is present is an adequate excitant of fear, and, since the whole object does not cause fear, that the part which is missing is normally an inhibiter or in some way prevents an innately determined response to the other part. Such reasoning will be found to lead rapidly to absurdities. Doubt is then cast on the original assumption, and the alternative conclusion is indicated that the determinant of certain strongly marked anthropoid fears is not any property of the sensory excitation alone but may have to be sought in some interaction of sensory events with other cerebral processes.

This argument depends on the accuracy of the analysis which has been made of the stimulating conditions in which fear of dismembered or inert bodies is observed. Other interpretations are possible, but seem either to beg the question or to amount to the same thing. (One might say, for example, that it is strangeness or mysteriousness that produces fear of a decapitated head and of an inert chimpanzee being carried by human beings. Actually, reference to strangeness only strengthens the preceding argument, as we shall see in a moment.) Nevertheless, it would be unwise to depend too strongly on the evidence of behavior into which so many complicating factors of experience may enter. Let us turn to fear of strangers (14) and of sudden noise (8). The theoretical interpretation suggested by fear of a dismembered body gains decisive support from these other observations and in turn makes their theoretical significance clearer.

The growing chimpanzee is persistently

afraid of strange persons, objects and places, although the response is not always predictable in the individual case. Hebb and Riesen (14) have shown that the fear of strangers by chimpanzee infants is spontaneous and cannot be accounted for as a conditioned response. Also, a slight change of clothing may produce fear of a familiar attendant who was not feared before. To assume that the form of the response on seeing something strange is controlled alone by some property of the sensory event is to assume that *any* visual excitation is primarily a cause of fear and that other responses are substituted merely by repetition of the stimulation. Fear of strangers would mean that the visual excitation from any human or chimpanzee face (strange chimpanzees are feared as much as strange men) or any pattern of clothing is an innately adequate excitant of fear; for any pattern whatever may be strange, depending on accidents of experience. The idea seems absurd in itself, and is definitely contradicted by observations of the behavior of an infant chimpanzee blindfolded from birth to the age of four months, when the avoidance of strangers by normal animals is beginning (Nissen [3]). In Senden's (35) comprehensive review of the literature on persons born blind and given their sight after infancy, there is no mention of fear aroused by the first visual form-perception; and Dennis (7) explicitly denies that fear occurs in these persons. Fear of a strange person is therefore not determined by a particular property of the sensory excitation, but by some discrepancy of the pattern from those which have been frequently experienced by the subject—by a complex relationship, that is, of the sensory event to preexistent cerebral processes.

A similar meaning lies in the fact noted by English (8) that a noise must be sudden to cause fear. When auditory intensity is built up gradually, the response is hard to elicit. The same is true of loss of support. An unexpected drop is the one that causes fear,

[3] Personal communication from Dr. H. W. Nissen. The experiment was not an investigation of emotional behavior, and detailed records on this point were not kept. But it is known with certainty that there was no avoidance evoked by the chimpanzee's first visual perception of human beings.

not one for which preparation has been made verbally or by playful swinging of infant subjects. Jones (21) has shown that unexpectedness is an essential feature of a number of fear-provoking situations. In all such fears the major determinant cannot be the afferent excitation alone but involves a relationship of that excitation to concurrent cerebral activity.

These facts actually raise no new theoretical issue. Their effect is to sharpen the definition of a problem which has been formulated in various ways by other writers. That both sensory and central processes are involved in the control of behavior and must be distinguished for theoretical purposes is implied by the concept of "operants" (Skinner, 37) and of "stimulus trace" (Hull, 16) no less than by the "expectancy" of Cowles and Nissen (6), Mowrer (34) and Hilgard and Marquis (15). It is the real problem of attention and of the selectivity of response to the several properties of a sensory event (Leeper, 27; Lashley, 26). The problem is made explicit by Hilgard and Marquis's "central process which seems relatively independent of afferent stimuli" (p. 275), Beach's (4) "central excitatory mechanism," and Morgan's (33) "central motive state." Every serious attempt in recent years to analyze the neural mechanisms of the more complex forms of behavior has found the need of distinguishing, as more or less independent factors, sensory and central states or processes; in other words, of denying that the direction of transmission of a sensory excitation is determined by the properties of that excitation alone, even when the stable changes of learning have been taken into account. This is thoroughly consistent also with modern electro-physiology. All parts of the brain are continuously active and there are reasons for believing that the activity may be self-maintaining, and even self-initiating (1, 18, 29, 30, 41). An afferent excitation does *not* arouse inactive tissue, but modifies an activity already in existence. The conclusion, therefore, that there are nonsensory factors in the determination of certain fears agrees with existing theory.

It must be added that the conclusion is not necessarily trivial. Current opinion recognizes the necessity of postulating central determinants of behavior but it has done so reluctantly, always with reference to a single, rather narrow aspect of behavioral theory, and apparently without recognizing how generally the necessity has actually cropped up in psychological analysis. The preceding discussion may do no more than suggest a change of emphasis, but the change is one which, as I shall try to show, has a considerable effect on theory. Besides drawing attention to facts of behavior which are usually forgotten, it reveals some order in the facts and makes possible a coherent hypothesis of the nature of fear.

Development of an Hypothesis

AVOIDANCE of strangers provides a possible starting point for a theory of the nature of fear. An essential feature of the stimulating conditions is the divergence of the object avoided from a familiar group of objects, while still having enough of their properties to fall within the same class. It is a most important fact that the fear or shyness does not develop at first vision, as the already cited data of Nissen, Senden (35) and Dennis (7) show. Common experience indicates also that the fear is minimized or absent if the growing infant has always been exposed to sight of a large number of persons. It is therefore dependent on the fact that certain perceptions have become habitual, a limited number of central neural reactions to the sight of human beings having been established with great specificity by repeated experience. The idea that there are such habits of perception was developed by Gibson (9) and further supported by later studies of the effect of set upon perception (5, 27, 43). A number of facts relating to the development of intelligence, and its changes with advancing age, have the same import (11, pp. 286, 289). From this point of view, it might be proposed that fear occurs when an object is seen which is like familiar objects in enough respects to arouse habitual processes of perception, but in other respects arouses incompatible processes.

Such a treatment of the fear of strangers would amount to an interference, incongruity or conflict theory. It might subsume fear of mutilated bodies as well, by classifying them as strange objects, and could be extended to cover fears due to pain and sudden loud noise, which obviously tend to disrupt concurrent psychological processes. But farther than this such a conflict theory will not go. There might be some difficulty in applying it even to the fear of strange objects, when the strangeness is apparently due to incompleteness in a familiar object (as with the chimpanzee's fear of a detached head); and conflict cannot account for causes of fear such as darkness (39) in which a sensory deficit is the effective condition, or nutritional disturbance (38).

Moreover, a fundamental question would remain as to the meaning of "conflict," and why an incompatibility between two perceptions should produce the incoördinations of emotional behavior. This is the crucial question, and in trying to answer it I believe we can find the possibility of a more comprehensive hypothesis, according to which conflict is only one of several ways in which a true source of fear occurs. If two perceptual processes, which cannot coexist, cannot even alternate without producing gross disturbances of behavior (which is what the conflict notion implies), ordinary unemotional behavior must depend on an essential temporal integration in cerebral processes, and fear may be a direct result of their disorganization. Let us ask what such ideas would involve.

It has already been seen that sensory and central processes contribute separately to the control of behavior. For convenience, let us designate the specific pattern of cellular activity throughout the thalamo-cortical system, at any one moment, as a "phase." Behavior is directly correlated with a phase sequence which is temporally organized (4), in part by the inherent properties of the system (the constitutional factor) and in part by the time relations of various afferent excitations in the past (the factor of experience). The spatial organization of each phase, the actual anatomical pattern of cells which are active at any moment, would be affected by the present afferent excitation also. Subjectively, the phase sequence would be identified with the train of thought and perception. Now each phase is determined by a neural interaction, between the preceding phase and the concurrent afferent excitations. Lorente de Nó's (29) discussion of the dynamics of neural action shows that two or more simultaneous neural events might reinforce each other's effects and contribute to a single, determinate pattern of subsequent cerebral activity; or on the contrary might be indeterminate, in the sense that slight changes of timing and intensity could lead to marked and sudden fluctuations of pattern. A phase sequence, that is, could be stable or unstable, and one can assume that vacillating, unpredictable and incoördinated behavior is the expression of unstable cerebral activity. Also, the effect of learning in general is to increase the predictability and coördination of behavior. The element of learning in emotional behavior will be discussed more specifically, but in the meantime we may speak of the cerebral processes controlling predictable, coördinated behavior as "organized," and recognize the tendency of learning to establish and maintain cerebral organization.

Disorganization could occur in several ways, some of which may be called conflict. (1) A sensory event might disrupt the concurrent phase sequence. The event might be one whose facilitation has been integrated into other phase sequences, and the disruptive only because it is "unexpected." If so the disruption would be brief, another well-organized phase sequence would be promptly established, and one would speak of the subject as having only been "startled." The disruption would be brief but it would occur; a well-organized phase could not be set up instantaneously, independent of facilitation from the preceding phase. On the other hand, the sensory event might fail to set up another organized sequence, and so initiate a prolonged disturbance; or might like loud noise, and especially pain, tend persistently to break down cerebral organization. (2) Simultaneous sensory events might have facilitations which are enough unlike to make the following phase sequence unstable, even though each event separately might be capable of integration with the concurrent phase. Evidently (1) and

(2) would be modes of conflict, one sensory-central, the other sensory-sensory.[4] But disorganization might also result (3) from the absence of a usually present sensory process. Cerebral organization involves learning. If a sensory activity A has always been present during adaptation to a sensory event B, facilitation from A would necessarily affect the final pattern of cellular activities which constitutes the adaptation to B, and might be essential to it. If so, B in the absence of A could again produce behavioral disturbance (if B without A occurs often enough, however, another adaptation would be established). Finally, (4) metabolic and structural changes in the central nervous system could obviously be a source of disorganization, by changing the time relations between the activities of individual cells, apart from any unusual conflict or sensory deficiency.

Attention must now be turned to the way in which cerebral processes tend to maintain their organization, in order to round out the picture of fear behavior. Whatever else may be true of it, avoidance certainly averts or minimizes disruptive stimulation. When we distinguish between the disruption and the processes tending to avert it, and assume that the degree of disruption may vary, we obtain the valuable result of seeing how a single mechanism of fear could on different occasions produce perfectly coördinated flight, a less coördinated avoidance accompanied by trembling and so on, startle, or the paralysis of terror: When cerebral disruption is extreme, it might presumably prevent any coördinated action, even flight.

It seems evident that the so-to-speak homeostatic processes which maintain the dynamic equilibrium of unemotional behavior are to a great extent processes of learning, operating in either of two ways. On the one hand there is negative adaptation to strange objects, which implies that a sensory-central

4 Logically, another category of "central-central" conflict would be possible, which might have some meaning with regard to emotional disturbances and anxiety arising from a conflict of ideas or beliefs. Such a concept might be applied to fear of socialism or of Catholics and emotional disturbances due to such purely intellectual ideas as those of Galileo or Darwin.

conflict may be banished by an effect of learning on the central organization alone. The sensory event remains the same, yet disturbance disappears. With still further exposure, the formerly strange object may become not merely tolerated but "liked" and "pleasant," which is to say that the originally disturbing sensory event now actively supports cerebral integration.

On the other hand, learning may contribute to this integration indirectly, by reinforcing a mode of behavior (avoidance) which minimizes or removes the disturbing sensation. The incoördinations of emotional behavior, its most characteristic feature, are unlearned; they are apt to be most marked on the first occasion on which they are aroused by any particular stimulus. But the coördinated element of the behavior tends to become more prominent on repetition of the stimulus and to increase, while the unlearned incoördination is decreasing. It thus appears that the coördinated avoidance which occurs in fear behavior of normal animals is mainly learned.

There is indeed a primitive innate avoidance (manifested, *e.g.*, in the flexion reflex of Sherrington's (36) spinal animals, and the cowering of Bard's (3) decerebrate cats), but the avoidance which operates most efficiently to maintain coördinated effector activity is acquired. In the normal mammal at least, simple avoidance appears as a conditioned response to cues which in the past have preceded a disruptive stimulation. When a disruptive event is sudden and without warning the response is never an uncomplicated avoidance, a smooth and economical coöperation of effector organs, but involves startle, trembling, sweating, vocalization and so on. The optimum toward which behavior tends, with repetition of such disturbances, is a response (to premonitory cues) which completely averts the disturbing sensory event. At this final stage of learning, avoidance is fully effective in maintaining integrated cerebral action, and no emotional component is left in the behavior. Thus avoidance without fear occurs. In the avoidance that does involve fear the learning process is not complete or premonitory cues have not been available, and the belated avoidance appears side by side with the excess of effector activity that justifies the inference of cerebral disorganization.

The reciprocal relationship of learning to the disruption of integrated behavior is most simply illustrated by an adult's unemotional avoidance of a hot stove which as an infant he may once have feared. Another illustration is provided by observation of adult chimpanzees where the course of learning in a very unusual social situation could be followed from its beginning. The experimenter, disguised with a grotesque false face and a change of clothing, approached each animal's cage wearing heavy gloves and acted the part of a very aggressive individual, instead of the cautious role one ordinarily takes with the chimpanzee. The results suggested an interpretation similar to that of Bridges (cited by Jones, 21) who concluded that an infant's fear develops out of primitive undifferentiated excitement. The first response by a number of animals was a generalized excitement and marked autonomic activity. An animal might be "friendly" and viciously aggressive, almost in the same breath, or show erection of hair and scream and yet solicit petting. Attack, flight and the friendly pattern alternated unpredictably. As the stimulus was repeated over a 5-weeks' period, the autonomic activity decreased and one or other of the various patterns dominated. Eventually each animal's behavior became predictable, but it appeared often to be a matter of chance whether the original disturbance would develop into fear, aggression or (less often) friendliness. When avoidance became dominant, the animal would move back out of reach while the experimenter was still distant, with a marked decrease of the excessive effector activity. Learning was clearly involved. We shall also see that the possibility, suggested by this example, that the learning may take more than one form, has a bearing on the theoretical relation of fear to other emotional patterns.

The hypothesis implicitly developed in this discussion can now be made explicit. The immediate source of fear is a disruption of a coördination, principally acquired, in the timing of cellular activities in the cerebrum. The disruption may be due to conflict, sensory deficit or constitutional change. With disruption there at once occur processes tending to restore the integration of cerebral activities; in fear these include either liminal or subliminal (13) activation of processes determining avoidance. Optimally, avoidance tends toward completely averting the cerebral disruption, and at this stage avoidance without fear would be said to occur.

Classification of Specific Fears

THE value and limitations of the hypothesis will be clearer if we next see how it would be related to specific causes of fear.

FEARS DUE TO "CONFLICT"

Here may be included fears induced by pain, loud noise, dead or mutilated bodies, and strange persons and animals. Pain and loud noise appear to have a primitive disrupting action, not psychologically analyzable nor dependent on any previous experience. To this extent fear of such things is in a special class. It is also noteworthy that there is little adaptation to the repetition of pain and sudden intense noise except in very special conditions (28).

Fear of the strange and of dead and mutilated bodies is included under the heading of conflict on the assumption that strange objects arouse incompatible perceptual and intellectual processes. If it should be concluded however that the effective condition is a perceptual deficit, fear of the strange should be included in the following category (2). Finally, fear of snakes and certain small mammals may belong either in this or the following category. Although some basis for including them in the present category might be proposed it would be much too speculative, and it is best to let such fears stand for the present as not fully accounted for.

FEARS DUE TO SENSORY DEFICIT.

Loss of support, darkness and solitude, as causes of fear, have in common an absence of customary stimulation.

Proprioceptive and pressure stimulation due to maintained position in space is practically always present, and it is plausible to

suppose that the afferent excitation from these sources would have an essential part in maintaining experientially organized, or habitual, modes of cerebral action. With loss of support, however, the proprioception accompanying maintenance of posture against gravity, and exteroception from the surfaces on which the body's weight rests, are decreased or abolished. Redistribution of blood pressure and changes of position of the viscera would no doubt also lead to positive stimulation, but it seems unlikely that this is an effective cause of fear, in the infant. In the adult of course such stimulation would have become conditioned by experience. (If it should be true that positive visceral stimulation is the main cause of fear in an infant dropped for the first time, the fear should be classed in the preceding category (1) as one of those aroused by an unaccustomed stimulation.)

Fears induced by darkness and solitude (39) do not occur with time relations such that the emotional excitation can be attributed to the positive visual activity of the "off-effect." The response appears to be a genuine reaction to deficit (25), intelligible only on the assumption of the present discussion that a "response" need have no direct sensory excitant. The violent attempts of the growing chimpanzee to avoid isolation, even in full daylight, seem to require a quite similar interpretation. Köhler (23) has shown that the effective condition here is the social deprivation, as such. Just as a few patterns of postural stimulation are a practically constant feature of the afferent influx to the brain, and visual stimulation during waking hours, so social perceptions are frequent (though intermittent) and might be expected to become an integral element in the organization of cerebral action patterns. It is important to note that this would be a function of experience, and that no fear of darkness or of being alone should be expected in the subject who has only infrequently experienced anything else. Such a subject would develop a different cerebral organization, in which the perceptions referred to would play no essential part. It is also implied that in early infancy neither darkness nor isolation would have any emotional effect; and that as psychological development continues the patterns of cerebral action might toward maturity become so stable as to be relatively independent of any particular set of perceptions. Some adults, or most adults in a particular culture, might have no fear of darkness and isolation.

CONSTITUTIONAL DISTURBANCES AND MATURATION

Spies *et al.* (38) have provided exceptionally clear evidence that the psychotic fears so frequently found in pellagra are, in some instances at least, directly due to nutritional disturbance (see also Jolliffe, 20). When the psychosis is acute (before irreversible neural damage has been done), fear of friends and relatives and of hallucinatory creatures may clear up dramatically upon administration of nicotinic acid. The patient regains insight rapidly, can recall his fears clearly, but also is puzzled at the lack of any incident that might have caused them. Controls made to exactly define the action of nicotinic acid rule out psychological influence as essential either to the mental illness or its cure. Such fears must be regarded as originating in a disturbance of the metabolism of the individual cell, changing (for example) the timing of its detonation cycle and thus its relationship to the activity of other cells. In other words, metabolic changes would have disrupted the orderly sequence of cerebral events which is postulated here as the basis of normal unemotional behavior.

It is also evident that endocrine factors might at times produce a similar effect, partly accounting for the increased shyness and emotional instability of adolescence. The gonadal hormones must be supposed to have a selective action on certain central neural cells (4, 25) changing their properties of excitability and thus disrupting to a greater or less degree the neural organizations into which those cells have entered. With the passage of time reorganization would occur and shyness would decrease.

I do not of course suggest that constitutional changes are the only cause of shyness, or even the main cause. In its most pronounced form it must be thought of simply as an avoidance of strangers; and the next most important factor, after the sight of a strange person, may well be the fact that as the child matures others begin to behave toward him in a different way, according to his age. The child is confronted by "strange" behavior, and situations which are strange to him. Thus shyness can be treated mainly as avoidance of the strange. It is not impossible however that structural and endocrine changes may also play a part in the emotional instabilities of youth. One thinks of maturation as slow and gradual; but there is actually little evidence on this point, and spurts of growth might well make a significant modification of cerebral organizations established by earlier experience. In general terms, such an approach makes intelligible the sporadic appearance of the "imaginative, subjective or anticipatory fears" classified as such by Jersild and Holmes (19). The fears referred to by Jersild and Holmes are markedly subject to maturation during a period of rapid and irregular growth, and when one observes them in the growing child it is characteristically hard to discover any sufficient cause in experience.

The Relationship of Fear to Rage and Other States

FEAR and rage are notoriously related, and it is impossible to frame any statement of the causes of rage (12) which would not on some points comprise causes of fear as well. The question, whether there is in fact any definite distinction, has been raised elsewhere (13). The hypothesis developed here suggests a kinship between the two emotions which may be put as follows:

The fundamental source of either emotion is of the same kind, a disruption of coördinated cerebral activity. Flight and aggression are two different modes of reaction tending to restore the dynamic equilibrium, or stability, of cerebral processes. The question may be left open at present whether there are different kinds of disturbance, one kind leading to rage, the other to fear. It seems almost certain that such a difference exists between extremes, but with no clear dichotomy; for in some situations, as I have suggested above, it appears to be a matter of chance whether aggression or flight will dominate behavior. Each of these modes of response tends to restore integrated cerebral action, one by modifying the disturbing source of stimulation, the other by removing the animal from it.

Fawning would be another mode of reaction which would tend to modify disruptive stimulation (by placating the source). It is evident also that the hypothesis of this paper opens a wide field of speculation concerning a number of socially and clinically familiar conditions, such as shame, grief, chronic depression and so on. To deal with these varied emotional disturbances, the first step would be to classify the source of disturbance as modifiable by the subject's responses, or unmodifiable; and to further classify the modifiable according to the mode of overt reaction which would be effective. Thus shame or grief would arise from unmodifiable conditions; fear primarily from situations which are (or appear to the subject to be) modifiable by retreat; and so on. Finally, neurosis and some forms of psychosis would be regarded as a chronic condition of cerebral disorganization which according to the hypothesis might be initiated either by severe and prolonged conflict, or by a metabolic disturbance.

It would be idle at present to carry speculation farther, but it has been worthwhile observing that a theoretical relationship of fear to other emotional patterns is provided. If the proposed hypothesis is on the right track, the details of the relationship will become evident when more is known of the physiology of the cerebrum.

Conclusions

THE conclusions of this paper may be put as follows:

1. Anthropoid fears of inert, mutilated or dismembered bodies are spontaneous: that is to say, although experience of a certain kind is a prerequisite and learning is definitely involved, the avoidance of such objects is not built up by association with a more primitive cause of fear.

2. These and a number of other fears are evidently not determined by a sensory event alone, and the behavior is not intelligible except on the assumption that its control is a joint product of sensory and "autonomous" central processes. Consequently no amount of analysis of the stimulating conditions alone can be expected to elucidate the nature of fear, or to lead to any useful generalization concerning its causes.

3. An adequate hypothesis of the nature of fear cannot be framed in psychological terms alone, but must utilize physiological concepts of cerebral action. No common psychological ground can be discovered for all the various causes of fear. What is there in common, for example, between the characteristically high level of the auditory and low level of visual stimulation which induces fear in children? or between fear of strangers, which decreases, and fear induced by pain, which tends to increase, with repetition?

The hypothesis developed here has made a considerable synthesis of formerly unrelated facts, although it remains vague on some crucial points. It proposes in brief that fear originates in the disruption of temporally and spatially organized cerebral activities; that fear is distinct from other emotions by the nature of the processes tending to restore cerebral equilibrium (that is, *via* flight); and classifies the sources of fear as involving (1) conflict, (2) sensory deficit or (3) constitutional change. By distinguishing between processes which break down and those which restore physiological organization in the cerebrum, the variability of fear behavior is accounted for.

The conceptions of neurophysiological action on which this is based were developed originally as an approach to other problems, and will be presented in detail elsewhere. When this is done, and the neurophysiological implications are made explicit, it may appear that a basis has been laid at last for an adequate theory of emotion and motivation— something which is lacking in psychology at present.

REFERENCES

1. ADRIAN, E. D. Electrical activity of the nervous system. *Arch. Neurol. Psychiatr.*, 1934, 32, 1125–1136.
2. BARD, P. On emotional expression after decortication with some remarks on certain theoretical views. *Psychol. Rev.*, 1934, 41, 309–329.
3. ———. Neural mechanisms in emotional and sexual behavior. *Psychosom. Med.*, 1942, 4, 171–172.
4. BEACH, F. A. Analysis of factors involved in the arousal, maintenance and manifestation of sexual excitement in male animals. *Psychosom. Med.*, 1942, 4, 173–198.
5. CARMICHAEL, L., HOGAN, H. P., & WALTER, A. A. An experimental study of the effect of language on the reproduction of visually perceived form. *J. exp. Psychol.*, 1932, 15, 73–86.
6. COWLES, J. T., & NISSEN, H. W. Reward-expectancy in delayed responses of chimpanzees. *J. comp. Psychol.*, 1937, 24, 345–358.
7. DENNIS, W. Congenital cataract and unlearned behavior. *J. genet. Psychol.*, 1934, 44, 340–350.
8. ENGLISH, H. B. Three cases of the "conditioned fear response." *J. abnorm. soc. Psychol.*, 1929, 24, 221–225.
9. GIBSON, J. J. The reproduction of visually perceived forms. *J. exp. Psychol.*, 1929, 12, 1–39.
10. HASLERUD, G. M. The effect of movement of stimulus objects upon avoidance reactions in chimpanzees. *J. comp. Psychol.*, 1938, 25, 507–528.
11. HEBB, D. O. The effect of early and late brain injury on test scores, and the nature of normal adult intelligence. *Proc. Amer. phil. Soc.*, 1942, 85, 275–292.
12. ———. The forms and conditions of chimpanzee anger. *Bull. Canad. Psychol. Assoc.*, 1945, 5, 32–35.
13. ———. Emotion in man and animal: An analysis of the intuitive processes of recognition. *Psychol. Rev.*, 1946, 53, 88–106.
14. ———, & RIESEN, A. H. The genesis of irrational fears. *Bull. Canad. Psychol. Assoc.*, 1943, 3, 49–50.
15. HILGARD, E. R., & MARQUIS, D. G. *Conditioning and learning.* New York: Appleton-Century, 1940.
16. HULL, C. L. *Principles of behavior: An introduction to behavior theory.* New York: Appleton-Century, 1943.
17. JACOBSEN, C. F., JACOBSEN, M. M., & YOSHIOKA, J. G. Development of an infant chimpanzee during her first year. *Comp. Psychol., Monog.*, 1932, 9, 1–94.
18. JASPER, H. H. Electrical signs of cortical activity. *Psychol. Bull.*, 1937, 34, 411–481.
19. JERSILD, A. T., & HOLMES, F. B. *Children's fears.* New York: Teachers College Bureau of Publications, 1935.
20. JOLLIFFE, N. The neuropsychiatric manifestations of vitamin deficiencies. *J. Mt. Sinai Hosp.*, 1942, 8, 658–667.
21. JONES, M. C. Emotional development. In *A handbook of child psychology*, 2nd ed. (C. Murchison, Ed.). Worcester, Mass.: Clark Univ. Press, 1933, 271–302.
22. JONES, H. E., & JONES, M. C. A study of fear. *Childhood Educ.*, 1928, 5, 136–143.
23. KÖHLER, W. *The mentality of apes.* New York: Harcourt, Brace, 1925.
24. LASHLEY, K. S. The thalamus and emotion. *Psychol. Rev.*, 1938, 45, 42–61.
25. ———. Experimental analysis of instinctive behavior. *Psychol. Rev.*, 1938, 45, 445–471.
26. ———. An examination of the "continuity theory" as applied to discrimination learning. *J. gen. Psychol.*, 1942, 26, 241–265.
27. LEEPER, R. A study of a neglected portion of the field of learning. The development of sensory organization. *J. genet. Psychol.*, 1935, 46, 41–75.
28. LIDDELL, H. S. Animal behavior studies bearing on the problem of pain. *Psychosom. Med.*, 1944, 6, 261–263.
29. LORENTE DE NÓ, R. Transmission of impulses through cranial motor nuclei. *J. Neurophysiol.*, 1939, 2, 402–464.
30. ———. Cerebral cortex: architecture. In *Physiology of the nervous system,* 2nd ed. (J. F. Fulton, Ed.). New York: Oxford Univ. Press, 1943, 274–301.
31. McCULLOCH, T. L., & HASLERUD, G. M. Affective responses of an infant chimpanzee reared in isolation from its kind. *J. comp. Psychol.*, 1939, 28, 437–445.
32. MASSERMAN, J. H. The hypothalamus in psychiatry. *Amer. J. Psychiatr.*, 1942, 98, 633–637.

33. MORGAN, C. T. *Physiological psychology.* New York: McGraw-Hill, 1943.

34. MOWRER, O. H. Preparatory set (expectancy) —a determinant in motivation and learning. *Psychol. Rev.,* 1938, 45, 62–91.

35. SENDEN, M. v. *Raum- und Gestaltauffassung bei operierten Blindgeborenen vor und nach der Operation.* Leipzig: Barth, 1932.

36. SHERRINGTON, C. S. *Integrative action of the nervous system.* New York: Scribner's, 1906.

37. SKINNER, B. F. *The behavior of organisms: An experimental analysis.* New York: Appleton-Century, 1938.

38. SPIES, T. D., ARING, C. D., GELPERIN, J., & BEAN, W. B. The mental symptoms of pellagra. Their relief with nicotinic acid. *Amer. J. med. Sci.,* 1938, 196, 461–475.

39. VALENTINE, C. W. The innate bases of fear. *J. genet. Psychol.,* 1930, 37, 394–419.

40. WATSON, J. B. *Behaviorism.* New York: Norton, 1924.

41. WEISS, P. Autonomous versus reflexogenous activity of the central nervous system. *Proc. Amer. phil. Soc.,* 1941, 84, 53–64.

42. YERKES, R. M., & YERKES, A. W. Nature and conditions of avoidance (fear) response in chimpanzee. *J. comp. Psychol.,* 1936, 21, 53–66.

43. ZANGWILL, O. L. A study of the significance of attitude in recognition. *Brit. J. Psychol.,* 1937, 28, 12–17.

JOHN B. WATSON *and* ROSALIE RAYNER

31. *Conditioned Emotional Reactions*

IN recent literature various speculations have been entered into concerning the possibility of conditioning various types of emotional response, but direct experimental evidence in support of such a view has been lacking. If the theory advanced by Watson and Morgan [1] to the effect that in infancy the original emotional reaction patterns are few, consisting so far as observed of fear, rage and love, then there must be some simple method by means of which the range of stimuli which can call out these emotions and their compounds is greatly increased. Otherwise, complexity in adult response could not be accounted for. These authors without adequate experimental evidence advanced the view that this range was increased by means of conditioned reflex factors. It was suggested there that the early home life of the child furnishes a laboratory situation for establishing conditioned emotional responses. The present authors have recently put the whole matter to an experimental test.

Experimental work has been done so far on only one child, Albert B. This infant was reared almost from birth in a hospital environment; his mother was a wet nurse in the Harriet Lane Home for Invalid Children. Albert's life was normal: he was healthy from birth and one of the best developed youngsters ever brought to the hospital, weighing twenty-one pounds at nine months of age. He was on the whole stolid and unemotional. His stability was one of the principal reasons for using him as a subject in this test. We felt that we could do him relatively little harm by carrying out such experiments as those outlined below.

At approximately nine months of age we ran him through the emotional tests that have become a part of our regular routine in determining whether fear reactions can be called out by other stimuli than sharp noises and the sudden removal of support. Tests of this type have been described by the senior author in another place.[2] In brief, the infant was confronted suddenly and for the first time successively with a white rat, a rabbit, a dog, a monkey, with masks with and without hair, cotton wool, burning newspapers, etc. A permanent record of Albert's reactions to these objects and situations has been preserved in a motion picture study. Manipulation was the most usual reaction called out. *At no time did this infant ever show fear in any situation.* These experimental records were confirmed by the casual observations of the mother and hospital attendants. No one had ever seen him in a state of fear and rage. The infant practically never cried.

Up to approximately nine months of age we had not tested him with loud sounds. The test to determine whether a fear reaction could be called out by a loud sound was made when he was eight months, twenty-six days of age. The sound was that made by striking a hammer upon a suspended steel bar four feet in length and three-fourths of an inch

1 "Emotional Reactions and Psychological Experimentation," *American Journal of Psychology,* April, 1917, Vol. 28, pp. 163–174.

2 "Psychology from the Standpoint of a Behaviorist," p. 202.

Reprinted by permission of the American Psychological Association from the *Journal of Experimental Psychology,* 1920, vol. 3, pp. 1–14.

in diameter. The laboratory notes are as follows:

One of the two experimenters caused the child to turn its head and fixate her moving hand; the other, stationed back of the child, struck the steel bar a sharp blow. The child started violently, his breathing was checked and the arms were raised in a characteristic manner. On the second stimulation the same thing occurred, and in addition the lips began to pucker and tremble. On the third stimulation the child broke into a sudden crying fit. This is the first time an emotional situation in the laboratory has produced any fear or even crying in Albert.

We had expected just these results on account of our work with other infants brought up under similar conditions. It is worth while to call attention to the fact that removal of support (dropping and jerking the blanket upon which the infant was lying) was tried exhaustively upon this infant on the same occasion. It was not effective in producing the fear response. This stimulus is effective in younger children. At what age such stimuli lose their potency in producing fear is not known. Nor is it known whether less placid children ever lose their fear of them. This probably depends upon the training the child gets. It is well known that children eagerly run to be tossed into the air and caught. On the other hand it is equally well known that in the adult fear responses are called out quite clearly by the sudden removal of support, if the individual is walking across a bridge, walking out upon a beam, etc. There is a wide field of study here which is aside from our present point.

The sound stimulus, thus, at nine months of age, gives us the means of testing several important factors. I. Can we condition fear of an animal, e.g., a white rat, by visually presenting it and simultaneously striking a steel bar? II. If such a conditioned emotional response can be established, will there be a transfer to other animals or other objects? III. What is the effect of time upon such conditioned emotional responses? IV. If after a reasonable period such emotional responses have not died out, what laboratory methods can be devised for their removal?

THE ESTABLISHMENT OF CONDITIONED EMOTIONAL RESPONSES

At first there was considerable hesitation upon our part in making the attempt to set up fear reactions experimentally. A certain responsibility attaches to such a procedure. We decided finally to make the attempt, comforting ourselves by the reflection that such attachments would arise anyway as soon as the child left the sheltered environment of the nursery for the rough and tumble of the home. We did not begin this work until Albert was eleven months, three days of age. Before attempting to set up a conditioned response we, as before, put him through all of the regular emotional tests. *Not the slightest sign of a fear response was obtained in any situation.*

The steps taken to condition emotional responses are shown in our laboratory notes.

11 Months 3 Days

1. White rat suddenly taken from the basket and presented to Albert. He began to reach for rat with left hand. Just as his hand touched the animal the bar was struck immediately behind his head. The infant jumped violently and fell forward, burying his face in the mattress. He did not cry, however.

2. Just as the right hand touched the rat the bar was again struck. Again the infant jumped violently, fell forward and began to whimper.

In order not to disturb the child too seriously no further tests were given for one week.

11 Months 10 Days

1. Rat presented suddenly without sound. There was steady fixation but no tendency at first to reach for it. The rat was then placed nearer, whereupon tentative reaching movements began with the right hand. When the rat nosed the infant's left hand, the hand was immediately withdrawn. He started to reach for the head of the animal with the forefinger of the left hand, but withdrew it suddenly before contact. It is thus seen that the two joint stimulations given the previous week were not without effect. He was tested with his blocks immediately afterwards to see if they shared in the process of conditioning. He began immediately to pick them up, dropping them, pounding them, etc. In the remainder of the tests the blocks were given frequently to quiet him and to test his general emotional state. They were always re-

moved from sight when the process of conditioning was under way.

2. Joint stimulation with rat and sound. Started, then fell over immediately to right side. No crying.

3. Joint stimulation. Fell to right side and rested upon hands, with head turned away from rat. No crying.

4. Joint stimulation. Same reaction.

5. Rat suddenly presented alone. Puckered face, whimpered and withdrew body sharply to the left.

6. Joint stimulation. Fell over immediately to right side and began to whimper.

7. Joint stimulation. Started violently and cried, but did not fall over.

8. Rat alone. The instant the rat was shown the baby began to cry. Almost instantly he turned sharply to the left, fell over on the left side, raised himself on all fours and began to crawl away so rapidly that he was caught with difficulty before reaching the edge of the table.

This was as convincing a case of a completely conditioned fear response as could have been theoretically pictured. In all, seven joint stimulations were given to bring about the complete reaction. It is not unlikely, had the sound been of greater intensity or of a more complex clang character, that the number of joint stimulations might have been materially reduced. Experiments designed to define the nature of the sounds that will serve best as emotional stimuli are under way.

WHEN A CONDITIONED EMOTIONAL
RESPONSE HAS BEEN ESTABLISHED
FOR ONE OBJECT, IS THERE A TRANSFER?

Five days later Albert was again brought back into the laboratory and tested as follows:

11 Months 15 Days

1. Tested first with blocks. He reached readily for them, playing with them as usual. This shows that there has been no general transfer to the room, table, blocks, etc.

2. Rat alone. Whimpered immediately, withdrew right hand and turned head and trunk away.

3. Blocks again offered. Played readily with them, smiling and gurgling.

4. Rat alone. Leaned over to the left side as far away from the rat as possible, then fell over, getting up on all fours and scurrying away as rapidly as possible.

5. Blocks again offered. Reached immediately for them, smiling and laughing as before.

The above preliminary test shows that the conditioned response to the rat had carried over completely for five days in which no tests were given. The question as to whether or not there is a transfer was next taken up.

6. Rabbit alone. The rabbit was suddenly placed on the mattress in front of him. The reaction was pronounced. Negative responses began at once. He leaned as far away from the animal as possible, whimpered, then burst into tears. When the rabbit was placed in contact with him he buried his face in the mattress, then got up on all fours and crawled away, crying as he went. This was a most convincing test.

7. The blocks were next given him, after an interval. He played with them as before. It was observed by four people that he played far more energetically with them than ever before. The blocks were raised high over his head and slammed down with a great deal of force.

8. Dog alone. The dog did not produce as violent a reaction as the rabbit. The moment fixation occurred the child shrank back and as the animal came near he attempted to get on all fours but did not cry at first. As soon as the dog passed out of his range of vision he became quiet. The dog was then made to approach the infant's head (he was lying down at the moment). Albert straightened up immediately, fell over to the opposite side and turned his head away. He then began to cry.

9. The blocks were again presented. He began immediately to play with them.

10. Fur coat (seal). Withdrew immediately to the left side and began to fret. Coat put close to him on the left side, he turned immediately, began to cry and tried to crawl away on all fours.

11. Cotton wool. The wool was presented in a paper package. At the end the cotton was not covered by the paper. It was placed first on his feet. He kicked it away but did not show the shock that the animals or fur coat produced in him. He then began to play with the paper, avoiding contact with the wool itself. He finally, under the impulse of the manipulative instinct, lost some of his negativism to the wool.

12. Just in play W. put his head down to see if Albert would play with his hair. Albert was

completely negative. Two other observers did the same thing. He began immediately to play with their hair. W. then brought the Santa Claus mask and presented it to Albert. He was again pronouncedly negative.

11 Months 20 Days

1. Blocks alone. Played with them as usual.

2. Rat alone. Withdrawal of the whole body, bending over to left side, no crying. Fixation and following with eyes. The response was much less marked than on first presentation the previous week. It was thought best to freshen up the reaction by another joint stimulation.

3. Just as the rat was placed on his hand the rod was struck. Reaction violent.

4. Rat alone. Fell over at once to left side. Reaction practically as strong as on former occasion but no crying.

5. Rat alone. Fell over to left side, got up on all fours and started to crawl away. On this occasion there was no crying, but strange to say, as he started away he began to gurgle and coo, even while leaning far over to the left side to avoid the rat.

6. Rabbit alone. Leaned over to left side as far as possible. Did not fall over. Began to whimper but reaction not so violent as on former occasions.

7. Blocks again offered. He reached for them immediately and began to play.

All of the tests so far discussed were carried out upon a table supplied with a mattress, located in a small, well-lighted darkroom. We wished to test next whether conditioned fear responses so set up would appear if the situation were markedly altered. We thought it best before making this test to freshen the reaction both to the rabbit and to the dog by showing them at the moment the steel bar was struck. It will be recalled that this was the first time any effort had been made to directly condition response to the dog and rabbit. The experimental notes are as follows:

8. The rabbit at first was given alone. The reaction was exactly as given in test (6) above. When the rabbit was left on Albert's knees for a long time he began tentatively to reach out and manipulate its fur with forefingers. While doing this the steel rod was struck. A violent fear reaction resulted.

9. Rabbit alone. Reaction wholly similar to that on trial (6) above.

10. Rabbit alone. Started immediately to whimper, holding hands far up, but did not cry. Conflicting tendency to manipulate very evident.

11. Dog alone. Began to whimper, shaking head from side to side, holding hands as far away from the animal as possible.

12. Dog and sound. The rod was struck just as the animal touched him. A violent negative reaction appeared. He began to whimper, turned to one side, fell over and started to get up on all fours.

13. Blocks. Played with them immediately and readily.

On this same day and immediately after the above experiment Albert was taken into the large well-lighted lecture room belonging to the laboratory. He was placed on a table in the center of the room immediately under the skylight. Four people were present. The situation was thus very different from that which obtained in the small darkroom.

1. Rat alone. No sudden fear reaction appeared at first. The hands, however, were held up and away from the animal. No positive manipulatory reactions appeared.

2. Rabbit alone. Fear reaction slight. Turned to left and kept face away from the animal but the reaction was never pronounced.

3. Dog alone. Turned away but did not fall over. Cried. Hands moved as far away from the animal as possible. Whimpered as long as the dog was present.

4. Rat alone. Slight negative reaction.

5. Rat and sound. It was thought best to freshen the reaction to the rat. The sound was given just as the rat was presented. Albert jumped violently but did not cry.

6. Rat alone. At first he did not show any negative reaction. When rat was placed nearer he began to show negative reaction by drawing back his body, raising his hands, whimpering, etc.

7. Blocks. Played with them immediately.

8. Rat alone. Pronounced withdrawal of body and whimpering.

9. Blocks. Played with them as before.

10. Rabbit alone. Pronounced reaction. Whimpered with arms held high, fell over backward and had to be caught.

11. Dog alone. At first the dog did not produce the pronounced reaction. The hands were

held high over the head, breathing was checked, but there was no crying. Just at this moment the dog, which had not barked before, barked three times loudly when only about six inches from the baby's face. Albert immediately fell over and broke into a wail that continued until the dog was removed. The sudden barking of the hitherto quiet dog produced a marked fear response in the adult observers!

From the above results it would seem that emotional transfers do take place. Furthermore it would seem that the number of transfers resulting from an experimentally produced conditioned emotional reaction may be very large. In our observations we had no means of testing the complete number of transfers which may have resulted.

THE EFFECT OF TIME
UPON CONDITIONED EMOTIONAL
RESPONSES

We have already shown that the conditioned emotional response will continue for a period of one week. It was desired to make the time test longer. In view of the imminence of Albert's departure from the hospital we could not make the interval longer than one month. Accordingly no further emotional experimentation was entered into for thirty-one days after the above test. During the month, however, Albert was brought weekly to the laboratory for tests upon right- and left-handedness, imitation, general development, etc. No emotional tests whatever were given and during the whole month his regular nursery routine was maintained in the Harriet Lane Home. The notes on the test given at the end of this period are as follows:

1 Year 21 Days

1. Santa Claus mask. Withdrawal, gurgling, then slapped at it without touching. When his hand was forced to touch it, he whimpered and cried. His hand was forced to touch it two more times. He whimpered and cried on both tests. He finally cried at the mere visual stimulus of the mask.

2. Fur coat. Wrinkled his nose and withdrew both hands, drew back the whole body and began to whimper as the coat was put nearer. Again there was the strife between withdrawal and the tendency to manipulate. Reached tentatively with left hand but drew back before contact had been made. In moving his body to one side his hand accidentally touched the coat. He began to cry at once, nodding his head in a very peculiar manner (this reaction was an entirely new one). Both hands were withdrawn as far as possible from the coat. The coat was then laid on his lap and he continued nodding his head and whimpering, withdrawing his body as far as possible, pushing the while at the coat with his feet but never touching it with his hands.

3. Fur coat. The coat was taken out of his sight and presented again at the end of a minute. He began immediately to fret, withdrawing his body and nodding his head as before.

4. Blocks. He began to play with them as usual.

5. The rat. He allowed the rat to crawl towards him without withdrawing. He sat very still and fixated it intently. Rat then touched his hand. Albert withdrew it immediately, then leaned back as far as possible but did not cry. When the rat was placed on his arm he withdrew his body and began to fret, nodding his head. The rat was then allowed to crawl against his chest. He first began to fret and then covered his eyes with both hands.

6. Blocks. Reaction normal.

7. The rabbit. The animal was placed directly in front of him. It was very quiet. Albert showed no avoiding reactions at first. After a few seconds he puckered up his face, began to nod his head and to look intently at the experimenter. He next began to push the rabbit away with his feet, withdrawing his body at the same time. Then as the rabbit came nearer he began pulling his feet away, nodding his head and wailing "da da." After about a minute he reached out tentatively and slowly and touched the rabbit's ear with his right hand, finally manipulating it. The rabbit was again placed in his lap. Again he began to fret and withdrew his hands. He reached out tentatively with his left hand and touched the animal, shuddered and withdrew the whole body. The experimenter then took hold of his left hand and laid it on the rabbit's back. Albert immediately withdrew his hand and began to suck his thumb. Again the rabbit was laid in his lap. He began to cry, covering his face with both hands.

8. Dog. The dog was very active. Albert fixated it intensely for a few seconds, sitting very still. He began to cry but did not fall over backwards as on his last contact with the dog. When

the dog was pushed closer to him he at first sat motionless, then began to cry, putting both hands over his face.

These experiments would seem to show conclusively that directly conditioned emotional responses as well as those conditioned by transfer persist, although with a certain loss in the intensity of the reaction, for a longer period than one month. Our view is that they persist and modify personality throughout life. It should be recalled again that Albert was of an extremely phlegmatic type. Had he been emotionally unstable probably both the directly conditioned response and those transferred would have persisted throughout the month unchanged in form.

"DETACHMENT" OR REMOVAL OF
CONDITIONED EMOTIONAL RESPONSES

Unfortunately Albert was taken from the hospital the day the above tests were made. Hence the opportunity of building up an experimental technique by means of which we could remove the conditioned emotional responses was denied us. Our own view, expressed above, which is possibly not very well grounded, is that these responses in the home environment are likely to persist indefinitely, unless an accidental method for removing them is hit upon. The importance of establishing some method must be apparent to all. Had the opportunity been at hand we should have tried out several methods, some of which we may mention.

1. Constantly confronting the child with those stimuli which called out the responses in the hopes that habituation would come in, corresponding to "fatigue" or reflex when differential reactions are to be set up. 2. By trying to "recondition" by showing objects calling out fear responses (visual) and simultaneously stimulating the erogenous zones (tactual). We should try first the lips, then the nipples and as a final resort the sex organs. 3. By trying to "recondition" by feeding the subject candy or other food just as the animal is shown. This method calls for the food control in the subject. 4. By building up "constructive" activities around the subject by imitation and by putting the hand through the motions of manipulation. At this age imitation of overt motor activity is strong, as our present but unpublished experimentation has shown.

Incidental Observations

THUMB SUCKING AS A COMPENSATORY
DEVICE FOR BLOCKING FEAR AND
NOXIOUS STIMULI

DURING the course of these experiments, especially in the final test, it was noticed that whenever Albert was on the verge of tears or emotionally upset generally he would continually thrust his thumb into his mouth. The moment the hand reached the mouth he became impervious to the stimuli producing fear. Again and again while the motion pictures were being made at the end of the thirty-day rest period, we had to remove the thumb from his mouth before the conditioned response could be obtained. This method of blocking noxious and emotional stimuli (fear and rage) through erogenous stimulation seems to persist from birth onward. Very often in our experiments upon the work adders with infants under ten days of age the same reaction appeared. When at work upon the adders both of the infant's arms are under slight restraint. Often rage appears. They begin to cry, thrashing their arms and legs about. If the finger gets into the mouth crying ceases at once. The organism thus apparently from birth, when under the influence of love stimuli, is blocked to all others.[3] This resort to sex stimulation when under the influence of noxious and emotional situations, or when the individual is restless and idle, persists throughout adolescent and adult life. Albert, at any rate, did not resort to thumb sucking except in the presence of such stimuli. Thumb sucking could immediately be checked by offering him his blocks.

3 The stimulus to love in infants according to our view is stroking of the skin, lips, nipples and sex organs, patting and rocking, picking up, etc. Patting and rocking (when not conditioned) are probably equivalent to actual stimulation of the sex organs. In adults of course, as every lover knows, vision, audition and olfaction soon become conditioned by joint stimulation with contact and kinaesthetic stimuli.

These invariably called out active manipulation instincts. It is worth while here to call attention to the fact that Freud's conception of the stimulation of erogenous zones as being the expression of an original "pleasure" seeking principle may be turned about and possibly described as a compensatory (and often conditioned) device for the blockage of noxious and fear and rage producing stimuli.

EQUAL PRIMACY OF FEAR, LOVE AND POSSIBLY RAGE

While in general the results of our experiment offer no particular points of conflict with Freudian concepts, one fact out of harmony with them should be emphasized. According to proper Freudians sex (or in our terminology, love) is the principal emotion in which conditioned responses arise which later limit and distort personality. We wish to take sharp issue with this view on the basis of the experimental evidence we have gathered. Fear is as primal a factor as love in influencing personality. Fear does not gather its potency in any derived manner from love. It belongs to the original and inherited nature of man. Probably the same may be true of rage although at present we are not so sure of this.

The Freudians twenty years from now, unless their hypotheses change, when they come to analyze Albert's fear of a sealskin coat—assuming that he comes to analysis at that age—will probably tease from him the recital of a dream which upon their analysis will show that Albert at three years of age attempted to play with the pubic hair of the mother and was scolded violently for it. (We are by no means denying that this might in some other case condition it.) If the analyst has sufficiently prepared Albert to accept such a dream when found as an explanation of his avoiding tendencies, and if the analyst has the authority and personality to put it over, Albert may be fully convinced that the dream was a true revealer of the factors which brought about the fear.

It is probable that many of the phobias in psychopathology are true conditioned emotional reactions either of the direct or the transferred type. One may possibly have to believe that such persistence of early conditioned responses will be found only in persons who are constitutionally inferior. Our argument is meant to be constructive. Emotional disturbances in adults cannot be traced back to sex alone. They must be retraced along at least three collateral lines—to conditioned and transferred responses set up in infancy and early youth in all three of the fundamental human emotions.

NEAL E. MILLER

32. Central Stimulation and Other New Approaches to Motivation and Reward

. . . THE focus of my paper will be on . . . determining how motivations and rewards produce their effects. While the immediate practical implications will not be . . . obvious, it is a well-known fact that the deeper understanding of basic phenomena almost always leads to significant practical applications, frequently being the necessary foundation for radical innovations.

You are well aware that problems of motivation and reward, which incidentally shade off into mood and temperament, have wide clinical, social, and educational implications. I believe we are at last developing new techniques for getting inside of the organism, manipulating and measuring some of the simpler, more basic things that are going on there, and thus are laying the foundations for fundamental advances in our understanding of the mechanisms of motivation and reward.

Combination of Behavioral and Physiological Techniques

THE recent spurt of fruitful research on the mechanisms of motivations has emerged as a result of the convergence of two lines of development. Physiologists, pharmacologists, and biochemists have been developing new and subtler tools for radically affecting and measuring organic processes. At the same time, experimental psychologists have been developing a variety of more effective techniques for measuring drives. The combination of techniques from these two sources is be-

ginning to yield results which have exciting potentialities.

In this brief presentation I can only sample a few of these results. . . .

AN EARLY STUDY OF HUNGER

Using the improved electrolytic technique for making lesions deep in the more primitive structures of the brain, Hetherington and Ranson (12) found that lesions in the region of the ventromedial nuclei of the hypothalamus would cause albino rats to overeat enormously so that . . . they became very fat. But Bailey, Stevenson, and I (25) used behavioral tests to show that these lesions do not necessarily always potentiate hunger. Although our rats would eat more, they would not work as hard for food. Furthermore, they were stopped by smaller doses of quinine. Thus the additional behavioral tests did not support the original inference of increased hunger drawn from the measure of amount of food consumed. It seemed more reasonable to assume that the lesion interfered with complete satiation.

In the foregoing study, the single test of amount of food consumed disagreed with the rate of bar pressing and a number of other behavioral measures. Other studies, summarized elsewhere (18), show that certain circumstances can affect the rate of bar pressing, so the results of this test will disagree with those of a number of different tests. Discrepancies among tests purporting to measure the same thing raise important problems which the aptitude testers have long since explored:

Reprinted by permission of the American Psychological Association and the author from the *American Psychologist*, 1958, vol. 13, pp. 100–08.

namely, problems of general versus specific factors, and of the purity of various measures of such factors.[1] But our main point for the moment is that it is prudent and extremely fruitful to use a variety of behavioral tests in studying a drive such as hunger. We are just beginning to cash in on the potentialities of these tests; to date most studies of the physiological mechanisms of hunger are still limited to the single measure of the amount of food consumed (17).

SAMPLE OF OTHER
BRAIN-LESION STUDIES

Lesions in the same general region as those producing overeating can markedly change the temperament of the rat. Anand and Brobeck (1) found that such lesions in the hypothalamus could make rats far more aggressive (a finding which Bailey, Stevenson, and I confirmed on our fingers) and that lesions in the region of the amygdala could abolish this hyperaggressiveness. Similarly, Brady and Nauta (6) have shown that lesions in the septal region can produce heightened startle responses and, with the interesting exception of conditioned suppression (CER), a variety of other indications of increased emotionality. An abstract by King (13) indicates that his paper shows that such emotionality can also be counteracted by lesions in the amygdaloid complex.

In addition to making the animals much tamer, lesions in the region of the amygdala can also produce marked hypersexuality. This is part of the classical Klüver-Bucy (14) syndrome which has been one of the points of departure for many excellent studies of the effects of brain lesions on motivation (e.g., 28, 30, 31, 33).

In the past, the combination of the ablation technique with behavioral tests has been found to be a powerful method for studying sensory, perceptual, and motor functions of the brain. The same combination is becoming a powerful technique for studying also the motivational and emotional functions of the brain. I have cited only a small sample out of the increasingly impressive population of sophisticated studies by able men in this field.

DRIVE ELICITED BY
ELECTRICAL STIMULATION

Electrical stimulation of specific points has been another classical technique for studying brain function. Originally, this technique was used to study motor effects on anaesthetized animals. In his classic work, Hess (11) refined this technique by permanently implanting electrodes in the brains of cats so that they could be stimulated in the normal unanaesthetized state. In addition to eliciting complex motor and postural responses, which were less like reflexes and more like acts, Hess discovered that stimulation in the hypothalamus produced a variety of apparently motivational effects such as rage, flight, and eating. His trail-blazing results, which were limited to naturalistic observation, have provided an excellent point of departure for recent studies using a variety of more rigorous behavioral tests.

Let me illustrate by brief excerpts from a film joined together by pieces of black leader to form a series of animated slides. First we see a cat with electrodes permanently implanted in his brain. As soon as he is stimulated, he lowers his head and starts lapping up water. This cat has Delgado-type electrodes ending in subminiature radio sockets so that the wires can be plugged into his head. The demonstration of drinking is very effective. But when the dish is moved a few inches to one side, the cat lowers his head and licks the floor. This simple test shows that we obviously are not eliciting normal thirst, but only a reflex licking response. Other less extreme examples require considerably more subtle tests.

Turning now to some work in collaboration with E. E. Coons, we see . . . a rat with electrodes placed in a region where stimulation elicits eating. This rat has been thoroughly satiated on food. Soon after stimulation is turned on, the rat starts to eat; soon after it is turned off, he stops. Again, the demonstration is very effective.

But . . . these rats, like Hess's cats, will sometimes also gnaw at inedible objects such

[1] For a discussion of the design required, but seldom used, to test for the unity and generality of intervening variables such as drives, see (20).

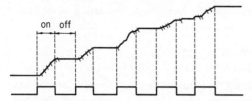

FIG. 1. Stimulation in the hypothalamus elicits the learned response of bar pressing in a satiated rat. Each bar press moves the pen up a little. The rat has been trained on a variable-interval schedule; each spike below the record indicates when a bar press actually delivers food.

as pieces of wood. Therefore, we wonder whether the centrally elicited eating has the properties of normal hunger or is mere reflex gnawing. As a test, we thoroughly trained rats, when thirsty, to get water from a spout above; and, when hungry, to get food by pushing aside a little hinged door below. Then, after thorough satiation, we tested the effects of electrical stimulation. . . . The stimulation can cause a moderately thirsty rat to leave the water spout where he has been drinking and go to a different place to perform the instrumental response of pushing back the hinged door which he has learned as a means of getting food. The fact that the rat stops drinking shows that the effects of stimulation are not mere indiscriminate activation. The fact that the stimulation elicits the learned response of pushing aside the hinged door shows that it has at least some of the more general motivating properties of normal hunger.

In order to make the results completely official, we also trained the rats, when hungry, to secure food by pressing a Skinner bar which delivered small pellets on a variable-interval schedule. FIG. 1 shows the effects of brain stimulation on a thoroughly satiated rat. (Each time the rat presses the bar, the recording lever moves upwards slightly. Each time a bar press actually delivers food, the pen draws a downward spike.) Horizontal sections of the cumulative record show that the satiated rat did relatively little work at the bar during two-minute periods of non-stimulation. The upward steps show that, during the two minutes when the stimulation

was on, the rat worked at the bar which occasionally delivered food. Thus we have further evidence that electrical stimulation in the areas that induce eating will also motivate the performance of learned instrumental responses that have been reinforced by food. The results are convincing pictorially; they also are statistically reliable.

Continuing our program of testing point-by-point whether the motivation elicited by the electrical stimulation of the brain has all of the properties of normal hunger, Coons and I found that its effects were not limited to the gnawing of solid foods; it caused a satiated rat to drink milk. In control tests the stimulation did not elicit similar sustained drinking of water. Furthermore, the stimulation could be used to motivate the rat to run a T maze with the termination of the stimulation serving as a reward to produce highly reliable choice of the endbox in which the stimulation was turned off. In short, the termination of centrally stimulated "hunger" by turning off the switch seems to have the same rewarding effects as the eating of food which ordinarily terminates normally elicited hunger.

Let us turn now to a different type of motivation: a pain-fear-like emotional disturbance which can be elicited by electrical stimulation in a number of regions deep in the brain (8). Does this emotional reaction have all of the functional properties of normally aroused pain and fear? Some of these properties are: (a) Pain and fear can motivate, and their termination reinforce, trial-and-error learning. (b) They can be used to establish a conditioned response. (c) They can serve as a punishment to establish an approach-avoidance conflict so that a hungry animal will avoid food.

The purpose of the experiments is to demonstrate point-by-point that central stimulation of the critical places in the brain has all of the foregoing properties.

. . . A cat, with chronic Delgado-type electrodes ending in subminiature tube sockets into which are plugged the wires bearing the stimulation, . . . first learned to rotate a paddle wheel to turn off electric shock. Then he was tested with brain stimulation. As soon as the stimulation was delivered, the cat became active and, after a few irrelevant responses, rotated the wheel which turned off the stimulation and thus rewarded the response of rotating the wheel. After a few trials, facilitated by transfer from the previous training, the cat learned to rotate the wheel as soon as the stimulation was turned on. . . .

In the next experiment, preliminary tests showed that a tone was a neutral stimulus which produced no obvious response. Then for a number of trials the tone was immediately followed by the brain stimulation which elicited wheel turning. After a few such trials, the wheel turning was conditioned: the tone alone, without brain stimulation, caused the cat to turn the wheel.

In the final experiment, we found that stimulation in the sensorimotor area of a hungry control cat, which was eating, produced a violent withdrawal from food; but even after repeated stimulation, the control animals promptly returned to eat. By contrast, experimental cats, stimulated once or twice with a lower voltage in the critical area of the brain, learned to avoid the food.

These experiments have shown that brain stimulation at critical points can have a number of the significant properties of normally elicited pain and fear. In addition to illustrating a general approach to the problem of investigating motivational factors elicited by electrical stimulation of the brain, experiments of the foregoing type may yield information which will help us in knowing where to place lesions in order to relieve certain hitherto hopeless patients from the acute misery of intractable pain.

Similar experiments on centrally aroused aggression have elicited a spectacular and relatively well-integrated cluster of symptoms of rage—hissing, spitting, clawing, etc.—which suggest that rage contains some integrated motor components different from fear (24). So far, however, Warren Roberts and I have confirmed Masserman's results (16) in that we have not been able to condition such responses. This raises an interesting question. Is anger a distinctive drive whose mechanisms we have simply failed to date to locate, or are

the motor components involved in rage organized without any separate, distinctive drive so that they must be motivated by other drives such as fear, hunger, or sex?

The results of these experiments are enough to illustrate that the combination of the physiological technique of electrical stimulation with various behavioral techniques for measuring the effects of such stimulation is turning out to be a powerful new tool for investigating the motivational functions of the brain.

REWARD EFFECTS OF ELECTRICAL STIMULATION

The combination of the techniques for stimulating the brains of unanaesthetized animals with those of exact behavioral testing led Olds and Milner (27) to a completely unexpected discovery. They found that electrical stimulation of certain areas of the brain would act as a powerful reward. This reward could be used to cause animals to choose the correct side of a T maze or to press a bar in a Skinner box. Often in the history of science, the unexpected discovery of a novel phenomenon, such as X-rays or radioactivity, has forced drastic revisions in current theory and ultimately led to important practical developments. While it is too early to be certain exactly how important will be the effects of this unexpected discovery by Olds and Milner, I suspect they will be considerable.

On the theoretical front, the rewarding effect of central stimulation tends to revive hedonistic theories of reinforcement. As I have pointed out elsewhere, however, the results known to date can be fitted in fairly well with any of the current theories of reinforcement, and the drive-reduction hypothesis suggests a number of interesting lines of investigation in the area of centrally rewarding effects (22). The important thing is that we have here a genuinely novel phenomenon and a completely new technique for investigating the mechanism of reward and its relationship to various drives.

This new discovery has touched off a flurry of research which is still mounting with positive acceleration. Olds (26) has shown that there are certain regions of the hypothalamus where the rate of bar pressing increases with hunger much as it would if the animals were receiving a food reward. In a slightly different area, the rate of bar pressing varies positively with sex—being reduced by castration and increased by androgen therapy. Furthermore, different drugs, such as tranquilizers, seem to have differential effects on the reward phenomenon elicited by stimulation in different parts of the brain. Thus, we probably have here a technique for learning more about how drugs affect different parts of the brain and also for screening drugs in order to discover ones that have more specific psychological effects.

PARADOXICAL DUAL EFFECTS

The experiments which I performed in collaboration with Delgado and Roberts (8) showed that stimulation of certain points in the brain can serve as a punishment. The experiments by Olds and Milner (27) showed that stimulation at other points of the brain can serve as a reward. One of my students, Roberts (29), has recently shown that stimulation in other places may paradoxically function first as a reward and then as a punishment. Bower and I (5) have described further work along this line.

. . . A rat with electrodes at a point in the anterior portion of the medial forebrain bundle which elicits these paradoxical dual effects [presses a] bar [that] turns the stimulation on. . . . Immediately after having pressed the bar the rat turns away and goes to rotate a wheel which terminates the stimulation, then he returns to press the bar again, continuing to repeat the sequence. I believe that this phenomenon may conceivably give us a technique for studying drugs that accentuate the positive rewarding function of the brain and minimize the negative punishing ones.

MOTIVATIONAL EFFECTS OF DRUGS

One of my students, Robert Kirschner, used an apparatus much like the one [described above] except that the bar and wheel were replaced by two bars diagonally across a corner from each other in order to equalize

the skill and effort required to turn the stimulation on or off. Studying the effects of methamphetamine and chlorpromazine, he found that 2 mg/k of the former and 4 mg/k of the latter produced roughly equivalent reductions in the total number of bar presses.

But, when the rewarding and aversive effects were analyzed separately, these two drugs had strikingly different effects. The methamphetamine increased the time to turn the stimulation off while decreasing the time to turn it on. By contrast, the chlorpromazine produced a great increase in the time to turn the stimulation on and also some increase in the time to turn it off. One interpretation of these results is that methamphetamine was accentuating the positive rewarding effects and minimizing the negative punishing ones— a result congruent with its clinical euphoric effects. Chlorpromazine seemed to be reducing reward more than the aversion—a result congruent with the fact that it sometimes causes patients to feel depressed.

The organic chemists are turning out thousands of new compounds and are able to produce at will slight modifications in known drugs. Similarly, the biochemists are learning more about vital hormones, enzymes, enzyme inhibitors, and other powerful agents of metabolism. But one of the chief bottlenecks to the discovery of superior psychotropic drugs is the difficulty in efficiently and safely testing for the psychological effects of all these new compounds. Perhaps this test, along with many other ingenious ones recently devised by experimental psychologists, will help us in finding drugs which have more potent therapeutic effects with fewer harmful side effects. Although the current enthusiasm for the tranquilizing drugs may have the same rocketing rise and frustrating fall as other "wonder cures" for schizophrenia, I believe that the recent signs of vigorous growth of a new infant science of psychopharmacology afford a reasonable ground for eventual hope.

For the rapid growth of psychopharmacology to be healthy, however, I believe that it should soon advance beyond the stage where a single test is widely used for screening merely on the basis of its face validity. The standards and methods of modern aptitude testing should be adapted to this new area. Batteries of tests should be tried out and validated, first by the criterion of internal consistency and eventually by the criterion of predicting clinically useful effects. Both screening tests and drugs might eventually be factor analyzed. At the same time that we are refining our screening instruments, we should also be conducting pure-science studies to analyze how well-known drugs achieve their psychological effects. We need to discover fundamental laws to develop a basic science of psychopharmacology. Such a science should provide a rational basis for practical applications to mental hygiene in the same way that organic chemistry provides a basis for the analysis and synthesis of new compounds (21).

In connection with the problem of drugs, let me emphasize that there is no necessary incompatibility between organic and functional approaches to the problem of mental disease.[2] As you know, I find it useful to describe neurosis and psychotherapy in terms of learning theory. But the book (9) which Dollard and I wrote on this topic contains a chapter on drugs and brain lesions. It is entirely possible that people differ, for example, in the strength of the innate mechanisms for fear, guilt, and anxiety just as they vary in physical size and strength. A person with unusually strong emotional mechanisms of this kind would be especially susceptible to learning strong fears and guilts by traumatic incidents. These unusually strong fears and guilts might directly elicit certain psychosomatic symptoms, produce strong conflicts, or motivate the learning of functional symptoms. It is quite conceivable that chronic medication by suitable drugs could reduce this special susceptibility to irrationally strong fears and guilts much as insulin enables the diabetic to tolerate a diet containing more carbohydrates.

Furthermore, drug effects have the great advantage over certain other forms of organic intervention in that they are reversible. Some interesting results have already been secured by combining the use of barbiturates

2 For a more detailed discussion, see (19).

with psychotherapy. It is conceivable that a superior drug will be produced which will be a much more effective aid to emotional re-education. Indeed, it is conceivable that radically improved results with certain forms of mental disease may be achieved by an unconventional combination of drug therapy, individual therapy, group therapy, training in social skills, and temporary manipulation of the environment.

BIOCHEMICAL STIMULATION

In addition to electrical techniques of stimulation, new biochemical techniques (which obviously have implications also for psychopharmacology) have recently been exploited. For example, Andersson (2) has shown that minute injections of salt solution into the region of the third ventricle can cause excessive drinking in goats. Conversely, our group has shown that minute injections of water into the brain can cause a thirsty cat to stop drinking. Furthermore, we have shown that the minute salt injections increase, while the water ones decrease, the rate of performing a learned response to get water. Therefore, these minute injections into the brain have some of the more general effects of normal increases or reductions of thirst (23).

Similarly, Alan Fisher (10) has shown that a minute injection of male hormone into a specific site in the brain can induce complex sexual, and in some instances maternal, behavior as though it had a motivating effect. Since similar effects were not produced by electrical stimulation of the same sites, there is reason to believe that, in some instances at least, the chemical stimulation may be more effective and selective than the electrical technique. Here again, we have a powerful new tool, the potentialities of which are just beginning to be explored.

ELECTRICAL RECORDING
OF BRAIN ACTIVITY

The converse of the stimulation technique is that of recording electrical activity of the brain and other parts of the nervous system. This technique has been used with great success in tracing sensory systems and has recently produced some quite exciting results which may help to explain the mechanism for the relationship between motivation and attention. For example, it has been found that stimulation of the reticular system in the brain can actually reduce the transmission of sensory impulses from the end organs and through lower relay centers, thus partially shielding the brain from certain sources of stimulation. As Livingston (15) has pointed out, this finding produces a radical change in our previous notions of sensory neurophysiology.

Can these new techniques be applied to other motivational phenomena? For example, Pavlov reports that, when a somewhat painful stimulus is made the conditioned stimulus for food, all of the obvious emotional responses to pain seem to drop out. By using suitable recording techniques, could we demonstrate that the pain impulses themselves are reduced before they reach the highest centers? Would we have an experimental method for producing and studying a phenomenon analogous to hysterical anaesthesia?

Although techniques for recording the electrical activity of the nervous system have been used very successfully in the study of sensory mechanisms, they have not been used much in the study of drive and reward. Here seems a promising new area of application, although there are technical difficulties to overcome. For example, if an animal's motor responses (which disturb electrical recording) were eliminated by one of the improved curare derivatives, such as flaxidil, would we find that the electrical activity in different tracts and centers of the brain is altered when the animal is hungry, thirsty, or suffering painful stimulation? What would be the effects of rewards such as water injected directly into the blood stream of a thirsty animal, if indeed it can be demonstrated that such injections function as a reward? Would there be any effects specific to stimulation of the brain at points where such stimulation is rewarding and different from those at points where it is neutral or aversive? Any such differences are likely to give us significant clues to the basic mechanisms of motivation and reward (22).

Other Promising Approaches

NOW fasten your seat belts for a final spurt through a number of different approaches for which the brevity of listing does not mean any inferiority in merit.

Recently Roger Russell's group has been studying the effects of what might be called biochemical lesions of the brain, while David Krech and Mark Rosenzweig have been pursuing the relationships among brain chemistry, heredity, and behavior. While these new lines of work have been aimed chiefly at cognitive functions, they could easily turn up facts which would lead directly into problems of motivation and reward.

Most of the studies I have sampled thus far have involved relatively direct approaches to the brain. The combination of exact behavioral tests with various "intermediate" techniques has also proved fruitful. Some of the techniques used in this way have been a fistula into the stomach, a cannula into a vein, a subcutaneous saline injection, enzyme inhibitors, and unusual substances which are similar to a metabolite in one respect but different in others. Programs involving such work are well under way in Mayer's laboratory at Harvard (3), Stellar's (32) at Pennsylvania, and our own laboratory at Yale (24). Similarly, Beach (4) and his students are introducing a greater variety of behavioral techniques into the study of sex.

Thus far, various approaches usually have been used in relative isolation. Additional advances may be expected when more use is made of systematic combinations of these approaches. For example, appropriately placed lesions might be used in the analysis of the systems involved in the drive or reward effect of brain stimulation or of the different effects of distending the stomach with either food or a balloon.

Finally, a completely different and highly promising development has been the use of behavioral techniques to bring new drives into the laboratory: first fear, then curiosity, and most recently social deprivation. We can and should extend the range of drives experimentally studied. But that is another story (20).

REFERENCES

1. ANAND, B. K., & BROBECK, J. R. Food intake and spontaneous activity of rats with lesions in the amygdaloid nuclei. *J. Neurophysiol.*, 1952, 15, 421–430.

2. ANDERSSON, B. The effect of injections of hypertonic NaCl solutions into different parts of the hypothalamus of goats. *Acta Physiol., Scand.*, 1953, 28, 188–201.

3. ANLIKER, J., & MAYER, J. The regulation of food intake: Some experiments relating behavioral, metabolic and morphologic aspects. *Amer. J. clin. Nutr.*, 1957, 5, 148–153.

4. BEACH, F. A. Characteristics of masculine "sex drive." In M. R. Jones (Ed.), *Nebraska symposium on motivation.* Lincoln: Univer. Nebraska Press, 1956.

5. BOWER, G., & MILLER, N. E. Paradoxical rewarding and aversive effects from stimulating the same place in a rat's brain. *Amer. Psychologist*, 1957, 12, 464. (Abstract)

6. BRADY, J. V., & NAUTA, W. J. H. Subcortical mechanisms in emotional behavior: The duration of affective changes following septal and habenular lesions in the albino rat. *J. comp. physiol. Psychol.*, 1955, 48, 412–420.

7. BROWN, J. The generalization of approach responses as a function of stimulus intensity and strength of motivation. *J. comp. Psychol.*, 1942, 33, 209–226.

8. DELGADO, J. M. R., ROBERTS, W. W., & MILLER, N. E. Learning motivated by electrical stimulation of the brain. *Amer. J. Physiol.*, 1954, 179, 587–593.

9. DOLLARD, J., & MILLER, N. E. *Personality and psychotherapy: An analysis in terms of learning, thinking and culture.* New York: McGraw-Hill, 1950.

10. FISHER, A. Maternal and sexual behavior induced by intracranial chemical stimulation. *Science*, 1956, 124, 228–229.

11. HESS, W. R. *Das Zwischenhirn: Syndrome, Lokalisationen, Functionen.* (2nd ed.) Basel: Schwabe, 1954.

12. HETHERINGTON, A. W., & RANSON, S. W. The relation of various hypothalamic lesions to adiposity in the rat. *J. comp. Neurol.*, 1942, 76, 475–499.

13. KING, F. A. Effects of amygdaloid lesions upon septal hyperemotionality in the rat.

Amer. Psychologist, 1957, 12, 466. (Abstract)

14. KLÜVER, H., & BUCY, P. C. Preliminary analysis of functions of the temporal lobes in monkeys. *Arch. Neurol. Psychiat.*, 1939, 42, 979–1000.

15. LIVINGSTON, R. B. Central control of afferent activity. In H. H. Jasper, et al. (Ed.), *Henry Ford hospital international symposium: Reticular formation of the brain.* Boston: Brown, in press.

16. MASSERMAN, J. H. Is the hypothalamus a center of emotion? *Psychosom. Med.*, 1941, 3, 3–25.

17. MILLER, N. E. Shortcomings of food consumption as a measure of hunger: Results from other behavioral techniques. *Ann. N.Y. Acad. Sci.*, 1955, 63, 141–143.

18. MILLER, N. E. Effects of drugs on motivation: The value of using a variety of measures. *Ann. N.Y. Acad. Sci.*, 1956, 65, 318–333.

19. MILLER, N. E. A psychologist speaks. In H. D. Kruse (Ed.), *Integrating the approaches to mental disease.* New York: Paul B. Hoeber, 1957.

20. MILLER, N. E. Liberalization of basic S-R concepts: Extensions to conflict behavior and social learning. In S. Koch (Ed.), *Psychology: A study of a science.* Vol. II. *General systematic formulations, learning and special processes.* New York: McGraw-Hill, in press.

21. MILLER, N. E. Objective techniques for studying motivational effects of drugs on animals. In S. Garattini & V. Ghetti (Eds.), *Psychotropic drugs.* Amsterdam: Elsevier; New York: Van Nostrand, 1957.

22. MILLER, N. E. Comments on the implications of the Olds reward effect for theories of reinforcement. In D. E. Sheer (Ed.), *Electrical stimulation of the brain: Subcortical integrative systems.* Houston: Univer. Texas Press, in press.

23. MILLER, N. E. Learning and performance motivated by direct stimulation of the brain. In D. E. Sheer (Ed.), *Electrical stimulation of the brain: Subcortical integrative systems.* Houston: Univer. Texas Press, in press.

24. MILLER, N. E. Experiments on motivation:

Studies combining psychological, physiological, and pharmacological techniques. *Science,* 1957, 126, 1271–1278.

25. MILLER, N. E., BAILEY, C. J., & STEVENSON, J. A. F. Decreased "hunger" but increased food intake resulting from hypothalamic lesions. *Science,* 1950, 112, 256–259.

26. OLDS, J. Self-stimulation of the brain: Used to study local effects of hunger, sex and drugs. *Science,* in press.

27. OLDS, J., & MILNER, P. Positive reinforcement produced by electrical stimulation of septal area and other regions of rat brain. *J. comp. physiol. Psychol.,* 1954, 47, 419–427.

28. PRIBRAM, K. H., & WEISKRANTZ, L. A comparison of the effects of medial and lateral cerebral resections on conditioned avoidance behavior in monkeys. *J. comp. physiol. Psychol.,* 1957, 50, 77–80.

29. ROBERTS, W. W. Both rewarding and punishing effects from stimulation of posterior hypothalamus with same electrodes at same intensity. *J. comp. physiol. Psychol.,* in press.

30. ROSVOLD, H. E., MIRSKY, A. F., & PRIBRAM, K. H. Influence of amygdalectomy on social behavior in monkeys. *J. comp. physiol. Psychol.,* 1954, 47, 173–178.

31. SCHREINER, L., & KLING, A. Rhinencephalon and behavior. *Amer. J. Physiol.,* 1956, 184, 486–490.

32. STELLAR, E. Physiological psychology. In P. R. Farnsworth (Ed.), *Annual review of psychology.* Vol. 8. Palo Alto, Calif.: Annual Reviews, Inc., 1957.

33. WATERHOUSE, I. K. Effects of prefrontal lobotomy on conditioned fear and food responses in monkeys. *J. comp. physiol. Psychol.,* 1957, 50, 81–88.

JUDSON S. BROWN *and* ALFRED JACOBS

33. The Role of Fear in the Motivation and Acquisition of Responses

A N important concept in a number of current theories of behavior is that the emotion of fear is (usually) a learned, anticipatory response to painful stimulation and that its significance as a behavior-determinant lies primarily in its motivational properties. The assumption that fear is a learned response stems from the fact that it can be elicited by (conditioned) stimuli which in the past have been closely associated with, or have been followed by, noxious (unconditioned) stimuli. The additional assumption that fear is (or produces) a drive, rests on the assertion that it exhibits certain of the major functional properties commonly attributed to primary drives such as hunger. Specifically, (1) the presence of fear is said to energize or motivate behavior, and (2) a reduction in fear is said to act as a reinforcement for the acquisition of new responses. Since the fear reaction is learned, the resulting drive is termed secondary or acquired to distinguish it from primary drives whose antecedent conditions are unlike those typically observed in learning situations.

This conception, which is essentially a translation of certain Freudian (4) ideas into stimulus-response terms, was first proposed by Mowrer (9). Subsequently, he and others have applied the notion to the interpretation of a variety of behavior and have carried out a number of experiments tending to support the hypothesis (3, 6, 8, 11, 12). A recent study by N. E. Miller (7), which apparently provides the most convincing confirmatory evidence, forms the point of departure for the present investigation.

The procedure employed by Miller may be summarized briefly as follows. The apparatus consisted of an oblong box, divided by a sliding door into two compartments, one white with a grid floor, the other black with a smooth floor. During preliminary training trials, rats were allowed to escape a shock in the white compartment by running into the black, the door being open. On subsequent learning trials, the animals were placed in the white side with the door closed, but with no shock on the grid. If an animal made the "correct" response of turning a small wheel (located over the door) within 100 sec., the door dropped and the rat could escape into the black compartment. If the response was not made within the allotted time, the animal was lifted out of the box to await its next trial. The results obtained on the learning trials indicated clearly that if the wheel-turning response occurred a few times early in the series it was then rapidly learned, apparently being reinforced by the reduction in fear accompanying escape into the black compartment. Thirteen out of 25 animals showed clear-cut evidence of learning the new response. On subsequent trials, when the wheel-turning response was made "incorrect" for these 13 rats, it extinguished rapidly, and a new "correct" response of pressing a bar to open the door was readily learned. Since no shock was administered on any of the learning trials, the results were interpreted as indicating that the fear aroused by the stimuli from the white compartment provided a drive which led to random activity and hence to the initial correct responses, and

Reprinted by permission of the American Psychological Association and the authors from the *Journal of Experimental Psychology*, 1949, vol. 39, pp. 747–59.

that the reduction in fear accompanying escape from the white box operated to reinforce the wheel-turning and bar-pressing responses.

Although Miller's interpretation of his results in terms of fear and its reduction appears quite plausible, there are other interpretations that merit consideration. One alternative is to assume that frustration, not fear, is the important drive in the situation and hence that frustration-reduction is the significant reinforcing event. According to this hypothesis, the interruption or blocking of any strong, on-going response produces a state of frustration or anger which functions as a drive. In Miller's experiment, the response which was blocked was that of running from the white box into the black, a response which had been powerfully reinforced by shock-reduction during the training trials. On the learning trials, when this response was prevented from occurring by the closed door, the hypothetical frustration drive might well have been aroused. This drive, like that of fear, could lead to the appearance of varied activity and, eventually, to the correct response of turning the wheel. Since the opening of the door would permit the resumption of the running response, there would follow an almost immediate reduction in frustration. As a consequence, the tendency to perform the wheel-turning response would be strengthened by this decrease in drive.

The two experiments reported herein were designed to control for this possible frustration factor by eliminating the locomotor response from the initial training situation. The general procedure employed in both studies involved a number of training trials during which rats were placed in an oblong box and given paired presentations of a neutral (conditioned) stimulus and an electric shock. On subsequent learning trials, the conditioned stimulus was presented without shock and an opportunity was provided for the animals to execute a new response of crossing from one side of the box to the other by jumping over a barrier. If the barrier-crossing response occurred, the conditioned stimulus was immediately terminated. Learning was estimated from the latencies of the barrier-crossing responses. In the case of both ex-

periments it was assumed that: (1) the pairing of the neutral stimulus and the shock would result in the development of a conditioned fear response; (2) the presence of fear would lead to varied responses, including that of crossing the barrier; and (3) the barrier-jumping reaction would be reinforced by the cessation of the conditioned stimulus and the consequent reduction in fear. It was also assumed that, since no specific escape response was reinforced by shock-reduction during training, the possibility of arousing frustration during the subsequent learning trials would be negligible. The two experiments differed with respect to certain details such as number of training trials, nature of the conditioned stimulus, and so on. These variations led to certain differences in the results which are believed to be of importance for interpretations of fear-motivated behavior.

Experiment I

APPARATUS

THE apparatus consisted of an oblong box 14 in. long, 5 in. wide, and 5 in. deep (inside dimensions), painted flat black and provided with a grid floor. The grid was constructed of ³⁄₃₂-in. brass rods, spaced at intervals of ⁷⁄₁₆ in. The lid of the box was constructed by tacking celluloid to a light wooden frame hinged to the upper edge of the box. A removable barrier extended two in. above the grid floor when in position.

The shocking current was obtained from a 75,000-ohm potentiometer wired as a voltage divider across the 500-volt secondary of a conventional radio power transformer. The voltage was applied to the grid through a fixed resistor of 0.3 megohm. The shock-voltage values given below represent readings from a 2000-ohm-per-volt a.c. voltmeter connected across the output leads of the potentiometer at all times.

The conditioned stimulus was the sound produced by a high-frequency buzzer (Speedex Type) operating on six volts a.c. The latencies of the barrier-crossing responses were measured with a stop-watch from the onset of the conditioned stimulus until an animal had crossed completely over the barrier.

The room was in almost complete darkness save for the illumination provided by a 10-watt lamp suspended about 18 in. directly above the center of the box.

SUBJECTS

Two groups of 10 rats, each consisting of eight hooded females and two albino males approximately 100 days old, were used as *S*s. Within each sex the animals were assigned to the two groups at random.

TRAINING PROCEDURE

The procedure followed during training was designed to produce a conditioned fear response in the animals of the experimental group, but not in those of the control group. Each animal of the fear group was placed in the apparatus (with barrier absent) and given 40 paired presentations of buzzer and shock, 10 per day for four successive days. The buzzer was sounded for either 2, 3, or 4 sec. before the shock and continued to sound with the shock for either 3, 4, or 5 sec. Individual trials were spaced at intervals of either 4, 5, or 6 min. The durations of buzzer, buzzer with shock, and inter-trial interval were selected at random from the above ranges and the same sequence was administered to all animals. At the conclusion of each day's training, each animal was left in the apparatus for 10 min. before being returned to its home cage. The shocks were 160 volts for the females and 180–200 volts for the larger males. Food and water were present at all times in the home cages. The animals in the control group were trained in exactly the same manner as were those in the experimental group, except that *no shocks were given the controls at any time.*

TESTING PROCEDURE

The two-in. barrier was introduced into the center of the box and each animal was given 40 learning trials, 10 on each of four successive days. On each learning trial, an animal was placed in the box and the buzzer was sounded *but no shock was presented.* When the rat jumped the hurdle, the buzzer was immediately turned off. On the first day, successive trials were given at five-min. intervals. If a response had not occurred by the end of a continuous three-min. sounding of the buzzer, the buzzer was turned off and two min. were allowed to pass before the next trial. On Days 2, 3, and 4, the trials were run at four-min. intervals, the buzzer being turned off when the response was completed, or after an interval of two min. if no response occurred. The initial trial of the first day was given five min. after an animal was placed in the box; on the other days the interval preceding the first trial was three min. As in the case of the training procedure, the animals were returned to their cages 10 min. after the last trial of a day. The control and experimental animals were treated in an identical manner throughout the learning session.

RESULTS

The outcome of the procedure followed in Experiment I is summarized in TABLE 1 where the mean log latencies (plus a constant of 1.0) for successive blocks of five learning trials have been listed for both the experimental and the control groups.

These values have also been plotted in FIG. 1. The individual response latencies (in sec.) were transformed into logarithms in order to normalize the data for statistical treatment. The constant was added so that the values obtained here could be plotted to the same

TABLE 1

Mean Log Latencies (Plus 1.0) for Successive Blocks of Five Learning Trials

	1–5	6–10	11–15	16–20	21–25	26–30	31–35	36–40
				TRIALS				
Control group	2.23	2.64	2.40	2.52	2.26	2.47	2.30	2.40
Exper. group	2.75	2.54	2.28	2.29	2.01	2.04	1.81	1.95

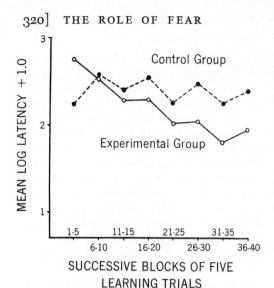

SUCCESSIVE BLOCKS OF FIVE
LEARNING TRIALS

FIG. 1. Latencies of barrier-crossing responses made by the experimental and control animals on successive blocks of five learning trials. The experimental animals were presumably fearful and show evidence of improved performance with fear-reduction as the reinforcement for the new response. The non-fearful controls show no improvement. These curves were plotted from the values listed in TABLE 1.

scale as those in the second experiment where a constant was added to avoid negative logarithms.

An examination of these statistics shows that the experimental animals exhibited a progressive decrease in the latency of the barrier-crossing response with successive non-shock trials. All but one of the experimental animals learned the new response with a fair degree of promptness. The one that did not learn made only one barrier-crossing response during the 40 test trials. The scores for this animal have not been included in the treatment of the data. That the decrease in latency shown by the group as a whole can scarcely be attributed to chance is indicated by the highly significant value of t obtained from a comparison of the means of the first and the last five trials of this group. This t-value is the first shown in TABLE 2. By comparison, the control animals (not shocked during training) showed no progressive decrease in latency during the course of the learning trials. In fact, their mean reaction latency on Trials 36–40 was longer than that on Trials 1–5, although the difference is not significant, as may be seen from the second entry in TABLE 2.

It is important to note, however, that although the fear-group animals showed clear evidence of learning the new response and were significantly faster than the controls on the last five trials (fourth entry, TABLE 2), they were significantly slower than the controls on the first five trials (third entry in TABLE 2). As a result of this reversal in the relative proficiencies of the two groups, a statistical comparison of the *overall means* of the two groups does not lead to the rejection of the null hypothesis (last value in TABLE 2).

One feature of the data that is of interest is the cyclic fluctuations in latency exhibited by both the control and experimental animals (FIG. 1). In the case of the controls, the mean latencies were longer on the last five trials of each day than on the first five. This suggests that exploratory tendencies were undergoing extinction during the course of each day's trials. Consistent with this interpretation is the fact that the controls also had

TABLE 2

A Summary of Tests of Significance Computed between Various Means for Both Experimental and Control Animals

TRIALS OR GROUPS COMPARED	t	d.f.	P
1. Trials 1–5 vs. 36–40 (exper.)	5.70	8	<.01
2. Trials 1–5 vs. 36–40 (cont.)	2.00	9	<.10, >.05
3. Exper. vs. cont.: trials 1–5	4.40	17	<.01
4. Exper. vs. cont.: trials 36–40	2.97	17	<.01
5. Exper. vs. cont.: mean of all trials	1.55	17	<.20, >.10

shorter latencies on the first five trials of each of the last three days than on the last five trials of each preceding day. Conceivably, this reflects the spontaneous recovery of the extinguished exploratory tendencies.

The cyclic fluctuations shown by the experimental animals were limited to the last three days of testing (Trials 11–40) and were less marked than those of the controls. These might also be attributed to the extinction and spontaneous recovery of exploratory behavior on the assumption that the exploratory tendencies were superimposed upon the gradually developing tendency to cross the barrier in response to the buzzer. It is quite possible, however, that processes of extinction and spontaneous recovery were actually taking place in the case of either the jumping response or the fear response, or both.

DISCUSSION

The major objective of the present study was to determine whether the rewarding and energizing functions commonly attributed to fear, but also ascribable in special cases to a drive resulting from the frustration of a locomotor response, would be exhibited under conditions unfavorable to the development of frustration. Since, in this experiment, clear evidence of learning was obtained under such conditions, it may be concluded that the *rewarding function* of fear-reduction receives additional experimental support, and that frustration, at least of the hypothesized variety, is apparently not an essential element.

It has been shown that the cessation of a normally neutral stimulus, after that stimulus has been repeatedly presented with a noxious one, acquires the property of strengthening new stimulus-response connections. In accounting for this empirical fact, it may be assumed that the pairing of the two stimuli results in the neutral one's becoming a conditioned stimulus which evokes a fear reaction. This reaction, which may be a fractional anticipatory component of the unconditioned response to the noxious stimulus, is presumed, perhaps by virtue of the stimulation it provides (8), to add an increment to the general drive level of the animal. As a consequence, any new reaction occurring in close

temporal proximity to the cessation of the fear response and the consequent drive reduction will be reinforced.

With respect to the *energizing function* of fear, it must be concluded that the present experiment yields no direct evidence that fear leads inevitably to an increase in random or exploratory movements. If such were the case, one would anticipate that the *initial* barrier-crossing responses of the fearful (experimental) animals would have been quicker than those of the controls, since on the first few trials, before any appreciable learning had occurred, the response latencies should reflect rather directly the tendency to make random movements. This expectation is not confirmed by the data. On the first trial, for example, the fearful animals were much slower than the controls, the mean log latencies for the two groups being 2.71 and 1.88 sec., respectively. And even at the end of the first five trials when the mean latency for the controls had risen to 2.23 sec. (five trials combined) the fearful group was still significantly inferior to the controls.

From qualitative observations of the behavior of our animals it seems probable that the initial response latencies of the experimental rats were long because these animals were more prone to "freeze" or crouch than were the non-fearful ones. In some instances, the fearful rats were fairly active when first placed into the apparatus but would immediately become immobile when the buzzer was sounded. It seems likely, therefore, that under the conditions of this study, fear was quite often accompanied by a reduction in random activity instead of by an increase in activity. Confirmatory evidence for these observations is provided by Miller (7), who reports marked crouching on the part of some of his animals, and by Arnold (1), who states categorically (though on the basis of only two or three studies) that fear is always accompanied by a reduction in somatic activity.

Although these findings appear to be inconsistent with the hypothesis that fear exhibits the energizing function of a drive, the hypothesis may be retained, provided one abandons the rather limited assumption that drives, when functioning as energizers, always lead to more vigorous overt or random action.[1] Thus, it may be supposed, as Hull (5) does, that the generalized drive state (D), to which all of the specific drives or needs contribute, combines in a multiplicative manner with the habit values of both learned and innate responses ($_sH_R$'s and $_sU_R$'s). Other things equal, the response which occurs is that having the strongest habit, irrespective of the specific drives which are the major contributors to the strength of D. If crouching is exhibited instead of random activity, then the strength of the crouching habit must be greater than that for random action, and the stronger the drive, the more intense the crouching will be. According to this conception, then, *the presence of fear may act as an energizer (by virtue of its contribution to D) and yet lead in certain instances to an increase in immobility*.

The question remains, of course, as to why the habit of crouching should be strong for fearful animals but not for non-fearful ones, or for ones highly motivated by hunger, thirst, etc. One answer, suggested by Miller (7), is that crouching occupies a dominant position in the hierarchy of innate responses to the stimuli accompanying (or arising from) fear. Hungry animals do not crouch because hunger-produced stimuli are different from fear-produced stimuli and are not innately associated with responses of immobility.

It is also possible that crouching is *learned* during the shock trials, and that it becomes conditioned to the fear stimuli, as well as to stimuli provided by the shock and the apparatus. Crouching or freezing would certainly be reinforced if they occurred at the time the shock was turned off or if they led in some way to either a complete or partial reduction of shock.[2] Although no systematic

observations were made of such behavior, the impression is strong that the initial reactions of the animals to shock were almost always ones of rather violent action. Immobility reactions never became dominant until after a number of shock trials had been administered. Similar observations of the learning of immobile reactions to escape shock have been made by Mowrer (10). We would conclude tentatively, therefore, that responses of crouching or standing still may well have been acquired during the course of the training trials in our experiment, and that in all probability these responses were conditioned to both external and internal stimuli by the reinforcing effect of reductions in shock intensity.[3]

Although in this experiment the evidence for learning appears to be relatively unambiguous, since the fearful animals were significantly superior to the controls when compared on the last five trials, it is possible that some of the drop in the curve of FIG. 1 for the fear group could have been due to factors other than learning. In particular, the initial fall of the curve, at least to the point where it crosses the control-group curve, might indi-

---

[1] It should be noted that although both Mowrer and Miller have, in general, restricted their treatments of the energizing function of fear to its role as a motivator of so-called random or trial-and-error behavior, neither of them has apparently held the view that random activity is the only variety of response that will be exhibited when the drive of fear is present. Such a view, however, of the energizing action of drives is rather commonly expressed in introductory treatments of motivation (see, e.g., Shaffer, 13, p. 89).

[2] A reduction in shock intensity would result if an animal's position led to an increase in contact area and a decrease in current density through the tissues of its feet. Or, complete elimination of shock could be effected by an animal's standing on its hind feet and touching only one side of the shock circuit. When such postures were adopted in this experiment, it was noted that marked increases could be produced in the shock voltage without disturbing the animals. This constitutes objective evidence that the animals were not feeling the shock at those times. On a few occasions it was even necessary to move an animal forcibly into a new position in the apparatus so that further shock trials could be given.

[3] It seems highly probable that, if crouching can be learned as a reaction to fear, animals could also be trained to be exceptionally active in the presence of fear by suitably reinforcing such activity. Confirmatory evidence for this possibility has been obtained in a previous experiment by one of the present authors (2). In that experiment, rats that had been given strong shocks at the end of a short straight alley, and who were therefore presumably quite fearful, exhibited vigorous avoidance responses when placed back into the alley even when no shock was present. In Miller's experiment discussed above, the initial training procedure was also such as to reinforce the tendency of his animals to be active when fearful. Such a tendency might be strengthened (by fear reduction) in the case of those animals that learned to escape, and extinguished in the case of those that failed to learn, thus permitting the crouching response to become dominant in the latter group.

cate merely that the freezing responses were becoming extinguished and that the level of general activity was increasing. An increase in activity level would be quite likely to lead to shorter response latencies. Thus it was felt that the interpretation of at least the first segment of the curve was difficult and that further experimentation was needed.

Experiment II

PURPOSE

THE second experiment was conducted to determine whether by modifying the procedure of the first, the degree of freezing exhibited by the fearful rats could be substantially reduced while maintaining fear at a sufficiently high level to enable it to serve in a reinforcing capacity. The changes in procedure were designed to reduce the opportunities for the animals to learn to crouch, and to make conditions more favorable for the learning of the new response. Specifically, the procedure of the second experiment when compared with that of the first involved (1) a reduction in the number of shock trials, (2) a change from steady shock to pulsating shock, (3) a change in the conditioned stimulus, (4) a modification of the learning procedure, making it unnecessary for the animals to shuttle back and forth in the apparatus, and (5) the introduction of an irrelevant (hunger) drive.

APPARATUS

The same basic apparatus described above was used. The box was modified to permit the introduction of a guillotine-type door which extended down through the top at the center and rested directly on the upper edge of the two-in. partition. This served to divide the box into two compartments of equal size and appearance.

Because of noticeable fluctuations in both the frequency and intensity of the buzzer used in Experiment I and because of its somewhat raucous sound, a new conditioned stimulus was introduced. This consisted of a light and tone presented together, both being interrupted 100 times per min. by a commutator on a small synchronous motor. The light was provided by an inside-frosted 10-watt lamp suspended 12 in. above the exact center of the box. The tone, generated by a resistance-capacitance oscillator and fed directly into a five-in. permanent magnet speaker, had a frequency of 2000 cycles and an intensity, measured at the top of the box, of about 70 db. above a reference level of 10^{-16} watts/cm.^{2} This compound stimulus of pulsating light and tone was employed in order to achieve distinctiveness without at the same time increasing intensity to the painful or slightly noxious level. The shock was the same as in Experiment I, except that the circuit was interrupted at the same rate as were the light and tone. This modification was introduced because exploratory work revealed that with intermittent shock there was apparently less chance that the animals would adopt a crouching position which would effectively reduce the shock intensity.

The latency of each response on the learning trials was measured by means of a Standard Electric Timer. The timer was started automatically when the guillotine door was lifted (to allow the animal to cross the barrier) and stopped when the door was lowered following a response.

SUBJECTS

The experimental and control groups each consisted of eight naive albino rats between 60 and 120 days of age. Five of the animals in each group were females, three were males. Within each sex, animals were assigned at random to the two groups.

TRAINING PROCEDURE

The purpose of the training trials, as in Experiment I, was to develop in the experimental animals a conditioned fear response to the tone-light stimulus. These animals received a total of 22 training trials (as contrasted with 40 in Experiment I): 10 trials were given on each of two successive days and two on the third day. The trials were alternated, half of them being administered in one compartment and half in the other. Each trial consisted of a nine-sec. presentation of the conditioned stimulus, with the interrupted shock presented during the last six sec. of the period. Nor-

TABLE 3

Mean Log Latencies (Plus 1.0) for Successive Blocks of Five Learning Trials

| | TRIALS | | | | | | | |
	1–5	6–10	11–15	16–20	21–25	26–30	31–35	36–40
Control group	2.09	2.26	2.14	2.35	2.10	2.39	2.19	2.50
Exper. group	2.02	1.50	1.23	0.94	1.08	1.19	1.10	1.25

mally, the shock was set at 150 volts, but occasionally it was raised to 180 if an animal showed no signs of receiving the shock. Successive training trials were run at intervals of three min. One min. after a trial, the animal was moved to the opposite compartment where the next trial followed in two min. After the last trials of the first two days, the animals remained in the box for two min. before being returned to their home cages. Two min. after the second trial of the third day, the animals were removed to a carrying cage, where they remained for five min. before being returned to the apparatus for the learning trials.

All animals were run under a 22-hour hunger drive. They were fed in separate feeding cages one hour after the completion of each day's trials. The purpose of the hunger drive was to raise the general activity level of the animals and hence to increase the probability that the desired response of crossing the barrier would occur promptly on the initial learning trials.

The procedure employed in the training of the control animals was identical with that described above for the experimentals, except that the controls were never shocked.

TESTING PROCEDURE

On each test (learning) trial an animal was placed in one of the compartments, whereupon the door was lifted and the light-tone stimulus was presented *without shock*. As soon as the response of crossing the hurdle occurred, the light and tone were shut off and the door was lowered. After the lapse of two min., the animal was returned to the first compartment for the next trial. In the event that the barrier-crossing response did not occur within one min., the light-tone stimulus

was terminated and the door was lowered, the animals being left in the compartment for an additional min. At the end of this period, they were lifted out of, and immediately replaced in, the same compartment and a new trial was begun. The test trials for both groups were identical, all animals receiving 40 trials, 10 on each of four successive days. The test trials for half of the animals in each group consisted in going *from* the compartment in which they had received their last training trial; the other half went *into* the compartment where the last training trial had been given.

RESULTS AND DISCUSSION

The major findings of the second experiment are summarized in TABLE 3, where the mean log latencies (plus 1.0) for successive blocks of five trials are given. These values are plotted in FIG. 2 to the same scale as that of FIG. 1. The results of tests of significance applied to the data are given in TABLE 4.

From the curves of FIG. 2, it is apparent that, in broad outline at least, the results of the second experiment parallel and confirm those of the first. All of the eight experimental animals learned the new response, and a comparison of the group means for the first and last blocks of five trials shows that the decrease in latency was highly significant. The control animals, by contrast, not only showed no improvement in performance, but instead showed a significant decrement. The general thesis concerning the reinforcing effect of fear-reduction thus receives additional experimental support.[4]

4 Since the control-group animals were never shocked, there is a possibility that the experimental animals learned to jump the barrier simply to escape from a compartment in which they had been shocked.

TABLE 4

Tests of the Significance of Differences Between Various Means
Obtained from the Experimental and Control Groups

TRIALS OR GROUPS COMPARED	t	d.f.	P
1. Trials 1–5 vs. 36–40 (exper.)	4.48	7	$<.01$
2. Trials 1–5 vs. 36–40 (cont.)	6.03	7	$<.01$
3. Exper. vs. cont.: trials 1–5	0.45	14	$<.70, >.60$
4. Exper. vs. cont.: trials 36–40	6.61	14	$<.01$
5. Exper. vs. cont.: mean of all trials	9.06	14	$<.01$

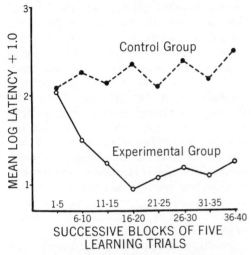

SUCCESSIVE BLOCKS OF FIVE
LEARNING TRIALS

FIG. 2. A graphic presentation of the values listed in TABLE 3. The resulting curves are comparable to those in FIG. 1, and reveal the marked superiority of the fearful experimental animals over the non-fearful controls in the learning of the barrier-crossing response in the second experiment.

When one compares the curves for the two control groups in the first and second experiments, it is seen that they are roughly alike in absolute height and both show similar cyclic fluctuations in latencies with successive blocks of trials. The two curves differ in that the one for the second control group starts at a lower point and ends at a higher point than that for the first group. The fact that the second group shows a significant increase in latency may be the result of differences between the two conditioned stimuli. The somewhat raucous buzzer in Experiment I could well have been annoying to the animals, and its cessation following a response might have functioned, therefore, as a reinforcing event. Such reinforcement would tend to counteract increases in response latency resulting from the weakening of exploratory tendencies.

A comparison of the two experimental groups reveals that the second showed a marked superiority (shorter latencies) over the first at all stages of learning. Furthermore, the second group differed much more widely from its comparable control group than did the first. Evidently the altered procedures of the second experiment led to more efficient learning. It is impossible, however, to determine from the data just which procedural modifications were primarily responsible for this increase in efficiency.

One feature of interest regarding the curves for the experimental groups is that the animals in the second experiment reached their maximum level of proficiency by the 20th trial and from then on exhibited a fairly progressive decline in performance. This was not the case in the first experiment. Although a statistical comparison of Trials 16–20 with Trials 36–40 for the second experimental group yielded a non-significant t of 1.7, six

The response might have been reinforced if, for some obscure reason, the cues of the escaped-into compartment aroused less anxiety than those of the escaped-from compartment. Subsequent to the preparation of this article, an additional control group of eight animals was run to test this possibility. These new animals were trained under precisely the same conditions as were the members of the experimental group in Experiment II. On the subsequent learning trials, however, both the light-tone stimulus and the shock were omitted. The performance of these animals was quite similar to that of the controls in Experiment II, no learning being exhibited. The mean log latencies (plus one) for successive blocks of five trials were 2.26, 2.22, 2.24, 2.56, 2.45, 2.52, 2.44, and 2.60.

of the eight animals had longer mean latencies on the later block of trials than on the earlier one. It is possible, therefore, that the barrier-crossing response was becoming extinguished in spite of the reinforcement provided by fear reduction. Such a decrement in performance could occur as the result of the accumulation of fatigue or work inhibition, even if the level of fear and the reinforcement it provided remained unchanged. But this seems somewhat unlikely, in view of the fact that the response was not especially effortful and the trials were spaced at intervals of a little over two minutes. On the other hand, the decrement in performance could be attributed to a partial extinction of the fear response with a consequent loss in its capacity to provide both an increment to the drive and adequate reinforcement for the jumping response. But if the fear did extinguish, the question immediately arises as to why the reinforcing property attributed to fear-reduction could apparently strengthen the jumping response but not the fear response itself. To our knowledge, there is as yet no completely satisfactory answer to this question; and any attempt to consider the problems which it raises concerning the acquisition and extinction of fear would take us far beyond the intended scope of the present paper.

One of the important outcomes of the second experiment is the manner in which the data bear, though somewhat obliquely, it is admitted, upon the problem of crouching discussed previously. In this regard, it should be noted that the mean scores on the first five-trial block for the experimental and control groups are almost identical, there being no statistical basis for the rejection of the null hypothesis. In the first experiment, however, the experimental group was significantly *inferior* to its comparable control group on the first five trials. Now, if the assumption is made that long response latencies on early trials are indicative of crouching (which was not, of course, measured directly) it follows that the animals in the second experiment crouched less (relative to their own controls) than did those in the first experiment. At first thought it might seem that such a reduction

in crouching could be attributed to the fact that the animals in the second study were hungry whereas those in the first were not; but this hypothesis may be rejected on the grounds that both the controls and the experimentals in the second study were tested under the same conditions of food deprivation. More reasonably, it could be argued that the degree of immobility in the second experiment diminished either because the fearful animals were less fearful (they received fewer shocks) or because the experimental conditions (pulsating shock, etc.) were less favorable for the learning of the freezing responses. In any event, it seems fairly certain that the experimental animals in the second study *were fearful,* since they readily acquired the new response when it was followed by the cessation of the fear-arousing conditioned stimulus, and *in spite of the presence of this fear they did not crouch more on the early trials than did their non-fearful controls.* Accordingly, we would surmise that fear is not always accompanied by crouching and that the procedural changes of the second experiment probably acted to diminish crouching by reducing the opportunities for its acquisition.

Finally, it should be pointed out that the lack of a significant difference between the performance of the experimental and control groups on the first five-trial block can be interpreted as indicating not only that fear is not always accompanied by crouching, but also that it does not always lead to an increase in general activity level. As in the case of the first experiment, it can be assumed that the *energizing function* of the acquired drive of fear is to intensify whatever responses are dominant, with both innate and acquired habits or predispositions being the determiners of response dominance. As a consequence, almost any degree of overt activity, ranging from vigorous action to rigid immobility, could be exhibited by fearful animals if the appropriate habits were present.

Summary and Conclusions

1. Two experiments have been described in which an investigation was made of the

assumption that fear functions as a drive to motivate or energize behavior and that fear-reduction serves as a reinforcing event in the learning of new responses. In both studies, the methods employed in establishing the fear reaction and in measuring its reinforcing properties were designed to minimize the possibility of arousing some other emotional state such as frustration of conflict to which the results might be attributed instead of to fear. The two experiments differed with respect to certain details of procedure, the results of which are believed to be of importance in the interpretation of fear-motivated behavior.

2. The general procedure of both studies involved a number of training trials during which rats were placed in an oblong box and given paired presentations of a conditioned stimulus and an electric shock. Control animals received the conditioned stimulus but not the shock. On subsequent learning trials the conditioned stimulus was presented alone to all animals and an opportunity was provided for them to perform a new response of crossing from one side of the box to the other by jumping over a central barrier. When the new response was made, the conditioned stimulus was immediately terminated.

3. The assumptions underlying this procedure were: (a) that the paired presentation of the conditioned stimulus and shock, even though no specific escape response was systematically reinforced, would lead to the development of a conditioned fear reaction elicitable by the conditioned stimulus alone; (b) that the conditioned fear would motivate the behavior of crossing the barrier; and (c) that the reduction in fear, occasioned by the cessation of the conditioned stimulus following the new response, would act to strengthen the tendency to perform that response.

4. Since in both experiments the fearful animals learned the new response, whereas their comparable controls did not, the conclusion is drawn that fear-reduction functions much like other drive-reductions to reinforce new responses. The data do not indicate, however, that fear, in spite of its apparent drive properties, is necessarily accompanied by an increase in overt activity. Instead, it appears that fear acts to intensify whatever response is dominant at the moment, whether it be a response of crouching or one of a more active variety. Although the determination of response dominance may be a function in part of innate factors, significant changes in the characteristics of the dominant response to fear can apparently occur as the result of learning.

REFERENCES

1. ARNOLD, MAGDA B. Physiological differentiation of emotional states. *Psychol. Rev.*, 1945, 52, 35–48.
2. BROWN, J. S. Gradients of approach and avoidance responses and their relation to level of motivation. *J. comp. physiol. Psychol.*, 1948, 41, 450–465.
3. FARBER, I. E. Response fixation under anxiety and non-anxiety conditions. *J. exp. Psychol.*, 1948, 38, 111–131.
4. FREUD, S. *The Problem of anxiety.* New York: Norton, 1936.
5. HULL, C. L. *Principles of behavior.* New York: Appleton-Century, 1943.
6. MAY, M. A. Experimentally acquired drives. *J. exp. Psychol.*, 1948, 38, 66–77.
7. MILLER, N. E. Studies of fear as an acquirable drive: I. Fear as motivation and fear-reduction as reinforcement in the learning of new responses. *J. exp. Psychol.*, 1948, 38, 89–101.
8. MILLER, N. E., & DOLLARD, J. *Social learning and imitation.* New Haven: Yale Univ. Press, 1941.
9. MOWRER, O. H. A stimulus-response analysis of anxiety and its role as a reinforcing agent. *Psychol. Rev.*, 1939, 46, 553–565.
10. MOWRER, O. H. An experimental analogue of "regression" with incidental observations on "reaction-formation." *J. abnorm. soc. Psychol.*, 1940, 35, 56–87.
11. MOWRER, O. H. Anxiety-reduction and learning. *J. exp. Psychol.*, 1940, 27, 497–516.
12. MOWRER, O. H., & LAMOREAUX, R. R. Fear as an intervening variable in avoidance conditioning. *J. comp. physiol. Psychol.*, 1946, 39, 29–50.
13. SHAFFER, L. F. *The psychology of adjustment.* Boston: Houghton Mifflin, 1936.

LEON FESTINGER *and* JAMES M. CARLSMITH

34. Cognitive Consequences of Forced Compliance

WHAT happens to a person's private opinion if he is forced to do or say something contrary to that opinion? Only recently has there been any experimental work related to this question. Two studies reported by Janis and King (1954; 1956) clearly showed that, at least under some conditions, the private opinion changes so as to bring it into closer correspondence with the overt behavior the person was forced to perform. Specifically, they showed that if a person is forced to improvise a speech supporting a point of view with which he disagrees, his private opinion moves toward the position advocated in the speech. The observed opinion change is greater than for persons who only hear the speech or for persons who read a prepared speech with emphasis solely on elocution and manner of delivery. The authors of these two studies explain their results mainly in terms of mental rehearsal and thinking up new arguments. In this way, they propose, the person who is forced to improvise a speech convinces himself. They present some evidence, which is not altogether conclusive, in support of this explanation. We will have more to say concerning this explanation in discussing the results of our experiment.

Kelman (1953) tried to pursue the matter further. He reasoned that if the person is induced to make an overt statement contrary to his private opinion by the offer of some reward, then the greater the reward offered, the greater should be the subsequent opinion change. His data, however, did not support this idea. He found, rather, that a large reward produced less subsequent opinion change than did a smaller reward. Actually, this finding by Kelman is consistent with the theory we will outline below but, for a number of reasons, is not conclusive. One of the major weaknesses of the data is that not all subjects in the experiment made an overt statement contrary to their private opinion in order to obtain the offered reward. What is more, as one might expect, the percentage of subjects who complied increased as the size of the offered reward increased. Thus, with self-selection of who did and who did not make the required overt statement and with varying percentages of subjects in the different conditions who did make the required statement, no interpretation of the data can be unequivocal.

Recently, Festinger (1957) proposed a theory concerning cognitive dissonance from which come a number of derivations about opinion change following forced compliance. Since these derivations are stated in detail by Festinger (1957, Ch. 4), we will here give only a brief outline of the reasoning.

Let us consider a person who privately holds opinion "X" but has, as a result of pressure brought to bear on him, publicly stated that he believes "not X."

1. This person has two cognitions which, psychologically, do not fit together: one of these is the knowledge that he believes "X," the other the knowledge that he has publicly stated that he believes "not X." If no factors

Reprinted by permission of the American Psychological Association and the authors from the *Journal of Abnormal and Social Psychology*, 1959, vol. 58, pp. 203–10.

other than his private opinion are considered, it would follow, at least in our culture, that if he believes "X" he would publicly state "X." Hence, his cognition of his private belief is dissonant with his cognition concerning his actual public statement.

2. Similarly, the knowledge that he has said "not X" is consonant with (does fit together with) those cognitive elements corresponding to the reasons, pressures, promises of rewards and/or threats of punishment which induced him to say "not X."

3. In evaluating the total magnitude of dissonance, one must take account of both dissonances and consonances. Let us think of the sum of all the dissonances involving some particular cognition as "D" and the sum of all the consonances as "C." Then we might think of the total magnitude of dissonance as being a function of "D" divided by "D" plus "C."

Let us then see what can be said about the total magnitude of dissonance in a person created by the knowledge that he said "not X" and really believes "X." With everything else held constant, this total magnitude of dissonance would decrease as the number and importance of the pressures which induced him to say "not X" increased.

Thus, if the overt behavior was brought about by, say, offers of reward or threats of punishment, the magnitude of dissonance is maximal if these promised rewards or threatened punishments were just barely sufficient to induce the person to say "not X." From this point on, as the promised rewards or threatened punishment become larger, the magnitude of dissonance becomes smaller.

4. One way in which the dissonance can be reduced is for the person to change his private opinion so as to bring it into correspondence with what he has said. One would consequently expect to observe such opinion change after a person has been forced or induced to say something contrary to his private opinion. Furthermore, since the pressure to reduce dissonance will be a function of the magnitude of the dissonance, the observed opinion change should be greatest when the pressure used to elicit the overt behavior is just sufficient to do it.

The present experiment was designed to test this derivation under controlled laboratory conditions. In the experiment we varied the amount of reward used to force persons to make a statement contrary to their private views. The prediction [from 3 and 4 above] is that the larger the reward given to the subject, the smaller will be the subsequent opinion change.

Procedure

SEVENTY-ONE male students in the introductory psychology course at Stanford University were used in the experiment. In this course, students are required to spend a certain number of hours as subjects (*S*s) in experiments. They choose among the available experiments by signing their names on a sheet posted on the bulletin board which states the nature of the experiment. The present experiment was listed as a two-hour experiment dealing with "Measures of Performance."

During the first week of the course, when the requirement of serving in experiments was announced and explained to the students, the instructor also told them about a study that the psychology department was conducting. He explained that, since they were required to serve in experiments, the department was conducting a study to evaluate these experiments in order to be able to improve them in the future. They were told that a sample of students would be interviewed after having served as *S*s. They were urged to cooperate in these interviews by being completely frank and honest. The importance of this announcement will become clear shortly. It enabled us to measure the opinions of our *S*s in a context not directly connected with our experiment and in which we could reasonably expect frank and honest expressions of opinion.

When the *S* arrived for the experiment on "Measures of Performance" he had to wait for a few minutes in the secretary's office. The experimenter (*E*) then came in, introduced himself to the *S* and, together, they walked into the laboratory room where the *E* said:

This experiment usually takes a little over an hour but, of course, we had to schedule it for two hours. Since we have that extra time, the introductory psychology people asked if they could interview some of our subjects. [Offhand and conversationally.] Did they announce that in class? I gather that they're interviewing some people who have been in experiments. I don't know much about it. Anyhow, they may want to interview you when you're through here.

With no further introduction or explanation the *S* was shown the first task, which involved putting 12 spools onto a tray, emptying the tray, refilling it with spools, and so on. He was told to use one hand and to work at his own speed. He did this for one-half hour. The *E* then removed the tray and spools and placed in front of the *S* a board containing 48 square pegs. His task was to turn each peg a quarter turn clockwise, then another quarter turn, and so on. He was told again to use one hand and to work at his own speed. The *S* worked at this task for another half hour.

While the *S* was working on these tasks, the *E* sat, with a stop watch in his hand, busily making notations on a sheet of paper. He did so in order to make it convincing that this was what the *E* was interested in and that these tasks, and how the *S* worked on them, was the total experiment. From our point of view the experiment had hardly started. The hour which the *S* spent working on the repetitive, monotonous tasks was intended to provide, for each *S* uniformly, an experience about which he would have a somewhat negative opinion.

After the half hour on the second task was over, the *E* conspicuously set the stop watch back to zero, put it away, pushed his chair back, lit a cigarette, and said:

O.K. Well, that's all we have in the experiment itself. I'd like to explain what this has been all about so you'll have some idea of why you were doing this. [*E* pauses.] Well, the way the experiment is set up is this. There are actually two groups in the experiment. In one, the group you were in, we bring the subject in and give him essentially no introduction to the experiment. That is, all we tell him is what he needs to know in order to do the tasks, and he has no idea of what the experiment is all about, or what it's going to be like, or anything like that. But in

the other group, we have a student that we've hired that works for us regularly, and what I do is take him into the next room where the subject is waiting—the same room you were waiting in before—and I introduce him as if he had just finished being a subject in the experiment. That is, I say: "This is so-and-so, who's just finished the experiment, and I've asked him to tell you a little of what it's about before you start." The fellow who works for us then, in conversation with the next subject, makes these points: [The *E* then produced a sheet headed "For Group B" which had written on it: It was very enjoyable, I had a lot of fun, I enjoyed myself, it was very interesting, it was intriguing, it was exciting. The *E* showed this to the *S* and then proceeded with his false explanation of the purpose of the experiment.] Now, of course, we have this student do this, because if the experimenter does it, it doesn't look as realistic, and what we're interested in doing is comparing how these two groups do on the experiment—the one with this previous expectation about the experiment, and the other, like yourself, with essentially none.

Up to this point the procedure was identical for *S*s in all conditions. From this point on they diverged somewhat. Three conditions were run, Control, One Dollar, and Twenty Dollars, as follows:

CONTROL CONDITION

The *E* continued:

Is that fairly clear? [Pause.] Look, that fellow [looks at watch] I was telling you about from the introductory psychology class said he would get here a couple of minutes from now. Would you mind waiting to see if he wants to talk to you? Fine. Why don't we go into the other room to wait? [The *E* left the *S* in the secretary's office for four minutes. He then returned and said:] O.K. Let's check and see if he does want to talk to you.

ONE AND TWENTY DOLLAR CONDITIONS

The *E* continued:

Is that fairly clear how it is set up and what we're trying to do? [Pause.] Now, I also have a sort of strange thing to ask you. The thing is this. [Long pause, some confusion and uncertainty in the following, with a degree of embarrassment on the part of the *E*. The manner of the *E* contrasted strongly with the preceding unhesitant and assured false explanation of the experiment. The point was to make it seem to the *S* that this was the first time the *E* had done this and that he felt unsure of himself.] The fellow who normally does this for us couldn't do it today—he just phoned in, and something or other came up for him—so we've been looking around for someone that we could hire to do it for us. You see, we've got another subject waiting [looks at watch] who is supposed to be in that other condition. Now Professor ———, who is in charge of this experiment, suggested that perhaps we could take a chance on your doing it for us. I'll tell you what we had in mind: the thing is, if you could do it for us now, then of course you would know how to do it, and if something like this should ever come up again, that is, the regular fellow couldn't make it, and we had a subject scheduled, it would be very reassuring to us to know that we had somebody else we could call on who knew how to do it. So, if you would be willing to do this for us, we'd like to hire you to do it now and then be on call in the future, if something like this should ever happen again. We can pay you a dollar (twenty dollars) for doing this for us, that is, for doing it now and then being on call. Do you think you could do that for us?

If the *S* hesitated, the *E* said things like, "It will only take a few minutes," "The regular person is pretty reliable; this is the first time he has missed," or "If we needed you we could phone you a day or two in advance; if you couldn't make it, of course, we wouldn't expect you to come." After the *S* agreed to do it, the *E* gave him the previously mentioned sheet of paper headed "For Group B" and asked him to read it through again. The *E* then paid the *S* one dollar (twenty dollars), made out a hand-written receipt form, and asked the *S* to sign it. He then said:

O.K., the way we'll do it is this. As I said, the next subject should be here by now. I think the next one is a girl. I'll take you into the next room and introduce you to her, saying that you've just finished the experiment and that we've asked you to tell her a little about it. And what we want you to do is just sit down and get into a conversation with her and try to get across the points on that sheet of paper. I'll leave you alone and come back after a couple of minutes. O.K.?

The *E* then took the *S* into the secretary's office where he had previously waited and where the next *S* was waiting. (The secretary had left the office.) He introduced the girl and the *S* to one another saying that the *S* had just finished the experiment and would tell her something about it. He then left saying he would return in a couple of minutes. The girl, an undergraduate hired for this role, said little until the *S* made some positive remarks about the experiment and then said that she was surprised because a friend of hers had taken the experiment the week before and had told her that it was boring and that she ought to try to get out of it. Most *S*s responded by saying something like "Oh, no, it's really very interesting. I'm sure you'll enjoy it." The girl, after this, listened quietly, accepting and agreeing to everything the *S* told her. The discussion between the *S* and the girl was recorded on a hidden tape recorder.

After two minutes the *E* returned, asked the girl to go into the experimental room, thanked the *S* for talking to the girl, wrote down his phone number to continue the fiction that we might call on him again in the future and then said: "Look, could we check and see if that fellow from introductory psychology wants to talk to you?"

From this point on, the procedure for all three conditions was once more identical. As the *E* and the *S* started to walk to the office where the interviewer was, the *E* said: "Thanks very much for working on those tasks for us. I hope you did enjoy it. Most of our subjects tell us afterward that they found it quite interesting. You get a chance to see how you react to the tasks and so forth." This short persuasive communication was made in all conditions in exactly the same way. The reason for doing it, theoretically, was to make it easier for anyone who wanted to persuade himself that the tasks had been, indeed, enjoyable.

When they arrived at the interviewer's office, the *E* asked the interviewer whether or not he wanted to talk to the *S*. The interviewer said yes, the *E* shook hands with the *S*, said good-bye, and left. The interviewer, of course, was always kept in complete ignorance of which condition the *S* was in. The interview consisted of four questions, on each of which the *S* was first encouraged to talk about the matter and was then asked to rate his opinion or reaction on an 11-point scale. The questions are as follows:

1. Were the tasks interesting and enjoyable? In what way? In what way were they not? Would you rate how you feel about them on a scale from −5 to +5 where −5 means they were extremely dull and boring, +5 means they were extremely interesting and enjoyable, and zero means they were neutral, neither interesting nor uninteresting.
2. Did the experiment give you an opportunity to learn about your own ability to perform these tasks? In what way? In what way not? Would you rate how you feel about this on a scale from 0 to 10 where 0 means you learned nothing and 10 means you learned a great deal.
3. From what you know about the experiment and the tasks involved in it, would you say the experiment was measuring anything important? That is, do you think the results may have scientific value? In what way? In what way not? Would you rate your opinion on this matter on a scale from 0 to 10 where 0 means the results have no scientific value or importance and 10 means they have a great deal of value and importance.
4. Would you have any desire to participate in another similar experiment? Why? Why not? Would you rate your desire to participate in a similar experiment again on a scale from −5 to +5, where −5 means you would definitely dislike to participate, +5 means you would definitely like to participate, and 0 means you have no particular feeling about it one way or the other.

As may be seen, the questions varied in how directly relevant they were to what the *S* had told the girl. This point will be discussed further in connection with the results.

At the close of the interview the *S* was asked what he thought the experiment was about and, following this, was asked directly whether or not he was suspicious of anything and, if so, what he was suspicious of. When the interview was over, the interviewer brought the *S* back to the experimental room where the *E* was waiting together with the

girl who had posed as the waiting *S*. (In the control condition, of course, the girl was not there.) The true purpose of the experiment was then explained to the *S* in detail, and the reasons for each of the various steps in the experiment were explained carefully in relation to the true purpose. All experimental *S*s in both One Dollar and Twenty Dollar conditions were asked, after this explanation, to return the money they had been given. All *S*s, without exception, were quite willing to return the money.

The data from 11 of the 71 *S*s in the experiment had to be discarded for the following reasons:

1. Five *S*s (three in the One Dollar and two in the Twenty Dollar condition) indicated in the interview that they were suspicious about having been paid to tell the girl the experiment was fun and suspected that that was the real purpose of the experiment.
2. Two *S*s (both in the One Dollar condition) told the girl that they had been hired, that the experiment was really boring but they were supposed to say it was fun.
3. Three *S*s (one in the One Dollar and two in the Twenty Dollar condition) refused to take the money and refused to be hired.
4. One *S* (in the One Dollar condition), immediately after having talked to the girl, demanded her phone number saying he would call her and explain things, and also told the *E* he wanted to wait until she was finished so he could tell her about it.

These 11 *S*s were, of course, run through the total experiment anyhow and the experiment was explained to them afterwards. Their data, however, are not included in the analysis.

SUMMARY OF DESIGN

There remain, for analysis, 20 *S*s in each of the three conditions. Let us review these briefly: 1. *Control condition.* These *S*s were treated identically in all respects to the *S*s in the experimental conditions, except that they were never asked to, and never did, tell the waiting girl that the experimental tasks were enjoyable and lots of fun. 2. *One Dollar* *condition.* These *S*s were hired for one dollar to tell a waiting *S* that tasks, which were really rather dull and boring, were interesting, enjoyable, and lots of fun. 3. *Twenty Dollar condition.* These *S*s were hired for twenty dollars to do the same thing.

Results

THE major results of the experiment are summarized in TABLE 1 which lists, separately for each of the three experimental conditions, the average rating which the *S*s gave at the end of each question on the interview. We will discuss each of the questions on the interview separately, because they were intended to measure different things. One other point before we proceed to examine the data. In all the comparisons, the Control condition should be regarded as a baseline from which to evaluate the results in the other two conditions. The Control condition gives us, essentially, the reactions of *S*s to the tasks and their opinions about the experiment as falsely explained to them, without the experimental introduction of dissonance. The data from the other conditions may be viewed, in a sense, as changes from this baseline.

HOW ENJOYABLE THE TASKS WERE

The average ratings on this question, presented in the first row of figures in TABLE 1, are the results most important to the experiment. These results are the ones most directly relevant to the specific dissonance which was experimentally created. It will be recalled

that the tasks were purposely arranged to be rather boring and monotonous. And, indeed, in the Control condition the average rating was −.45, somewhat on the negative side of the neutral point.

In the other two conditions, however, the *S*s told someone that these tasks were interesting and enjoyable. The resulting dissonance could, of course, most directly be reduced by persuading themselves that the tasks were, indeed, interesting and enjoyable. In the One Dollar condition, since the magnitude of dissonance was high, the pressure to reduce this dissonance would also be high. In this condition, the average rating was +1.35, considerably on the positive side and significantly different from the Control condition at the .02 level [1] ($t = 2.48$).

In the Twenty Dollar condition, where less dissonance was created experimentally because of the greater importance of the consonant relations, there is correspondingly less evidence of dissonance reduction. The average rating in this condition is only −.05, slightly and not significantly higher than the Control condition. The difference between the One Dollar and Twenty Dollar conditions is significant at the .03 level ($t = 2.22$). In short, when an *S* was induced, by offer of reward, to say something contrary to his private opinion, this private opinion tended to change so as to correspond more closely with what he had said. The greater the reward

[1] All statistical tests referred to in this paper are two-tailed.

TABLE 1

Average Ratings on Interview Questions for Each Condition

| | EXPERIMENTAL CONDITION | | |
QUESTION ON INTERVIEW	Control ($N = 20$)	One Dollar ($N = 20$)	Twenty Dollars ($N = 20$)
How enjoyable tasks were (rated from −5 to +5)	−.45	+1.35	−.05
How much they learned (rated from 0 to 10)	3.08	2.80	3.15
Scientific importance (rated from 0 to 10)	5.60	6.45	5.18
Participate in similar exp. (rated from −5 to +5)	−.62	+1.20	−.25

offered (beyond what was necessary to elicit the behavior) the smaller was the effect.

DESIRE TO PARTICIPATE IN A SIMILAR EXPERIMENT

The results from this question are shown in the last row of TABLE 1. This question is less directly related to the dissonance that was experimentally created for the Ss. Certainly, the more interesting and enjoyable they felt the tasks were, the greater would be their desire to participate in a similar experiment. But other factors would enter also. Hence, one would expect the results on this question to be very similar to the results on "how enjoyable the tasks were" but weaker. Actually, the results, as may be seen in the table, are in exactly the same direction, and the magnitude of the mean differences is fully as large as on the first question. The variability is greater, however, and the differences do not yield high levels of statistical significance. The difference between the One Dollar condition (+1.20) and the Control condition −.62) is significant at the .08 level ($t = 1.78$). The difference between the One Dollar condition and the Twenty Dollar condition (−.25) reaches only the .15 level of significance ($t = 1.46$).

THE SCIENTIFIC IMPORTANCE OF THE EXPERIMENT

This question was included because there was a chance that differences might emerge. There are, after all, other ways in which the experimentally created dissonance could be reduced. For example, one way would be for the S to magnify for himself the value of the reward he obtained. This, however, was unlikely in this experiment because money was used for the reward and it is undoubtedly difficult to convince oneself that one dollar is more than it really is. There is another possible way, however. The Ss were given a very good reason, in addition to being paid, for saying what they did to the waiting girl. The Ss were told it was necessary for the experiment. The dissonance could, consequently, be reduced by magnifying the importance of this cognition. The more scientifically important they considered the experiment to be, the less was the total magnitude of dissonance.

It is possible, then, that the results on this question, shown in the third row of figures in TABLE 1, might reflect dissonance reduction.

The results are weakly in line with what one would expect if the dissonance were somewhat reduced in this manner. The One Dollar condition is higher than the other two. The difference between the One and Twenty Dollar conditions reaches the .08 level of significance on a two-tailed test ($t = 1.79$). The difference between the One Dollar and Control conditions is not impressive at all ($t = 1.21$). The result that the Twenty Dollar condition is actually lower than the Control condition is undoubtedly a matter of chance ($t = 0.58$).

HOW MUCH THEY LEARNED FROM THE EXPERIMENT

The results on this question are shown in the second row of figures in TABLE 1. The question was included because, as far as we could see, it had nothing to do with the dissonance that was experimentally created and could not be used for dissonance reduction. One would then expect no differences at all among the three conditions. We felt it was important to show that the effect was not a completely general one but was specific to the content of the dissonance which was created. As can be readily seen in TABLE 1, there are only negligible differences among conditions. The highest t value for any of these differences is only 0.48.

Discussion of a Possible Alternative Explanation

WE mentioned in the introduction that Janis and King (1954; 1956) in explaining their findings, proposed an explanation in terms of the self-convincing effect of mental rehearsal and thinking up new arguments by the person who had to improvise a speech. Kelman (1953), in the previously mentioned study, in attempting to explain the unexpected finding that the persons who complied in the moderate reward condition changed their opinion more than in the high reward condition, also proposed the same kind of explanation. If the results of our experiment are to be taken as strong corroboration of the theory of cognitive dissonance, this possible alternative explanation must be dealt with.

Specifically, as applied to our results, this alternative explanation would maintain that perhaps, for some reason, the Ss in the One Dollar condition worked harder at telling the waiting girl that the tasks were fun and enjoyable. That is, in the One Dollar condition they may have rehearsed it more mentally, thought up more ways of saying it, may have said it more convincingly, and so on. Why this might have been the case is, of course, not immediately apparent. One might expect that, in the Twenty Dollar condition, having been paid more, they would try to do a better job of it than in the One Dollar condition. But nevertheless, the possibility exists that the Ss in the One Dollar condition may have improvised more.

Because of the desirability of investigating this possible alternative explanation, we recorded on a tape recorder the conversation between each S and the girl. These recordings were transcribed and then rated, by two independent raters, on five dimensions. The ratings were, of course, done in ignorance of which condition each S was in. The reliabilities of these ratings, that is, the correlations between the two independent raters, ranged from .61 to .88, with an average reliability of .71. The five ratings were:

1. The content of what the S said *before* the girl made the remark that her friend told her it was boring. The stronger the S's positive statements about the tasks, and the more ways in which he said they were interesting

and enjoyable, the higher the rating.

2. The content of what the S said *after* the girl made the above-mentioned remark. This was rated in the same way as for the content before the remark.

3. A similar rating of the over-all content of what the S said.

4. A rating of how persuasive and convincing the S was in what he said and the way in which he said it.

5. A rating of the amount of time in the discussion that the S spent discussing the tasks as opposed to going off into irrelevant things.

The mean ratings for the One Dollar and Twenty Dollar conditions, averaging the ratings of the two independent raters, are presented in TABLE 2. It is clear from examining the table that, in all cases, the Twenty Dollar condition is slightly higher. The differences are small, however, and only on the rating of "amount of time" does the difference between the two conditions even approach significance. We are certainly justified in concluding that the Ss in the One Dollar condition did not improvise more nor act more convincingly. Hence, the alternative explanation discussed above cannot account for the findings.

Summary

RECENTLY, Festinger (1957) has proposed a theory concerning cognitive dissonance. Two derivations from this theory are tested here. These are:

1. If a person is induced to do or say something which is contrary to his private opinion, there will be a tendency for him to change

TABLE 2

Average Ratings of Discussion between Subject and Girl

| | CONDITION | | |
DIMENSION RATED	One Dollar	Twenty Dollars	Value of t
Content before remark by girl (rated from 0 to 5)	2.26	2.62	1.08
Content after remark by girl (rated from 0 to 5)	1.63	1.75	0.11
Over-all content (rated from 0 to 5)	1.89	2.19	1.08
Persuasiveness and conviction (rated from 0 to 10)	4.79	5.50	0.99
Time spent on topic (rated from 0 to 10)	6.74	8.19	1.80

his opinion so as to bring it into correspondence with what he has done or said.

2. The larger the pressure used to elicit the overt behavior (beyond the minimum needed to elicit it) the weaker will be the above-mentioned tendency.

A laboratory experiment was designed to test these derivations. Subjects were subjected to a boring experience and then paid to tell someone that the experience had been interesting and enjoyable. The amount of money paid the subject was varied. The private opinions of the subjects concerning the experiences were then determined.

The results strongly corroborate the theory that was tested.

REFERENCES

FESTINGER, L. *A theory of cognitive dissonance.* Evanston, Ill.: Row, Peterson, 1957.

JANIS, I. L., & KING, B. T. The influence of role-playing on opinion change. *J. abnorm. soc. Psychol.,* 1954, 49, 211–218.

KELMAN, H. Attitude change as a function of response restriction. *Hum. Relat.,* 1953, 6, 185–214.

KING, B. T., & JANIS, I. L. Comparison of the effectiveness of improvised versus non-improvised role-playing in producing opinion changes. *Hum. Relat.,* 1956, 9, 177–186.

NEAL E. MILLER

35. *Theory and Experiment Relating Psychoanalytic Displacement to Stimulus-Response Generalization*

Diverse Origin of the Two Concepts

THE concept of displacement comes from the clinic, that of generalization from the laboratory. The experiments and hypotheses to be described in this paper were devised in an attempt to relate these two concepts and to begin the formulation of a theory of displacement in terms of principles of learning.

Freud was led to the concept of displacement by applying the free association method to the analysis of material appearing in dreams (6, 7). Though the mechanism of displacement seems to be especially operative in the realm of dreams, other examples are easier to expound. A problem child is a nuisance because he pinches, bites, and scratches his little playmates at school and harasses the teacher in a variety of ingenious ways. Investigation reveals that in all probability the fault lies not in the playground situation at school but rather in the home situation. He hates his foster parents. Formerly, he attempted to pinch, bite, and scratch these foster parents, but was forced to desist. Later he commenced to plague his schoolmates in this manner. After the home situation is cleared up, the trouble on the playground disappears. This transfer of aggression from the home situation to the school is called displacement.

A more familiar example is that of the man who, when severely frustrated at the office by business or professional rivals and unable to revenge himself directly, may come home and make scapegoats of members of his family.

According to an hypothesis especially elaborated upon in *Frustration and Aggression* (4) and refined in later publications (15, 19, 24), the irrational component of latent aggression against out-groups which easily flares into outbursts of race persecution and war is produced by the mechanism of displacement rather than by an instinct of aggression. According to this hypothesis, the out-groupers may be not only the target for the direct aggression which they arouse by competition with the in-groupers, but also may be the scapegoat for strong aggression which is first aroused by friction within the in-group, then suppressed by in-group taboos and conveniently displaced to members of the out-group.

Finally, displacement is involved in transference which is a crucial factor in psychoanalytic therapy. In transference the patient irrationally displaces to the analyst love and hate which have their real origin elsewhere.

The concept of generalization grew out of the work in Pavlov's laboratory. In a typical experiment a hungry dog is placed in a sound-proof room and harnessed to a device which electrically records the dripping of his saliva (21). Then a tone of a specific pitch is sounded a number of times always immediately followed by food until the dog has been conditioned to salivate to the sound of the tone alone. Next the dog is presented for the first time in the training situation with tones

Reprinted by permission of the American Psychological Association and the author from the *Journal of Abnormal and Social Psychology*, 1948, vol. 43, pp. 155–78.

of different pitches and it is found that he salivates immediately to these new tones also. This transfer of the response from the original to the new tones is called generalization. It is further found that the more similar the new tone is to the pitch of the originally conditioned one, the larger is the response to the new tone. This greater transfer the more similar the new tone is called a gradient of generalization.

From the out-group aggression and the analysis of the bizarre dreams of Freud's patients to the electric recording of the salivation of dogs in Pavlov's soundproof laboratory seems to be a huge leap. The following experiments were designed to cast the first rope of a slender bridge across that chasm.

Experiment on Object Displacement or Generalization

IN the first stage of the first experiment albino rats were trained to strike at each other. They were placed two at a time in an enclosure, the floor of which was a grid. Through this grid they were given an electric shock sufficiently strong to keep them active. Their random acts were observed through a glass window on one side of the enclosure. When they by chance happened to approach each other in a sparring position similar to that used by rats in fighting, the shock was abruptly turned off. Thus the act of sparring was rewarded by escape from shock. After a minute without shock the current was turned on again and the animals given another trial. As training progressed, they were required to strike at each other before the shock was turned off. Training was continued till the habit of striking was thoroughly established. . . .

After this training, the animals were given test trials in which a small celluloid doll was placed in the arena along with each pair of rats. . . . The animals struck at each other when the shock was turned on, and not at the doll. In different test trials, the animals were placed *one at a time* in the same apparatus. Under these conditions they tended to strike at the doll when the shock was turned on. . . .

Twelve animals were trained and given both tests. For half of them the first test was the one with the other rat and the doll both present, for the other half, the one with the doll alone. When another rat was present only one of the twelve struck at the doll, and this one then immediately turned to strike at the other rat. If the tendencies to strike the other rat and the doll were equally strong, half of the animals would be expected to strike at each. Instead, eleven out of the twelve animals struck at the other rat. Using chi-square corrected for discontinuity, it can be calculated that a difference of this size would be expected by chance less than one time in a hundred. Therefore, we may conclude that when another rat and the doll were both present, the stronger tendency was to strike at the other rat.

When the animals which had been trained to strike the other rat were placed into the arena alone with the doll and given an electric shock, six of them knocked it down by striking at it; the other six pushed it over in various irrelevant ways such as bumping it head on in the course of running around the cage. In order to show that the tendency to strike the doll when no other rat was present was produced by the previous training to strike at another rat (i.e., would not have been produced by electric shock without this training), a control group of twelve untrained animals was tested one at a time under exactly similar conditions. Only one out of the control group struck at the doll before knocking it down in various irrelevant ways. By means of chi-square corrected for discontinuity it was calculated that a difference of this size in favor of the experimental group would be expected by chance less than five times in a hundred. This indicates that the tendency to knock the doll down by striking at it was a function of previous training to strike at another rat.

Similarity between Object Displacement and Stimulus Generalization

WHEN rats trained to strike the other animal were prevented from doing this by the absence of that animal, they tended to strike the doll. Viewed in Freudian terms this might be taken to indicate displacement. If one can call the original response of striking the other rat aggression, then this aggression has been displaced to the doll which might be called a scapegoat. However, it is not necessary to go this far; it will be safer to say that some pattern of response, as yet undesignated, has been displaced from the other rat to the doll.[1]

But exactly the same phenomenon may be described equally as well in stimulus-response terms as transfer of training, or, in other words, generalization. This is clearly illustrated in FIGURE 1. The first data are from a typical experiment on conditioning (10). A tone of the pitch of 153 double vibrations per second is presented to college students and always followed by electric shock until a conditioned galvanic skin response has been established. Then this tone and other tones are presented without shock. The largest response is to the tone originally conditioned, the next largest to the most similar tone and the smallest to the least similar tone. This is a gradient of generalization.

The experiment on displacement may be analyzed in exactly the same way. The response of striking was originally established to the stimulus of another rat, the partner. Thus the stimulus of the partner will evoke the strongest response and, assuming the doll to present a different stimulus pattern, it will evoke a weaker response. Therefore, when a rat is confronted simultaneously with the stimuli of the partner and the doll, the stronger response to the partner will win out and he will strike at the partner rather than at the doll. When the partner is absent, however, the stimulus of the doll is more similar to the original stimulus than is the stimulus of the wall. Hence, the stimulus of the doll evokes the stronger response; the rat strikes at the doll rather than at the wall.

Another experiment (18) on human sub-

1 In classroom demonstrations the author has repeatedly shown that if animals are trained to bite a rubber tube as soon as an electric shock is turned on and then tested with shock but without the tube being present, they are (a) more likely to bite other objects similar to the tube than to bite grossly dissimilar objects, and (b) much more likely to bite such objects than are animals given an electric shock without any previous training of any kind.

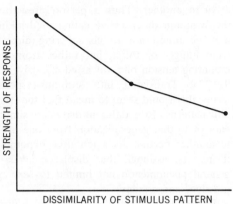

Tones:	153~	468~	1000~
Objects:	White Rat	Doll	Wall
Drives:	Thirst	Hunger	Satiation
	+	+	+
	(Alley)	(Alley)	(Alley)

FIG. 1. The parallel between displacement and generalization. The strength of the direct responses to the stimulus pattern involved in the original learning is represented by the first point on the left; the strengths of the weaker displaced, or generalized, responses are represented by the other two points. The particular values selected to illustrate a gradient of generalization in this diagram are from a typical experiment on the generalization of a conditioned galvanic skin response to tones of different pitches (10).

jects has been analyzed in a similar way. In this experiment it was found that subjects who had been angered by frustrations imposed upon them by members of their own country expressed less favorable attitudes toward faraway foreigners who could not possibly have been responsible for their plight. In this case one may assume that the members of the out-group were sufficiently similar as stimulus objects to the members of the in-group so that the response of aggression generalized from the one to the other.

Drive Generalization or Displacement from Hunger to Thirst

TRANSFERS from one external stimulus to another have been dealt with. According to psychoanalytic observations, however, displacement may occur not only from one external object to another, but also from one drive to another. Thus a person presenting the symptom of excessive eating or drinking may be found not to be suffering directly from hunger or thirst, but rather from the mounting tension of a thwarted sex drive (3, 9, 22). Translated into stimulus-response terms, this would seem to mean that the stimulus patterns of the different drives are similar enough so that generalization from one drive to another occurs. As a tentative hypothesis it may be assumed that displacement is a general phenomenon not limited to sex, aggression, and anxiety.

FIGURE 1 illustrates the way in which drive displacement may be produced by generalization. It is assumed that thirsty animals have learned to run down an alley to drink water, and are then given tests in this alley under three different conditions of drive: thirsty, not thirsty but hungry, neither thirsty nor hungry. The stimuli in these test situations have varying degrees of similarity to those involved in the original learning. The first, thirst plus alley, is identical. The second contains as identical elements all the stimuli in the alley and some from the hunger drive, which it is assumed is not completely distinctive from thirst. The third contains only the identical elements involved in the alley. The way in which this parallels the sequence of tones of different pitches is illustrated in FIGURE 1. When the animals are tested without either thirst or hunger, the stimuli in the alley will be expected to mediate some generalization of the responses of running and drinking; when they are not thirsty but hungry, more generalization should occur.

An experiment was performed to test these expectations. Thirty thirsty animals were trained to run down an alley 6 feet long to drink water from a tube supplied by a burette graduated in tenths of a cc. Motivated by a 45-hour water deprivation,[2] the animals were given five trials a day every other day to a total of 50 trials. After this training, they were deprived of water for another 45 hours and then all given water in their cages for one hour. At the end of this period they were

lured over to the water bottle till they would consistently turn away and refuse to drink. Half of them had been deprived of food and so were hungry; the other half received wet food and were not hungry.

FIGURE 2 presents the results of the hungry and non-hungry groups when tested in the alley immediately after having refused water in their cages. It can be seen that, exactly as demanded by the hypothesis, both groups show a tendency to run the alley and even to drink, and that the hungry group manifests the stronger response by requiring less time to run the alley and by drinking more water. A statistical analysis indicates that the difference in running time and in amount of water drunk would be expected by chance less than two times in a hundred and three in a thousand, respectively. This demonstrates that hunger and thirst have a certain functional equivalence, which may be called either generalization or displacement.[3]

3 *Technical notes:* In this experiment the generalization may have been facilitated by the fact that, since thirsty animals stop eating dry food, they may have been somewhat hungry as well as thirsty while they were being trained to run the alley for water. To the extent that this was true, the hunger drive would be a stimulus element common to the training and testing situation during the non-thirsty tests of the experimental and not during these tests of the control group.

The faster running and more drinking of the hungry group was deduced from the principle of generalization; it is also in line with Hull's (11) postulate 7, which states: "Any habit strength ($S^H R$) is sensitized into reaction potentiality ($S^H R$) by all primary drives active within an organism at a given time, the magnitude of this potentiality being a product obtained by multiplying an increasing function of $S^H R$ by an increasing function of D."

Kendler (12) has demonstrated a possibly similar facilitating effect of weak thirst on habits established by using food as a reward for hungry animals. He used resistance to extinction as his measure of habit strength and had both the relevant and irrelevant drives present during both the training and extinction. In his experiment, as well as in one by Siegel (25), stronger thirst apparently interfered with the habit. This seems to be in line with the fact that hungry animals will not eat dry food when they are very thirsty. In the present experiment the effect of hunger on a thirst-motivated habit was chosen for study (instead of the opposite relationship) in order to avoid any interference of this kind which might possibly override the effect being studied. It should also be kept in mind that in Kendler's and Siegel's experiments the two drives were both present during training and testing, while in the present one the irrelevant drive was absent during training (or possibly weakly present because the thirst tended to

2 Because this experiment was run during the summer when the humidity in New Haven is usually high, the drive was only fairly strong.

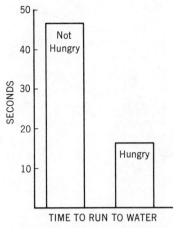 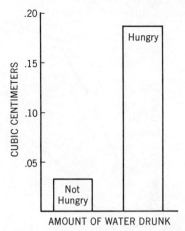

TIME TO RUN TO WATER   AMOUNT OF WATER DRUNK

FIG. 2. Effect of hunger on water-getting habit of non-thirsty animals. Thirsty rats were trained to run an alley to secure water. Then they were completely satiated on water in their home cages and it was found that they would run down the alley faster and drink more if tested when hungry than if tested when not hungry.

It seems likely that a similar type of drive interaction is relevant to the development of the human sex drive. Freud maintains that during infancy sex is an anaclitic drive (*Anlehnungstrieb*), dependent on the more primary drives involved in the nursing and care of the child. In the light of the results of the experiment which has just been described, it seems likely that, as the sex drive begins to emerge in the child, there should be some tendency for it to motivate responses which have been successful in satisfying other drives and for these responses to be directed toward the stimulus object which had been most frequently involved in satisfying those drives, namely, the mother.

Confirmation of Additional Deductions

THE principle of generalization was useful in predicting these results. Additional stimulus-response principles should also be applicable to the same situation. During the original training, the responses of running and drinking were reinforced by a reduction in the strength of the thirst stimulus. During the

___
stop the animals from eating dry food) and the relevant drive was absent during testing. It seems likely that the weaker effects of the irrelevant drive will be less likely to be masked when the stronger effects of the relevant one are absent.

test trials, however, thirst is already reduced to a minimum so that little if any reduction and hence little if any primary reinforcement can occur. Thus a succession of such non-reinforced trials should, according to the principle of experimental extinction, produce a decrement in the strength of response. If this decrement is indeed produced by extinction it should be subject to spontaneous recovery, that is, a rest interval should partially restore the strength of response. After the rest interval a second succession of non-reinforced trials will, of course, be expected to produce a second decrement in the response.

The data in FIGURE 3 demonstrate that both extinction and recovery occur. A succession of non-thirsty trials produces a decrement in response indicated by longer running times. An interval of one day produces recovery despite the fact that the animals have been thoroughly satiated again in their cages. A second succession of trials produces a second extinction. In FIGURE 4 it can be seen that the same pattern applies to the amount of water consumed, first extinction indicated by less drinking, then recovery, then some further extinction. These data indicate that the principles of extinction and recovery apply not only to situations where non-reinforcement occurs by virtue of absence of the appropriate

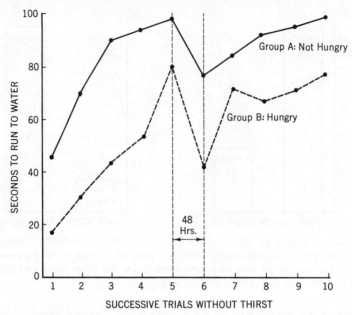

FIG. 3. Experimental extinction and spontaneous recovery measured by running time during a series of trials with water present but thirst absent. Animals trained to run for water and tested when not thirsty showed experimental extinction by a progressive increase in time scores and spontaneous recovery by a decrease after a 48-hour interval and resatiation. The animals with an irrelevant drive, hunger, ran faster than those without it.

reward to be consumed but also where non-reinforcement occurs by virtue of absence of the appropriate drive to be reduced.

Finally, it should be noted that the tendency for the hungry animals to run faster and drink more than the non-hungry ones persists through all of the ten trials.

Generalization or Displacement from Pain and Fear to Hunger

IT is perhaps not surprising that there should be transfer between the particular stimuli of hunger and thirst, but would there be any generalization between two stimuli which might appear to be far more dissimilar, such as hunger and fear? There is some clinical evidence for such a dynamic relationship. With some people overeating seems to be motivated by fear; they worry themselves fat.

The next experiment determines whether responses originally established on the basis of hunger will generalize to pain and fear. In addition to verifying the clinical observations,

this experiment avoids a source of ambiguity in the interpretation of the preceding one. In that experiment it might be argued that the sole reason for the better performance of the hungry animals was that they were not inhibited by the effects of a full stomach. When either pain or fear is used in the test for drive generalization, this type of explanation is impossible.

The response originally established on the basis of hunger was running on a T-maze and turning in the correct direction to get food. The painful stimulus was an electric shock of one second's duration and 5 ma. strength, held constant by a vacuum tube device. In the first stage of the experiment hungry rats were trained on a T-maze to turn in the correct direction to get a pellet of wet food. In order to make the choice as distinctive as possible, a 60-watt desk lamp was suspended one meter above the end of the right-hand arm of the T. The maze was made of elevated strips of wood 6 cms. wide. From the start to choice point was 25 cms., and from there

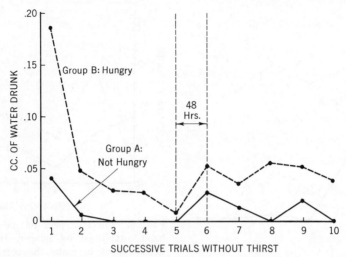

F ɪ ɢ. 4. Experimental extinction and spontaneous recovery measured by amount of water drunk during a series of trials after satiation on water. Animals trained to run down an alley for water and then allowed to drink water in the home cage till they consistently refused it showed experimental extinction by a progressive decrease in the amount of water drunk in the alley, and spontaneous recovery by an increase. The animals with an irrelevant drive, hunger, drank more than those without it.

to the end of each arm, 50 cms. So that electric shock could be administered as a painful stimulus in the second stage of the experiment, all the pathways had been boiled in paraffin and were wrapped with a grid of stainless steel wires spaced 1 cm. apart.

Twenty-three male albino rats were used. For twelve the reward was on the end of the right arm of the maze, for eleven, on the left. The animals were given three trials a day. So that their hunger drive would be at a high level on the next day, they were given only dry food without water for an hour after each day's run. Then the food was removed and the water restored. Training was continued until the animal had reached a criterion of nine correct turns out of ten.

After reaching this criterion, the animals were put through a preliminary experiment which involved one test trial on the maze when satiated, four days of retraining, and another test trial on the maze when satiated. For half of these animals the first test was immediately after having received an electric shock (5 ma. for 1 second) on a grid away from the maze and the second test was without shock; for the other half these procedures

were reversed. The results were in line with theoretical expectations. When satiated the animals were slowed down, but they did run and take the correct turn. These results were highly reliable. After just having received shock they were not slowed down as much as when tested without shock. This difference could have been produced by chance one time in ten.

In order to secure a more clear-cut difference between the shock and non-shock groups the animals were given four additional days' retraining, satiated as before, and given a series of tests with shock administered directly on the maze. After satiation all animals were given one trial without shock. Then twelve of them received five trials on which immediately after being placed at the starting point they received an electric shock lasting for one second *irrespective of what they did on the maze*. After this they received another non-shock test. Trials were given at 15-minute intervals. As a control eleven animals received similar trials without shock.

Complete satiation was accomplished before the test by placing the hungry animal for one hour in a cage containing wet food. After

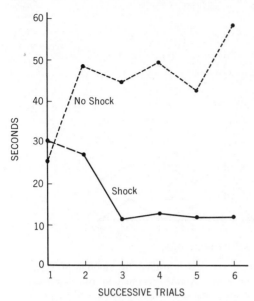

FIG. 5. Effect of pain on the speed of performance of a habit established by hunger. Hungry animals were trained to run a T-maze for food and given a series of test trials when completely satiated. For one group an electric shock of one second's duration was introduced on trials two through six. The animals receiving this shock ran faster than those without it.

that the experimenter placed the animal with a supply of wet food on one of the elevated perches used to hold the rats between training trials and left it there until it had turned away three consecutive times from additional wet food offered on a spoon.

The results are presented in FIGURES 5 and 6. It can be seen that in the control group, which did not receive shock, the response of running correctly to food when satiated occurred at first and then tended to extinguish.[4]

---

4 The definite tendency of the control animals in this and the preceding experiment to perform the habit for a few trials after being thoroughly satiated is different from the results reported by Koch and Daniel (13). It seems possible that the lack of performance after satiation in their experiment may have been produced by the fact that while they used hard dry pellets as a reward during training, they satiated their animals with wet mash which seems to be a more preferred food. Since they used a different type of habit, bar pressing, differences in the stimuli and responses may also have been involved. Anderson (1), using a maze, one trial a day, and allowing his animals to recover from their hunger more

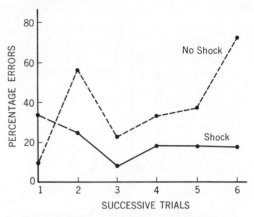

FIG. 6. Effect of pain on the accuracy of a habit established by hunger. Hungry animals were trained to make the correct turn on a T-maze to secure food. Then they were given six test trials when completely satiated. For one group an electric shock which lasted for one second no matter what the animal did on the maze was administered on trials two through six The animals with this shock made fewer errors than those without it.

In both the time and error scores the difference between the first and sixth trials would be expected by chance less than one time in a thousand.

The experimental group, on the first trial, which was without shock, was slightly but not significantly poorer than the control. On the second trial, during which the experimental animals received their first shock, they ran faster and made fewer errors than the controls. On this trial the differences in either time or errors would be expected by chance only two times in a hundred. By the sixth trial the differences had increased to a point where they would be expected by chance less than two times in a thousand.

The number of errors made by the animals in the experimental group was not only smaller than that of the controls; it was also reliably less than the 50 per cent which would be expected by chance. Thus the shock elicited the habit previously learned on the basis of

---

gradually so that they were not over-stuffed, reports very considerable persistence of maze running despite satiation.

hunger rather than mere random running. This demonstrates generalization from hunger to pain.[5]

When the animals that had just received the series of shocks on the maze were given an additional test trial without shock, they continued to make fewer errors and run faster than the controls. The differences are of a magnitude to be expected by chance less than two times in a hundred and one in a thousand, respectively. This demonstrates that the habit generalized from hunger to pain could also be maintained by fear.

Prevention by Absence versus Inhibition by Conflict

IN all of these experiments the animals were prevented from performing the direct response during the test for displacement by the absence of an appropriate goal. In the first experiment animals trained to escape shock by striking at another rat were prevented from doing this by the absence of that rat. In the second experiment, hungry animals were prevented from eating by the absence of food, and in the third, there was no way to escape a one-second shock on the maze.

In clinical examples of displacement the direct response is also sometimes prevented by absence of the appropriate object, as when one is angered by a message left by the chief but unable to say anything to him because he has already left town.

In many other cases, the direct response is prevented not by absence of the appropriate object, but by conflict; the chief is physically present but direct aggression against him is prevented by fear and then displaced to the office boy. In order to parallel this situation in the tests for striking displaced to the doll, the experimenter would have had to leave both rats in the compartment, but teach one

5 This generalization may be based indirectly on stimuli produced by similar states of muscular tension elicited by both drives, rather than upon common elements directly present in the drives themselves. In other words, one of the reasons the animals make fewer errors when shocked may be that their tense, fast running creates cues which make the situation more like that in which they learned the maze while hungry.

of them to bite so severely that the other would avoid striking at it.

But if the other rat and the doll are similar enough for striking to generalize from one to the other, the avoidance preventing striking will also be expected to generalize. Similarly, the fear inhibiting aggression should tend to generalize from the chief to the office boy. It is obvious that if the inhibiting responses generalize as much as (or more than) the responses which they inhibit, the latter will be just as inhibited in the new displacement situation as they were in the original direct one. Therefore, displacement can occur only if the tendencies opposing the occurrence of the response generalize less strongly than the response itself. In other words, in order to be able to deduce displacement in this type of situation, one must assume that the gradient of generalization falls off at a faster rate for the inhibiting tendencies than for the responses which they inhibit.

Such an assumption is made plausible by the fact that experimental work on conflict (17) has demonstrated that if a hungry animal is first trained to find food at the end of an alley and then given an electric shock there, the tendency to avoid that place is weakened by distance more than the approach to food which it inhibits. In other words, the spatial gradient of avoidance is steeper than that of approach. The present assumption is that an analogous difference exists in non-spatial dimensions of stimulus generalization. This has not yet been experimentally tested.

Basic Assumptions and Deductions

LET us summarize and then proceed to further implications. Five assumptions are needed to deduce the tendency for displacement to occur in situations in which the direct response to the original stimulus is prevented by conflict. These are: (1) that the direct response to the original stimulus generalizes to other similar stimuli, with the amount of generalization becoming smaller the less similar the stimuli; (2) that the response which conflicts with the occurrence of the direct response to the original stimulus also gen-

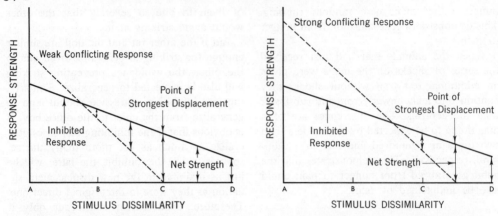

FIG. 7. Displacement produced by greater steepness in the gradient of generalization of the conflicting response (assuming linearity). It can be seen that displaced responses can occur and that the strongest displaced response will be expected at an intermediate point, *C* in the diagram on the left. Increasing the strength of the conflicting response weakens the strongest displaced response and causes it to be elicited by less similar stimuli, those between *C* and *D* in the diagram to the right. Although straight lines were used in order to simplify these diagrams, FIGURE 8 shows that the deductions are not dependent upon the assumption of linearity.

eralizes to other similar stimuli, becoming weaker the less similar the stimuli; (*3*) that the gradient of generalization of the conflicting response falls off more steeply with dissimilarity than does that of the original response which it inhibits; (*4*) that when two or more incompatible responses are simultaneously excited, the one with the greatest net strength will be the one which will occur; and (*5*) that the net strength of a response will be its strength minus that of any response incompatible with it which is excited at the same time. The first three of these assumptions have already been discussed; the fourth is a general assumption in behavior theory (11), and the fifth involves a type of complex response interaction which has not yet been subjected to experimental analysis. In addition to these assumptions, two more will be useful in dealing with other aspects of the problem. One of these is (*6*) that an increase in the drive involved in either type of gradient will raise the overall height of that gradient. Evidence supporting such an assumption has been secured by Judson Brown (2). The final assumption is (*7*) that gradients of generalization approximate the form of negative growth curves. This is much more specific than the first two assumptions and is needed only

for certain of the deductions. Professor Hull (11) has found a similar assumption useful in dealing with other types of data.

The operation of the factors involved in these assumptions is illustrated graphically in FIGURES 7, 8, 9. It can be seen that these assumptions do more than account for the mere fact that displacement can occur; they allow one to make the following specific deductions:

1. *When the direct response to the original stimulus is prevented by the absence of that stimulus, displaced responses will occur to other similar stimuli and the strongest displaced response will occur to the most similar stimulus present.* This follows directly from the first assumption and is illustrated in FIGURE 1. It is also illustrated by the solid line representing the inhibited response in FIGURE 7, if all the other features of that diagram are ignored.

Corollary: If the direct response to the original stimulus is prevented by the absence of that stimulus and the situation is such that responding to a given stimulus is incompatible with responding to other stimuli, the response will be most likely to be made to the most similar of the stimuli present. This corollary

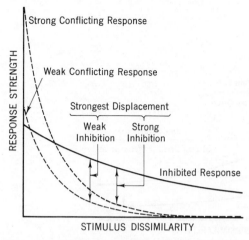

FIG. 8. Effect of strength of conflicting response upon displacement (assuming that gradients of generalization are negative growth curves). Increasing the strength of the conflicting response weakens the strength of the displaced responses and causes the point at which the strongest displaced response is elicited to be moved to stimuli which are less similar to those originally eliciting the direct response. FIGURE 7 shows that these same effects will also be produced by linear gradients; the only difference is that when the gradients are curvilinear the conflicting responses are above zero strength at the point at which strongest displacement is elicited.

and the ones to the following deductions deal with object choice. For example, other things equal, a girl who is prevented from marrying her sweetheart by his death and who has completely recovered from her grief and other possibly negative factors, will be expected to prefer the suitor who is most similar to him, ideally his identical twin. This follows from the preceding deduction and assumption 4.

2. *When the direct response to the original stimulus is prevented by conflict, the strongest displaced response will occur to stimuli which have an intermediate degree of similarity to the original one.* In the diagram on the left side of FIGURE 7, these are the stimuli at point *C*; it can be seen that those which are more similar, *B*, or less similar, *D*, elicit responses of weaker net strength.

Corollary: If the direct response to the original stimulus is prevented by conflict and

the situation is such that responding to a given stimulus is incompatible with responding to other stimuli, the displaced response will be most likely to occur to stimuli which have an intermediate degree of similarity to the original one. Thus a girl who is prevented from marrying her sweetheart by a violent quarrel would be expected to prefer someone not completely similar but not completely different. This follows from the preceding deduction and assumption 4.

3. *If the relative strength of the inhibitory response is increased, the point of strongest displacement will shift in the direction of stimuli which are less similar to the original one eliciting the direct response.* This is illustrated by the comparison between the two parts of FIGURE 7. With weak inhibition, the strongest net response occurs at point *C*; with stronger inhibition it occurs between *C* and *D*.

Corollary: If the direct response to the original stimulus is prevented by conflict and the situation is such that responding to one stimulus is incompatible with responding to others, the stimulus responded to will be less similar the stronger the inhibition involved. In other words, the more unhappy the girl's experience with her previous lover, the less similar should be her choice of a second object. This follows the preceding deduction and assumption 4.

4. *If the strength of the drive motivating the direct response to the original stimulus is held constant, the strength of a displaced response will be weaker than the direct response to the original stimulus would be if it were not prevented by the absence of that stimulus or by conflict with any inhibition.* This follows from the first assumption, which is that the gradient of generalization has a downward slope.

5. *If the strength of the drive motivating the direct response to the original stimulus is held constant, the strength of the displaced response will be greater when the direct response to the original stimulus is prevented by the absence of that stimulus (provided other very similar stimulus objects are present) and progressively weaker the stronger the inhibition involved.* This follows from the

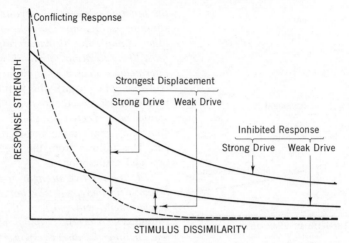

FIG. 9. Effect of strength of drive upon displacement (assuming that gradients of generalization are negative growth curves). By raising the height of the whole gradient of generalization, increasing the strength of the drive motivating the inhibited response will increase the strength of the strongest displaced response and cause the points at which the strongest displaced response is elicited to be moved in the direction of the stimuli more similar to those originally eliciting the direct response. The second of these effects is the only one of those illustrated in these diagrams which would not be produced by linear gradients.

fact that inhibition weakens the response and causes the strongest net response to occur to dissimilar stimuli which are at a lower point on the gradient of generalization. Thus it can be seen that the net strength of the response at the point of strongest displacement is less on the right side of FIGURE 7.

Corollary: If the inhibition is strong enough so that the two gradients do not cross, no displaced response will occur.

Note: A comparison of FIGURES 7 and 8 shows that all of the foregoing deductions and corollaries may be derived equally well from either the assumption that the gradient of generalization is linear or that it is a negative growth curve.

6. *If the drive motivating the direct response to the original stimulus is increased, the strength of all displaced responses will be increased.* This follows from assumption 6 and is illustrated in FIGURE 9.

7. *If the strength of the drive motivating the direct response to the original stimulus is increased, it will be possible for increasingly dissimilar stimuli to elicit displaced responses.* This should occur irrespective of whether the direct response was prevented by absence or

conflict. It follows from assumption 6 and may be illustrated by introducing a response threshold (and extrapolating the curves) in FIGURE 9. If a response threshold is introduced parallel to and above the base line of this figure, it is obvious that the lower of the two solid curves will fall below this threshold before the upper one does.

8. *In situations in which the direct response to the original stimulus is prevented by conflict, increasing the strength of the drive to the inhibited response will shift the point of strongest displacement in the direction of stimuli which are more similar to the original one eliciting the direct response.* This is illustrated in FIGURE 9; it is the only one of the deductions which does not hold for the assumption of linear gradients as well as for that of growth curves.

Corollary: Increasing the drive to the inhibited response will shift object choice in the direction of stimuli more similar to the original one eliciting the direct response.

In order to simplify the exposition, the foregoing deductions have used generalization gradients which were represented as either linear or as negative growth curves. These deductions are not, however, limited to the assumption of these particular forms of gradients. Within the range of stimuli included in the generalization gradient, deductions 1 and 4 will hold for any form of curve which has a negative slope throughout. For all such curves, deductions 5, 6, and 7 will also hold provided that any increase in the strength of response produces some increase in the height of all points and, if the curve intercepts the base line, moves this intercept farther out to the right. The second deduction will hold for any monotonic curves which have negative slopes throughout, cross only once, and cannot go below the base line of zero. The third applies to the same types of curves as the second provided that, when the strength of the response to the original stimulus is increased, (a) if the gradient is linear or convex, some increase is produced in the height of all points and the point at which it intercepts the base line is moved out farther, and (b) if the gradients are concave, the amount of absolute increase at any point is some positive function of the original height of the curve at that point. The eighth deduction requires the same stipulations as the third but does not hold for linear or convex gradients.

A few of the implications of these deductions will be briefly discussed. According to the first deduction, displacement caused by absence of the appropriate stimulus object should follow the pattern of stimulus generalization, with the strongest responses being to the most similar stimuli present. According to the second deduction, displacement caused by conflict should follow a different pattern, with the strongest responses occurring to stimuli of an intermediate degree of similarity. Since many clinical cases are of the latter type and seem to follow that pattern, this difference may have been one of the factors tending to prevent investigators from identifying displacement with generalization. It is interesting to note that this difference is not incompatible with the assumption that generalization is the primary process involved. In fact, it was deduced as a

factor which emerges from the interaction of the gradients of generalization of two competing responses.

The last three deductions (6, 7, and 8) become especially important in the light of the fact that there seem to be many situations in which the prevention of the direct response to the original stimulus causes the drive motivating that response to continue to mount because the displaced responses are either less efficient or completely ineffective in reducing that drive. Under such circumstances it will be possible for the displaced response to be stronger than the direct one was before its prevention caused the drive to mount. This is illustrated in FIGURE 9.

Finally, in addition to a mounting drive, it seems possible that the strength of a displaced response may be increased by two factors of a somewhat different kind. In the first place, the conflict between the direct response and the responses inhibiting it may cause tension producing strong stimuli which have the dynamogenic effect of facilitating whatever response finally does occur, much as locking the hands and pulling strongly in opposite directions will facilitate the knee jerk. Such an effect of conflict has been posited by Miller and Stevenson (20) and measured by Finger (5). In the second place, it is possible that, when generalized to a different stimulus situation and probably also modified by response generalization, the two competing tendencies may no longer be as incompatible as they were in the original situation. In that case certain elements of the two generalized responses may summate instead of conflicting. Compromise responses of this type have been discussed in somewhat more detail in a previous article (17).

Factors Influencing the Relative Steepness of Gradients

IT seems possible that the gradient of generalization for the inhibiting response may be steeper than that of the inhibited one in some types of situations but not in others. In this case one would expect displacement to occur in some types of situations but not in others.

In order to predict when displacement will occur, one would have to know what factors are responsible for the relative steepness of the two gradients. It seems likely that there are at least two such factors: (1) learning and (2) the degree to which the drive involved is dependent on external cues.

Experiments on discrimination show that the steepness of gradients of generalization can be modified by learning. If aggression against the scapegoat is not punished, this will extinguish the generalized inhibition and steepen that gradient. Similarly, if the expression of aggression against the scapegoat is rewarding, this will strengthen the generalized aggression and flatten that gradient. Under these conditions the greater steepness of the gradient of inhibition could be the result of a learned discrimination.

Another factor influencing the relative steepness could be the degree to which the drive motivating the response is dependent upon external cues. If the motivation is an acquired drive, such as fear of a given situation, it will be most strongly aroused by the cues in that situation, and less strongly aroused by other similar cues. Therefore, when the subject is confronted with cues which are somewhat similar to the original ones, the gradient of generalization will have a double effect: it will weaken not only the specific responses involved (for example, withdrawal) but also the fear motivating these responses. This double effect will cause the strength of the inhibiting response to fall off more rapidly. On the other hand, if the drive is a primary one, more dependent upon physiological factors, it will be less influenced by the cues and hence its strength will be more nearly the same in different stimulus situations. The factor of generalization will operate only on the tendency to respond and will not also affect the strength of motivation. Therefore, whenever the drive motivating the direct response to the original stimulus is relatively less dependent upon external cues than the one motivating the inhibiting response, the gradient of generalization of the direct response should not be as steep as that of the inhibiting response.

Deduction of the Functional Difference between Consciously and Unconsciously Determined Behavior

ACCORDING to Freud, the unconscious is the unverbalized. To quote him:

> It strikes us all at once that now we know what is the difference between a conscious and an unconscious idea. The two are not, as we supposed, different records of the same content situate in different parts of the mind, nor yet different functional states of cathexis in the same part; but the conscious idea comprises a concrete idea plus the verbal idea corresponding to it, whilst the unconscious idea is that of the thing alone . . . Now, too, we are in a position to state precisely what it is that repression denies to the rejected idea in the transference neuroses—namely, translation of the idea into words which are to remain attached to the object.[6]

Thus, according to Freud, the effects of memory traces of events occurring before the age at which the child learned to talk are automatically unconscious. Material that once was conscious becomes unconscious when the verbal part of the response pattern is repressed.[7]

In man, according to stimulus-response theory, it is primarily the verbal responses (with some assistance from other stimulus-producing responses) which mediate the higher mental processes (11, 19).[8] Therefore, the absence of these verbal responses should

6 Freud, S., *The unconscious,* (1915) in *Collected Papers,* Vol. IV, pp. 133–134.

7 See also Sears (23).

8 Saying that verbal and other stimulus-producing responses play an essential role in the higher mental processes does not deny the fact that the organism must possess certain greater capacities, the exact nature of which is still unknown, before such responses can operate in this way. The anatomical locus of these verbal thoughts and other stimulus-producing responses—whether they involve peripheral contractions of vocal cords or central activities within the brain—is unimportant as long as they are learned in the same way that saying a word is and can serve as cues in the same way that hearing oneself say a word does. They will be called stimulus-producing responses whenever they seem to have the functional properties of stimuli and to obey the laws of responses (19).

make unconsciously determined behavior less intelligent than that which is conscious. This is exactly what Freud has observed. The therapeutic effect of making the unconscious conscious arises from the fact that conscious behavior is more intelligent.

A more thorough discussion of the details of this difference, the way repression is learned, and the implications for psychotherapy is being prepared by the author in collaboration with John Dollard. The present discussion will be limited to the problem as it affects displacement.

According to stimulus-response theory, learning to respond with highly distinctive names to similar stimulus situations should tend to lessen the generalization of other responses from one of these situations to another since the stimuli produced by responding with the distinctive name will tend to increase the differences in the stimulus patterns of the two situations. Increased differentiation based on this mechanism has been called acquired distinctiveness of cues (19).

On the other hand, if the individual learns to respond to two quite different situations with the same verbal response, the stimuli produced by this response will be a common element mediating an increased amount of generalization from one situation to the other. This has been called acquired equivalence of cues (19), or secondary generalization (11).

The removal of all verbal responses by repression, therefore, will be expected to have a dual effect: (1) in cases where similar objects or situations are labeled differently, repression will remove the basis for acquired distinctiveness and increase the amount of primary generalization; and (2) in cases in which different objects or situations are given the same name, repression will remove the basis for acquired equivalence and thus decrease the amount of secondary generalization. In other words, there should be more primary and less secondary generalization in the unconscious.

The function of the mechanisms for acquired equivalence and acquired distinctiveness is to allow the patterns based on the innate characteristics of cues to be refined in the light of experience and thus to become better adapted to the particular conditions of a specific environment. In the social life of man, the importance of these mechanisms is enormously magnified by the influence of culture. The discriminations and generalizations which have been found useful through generations of trial and error are imbedded in the language which is taught to each new member of society. For example, in our society, where discriminating different stages in the ripeness of cocoanuts is not important, we have only two phrases, green and ripe cocoanuts, while among the Cook Islanders in Polynesia, in whose economy they play a paramount role as a source of food, drink, and fiber, there are twelve distinctive words and phrases each describing a different stage in the maturity of this nut (8). Learning to use these words to describe the state of the cocoanut correctly will be expected to be of great assistance in subsequent behavior where these discriminations are important.

Since socially important discriminations are facilitated by giving different names to the situations or objects which should be discriminated, the removal of these verbal responses by repression should interfere with the discrimination and allow primary generalization to occur wherever the stimuli in the situations are superficially similar. This generalization will be maladaptive and is likely to be called displacement. In other words there should be more displacement in the unconscious. Freud's observations indicate that this is exactly what occurs.

Similarly, socially acceptable generalizations are likely to be facilitated by the habit of applying the same words to those aspects of the two situations which are functionally equivalent. Adaptive generalizations mediated in this way are, however, not referred to as displacement, but as insight or reasoning. They should be greatly reduced when the verbal responses are removed by repression.

The process can become more complicated

when, as is usually the case, some verbal responses are removed and others remain. For example, Mr. Johnson, a somewhat neurotic and intensely ambitious middle-class social climber moved into an upper-class neighborhood near the Bartletts, an upper-class family with whom he had previous business contact. The Bartletts were the only family who gave any recognition of Johnson's arrival in the neighborhood and the whole program of obtaining social acceptance seemed to depend on them.

But on the few occasions when the Bartletts invited the Johnsons over it was all too clear that their role was more one of entertainers than of guests. Painful snubbing aroused fierce aggression, which Mr. Johnson did not dare express because it would completely ruin his best chance for mobility. The overt responses of performing the aggressive acts and saying the bitter words were therefore suppressed. But even saying the words to himself caused so much anxiety that he was motivated to stop saying such words to himself and, whenever he stopped, was strongly reinforced, by a drop in the intense anxiety which they elicited. Thus he became unable to say to himself that he was angry at Mr. Bartlett, or, in other words, repressed his anger.[9, 10]

One day Mr. Johnson saw the Bartlett dog running across one of his newly planted flower beds. In addition to the mild aggression which the sight of an ordinary dog doing this would be expected to arouse, he thought of it as the Bartlett dog and the mental stimulus of these words aroused burning anger which, however, was not labeled as anger at Bartlett. Feeling very angry, he picked up a large stone and threw it violently at the dog.

In this case Mr. Johnson's anger was aroused by a verbal response, thinking of the Bartletts when he saw their dog. Since

9 This repression was probably dependent on patterns which had been established during infancy when his helplessness made him subject to stronger drives.

10 The stimulus-response description of the way in which repression is motivated and reinforced was worked out in collaboration with John Dollard. For experimental evidence that a reduction in the acquirable drive of anxiety can serve as a powerful reinforcing agent, see (16).

this particular verbal response was not repressed, it could mediate the generalization of anger from Mr. Bartlett and his snubs to his dog. Since no verbal response of the type, "I am sore at Bartlett," occurred, Mr. Johnson was not conscious of the source of the aggression. If he had said to himself, "I am sore at Bartlett," throwing the large rock so violently at the dog would have seemed illogical as a result of his previous training to respond to words grouped into sentences of this kind and unfair in the light of his social training to limit punishment to those labeled as deserving it.

In this case it is not the single word as a stimulus which is crucial but rather the subject-verb-object relationship of a group of words. Though sentences are obviously responded to in this way, the details of how responses to patterns of this kind are learned have not yet been thoroughly studied.

To summarize, the repression of verbal responses specifying the source of aggression may remove a basis for discrimination and allow the illogical generalization, or displacement, of that aggression to be mediated by a different verbal response which is not repressed. In the illustration, displacement was facilitated by the fact that Mr. Johnson was conscious of the fact that it was the Bartlett dog but unconscious of the fact that he was angry at Mr. Bartlett.

Summary

1. Pairs of albino rats were trained by trial and error to commence striking at each other, like they do when fighting, as soon as an electric shock was turned on. This behavior was reinforced by turning off the shock when the animals started striking vigorously. In test trials they were placed in the apparatus along with a celluloid doll. When tested in pairs they struck at each other, but when no other rat was present, they struck at the doll. In psychoanalytic terms this might be described as displacement and in stimulus-response ones as generalization from the other rat to the doll.

2. On the assumption that the stimulus patterns involved in the different drives are not completely dissimilar, it was deduced that a

certain amount of generalization, or displacement, should occur from one drive to another. This deduction was confirmed by the following experiments:

a. Rats motivated by thirst and rewarded by water were trained to run down a short alley. They were then completely satiated on water in their home cages and tested in the alley under one of two conditions: hungry or not hungry. Those tested with the irrelevant drive of hunger ran faster and drank more water than those tested without it.

b. Hungry rats were trained to take the correct turn on a T-maze in order to secure food and tested after being completely satiated away from the maze. Those tested with an electric shock on the maze, which lasted for one second irrespective of what they did, ran faster and made fewer errors than those tested without this irrelevant drive. The fear persisting after a series of shocked trials caused the experimental animals to continue to run faster and more accurately than their controls.

3. In both of the above studies, experimental extinction was observed during a series of trials with reward present but drive absent. When the animals in the first study were satiated and tested again after an interval of 48 hours, spontaneous recovery was indicated by an increase in the speed of running and in the amount of water consumed.

4. In a further analysis, the situation in which the direct response to the original stimulus-object is prevented by the absence of that object was contrasted with the one in which the direct response to the original stimulus is prevented by conflict. It was shown that displacement would be expected in the latter type of situation only if the gradient of generalization of the conflicting responses is steeper than that of the responses which they inhibit. On the basis of this and other stimulus-response assumptions, the following deductions were made:

a. When the direct response to the original stimulus is prevented by the absence of that stimulus, displaced responses will occur to other similar stimuli and the strongest displaced response will occur to the most similar stimulus present.

b. When the direct response to the original stimulus is prevented by conflict, displaced responses can occur and the strongest displaced response will occur to stimuli which have an intermediate degree of similarity to the original one.

c. If the relative strength of the inhibitory response is increased, the point of strongest displacement will shift in the direction of stimuli which are less similar to the original one eliciting the direct response.

d. If the strength of the drive motivating the direct response to the original stimulus is held constant, the strength of the displaced response will be weaker than the direct response to the original stimulus would be if it were not prevented by absence and/or if no conflict were present.

e. If the strength of the drive motivating the direct response to the original stimulus is held constant, the strength of the displaced response will be greater when the direct response to the original stimulus is prevented by the absence of that stimulus (provided other very similar stimulus objects are present) and progressively weaker the stronger the inhibition involved.

f. If the drive motivating the direct response to the original stimulus is increased, the strength of all displaced responses will be increased. (Thus, if the displaced response is less effective than the direct one in reducing the drive, it may continue to mount so that the displaced response becomes stronger than the original direct one.)

g. If the strength of the drive motivating the direct response to the original stimulus is increased, it will be possible for increasingly dissimilar stimuli to elicit displaced responses.

h. In situations in which the direct response to the original stimulus is prevented by conflict, increasing the strength of the drive to that response will shift the point of strongest displacement in the direction of stimuli which are more similar to the original one eliciting the direct response.

5. It was deduced that the gradient of generalization for the conflicting response should tend to be steeper than that for the direct one when:

a. The direct response is punished and the displaced one is not, and/or

b. The drive motivating the direct response to the original stimulus is relatively less dependent upon external cues than the one motivating the conflicting response.

6. A stimulus-response analysis of the difference between consciously and unconsciously determined behavior indicated why the latter should be less adaptive and exhibit more displacement.

REFERENCES

1. ANDERSON, E. E. The externalization of drive: III. Maze learning by non-rewarded and by satiated rats. *J. gen. Psychol.*, 1941, 59, 397–426.

2. BROWN, J. S. The generalization of approach responses as a function of stimulus intensity and strength of motivation. *J. comp. Psychol.*, 1942, 33, 209–226.

3. CORIAT, I. H. Sex and hunger. *Psychoanal. Rev.*, 1921, 8, 375–381.

4. DOLLARD, J., et al. *Frustration and aggression.* New Haven: Yale University Press, 1939.

5. FINGER, F. W. Quantitative studies of "conflict": I. Variations in latency and strength of the rat's response in a discrimination-jumping situation. *J. comp. Psychol.*, 1941, 31, 97–127.

6. FREUD, S. *A general introduction to psychoanalysis.* (Authorized translation, with a preface by G. S. Hall.) New York: Boni and Liveright, 1920.

7. FREUD, S. *The interpretation of dreams.* (Introduction by A. A. Brill.) London: Allen and Unwin; New York: Macmillan, 1927.

8. HIROA, T. R. Ethnology of Ranihiki and Rakahanga. *B. P. Bishop Museum Bull.*, 1932, 99.

9. HOCHMAN, S. Mental and psychological factors in obesity. *Med Rec.*, 1938, 148, 108–111.

10. HOVLAND, C. I. The generalization of conditioned responses. I. The sensory generalization of conditioned responses with varying frequencies of tone. *J. gen. Psychol.*, 1937, 17, 125–148.

11. HULL, C. L. *Principles of behavior.* New York: Appleton-Century, 1943.

12. KENDLER, H. H. Drive interaction: I. Learning as a function of the simultaneous presence of the hunger and thirst drives. *J. exp. Psychol.*, 1945, 35, 96–109.

13. KOCH, S., & DANIEL, W. F. The effect of satiation on the behavior mediated by a habit of maximum strength. *J. exp. Psychol.*, 1945, 35, 167–187.

14. MILLER, N. E. Experiments relating Freudian displacement to generalization of conditioning. *Psychol. Bull.*, 1939, 36, 516–517.

15. MILLER, N. E. The frustration-aggression hypothesis. *Psychol. Rev.*, 1941, 48, 337–342.

16. MILLER, N. E. Studies of fear as an acquirable drive: I. Fear as motivation and fear-reduction as reinforcement in the learning of new responses. *J. exp. Psychol.*, 1948, 38, 89–101.

17. MILLER, N. E. Experimental studies of conflict. In J. McV. Hunt, edit., *Personality and the behavior disorders.* New York: Ronald Press, 1944.

18. MILLER, N. E., & BUGELSKI, R. Minor studies of aggression: II. The influence of frustrations imposed by the in-group on attitudes expressed toward out-groups. *J. Psychol.*, 1948, 25, 437–442.

19. MILLER, N. E., & DOLLARD, J. *Social learning and imitation.* New Haven: Yale University Press, 1941.

20. MILLER, N. E., & STEVENSON, S. S. Agitated behavior of rats during experimental extinction and a curve of spontaneous recovery. *J. comp. Psychol.*, 1936, 21, 205–231.

21. PAVLOV, I. P. *Conditioned reflexes.* (Trans. by G. V. Anrep.) London: Oxford University Press, 1927.

22. SAUL, L. J. Physiological effects of emotional tension. In J. McV. Hunt, edit., *Personality and the behavior disorders.* New York: Ronald Press, 1944.

23. SEARS, R. R. Functional abnormalities of memory with special reference to amnesia. *Psychol. Bull.*, 1936, 33, 229–274.

24. SEARS, R. R. Non-aggressive reactions to frustration. *Psychol. Rev.*, 1941, 48, 343–346.

25. SIEGEL, P. S. Alien drive, habit strength, and resistance to extinction. *J. comp. Psychol.*, 1946, 39, 307–317.

SEYMOUR FESHBACH

36. *The Drive-Reducing Function of Fantasy Behavior*

THE primary object of this research is to investigate the hypothesis that fantasy will reduce the strength of a motive by means of symbolic satisfaction. Current interest in fantasy as a form of behavior stems primarily from: (*a*) the emphasis placed by psychoanalysis on the role of fantasy in human adjustment, (*b*) the widespread use of the Thematic Apperception Test as a diagnostic instrument, and (*c*) recent studies exploring the effects of experimentally induced drives upon various cognitive processes including fantasy. These latter investigations have in general confirmed the assumption that ungratified needs are reflected in fantasy. However an unresolved and neglected problem is whether fantasy behavior to any degree satisfies these needs.

Psychoanalysts have long maintained that fantasies including dreams, daydreams, myths, and artistic productions represent wish fulfillment. According to Freud, "unsatisfied wishes are the driving power behind phantasies; every separate phantasy contains the fulfillment of a wish, and improves on unsatisfactory reality" (7, p. 176). More recently Symonds (12), writing from the psychoanalytic standpoint, clearly suggests that goal responses expressed in fantasy may be drive reducing. The latter hypothesis is compatible with a behavior theory which holds that self-initiated verbal responses may have secondary reward value and thus reinforce the tendency to repeat those responses when stimulated by the drive which had originally occasioned them. Some such hypothesis is suggested by a reinforcement theory in explaining the persistence of certain forms of fantasy behavior as, for example, that found in obsessional neurosis.

Although the hypothesis that fantasy behavior has a substitute or compensatory function is widely entertained (1, 6, 13), it is by no means universally accepted. McClelland *et al.* (2, 9) have explicitly doubted its validity on the basis of indirect inference from the content of TAT-type fantasies. A study by Wittenborn and Eron (14), also based on TAT fantasies, finds some substantiation for a drive-reduction hypothesis in the pattern of intercorrelations among certain features of TAT responses. However, positive or negative evidence directly bearing upon the hypothesis is lacking.

Experimental studies of substitute behavior, conducted chiefly by Lewin and his students, have touched upon this problem (3, 5, 8, 10). Some of their results suggest that, with the exception of "play" situations, fantasy completion of interrupted or insoluble tasks has little, if any, substitute value. However, the exclusive use of the resumption technique as a measure of drive strength and of the interrupted-task technique as the primary method of inducing motivation (in addition to inadequate experimental procedures) greatly limits the generality of their findings. An experimental approach using more sensitive and direct measures of drive strength, and inducing drives with possibly wider theoretical and practical implications, seems necessary.

In addition, in order to demonstrate the

Reprinted by permission of the American Psychological Association and the author from the *Journal of Abnormal and Social Psychology*, 1955, vol. 51, pp. 3–11.

phenomenon of drive reduction as an effect of fantasy behavior, it seems desirable to use a drive which by reason of theory and experience seems likely to be measurably reduced by fantasy; i.e., a psychogenic as contrasted to a physiologically rooted drive. With these considerations in mind, the present research is designed to test the following hypothesis: Fantasy expression of hostility will partially reduce situationally induced aggression. Ideally, this hypothesis might be tested by inducing aggressive drive, measuring the strength of the drive induced and, after an interpolated fantasy activity, measuring the strength of aggressive drive a second time. The decrement in aggression from the first occasion to the second would provide the most direct test of the hypothesis. There are practical difficulties in carrying out this design. For one thing, it is difficult to find measures of aggression that can be meaningfully applied twice within a short period of time. Secondly, in preliminary work, the subjects (Ss) would not accept the situation when the measures of aggression were given directly after aggression was aroused.

For these reasons the drive-reduction hypothesis is to be tested by comparing the strength of aggressive drive (at the end of the experimental session) in two groups, one of which receives the opportunity to express hostile fantasy while the other engages in nonfantasy or control activities. The actual test is then simply a measure of the subsequent difference in aggression between these two groups. The specific prediction is that the fantasy group will be less aggressive than the control group. The predicted difference is just as pertinent to the drive-reduction hypothesis as the ideal test previously described, even though the measure is one of end effect and relative difference rather than of absolute change in each group.

Method

THE Ss were all members of introductory psychology classes at a large metropolitan college. Classes were randomly assigned to one of three experimental treatments: (a) arousal of aggression and interpolation of

fantasy activity (Insult Fantasy group); (b) arousal of aggression and interpolation of nonfantasy activities (Insult Control group); (c) nonarousal of aggression and interpolation of fantasy activities (Noninsult Fantasy group). The Insult Fantasy group consisted of 123 Ss (five classes), the Insult Control group of 56 Ss (three classes), and the Noninsult Fantasy group of 78 Ss (three classes).[1] In the total group there were approximately twice as many men as women. However, the sex ratio from class to class varied considerably.

Aggression was aroused by the experimenter (E), who assumed an insulting attitude toward a class of college students. The interpolated activities provided one group of insulted Ss the opportunity to express their hostility in fantasy (Insult Fantasy group), whereas the activities in which a comparable group of insulted Ss were engaged permitted little or no opportunity for fantasy (Insult Control group). These two groups were then compared on subsequent measures of hostility toward E and the experiment to determine if the fantasy experience resulted in less aggression than did the nonfantasy activity.

The Noninsult Fantasy group engaged in the same fantasy activity as did the Insult Fantasy group and received the same measures of aggression as did the two Insult groups. Comparison between the Noninsult and Insult groups on these measures would indicate whether E's insulting attitude actually did arouse aggression in the insulted groups and at the same time would establish the validity and usefulness of the measures of aggression with respect to the principal comparison between the Insult Fantasy and Insult Control groups.

PROCEDURE

Two Es were used in carrying out the study. The individual who acted as the principal

---

1 These are the Ss who remained after eliminating from all Insult groups 23 Ss who in class discussions held several days after the experiment said they knew the insulting attitude of E was feigned. Because of administrative limitations, classes, not Ss, were assigned at random to the various experimental treatments.

E^2 was carefully selected for his ability to arouse the hostility of Ss in the Insult groups without their realizing that his remarks were deliberately intended to achieve that end. The writer acted as his assistant in each of the 11 classes which participated in the study.

The E was briefly introduced to the class by its instructor, who left the classroom and did not return until near the end of the period. Administration of the experimental procedures consumed one 50-minute class period and all the classes were seen within a four-day period.

After the instructor left the classroom, E, in an authoritarian, arrogant manner, made several derogatory remarks about the motivation, ability, and level of maturity of the student body of the college. For example, he made such comments as "Now I realize that you _____ College students, or should I say _____ College grinds have few academic interests outside of your concern for grades . . . if you will try to look beyond your limited horizons, your cooperation will be useful. In other words, I'd like you to act like adults rather than adolescents." [3] The Noninsult classes received a friendly introduction designed to gain their cooperation.

FANTASY-NONFANTASY VARIABLE

The E who acted as insulter did not know whether the insulted class was to be in the Fantasy or Control group until after he made his insulting comments. After making his introductory remarks, he opened a folder from which he read the instructions for the particular activity to be given. This procedure was followed so as to eliminate the possibility that E's behavior could be biased by foreknowledge of whether the class was to be in the Fantasy or Control group.

Four TAT pictures (4, 18GF, 7BM, and 12M) were presented by means of a slide projector to the Noninsult Fantasy and Insult Fantasy groups. The order in which the pictures were given was systematically varied. The instructions and procedure for administration of the group TAT followed those used by McClelland, Clark, et al.; these instructions present the TAT as an achievement task which involves the construction of an interesting and dramatic story under specific time limitations. The TAT was given as a test of ability, and in this respect is like the nonfantasy activities administered to the Control group.

The Insult Control classes received tests which offered little, if any, opportunity for fantasy. Each class was given a different nonfantasy activity which consumed the same amount of time as the TAT procedure. The nonfantasy activity was varied in an attempt to control for possible differences in preference for the fantasy vs. the nonfantasy activity. Had only one nonfantasy activity been used in all three classes in the Control group, then one might argue that if the Fantasy group subsequently displayed less aggression than the Control group, the difference could be due to the negative characteristics of the nonfantasy activity. Two of the Control classes were given standard tests; one Series AA of the Revised Minnesota Paper Form Board Test, and the second, Parts 1 through 4 of the General Clerical Aptitude Test. The instructions for the tests were abridged so as to correspond in length with those given for the TAT. The remaining class was given a "picture description test" which required a one-sentence description of each of a series of slides projected on a screen. These slides consisted of scenic photographs and paintings in which architectural forms predominated.

MEASURES OF AGGRESSION

Subsequent to the interpolated activity all groups were administered a slightly modified version of the Rotter-Willerman (11) form of the Sentence Completion Test. The instructor then returned, and the Es left the class-

---

2 The writer is very much indebted to John Dickinson, at the time a graduate law student, whose caustic skills and courtroom demeanor were very effective in antagonizing the students and at the same time restraining them from overt aggressive behavior.

3 A full account of all procedures including measures of aggression has been deposited with the American Documentation Institute. Order Document No. 4244 from the ADI Auxiliary Publications Project, Photoduplication Service, Library of Congress, Washington 25, D. C., remitting in advance $2.50 for 6 $\times$ 8 in. photoprints or $1.75 for 35 mm. microfilm. Make checks payable to Chief, Photoduplication Service, Library of Congress.

room. The instructor informed the class that the faculty was interested in reactions of the students to having research take up class time. He then administered to the class a questionnaire consisting of eight items dealing with attitudes toward the experimenter, experiment, and psychological research.

Results

EFFECTS OF THE INSULTING BEHAVIOR OF "E"

The attitude questionnaire. The attitude questionnaire administered by the instructor at the close of the class hour is the most explicit and direct measure of aggression toward E. If the insulting attitude assumed by E had the intended effect of arousing hostility toward him, then this effect should be reflected by the responses of the insulted Ss on the questionnaire.

The Insult and Noninsult groups [4] were initially compared on each question separately. For the first six items, each of which had six alternatives, comparisons are based on the proportion of Ss selecting the most aggressive alternatives, points 5 and 6 on the six-point scale. Preliminary experiments had indicated that the best discrimination between insulted and noninsulted groups would probably be obtained in this way. For the remaining questions, which had only two possible answers, "yes" and "no," the differences are based on the proportion of people who gave the more aggressive of the two answers. The Insult groups display considerably more aggression on the questionnaire than the Noninsult group. The differences between the Noninsult and Insult Fantasy groups are significant for five of the eight questions, and differences between the Noninsult and Insult Control groups are significant for seven of the eight questions.

In addition to the item analysis, a more

general measure of aggression was obtained based on the first six items by assigning scores to each response, the least aggressive choice receiving a score of 1 and the most aggressive choice receiving a score of 6. A second measure was based only on the three questions dealing with attitudes toward E (items 3, 5, and 6). The third measure was based on the two questions concerning evaluation of the experiment (items 2 and 4).[5] On all three of these measures there are highly significant differences between the Insult groups and the Noninsult group.

The results of both the item comparisons and the over-all scores confirm the existence of the intended effect of the insult variable. As anticipated, the insulted Ss are much more critical of the study and much more hostile toward E than Ss who were not insulted.

The Sentence Completion Test. The responses to this test were scored for aggression according to a detailed scoring scheme [6] based primarily on distinctions according to the object of aggression and the form in which the aggression was expressed. The most important categories were: (*a*) aggression toward E; (*b*) aggression expressed toward possible substitutes for E (teachers, research workers); (*c*) aggression toward the test situation; (*d*) aggression expressed toward possible substitutes for the test situation (tests in general, experiments, college); (*e*) general aggression (aggression toward people, institutions, or practices). Within each of the above categories a distinction was made between emotional and objective aggression. The former was denoted by such terms as hate, dislike, detest, while the latter referred to criticism of the objects specified in each category. Emotional aggression was conceived to be a more direct expression of hostility than objective aggression.

An analysis was made of the percentage of

4 In order to avoid repetition of tables, the Noninsult Fantasy group data are presented in the section of the results concerned with differences between the Insult Fantasy and Insult Control groups. For those interested in the specific numerical results pertinent to the responses of the Noninsult Fantasy group on the questionnaire, reference can be made to TABLES 1 and 2.

5 Question 1 was omitted from these two more specific measures because it could not be unambiguously assigned to either one.

6 A study of the reliability of the scoring categories based on 30 Ss selected at random was carried out with another psychologist. The tests were independently scored. There was disagreement in scoring of only seven sentences.

*S*s having one or more responses in each scoring category.[7] Only three categories yielded differences in aggression between the Noninsult group and either of the Insult groups significant at the .05 level or above.[8] These categories—1, 2Em, and 3—deal, respectively, with aggression toward *E*, emotional aggression toward possible substitutes for *E*, and aggression toward the test. There is no significant difference in category 5 which repre-

sents aggression toward individuals who do not show any manifest similarity to *E*. The results provide tentative evidence of a gradient of generalization—aggression toward objects being a decreasing function of their similarity to the original instigator of the aggression in this situation.

The analysis of the attitude questionnaire and the Sentence Completion Test has demonstrated that both are sensitive to the arousal of aggression by the insulting comments of *E* and can therefore be used to test differences in aggression between the Insult Fantasy and Insult Control groups.

EFFECT OF FANTASY

The attitude questionnaire. The results of the item analysis of the attitude questionnaire are presented in TABLE 1. Inspection of the

[7] Due to lack of time, one class in the Noninsult Fantasy group and one class in the Insult Fantasy group failed to complete the test. These classes are not included in the analysis of the results for the Sentence Completion Test. A second class in the Insult Fantasy group was eliminated from this analysis in order to equate the proportion of the two sexes in each experimental group.

[8] The data are presented in TABLE 4. Yates's correction for continuity was used in all chi-square tests of independence.

TABLE 1

Percentage of Subjects in Each Group Giving Extreme Aggressive Responses
on the Attitude Questionnaire

QUESTION	RESPONSE	NON-INSULT FANTASY ($N = 78$)	INSULT FANTASY ($N = 107$)	INSULT CONTROL ($N = 56$)	DIFF. IC − IF	t	p
1. How much did you like participating in the study just recently conducted?	very irritated and extremely irritated	0	9.3	25.0	15.7	2.7	$<.004$
2. How worth while was it to participate in the study just recently conducted?	considerable and complete waste of time	6.4	15.9	19.7	3.8	0.62	$<.27$
3. If you were asked by the Experimenter to volunteer for another study he was conducting, would you volunteer?	probably not, definitely not	6.4	32.7	50.0	17.3	2.15	$<.02$
4. In your opinion, how much of a contribution will this study make to the field of psychology?	very little, none	11.5	26.1	30.4	4.3	0.63	$<.27$
5. In your opinion, how competent was the psychologist who conducted the experiment in which you participated?	very incompetent and extremely incompetent	3.8	21.5	35.7	14.2	1.95	$<.03$
6. What is your reaction now to the psychologist who conducted this experiment? How much do you like or dislike him?	dislike very much	0	42.0	57.2	15.2	1.85	$<.04$
7. Is there anything you disliked about the experiment?	yes	42.0	73.0	82.0	9.0	1.3	$<.10$
8. Several experiments are going to be conducted by the psychology department. Are you willing to volunteer?	no	56.0	56.0	66.0	10.0	1.2	$<.12$

table reveals that on every item the Insult Control group is more aggressive than the Fantasy group.[9] The smallest differences, not statistically significant, are on questions which deal with attitudes toward the study. The differences on questions which deal explicitly with attitudes toward E are much larger and are also statistically significant.[10] The consistently lower amount of aggression displayed by the Insult Fantasy group is in accord with the hypothesis that aggression expressed in fantasy behavior will reduce aggressive motivation.

The means of the Insult Fantasy and Insult Control groups on the more general measures based on the attitude questionnaire are given in TABLE 2. The differences between the two insulted groups indicated by the item comparisons are borne out by this method of analysis. The over-all aggression scores of the Insult Control group are significantly higher than those of the Insult Fantasy group. For the measure reflecting only aggression toward E this difference is significant at the .01 level. For the measure based on the criticism of the experiment, the difference is in the

same direction but is small and not statistically significant.

The conclusions stated thus far about the statistical significance of the results have been reached by treating each individual as an independent case. However, it is possible that differences in E's behavior, in the several classes in which he tried to keep his behavior constant, may have caused all the members of one class to vary from the others uniformly. To control for this possibility, another significance test of the difference between the two Insult groups was made using only the class means to constitute the sample. The comparison was based on the class means of the men only because of the varying proportions of women in different classes, and their tendency to have lower aggression scores than the men. The results of this analysis are presented in TABLE 3. All differences are in the predicted direction, thus confirming the findings reported above. The difference in over-all aggression between the insult Fantasy and Insult Control groups approaches significance, while the difference based on attitudes toward E is significant at the .05 level of confidence. Also, the difference based

9 The number of women in the Insult Fantasy group was reduced in order to equate the proportion of the two sexes in each experimental group. Since the women displayed less aggression than the men, a higher proportion of women in the Insult Fantasy group would tend to lower the mean aggression scores of that group. Cases to be eliminated were selected by use of a table of random numbers.

10 The p values reported in this paper, with the exception of the Sentence Completion Test analysis,

are based on a one-tailed test of significance. The one-tailed test is used where specific predictions of the direction of the anticipated difference were made. In the case of the Sentence Completion Test, the predictions were not specific enough to indicate on which of the scoring categories the Fantasy group would show less aggression than the Nonfantasy group.

TABLE 2

Mean Aggression Scores of Each Group on the Attitude Questionnaire

GROUP	TOTAL AGGRESSION (all 6 items)	PERSONAL AGGRESSION TOWARD E (items 3, 5, 6)	AGGRESSIVE EVALUATION OF THE EXPERIMENT (items 2 and 4)
Noninsult fantasy ($N = 78$)	14.92	7.04	5.96
Insult fantasy ($N = 107$)	21.17	11.47	7.03
Insult control ($N = 56$)	23.09	12.88	7.23
Difference (IC − IF)	1.92	1.41	.20
t	2.02	2.49	.56
p	<.025	<.01	<.29

TABLE 3

Mean Aggression Scores on the Attitude
Questionnaire of Men in Each Class
in the Insult Groups

GROUP	TOTAL AGGRESSION (all 6 items)	PERSONAL AGGRESSION TOWARD E (items 3, 5, 6)	AGGRESSIVE EVALUATION OF THE EXPERIMENT (items 2 and 4)
Insult fantasy			
Class D	23.04	11.83	7.15
Class E	21.95	11.81	7.00
Class F	20.14	11.00	6.85
Class G	22.19	12.62	7.06
Class H	18.10	9.60	6.70
Mean	21.08	11.37	6.95
Insult control			
Class J	23.13	12.47	7.33
Class K	23.13	12.88	7.25
Class L	23.80	13.40	7.50
Mean of classes	23.35	12.92	7.36
Difference between mean of classes	2.27	1.55	0.41
t	1.91	2.01	3.37
p	<.06	<.05	<.01

on evaluation of the study is significant at the .01 level.

The Sentence Completion Test. The results of a chi-square analysis of the percentage of Ss having one or more responses in each of the aggression categories are reported in TABLE 4.

The most relevant measures for comparing the two Insult groups are categories 1, 2Em, and 3, which, since they discriminate between the Insult and Noninsult groups, are the most indicative of aggression. On each of these three measures, the Insult Control group displays more hostility than the Insult Fantasy Ss. The difference is significant at the .05 level for category 2Em and is not statistically significant for the other categories. If one computes for each individual the number of aggressive responses based on all three categories, the differences between the Insult Con-

trol and Insult Fantasy groups are considerably enhanced. The results of this comparison are presented in TABLE 5 and show the Insult Fantasy group to have significantly less hostility than the Insult Control group. Thus the differences in aggression found between the two groups on the attitude questionnaire are confirmed by the Sentence Completion Test.

FANTASY DATA

The effect of the insults upon the fantasy responses. The TAT stories were coded to conceal identity of Ss and the experimental treatment and then rated on a five-point rating scale of aggression, a rating of five being given to the most aggressive fantasy. The results of the ratings are presented in TABLE 6. The stories of the Insult Fantasy group are consistently more aggressive than those of the Noninsult Fantasy group. However, the

TABLE 4

Percentage of Subjects in Each Group Having One or More
Aggressive Responses in Each Scoring Category
on the Sentence Completion Test

SCORING CATEGORY	NON-INSULT FANTASY ($N = 51$)	INSULT FANTASY ($N = 76$)	INSULT CONTROL ($N = 55$)	χ^2 (IF, IC)	p *
1. Aggression toward E					
Emotional	2	13	24		
Objective	0	3	2		
Combined	2	13	25	2.46	>.13
2. Aggression toward E substitute					
Emotional	4	5	18	4.31	>.05
Objective	18	18	7	2.47	>.13
Combined	21	23	25		
3. Aggression toward test					
Emotional	0	8	11		
Objective	4	13	18		
Combined	4	17	25	.95	>.35
4. Aggression toward test substitute					
Emotional	6	5	4		
Objective	24	32	16	3.13	>.09
Combined	26	32	20		
5. Aggression toward individuals other than those included under categories 1 and 2					
Emotional	21	24	24		
Objective	16	22	15		
Combined	28	34	36		

* The p values are based on two-tailed tests of significance.

differences are small and only for Card 18 GF is the mean difference significant. The difference between the two groups in total mean aggression scores based on all four cards is also small but is statistically significant.

The insulted Ss did then express more hostility in fantasy than the noninsulted Ss. This difference is consistent with an interpretation

TABLE 5

Percentage Frequency Distributions of Insult Groups for Scores Based on Categories 1, 2E, and 3 on Sentence Completion Test

AGGRESSION SCORE	INSULT FANTASY ($N = 76$)	INSULT CONTROL ($N = 55$)
0	71	45
1	17	22
2	5	15
>2	7	18

Note: Dichotomizing between 0 and 1, $x^2 = 7.7$; $p < .01$; dichotomizing between 1 and 2, $x^2 = 7.3$; $p < .01$.

TABLE 6

Comparisons Between Insult Fantasy and Noninsult Fantasy Groups on Mean Aggression Ratings on the TAT Stories

PICTURE	NON-INSULT FANTASY	INSULT FANTASY	t	p
4	2.07	2.23	1.0	<.17
18GF	2.09	2.44	2.2	<.02
7BM	1.72	1.89	1.3	<.10
12M	1.95	2.06	0.7	<.25
Total (all 4 pictures)	7.83	8.62	2.1	<.02

of the main findings, reported in the previous section, as due to reduction of aggressive drive by aggressive fantasy.

The relationship between aggression in fantasy and aggression toward E. A negative correlation between aggression in fantasy and subsequent aggression toward E would tend to support the major hypothesis but is not a critical test. A Pearson r was calculated between over-all aggression on the attitude questionnaire and aggression as rated from the TAT fantasies. The correlation for the Insult Fantasy group is $-.25$ and is significant at the .01 level of confidence. The corresponding correlation for the Noninsult Fantasy group is $-.15$ which is not significantly greater than zero. The two correlations are not, however, significantly different from each other. The relationship between aggression in fantasy and subsequent aggression toward E is in a direction, then, which tends to support the hypothesis of a drive-reducing effect of fantasy.

Discussion

THE experimental findings confirm the major prediction based on the drive-reduction hypothesis, namely, that those Ss who were insulted by an E and were given the opportunity to express their aggression in fantasy would subsequently display less hostility toward E than a comparable insulted group which engaged in nonfantasy activities. The fact that two different and independent measures of drive strength, the attitude questionnaire and the Sentence Completion Test, yielded similar results increases confidence in the genuineness of the phenomenon. These measures are different in several important respects. The expression of aggression on the attitude questionnaire was sanctioned for all groups by the instructor, who encouraged the students to reveal their feelings about experiments in which they had been participants. In addition, the range of alternatives to each question gave tacit sanction to the holding of extreme attitudes about E. On the other hand, the Sentence Completion Test involved the spontaneous expression of aggressive feelings toward E despite the knowledge that the test responses would be available to him.

The question arises as to possible alternative explanations of the difference in hostility between the two insulted groups. One might argue that the difference is a result of an increment in hostility in the Control group rather than a decrement in the Fantasy group. Such an increment could conceivably arise from differences in the frustrating qualities of the control and fantasy activities, the former supposedly being more frustrating. An effort was made to control this factor in the experimental design by varying the nature of the nonfantasy task. There is no a priori reason for assuming that the control activities are any more or less demanding than the activity of constructing TAT stories which is presented as an achievement task. Moreover, because the variation of class means in the Insult Control group is very small and the statistical analysis based on class means takes account of the effect of possible differences in the frustrating character of the particular task used in each class, the obtained difference cannot be attributed to an assumed frustrating quality of just one or two of the control tasks.

Any obvious frustration produced by the control activities should be reflected on the measures of aggression. In response to a question on the attitude questionnaire requesting the students to indicate if there was anything about the experiment they disliked, 82 per cent of the Insult Control group and 73 per cent of the Insult Fantasy group expressed dislike of some aspect of the experiment including the E. An analysis of these spontaneous comments revealed that, of those who expressed some criticism, 16 per cent of the Insult Fantasy group criticized the fantasy activity while only 11 per cent of the Insult Control group criticized the control activities.[11] Thus, in addition to the a priori argument, there is no empirical evidence to

11 Even in the Noninsult Fantasy group, 14 per cent of of Ss (33 per cent of those who expressed some dislike of the experiment) criticized the fantasy task. They complained of insufficient time in which to complete the stories and of having to do too much writing.

indicate that the control tasks are more frustrating than the fantasy task.

One must look then to the fantasy activity as the cause of the significant difference in aggression between the Fantasy and Control groups. The most direct explanation of this difference is the reduction of hostility by means of aggressive fantasy. A possible alternative to the drive-reduction hypothesis is one that assumes that guilt and not drive reduction is the primary mechanism responsible for the lowered aggression in the fantasy group. Here it would be supposed that the evocation of aggressive fantasy aroused guilt responses which generalized to subsequent expressions of hostility on the tests of aggression and tended to inhibit aggressive responses on those tests.

The experimental data provide some basis for rejecting the assumption that guilt is the important mediating mechanism. If guilt were the crucial factor, then one would expect the increase in hostile fantasy in the Insult group to be associated with an increase in expression of guilt. The TAT stories were analyzed for indications of guilt in regard to aggressive expression. The difference in expression of guilt between the Insult Fantasy and Noninsult Fantasy groups was slight and insignificant. In addition, the Sentence Completion Test was scored for self-aggressive responses, which might be taken as an index of guilt. The frequency of such responses was very low in all experimental groups, and the small differences among the groups were insignificant.

The drive-reduction hypothesis seems the simplest and also the most suited to account for the differences between the Fantasy and Control groups. A basic assumption underlying this hypothesis is that fantasy expression is a form of behavior that follows the same behavioral principles that have been derived from motor phenomena. Fantasy or imaginative behavior, like other forms of behavior, can serve as a substitute goal response when the most adequate goal response cannot be made. In the present experiment, Ss could not give vent to their hostility directly because of social inhibiting factors, fear of possible punishment from an authority figure,

or lack of adequate opportunity. The Fantasy group Ss, however, were given an opportunity for indirect expression of hostility in their fantasy constructions.

Fantasy responses may acquire reward value, i.e., become drive reducing in at least two ways: (a) through response generalization from direct, overt aggression or (b) through a gradient of reward; if in the past covert aggressive thoughts and wishes preceded and/or accompanied overt aggressive responses which were reinforced, these preceding covert verbal responses may acquire secondary reinforcing properties.

This interpretation is compatible with a more general hypothesis relating verbal behavior and drive reduction which has been developed by Dollard and Miller (4). In explaining various abnormal phenomena such as delusional fantasies, these authors emphasize the reduction of anxiety as the primary reinforcement of the delusional responses. The results of the present study suggest that these delusional responses may also reduce the drive, e.g., aggression, which is eliciting anxiety.

As viewed here, fantasy behavior is an adjustment mechanism which can serve to reduce tensions and provide substitute goal satisfactions. It may function as an outlet for socially unacceptable motives and frustrated achievement strivings. The effects of fantasy are likely to depend on a number of factors such as the particular drive, the type of fantasy, and individual predisposition. For example, one might expect that fantasy behavior would be less effective in reducing such primary drives as pain, hunger, and thirst. Spontaneous fantasy, as in daydreams, may be more effective than induced fantasy, as represented by TAT stories, in reducing motivation. This might occur because, in the former case, the fantasy responses are more similar to those present in the real-life situation. Finally, in some individuals fantasy might conceivably increase rather than decrease drive. Thus rehearsal of undisguised aggressive thoughts might augment the aggressive motives of people who characteristically express their hostility in direct, overt behavior and consequently have not learned to use fantasy as a means of discharging their aggression. The extent of drive reduction produced by fantasy under various circumstances is a problem to be solved by future research.

Summary and Conclusions

THE purpose of this study was to investigate the hypothesis that the expression of aggression in fantasy will serve to partially reduce aggressive drive.

This hypothesis was tested by experimentally inducing aggression by insulting a group of students, interpolating a fantasy or nonfantasy activity, and subsequently measuring the strength of the aggressive drive. Another group was not insulted but was administered the fantasy activity and the subsequent tests of aggression in order to provide a means of validating the measures of aggression used.

The results are consistent with the drive-reduction hypothesis:

1. The insulted group which had an opportunity to express aggression in fantasy subsequently displayed significantly less aggression toward E than did the control group which engaged in nonfantasy activities. This difference was found with two independent and valid measures of aggression.

2. A significant negative correlation was found between the amount of aggression expressed in fantasy and subsequent aggression toward E for the insulted group which had engaged in fantasy.

3. The insulted Ss expressed significantly more aggression in their fantasies than did the noninsulted Ss.

REFERENCES

1. ALLPORT, G. W. *Personality.* New York: Holt, 1937.
2. ATKINSON, J. W., & MCCLELLAND, D. C. The projective expression of needs: II. The effect of different intensities of the hunger drive on thematic apperception. *J. exp. Psychol.,* 1948, 38, 643–658.
3. DEMBO, TAMARA. Anger as a problem of dynamics. In Translations of eight experimental studies in personality directed by Kurt Lewin. Unpublished manuscript, Yale Univer. Library, 1940.
4. DOLLARD, J., & MILLER, N. *Personality and psychotherapy.* New York: McGraw-Hill, 1950.
5. ESCALONA, SIBYLLE. Play and substitute satisfaction. In R. G. Barker, J. S. Kounin, & H. F. Wright (Eds.), *Child behavior and development.* New York: McGraw-Hill, 1943. Pp. 363–378.
6. FREUD, ANNA. *The ego and mechanisms of defense.* New York: International Universities Press, 1946.
7. FREUD, S. The relation of the poet to daydreaming. In *Collected papers.* Vol. IV. London: Hogarth, 1949. Pp. 173–183.
8. LEWIN, K. *A dynamic theory of personality.* New York: McGraw-Hill, 1935.
9. MCCLELLAND, D. C., CLARK, R. A., ROBY, T. B., & ATKINSON, J. W. The projective expression of needs: IV. The effect of the need for achievement on thematic apperception. *J. exp. Psychol.,* 1949, 39, 242–255.
10. MAHLER, W. Studies of the substitute function of different levels of reality. In Translations of eight experimental studies in personality directed by Kurt Lewin. Unpublished manuscript, Yale Univer. Library, 1940.
11. ROTTER, J. B., & WILLERMAN, B. The Incomplete Sentence Test as a method of studying personality. *J. consult. Psychol.,* 1947, 11, 43–48.
12. SYMONDS, P. M. *The dynamics of human adjustment.* New York: D. Appleton-Century, 1946.
13. TOMKINS, S. S. *The Thematic Apperception Test.* New York: Grune & Stratton, 1947.
14. WITTENBORN, J. R., & ERON, L. D. An application of drive theory to TAT responses. *J. consult. Psychol.,* 1951, 15, 45–50.

WILLIAM DEMENT

37. The Effect of Dream Deprivation

ABOUT a year ago, a research program was initiated at the Mount Sinai Hospital which aimed at assessing the basic function and significance of dreaming. The experiments have been arduous and time-consuming and are still in progress. However, the results of the first series have been quite uniform, and because of the length of the program, it has been decided to issue this preliminary report.

In recent years, a body of evidence has accumulated which demonstrates that dreaming occurs in association with periods of rapid, binocularly synchronous eye movements (1–3). Furthermore, the amount and directional patterning of these eye movements and the associated dream *content* are related in such a way as to strongly suggest that the eye movements represent scanning movements made by the dreamer as he watches the events of the dream (3). In a study of undisturbed sleep (4), the eye-movement periods were observed to occur regularly throughout the night in association with the lightest phases of a cyclic variation in depth of sleep, as measured by the electroencephalograph. The length of individual cycles averaged about 90 minutes, and the mean duration of single periods of eye movement was about 20 minutes. Thus, a typical night's sleep includes four or five periods of dreaming, which account for about 20 percent of the total sleep time.

One of the most striking facts apparent in all the works cited above was that a very much greater amount of dreaming occurs normally than had heretofore been realized— greater both from the standpoint of frequency

and duration in a single night of sleep and in the invariability of its occurrence from night to night. In other words, dreaming appears to be an intrinsic part of normal sleep and, as such, although the dreams are not usually recalled, occurs every night in every sleeping person.

A consideration of this aspect of dreaming leads more or less inevitably to the formulation of certain rather fundamental questions. Since there appear to be no exceptions to the nightly occurrence of a substantial amount of dreaming in every sleeping person, it might be asked whether or not this amount of dreaming is in some way a necessary and vital part of our existence. Would it be possible for human beings to continue functioning normally if their dream life were completely or partially suppressed? Should dreaming be considered necessary in a psychological sense or a physiological sense or both?

The obvious attack on these problems was to study subjects who had somehow been deprived of the opportunity to dream. After a few unsuccessful preliminary trials with depressant drugs, it was decided to use the somewhat drastic method of awakening sleeping subjects immediately after the onset of dreaming and to continue this procedure throughout the night, so that each dream period would be artificially terminated right at its beginning.

Subjects and Method

THE data in this article are from the first eight subjects in the research program, all males, ranging in age from 23 to 32. Eye

Reprinted by permission of the American Association for the Advancemenet of Science and the author from *Science*, 1960, vol. 131, pp. 1705–07.

movements and accompanying low-voltage, nonspindling electroencephalographic patterns (4) were used as the objective criteria of dreaming. The technique by which these variables are recorded, and their precise relationship to dreaming, have been extensively discussed elsewhere (2, 4). Briefly, the subjects came to the laboratory at about their usual bedtime. Small silver-disk electrodes were carefully attached near their eyes and on their scalps; then the subjects went to sleep in a quiet, dark room in the laboratory. Lead wires ran from the electrodes to apparatus in an adjacent room upon which the electrical potentials of eye movements and brain waves were recorded continuously throughout the night.

Eye movements and brain waves of each subject were recorded throughout a series of undisturbed nights of sleep, to evaluate his base-line total nightly dream time and over-all sleep pattern. After this, recordings were made throughout a number of nights in which the subject was awakened by the experimenter every time the eye-movement and electroencephalographic recordings indicated that he had begun to dream. These "dream-deprivation" nights were always consecutive. Furthermore, the subjects were requested not to sleep at any other time. Obviously, if subjects were allowed to nap, or to sleep at home on any night in the dream-deprivation period, an unknown amount of dreaming would take place, offsetting the effects of the deprivation. On the first night immediately after the period of dream deprivation, and for several consecutive nights thereafter, the subject was allowed to sleep without disturbance. These nights were designated "recovery nights." The subject then had a varying number of nights off, after which he returned for another series of interrupted nights which exactly duplicated the dream-deprivation series in number of nights and number of awakenings per night. The only difference was that the subject was awakened in the intervals between eye-movement (dream) periods. Whenever a dream period began, the subject was allowed to sleep on without interruption, and was awakened only after the dream had ended spontaneously. Next, the subject had

a number of recovery nights of undisturbed sleep equal to the number of recovery nights in his original dream-deprivation series. Altogether, as many as 20 to 30 all-night recordings were made for each subject, most of them on consecutive nights. Since, for the most part, tests could be made on only one subject at a time, and since a minute-by-minute all-night vigil was required of the experimenter to catch each dream episode immediately at its onset, it can be understood why the experiments have been called arduous and time-consuming.

TABLE 1 summarizes most of the pertinent data. As can be seen, the total number of base-line nights for the eight subjects was 40. The mean sleep time for the 40 nights was 7 hours and 2 minutes, the mean total nightly dream time was 82 minutes, and the mean percentage of dream time (total dream time to total sleep time $\times$ 100) was 19.4. Since total sleep time was not held absolutely constant, percentage figures were routinely calculated as a check on the possibility that differences in total nightly dream time were due to differences in total sleep time. Actually, this is not a plausible explanation for any but quite small differences in dream time, because the range of values for total sleep time for each subject turned out to be very narrow throughout the entire study. When averaged in terms of individuals rather than nights, the means were: total sleep time, 6 hours 50 minutes; total dream time, 80 minutes; percentage of dream time, 19.5; this indicates that the figures were not skewed by the disparate number of base-line nights per subject. The remarkable uniformity of the findings for individual nights is demonstrated by the fact that the standard deviation of the total nightly dream time was only plus or minus 7 minutes.

Progressive Increase in Dream "Attempts"

THE number of consecutive nights of dream deprivation arbitrarily selected as a condition of the study was five. However, one subject left the study in a flurry of obviously contrived excuses after only three nights, and

TABLE 1

Summary of Experimental Results: *TST,* Total Sleep Time; *TDT,* Total Dream Time

MEAN AND RANGE, BASE-LINE NIGHTS			DREAM-DEPRI-VATION NIGHTS	AWAKENINGS		DREAM-DEPRIVATION RECOVERY NIGHTS FIRST NIGHT				FIRST CONTROL RECOVERY NIGHT		
TST	TDT	Per-cent		First Night	Last Night	No.	TST	TDT	Per-cent	TST	TDT	Per-cent
Subject W. T. (4 base-line nights)												
6^h36^m 6^h24^m–6^h48^m	1^h17^m 1^h10^m–1^h21^m	19.5 17.0–21.3	5	8	14	1	6^h43^m	2^h17^m	34.0	6^h50^m	1^h04^m	15.6
Subject H. S. (5 base-line nights)												
7^h27^m 7^h07^m–7^h58^m	1^h24^m 1^h07^m–1^h38^m	18.8 15.4–21.8	7	7	24	2	8^h02^m	2^h45^m	34.2	8^h00^m	1^h49^m	22.7
Subject N. W. (7 base-line nights)												
6^h39^m 5^h50^m–7^h10^m	1^h18^m 1^h11^m–1^h27^m	19.5 17.4–22.4	5	11	30	5	6^h46^m	1^h12^m	17.8	7^h10^m	1^h28^m	20.2
Subject B. M. (6 base-line nights)												
6^h59^m 6^h28^m–7^h38^m	1^h18^m 0^h58^m–1^h35^m	18.6 14.8–22.2	5	7	23	5	7^h25^m	1^h58^m	26.3	7^h48^m	1^h28^m	18.8
Subject R. G. (10 base-line nights)												
7^h26^m 7^h00^m–7^h57^m	1^h26^m 1^h13^m–1^h46^m	19.3 16.9–22.7	5	10	20	5	7^h14^m	2^h08^m	29.5	7^h18^m	1^h55^m	26.3
Subject W. D. (4 base-line nights)												
6^h29^m 5^h38^m–7^h22^m	1^h21^m 1^h08^m–1^h32^m	20.8 17.8–23.4	4	13	20	3	8^h53^m	2^h35^m	29.0			
Subject S. M. (2 base-line nights)												
6^h41^m 6^h18^m–7^h04^m	1^h12^m 1^h01^m–1^h23^m	17.9 16.2–19.3	4	22	30	6	5^h08^m 6^h32^m*	1^h01^m 1^h50^m*	19.8 28.1*	6^h40^m	1^h07^m	16.8
Subject W. G. (2 base-line nights)												
6^h16^m 6^h08^m–6^h24^m	1^h22^m 1^h17^m–1^h27^m	20.8 20.7–20.9	3	9	13							

* Second recovery night (see text).

two subjects insisted on stopping after four nights but consented to continue with the recovery nights and the remainder of the schedule. One subject was pushed to seven nights. During each awakening the subjects were required to sit up in bed and remain fully awake for several minutes. On the first nights of dream deprivation, the return to sleep generally initiated a new sleep cycle, and the next dream period was postponed for the expected amount of time. However, on subsequent nights the number of forced awakenings required to suppress dreaming steadily mounted. Or, to put it another way, there was a progressive increase in the number of attempts to dream. The number of awakenings required on the first and last nights of deprivation are listed in TABLE 1. *All* the subjects showed this progressive increase, although there was considerable variation in the starting number and the amount of the increase. An important point is that each awakening was preceded by a minute or two of dreaming. This represented the time required for the experimenter to judge the emerging record and make the decision to awaken the subject after he first noticed the beginning of eye movements. In some cases the time was a little longer, as when an eye-movement period started while the experimenter was looking away from the recording apparatus. It is apparent from this that the method employed did not constitute absolute dream deprivation but, rather, about a 65- to 75-percent deprivation, as it turned out.

Nightly Dream Time Elevated after Deprivation

THE data on the first night of the dream-deprivation recovery period are summarized for each subject in TABLE 1. As was mentioned, one subject had quit the study. The mean total dream time on the first recovery night was 112 minutes, or 26.6 percent of the total mean sleep time. If the results for two subjects who did not show marked increases on the first recovery night are excluded, the mean dream time is 127 minutes or 29 percent, which represents a 50-percent increase over the group base-line mean. For all seven subjects together, on the first recovery night the increase in percentage of dream time over the base-line mean (TABLE 1, col. 3, mean percentage figures; col. 10, first recovery night percentages) was significant at the $p < .05$ level in a one-tail Wilcoxin matched-pairs signed-ranks test (5).

It is important to mention, however, that one (S.M. in TABLE 1) of the two subjects alluded to above as exceptions was not really an exception because, although he had only 1 hour 1 minute of dreaming on his first recovery night, he showed a marked increase on *four* subsequent nights. His failure to show a rise on the first recovery night was in all likelihood due to the fact that he had imbibed several cocktails at a party before coming to the laboratory so that the expected increase in dream time was offset by the depressing effect of the alcohol. The other one of the two subjects (N.W. in TABLE 1) failed to show a significant increase in dream time on any of five consecutive recovery nights and therefore must be considered the single exception to the over-all results. Even so, it is hard to reconcile his lack of increase in dream time on recovery nights with the fact that during the actual period of dream deprivation he showed the largest build-up in number of awakenings required to suppress dreaming (eleven to thirty) of any subject

in this group. One may only suggest that, although he was strongly affected by the dream loss, he could not increase his dream time on recovery nights because of an unusually stable basic sleep cycle that resisted modification.

The number of consecutive recovery nights for each subject in this series of tests was too small in some cases, mainly because it was naively supposed at the beginning of the study that an increase in dream time, if it occurred, would last only one or two nights. One subject had only one recovery night, another two, and another three. The dream time was markedly elevated above the base-line on all these nights. For how many additional nights each of these three subjects would have maintained an elevation in dream time can only be surmised in the absence of objective data. All of the remaining four subjects had five consecutive recovery nights. One was the single subject who showed no increase, two were nearing the base-line dream time by the fifth night, and one still showed marked elevation in dream time. From this admittedly incomplete sample it appears that about five nights of increased dreaming usually follow four or five nights of dream suppression achieved by the method of this study.

Effect Not Due to Awakening

SIX of the subjects underwent the series of control awakenings—that is, awakenings during non-dream periods. This series exactly duplicated the dream-deprivation series for each subject in number of nights, total number of awakenings, and total number of awakenings per successive night. The dream time on these nights was slightly below base-line levels as a rule. The purpose of this series was, of course, to see if the findings following dream deprivation were solely an effect of the multiple awakenings. Data for the first recovery nights after nights of control awakenings are included in TABLE 1. There was no significant increase for the group. The mean dream time was 88 minutes, and the mean percentage was 20.1. Subsequent recovery nights in this series also failed to show the marked rise in dream time that was observed after nights of dream deprivation. A moderate increase found on four out of a total of 24 recovery nights for the individuals in the control-awakening group was felt to be a response to the slight reduction in dream time on control-awakening nights.

Behavioral Changes

PSYCHOLOGICAL disturbances such as anxiety, irritability, and difficulty in concentrating developed during the period of dream deprivation, but these were not catastrophic. One subject, as was mentioned above, quit the study in an apparent panic, and two subjects insisted on stopping one night short of the goal of five nights of dream deprivation, presumably because the stress was too great. At least one subject exhibited serious anxiety and agitation. Five subjects developed a marked increase in appetite during the period of dream deprivation; this observation was supported by daily weight measurements

which showed a gain in weight of 3 to 5 pounds in three of the subjects. The psychological changes disappeared as soon as the subjects were allowed to dream. The most important fact was that *none* of the observed changes were seen during the period of control awakenings.

The results have been tentatively interpreted as indicating that a certain amount of dreaming each night is a necessity. It is as though a pressure to dream builds up with the accruing dream deficit during successive dream-deprivation nights—a pressure which is first evident in the increasing frequency of attempts to dream and then, during the recovery period, in the marked increase in total dream time and percentage of dream time. The fact that this increase may be maintained over four or more successive recovery nights suggests that there is a more or less quantitative compensation for the deficit. It is possible that if the dream suppression were carried on long enough, a serious disruption of the personality would result.

REFERENCES AND NOTES

1. E. ASERINSKY AND N. KLEITMAN, *J. Appl. Physiol.* 8, 1 (1955); W. Dement and E. Wolpert, *J. Nervous Mental Disease* 126, 568 (1958); D. Goodenough, A. Shapiro, M. Holden, L. Steinschriber, *J. Abnormal Social Psychol.* 59, 295 (1959); E. Wolpert and H. Trosman, *A.M.A. Arch. Neurol. Psychiat.* 79, 603 (1958).

2. W. DEMENT, *J. Nervous Mental Disease* 122, 263 (1955).

3. ——— AND N. KLEITMAN, *J. Exptl. Psychol.* 53, 339 (1957); W. Dement and E. Wolpert, *ibid.* 55, 543 (1958).

4. W. DEMENT AND N. KLEITMAN, *Electroencephalog. and Clin. Neurophysiol.* 9, 673 (1957).

5. S. SIEGEL, *Nonparametric Statistics for the Behavioral Sciences* (McGraw-Hill, New York, 1956).

SECTION VIII

Personality

IT IS a well-known paradox that people are, at the same time, very much the same and yet strikingly different. Their differences arise partly from the uniqueness of each individual's personality structure, which is determined by the interaction of his particular hereditary tendencies with environmental and social influences. The articles in this section represent typical attempts by psychologists to discover, first, just how personality traits are established, and, second, what methods can best be used for personality assessment.

The first two selections, "The Genetic Theory of Schizophrenia" by Franz J. Kallmann and "Heredity in the Functional Psychoses" by Ralph Rosenberg, concern the inheritance of psychoses. Kallmann, using the twin family method, found that true schizophrenia does not develop under normal conditions unless a predisposition to it has been inherited by a person from both parents; furthermore, a person's chances of developing schizophrenia increase in proportion to the degree of his blood relationship to a schizophrenic. Rosenberg reviews the four methods available for determining the influence of heredity: Galton's family history method, Mendel's method, the combination method, and the study of the mental status of twins. He finds the first three fallacious or irrelevant to the study of functional psychoses; the results obtained through use of the fourth, he says, indicate that environment may indeed play a larger role in the development of such psychoses than heredity does.

"The Achievement Syndrome" by Bernard C. Rosen illustrates how environment can influence personality development. Rosen suggests that the reason upward mobility is greater in the middle than in the lower classes may be that, because of parental encouragement, children in the middle class tend to have more achievement motivation (the internal impetus to excel) and to value behavior aimed at achievement more highly than children in the lower class.

In assessing personality, psychologists must decide both what kinds of tests to use and how to interpret the results. In "Exploring the Psychoanalytic Theory of the 'Oral Character,'" Gerald S. Blum and Daniel R. Miller examine the feasibility of testing psychonanalytic theory through conventional psychological methods. They tested hypotheses concerning oral behavior in a group of eight-year-olds and concluded that the overall results hold promise for the investigation of psychoanalytic theory through traditional techniques.

Douglas N. Jackson and Samuel Messick point out in "Content and Style in Personality Assessment" that how a person responds to a certain test item is as important as what his response is. Some people are inclined to be overly acquiescent, to overgeneralize, or to respond in socially desirable ways; others tend in *opposite directions. These different "styles" account for a large proportion of the response variation on several of the standard personality scales, indicating that it is important to design assessment techniques which will evoke important styles of response. In this way the style as well as the content of the responses may be included in the picture the test provides of a subject's personality.*

FRANZ J. KALLMANN

38. *The Genetic Theory of Schizophrenia*

DESPITE notable changes in the attitude of contemporary psychiatry toward the constitutional problems of psychosomatic medicine, there is still a tendency to perpetuate the genetic theory of schizophrenia as a controversial issue.

Some arguments thrive largely on dialectic grounds and, from a scientific standpoint, are more apparent than real. Others are based on preconceptions which are kept alive by an ambiguous terminology and the pardonable tendency either to oversimplify a complex causality or to mistake it for obscurity. A main source of misunderstanding is the erroneous belief that acceptance of causation by heredity would be incompatible with general psychological theories of a descriptive or analytical nature, or that it might lead to a depreciation of present educational and therapeutic standards. Evidently, there is no point in presenting evidence of the inheritance of schizophrenia, if in subsequent statements the etiology of schizophrenic psychoses is likely to be listed as unknown, or if reservations are made regarding a similar psychotic syndrome labeled dementia praecox, or if the given genetic mechanism is finally dismissed as unessential or non-Mendelian.

From a genetic point of view, the main question to be clarified is whether or not the capacity for developing a true schizophrenic psychosis is somehow controlled by inherited, predispositional elements. In order to settle this problem beyond any reasonable doubt, only three types of investigative procedure are available. They are:

1. The pedigree or family history method,
2. The contingency method of statistical prediction, and
3. The twin study method.

The investigation of individual *family histories* is the oldest, simplest, and most popular method of recording familial occurrence of an apparently hereditary trait. Such a pedigree is often impressive to behold and sometimes as suggestive of the operation of heredity as is true with respect to the family unit presented in FIG. 1. If the mating of two psychotic parents is found, under certain circumstances, to be capable of giving rise to seven definite cases of schizophrenia among the offspring, that is, in all the children of this union who reached the age of maturity, it would seem inadequate to disregard the possible significance of the biological factor prerequisite for inheritance, namely, consanguinity. On the basis of this single observation, however, the genetic hypothesis would be no more conclusive than either the assumption of *folie à neuf* due to "psychic contagion" or the supposition that the psychosis of the father of this remarkable sibship was not "inherited" because his parents had apparently been ordinary first cousins without schizophrenia.

Obviously, the general usefulness of the pedigree method is limited to the study of relatively rare unit characters which are easily traced and fairly constant in their clinical appearance. In more common traits and especially in irregularly expressed anomalies such

Address read at the 102nd annual meeting of the American Psychiatric Association, Chicago, Ill., May 27–30, 1946. Reprinted by permission of the American Psychiatric Association and the author from *American Journal of Psychiatry*, 1946, vol. 9, pp. 309–22.

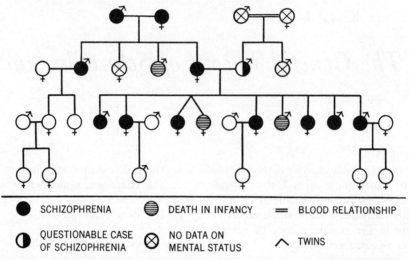

| ● SCHIZOPHRENIA | ⊜ DEATH IN INFANCY | = BLOOD RELATIONSHIP |
| ◐ QUESTIONABLE CASE OF SCHIZOPHRENIA | ⊗ NO DATA ON MENTAL STATUS | ∧ TWINS |

FIG. 1. Pedigree of a family showing unusual accumulation of schizophrenic cases.

as schizophrenia, it is necessary to employ statistical methods which demonstrate more clearly the effect of blood relationship.

This objective is accomplished by the *contingency method,* which compares the morbidity rates for representative samples of consanguineous and non-consanguineous groups. The results of such a procedure will indicate whether or not a given anomaly occurs more frequently in blood relatives of unselected index cases than is to be expected in the light of the normal average distribution of the trait in the general population. The available morbidity figures for schizophrenia, obtained with the contingency method, are summarized in TABLE 1. The rates refer to different population and consanguinity groups and may have been compiled with different degrees of statistical accuracy. The samples differ in size as well as in uniformity, and many of them seem to have lived under socioeconomic conditions which cannot be compared directly.

However, one essential point has been confirmed by all of these studies, namely, that the incidence of schizophrenia tends to be higher in blood relatives of schizophrenic index cases than it is in the general population. Concerning the offspring of schizophrenic index cases it has been shown that their morbidity rates range from 16.4 to 68.1

per cent, that is, from nineteen to about eighty times average expectancy, according to whether one or both of their parents are schizophrenic (FIG. 2). It is to be verified, therefore, that the chance of developing schizophrenia in comparable environments increases in direct proportion to the degree of blood relationship to a schizophrenic index case. If such evidence can be supplied, intransigent supporters of purely environmental theories should be expected to demonstrate with equally precise methods that a consistent increase in morbidity is found associated with particular environmental circumstances *in the absence* of consanguinity.

In order to establish the hereditary nature of a psychosis beyond the possibility of random contingency and in relation to the interaction of predispositional genetic elements and various precipitating or perpetuating influences acting from without, the best available procedure is the *twin study method* in conjunction with an ordinary sibling study. Such a combination method [1] has been adopted in our long-range studies of specific

[1] A more detailed description of the method can be found in a previous report of F. J. Kallmann and D. Reisner, "Twin Studies on Genetic Variations in Resistance to Tuberculosis," *Journal of Heredity,* Vol. 34, No. 9.

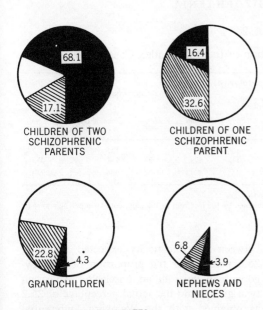

CHILDREN OF TWO
SCHIZOPHRENIC
PARENTS

68.1

17.1

CHILDREN OF ONE
SCHIZOPHRENIC
PARENT

16.4

32.6

GRANDCHILDREN

22.8

4.3

NEPHEWS AND
NIECES

6.8

3.9

GENERAL POPULATION RATES:

■ SCHIZOPHRENIA = 0.85 PER CENT

▨ SCHIZOID PERSONALITY = 2.9 PER CENT

FIG. 2. Expectation of schizophrenia and schizoid personality in descendants of schizophrenics.

STEP-SIBLINGS   HALF-SIBLINGS   SIBLINGS

OPPOSITE-SEXED   SAME-SEXED   MONOZYGOTIC
DIZYGOTIC TWINS   DIZYGOTIC TWINS   TWINS

FIG. 3. Degree of consanguinity in twin family method.

behavior disorders and has been called by us "Twin Family Method" (FIG. 3). This approach provides six distinct categories of sibship groups reared under comparable environmental conditions; namely, monozygotic twins, dizygotic twins of the same sex, dizygotic twins of opposite sex, full siblings, half-siblings, and step-siblings. If the assumed genetic factor exists and the part played by the twinning factor is negligible, the statistical expectation will be that the morbidity rates for full siblings and dizygotic twin partners should be about the same, but they should clearly differ from the rates for the other sibship groups.

One-egg twins are expected to show the highest concordance rate for a genetically determined disorder, even if brought up in different environments. Two-egg twins may be either of the same or of opposite sex, but genetically they are no more alike than any other pair of brothers and sisters who are born at different times. Half-siblings with only one parent in common should be about midway between the full siblings and the non-consanguineous step-siblings, if the given morbidity depends on the closeness of blood

TABLE 1

Schizophrenia Rates Obtained with the Contingency Method of Statistical Prediction

	INCIDENCE OF SCHIZOPHRENIA IN GENERAL POPULATION	INCIDENCE OF SCHIZOPHRENIA IN CONSANGUINEOUS GROUPS RELATED TO:										
		One ordinary index case of schizophrenia							Two ordinary index cases		One twin index case	
		Nephews and nieces	First cousins	Grand-children	Half-siblings	Parents	Full siblings	Children	Siblings	Children	Di-zygotic cotwins	Mono-zygotic cotwins
Previous morbidity studies of Kallmann	.85	3.9		4.3	7.6	10.3	11.5	16.4	20.5	68.1	12.5	81.7
Range of morbidity rates of other investigators	.3–1.5	1.4–3.9	2.6			7.1–9.3	4.5–11.7	8.3–9.7	20.0	53.0	14.9	68.3

TABLE 2

Racial and Diagnostic Distribution of the Twin Index Cases

| | ALL SCHIZOPHRENIC TWIN INDEX CASES REPORTED * | | | | | | | ALL COMPLETE INDEX PAIRS STUDIED † | | | |
| | Marital status | | Racial distribution | | Diagnostic distribution | | | | Dizygotic | | |
	Single	Married	White	Non-white	Nuclear	Periph-eral	Total number	Mono-zygotic	Same sex	Opposite sex	Total number
Male	292	70	337	25	253	109	362	75	132	22½	317½
Female	266	166	405	27	290	142	432	99	164	22½	373½
Total number	558	236	742	52	543	251	794	174	296	221	691

* Without index cases whose cotwins were unavailable at the age of 15 years.
† The difference between 794 index cases and 691 index pairs is explained by the fact that in 103 pairs both twin partners were reported as index cases and acceptable as such.

relationship rather than on the similarity in environment.

In order to obtain statistically representative material for the application of this method, our survey was organized on a state-wide basis. The twin index cases (TABLE 2) were collected from the resident populations and new admissions of all mental hospitals under the supervision of the New York State Department of Mental Hygiene. The danger of bias on account of technical selective factors in the sampling of the material was avoided by referring the determination of the twin index cases to the staffs of the hospitals cooperating in the survey. The only criteria for selection were that the reported cases be born by multiple birth and that they had been admitted with a diagnosis of mental disease.

The classifications of both schizophrenia and zygosity were made on the basis of personal investigation and extended observation. The twin diagnosis was based on findings obtained with the similarity method, since it is known now that monozygotic twins are not necessarily monochorial. The statistical analysis was limited to the families of 794 schizophrenic twin index cases whose cotwins were available for examination at the age of fifteen years. These index cases were reported within a period of nine years by twenty institutions, which in 1945 had a total resident population of 73,252 patients with 47,929 schizophrenics and 12,316 new admissions.

The random sampling of the 691 index pairs is indicated by the close correspondence between the statistically expected figure of 25.6 percent for the proportion of monozygotic twin pairs in an unselected American twin group, and the actual percentage of 25.2 as obtained with the Weinberg Differential Method for the present study. It is in accordance with expectation that the main deficit is on the part of dizygotic twins of opposite sex. Altogether, there are 174 monozygotic and 517 dizygotic index pairs with schizophrenia in at least one member or, more precisely, 691 pairs constituted by 1,382 twins, of whom 794 were legitimate index cases. Of the dizygotic sets, 296 are same-sexed and 221 are opposite-sexed.

The excess of female over male index cases is almost 20 percent. The ratio of white to non-white index cases is about 14:1. Approximately 70 percent of the index cases are unmarried. The proportion of nuclear cases, characterized by hebephrenic or catatonic psychoses with the tendency to progression and deterioration, amounts to 68 percent.

The various groups of relatives included in the analysis of these 691 twin index families are identified in TABLE 3. There are 1,382 twins, 2,741 full siblings, 134 half-siblings, 74 step-siblings, 1,191 parents and 254 marriage partners of twin patients, making a total of 5,776 persons who have been uniformly classified according to their mental, social and genealogical conditions.

The collective schizophrenia rates for the different relationship groups are compared in TABLE 4. The variations in age distribution have been corrected by the use of the

TABLE 3

Number and Relationship of the Persons Included in the Survey

	TWINS	FULL SIBLINGS	HALF-SIBLINGS	STEP-SIBLINGS	PARENTS	HUSBANDS AND WIVES OF INDEX CASES	TOTAL NUMBER
Living	1,198	1,682	84	47	618	221	3,850
Dead	184	1,059	50	27	573	33	1,926
Total number	1,382	2,741	134	74	1,191	254	5,776

"Abridged Weinberg Method." The resulting morbidity rates are average expectancy figures valid for persons above the chief manifestation period, which in this study was assumed to extend from the age of fifteen to forty-four.

Regardless of whether the uncorrected or corrected rates are taken into account, they are in definite accordance with genetic expectation regarding both schizophrenia and schizoid personality. The corrected schizophrenia rate for full siblings amounts to 14.3 percent, corresponding closely with the collective concordance rate for dizygotic twin pairs (14.7 percent), although it clearly exceeds the rate for half-siblings (7.0 percent). A comparison with our previous sibship figures reveals only minor variations which seem sufficiently explained by the different sampling procedures of sibship and descent studies. Our previous schizophrenia rates

were 7.6 percent for half-siblings, 11.5 percent for full siblings, and 12.5 percent for dizygotic cotwins.

The newly obtained morbidity figures for step-siblings and marriage partners of schizophrenic index cases are 1.8 and 2.1 percent, respectively, showing a small excess over the general population rate of 0.85 per cent. So far as this excess is statistically significant, it is referable to the effect of mate selection rather than an expression of socially induced insanity.

By contrast, the difference in concordance between two-egg and one-egg twin partners ranges from 14.7 to 85.8 percent. An almost equally striking difference remains, if the comparison is limited to the groups of same-sexed dizygotic and separated monozygotic twin pairs (FIG. 4). Their morbidity rates vary from 17.6 to 77.6 percent, and this difference is still so pronounced that explana-

TABLE 4

Incidence of Schizophrenia and Schizoid Personality in the Twin Index Families

	RELATIONSHIP TO SCHIZOPHRENIC TWIN INDEX CASES						
	Parents	Husbands and wives	Step-siblings	Half-siblings	Full siblings	Dizygotic cotwins	Monozygotic cotwins
Statistically uncorrected rates							
Number of persons	1191	254	85	134	2741	517	174
Cases of schizophrenia	108	5	1	4	205	53	120
Incidence of schizophrenia *	9.1	2.0	1.4	4.5	10.2	10.3	69.0
Corrected morbidity rates							
Schizophrenia †	9.2	2.1	1.8	7.0	14.3	14.7	85.8
Schizoid personality	34.8	3.1	2.7	12.5	31.5	23.0	20.7

* Related to all cases of schizophrenia and to all persons over age 15.
† Related only to definite cases of schizophrenia and to half of the persons in the age group 15–44 (plus all persons over age 44).

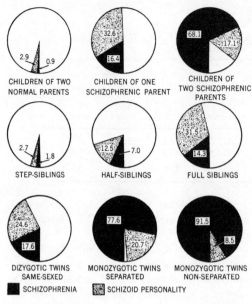

FIG. 4. Expectancy of schizophrenia and schizoid personality in blood relatives of schizophrenic twin index cases.

tions on non-genetic grounds are very difficult to uphold. The total morbidity distribution as summarized in FIG. 4 is a rather clear indication that the chance of developing schizophrenia increases in proportion to the degree of consanguinity to a schizophrenic index case. The only other syndrome showing a significant increase in the index families is that of schizoid personality changes, whose genetically heterogeneous nature has been discussed in previous reports.

Concerning the total morbidity rate of 85.8 percent for monozygotic cotwins it should be borne in mind that the figure expresses the chance of developing schizophrenia in a comparable environment for any person that has survived the age of forty-four and is genetically identical with a schizophrenic index case, but is not distinguished by the fact of having been selected as the child of such an index case. The last point needs particular emphasis, since it apparently explains the difference between the morbidity rates of 68.1 and 85.8 percent as found for the children of two schizophrenic parents and for the monozygotic cotwins of schizophrenic index cases, respectively. In fact, it is only by a

comparison of these two figures that a satisfactory estimate can be obtained of the extent of biased sampling in a morbidity study dealing with children of schizophrenic index cases. In order to provide such a sample, schizophrenics must have had a chance of getting married and producing offspring.

According to our previous fertility studies (FIG. 5), the total reproductive rate of schizophrenic index cases is not more than about half that of a comparable general population. However, the decrease in fertility is much more pronounced in the nuclear group of schizophrenia, comprising the deteriorating types of hebephrenia and catatonia, than it is in the paranoid and simple cases. The consequence is that milder schizophrenic cases have a better chance of reproducing a schizophrenic child than have the more severe cases. If the children of one schizophrenic parent will often be the offspring of patients with lessened severity of their symptoms, the children of two schizophrenic parents may be expected to represent an even greater selection of potential schizophrenics in the direction of a highly resistant constitution. Obviously, such a process of natural selection does not operate in persons who have only the distinction of being the monozygotic cotwins of schizophrenic twin index cases.

Clinically it is very important that neither the offspring of two schizophrenic parents nor the monozygotic cotwins of schizophrenic index cases have a morbidity rate of 100 percent as would be expected theoretically in regard to a strictly hereditary trait. This observation indicates a limited expressivity of the main genetic factor controlling schizophrenia, but it should not be misinterpreted in the sense that the extent of the deficit is an adequate measure of the part played by non-genetic agents in the production of a schizophrenic psychosis. From a biological standpoint, the finding classifies schizophrenia as both preventable and potentially curable. The implication is that the main schizophrenic genotype is not fully expressed either in the absence of any particular factor of a precipitating nature or in the presence of strong constitutional defense mechanisms which in turn are partially determined by

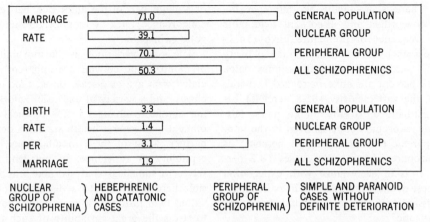

FIG. 5. Marriage and birth rates of schizophrenic hospital patients.

heredity. The statistical difference between observed and expected morbidity rates for unquestionably homozygous carriers of the schizophrenic genotype does not mean, however, that heredity is effective in only 70 to 85 percent of schizophrenic cases, or that it is essential merely to the extent of 70 to 85 percent in any one case.

In order to exclude the possibility that the entire difference in morbidity between monozygotic and dizygotic cotwins might be sufficiently *explained by factors other than genetic,* it is necessary to analyze the morbidity rates for the various sibship groups in relation to any developmental or environmental circumstances peculiar to twins and siblings. In this evaluation of significant similarities and dissimilarities in the life conditions of various relationship groups in our index families, a credible explanation should be sought especially for a finding which is never accounted for by exponents of purely "cultural" theories of schizophrenia. This rather striking observation is that over 85 percent of our groups of siblings and dizygotic cotwins did *not* develop schizophrenia, although about 10 percent of them had a schizophrenic parent, all of them had a schizophrenic brother or sister, and a large proportion shared the same environment with these schizophrenics before and after birth.

For anatomical reasons, prematurity of birth, instrumental delivery and reversal in handedness are more common in twins than in single-born individuals. It is shown in TABLE 5, however, that no one of these factors has any bearing on the occurrence of schizophrenia in persons who happen to be

TABLE 5

Handedness and Instrumental Delivery in the Twin Index Pairs

| | SIMILARITY OF DELIVERY AND HANDEDNESS IN TWIN PARTNERS | | | | | DISSIMILARITY OF INSTRUMENTAL DELIVERY AND HANDEDNESS IN TWIN PARTNERS | | | |
| | | | | | | Instrumental delivery in: | | Left-handedness in: | |
	Normal delivery	Pre-mature birth	Instru-mental delivery	Right-handed-ness	Left-handed-ness	Schizo-phrenic twin	Non-schizo-phrenic twin	Schizo-phrenic twin	Non-schizo-phrenic twin
Both twin partners schizophrenic	79.6	14.3	4.1	72.1	2.5	2.0		25.5 *	
One twin partner schizophrenic	76.2	15.4	4.2	81.8	0.9	2.4	1.8	8.2	9.1
All twin index pairs	77.1	15.1	4.2	67.4	1.2	2.3	1.3	12.9	6.6

* Of 41 twin pairs in whom only one of the two schizophrenic twin partners was found to be left-handed, 33 pairs were monozygotic.

twins. There is practically no difference between concordant and discordant twin pairs in the frequency of premature birth (14.3–15.4 percent) or of instrumental delivery (4.1–4.2 percent). In discordant index pairs, over 82 percent are alike in regard to handedness, the vast majority (81.8 percent) being right-handed. In the unlike pairs, left-handedness occurs about as often in the non-schizophrenic twin partners (9.1 percent) as in schizophrenic twin index cases (8.2 percent). It is in accordance with expectation that most of the concordant twin pairs showing dissimilarity as to left-handedness are monozygotic.

The collective morbidity rates for the cotwins are modified by a variety of secondary factors, genetic as well as non-genetic, but certainly not to an extent which would explain the marked difference between the two types of twins. Variation in relation to the sex factor cannot exist in monozygotic twin pairs and is of equally limited extent in the groups of siblings and dizygotic twins. The range of the former group is from 12.3 to 16.1 percent, and that of the latter group from 10.3 to 17.6 percent (TABLE 6). The difference in morbidity remains constant regardless of whether the siblings and cotwins are male or female. This sex variation is an indication that fraternals belonging to the same sex as a given index case have a greater chance of being alike in any particular circumstances which may favor the manifestation of the schizophrenic genotype. It is clear, however, that these sex variations are by no means extensive enough to permit a non-genetic explanation for the entire difference,

or a major part of the difference, between the concordance rates of monozygotic and dizygotic twin pairs.

The main variations in the morbidity rate of monozygotic cotwins are apparently associated with age at disease onset, type of psychosis, and a variety of extrinsic factors causing significant changes in the physical development and general health status of one twin partner. Most of these modifications in susceptibility or resistance do not lend themselves to statistical analysis, and it is impossible here to enter into a discussion of individual twin histories. It is essential, however, to stress the great variability of such contingent influences, because it is this point which makes the etiology of schizophrenic processes so complex and a carefully adapted program of constructive therapeutic measures so important. Many of our twin histories indicate that incidental factors such as pregnancy, intercurrent disease, or a reducing diet which may have been responsible for the crucial difference between health and psychosis in one twin pair, will not have the same vital effect in others.

The morbidity rate for monozygotic cotwins varies from 77.6 to 91.5 percent for those twin partners who were or were not separated for over five years prior to disease onset in the index twin (TABLE 7). It has already been emphasized that this statistical difference is no adequate expression of the relative effect of extraneous circumstances on the development of schizophrenia in genetically alike persons. Separation is no exact measure of dissimilarity in regard to environmental agents precipitating schizo-

TABLE 6

Variations in the Schizophrenia Rates of Siblings and Twin Partners
According to Sex and the Similarity or Dissimilarity in Environment

| | SIBLINGS OF TWIN INDEX CASES | | | DIZYGOTIC COTWINS | | | MONOZYGOTIC COTWINS | | |
	Male	Female	Total number	Male	Female	Total number	Separated	Non-separated	Total number
Same-sexed	15.9	16.3	16.1	17.4	17.7	17.6	77.6	91.5	85.8
Opposite-sexed	12.5	12.0	12.3	10.5	10.2	10.3			
Total number	14.0	14.5	14.3	14.3	14.9	14.7	77.6	91.5	85.8

TABLE 7

Concordance as to Schizophrenia in Separated and Non-Separated Pairs of
Monozygotic Twins

	SEPARATED * PAIRS	NON-SEPARATED PAIRS	TOTAL NUMBER
Number of cotwins	59	115	174
Corrected morbidity rate of cotwins	77.6	91.5	85.8

* Separated for five years or more prior to the onset of schizophrenia in the index twin.

phrenia. There are numerous factors of potential etiological significance, which are practically universal. In fact, our group of separated one-egg pairs includes twins who developed schizophrenia at almost the same time, although their separation took place soon after birth and led to apparently very different life conditions.

Conversely, even with similar environment it cannot be expected that the time of onset of a schizophrenic psychosis in genetically identical persons will be exactly the same. It is shown in TABLE 8 that simultaneous occurrence of schizophrenia is found in only 17.6 percent of monozygotic twin pairs. In about one-half of the index pairs (52.9 percent) there is a difference of one month to four years, and in over one-quarter the difference may be from four to twelve years. Psychobiologically it is of interest to note that significant dissimilarities in symptomatology are observed only in twin partners who show a definite variation in age of onset.

The age discrepancies between twin partners remain about the same if the comparison is based on the dates of first admission. The average age at disease onset is 22.1 years for the index twins, and 25.6 years for the cotwins.

There are also certain differences in the period of time during which either the twin partners were under observation before they were classified as concordant or discordant as to schizophrenia, or during which the concordant pairs had been separated before the index twins developed their psychosis. A glance at TABLE 9 will reveal, however, that these differences are entirely insufficient to explain the variations in morbidity between one-egg and two-egg types of twins. The separated concordant twins had lived apart for an average of 11.8 years before disease onset in the first twin, and the discordant index pairs had reached a total average age of thirty-three years at the time of their examination for this survey. All categories of cotwins had at that time been discordant for over eight years since the development of schizophrenia in the index cases.

It is more significant that similarity and dissimilarity of environment are almost equally

TABLE 8

Variations in the Average Age at Disease Onset and First Admission of the
Monozygotic Twin Index Pairs Concordant as to Schizophrenia

	AVERAGE AGE IN YEARS			PERCENTAGE OF TWIN PAIRS SHOWING DIFFERENCES IN AGE AT ONSET OF SCHIZOPHRENIA					
	First twin	Second twin	Difference between twin partners	No difference	0.1–4 years	4.1–8 years	8.1–12 years	12.1–16 years	16.1–20 years
Onset of disease	22.1	25.6	3.5	17.6	52.9	18.6	10.8		
First admission	26.0	30.3	4.3	26.5	38.2	21.6	7.8	3.9	2.0

TABLE 9

Distribution of Concordance and Discordance in Twin Index Pairs in Relation to Disease Onset and Environment

	NUMBER OF INDEX PAIRS		AVERAGE DURATION IN YEARS		DISCORDANT PAIRS IN PERCENT	
	Concordant	Discordant	Separation in concordant pairs	Discordance in concordant pairs	With similar environment	With dissimilar environment
Monozygotic	120	54	11.1	8.5	61.1	38.9
Dizygotic same-sexed	34	262	12.9	12.5	57.3	42.7
Dizygotic	13	208	13.8	11.1	50.5	49.5
opposite-sexed	167	524	11.8	11.5	5.50	45.0

distributed among the discordant index pairs. The ratio for all discordant pairs is 5.5:4.5, and that for monozygotic pairs alone is 6:4.

Additional evidence against a simple correlation between closeness of blood relationship and increasing similarity in environment with correspondingly intensified pressure toward development of a psychosis is obtained by an investigation of the distribution of concordance and discordance in similar and dissimilar environments in both groups of index pairs (TABLE 10). This analysis indicates that 22.4 percent of all monozygotic pairs are concordant without similar environment, and that 49.3 percent of all dizygotic twin partners remain discordant although they have been exposed to the same environment as an index case.

It may be of some interest that the concordance rate of monozygotic pairs varies from 65.0 to 71.1 percent according to dissimilarity or similarity of environment, while there is no corresponding increase in the dizygotic group (10.8–7.6 percent). There can be no doubt, however, that any such variation in relation to environment does not suffice to explain a ratio of 1:6 or 14.7:85.8 percent, as has been obtained for the morbidity rates of dizygotic and monozygotic twin partners.

That heredity determines the individual capacity for development and control of a schizophrenic psychosis is demonstrated still more clearly, if the similarities in extent and outcome of the disease are taken as further criteria of comparison. This is the objective of the remaining tabulations (TABLES 11 and 12 and FIG. 6) which compare the cotwin

TABLE 10

Relationship between Similarity or Dissimilarity in Environment and Concordance or Discordance as to Schizophrenia in the Twin Index Pairs

	COTWINS WITH SIMILAR ENVIRONMENT			COTWINS WITH DISSIMILAR ENVIRONMENT				ALL COTWINS Rate of cotwins in percent:	
	Number of cotwins	Rate of cotwins in percent:		Number of cotwins	Rate of cotwins in percent:		Total number	Concordant with dissimilar environment	Discordant with similar environment
		Concordant	Discordant		Concordant	Discordant			
Monozygotic	114	71.1	28.9	60	65.0	35.0	174	22.4	19.0
Dizygotic	276	7.6	92.4	241	10.8	89.2	517	5.0	49.3
Total number	390	26.2	73.8	301	21.6	78.4	691	9.4	41.7

TABLE 11

Distribution of Concordance in Relation to Similarity of Environment and
Clinical Course of Schizophrenia

		CONCORDANT PAIRS IN PERCENT			
	Not separated	Separated-similar environment	Separated-dissimilar environment	Completely * concordant	Incompletely * concordant
Monozygotic	50.8	16.7	32.5	67.5	32.5
Dizygotic	42.5	2.1	55.3	6.4	66.0
All twin index pairs	48.5	12.6	38.9	50.3	49.7

* As related to the following four classifications:
  Group   I: No schizophrenia despite similar environment.
  Group II: Schizophrenia with little or no deterioration (recovery).
  Group III: Schizophrenia with medium deterioration.
  Group IV: Schizophrenia with extreme deterioration.

groups with completely and incompletely similar or dissimilar behavior to schizophrenia, instead of comparing the twin groups with and without psychotic symptoms as was done by the use of morbidity rates.

Complete similarity has been assumed when both twins either recovered from a mild psychosis with little or no defect (Group II) or reached about the same degree of medium (Group III) or extreme deterioration (Group IV). On the basis of this classification, complete concordance is found in 67.5 percent of the concordant one-egg twin pairs, but only in 6.4 percent of the dizygotic pairs (TABLE 11).

Complete dissimilarity means that the co-twins developed no psychosis despite similar environment (Group I), while the index twins showed an extremely deteriorating type of psychosis. Such a difference does not occur in the group of monozygotic twins, but it ensues in about every sixth dizygotic pair under dissimilar environmental conditions (TABLE 12). This finding implies that the chance of a rapidly progressive psychosis (low resistance) is practically zero for a schizophrenic patient who is the monozygotic twin of, or genetically identical with, a person who remains free of schizophrenic manifestations under similar environmental circumstances. However, the chance of developing a very destructive type of psychosis is 1:3.5, if the person is merely the patient's

sibling or dizygotic twin, which means that he is as likely to differ in the inherited elements for a satisfactory resistance as are two brothers or sisters.

In comparing the total groups with dissimilar and similar behavior to schizophrenia, incomplete similarity denotes a difference of only one step between two of the four subgroups; and incomplete dissimilarity, a difference of two steps. This comparison yields a ratio of 3:55 for the monozygotic pairs, and a ratio of 3:1 for the dizygotic pairs. The difference in similarity of resistance be-

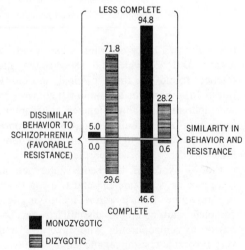

FIG. 6. Rates of similar and dissimilar resistance to schizophrenia.

TABLE 12

Variations in Resistance to Schizophrenia in the Twin Index Pairs

DEGREE OF RESISTANCE TO SCHIZO-PHRENIA	CLINICAL BEHAVIOR TO SCHIZOPHRENIA IN TWIN INDEX PAIRS				NUMBER OF TWIN PAIRS	
	First Twin		Second Twin			
	Sub-groups	Clinical classification	Sub-groups	Clinical classification	Mono-zygotic	Di-zygotic
Complete dissimilarity	IV	Extremely deteriorating type of schizophrenia	I	No schizophrenia despite similar environment	0	91
	IV	Extremely deteriorating type of schizophrenia	Ia	No schizophrenia with dissimilar environment	0	62
Less complete dissimilarity	IV	Extremely deteriorating type of schizophrenia	II	Schizophrenia with little or no deterioration	9	21
	III	Schizophrenia with medium deterioration	I, Ia	No schizophrenia (regardless of environment)	0	197
Complete similarity	II	Schizophrenia with little or no deterioration (recovery)	II	Schizophrenia with little or no deterioration	19	2
	III	Schizophrenia with medium deterioration	III	Schizophrenia with medium deterioration	33	0
	IV	Schizophrenia with extreme deterioration	IV	Schizophrenia with extreme deterioration	29	1
Less complete similarity	II	Schizophrenia with little or no deterioration	I, Ia	No schizophrenia	54	120
	III	Schizophrenia with medium deterioration	II	Schizophrenia with little or no deterioration	20	14
	IV	Schizophrenia with extreme deterioration	III	Schizophrenia with medium deterioration	10	9
Total number of pairs		All dissimilar pairs			9	371
		All similar pairs			165	146
		Grand total			174	517
Ratio		No schizophrenia to extremely deteriorating schizophrenia			0 : 174	1 : 2.5
		Dissimilar resistance to similar resistance			3 : 55	3 : 1

tween the two types of twins is expressed by a ratio of 1:55, which far exceeds the difference found in their original morbidity rates. In other words, similar behavior to schizophrenia is about eighteen times more frequent than dissimilar behavior in monozygotic twins, although dissimilarity predominates in dizygotic twin partners.

FIG. 6 expresses the same difference in resistance between one-egg and two-egg twins in rates rather than in ratios, identifying less complete and complete dissimilarity in behavior to schizophrenia with favorable and very favorable resistance, and similar behavior in the deteriorating subgroups with insufficient resistance. In the monozygotic group, five out of 100 cotwins of schizophrenic index cases show a tendency to favorable resistance and none shows very favorable resistance, if their twin partners are insufficiently resistant. In the dizygotic group, however, favorable resistance is seen in seventy-two out of 100 cotwins of insufficiently resistant index cases, and very favorable resistance in about 30.

This finding indicates that *constitutional resistance* to the main genotype of schizophrenia is determined by a genetic mechanism which is probably non-specific and certainly multifactorial. Taking into account the results of biometric investigations, there is reason to believe that this constitutional defense mechanism is a graded character and somehow correlated with the morphological development of mesodermal elements. For various reasons it does not seem likely, however, that the genetic mechanisms controlling susceptibility and lack of resistance to schizophrenia, that is, the ability to develop a schizophrenic psychosis and the inability to counteract the progression of the disease, are entirely identical with each other. If they are identifiable, it is possible without qualification to accept the recent suggestions of Penrose and Luxenburger that inheritance of schizophrenia may be "the result of many factors."

As far as the *specific predisposition* to schizophrenia is concerned, that is, the inherited capacity for responding to certain stimuli with a schizophrenic type of reaction, the findings of the present study are conclusively in favor of the genetic theory. Our conclusion is that this predisposition depends on the presence of a specific genetic factor which is believed by us to be recessive and autosomal.

The hypothesis of recessiveness is borne out by the taint distribution in the ancestry of our index cases and by an excess of consanguineous marriages among their parents. Of 211 twin index pairs without schizophrenia in their known ancestry, twelve sets (5.7 percent) originated from consanguineous parental matings. Of the remaining index pairs, 95 were found to have a schizophrenic parent; 283 had no schizophrenic parent, but schizophrenic cases in the collateral lines of ancestry; and in 102 pairs the available information about the ancestors was considered inadequate. This excess of consanguineous parental marriages in the present survey appears quite convincing, even if a part of it may be due to the fact that our index cases are twins.

Psychiatrically it should be evident that the *genetic theory of schizophrenia* as it may be formulated on the basis of experiment-like observations with the twin family method, does not confute any psychological concepts of a descriptive or analytical nature, if these concepts are adequately defined and applied. There is no genetic reason why the manifes-

tations of a schizophrenic psychosis should not be described in terms of narcissistic regression or of varying biological changes such as defective homeostasis or general immaturity in the metabolic responses to stimuli. Genetically it is also perfectly legitimate to interpret schizophrenic reactions as the expression either of faulty habit formations or of progressive maladaptation to disrupted family relations. The genetic theory explains only *why* these various phenomena occur in a particular member of a particular family at a particular time.

The general meaning of this genetic explanation is that a true schizophrenic psychosis is not developed under usual human life conditions unless a particular predisposition has been inherited by a person from both parents. Genetically it is also implied that resistance to a progressive psychosis does not break down without certain inherited deficiencies in constitutional defense mechanisms, the final outcome of the disease being the result of intricate interactions of varying genetic and environmental influences. Another genetic implication is that a schizophrenic psychosis can be both prevented and cured. The prerequisite is that the psychosomatic elements, which may act as predispositional, precipitating or perpetuating agents in such a psychosis, are morphologically identified, and that the complex interplay of etiologic and compensatory mechanisms is fully understood. Pragmatic speculation will be no aid in reaching this goal.

Summary

1. The methods available for genetic investigations in man are the pedigree or family history method, the contingency method of statistical prediction, and the twin study method.

2. A study of the relative effects of hereditary and environmental factors in the development and outcome of schizophrenia was undertaken by means of the "Twin Family Method." The study was organized with the cooperation of all mental hospitals under the supervision of the New York State Department of Mental Hygiene. The total number

of schizophrenic twin index cases, whose co-twins were available for examination at the age of fifteen years, was 794.

3. In addition to 1,382 twins, the 691 twin index families used for statistical analysis include 2,741 full siblings, 134 half-siblings, 74 step-siblings, 1,191 parents, and 254 marriage partners of twin patients. The random sampling of these twin index pairs is indicated by the distribution of 174 monozygotic and 517 dizygotic pairs, yielding a ratio of about 1:3.

4. The morbidity rates obtained with the "Abridged Weinberg Method" are in line with the genetic theory of schizophrenia. They amount to 1.8 percent for the step-siblings; 2.1 percent for the marriage partners; 7.0 percent for the half-siblings; 9.2 percent for the parents; 14.3 percent for the full-siblings; 4.7 percent for the dizygotic cotwins; and 85.8 percent for the monozygotic cotwins. This morbidity distribution indicates that the chance of developing schizophrenia in comparable environments increases in proportion to the degree of blood relationship to a schizophrenic index case.

5. The differences in morbidity among the various sibship groups of the index families cannot be explained by a simple correlation between closeness of blood relationship and increasing similarity in environment. The morbidity rates for opposite-sexed and same-sexed two-egg twin partners vary only from 10.3 to 17.6 percent, and those for non-separated and separated one-egg twin partners from 77.6 to 91.5 percent. The difference in morbidity between dizygotic and monozygotic cotwins approximates the ratio of 1:6. An analysis of common environmental factors before and after birth excludes the possibility of explaining this difference on non-genetic grounds.

6. The difference between dizygotic and monozygotic cotwins increases to a ratio of 1:55, if the similarities in the course and outcome of schizophrenia are taken as additional criteria of comparison. This finding indicates that constitutional inability to resist the progression of a schizophrenic psychosis is determined by a genetic mechanism which seems to be non-specific and multifactorial.

7. The predisposition to schizophrenia, that is, the ability to respond to certain stimuli with a schizophrenic type of reaction, depends on the presence of a specific genetic factor which is probably recessive and autosomal.

8. The genetic theory of schizophrenia does not invalidate any psychological theories of a descriptive or analytical nature. It is equally compatible with the psychiatric concept that schizophrenia can be prevented as well as cured.

BIBLIOGRAPHY

1. GRALNIK, A. The Carrington family. Psychiat. Quart., 17:2, 1943.
2. HOSKINS, R. G. The biology of schizophrenia. The Salmon Memorial Lectures, New York, 1945.
3. KALLMANN, F. J. The genetics of schizophrenia. New York, 1938, J. J. Augustin.
4. KALLMANN, F. J. The scientific goal in the prevention of hereditary mental disease. Proc. of Seventh International Genetical Congress, Edinburgh, 1939, Cambridge University Press.
5. KALLMANN, F. J., and BARRERA, S. E. The heredoconstitutional mechanisms of predisposition and resistance to schizophrenia. Am. J. Psychiat., 98:4, 1942.
6. KALLMANN, F. J., and REISNER, D. Twin studies on the significance of genetic factors in tuberculosis. Am. Rev. Tuberc., 47:6, 1943.
7. LUXENBURGER, H. Erbpathologie der Schizophrenie. Part II, Vol. II of Guett's Handbuch der Erbkrankheiten. Leipzig, 1940, G. Thieme.
8. MYERSON, A. Some trends of psychiatry. Am. J. Psychiat., Cent. Anniv. Iss., 1944.
9. PENROSE, L. S. Heredity. Part IV, Vol. I of Hunt's Handbook, Personality and the Behavior Disorders. New York, 1944, Ronald Press Co.
10. POLLOCK, H. M., MALZBERG, B., and FULLER, R. G. Heredity and environmental factors

in the causation of manic-depressive psychoses and dementia praecox. Utica, 1939,
State Hospital Press.

11. ROSANOFF, A. J., HANDY, L. M., ROSANOFF
PLESSET, I., and BRUSH, S. The etiology of
so-called schizophrenic psychoses. Am. J.
Psychiat., 91:247, 1934.

12. ROSENBERG, R. Heredity in the functional
psychoses. Am. J. Psychiat., 101:2, 1944.

13. SLATER, E. Genetics in psychiatry. J. Ment.
Sci., 90:3, 1944.

14. STRECKER, E. A. Fundamentals of psychiatry.
Philadelphia, 1945, J. B. Lippincott Co.

15. WEINBERG, W. Zur Probandenmethode und
zu ihrem Ersatz. Ztschr. Neurol., 123:809,
1930.

RALPH ROSENBERG

39. *Heredity in the Functional Psychoses*

THUS far, four methods have been used for the study of heredity. First in historical order is Sir Francis Galton's family history method, introduced about the middle of the 19th century. Next came Mendel's experimental method which appeared in 1900 and is still in use. The third or combination method arose about 1910 and constitutes an attempt to apply Mendel's laws to family histories. This method has had limited success and is sometimes used today. The fourth is the identical twin method. This approach has only been in vogue during the last two decades; but its statistical series, though small, is quite significant. These four methods will be dealt with in chronological sequence.

Galton's method of studying inheritance is of utmost importance to us, for it is the family history method used in present day psychiatry. The method originated in Galton's fertile imagination in the 1860's. At that time the scientific method was very different from that of today. It was dominated by Charles Darwin, Galton's brilliant cousin. Darwin's method was purely observational. His masterpiece, "The Origin of Species," was a list of observations with his theoretical attempts to explain the observations. The experimental method, as we use it now, was almost nonexistent. Influenced by the methods of his time, Galton collected exhaustive observations on the recurrence of selected traits in certain families. He concluded that the traits must be hereditary because they recurred in some families and not in others.

Among his family history studies of natural inheritance, we find a monograph called "Noteworthy Families." In it "The brief biographical notices of 66 noteworthy families . . . are compiled from replies to a circular issued . . . in the spring of 1904 to all living fellows of the Royal Society." Judging by the replies to the circulars, all the family trees studied revealed many men distinguished in the arts and sciences. Eight members of the Darwin family were listed as famous. Galton included himself in this constellation as cousin of Charles Darwin. He concluded from this study that superior intelligence must be inherited because it recurred in generation after generation of the same families. The test of intelligence, of course, was membership in the Royal Society. One wonders how many London slum denizens would have become distinguished in the arts and sciences had they the educational opportunities afforded these sons of the English upper classes.

In his "Hereditary Genius," Galton expanded the family history method. He observed entire populations and then estimated the level of their hereditary intelligence. By this inaccurate method he concluded that the hereditary intelligence of Londoners was inferior to that of English north country folk. His only evidence was that "It is perfectly distressing to me to witness the bedraggled, drudged, mean look of the mass of individuals . . . that one meets in the streets of London. The conditions of their life seem too hard for their constitutions." One wonders whether their 16 hour day and subminimal diet would not be too hard for everyone's "constitution."

The intrinsic fallacy of Galton's observational method is shown in our changing concepts of tuberculosis. Previous to 1882 tuberculosis was believed to be due to heredity. Many families were found in which tubercu-

Reprinted by permission of the American Psychiatric Association and the author from the *American Journal of Psychiatry*, 1944, vol. 7, pp. 157–65.

losis occurred generation after generation, families were found in which many or all of the siblings had the disease. Such family histories branded these families as having the "scrofulous diathesis," *i.e.,* of being tainted stock which contained tuberculosis, slenderness, fainting spells and rickets. The recurrence of these traits in generation after generation does not prove their hereditary nature. This is the type of evidence we have today for the inheritance of insanity—mere recurrence in the family history. To the modern physician, tuberculosis, slenderness and rickets mean slum environment, not poor heredity. To the modern psychiatrist, generation after generation of insanity means schizoid or manic parents imposing their unreasonable attitudes on children who warp under the family tensions. These children in turn impress their twisted views on their children and so on down the generations. The process is environmental. The proof is that these repressed traumatic memories can be recovered, if we but listen to our patients.

To return to the original point, in 1882 Koch discovered the tubercle bacillus. The hereditarians refused to surrender. Instead, they advanced the hypothesis that tuberculosis is due to a hereditary susceptibility of the lungs to the bacillus. Suffice to say there has never been a single bit of experimental evidence to show that one human being is more susceptible to a measured dose of tubercle bacilli than another. The hereditarians have discreetly ceased talking of the inheritance of rickets. It used to occur in generation after generation of the same family. It was absent in other families generation after generation.

One or two other examples will suffice to show the fundamental fallacy of Galton's family history method. The first is pellagra. Before Goldberger, it would have been easy to prove that this psychosis was due to the hereditary defects of a tainted family stock. This follows automatically from the fact that the disease occurred in certain families generation after generation and did not occur in other families at all. The fact that lower class families had the disease would support the theory that it was due to tainted stock—for

the lower classes were thought to have poor heredity. Conversely, the upper classes seldom showed the disease. This must, of course, be due to their superior heredity. Goldberger's discovery of the p-p factor upset this view, and the discovery of nicotinic acid completely demolished it.

Feeblemindedness is a third example of the fallacy of the family history method. This condition has long been considered a classic example of the inheritance of a mental disorder. In recent times this concept has largely won support from Goddard's famous study of the Kallikak family. This work opens with an account of Deborah Kallikak, a patient in Goddard's institution at Vineland. Goddard traced Deborah's ancestry through a long line of defectives to the union of Martin Kallikak and a "nameless feebleminded girl" in the days of the American Revolution. Martin united himself first with this nameless feebleminded girl, and started a long row of feebleminded syphilitics and alcoholics. Then, reforming, he married a girl of Puritan stock, and started a long row of descendants, not a single one of whom was immoral, syphilitic, alcoholic, insane, criminal or feebleminded. One doubts Goddard's definite diagnosis that this or that post-Revolutionary War ancestor was an idiot, an imbecile or a high-grade moron. Intelligence tests were not devised until much later. Goddard concludes that feeblemindedness is inherited from tainted stock. He made no attempt to discover whether the supposed feeblemindedness of an unknown ancestor was due to cerebral agenesis, epidemic meningitis, birth trauma, congenital lues, hypothyroidism, Mongolian idiocy, amaurosis, Schilder's disease, sensory deprivation, encephalitis, congenital hydrocephaly, microcephaly or tuberous sclerosis. It is evident that 13 separate clinical entities cannot be inherited as a single Mendelian character. Again, Goddard labeled certain ancestors syphilitic, but these ancestors died decades before the Wassermann reaction was discovered, and decades before general paresis was discovered to be syphilitic. Having diagnosed syphilis in persons dead for generations, Goddard intimates that the infection is a sign of poor stock. There is no proof that Martin Kallikak is actually the father in question. If the girl were as feebleminded as indicated, Martin might well be but one of a dozen possible fathers. This one error would invalidate the entire hereditary study. Any family tree investigation must be looked upon as inaccurate, for the more remote the ancestor, the less accurate our knowledge of him must be.

Oftentimes, we "know from observation" that certain human traits are hereditary in various families and races. Take, for example, the question of human height. Ordinarily one takes for granted that Scandinavians are tall and Japanese are short and that this is an inherited character. One takes for granted that tall parents will have tall children and vice versa and that this family character is inherited. However, Franz Boas (1) (1911) found that children born in this country were taller than children born in Europe of the same parents. Others have shown that Japanese children born in this country of pure blooded Japanese parents are about 1 inch taller than the parents. The children of these children, though still 100 per cent Japanese blood, are in turn about 1 inch taller than their parents and 2 inches taller than their grandparents. The same process holds true for Orthodox Jewish immigrants whose religion prevents outbreeding. Though the heredity is the same, the height increases about 1 inch per generation.

A study made at Harvard University (2, 3) disclosed that 1166 undergraduates averaged 1.4 inches taller than their alumni fathers. It will thus be seen that height, which is usually thought to be hereditary, is in fact determined by environment. The precise factor in the environment which determines height is not known, but there is good reason to believe that diet plays the controlling role. One can see how the poor dietary habits of short parents might automatically condition the eating habits of the children and make them short as well. This summarizes the underlying error in Galton's statistical method. It cannot, by family observation alone, or by statistics derived therefrom, determine whether a trait is due to heredity

or environment, for both are similar in the same family and both are likely to create similarities among the members of that family. It seems advisable to drop this obsolete family history method from our present day psychiatric armamentarium.

We turn now to the second method. In 1866 an obscure Austrian monk named Gregor Mendel gave the world the first accurate method ever developed for the study of heredity. The method lay buried in obscurity until 1900 when it was unearthed simultaneously by Correns of Germany, DeVries of Holland and Von Tschermak of Austria. Gregor Mendel clearly realized that both heredity and environment are variables which influence an individual. He therefore devised experiments in which the environment was kept as constant as he could possibly make it, while he varied the heredity. He concluded that since the environment was constant, variation in the offspring must be due to his experimental variation in the heredity. It might not be amiss to review some of the experiments of Mendel and his successors.

Mendel's first experiment is shown in Fig. 1. It consisted in mating round and wrinkled garden peas. Fortunately the shape of a green pea depends on a single chromosome. This is the simplest type of inheritance and such single chromosome differences between parents produce monohybrids. Fig. 1 shows the derivation of the famous 3 to 1 Mendelian ratio of three round to one wrinkled. This formula, of course, is a general biological law for the behavior of one chromosome inheritance. It will be noticed that several essentials of Mendel's method are concealed in this simple diagram. First, P, the parent generation, consists of pure stock of known genetic constitution. Next, F 1, the first filial or experimental generation, consists of siblings all alike. The second filial generation (known as F 2) is produced by a brother and sister mating of F 1 individuals. The environment has been kept absolutely constant while these mating experiments are being conducted. Under these conditions and only under these conditions is the characteristic 3 to 1 ratio unearthed. TABLE 1 shows the size of the series of plants needed to approximate the theoretical ratio. Only when similarly conducted experiments show a 3 to 1 ratio in F 2 can we prove a certain character to be inherited by a 1-chromosome mechanism. Only by the demonstration of the genetic mechanism can Mendel's method be used to prove conclusively that a character is hereditary.

FIG. 2 shows an exception to Mendel's 3 to 1 monohybrid ratio. Cuénot mated yellow mice to try to produce pure yellow stock Y Y. The offspring were 2 yellow which did not breed true to 1 black which did. He rightly inferred that the chromosome containing the yellow gene also had a lethal gene incapable of killing by itself, but capable of killing the embryo when both alleles (paired chromosomes) had the same gene. In other words, when the animal was homozygous for the lethal gene (had the gene in both dominant and recessive chromosome) death was produced. When the animal was heterozygous for the gene (had the gene in only 1 of the pair) the animal lived. It may thus be seen that an animal may inherit the capacity to be born dead and may transmit the character to its offspring. Cuénot proved the point by dissecting the pregnant uteri of his mice and discovering ¼ yellow dead, ½ yellow alive and ¼ black alive. The latter 2 groups provide the 2 to 1 ratio in the offspring.

Another interesting variation of Mendel's 3:1 monohybrid is a cross between red and ivory snapdragons. The offspring are red if grown in bright light and ivory if grown in dim light. Similarly, the gene for duplicated legs in Drosophila Melanogaster (the fruit fly) produces its effect only if the fly is reared at low temperature. In the same fashion, the

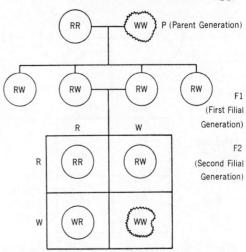

FIG. 1. Monohybrid. (Parents differ in 1 character.) In F 2 three peas are round. Two of them have wrinkled recessives. These two have the dominant morphology (round) but can transmit wrinkles (W being a recessive gene) to their offspring. The one W W is wrinkled and can only transmit wrinkles to its offspring. The gross morphology of 3 round to 1 wrinkled in F 2 is the classical Mendelian 3:1 ratio for a character determined by 1 gene.

genes for vestigial wings, bar eyes, etc., produce different effects at different temperatures. These instances reiterate the basic fact that Mendel's laws can only be applied to completely controlled environments constant for all the experimental plants or animals used.

Let us consider the next most complicated genetic mechanism—that in which the parents differ in 2 chromosomes. FIG. 3 shows the basic experiment. A round yellow pea is crossed with a green wrinkled pea. The offspring (F 1) all look yellow and round because these characters are dominant. How-

TABLE 1

Mendel as Quoted in Walters' "Genetics"

CHARACTER	NUMBER DOMINANTS	NUMBER RECESSIVES	PHENOTYPIC RATIOS F 2
Form of seed	5474 smooth	1850 wrinkled	2.96 : 1
Color of cotyledons	6022 yellow	2001 green	3.01 : 1
Length of vine	787 tall	277 dwarf	2.84 : 1
Color pods	428 green	152 yellow	2.82 : 1

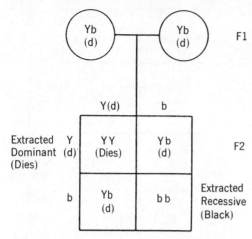

FIG. 2. This figure shows the effect of a lethal linked dominant in modifying the 3:1 ratio to 2:1. The extracted dominant Y Y contains two lethal genes and dies in utero.

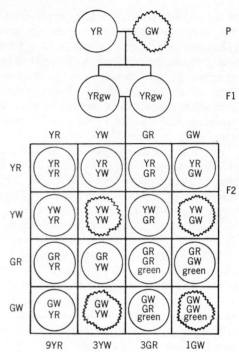

FIG. 3. Dihybrid P differs in 2 characters. Dihybrid ratio 9:3:3:1.

ever, F 1 contains 2 recessive genes which cannot be discovered by inspecting the peas. When brother and sister are mated to form the F 2 generation, 4 differently appearing kinds of peas are produced in the characteristic dihybrid Mendelian ratio of 9 yellow round, 3 yellow wrinkled, 3 green round, 1 green wrinkled. The appearance of a 9:3:3:1 ratio in F 2 proves the characters to be hereditary and proves 2 chromosomes are involved. The 1 green wrinkled pea is of profound interest to psychiatrists. At this point, let us be content to note that only 1 "child" in 16 resembled the green wrinkled parent.

There are numerous exceptions to the classical 9:3:3:1 dihybrid Mendelian ratio. The checkerboard in FIG. 4 shows how the mating of two white flowers produced all purple flowers in F 1 and a ratio of 9 purple to 7 white in F 2. This occurs because the dominant C chromosome produces white unless it coexists with the dominant P chromosome. The effect of these interacting dominants is the addition of the last 3 factors of the classical 9:3:3:1 to produce a 9:7 ratio. Another exception is the mating of two round summer squashes of different ancestry. The checkerboard in FIG. 5 gives us the amazing information that two round parents produced all disc shaped children in F 1 and ¹⁄₁₆ of the

F 2 children were elongate! These elongate children do not resemble any of their ancestors, yet their character is determined by heredity. This fact is worth considering when we look for a family history of insanity in our patients. Were schizophrenia inherited by some such mechanism, it might appear in a patient and in none of his ancestors. Since it appears in one of 16 of the children, and the average family has 2 or 3 children, the patient might be the only one of an enormous family to inherit the psychosis.

Another exception to the classical Mendelian 9:3:3:1 dihybrid ratio is the mechanism for the grey coat color of rodents. The C gene is necessary for the development of any color, its absence produces an albino. A is the gene for grey. Gene C produces grey if it coexists with dominant A, but produces black if it is not. Thus the effect of gene C depends upon the presence or absence of other genes. Similar interaction of genes complicates hereditary mechanisms beyond description. Dozens of exceptions and varia-

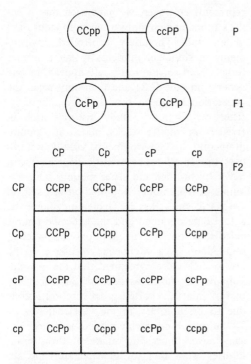

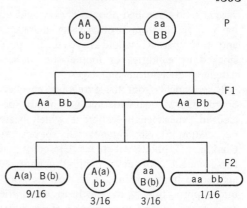

FIG. 5. (a) = A or a

The interaction of gene A with gene B produces a disc squash.

Gene A or gene B produces round squash.

The absence of either dominant produces elongate fruit.

Since there are two round groups in F 2, the ratio is modified to 9:6:1.

FIG. 4. The diagram shows how interacting dominants modify the classical 9:3:3:1 Mendelian ratio to 9:7.

Both parents are white because each contains only 1 type of dominant.

All F 1 are purple because each contains both interacting dominants.

In F 2 nine contain CP and are purple, seven do not and are white.

tions of the dihybrid 9:3:3:1 ratio have been discovered.

The next most complicated genetic problem is the inheritance of a character dependent on 3 genes. The Mendelian checkerboard shows 7 kinds of F 2 progeny. The first kind has 27 children, 3 kinds have 9 children each, 3 kinds have 3 each, and 1 individual is unique. One could cull hundreds of exceptions from the genetic literature in which the classic 27:9:9:9:3:3:3:1 ratio is modified by gene interaction. The description of these exceptions would take volumes. They would constitute a tiny fragment of a simple problem in genetics. Man has 24 pairs of chromosomes and each chromosome probably has at least 10 genes. One can but admire Walters'

(4) understatement when he says, "With 24 pairs of chromosomes in man there are, assuming independent assortment 281, 474, 976, 710, 656 different possible combinations, while the many different ways in which the genes within the chromosomes may change their alignment and cross over, increases this number beyond imagination."

Morgan has discovered that the eye color of the fruit fly is determined by 7 genes. Let us suppose that the functional psychoses are inherited by as simple a mechanism as the eye color of the fruit fly. The Mendelian checkerboard for a 7-gene process would contain over 11,000 squares. The F 2 ratio would not be the simple 3 to 1 ratio of the 1 gene mechanism. It would be 1 class of 2189 individuals to 7 classes of 729 each, 35 classes of 9 individuals each, 37 classes of 27 individuals each, 21 classes of 9 individuals each, 7 classes of 3 individuals each and 1 unique individual. Reference to TABLE 1 will show that the theoretically computed 3 to 1 ratio was not actually achieved with 4 progeny. In fact, a series of almost 600 children was necessary to approximate that simple ratio. About 100,000 children would have to be bred experimentally to test the complex

7-gene ratio described above. They would all have to result from brother-sister marriages and their parents would have to be pure stocked by centuries of mother-son, father-daughter, uncle-niece marriages.

It is evident from the foregoing checkerboards that Mendel's method is a highly specialized experimental technique which bears no relation to our patients whatsoever. As Conklin (5) points out in his "Heredity and Environment" Mendel's method cannot be applied to human beings, first, because it requires pure stock with which to begin the experiment and no pure human stock exists (Hitler's "Nordics" to the contrary notwithstanding). The average Englishman, for example, has Norse, Saxon, Angle, Teuton, Norman, Welsh, Irish, Scottish, Roman and Druid blood. Second, Mendel's method cannot be applied to human beings because it is strictly and solely an experimental method based exclusively on experimental matings. Third, Mendel's method cannot be applied to human beings because the number of offspring is too small to construct a statistical matrix to discover the ratio (and from that the mechanism which proves the character to be hereditary). Fourth, Mendel's method cannot be applied to human beings because it predicates an absolutely uniform and controlled environment while the heredity is being varied. The dynamic schools of psychiatry have amply demonstrated that no two human beings can possibly have precisely the same likes, dislikes, attitudes, fears, loves and that these characteristics are derived from various experiences (*i.e.,* different environments). No method has yet been devised which can keep a large number of human beings' psychological environments identical throughout every second of their lifetimes.

Let us now consider the third method devised for the study of heredity. This is the combination method. In this method family histories are studied and the frequency of occurrence of certain traits is noted. An attempt is then made to fit the ratio of occurrence and non-occurrence into a classical Mendelian ratio. This is supposed to prove the trait to be hereditary and dependent on whatever number of chromosomes the ratio happens to represent. However, we have seen that Mendel's ratios appear only when pure stocks are mated under precisely controlled environments in sufficient numbers to get a proper series. Even so, the ratio only appears in one generation (the F 2) and then only when the generation has been produced by a brother-sister mating. Our family histories are derived from impure stocks, mated at random, in uncontrolled environments, usually in numbers too small to be statistically significant, never by brother and sister matings. One example of the combination method will suffice. Goddard states that in feeblemindedness the actual data obtained and the expected figures calculated on the assumption that feeblemindedness is a Mendelian recessive (3:1) are in such close agreement that the assumption may be taken as verified. Suffice to say that Wilmarth reported gross cerebral lesions due to brain injury in the vast majority of 70 autopsies on feebleminded patients. We shall never know how many of these brain injuries were due to improper forceps application, how many to rachitic pelves, how many to an oversized child, how many to difficult labor in primiparae, how many to postnatal trauma. We do know that the feeblemindednes was due to the environment and that it is useless to look for Mendelian ratios in the family histories of our insane patients. In other words, the combination method has all the fallacies of Galton's family history method—it cannot by observation alone tell hereditary from environmental causes.

The fourth method for studying heredity is the study of identical twins. Conveniently, these amazing individuals have precisely identical heredities. If both of a pair of twins developed the same psychosis, we would be prone to blame it on their identical heredity. But what if both suffered the trauma of desertion by the mother? What if both suffered the trauma of bullying by the father or an elder brother? What if both had unresolved Oedipus situations due to an oversolicitous mother?

One of the best twin studies is that of Rosanoff et al. (6). They studied 142 pairs of twins of whom one or both had schizophrenia. The following table compares their

TABLE 2

Rosanoff et al. and Humm

	IDENTICAL TWINS	SAME SEX TWINS NOT IDENTICAL	OPPOSITE SEX TWINS NOT IDENTICAL	HUMM ORDINARY SIBLINGS
Both schizophrenic	68 per cent	20 per cent	10 per cent	3.1 per cent
Number studied	41 pairs	53 pairs	48 pairs	

results with Humm's (7) study of schizophrenia in ordinary siblings:

Of the 41 pairs of identical twins, schizophrenia occurred in both of 68 per cent of the pairs. In 32 per cent of the twin pairs, only one twin developed schizophrenia. Yet each pair of twins had identical chromosomes. Obviously heredity cannot produce schizophrenia in one twin and not in the other. One could argue that the other twin might get schizophrenia if we waited long enough. Histories of such twins do not bear this out. Those who have known identical twins notice that they are inseparable companions. They like to wear identical clothes, go to the same schools, attend the same classes, have the same amusements. The psychological motive for always appearing together is evident. Each twin alone is just an ordinary child. When the twins are together they are pointed out as remarkable, and easily gain the center of attention. Alfred Adler and many others have shown that this striving for the limelight is a major force in human behavior. Identical twins, then, are constantly together; that is, their environments are much more alike than those of ordinary siblings. Small wonder that when the environment is poor, both succumb to schizophrenia in 68 per cent.

In the second group (same sex twins not identical), schizophrenia occurs in both twins in only 20 per cent. The heredity of these twins is the same as that of ordinary siblings. Yet Humm has shown that two ordinary siblings get schizophrenia in only 3 per cent. Since the hereditary variation is the same in both sibling groups, it follows that the difference between 20 per cent and 3 per cent must be the measure of environmental difference! In the third group (opposite sex twins not

identical) schizophrenia occurs in both twins in only 10 per cent. Again, the heredity of these twins is the same as that of ordinary siblings. The difference between the same sex twins (20 per cent), opposite sex twins (10 per cent) and ordinary siblings (3 per cent) is the measure of environmental difference, since the hereditary relationships are the same in all three groups.

Summary

To date four methods have been devised for the study of heredity. The first is Galton's family history method. Several generations of clinical experience have shown that this method is fallacious because mere observation alone cannot differentiate hereditary from environmental causes. On the basis of their fallacious statistical studies, the Galtonians have come to incorrect conclusions such as the inheritability of rickets, tuberculosis and pellagra. It is evident that the mere recurrence of a certain trait in the same family does not prove that trait to be hereditary. This follows automatically from the fact that members of the same family have similar environments. Unfortunately, this obsolete family history method is often used today. The second method was introduced by Mendel. This [is] a purely experimental technique which necessitates pure stock for the parent generation, a completely controlled environment, inbreeding of brother and sister and a sufficiently large number of F 2 progeny to bring out the characteristic Mendelian ratio. Only by the experimental demonstration of the F 2 ratio can this method prove a character to be hereditary. For functional psychoses none of the conditions necessary for a Mendelian experiment can be achieved in human beings. The method, therefore, can give us no information as to whether or not these psychoses are inherited. The third method widely used for the study of heredity in mental diseases is the combination method. This method seeks to find the characteristic F 2 Mendelian ratios in family histories. We have seen that these ratios appear only in certain stages of a very highly specialized experimental technique. Occasionally a characteristic ratio can be found in simple 1-gene diseases like Huntington's chorea and polydactyly. It is a grave error to reason from this analogy that the discovery of a characteristic ratio in a few families necessarily proves the character to be hereditary. A casual inspection of family histories of mental patients shows that no such simple mechanism could possibly be involved. Goddard's classical error of trying to prove feeblemindedness to be hereditary by this method is a typical example of the uselessness of the method for psychiatric disorders. The fourth method is the study of the mental status of twins. Although the heredity is the same in identical twins, the mere discovery of two twins with the same mental disorder does not prove the mental disorder to be hereditary. Since twins are more likely to have similar environments than are ordinary individuals, similarities in environment seem to be the cause of such simultaneous appearance of functional psychoses. If heredity were the cause of the psychosis, it would be impossible for only one twin to be affected. In Rosanoff's study of 41 pairs of identical twins, only one twin was affected in 32 per cent of the pairs. This is substantial evidence against a hereditary etiology of schizophrenia. The other three groups of cases summarized in FIG. 7 are ordinary siblings. They have identical hereditary relationships. The declining double schizophrenia rate in these three groups (20 per cent, 10 per cent, 3 per cent) must be due to environmental difference.

Conclusion

THERE are four methods for studying heredity as a possible etiology in the functional psychoses. The first three are either fallacious or irrelevant. The fourth, the twin method, strongly indicates that heredity plays no part in these psychoses. In fact, our poor therapeutic results in the functional psychoses seem to be due to our neglect of the environmental (dynamic) schools of psychiatry.

BIBLIOGRAPHY

1. BOAS, F. Changes in bodily form of descendants of immigrants. Washington, Gov. Prtg. Off., 1911. (United States Immigration Commission. Reports V. 38.)
2. HOOTON, E. A. Harvard Alumni Bull., 33:994, 1931.
3. BOWLES, G. T. New types of old Americans at Harvard. Cambridge University Press, 1932.
4. WALTERS, H. E. Genetics, p. 300. 4th Ed., 1938. Macmillan, N. Y.
5. CONKLIN, E. G. Heredity and environment in the development of man, pp. 288, 290. Princeton University Press, 1915.
6. ROSANOFF, et al. Am. J. Psychiat., 91:247, Sept. 1943.
7. HUMM, D. G. Am. J. Psychiat., 12:239, Sept. 1932.

BERNARD C. ROSEN

40. The Achievement Syndrome: A Psychocultural Dimension of Social Stratification

THE empirical generalization that upward mobility is greater among members of the middle class than those of the lower strata has been explained in several alternative ways.[1] It has been suggested, for example, that social strata possess different physical characteristics which affect mobility, that as a result of certain selective processes persons in the upper and middle strata are, on the average, more intelligent, healthier, and more attractive than those in the lower strata.[2] More frequently, differential mobility is described as a function of the relative opportunities available to individuals in the social structure. This structural dimension of stratification is explicit in the "life chances" hypothesis in which it is argued that money, specialized training, and prestigeful contacts—factors which affect access to high position—are relatively inaccessible to individuals in the lower social strata.[3] Such explanations are relevant and consistent with one another. They

lack exhaustiveness, however, since neither explanation takes into account the possibility that there may be psychological and cultural factors which affect social mobility by influencing the individual's willingness to develop and exploit his talent, intelligence, and opportunities.

It is the thesis of this paper that class differential rates of vertical mobility may be explicated also in terms of a psychocultural dimension of stratification, that is, as a function of differences in the motives and values of social classes.[4] More specifically, this study examines empirically the notion (long current in sociology, but for which there is as yet insufficient empirical verification) that social classes in American society are characterized by a dissimilar concern with achievement, particularly as it is expressed in the

1 Cf. N. Rogoff, *Recent Trends in Occupational Mobility*, Glencoe: The Free Press, 1953; K. B. Mayer, *Class and Society*, New York: Doubleday, 1955; R. Albrecht, "Social Class in Old Age," *Social Forces*, 29 (May, 1951), pp. 400–405.

2 Cf. P. Sorokin, *Social Mobility*, New York: Harper and Bros., 1927. For the relationship of intelligence to social mobility, see C. A. Anderson, *et al.*, "Intelligence and Occupational Mobility," *Journal of Political Economy*, 60 (June, 1952), pp. 218–239.

3 Factors of this sort have been abundantly studied. See H. Pfautz, "The Current Literature on Social Stratification: Critique and Bibliography," *American Journal of Sociology*, 58 (January, 1953), especially pages 401–404.

4 A review of recent investigations of some psychocultural dimensions of social stratification can be found in H. Pfautz, *op. cit.* While a number of personality correlates of social class have been delineated, there have been no studies of the relationship of class to the achievement motive as such, though C. W. Mills' notion of the "competitive personality" comes closest to approximating the personality characteristic examined in this study. See his *White Collar*, New York: Oxford University Press, 1953. Of the many studies of the cultural correlates of social class, two which have particular relevance for the problem examined in this paper are H. Hyman, "The Value System of Different Classes: A Social Psychological Contribution to the Analysis of Stratification," in R. Bendix and S. Lipset (editors), *Class, Status and Power*, Glencoe: The Free Press, 1953; and T. Parsons, "A Revised Analytical Approach to the Theory of Social Stratification," in Bendix and Lipset, *op. cit.*

Reprinted by permission of the American Sociological Association and the author from the *American Sociological Review*, 1956, vol. 21, pp. 203–11.

striving for status through social mobility.[5] It is hypothesized that social classes possess to a disparate extent two components of this achievement orientation. The first is a psychological factor involving a personality characteristic called *achievement motivation* (or, in Murray's terminology, *need achievement*) which provides an internal impetus to excel. The second is a cultural factor consisting of certain *value orientations* which define and implement achievement motivated behavior. Both of these factors are related to achievement; their incidence, we suggest, is greater among persons of the middle class than those in the lower class.

The task of this paper is threefold: (1) to make a preliminary attempt at determining whether social strata are dissimilar with respect to these two factors by examining their incidence among a group of randomly selected adolescents stratified by social position, (2) to indicate the significance of these factors for differential occupational achievement, and (3) to suggest some class related origins of achievement motivation and values.

Research Procedure

THE universe from which the study sample was drawn is the entire male population of sophomores in two large public high schools in the New Haven area. This group was stratified by the social position of the main wage-earner in the family (in most cases the father) through data secured by questionnaire and according to a scheme developed by Hollingshead.[6] His Index of Social Position utilizes three factors: (1) occupation, (2) education, and (3) ecological area of residence. Each factor is scaled and as-

signed a weight determined by a standard regression equation. The combined scores group themselves in five clusters (social strata) and to each of these a numerical index is assigned. The highest status group is labeled Class I; the others follow in numerical order, Class V being the lowest. Respondents were drawn randomly from each stratum: 5 subjects from Class I (the entire Class I Sophomore population in the two schools), 25 from Class II, and 30 each from Classes III, IV, and V. In all there are 120 subjects, all of them white, ages 14 through 16; the modal age is 15.

It was hypothesized that social strata are dissimilar with respect to two factors related to achievement: that is, achievement motivation and achievement value orientation. By achievement motivation we mean an anticipation of an increase in affect aroused by cues in situations involving standards of excellence. The behavior of people highly motivated for achievement is persistent striving activity, aimed at attaining a high goal in some area involving competition with a standard of excellence. In relation to these standards of excellence the achievement oriented person directs his efforts towards obtaining the pleasure of success and avoiding the pain of failure. Value orientations are defined (following the manner described in William's *American Society*) as meaningful and affectively charged modes of organizing behavior, as principles that guide human conduct. They establish the criteria which influence the individual's preferences and goals; they act as spectacles through which the individual sees himself and his environment. Two techniques were employed to measure these factors. A projective test (a technique which does not rely upon the person's self-knowledge) was used to measure the adolescent's achievement motivation; the direct questionnaire was used to measure his values.

The personality correlate of achievement called "achievement motivation" has been investigated by McClelland and his associates.[7] Using a Thematic Apperception Test type

---

5 A. Green in his introductory text, *Sociology,* New York: McGraw-Hill, 1952, regards the middle class' high level of achievement drive, as expressed through status striving, as its single most pronounced characteristic. However, the data to support this conclusion are largely of an anecdotal, or highly qualitative nature. See C. W. Mills, *op. cit.;* A. Davis, B. Gardner, and M. Gardner, *Deep South,* Chicago: University of Chicago Press, 1941.

6 For a fuller exposition of this scheme, see A. Hollingshead and F. C. Redlich, "Social Stratification and Psychiatric Disorders," *American Sociological Review,* 18 (April, 1953), pp. 163–169.

7 D. McClelland, J. Atkinson, R. Clark, and E. Lowell, *The Achievement Motive,* New York: Appleton-Century-Crofts, 1953.

measure, they have developed a projective test whose scoring system is designed to detect and measure the degree to which a person thinks about and is emotionally involved in competitive task behavior that is evaluated against a standard of excellence. As is customary in the TAT testing procedure, the subject is presented with a set of fairly ambiguous pictures and asked to tell a story about each of them. His imaginative responses are then scored for evidences of achievement motivation. Two criteria must be satisfied before a story can be scored as containing achievement imagery. First, the events and people in the stories must show some evaluation of individual performance in relation to and competition with a standard of excellence, e.g.: "The boy has done a good job in the exam." Second, some affect, neither positive or negative, must be connected with the evaluated performance, e.g.: "He is unhappy because he lost the essay contest." It is the assumption of the test that the more the individual shows indications of evaluated performance connected with affect in unstructured situations the greater the degree in which achievement motivation is part of his personality.

This projective test was administered to the subjects in the following standardized way. Subjects were assembled during the school day in small groups (20 to 30 persons) in a school room equipped with a screen and a slide projector. The test administrator explained to the students that they were going to see a series of pictures and that their task was to write a story about each picture. In his instructions to the subjects the administrator made no effort to manipulate the motive of the students. Since all testing was done in the school, it was expected that each boy would bring to the test his normal achievement motivation level induced by the cues of the school. The same administrator was used throughout the tests.[8]

Following the test, the subjects were asked to fill out a structured questionnaire, part of which contained items (the content of which is described in a later section of this paper) designed to index their value orientations. These items took the form of statements with which the subjects were asked to agree or disagree, and are centered around certain kinds of values that we felt are related to scholastic and vocational achievement.

Research Findings

SOCIAL STRATIFICATION AND THE ACHIEVEMENT MOTIVE

THE findings of this study support the hypothesis that social strata differ from one another in the degree to which the achievement motive is characteristic of their members. Furthermore, the data indicate that members of the middle class tend to have considerably higher need achievement scores than individuals in the lower social strata. Plotted on a graph, the mean achievement scores of the social classes fall along a regression curve: the highest mean score in Class II (the group most likely to be described as middle class when the trichotomy of upper, middle, and lower class is used), a somewhat lower score in Class I, and progressively lower scores in an almost linear fashion in Classes III, IV, and V. Reading in numerical order from Class I to V, the mean score for each class is 8.40, 8.68, 4.97, 3.40, and 1.87. The mean score for Class II is more than four times as great as the score for Class V.[9]

---

8 Experiments have shown that motivation scores vary with the conditions under which the test is given. The kind of instructions preceding the test are known to affect the test scores. These instructions are basically of three kinds: *achievement-oriented* instructions which produce cues aimed at increasing the score; *relaxed* instructions which tend to de-emphasize the arousal of the motive; and *neutral* instructions that are aimed at obtaining a measure of the normal level of motivation a subject brings to a situation. Instructions used in this study were of the neutral type. The impact of the school situation had upon the scores is unknown, but we believe that in effect this factor was controlled since all subjects were tested in the same situation. Further information on the various methods for administering this test, and their significance for the test results, can be found in D. McClelland, *et al., op. cit.,* Ch. 3. The test protocols were scored by two judges. The Pearson product moment correlation between the two scorings was plus .89, an estimate of scoring reliability similar to those reported in earlier studies with this measure.

9 In a study of personality and value differences between upper-class Harvard freshmen (private school graduates) and middle-class freshmen (pub-

TABLE 1

Achievement Motivation by Social Class
(in Percentages)

ACHIEVEMENT MOTIVATION SCORE	SOCIAL CLASS			
	I and II	III	IV	V
Low	17	57	70	77
High	83	43	30	23
Number	(30)	(30)	(30)	(30)

χ^2: 26.6.
$P < .001$.

A test of the statistical significance of this association between social position and achievement motivation is shown in TABLE 1. In order to simplify presentation, subjects whose scores fall below the approximate median for the entire sample are categorized as having low achievement motivation; [10] Classes I and II are collapsed into one group because of the scarcity of cases in Class I.[11] The data indicate a clear relationship between social position and motivation score. For example, 83 per cent of the subjects in Classes I and II have high motivation scores, as compared with 23 per cent in Class V, a difference that is statistically significant at the .001 level.

lic school graduates), C. McArthur, "Personality Differences Between Middle and Upper Classes," *Journal of Abnormal and Social Psychology,* 50 (March, 1955), pp. 247–254, found that the need achievement level of the middle-class was significantly higher than that of the upper-class. The difference between the two groups in the writer's study was in the same direction noted by McArthur, but was not statistically significant. However, since sampling methods, TAT pictures, and scoring procedures used in the two studies are different, the data are not comparable.

10 Four pictures were used in this study. The approximate median score for the entire sample was +4. Sixty-six subjects have a score of +4 or less; fifty-four subjects a score of +5 or more. Scores ranged from −4 to +15. It should be understood that the terms "high" and "low" used in this study do not refer to absolute standards but to relative ranks for individuals in this sample. As yet there are not sufficient data to permit the setting up of norms for broad cross-sections of the population for either achievement motivation or value orientation.

11 Analysis of the data in which persons in Classes I and II are examined together in one cell or part reveals that the conclusions noted above are not affected when the cells are collapsed.

SOCIAL STRATIFICATION AND
VALUE ORIENTATION

In itself the achievement motive is not a sufficient cause of upward mobility. Obviously the lack of innate capacity and/or structural opportunities may frustrate the achievement drive, but in addition there are cultural factors which are related to mobility. Among these factors are certain values which affect mobility in that they provide a definition of goals, focus the attention of the individual on achievement, and prepare him to translate motive into action. For example, before the achievement motive can be translated into the kinds of action that are conducive to culturally defined achievement (and hence operate as a factor in social mobility), there must be some definition of the kinds of situations in which achievement is expected and of the goals to which one should or may aspire.

Achievement oriented situations and goals are not defined by the achievement motive; it may provide the impetus to excel, but it does not delineate the areas in which such excellence should or may take place. Achievement motivation can be expressed through a wide range of behavior, some of which may not be conducive to social mobility in our society. The achievement motive can be, and perhaps frequently is, expressed through non-vocational behavior, for example lay religious activity of an individual whose drive to excel finds release through piety or mastery of sacred literature; or it may find an outlet in non-professional "hobby-type" behavior. Even when expressed through vocational activity, the achievement motive may be canalized into culturally defined deviant occupations (e.g. the criminal), or into low status vocations (e.g. the individual whose achievement drive is expressed and satisfied through his desire to be the *best* welder among his peers). Whether the individual will elect to strive for success in situations which facilitate mobility in our society will, in part, be determined by his values.

Furthermore, before the achievement motive can be expressed in culturally defined success behavior, there needs to be more than a desire to achieve success; there must also be some awareness of and willingness to undertake the steps necessary for achievement. Such steps involve, among other things, a preparedness to plan, to work, and to make sacrifices. Whether the individual will understand their importance and accept them will, in part, be affected by his values. It must follow, therefore, that differential inter-class rates of mobility cannot be entirely explained as a function of differences in achievement motivation; social classes must also be shown to differ in their possession of these implementary values necessary to achievement.

The notion that social classes possess dissimilar values as part of their distinctive sub-cultures has been suggested by a number of investigators, for example, the Kluckhohns, who have delineated a wide range of differences in the value systems of social strata in American society.[12] In Florence Kluckhohn's schema [13] these values are part of a configuration of value orientations which grow out of man's effort to solve five basic problems that are everywhere immanent in the human situation. While all five of Kluckhohn's orientations are relevant to the problem of achievement, three were selected as especially pertinent for examination in this study: (1) what is the accepted approach to the problem of mastering one's physical and social environment, (2) what is the significant time dimension, and (3) what is the dominant modality of relationship of the individual to his kin. We were interested in determining whether social classes are dissimilar in their possession of these orientations. A brief description of their content (modified somewhat from the way in which they appear in the Kluckhohn schema), and examples of

12 C. Kluckhohn and F. Kluckhohn, "American Culture: Generalized Orientations and Class Patterns" in *Conflicts of Power in Modern Culture,* edited by L. Bryson, *et al.,* Harper and Bros., 1947. See also, M. Gordon, "*Kitty Foyle* and the Concept of Class as Culture," *American Journal of Sociology,* 53 (November, 1947), pp. 210–217. Other investigators are cited in H. Pfautz, *op. cit.,* pp. 403–404.

13 F. Kluckhohn, "Dominant and Substitute Profiles of Cultural Orientations: Their Significance for the Analysis of Social Stratification," *Social Forces,* 28 (May, 1950), pp. 376–393.

the items used to index each of them, are as follows: [14]

1. *Activistic-passivistic orientation* concerns the extent to which a society or sub-group encourages the individual to believe in the possibility of his manipulating the physical and social environment to his advantage. In an activistic society the individual is encouraged to believe that it is both possible and necessary for him to improve his status, whereas a passivistic-orientation promotes the acceptance of the notion that individual efforts to achieve mobility are relatively futile.

Item 1. "All I want out of life in the way of a career is a secure, not too difficult job, with enough pay to afford a nice car and eventually a home of my own."

Item 2. "When a man is born the success he is going to have is already in the cards, so he might just as well accept it and not fight against it."

2. *Present-future orientation* concerns a society's attitude toward time and its impact upon behavior. A present-oriented society stresses the merit of living in the present with an emphasis upon immediate gratifications; a future-oriented society urges the individual to believe that planning and present sacrifices are worthwhile, or morally obligatory, in order to insure future gains.

14 In all fourteen items were used to index certain of the adolescent's values and perceptions. The nine additional items are as follows:

1. Even though parents often seem too strict, when a person gets older he will realize it was beneficial.
2. If my parents told me to stop seeing a friend of my own sex, I'd see that friend anyway.
3. Parents seem to believe that you can't take the opinion of a teenager seriously.
4. Parents would be greatly upset if their son ended up doing factory work.
5. It's silly for a teenager to put money in a car when the money could be used to get started in a business or for an education.
6. The best kind of job is one where you are part of an organization all working together, even if you don't get individual credit.
7. Education and learning are more important in determining a person's happiness than money and what it will buy.
8. When the time comes for a boy to take a job, he should stay near his parents even if it means giving up a good job.
9. Even when teenagers get married their main loyalty still belongs to their mother and father.

Item 3. "Planning only makes a person unhappy since your plans hardly ever work out anyway."

Item 4. "Nowadays with world conditions the way they are the wise person lives for to-day and lets tomorrow take care of itself."

3. *Familistic-individualistic orientation* concerns the relationship of the individual to his kin. One aspect of this orientation is the importance given to the maintenance of physical proximity to the family of orientation. In a familistically-oriented society the individual is not urged, or perhaps not permitted, to acquire independence of family ties. An individualistically-oriented society does not expect the individual to maintain the kinds of affective ties which will impede his mobility.

Item 5. "Nothing in life is worth the sacrifice of moving away from your parents."

Responses which indicate an activistic, future-oriented, individualistic point of view (the answer "disagree" to these items) are considered those which reflect values most likely to facilitate achievement and social mobility. These items were used to form a value index, and a score was derived for each subject by giving a point for each achievement oriented response.

An analysis of the data supports the hypothesis that the middle class is characterized by a larger proportion of persons with achievement oriented values than are the lower social strata. The plotting of mean value scores for each class reveals an almost linear relationship between social position and values: the higher the class the higher the value score. Thus the mean scores for the five social strata are in descending order, with Class I first and Class V last, 4.6, 4.1, 3.8, 3.0 and 2.5. This relationship is shown to be statistically significant in TABLE 2 in which social position is cross-tabulated with value score. To simplify presentation value scores are dichotomized: respondents whose score falls above the approximate median for the entire sample are designated as having a high score. The data reveal that of those adolescents in Class I or II, 77 per cent score high on the value scale, as compared with 17 per cent of the

TABLE 2

Value Orientations by Social Class (in Percentages)

VALUE SCORE	SOCIAL CLASS			
	I and II	III	IV	V
Low	23	30	67	83
High	77	70	33	17
Number	(30)	(30)	(30)	(30)

χ^2: 28.9.
$P < .001.$

adolescents in Class V. For the entire table, the probability of this level of association occurring by chance is less than one out of a thousand.

ACHIEVEMENT CORRELATES OF ACHIEVEMENT MOTIVATION AND VALUES

Achievement motivation and value orientation were found to be related to different kinds of behavior that affect social mobility. We have stated that the achievement motive expresses itself in concern with performance evaluated against a standard of excellence. In the school situation this performance may be canalized within the framework of scholastic achievement. That this is probably frequently the case can be seen in TABLE 3 in which motivation scores are cross-tabulated with average school grades. The data show that subjects with high motivation scores are proportionately more likely to achieve grades of "B" or better than are adolescents with

TABLE 3

Average School Grade by Achievement Motivation (in Percentages)

AVERAGE SCHOOL GRADE	ACHIEVEMENT MOTIVA-TION SCORE		VALUE ORIENTA-TION SCORE	
	High	Low	High	Low
"B" or above	69	35	54	46
"C" or below	31	65	46	54
Number	(54)	(66)	(59)	(61)

χ^2: 13.5.　　　　χ^2: .833.
$P < .001.$　　　　$P > .30.$

low motivation scores: 69 per cent of the former as against 35 per cent of the latter. Value scores, however, proved not to be related to academic achievement, although they are associated with a kind of behavior that is, if not in itself an act of achievement, at least a factor in social mobility in our society. It was found that the individual's value score, but *not* his motivation score, is related to educational aspiration. Thus the data in TABLE 4 indicate that subjects with high value scores are proportionately more likely to want to go to college than are those with low scores: 61 per cent of the former as compared with 33 per cent of the latter. The relationships between motivation and grades, and between values and aspiration level are statistically significant at the .001 level.

Since high need achievement and value scores tend to occur more frequently among members of the upper and middle than in the lower strata, it is not surprising to find that social strata are different in their academic achievement and educational aspiration levels. This is particularly marked in the case of educational aspiration level, which was found to be considerably higher for adolescents in the upper and middle strata than for those in the lower strata. Thus when subjects were asked, "If you could arrange things to suit yourself, how far would you go in school?" 92 per cent of respondents in the combined category of stratas I, II, and III

TABLE 4

School Aspiration by Value Orientation (in Percentages)

SCHOOL ASPIRATION	VALUE ORIENTA- TION SCORE High	Low	ACHIEVEMENT MOTIVA- TION SCORE High	Low
Aspires to go to college	61	33	51	46
Does not aspire to go to college	39	67	49	54
Number	(59)	(61)	(54)	(66)

χ^2: 13.3.
$P < .001.$

χ^2: 1.2.
$P > .20.$

TABLE 5

Value Score by Aspiration Level and Social Class (in Percentages)

	SOCIAL CLASS			
	I-II-III		IV-V	
VALUE SCORE	Under- Aspirers	Other- Aspirers	Over- Aspirers	Other- Aspirers
Low	57	23	65	79
High	43	77	35	21
Number	(7)	(53 *)	(17)	(43 †)

* Includes those individuals whose aspiration level represents the modal choice for their status group.

† Includes those subjects whose aspiration level is below or at the modal choice for their group.

aspired to continue their education beyond high school, either in college or in a technical school; whereas of the combined stratas IV-V only 47 per cent aspired to go beyond high school.[15]

The hypothesis that this differential in education aspiration is, in part at least, a function of value orientation differences is supported by the data shown in TABLE 5 in which under- and over-aspirers are examined. Under-aspirers are those respondents in strata I, II, or III whose educational aspiration level is lower than the modality for their group (i.e. those who do not aspire to go beyond high school); over-aspirers are those adolescents in strata IV-V whose aspiration level is higher than the norm for their group (i.e. those who aspire to go beyond high school). The data in TABLE 5 in which over- and under-aspirers are compared with one another, and with other members of their class, in terms of their value scores show a clear relationship between over-under-aspiration level and value orientations. Thus fewer under-aspirers have high value scores than do other members of their strata—43 per cent of the former as compared with 77 per cent of the latter; whereas over-aspirers are more likely to have high value scores than are other members of their

15 Class differentials in educational aspiration level have been noted by a number of investigators. See, for example, J. A. Kahl, "Educational and Occupational Aspirations of 'Common Man' Boys," *Harvard Educational Review*, 23 (Summer, 1953), pp. 186–203.

class—35 per cent as compared with 21 per cent. Furthermore, the class differences in value scores shown in TABLE 2 virtually disappear when aspiration level is held constant: an earlier difference of more than 40 per cent between categories I-II-III and IV-V is reduced to 8 per cent when over- and under-aspirers are compared with one another; whereas it is increased when the "other" categories are compared.

The relationship between academic achievement (as measured by average grades) and social class appears to reflect to a considerable extent strata differentials in achievement motivation. Class differences in academic achievement which appear significant on first inspection (e.g., 17 per cent of the subjects in the combined category of Classes I-II-III have average grades of "A"; only 3 per cent of those Classes IV-V have grades this high; also 54 per cent of the former have average grades of "B" or higher, as compared with 42 per cent of the lower status category) are markedly altered when need achievement score is introduced as a test variable. As can be seen in TABLE 6 the earlier relationship between class and grades is virtually erased for those with low achievement motivation and slightly reversed for those with high motivation. However, although the differences *between* strata are reduced to a statistically insignificant level, *within* strata differences between individuals with high and low motivation scores remain, thus pointing up the relationship between motivation and academic achievement.

Achievement motivation and achievement oriented values are not, of course, the only factors related to academic success and educational aspiration. The fact that *all* the cells

in the contingency tables described here contain some cases clearly indicates that other variables are at work. Among these variables may be such factors as sibling rivalry, the operation of ego defense mechanisms, or motives other than need achievement, for example, the need for power. Furthermore, social classes may be dissimilar in ways other than in their motives or values, and these differences can have significance for achievement. Classes are said to be different in manners, richness of cultural-esthetic experiences, and possibly with respect to intelligence, to a general sense of well being, power, and past history of successful endeavor. All of these factors may contribute to differential class rates of mobility by affecting academic and vocational success and aspiration level. The task of this paper, however, has been to focus upon the factors of achievement motivation and values, although probably in the empirical situation many of the above factors are operative and interactive at the same time.

Whatever the importance present and future studies may show the other factors listed above to have for achievement, the fact remains that this study reveals a significant relationship between achievement motivation and grades, and between values and educational aspiration. This fact is of more than academic interest. There is a nexus, though it is of course not a perfect one, between educational and vocational achievement in our society. Furthermore, the college degree is becoming an increasingly important prerequisite for movement into prestigeful and lucrative jobs; hence an aspiration level which precludes college training may seriously affect an individual's opportunity for social mobility. Since we have shown that achievement oriented motives and values are more characteristic of the middle than the lower strata, it is reasonable to suggest that these variables are, in part at least, factors which tend to create differential class rates of social mobility.

TABLE 6

School Grades by Achievement Motivation and Social Class (in Percentages)

AVERAGE SCHOOL GRADES	SOCIAL CLASS			
	I-II-III		IV-V	
	High	Low	High	Low
"B" or above	66	32	75	36
"C" or below	34	68	25	64
Number	(38)	(22)	(16)	(44)

CLASS RELATED ORIGINS OF
ACHIEVEMENT MOTIVATION AND VALUES

The achievement motive and values examined here, while related, represent genuinely different components of the achievement syndrome, not only in their correlates but also in their origins. Value orientations, because they tend to be on a conceptual level, are probably acquired in that stage of the child's cultural training when verbal communication of a fairly complex nature is possible. Achievement motivation, on the other hand, probably has its origins in certain kinds of parent-child interaction that occur early in the child's life and are likely to be emotional and unverbalized. Analytically, then, the learning of achievement oriented values can be independent of the acquisition of the achievement motive, though empirically they often occur together.

Several empirical studies have shown that achievement motivation is most likely to be high when the child is urged to obtain, and rewarded for achieving, independence and mastery, accompanied by few restrictions after mastery has been acquired.[16] Winterbottom's study,[17] for example, indicates that mothers of children with high achievement motivation differ from mothers of children who have low motivation in that they: (1) make more demands (particularly for evidences of independence, maturity, and achievement) at early ages; and (2) give more intense and frequent rewards for fulfilled demands.

These are the patterns which are believed to be especially characteristic of middle-class families, although it must be emphasized that the data to substantiate this conclusion are still tentative and often conflicting and that child-rearing practices, like other aspects of American culture, are in constant flux.[18] From babyhood on much of the middle-class

16 D. McClelland, et al., op. cit., Ch. 9.

17 M. Winterbottom, "The Relationship of Childhood Training in Independence to Achievement Motivation," University of Michigan Ph.D. Dissertation, 1953.

18 The uncertain character of data relating to class differences in child rearing is pointed up in the article, R. J. Havighurst and A. Davis, "A Comparison of the Chicago and Harvard Studies of Social Class Differences in Child Rearing," *American Sociological Review*, 20 (August, 1955), pp. 438–442. See also, M. C. Erickson, "Social Status and Child-rearing Practices," in T. Newcomb and E. Hartley (editors), *Readings in Social Psychology*, New York: Holt, 1947; A. Davis, *Social-class Influences Upon Learning*, Cambridge: Harvard University Press, 1951.

child's affect is likely to be associated with achievement related behavior structured for him by the training practices and values of his parents. In the pre-school period the tendency for middle-class parents to make early demands upon their children is reflected in such practices as early toilet training and the intense concern with cleanliness. As the child grows he is frequently urged and encouraged to demonstrate his developing maturity (e.g., early walking, talking, and self-care). Signs of precocity are signals for intense parental pride and often lavish rewards. It is precisely this atmosphere which provides, if Winterbottom is corect, a most fertile environment for the growth of the achievement motive.

When the child starts his formal schooling, the achievement oriented demands and values of his parents tend to be focussed on the school situation. From the beginning of his school career the middle-class child is more likely than his lower-class counterpart to have standards of excellence in scholastic behavior set for him by his parents. In fact, the relatively higher position which scholastic attainment has in the middle-class than in the lower-class value system means that more frequently for the middle- than for the lower-class child parental demands and expectations, as well as rewards and punishments, will center around school performance.

Associated with the stress on scholastic achievement are other achievement oriented values that are more characteristic of the middle than the lower class. While it is probably true that the notion that success is desirable and possible is widespread in our society, the implementary values—those which encouraged behavior that facilitate achievement—have long been more associated with the culture of the middle than of the lower class. Middle-class children are more likely to be taught not only to believe in success, but also to be willing to take those steps that make achievement possible: in short, to embrace the achievement value system which states that given the willingness to work hard, plan and make the proper sacrifices, an individual should be able to manipulate his environment so as to ensure eventual success.

GERALD S. BLUM *and* DANIEL R. MILLER

41. Exploring the Psychoanalytic Theory of the "Oral Character"

I N these days of sophisticated discussion on how to study psychoanalytic theory we feel somewhat defensive concerning the methods we are about to describe. Not only did we confine ourselves to conventional techniques in psychology's stockpile but we used as many as we could. This approach was designed to test whether the theory *can* be phrased in operational terms amenable to traditional types of experimentation.

The topic we chose to investigate was the theory of "oral character." On one hand, there is sufficient agreement in the psychoanalytic literature to provide a starting point from which to formulate hypotheses. On the other, this aspect of the theory is admittedly incomplete. The combination made the area seem especially promising for experimental exploration.

Various clinical manifestations of oral passivity are summarized by Fromm in the following selected excerpts describing what he calls the "receptive orientation":

In the receptive orientation a person feels "the source of all good" to be outside, and he believes that the only way to get what he wants—be it something material, be it affection, love, knowledge, pleasure—is to receive it from that outside source. In this orientation the problem of love is almost exclusively that of "being loved" and not that of loving. . . . They are exceedingly sensitive to any withdrawal or rebuff they experience on the part of the loved person. . . . It is characteristic of these people that their first thought is to find somebody else to give them needed information rather than to make even the smallest effort of their own . . . they are always

in search of a "magic helper." They show a particular kind of loyalty, at the bottom of which is the gratitude for the hand that feeds them and the fear of ever losing it. Since they need many hands to feel secure, they have to be loyal to numerous people. It is difficult for them to say "no," and they are easily caught between conflicting loyalties and promises. Since they cannot say "no," they love to say "yes" to everything and everybody, and the resulting paralysis of their critical abilities makes them increasingly dependent on others.

They are dependent not only on authorities for knowledge and help but on people in general for any kind of support. They feel lost when alone because they feel that they cannot do anything without help. . . .

This receptive type has great fondness for food and drink. These persons tend to overcome anxiety and depression by eating or drinking. The mouth is an especially prominent feature, often the most expressive one; the lips tend to be open, as if in a state of continuous expectation of being fed. In their dreams, being fed is a frequent symbol of being loved; being starved, an expression of frustration or disappointment. . . .[1]

Collection of Data

H AVING delimited our field of investigation, we were then faced with decisions concerning subjects and specific techniques. In regard to subjects, we chose to work with humans rather than animals. Generalizations from animal behavior are largely by way of analogy. Furthermore, the complexities of inter-

[1] From *Man for Himself* by Erich Fromm. Copyright 1947 by Erich Fromm. Reprinted by permission of Holt, Rinehart and Winston, Inc.

Reprinted by permission of the Duke University Press and the authors from the *Journal of Personality*, 1952, vol. 20, 287–304.

personal relationships cannot be fully duplicated in animal work. A second decision concerned normal versus abnormal subjects. We chose the former because of the frequently heard objection that a theory derived largely from abnormal subjects must be shown to be applicable to normals. A third decision involved the desired age level of the subjects. The selection finally centered on eight-year-olds, since children in the latency period have the double advantage of being relatively free of the rampant psychosexual conflicts of earlier childhood on one hand, and of crystallized adult defenses on the other. The experimental group consisted of the eighteen boys and girls in the third grade at the University of Michigan during 1948–49.

To test the hypotheses formulated from the literature, we first had to select a criterion measure of orality. This operational definition consisted of nonpurposive mouth movements recorded at various times over the three-week period of the research. Trained observers followed the children individually during eight two-minute intervals as part of a time-sampling procedure. They tallied such oral activities as thumb-sucking, licking the lips, tongue-rolling, and bubbling. In addition to these routine classroom observations, the same activities were noted in an experiment on boredom tolerance (see Section X). All children were ranked on both measures and a final average ranking computed.[2]

Data on the dependent variables were collected by the following methods: teacher ratings, time-sampling, sociometrics, and experimental situations. Wherever feasible, we employed several approaches to test each hypothesis. Since the theory postulates that all individuals fall along a continuum of orality, rank-order correlations (corrected for ties) were calculated to measure the association between variable and criterion.

Testing the Hypotheses

EACH of the following sections presents the statement of a hypothesis, the design worked out to test it, and the subsequent results.

2 These two measures of mouth movements correlated .61 with each other.

EXTREME INTEREST IN FOOD

A. *Hypothesis*

Since the oral character is emotionally involved with eating beyond the dictates of simple hunger, he will consume extreme amounts of oral supplies and evince great interest in related activities. Accordingly, positive correlations are predicted between the orality criterion (mouth movements) and variables measuring interest in food.

B. *Methods*

1. Ice cream consumption. Our measure of consumption of oral supplies was the amount of ice cream eaten after hunger satiation. The children all ate lunch together. The meal, provided by the school, was dietetically planned and ample for all the children. Upon conclusion of a short rest period which followed lunch, they were offered an unlimited supply of vanilla ice cream contained in one-ounce paper cups packaged especially for the study. The carton of ice cream was placed on a table in the center of the room by a female graduate student who supervised the distribution of cups. Each child was allowed to take one whenever he wished. However, only one cup at a time was permitted and that in return for an empty one. No limit was placed on how much a child ate. The carton was kept in the room for the entire forty minutes devoted to arts and crafts, during which period observers recorded the exact number of cups consumed by each child. This procedure was repeated daily over three weeks. From these data averages were computed. The range in any one day's session was quite startling, varying all the way from no cups to thirty-nine for a single child. The absence of any parental complaints concerning illness or lack of appetite was a pleasant surprise in view of the inability of the observers, even at the end of the most frustrating days of the experiment, to

eat more than five or six cups without discomfort.

2. Eagerness at lunch time. The regular teacher and five practice teachers were given a scale describing various kinds of behavior typical of oral children. They were asked to write the names of the children who occurred to them spontaneously as they read each of fourteen items.[3] At the completion of the form they were asked to reconsider each item and to increase all shorter lists of names to five. Among the questions was: "Which children appear most impatient to eat at lunch time, as if eating were particularly important to them?"

C. Results

MOUTH MOVEMENTS

1. Ice cream	.52	$P < .05$
2. Eagerness at lunch time	.51	$P < .05$

These figures strongly support the predicted association between orality (mouth movements) and interest in food.

NEED FOR LIKING AND APPROVAL

A. Hypothesis

In terms of the theory, a significant rela-

[3] Following is the complete list of questions: (1) Which children do you think get discouraged or give up most easily when something is difficult for them? (2) Which children do you think are most able to take care of themselves without the help of adults or other children? (3) Which children get the blues most often? (4) Which children would you most like to take with you on a two-week vacation? (5) Which children tend to ask the teacher for help most often, even when they know how to do the task? (6) Which children are most eager to have other children like them? (7) Which children display their affections most openly to the teachers? (8) Which children's feelings seem to be most easily hurt? (9) Which children seem to be always eager to help even when they are inconvenienced? (10) Which children seem to accept the suggestions of others almost without thinking twice? (11) Which children appear most impatient to eat at lunch time, as if eating were particularly important to them? (12) Which children make a special effort to get the teachers to like them? (13) Which children would you least like to take with you on a two-week vacation? (14) Which children seem most concerned with giving and receiving things?

tionship should be found between degree of orality and the need for liking and approval.

B. Methods

1. "Which children are most eager to have other children like them?" (Teacher item 6)
2. "Which children make a special effort to get the teachers to like them?" (Teacher item 12)
3. Approaches to teachers for approval. (Time-sampling item)
4. Approaches to children for approval. (Time-sampling item)
5. Attention to observers. (Time-sampling item)

MOUTH MOVEMENTS

1. Eagerness for others' liking	.68	$P < .01$
2. Efforts for teachers' liking	.10	N S[4]
3. Approaches to teachers for approval	.44	$P < .10$
4. Approaches to children for approval	.24	N S
5. Attention to observers	.36	$P < .20$

Viewing these correlations as a whole, the hypothesis seems to be fairly well supported. Although only two are significant beyond the 10 per cent level, all are in the positive direction.

DEPENDENCY

A. Hypothesis

Closely allied to the preceding hypothesis is the prediction of a positive correlation between orality and dependency.

B. Methods

1. "Which children do you think are most able to take care of themselves without the help of adults or other children?" (Teacher item 2)
2. "Which children tend to ask the teacher for help most often, even when they know how to do the task?" (Teacher item 5)

[4] Not significant.

C. Results

MOUTH MOVEMENTS

1. Doesn't take care of self	.50	P < .05
2. Asks teachers' help	.10	N S

These results tend to be equivocal, with one correlation being significant and the other not.

CONCERN OVER GIVING AND RECEIVING

A. Hypothesis

Since gifts represent a form of "supplies" to the oral character, it is predicted that concern over giving and receiving varies with degree of orality.

B. Methods

1. "Which children seem most concerned with giving and receiving things?" (Teacher item 14)

2. Generosity without promise of supplies in return. A related prediction held that oral children would be reluctant to give unless attractive supplies were forthcoming. After the distribution of ice cream on the second gift day (see Section 3 immediately following) the class was allowed to use the colored pencils in a drawing period. Shortly before the end of this session, a strange adult wearing a large, yellow badge marked "Pencil Drive" entered the room and made a very stirring appeal to give as many pencils as possible to the poor children of the neighborhood. Each child then went behind a screen and secretly deposited his pencils in the slot of a colorful box marked "Pencil Drive." All the new pencils had been marked with pin points, so that the contributions of each subject were readily identifiable. Unfortunately, this coding system was of little aid since only three in the entire class gave new pencils. The rest of the collection consisted of a variegated assortment of battered, chewed-up stumps with broken points—all without identification marks. In order to locate the pencil contributors, a new procedure was developed which provided the basis for the added experiment described in Section 4 following.

3. Gifts as the equivalent of food. The term "oral supplies" connotes, in addition to food, tokens of personal recognition. It was hypothesized that, if gifts and food are equivalent supplies, receipt of gifts should result in a diminution of ice cream consumption for the group as a whole. On one occasion the children were each given a box of crayons; another time they received seven colored pencils which they had chosen as their most desired gift in a rating session the preceding day.

4. Guilt over not giving. The theory leads to the prediction that guilt, typically experienced as a deprivation of supplies, should bring about an increase in the consumption of ice cream. The day after the pencil drive, the teacher agreed to deliver a stern lecture telling how ashamed she was of their stinginess. She was so effective that, before she finished, one boy blurted out that he had meant to give more new pencils and ran to the box to deposit a few. Next the teacher asked the group to retrieve their donations and observers tallied the number of pencils each pupil took back, which provided the data missing in Section 2 immediately above. Shortly afterward the ice cream was distributed and the number of cups counted as usual.

To relieve the guilt, the pencil solicitor returned later to proclaim happily that the school drive had been 100 per cent successful. He then apologized for not having announced previously that old pencils were not wanted.

C. Results

MOUTH MOVEMENTS

1. Concern over giving and receiving	.46	P < .10
2. Lack of generosity	.22	N S

3. Gifts as the equivalent of food. On the crayon day, 14 of the 16 subjects decreased in the number of cups consumed ($X^2 = 9.00$, $P < .01$); and on the pencil day, 12 out of 15 dropped ($X^2 = 5.40$, $P < .02$).

4. Guilt over not giving. While there were no significant increases in the actual amount of ice cream consumed after the "guilt" lecture, certain qualitative observations were noted. The five most oral children in the group sat on the table next to the ice cream carton throughout the whole period, in contrast to their usual wandering around the room. Since they had apparently been eating up to maximum physical capacity, it was virtually impossible for them to eat significantly more cups than before. Another exceptional feature was the fact that none of the ice cream was left over this time.

Considering the above experiments as a whole, there seems to be fair support for the hypothesis that orality is related to concern over giving and receiving.

NEED TO BE INGRATIATING

A. *Hypothesis*
The oral character, by virtue of his never-ending search for love and approval, tends to behave towards others in a very ingratiating manner.

B. *Methods*
1. "Which children display their affections most openly to the teachers?" (Teacher item 7)
2. "Which children seem to be always eager to help even when they are inconvenienced?" (Teacher item 9)
3. Going out of way to do favors. (Time-sampling item)

C. *Results*

MOUTH MOVEMENTS		
1. Displays affection openly	−.28	N S
2. Always eager to help	−.24	N S
3. Goes out of way to do favors	.16	N S

These results clearly negate the predicted association between orality and the need to be ingratiating.

SOCIAL ISOLATION

A. *Hypothesis*
According to the theory, the oral character should be infrequently chosen by his peers in view of his passivity, his excessive demands for attention, and his hostility when these demands are not gratified.

B. *Methods*
In a private interview each child was asked to answer a number of sociometric questions to determine his favorites among his classmates: (1) "Which children in your classroom do you like best?" (2) "Which of the children in your classroom would you most like to invite to a party?" (3) "Which teachers do you like the most?" [5] (4) "Which children in your class are you good friends with?" Class members were then ranked according to the number of times their names had been mentioned.

C. *Results*

MOUTH MOVEMENTS		
1. Social isolation	.68	P < .01

This correlation strongly supports the theoretical deduction that orality and social isolation go hand in hand.

INABILITY TO DIVIDE LOYALTIES

A. *Hypothesis*
The theory leads to the hypothesis that the more oral child has greater difficulty choosing between two friends, inasmuch as both represent potential sources of supply.

B. *Methods*
Several days after the sociometric ratings a measure of divided loyalty was obtained. Each child was interviewed individually and asked to make a number of choices between his two best friends as noted on

5 Included only for use in Section VII.

the sociometric ratings and also between his two best-liked teachers. The interviewer recorded decision time plus comments, actions, and expressive movements. The protocols were then rated blindly by three judges for degree of indecision.

C. Results

MOUTH MOVEMENTS

1. Inability to divide loyalties	−.28	N S

The correlation of this variable with the criterion contradicts the hypothesized association between orality and the inability to divide loyalties.

SUGGESTIBILITY

A. Hypothesis

From the theory it was anticipated that the oral child, in view of his excessive need for love and approval, would be suggestible in the presence of a potentially supply-giving adult.

B. Methods

1. Upon his arrival in the testing room, the child was told: "We have some things which we want you to help us try out in order to see if they are right for school children of your age." The experiment consisted of three parts: tasting a hypothetical cherry flavor in candy, smelling perfume from a bottle of water, and feeling nonexistent vibrations in a metal rod attached to some apparatus.
2. "Which children seem to accept the suggestions of others almost without thinking twice?" (Teacher item 10)

C. Results

MOUTH MOVEMENTS

1. Taste	.50	P < .05
Touch	.00	N S
Smell	.03	N S
2. Accepts suggestions	.11	N S

Except for taste, suggestibility does not appear to be related to degree of orality.

The discrepancy between results with taste and with the other items is most easily accounted for by the specifically oral quality of the taste measure.

DEPRESSIVE TENDENCIES

A. Hypothesis

Self-esteem in the oral child is presumed to depend upon external sources of love or supplies. Therefore, the unavoidable frustration of oral demands is said to be experienced as a feeling of emptiness or depression.

B. Methods

1. "Which children do you think get discouraged or give up most easily when something is difficult for them?" (Teacher item 1)
2. "Which children get the blues most often?" (Teacher item 3)
3. "Which children's feelings seem to be most easily hurt?" (Teacher item 8)

C. Results

MOUTH MOVEMENTS

1. Get discouraged	.32	P < .20
2. Get the blues	.05	N S
3. Feelings easily hurt	.13	N S

The low correlations between mouth movements and personality characteristics relevant to depression do not support the theoretical prediction.

BOREDOM TOLERANCE

A. Hypothesis

Boredom is assumed to be especially disturbing to the oral child because it signifies a lack of available supplies. Therefore he would be expected to show very little tolerance for a boring, unrewarded activity.

B. Methods

In this experiment the child was taken into a room where he was shown a large sheaf of papers containing lines of X's and O's. The examiner then said: "Your class is being compared with another class in another town to see which class can cross out the most circles." After giving the instructions, the examiner added: "There are several pages [the examiner leafed through all the sheets]. Don't write your name on the paper. We don't care how much you yourself can do, but how much the class can do. All right, you may begin."

The examiner then left the room. As soon as the child began, an observer casually entered the room, sat at a distance, and recorded all the actions of the subject, such as number of mouth movements and work interruptions. The child was stopped after twenty minutes. Ranks were based on number of lines completed. As mentioned previously, this experiment also contributed to the criterion measure of nonbiting mouth movements, which were tallied throughout.

C. Results

MOUTH MOVEMENTS

1. Boredom tolerance	.45	P < .10

While not very high, this figure does provide some support for the prediction that orality and boredom tolerance are positively associated.

SUMMARY OF RESULTS

Ten hypotheses concerning oral character structure have been tested. The results are summarized in the table at the foot of the page.

The goal of this phase of the research is to check the existing status of the theory, and to make revisions wherever dictated by

the evidence. The above data represent the initial tests of hypotheses deduced from the psychoanalytic literature on orality. In general, a fair number of predictions have been supported, some remain questionable, and still others are clearly not supported. Before evaluating specific hypotheses, however, we prefer to await the returns from successive attempts to measure the same variables. It is very possible that any one of the significant correlations may still reflect the influence of chance factors. Too, any one of the insignificant findings may be a function of faulty experimentation rather than incorrect theory. Both of these possibilities suggest the necessity for repeated research along similar lines. Apart from the fate of specific hypotheses, the over-all results hold promise for the investigation of psychoanalytic theory by conventional psychological methods.

Related Empirical Observations

INTERCORRELATIONS OF
MAJOR VARIABLES

In addition to providing data concerning specific hypotheses, the study lends itself to an over-all analysis of correlations among the major variables. This supplementary approach seems worth while in view of the postulated communality of the variables. If each variable really measures oral passivity, the table of intercorrelations should demonstrate positive relationships beyond chance expectancy. These data, grouped according to pure oral measures, experimental situations, and behavioral measures, are shown in TABLE 1.

From TABLE 2 we see that the total numbers of significant positive correlations at the

STRONG SUPPORT	FAIR SUPPORT	UNSUPPORTED	EQUIVOCAL
1. Extreme interest in food 2. Social isolation	1. Need for liking and approval 2. Concern over giving and receiving 3. Boredom tolerance	1. Dependency 2. Suggestibility	1. Need to be ingratiating 2. Inability to divide loyalties 3. Depressive tendencies

TABLE 1

Intercorrelations of Major Variables

	PURE ORAL MEASURES				PERSONALITY — EXPERIMENTAL SITUATIONS					BEHAVIORAL MEASURES	
Ice Cream	Eagerness at Lunch (T.R.)	Mouth Activity (T.S.)	Mouth Activity (B.T.)	Suggestibility	Boredom Tolerance	Divided Loyalty	Generosity	Sociometrics	Combined Teacher Ratings[1]	Combined Time Samples[2]
	19	67 ‡	32	30	31	−07	−29	40 *	−09	43 *
		41 *	50 †	11	34	−18	15	44 *	20	01
			61 ‡	04	39	−21	19	61 ‡	15	55 †
				25	44 *	−18	32	71 ‡	20	17
					12	44 *	−33	36	07	−11
						04	25	35	10	−04
							−33	03	04	−31
								18	45 *	09
									23	12
										−01

* = P < .10.
† = P < .05.
‡ = P < .01.

[1] Does not include 2 [Eagerness at Lunch (T.R.)]
[2] Does not include 3 [Mouth Activity (T.S.)]

10 per cent, 5 per cent, and 1 per cent levels clearly exceed the chance expectancies. These results suggest the possible existence of a general "factor" of orality.

COMPARATIVE EVALUATION OF METHODOLOGICAL APPROACHES

TABLE 3 presents a breakdown of the personality variables into two general types—experimental situations and behavioral measures. The number of significant correlations for each type with the major variables suggests a probable difference in their relative efficacy. It is true that the same operational variables are not measured in both types.

TABLE 2

Number of Significant Positive Correlations among Major Variables

PROBABILITY LEVEL	NUMBER EXPECTED BY CHANCE	NUMBER OBTAINED
.10	2.75	13
.05	1.38	6
.01	0.28	4

Nevertheless, the large number of significant behavioral correlations warrants speculation concerning possible causes. Three alternative explanations come to mind. One, the experimental designs were adequate and the negative results are a contradiction of the hypotheses. This possibility does not seem very plausible in light of the positive theoretical findings with other techniques. Two, the hypotheses are valid and the designs inadequate. No evidence exists for rejecting this alternative, but the marked discrepancy between results with the two approaches, both of which were carefully designed and pretested, leads us to question the explanation. Three, the difficulty lies, not in experimental design or theory, but in unreliability inherent in the settings in which the experiments were conducted. The number of observations involved in the experiments were necessarily limited to one session, whereas the behavioral measures were usually accumulated over several time periods. Unavoidable and unpredictable obstacles are bound to arise in the course of experimentation in a natural setting, such as a schoolroom, where the success of each

TABLE 3

Personality Measures Broken Down by the Type of Approach vs. Major Variables

PERSONALITY MEASURES	PROBABILITY LEVEL	NUMBER POSITIVE CORRELATIONS EXPECTED BY CHANCE	NUMBER OBTAINED
Experimental	.10	1.70	3
situations	.05	0.85	0
	.01	0.17	0
Behavioral	.10	1.35	7
measures	.05	0.68	3
	.01	0.14	2

design hinges upon the precision and co-operation of a large number of individuals.

Cases in point are the Love Withdrawal and Can't Say No experiments, both of which had to be abandoned. The hypothesis in the former stated that the oral child should be highly sensitive to withdrawal of love. The "ice-cream lady" first asked the children in the class to make drawings using themes of their own choice. When the drawings were finished she circulated around the room, praising them all freely. Then she instructed the group to draw a house, each child individually to bring his drawing to her upon its completion. She lauded half of the drawings, and held them up before the class while commenting on their merits and naming the artists. The other half were received with casual indifference but no criticism. This was the love withdrawal procedure. Finally, she asked the class to draw a picture of a child. The aim of the experiment was to determine the effects of the withdrawal of love upon both drawings and behavior as recorded by observers.

The experiment was to have been repeated several days later, with a reversal of the treatment of the previously praised and ignored halves. In the actual administration it turned out to be impossible to maintain any kind of order in the class. The children were all excited about an Indian play which they had performed that day before the entire school, and their drum-pounding and war-whooping precluded any systematic, experimental procedure.

The Can't Say No hypothesis dealt with the inability of the oral character to refuse requests from adults for fear of losing their approval. Nine observers entered the library while the class was listening to a fascinating record. Each observer approached a child, tapped him on the shoulder, and said in a neutral tone: "Come with me." The reactions to this request were later reported in detail. Like the preceding experiment this one was disrupted by an unforeseen complication. At the last minute the librarian was unable to schedule a record session when the other nine children in the group were to be asked to leave.

In contrast to the above illustrative experiments, the cumulative behavioral measures, on the other hand, were not as susceptible to unforeseen disruptions, since accidental influences on any one day tended to average out in the course of time. For example, differences occurred when ice cream was delivered late, yet this did not seriously alter the final ranking of subjects on the number of cups consumed.

From these speculations, it seems preferable that research designs, when dealing with something as complex as character structure, involve a series of measurements over a period of time.

EXPLORATION OF PROJECTIVE INSTRUMENTS

The following four projective techniques were included to explore their suitability as meas-

TABLE 4

Correlations of Projective Methods with Major Variables

	PURE ORAL MEASURES				PERSONALITY EXPERIMENTAL SITUATIONS				BEHAVIORAL MEASURES		
	Ice cream	Eager-ness at Lunch (T.R.)	Mouth Activ-ity (T.S.)	Mouth Activ-ity (B.T.)	Sug-gesti-bility	Bore-dom Toler-ance	Divided Loyalty	Gen-erosity	Socio-metrics	Com-bined Teacher Ratings	Com-bined Time Samples
Rorschach (objective)	28	19	20	−05	11	41	−03	−11	−13	−10	45
TAT (objective)	−40	−58	−34	−59	01	−37	33	−21	05	−02	−05
Story completion (objective)	−11	−45	−29	−36	08	−20	60	−06	−11	−12	−05
Story completion (interpretive)	47	06	33	48	40	37	23	−34	19	−12	06
Blacky (interpretive)	21	−23	16	25	41	−06	16	−20	28	15	21

ures of orality: the Rorschach Test (7), Thematic Apperception Test (6), Blacky Pictures (1, 2) and a specially constructed Story Completion Test which had been found to be significantly related to sociometric status in a previous study (5). Since there had been no previous applications of the techniques to this topic and age range, attempts at explicit prediction were not made.

TABLE 4 presents the correlations of the various projective methods with the major variables. Analysis of the projectives can be grouped under two broad headings, objective and interpretive. The Rorschach, TAT, and Story Completion (Objective) were all scored by counting the number of oral references, e.g., "food," "hunger," "eating," etc. The Blacky and Story Completion (Interpretive) protocols were ranked according to global impressions of oral passivity. While none of the correlations is very high, it should be noted that the "objective" approach yielded 22 negative and 11 positive correlations, whereas the "interpretive" produced only 5 negative and 17 positive ($X^2 = 10.19$ $P < .01$). Whether this difference can legitimately be attributed to type of scoring approach can be answered only by further investigation.

Summary

THIS project was designed to explore the feasibility of testing psychoanalytic theory by conventional psychological methods. Hypotheses concerning the "oral character," deduced from statements in the literature, were examined by means of teacher ratings, time-samplings, sociometrics, and experimental situations conducted in a third-grade class. The operational definition of orality consisted of nonpurposive mouth movements recorded by observers. The eighteen subjects were ranked on the criterion and on a series of variables related to specific hypotheses.

The resulting correlations lent strong support to hypotheses dealing with (*a*) extreme interest in food, and (*b*) social isolation. Fair support was given (*a*) need for liking and approval, (*b*) concern over giving and receiving, and (*c*) boredom tolerance. Unsupported hypotheses were (*a*) need to be ingratiating, (*b*) inability to divide loyalties, and (*c*) depressive tendencies; while remaining equivocal were (*a*) dependency and (*b*) suggestibility. Apart from the currently tentative nature of these specific findings, the over-all results were interpreted as holding promise for the investigation of psychoanalytic theory by traditional techniques.

REFERENCES

1. BLUM, G. S. A study of the psychoanalytic theory of psychosexual development. *Genet. Psychol. Monogr.,* 1949, 39, 3–99.

2. BLUM, G. S. *The Blacky Pictures: a technique for the exploration of personality dynamics.* New York: The Psychological Corporation, 1950.

3. FENICHEL, O. *The psychoanalytic theory of neurosis.* New York: W. W. Norton and Co., 1945.

4. MILLER, D. R., and HUTT, M. L. Value interiorization and personality development. *J. soc. Issues,* 1949, 5, No. 4, 2–30.

5. MILLER, D. R., and STINE, M. E. The Prediction of Social Acceptance by Means of Psychoanalytic Concepts. *J. Pers.,* 1951, 20, 162–174.

6. MURRAY, H. A. *Thematic Apperception Test manual.* Cambridge: Harvard University Press, 1943.

7. RORSCHACH, H. *Psychodiagnostics* (translation). Bern: Hans Huber, 1942.

8. THOMPSON, C. *Psychoanalysis: evaluation and development.* New York: Hermitage House, 1950.

9. THORNTON, G. R. The significance of rank-difference coefficients of correlation. *Psychometrika,* 1943, 8, No. 4, 211–222.

DOUGLAS N. JACKSON *and* SAMUEL MESSICK

42. Content and Style in Personality Assessment

I<small>N</small> personality theory a ubiquitous and fundamental distinction may be drawn between the interpretation of behavior in terms of (*a*) the *content* of "needs" and of cognitive structures generally and in terms of (*b*) characteristic *styles* of response and action. The separation of these two components of personality organization has taken a variety of forms in the hands of different theorists, as in the Allport-Vernon (2) *Studies in Expressive Movements,* in Murphy's (47) scholarly discussion of continuity in personality structure, in Klein's (40) distinction between needs and control processes, and in Vernon's (54) distinction between adaptive and expressive behavior. One may legitimately ask not only *what* a person says or does (the particular content of his statements and actions) but *how* he acts (his characteristic *mode* or *style* of expression).

What is conceptually a relatively sharp distinction is typically blurred and confounded in a particular concrete act; the what and how are fused in a given goal-directed response. An obsequious person indicates his deference not only by the act of yielding, but by the tone of his voice in performing the yielding act. Because content and style are intermixed in a given behavior sequence, and because there is often a theoretical predilection for content components, style is often overlooked in personality assessment. Also, the measurement of content appears to be more direct and unambiguous than the assessment of stylistic dimensions of personality. It is possible, for example, to ask a

person what his attitude is on a given topic, or to draw inferences about his need patterns from his reported likes and dislikes (51). The obviousness of such devices, while helpful from the viewpoint of labeling what one hopes one is measuring, also permits respondents to distort their scores if they so desire (32), something which is less likely to occur in the assessment of style.

In considering the general distinction between content and style, those methods of personality and attitude assessment which are based upon printed questionnaires of one form or another will be emphasized. While the complementary constructs of content and style have special relevance to questionnaire items, where the response-evoking properties of the particular item *form* may contribute markedly to response variance above and beyond the contribution of *content,* the distinction might also be applied usefully to other areas of personality assessment. For example, three possible applications are to perceptual and cognitive style as in the work of Thurstone (52), Witkin (58), Klein (39, 40), Gardner (21), and others (34); to achievement and aptitude testing (28, 32, 60); and to the perception of personality (2, 38, 54, 59).

The present discussion attempts to do two things: first, to present some evidence showing the important and subtle influences upon responses of stylistic components of item form; and, second, to illustrate how reliable measures of potentially useful stylistic dimensions may be generated from character-

Reprinted by permission of the American Psychological Association and the authors from the *Psychological Bulletin,* 1958, vol. 55, pp. 243–51.

istic responses to the form of personality and attitude items as distinct from measures of content.

Personality Style and Response Set

TRADITIONALLY, responses to a particular item or set of items are assumed to provide information about the respondent in terms of the item *content*. If, for example, a person agrees with the statement, "Under no conditions is war justified," or answers "true" to the item, "I have more trouble concentrating than others seem to have," it is commonly assumed that these responses, if consistent, will indicate respectively something about the person's attitude toward war or his mental state. Under these conditions response determinants such as the subjects' generalized tendency to agree are legitimately considered as sources of cumulative error, Cronbach's (13, 14) familiar "response sets." While Cronbach's emphasis was that response sets often lead to errors of interpretation in the logical validity of tests, he also indicated that these response tendencies might not always be temporary and trivial, but may have a stable and valid component which reflects a consistent individual style or personality trait. While recognizing Cronbach's contribution in describing the phenomenon, it is preferable for the present purposes to change the label from "response set" to components of *style*. This change in terms emphasizes the fact that for certain purposes in personality assessment opportunities for the expression of personal modes for responding should be enhanced and capitalized upon, rather than considered as sources of error to be avoided or minimized. This change also avoids the ambiguity inherent in the concept of "set" (22).

Characteristic Styles in Personality and Attitude Questionnaires

AMONG the more prominent response styles usually evoked by questionnaire items are response acquiescence, overgeneralization, a tendency to respond in a socially desirable way, and the complementary tendencies to respond negativistically, critically, and in a socially undesirable or idiosyncratic manner. Some pertinent illustrations will be drawn of how each of these, operating singly and in combination, may influence the interpretation of responses to psychological tests. Alternative procedures for evaluating these stylistic variables will then be discussed.

RESPONSE ACQUIESCENCE AND AUTHORITARIANISM

It has been long recognized that a subject who agrees with a personality or attitude item stated in a positive form may not necessarily disagree with its logical opposite, but may instead show a fairly general tendency toward agreement or disagreement. Studies by Rundquist and Sletto (49), by Lorge (42), and reviews by Cronbach (13, 14), Berg (8), and Messick and Jackson (45), indicate that response acquiescence is widespread and pervasive over a wide variety of item content and most pronounced when content is highly ambiguous or imaginary. Berg (8, 9) has suggested that acquiescence is a modal response in our culture when the issue before the respondents is unimportant or nonexistent.

The operation of such stylistic tendencies should be taken into account in the course of personality measurement. If a particular *content* area is to be assessed, it is at least necessary to introduce into the scaling procedure appropriate experimental controls for acquiescence, or else reconcile oneself to interpretive equivocality due to the confounding of content and style in a single measure. Other response determinants besides acquiescence, however, must be controlled before characteristics may be unequivocally attributed to respondents on the basis of item content. Messick and Jackson (45) have discussed alternative methods for reducing this ambiguity of interpretation in the measurement of authoritarian attitudes.[1]

---

[1] Gage, Leavitt, and Stone (20) have argued that confounding content and style in the F scale, far from being a source of error, is fortunate, because acquiescence contributes to the empirical validity of the F scale as assessed by independent ratings of authoritarian behavior. If the aim is merely to predict authoritarianism as a criterion, like predicting the success of salesmen, this argument might be

Even though much of the recent research with the California F scale (1) has been of a methodological and critical nature, it nevertheless yields some important information on the relationship between content and style. A number of investigators (5, 46, 36, 37, 41, 45) have independently correlated scores based on the California F scale, in which all of the items are so worded that agreement is always scored in the authoritarian direction, with scores based on logically reversed F-scale items. These correlations were not found to be high and negative, as would be expected from consistent responses to item content. With one reversed F scale (36), significant positive correlations in the acquiescence rather than the content direction were obtained. Furthermore, there is evidence (37) that previously obtained relationships between personality variables and the F scale, formerly thought to be interpretable in terms of correlates of authoritarian ideology or content, may need reinterpretation in terms of consistencies in style. The most recent study requiring such reinterpretation is one by Gilbert and Levinson (23), in which a scale purportedly measuring "custodial mental illness ideology" was constructed, with 17 of 20 items requiring agreement to be scored as "custodial ideology." A high correlation between the "custodial ideology" scale and the F scale was used to support the conclusion that "preference for a custodialistic orientation is part of a broader pattern of personal authoritarianism." But Howard and Sommer in a replication [2] found that "custodialism" correlated significantly with agreements to both the original and the Jackson-Messick (36) reversed F scales, which would seem to indicate that style rather than content is of primary importance in this instance.

Christie, Havel, and Seidenberg (12) have shown that it is possible in some samples to

obtain a correlation between reversed and original F-scale items significant in the content direction. Jackson, Messick, and Solley (37) had previously reported a correlation of +.35 between agreements to original and to reversed F-scale items. What accounts for this apparently considerable discrepancy? One set of investigators predicted and obtained a correlation significant in the acquiescence direction, while another, with a different reversed F scale, predicted and obtained a correlation in the content direction. The answer to this question requires a consideration of more than differences in the content of the two reversed F scales; the form of the items must be examined. Jackson and Messick (36) indicated that the original, extremely worded, cliché-ridden style of the F scale was retained in their reversals, while Christie, Havel, and Seidenberg (12) explicitly avoided the sweeping generalizations found in the originals and substituted much more cautious statements. It is likely that this difference in item form accounts for the different results of the two sets of investigators. It appears that the tendency to endorse statements containing phrases such as "every person," "no person," "all," "most important," "complete certainty," "never," "must," etc., is a general one, which may act independently of the content. This response style to overgeneralize may contribute to relationships between the F scale and cognitive variables like rigidity (37) and perceptual intolerance for ambiguity (18). It probably also partially accounts for the frequent observation that verbally elicited ethnic attitudes tend to be highly intercorrelated (10), even, for example, in Hartley's (30) study where the "groups" were nonexistent and no previous attitude or "cognitive structure" could be assumed to exist. An appraisal of variance associated with aspects of authoritarian content on one hand, and stylistic components like response acquiescence and overgeneralization on the other, would seem to require at least four sets of items: an extremely worded original and reversed F scale and a probabilistic original and reversed F scale. It is suspected that subjects endorsing probabilistic F-scale items would not show as much of the "authoritarian's" intolerance for

---

legitimate as long as the criterion did not change. But if one hopes to understand the various components of a dynamic construct like authoritarianism, conglomerate indices containing both content and style will not suffice and will confuse the issues (45).

[2] Howard, T. W., & Sommer, R. "A Critical Examination of 'Ideology, Personality, and Institutional Policy in the Mental Hospital.'" Unpublished manuscript.

ambiguity as might be expected, although some relationship between authoritarian ideology and response style might still be obtained.

RESPONSE ACQUIESCENCE IN PERSONALITY INVENTORIES

The distinct roles of content and style should also be noted in responses to personality inventories, especially those "true-false" devices like the MMPI developed by the empirical selection of discriminating items. While few, if any, investigators have ever explicitly assumed that the total number of empirically derived scales was the most parsimonious way of summarizing the common variance of an inventory, the use of a large number of separate scales as, for example, in the 9 clinical scales of the MMPI or the 18 scales of Gough's California Psychological Inventory, is justified by the extent to which each makes some independent contribution to the assessment problem not made by the other scales.[3] If there is a great deal of common variance among the various scales, this redundancy limits their efficiency.

There is considerable evidence that a very few factors account for the major proportion of the variance on personality inventories of the "true-false" variety. Wheeler, Little, and Lehner (57), for example, reported a factor analysis of MMPI scales in which only two major factors and one minor factor were identified. In the light of accumulating evidence it seems likely that the *major common factors in personality inventories of the true-false or agree-disagree type,* such as the MMPI and the California Psychological Inventory, *are interpretable primarily in terms of style rather than specific item content.*

One line of departure from which it is possible to evaluate the role of acquiescence

in personality inventories is to consider the percentage of items keyed "true" in each scale as an index of the extent to which that scale elicits response acquiescence. Jackson (33) did this with the California Psychological Inventory, computing rank order correlations between the percentage "true" in each scale and the scale's correlation with outside personality measures shown previously to reflect acquiescence. A number of high and significant correlations with such unidirectional scales as the California F scale and the MMPI K scale suggests strongly that acquiescence is a major source of variance in the CPI.

Messick and Jackson [4] have obtained evidence of a similar nature for the MMPI. They obtained rank order correlations in the seventies between each scale's percentage "true" and its loading on the first factor as reported in each of several factor analytic studies. Preliminary results suggest that the first factor of the MMPI is interpretable in terms of acquiescence. Equally striking is a recent factor analytic study by Welsh (55), who sought to obtain pure-factor MMPI scales through a variant of the internal consistency method. He was rather successful in developing two such scales, labeled A (for anxiety) and R (for repression), which loaded highly on the first and second factors, respectively. The remarkable thing about these scales is that all but one of the 39 items measuring the first factor are keyed "true," while all 40 items for the second pure factor scale are keyed "false." Even though Welsh's two scales are predominantly unidirectional, one in the "true," and the other in the "false" direction, they yield only low negative correlations with each other. This would lead one properly to reject the notion that a simple response set was sufficient to account for all of the variance in the two scales. Nevertheless, each scale does seem to have an acquiescence component, for such a distribution of "true" and "false" items would be unlikely to occur by chance, and Jackson (33) has shown that correlations based on both scales correlated significantly with percentage keyed

---

3 The MMPI was advanced initially as an aid in the prediction of psychiatric diagnoses. In practice it is rarely so used in any literal sense, which is fortunate, as the research evidence (e.g., 7, 48) indicates that predictions of specific diagnoses generally cannot be made with certainty. Rather, the original purpose of the MMPI, prediction, has come to be modified so that now scores, singly or in combination, are used to draw inferences about characteristics of respondents (56). Somewhat different notions of validity (15) and a different mathematical model (27, 53) are necessary in the latter case.

4 Messick, S. J., & Jackson, D. N. "Response Style and Factorial Interpretation of the MMPI." In preparation.

"true" in each CPI scale. Thus, careful consideration must be given to the possibility that response acquiescence is interacting with another variable, either of content or of style, and that responses are determined in part by this interaction. As with the F scale, where acquiescence operates most strikingly in conjunction with statements in the form of sweeping generalizations, it may be that acquiescence on the MMPI is elicited differentially by certain content categories, or in relation with another stylistic component.

The specific source of the variables which appear to moderate (50) the operation of response acquiescence in the MMPI is obviously a complicated research problem which awaits more evidence for a definitive answer. One very promising lead, however, is encountered in another important stylistic determinant of test-taking behavior, the general tendency to endorse socially desirable or socially undesirable statements about oneself. This stylistic reesponse tendency on the part of individuals should be distinguished from the judged characteristics of desirable and undesirable item content. There is considerable evidence that this tendency is general and is related to a tendency to respond in an idiosyncratic or atypical manner. Edwards (16) has reported a correlation of .87 between judged social desirability scale values and the proportion of respondents independently endorsing them. Hanley (29) obtained correlations of .82 and .89 respectively between probability of endorsement and social desirability ratings for samples of items from the MMPI D and Sc scales. Fordyce (17) correlated with the MMPI clinical scales a set of MMPI items judged to be socially desirable. His obtained correlations were high, ranging from $-.38$ to $-.91$. Although these coefficients indicate the importance of social desirability in scales like the MMPI, they also reflect the influence of response acquiescence, since the social desirability scale contained a disproportionate number of items keyed false. Jackson (33) showed that a combination of ranked indices of response acquiescence and social desirability on scales of the California Psychological Inventory was related to the rank of each scale's correlation with the

MMPI K scale to the extent of $r_s = .86$. This value was higher than the correlation of either response style operating singly, suggesting the possibility of summative effects of response acquiescence and social desirability.

Berg (8, 9), granting that there are modal response patterns, suggested that individual differences, particularly deviations, may be revealing of personality style. Berg hypothesized that deviant behavior tends to be general and not specific to any particular content area. Barnes (3, 4), appraising the Berg deviation hypothesis in the MMPI, shed important light on the relation between an acquiescent style and idiosyncratic responses. Barnes demonstrated a close correspondence between Wheeler, Little, and Lehner's (57) first or "psychotic" factor and total number of items answered deviantly true, and between their second or "neurotic" factor and total number of items answered deviantly false. Although response acquiescence and the tendency to respond in a socially undesirable or deviant manner are confounded in Barnes' analysis, these results strongly support the notion that items judged low in social desirability evoke different tendencies toward acquiescence, as compared with items judged high in social desirability. This interpretation appears consistent with Welsh's (55) data, where the first pure factor scale, composed of 38 "true" items out of 39, contains many socially undesirable statements, while the second pure factor scale, where all the items are keyed false, seems to consist predominantly of neutral or somewhat socially desirable statements. Here again, a consistent response style to acquiesce seems to be elicited differentially by a variety of self-deprecatory statements on the one hand, while, alternatively, neutral or mildly socially desirable statements evoke consistent differential tendencies to disagree or to be negativistic.

Whether there are consistencies attributable to content after allowing for style in these first two factors or, indeed, in any obtained scores on the present form of the MMPI is an important research question, as is the relation between various content and stylistic factors and psychopathology. If Berg (8) is correct, if one might just as well use abstract drawings (3) as items to discriminate empirically psychiatric patients from normals, then it may be that content is less important and style more important than previously supposed. If this is the case, then past attempts to draw conclusions about respondents on the basis of their answers to uncontrolled item content are suspect. If, on the other hand, consistencies in content can be demonstrated above and beyond components of style, it is extremely important that measures of these content variables make adequate use of proper experimental controls to avoid as far as possible confounding with style. Use of recent advances in scaling theory (27, 53) might be helpful.

Measuring Personality Styles

IN approaching the problem of the assessment of style, a curious dilemma presents itself. On the one hand, it is easy to show that most personality tests are loaded with stylistic components, but on the other hand, good measuring devices for these dimensions do not exist, largely because few research workers have attempted explicitly to devise such scales. Typically, a single measure, like the California F scale, the MMPI K scale, or Bass's (6) collection of aphorisms, has been offered as an index of a response style, acquiescence, for example. Little thought is given to the fact that these measures may not only contain several dimensions of content, but of style as well, thus limiting their usefulness as indices of any particular style. Thus, Fordyce (17) has suggested that the MMPI K scale reflects tendencies to respond in a socially desirable manner, while Fricke (19) has argued that the K scale reflects acquiescence. Evidence from each of the two authors is convincing, and, indeed, Jackson's study (33) supports the notion that the K scale contains both acquiescence and social desirability variance. It may reflect other things as well, but this confounding is not conducive to its use as a measure of one particular style. The same criticism might be leveled at the California F scale, at Edwards' (16) social desirability scale, and at Bass's (6) social acquiescence scale, all of which seem to confound response acquiescence with social desirability.

One way to construct measures of such styles as acquiescence or overgeneralization would involve selection of items extremely heterogeneous in content. Experimentally independent measures of each style would, of course, be desirable. Since a response style to answer in a socially desirable or undesirable direction seems to be omnipresent, it is hard to avoid in measures of other styles. Rather than attempting to develop items all at one level of social desirability, it might be better to vary social desirability systematically and to observe its relationships and interactions with other variables. Helmstadter (31) has described procedures for obtaining separate scores for different components of a test, some of which would be especially relevant to a situation in which one had already obtained social desirability scale values. Although social desirability has been assumed to be one-dimensional, it is easy to conceive of distinct, but perhaps correlated, dimensions consisting of items reflecting irresponsibility, psychiatric bizarreness, or hostility. The selection of sets of items for different dimensions of judged social desirability would be facilitated by the application of recent advances in multidimensional scaling (44). Such refinements as separating out the components of social desirability would do much to clarify response determinants and might put personality evaluation upon a more rigorous basis than has previously been thought possible.

Although the emphasis in this paper has been on some of the more conspicuous stylistic determinants encountered in common personality tests, there are many other possible measures of style that might be derived from personality theory. For example, a tendency to express a liking for diverse things, although it might be response acquiescence in a new disguise, might also represent greater cognitive differentiation or capacity to invest energy freely in objects in one's environment. Such general expressions of "like" and "dislike" have been found to be reliable. On one set of 300 items dealing with diverse activities (51), the corrected split-half reliability of the tendency to respond "like" was .86. With a paucity of evidence on these issues, the alternative to such conjecture is carefully planned research, for which there is an obvious need. There are many other research opportunities for the measurement of style, such as asking respondents to select from among two or more personality, attitude, or achievement items, equal in valence or correctness, but couched in different phrasings—perhaps one elaborate and pedantic, one simple, and one containing slang. Preferred modes or styles of expression might also be readily evaluated by techniques disguised as achievement tests (32). In this context, it would be interesting to evaluate personality correlates of such attributes as tolerance for logical contradictions within a passage, of a tendency to gamble on achievement tests (28, 54), and a variety of other consistent modes of response. Similarly, further research is needed to evaluate Jackson's (34, 35) hypothesis that respondents who acquiesce consistently manifest a lower level of cognitive energy in other situations.

Summary

IT has been suggested that stylistic determinants, such as acquiescence, overgeneralization, and a tendency to respond in a socially undesirable manner, as distinct from specific content, account for a large proportion of response variance on some personality scales, particularly the California F scale, the MMPI, and the California Psychological Inventory. In developing and evaluating measures of style it is important to select not only those measures which have appeared by accident on already established tests, but to design assessment techniques explicitly to evoke theoretically important styles of response. Research involving response style may contribute to a more systematic measurement in personality and may pay off handsomely in helping to further the common ground between personality theory and personality assessment.

REFERENCES

1. ADORNO, T. W., FRENKEL-BRUNSWIK, ELSE, LEVINSON, D. J., & SANFORD, R. N. *The authoritarian personality.* New York: Harper, 1950.
2. ALLPORT, G. W., & VERNON, P. E. *Studies in expressive movements.* New York: Macmillan, 1932.
3. BARNES, E. H. Response bias in the MMPI. *J. consult. Psychol.,* 1956, 20, 371–374.
4. BARNES, E. H. Factors, response bias, and the MMPI. *J. consult. Psychol.,* 1957, 20, 419–421.
5. BASS, B. M. Authoritarianism or acquiescence? *J. abnorm. soc. Psychol.,* 1955, 51, 611–623.
6. BASS, B. M. Development and evaluation of of a scale for measuring social acquiescence. *J. abnorm. soc. Psychol.,* 1956, 53, 296–299.
7. BENTON, A. L. The MMPI in clinical practice. *J. nerv. ment. Disease,* 1945, 102, 416–420.
8. BERG, I. A. Response bias and personality: the deviation hypothesis. *J. Psychol.,* 1955, 40, 61–72.
9. BERG, I., & RAPAPORT, G. M. Response bias in an unstructured questionnaire. *J. Psychol.,* 1954, 38, 475–481.
10. CAMPBELL, D. T., & McCANDLESS, B. R. Ethnocentrism, xenophobia, and personality. *Hum. Relat.,* 1951, 4, 185–192.
11. CHAPMAN, L. J., & CAMPBELL, D. T. Response set in the F scale. *J. abnorm. soc. Psychol.,* 1957, 54, 129–132.
12. CHRISTIE, R., HAVEL, JOAN, & SEIDENBERG, B. Is the F scale irreversible? *J. abnorm. soc. Psychol.,* 1958, 56, 143–159.
13. CRONBACH, L. J. Response sets and test validity. *Educ. psychol. Measmt,* 1946, 6, 475–494.
14. CRONBACH, L. J. Further evidence on response sets and test design. *Educ. psychol. Measmt.,* 1950, 10, 3–31.
15. CRONBACH, L. J., & MEEHL, P. E. Construct validity in psychological testing. *Psychol. Bull.,* 1955, 52, 281–302.
16. EDWARDS, A. L. The relationship between the judged desirability of a trait and the probability that the trait will be endorsed. *J. appl. Psychol.,* 1953, 37, 90–93.

17. FORDYCE, W. E. Social desirability in the MMPI. *J. consult. Psychol.,* 1956, 20, 171–175.

18. FRENKEL-BRUNSWIK, ELSE. Intolerance of ambiguity as an emotional and perceptual personality variable. *J. Pers.,* 1949, 18, 108–143.

19. FRICKE, B. G. Response set as a suppressor variable in the OAIS and MMPI. *J. consult. Psychol.,* 1956, 20, 161–169.

20. GAGE, N. L., LEAVITT, G. S., & STONE, G. C. The psychological meaning of acquiescence set for authoritarianism. *J. abnorm. soc. Psychol.,* 1957, 55, 98–103.

21. GARDNER, R. W. Cognitive styles in categorizing behavior. *J. Pers.,* 1953, 22, 214–223.

22. GIBSON, J. J. A critical review of the concept of set in contemporary experimental psychology. *Psychol. Bull.,* 1941, 38, 781–817.

23. GILBERT, DORIS C., & LEVINSON, D. J. Ideology, personality, and institutional policy in the mental hospital. *J. abnorm. soc. Psychol.,* 1956, 53, 263–271.

24. GOUGH, H. G. Studies of social intolerance: I–IV. *J. soc. Psychol.,* 1951, 33, 237–271.

25. GOUGH, H. G. Predicting social participation. *J. soc. Psychol.,* 1952, 35, 227–233.

26. GOUGH, H. G. *California Psychological Inventory Manual.* Palo Alto: Consulting Psychologist Press, 1957.

27. GREEN, B. F. Attitude measurement. In G. Lindzey (Ed.), *Handbook of social psychology,* Vol. I. Cambridge: Addison-Wesley, 1954.

28. GUILFORD, J. P., & LACEY, J. I. (Eds.) *Printed classification tests.* Washington: U.S. Government Printing Office, 1947.

29. HANLEY, C. Social desirability and responses to items from three MMPI scales: D, Sc, and K. *J. appl. Psychol.,* 1956, 40, 324–328.

30. HARTLEY, E. L. *Problems in prejudice.* New York: Kings Crown Press, 1946.

31. HELMSTADTER, G. C. Procedures for obtaining separate set and content components of a test score. *Psychometrika,* 1957, 22, 381–394.

32. HILLS, J. R. Objective tests of personality for practical use. Princeton, N. J.: Educational Testing Service Research Memorandum 57–4, 1957. (Multilithed report.)

33. JACKSON, D. N. Response acquiescence in the California Psychological Inventory.

Amer. Psychologist, 1957, 12, 412–413. (Abstract).

34. JACKSON, D. N. Independence and resistance to perceptual field forces. *J. abnorm. soc. Psychol.,* in press.

35. JACKSON, D. N. Cognitive energy level, response acquiescence, and authoritarianism. *J. soc. Psychol.,* in press.

36. JACKSON, D. N., & MESSICK, S. J. A note on ethnocentrism and acquiescent response sets. *J. abnorm. soc. Psychol.,* 1957, 54, 132–134.

37. JACKSON, D. N., MESSICK, S. J., & SOLLEY, C. M. How "rigid" is the "authoritarian"? *J. abnorm. soc. Psychol.,* 1957, 54, 137–140.

38. JACKSON, D. N., MESSICK, S. J., & SOLLEY, C. M. A multidimensional scaling approach to the perception of personality. *J. Psychol.,* 1957, 44, 311–318.

39. KLEIN, G. S. The Menninger Foundation research on perception and personality. 1947–1952: a review. *Bull. Menninger Clin.,* 1953, 17, 93–99.

40. KLEIN, G. S. Need and regulation. In M. R. Jones (Ed.), *Nebraska Symposium on Motivation.* Lincoln: Univer. Nebraska Press, 1954.

41. LEAVITT, H. J., HAX, H., & ROCHE, J. H. "Authoritarianism" and agreement with things authoritative. *J. Psychol.,* 1955, 40, 215–221.

42. LORGE, I. Gen-like: Halo or reality? *Psychol. Bull.,* 1937, 34, 545–546.

43. MEEHL, P. E. The dynamics of "structured" personality tests. *J. clin. Psychol.,* 1945, 1, 296–303.

44. MESSICK, S. J. Some recent theoretical developments in multidimensional scaling. *Educ. psychol. Measmt,* 1956, 16, 82–100.

45. MESSICK, S. J., & JACKSON, D. N. The measurement of authoritarian attitudes. *Educ. psychol. Measmt,* in press.

46. MESSICK, S. J., & JACKSON, D. N. Authoritarianism or acquiescence in Bass's data. *J. abnorm. soc. Psychol.,* 1957, 54, 424–426.

47. MURPHY, G. *Personality.* New York: Harper, 1947.

48. RUBIN, H. Validity of a critical-item scale for schizophrenia on the MMPI. *J. consult. Psychol.,* 1954, 18, 219–220.

49. RUNDQUIST, E. A., & SLETTO, R. F. *Personality in the depression.* Minneapolis: Univer. of Minnesota Press, 1936.

50. SAUNDERS, D. R. Moderator variables in pre-

diction. *Educ. psychol. Measmt.*, 1956, 16, 209–222.

51. STERN, G. G., STEIN, M. I., & BLOOM, B. S. *Methods in personality assessment.* Glencoe, Ill.: Free Press, 1956.

52. THURSTONE, L. L. *A factorial study of perception.* Chicago: Univer. Chicago Press, 1944.

53. TORGERSON, W. S. *Theory and methods of scaling.* New York: Wiley, in press.

54. VERNON, P. E. *Personality tests and assessments.* New York: Holt, 1953.

55. WELSH, G. S. Factor dimensions A and R. In G. S. Welsh and W. G. Dahlstrom (Eds.), *Basic readings on the MMPI.* Minneapolis: Univer. of Minn. Press, 1956. Pp. 264–281.

56. WELSH, G. S., & DAHLSTROM, W. G. (Eds.) *Basic readings on the MMPI.* Minneapolis: Univer. of Minn. Press, 1956. Pp. 290–337.

57. WHEELER, W. M., LITTLE, K. B., & LEHNER, G. F. J. The internal structure of the MMPI. *J. consult. Psychol.*, 1951, 15, 134–141.

58. WITKIN, H. A., LEWIS, H. B., HERTZMAN, M., MACHOVER, K., MEISSNER, P. B., & WAPNER, S. *Personality through perception.* New York: Harper, 1954.

59. WOLFF, W. *Expression of personality.* New York: Harper, 1943.

60. ZIMMERMAN, W. S. The influence of item complexity upon the factor composition of a spatial visualization test. *Educ. psychol. Measmt,* 1954, 14, 106–119.

SECTION IX

Intelligence

SINCE the first intelligence test (known today as the Stanford-Binet scale) was originated by Alfred Binet in 1905, the intelligence quotient, or I.Q., has become almost synonymous with intelligence itself. This fact alone indicates the importance of the Stanford-Binet index; however, as the articles that follow will show, intelligence tests raise almost as many questions concerning the nature of intelligence and intelligence testing as they answer. To what extent is intelligence genetically determined? Do a child's environment and culture influence his intelligence, or only his performance on I.Q. tests? Can tests be devised which are reliable for all children, regardless of background? How is creativity related to intelligence, and how adequately is it measured through current testing methods?

In "The Inheritance of Mental Ability," Cyril Burt reviews the evidence psychologists have gathered on whether intelligence is indeed inherited, how it is inherited, and the relative importance of genetic and environmental factors. Although he reports that intelligence is largely determined by genetic factors, his findings indicate that experience also plays an important role in its development. For example, as Robert D. Hess shows in "Controlling Culture Influence in Mental Testing," children from higher socio-economic classes regularly score higher on the standard intelligence tests than children from low-status groups. His data show, however, that these differences are substantially reduced when "culture-fair" tests of mental ability are used; in other words, the discrepancies in scores tend to indicate culturally biased items in the intelligence tests rather than higher intelligence in the high-status children.

It is extremely difficult to determine the exact relationship between creativity and intelligence: a high or low score on a standard I.Q. test is sometimes, but by no means always, accompanied by a corresponding degree of creativity. In "Potentiality for Creativity and Its Measure," J. P. Guilford points out that the creative person must be able to manipulate and elaborate on the information he possesses in order to produce new ideas. Since the standard intelligence tests do little to measure creativity, Guilford suggests that psychologists try to discover, as rapidly as possible, how the tests may be revised. He urges for the present that creativity not be overlooked; it can be measured informally through, for example, such biographical signs of creative promise as scientific investigation, composing, and writing initiated by the child himself.

CYRIL BURT

43. *The Inheritance of Mental Ability*

The Genetic Component

HERE three distinct questions seem to be involved: (*a*) what evidence is there for the *fact* of inheritance, (*b*) what precisely is the *mode* in which intelligence is inherited, and (*c*) what is the *relative importance* of the genetic factor as compared with the environmental?

THE FACT

In controversies about the facts of mental heredity most critics have tended to assume that the two causal agencies commonly discussed—heredity and environment—are not merely antithetical but mutually exclusive. The environmentalists apparently suppose that, once they have shown that intelligence tests are affected by environment, it follows that all differences in intelligence are due to nothing but environment. Similarly the thorough-going hereditarian is apt to talk as though he believed that differences in intelligence were due to nothing but genetic constitution. This is the old familiar fallacy which I am tempted to label "nothing-buttery." In point of fact, with a few rare exceptions, like eye colour or serological differences in the blood, every observable characteristic that geneticists have studied has proved to be the product of the joint action of both heredity and environment. There are, in short, no such things as hereditary characters: there are only hereditary tendencies.

Now, where two contributory factors, such as heredity and environment, are likely to be involved, the obvious procedure will be to keep first one and then the other as constant as possible, and observe the results in either case.

Uniform environment. As psychological consultant to the London County Council, I had free access to orphanages and other residential institutions, and to the private files of case records giving the history of the various inmates. My co-workers and I were thus able to study large numbers of children who had been transferred thither during the earliest weeks of infancy, and had been brought up in an environment that was much the same for all. To our surprise we found that individual differences in intelligence, so far from being diminished, varied over an unusually wide range. In the majority of cases, they appeared to be correlated with differences in the intelligence of one or both of the parents. Some of the most striking instances were those of illegitimate children of high ability: often the father (so the case records showed) had been a casual acquaintance, of a social and intellectual status well above that of the mother, and had taken no further interest in the child. In such cases it is out of the question to attribute the high intelligence of the child to the special cultural opportunities furnished by the home environment, since his only home has been the institution.[1]

[1] Details are given in the various *Annual Reports of the Psychologist to the London County Council* (2) and are summarized in (4). In the recent symposium on *Quantitative Inheritance* (15), Woolf, quoting a later paper of mine, regrets that I have "based such far reaching conclusions on the study by Barbara Burks . . . covering only 214 foster

Reprinted with abridgment by permission of the American Psychological Association and the author from the *American Psychologist*, 1958, vol. 13, pp. 5–10; 15.
In the material which has been cut from this article, Dr. Burt briefly discussed some arguments pertaining to the problem of whether intelligence is due to heredity or environment. He also discussed the hypothesis of general ability versus special abilities in man.—Ed.

TABLE 1

Correlations between Mental and Scholastic Assessments

	IDENTICAL TWINS REARED TOGETHER	IDENTICAL TWINS REARED APART	NON-IDENTICAL TWINS REARED TOGETHER	SIBLINGS REARED TOGETHER	SIBLINGS REARED APART	UNRELATED CHILDREN REARED TOGETHER
Mental "Intelligence"						
Group Test	.944	.771	.542	.515	.441	.281
Individual Test	.921	.843	.526	.491	.463	.252
Final Assessment	.925	.876	.551	.538	.517	.269
Scholastic Attainments						
General	.898	.681	.831	.814	.526	.535
Reading and Spelling	.944	.647	.915	.853	.490	.548
Arithmetic	.862	.723	.748	.769	.563	.476

Uniform heredity. To secure cases in which the children's genetic endowment is the same, we may turn to assessments obtained from monozygotic or "identical" twins. The mother is not infrequently unable or unwilling to bring up two children at the same time, and one twin is consequently sent to a relative or to a foster home. Owing to the strong popular prejudice against separating twins, she not unnaturally tries, as a rule, to keep these arrangements secret. But patient and tactful inquiries show that cases of twins brought up in different environments almost from birth are in fact much commoner than is usually believed. We have now collected over 30 such cases (4, 6). I reproduce the more important correlations for the twins in TABLE 1 and have added for comparison corresponding coefficients obtained from other pairs, both related and unrelated. As regards intelligence the outstanding feature is the high correlation between the final assessments for the monozygotic twins, even when reared apart: it is almost as high as the correlation between two successive testings for the same individuals. On the other hand, with school attainments the correlations are much lower for twins reared separately than for twins reared together in the same home.

children" (1). But the principal basis for my own conclusion was a series of investigations in residential schools under the LCC covering in the course of years over 600 cases. I cited Burks' inquiry merely to show how an independent investigator in a different country had arrived at much the same figures as my own.

Several of our critics—Heim and Maddox, for example—have cited the account of analogous cases (described by Newman and others) as proving that intelligence is dependent on environment. Thus, to take an oft-quoted pair, "Helen," who had been trained as a teacher, scored with the Stanford-Binet tests an I.Q. of 116; whereas her twin sister, "Gladys," brought up for much of her childhood in an isolated district of the Canadian Rockies, scored only 92. But, says Newman, her score

. . . was higher than we might expect considering her scant education; and . . . it seems certain that the great deficiency in education had inhibited the development of the rather high grade of mental ability with which she was *endowed by heredity* (13, pp. 136–144).

Thus Newman's interpretation in no way conflicts with ours.

It is sometimes alleged (12) that, since twins are born at the same time, the intrauterine environment must have been the same for both before birth, even if later on their environments differ widely, and that quite conceivably it is the former that is crucial. As it happens, however, this rather gratuitous assumption reverses the actual facts. Embryological and obstetric records show that, particularly with twins developed from split ova, the position of each in the uterus, and the subsequent development, is liable to differ widely (7, pp. 123ff. and refs.).

I think, therefore, that it may be safely said that, apart from the influence of some preconceived theory, few psychologists nowadays would be inclined to contest the mere fact of mental inheritance: the most that can be plausibly alleged is that its influence is comparatively slight and distinctly elusive.

THE MODE OF INHERITANCE

The majority of those who still question the importance of mental inheritance, and many of those who support it, seem by preference to adopt entirely antiquated notions of the way in which inheritable characteristics are transmitted. If, as I have maintained, mental capacities are dependent on the physical characteristics of the brain (or, to speak a little more precisely, on the structural and biochemical qualities of the nervous system), then we should expect those capacities to be inherited in accordance with the same principles that govern the inheritance of physical characteristics; and these principles (except for obscure and apparently exceptional instances of extranuclear heredity) are essentially those commonly associated with the name of Mendel. Many British psychologists, however, feel a strong and not unreasonable prejudice against applying "atomistic theories like Mendel's" to explain the facts of mental life, and consequently, so far as they admit the possibility of mental inheritance at all, still cling to the old Darwinian principle of blended inheritance. On this view heredity means "the tendency of like to beget like" (the definition quoted by one of them from the Oxford English Dictionary). As a result, they commonly assume that the arguments for inheritance must consist in demonstrating resemblances between the parent and his children by means of correlations. When the two parents differ, then the child is still expected to consist in an intermediate blend of both.

The approach of the modern geneticist is the reverse of all this. As he views it, the real problem is rather to explain why in so many instances "like begets unlike." Both for the environmentalist and for the believer in blended inheritance, one of the most puzzling phenomena is the appearance, not merely of extremely dull children in the families of the well-to-do professional classes, but also of extremely bright children in families where both the cultural and the economic conditions of the parents would, one might imagine, condemn every child to hopeless failure. With the Mendelian hypothesis these anomalies are just what we should anticipate. However, the few critics who are familiar with the Mendelian explanation appear, as a rule, to suppose that it can apply only to discontinuous variations; and point out that intelligence, like stature, exhibits not discontinuous but continuous or graded variation. Hence, so they contend (sometimes citing the experiments of De Vries on "pure lines"), the apparent differences in intelligence between one individual and another must be due almost entirely to differences in environmental conditions.

Mendel himself was the first to indicate how his theory could be extended to account for this particular difficulty. When supplementing his experiments on the hybridization of peas by hybridizing beans, and (as before) crossing white flowered plants with purple, he found, that, whereas with peas the two types always sorted out with no hint of any intermediate color, with beans the offspring displayed "a whole range of hues from white to deep purple." This, he suggested, might be explained by postulating that with beans the color was determined, not by a single pair of alternative factors, but by a number of such pairs, each positive factor, when present, contributing a small additional amount of color. And if, as before, the recombinations are the effects of chance unions, then the resulting frequencies would obviously approximate to those of the normal curve.

However, in our early surveys of London children (2, 3), we found that, when complete age groups were tested, the distribution of intelligence departed significantly from that of a perfect normal curve: there was a swollen tail at the lower end, due to an excess of mental defectives, and a smaller enlargement at the upper end. This and other considerations led me to put forward the tentative hypothesis that innate variations in intelligence are due partly to unifactor and partly to multifactor inheritance: i.e., they result from Mendelian factors of two main kinds (no doubt overlapping), viz., (*a*) major genes responsible for comparatively *large* deviations, usually of an abnormal type, and (*b*) multiple genes whose effects are *small, similar,* and *cumulative.*

Karl Pearson (14) endeavoured to test the Mendelian theory in its multifactorial form by comparing its implications with actual figures obtained for height, arm length, and similar physical measurements, collected by himself and Alice Lee, from over 2,000 students and their relatives. The expected correlations which he deduced for various degrees of kinship were in every case far smaller than the observed coefficients. He therefore emphatically rejected the hypothesis of Mendelian inheritance, and fell back on the older theory of blending. However, in deriving his formulae and his expected values, Pearson relied on an oversimplified model. Contrary to what we now know to be the case, he assumed that the effect of assortative mating—the tendency of like to marry like—could be ignored as negligible, and that dominance would in every case be perfect. Ronald Fisher has since undertaken the rather formidable task of deducing more appropriate formulae, which allow for these and other complicating factors (9). And with these refinements the calculated correlations fit Pearson's own figures as well as could be wished.

My colleagues and I have applied Fisher's methods (suitably modified) to assessments for intelligence (7). The data were secured in the course of surveys of the entire school population in a representative London borough, and covered nearly 1,000 pairs of siblings, together with ratings for parents, and (so far as they were accessible) grandparents, uncles and aunts, and first cousins. The final assessments for the children were obtained by submitting the marks from the group tests to the judgment of the teachers who knew the children best: where the teacher disagreed with the verdict of the marks, the child was interviewed personally, and subjected to further tests, often on several successive occasions. The assessments for the adult members of the family were naturally far less accurate. Nevertheless, in almost every case the correlations computed from the actual data agreed with the theoretical values deduced from the multifactorial hypothesis far better than with the values deduced from any other hypothesis hitherto put forward. The only appreciable discrepancy occurred in the case of first cousins. Here, as for stature, the observed correlation for intelligence is larger than the theoretical; but the difference is not statistically significant, and could readily be explained if (as has been suggested above) variations in intelligence are affected by a few major genes as well as by numerous minor genes. I may add that on sorting out figures for cousins of maternal, paternal, and mixed kinship there is also some slight evidence suggestive of sex linkage.

THE RELATIVE INFLUENCE OF HEREDITY AND ENVIRONMENT

In practical work, however, the question most frequently raised is not whether differences in intelligence are inherited, nor even how they are inherited, but rather what is the relative influence of heredity as compared with environment. To an omnibus inquiry like this there can be no single answer. We can only try to determine, for this or that type of environment, for this or that population, and for this or that type of assessment, how far the observable results appear to be influenced by each of the two main groups of factors.

As Fisher's analysis has shown, formulae analogous to those used to deduce the expected correlations from the theoretical variances can also be devised for deducing the amount of the constituent variances from the observed correlations. I have ventured to amplify Fisher's methods (mainly on the lines of later work by Mather and Sewall Wright) so as to allow for unreliability and for the systematic effects of environment, i.e., of environmental influences which are correlated with those of heredity, as well as for random effects. The genetic contribution may be regarded as comprising two distinguishable portions: that due to the "fixable" component (or, as Fisher expresses it, to the "essential genotypes") and that due to the "nonfixable" (i.e., deviations due to dominance and similar influences). The data analysed consist of (a) the marks obtained from intelligence tests of the ordinary type taken just as they stand and (b) adjusted assessments obtained by the supplementary methods already described (7).

From TABLE 2 it will be seen that, with the crude test results, taken just as they stand, nearly 23% of the total variance appears due to nongenetic influences, i.e., to environment or to unreliability, and about 77% to genetic factors; with the adjusted assessments only about 12% (or slightly more) is apparently due to nongenetic influences and 88% to genetic factors. This of course means that the common practice of relying on tests alone— usually a group test applied once only—is by no means a satisfactory method of assessing a child's innate ability. Better assessments are obtained by submitting the test scores to the teachers for criticism or correction, and where necessary adjusting them by the methods described above. But such intensive inquiries would be too costly for routine use except in borderline cases.

Environment appears to influence the test results chiefly in three ways: (a) the cultural amenities of the home and the educational opportunities provided by the school can undoubtedly affect a child's performance in intelligence tests of the ordinary type, since so often they demand an acquired facility with abstract and verbal modes of expression; (b) quite apart from what the child may learn,

the constant presence of an intellectual background may stimulate (or seem to stimulate) his latent powers by inculcating a keener motivation, a stronger interest in intellectual things, and a habit of accurate, speedy, and diligent work; (c) in a few rare cases illness or malnutrition during the prenatal or early postnatal stages may, almost from the very start, permanently impair the development of the child's central nervous system. The adjusted assessments may do much towards eliminating the irrelevant effects of the first two conditions; but it is doubtful whether they can adequately allow for the last.

Limitations Involved in These Conclusions

As in almost all scientific investigations, the hypothetical model which has formed the basis of our inquiry involves of necessity certain minor simplifications. In particular we have assumed, for purposes of calculation, a sharp distinction between the "major genes" of unifactor inheritance and the "polygenes" of multifactor inheritance, and have treated the latter as contributing equal and additive doses to the sum total of each child's innate intelligence. We have then supposed that the effects of the former would on the whole be excluded if the few obviously pathological cases (mostly found in special schools or institutions) were omitted from our final calculations. However, these assumptions have led several critics to accuse us of

. . . disrupting the individual personality into atomic bits and discrete pieces which have subsequently to be joined together like a mosaic. . . . Personality [it is argued] is not a mosaic but a seamless whole, and hence the entire Mendelian hypothesis with its particulate genes, each producing a unit-character or adding another unit to the same character, is quite inapplicable to the facts of conscious behavior, and therefore to the study of mental capacity.

Objections of this kind could of course be used just as well to prove that a neuronic theory of the central nervous system is incompatible with the facts of conscious behaviour or of individual variations in ability, since

TABLE 2

Analysis of Variance for Assessments of Intelligence

SOURCE	UNADJUSTED TEST SCORES	ADJUSTED ASSESSMENTS
Genetic component		
Fixable	40.51	47.92
Nonfixable	16.65	21.73
Assortative mating	19.90	17.91
Environment		
Systematic	10.60	1.43
Random	5.91	5.77
Unreliability	6.43	5.24
Total	100.00	100.00

nerve cells or "neural bonds" are equally "particulate." Nevertheless, even those neurologists who prefer to start from a "field theory" do not wholly reject the neuronic hypothesis (cf. 16). In both cases the difficulties raised owe their force chiefly to the fact that there is a vast series of elusive processes intervening between theory and observable results which the critic is exceedingly apt to forget. Moreover, criticisms like those just cited plainly rest on an obsolete version of the Mendelian doctrine. No geneticist today, I imagine, accepts the hypothesis of the autonomous corpuscular gene; and the genotypic endowment of the individual can only affect the phenotypic resultant through the mediation of innumerable obscure biochemical steps.

In our original papers Howard and I tried carefully to guard against recurrent objections of this type. As we pointed out, the phrase "multiple factors" may be used to cover either (a) relatively numerous loci each with only two allelomorphs or (b) a single locus (or relatively few loci) each with numerous allelomorphs, or possibly (c) some combination of the two. Hypothesis b by itself would hardly seem to fit the facts. We are inclined to think that factors of all the various types may be operative in varying degrees, and that the attempt to classify factors or genes should not be too severely pressed.

We further assumed that in all probability the influence of such factors on the individual's observable intelligence was mainly the indirect result of their influence on the development of his central nervous system, and was presumably effected by modifying growth rates. And we expressly stated that the ultimate influence of any one "gene" upon intelligence might be but one of its multifarious consequences, and possibly a comparatively remote consequence at that. Some genes may have a larger share in the final result; others a smaller; and the rough classification of genes

into "major" genes and "minor" was adopted primarily with a view to simplifying our general discussion.[2] We ourselves find the "theory of chromosomal hierarchy," advanced by Goldschmidt (11), especially attractive as a basis for the ultimate hierarchical differentiation of mental ability.

However, this is not the place to enlarge on these speculative interpretations. We fully admit that the simplifications involved in our hypothetical model mean that the figures finally deduced can be no more than approximations. But we maintain that the error of approximation, however large, will nevertheless be smaller than the amount of "unreliability" inevitably involved in all such measurements.

In any case we must repeat that the conclusions reached are at best only valid in reference to the particular conditions under which they were obtained. They would not necessarily hold good (a) of other mental traits, (b) of different methods of assessment, (c) of a population of a different genetic composition, or (d) of a population at a different cultural level: much less would they hold good if there were any subsequent change (e) in the present distribution of environmental and genetic characteristics, or (f) in the influences affecting their mutual interaction.[3]

2 If Mather's view that "the major genes occur only in euchromatin, while heterochromatin contains only polygenes" (15, p. 151 and refs.) is eventually confirmed, there would be more adequate grounds for retaining a sharp distinction between the two modes of inheritance. However, this view is not universally accepted. For an alternative interpretation of the experimental results on which Mather largely relies, see the papers by Reeve and Robertson quoted in our article (12, p. 116). These writers incline more to what in the text I have called hypothesis b. But, as Howard and I contended, their alternative interpretation would affect only the method, not the results, of our statistical deductions.

3 A more detailed reply to the criticisms urged by Woolf, Heim, and Maddox will appear in the forthcoming issue of the Brit. J. statist. Psychol., 10, Part i.

REFERENCES

1. BURKS, BARBARA. *27th Yearbook National Society for the Study of Education*, 1928, 1, 219.

2. BURT, C. *Annual reports of the psychologist to the London County Council*. London: London County Council, 1914–1931.

3. BURT, C. *The distribution and relations of educational abilities*. London: P. S. King & Son, 1917.

4. BURT, C. Ability and income. *Brit. J. educ. Psychol.*, 1943, 13, 83–98.

5. BURT, C. The differentiation of intellectual ability. *Brit. J. educ. Psychol.*, 1954, 24, 76–90.

6. BURT, C. The evidence for the concept of intelligence. *Brit. J. educ. Psychol.*, 1955, 25, 158–177.

7. BURT, C., & HOWARD, M. The multifactorial theory of inheritance and its application to intelligence. *Brit. J. statist. Psychol.*, 1956, 9, 95–131.

8. DARLINGTON, C. D., & MATHER, K. *The elements of genetics*. London: Allen & Unwin, 1949.

9. FISHER, R. A. Correlation between relatives on the supposition of Mendelian inheritance. *Trans. roy. Soc., Edin.*, 1918, 52, 399–433.

10. GOLDSCHMIDT, R. B. *Theoretical genetics*. Univer. California Press, 1955.

11. MADDOX, H. Nature-nurture balance sheets. *Brit. J. educ. Psychol.*, 1957, 27, 166–175.

12. NEWMAN, H. H. *Twins and super-twins*. London: Hutchinson, 1942.

13. PEARSON, K. On a generalized theory of alternative inheritance with special reference to Mendel's laws. *Phil. Trans.*, 1904, 203, 53–87.

14. REEVE, F. C. R., & WADDINGTON, C. H. (Ed.) *Quantitative inheritance*. London: H. M. Stationery Office, 1952.

15. SHOLL, D. A. *The organization of the cerebral cortex*. London: Methuen, 1956.

ROBERT D. HESS

44. *Controlling Culture Influence in Mental Testing: An Experimental Test*

SIGNIFICANT differences in mental test performance between high and low socio-economic populations in the United States and Europe are well documented in the literature and consistently show a superiority in test scores of high-status samples. While this evidence for differential test performance by socio-economic level is indisputable, there have been traditional disagreements over the conclusions that reasonably may be drawn from these research reports. Proponents may be found for each of these three points of view: (1) the superior test performance of high socio-economic groups represents a *genetic superiority* in intelligence; (2) the superior performance of the high-status samples indicates a true difference in intelligence—a difference which results from *environmental* rather than genetic factors; and (3) the differential performance of high- and low-status levels arises from cultural factors within the testing instruments and testing situation themselves and *do not necessarily* reflect either genetic or environmental differences in intelligence *between groups*. The implications that follow from these separate points of view are sharply divergent in their significance for educational practice and curriculum development.

Allison Davis and his associates have recently advanced the last of the conclusions mentioned above.[1] Davis argues that behavior

requisite for successful achievement on intelligence test items is, to a very great extent, culturally learned, and that the cultural background of the high-status child, as compared with that of a low-status child, is more adequate preparation for appropriate response to a test which is highly saturated with "middle-class" symbols, problems, vocabulary, and objects. This situation, according to Davis, creates a bias in favor of high-status pupils which leads to higher test scores, on the average, for the pupil from high socio-economic levels.

When cultural dissimilarities exist between samples under investigation, it follows from Davis' position that relative mental ability of the groups can be evaluated only if the test items represent cultural experience and training equally familiar, on the average, to the groups involved.

Davis and Eells have conducted intensive research on the problem of cultural bias in several standard group intelligence tests. While their research establishes that cultural bias does exist in certain current tests, it presents at least two additional problems: (1) is it possible to construct a culturally unbiased test of intelligence, and (2) if such a test were constructed, to what extent would it reduce the socio-economic differential on test performance now observed on standard intelligence tests?

The research reported here dealt with these two problems. It represents an attempt to develop a test of mental ability which would control cultural variables with respect to

[1] For a more complete presentation of this argument, see Eell, K., Davis, A., et al., *Intelligence and Cultural Differences*. Chicago: University of Chicago Press, 1951.

Reprinted by permission of Dembar Publications, Inc., and the author from the *Journal of Educational Research*, 1955–56, vol. 49, pp. 53–58.

socio-economic status of high- and low-status samples drawn from an American metropolitan area. Cultural factors were to be controlled by constructing the test around experiences which were equally common or familiar to the groups to be tested. This procedure does not include any assumptions as to the relative performance of high- and low-status samples on such a test; rather, it attempts to provide an instrument which could be used to measure group differences in mental ability rather than group differences in both cultural background and mental ability.

The selection and construction of test items was possibly the most crucial aspect of the study. In addition to the obvious requirement that the problems present mental tasks, two criteria were utilized in initial choice: (1) the problems should represent as closely as possible real life situations rather than academic tasks; (2) the problems, vocabulary employed in instructions, materials, and motivation should offer no cultural advantage to any group to be tested.

These criteria obviously demanded firsthand knowledge of the games, work, and other extra-school activities of children from high and low socio-economic status levels. The research staff depended upon three sources for this knowledge: studies conducted by sociologists and cultural anthropologists on socio-economic differences in contemporary American culture; detailed interviews with children from these areas, taken in the home over a

period of months; and observations by the research staff members of the out-of-school activities of children in the areas of the city where testing was to be conducted.

Before the testing project began, a group of twenty-four items was devised on the basis of equal familiarity with materials, symbols, verbal content of instructions, similarity to real-life situations, and intrinsic motivation. The items were administered individually. Of the twenty-four items, eight were discarded during the project because of inappropriate level of difficulty, scoring problems, or other administrative faults; sixteen items, which were administered to each subject at each age level, were regarded as the experimental test proper.[2]

The test was administered by trained graduate students. Sessions were thirty to forty minutes in length, depending on the age and level of interest of the subject. Two or three such sessions were required to administer the entire group of twenty-four items. This time gradually diminished as items were dropped from the test. The final test of sixteen items required forty minutes to one hour, depending upon the age and working speed of the subject. Each subject was allowed to proceed at his own speed. Testers were urged to establish rapport with the subject and to encourage

2 At no time either in constructing items before testing or eliminating items after testing, was social status differential used as a criterion for including or excluding an item. Thus the experimental test does not represent a group of items selected as relatively unbiased on the basis of previous testing.

TABLE 1

Size and Composition of the Experimental Sample

| | STATUS LEVEL | | | | | | | | |
| | High (White) | | | Low (White) | | | Low (Negro) | | |
AGE	Male	Female	Total	Male	Female	Total	Male	Female	Total
6½	25	27	52	23	20	43	21	23	44
7½	24	22	46	22	22	44	24	23	47
8½	22	24	46	22	22	44	22	22	44
9½	21	23	44	25	22	47	22	22	44
TOTALS	92	96	188	92	86	178	89	90	179

TABLE 2

Mean Mental Age (Standard Tests) by Status Level and Age and Significant
Difference between Status Level by Age

				SIGNIFICANCE OF DIFFERENCES (t)			
				High vs. Low White		High White vs. Low Negro	
AGE	HIGH STATUS WHITE	LOW STATUS WHITE	LOW STATUS NEGRO	Diff.	t	Diff.	t
(1)	(2)	(3)	(4)	(5)	(6)	(7)	(8)
6½	7.22	6.44	5.67	.78	5.21 **	1.55	8.16 **
7½	8.12	7.68	6.88	.44	2.87 **	1.24	7.47 **
8½	9.24	8.86	7.46	.38	2.36 *	1.78	9.24 **
9½	10.55	9.78	8.88	.77	4.80 **	1.67	9.33

* Significant at .05.
** Significant at .01.

maximum performance on the part of the child.

The sample was comprised of 545 elementary school pupils between the age of six and one-half and nine and one-half years of age. It included three groups, selected on the basis of occupation of male parent: high socio-economic white children whose parents were from professional and managerial occupational levels; low socio-economic status white children whose parents were from unskilled and semi-skilled occupational levels; and low-status Negro children whose parents were unskilled or unemployed.

Approximately equal numbers of both males and females were selected for testing. Subjects were tested at four chronological age points: six and one-half, seven and one-half, eight and one-half, and nine and one-half years. The composition of the sample is given in TABLE 1.

In line with the general hypothesis of the study that the test would reduce socio-economic status differences on current test scores, it was necessary to determine the relative standing of the three groups on standard intelligence tests. This information was taken from the school records and calculated in terms of mental age. Means were computed for each age-status cell and significance of differences between the high-status white group and the other groups were calculated. The performance of the high-status white group was significantly superior to both low-status groups at each age level (see TABLE 2). Similar status differences were found on achievement test scores.

The Experimental Test Results

THE raw scores of the status-age groups on the experimental test do not confirm the standard test score differences (see TABLE 3). Differences between the two white groups are insignificant at all age levels; differences between the high-status white and low-status Negro groups are significant at all age levels but are reduced in comparison with the mental age differences.

Although group differences are reduced between the high- and low-status levels, individual variation is not depressed by the experimental test. Computed for status-age groups separately, the standard deviation ranged from 5.4 to 8.75, with fifty percent of the sigmas above 7.35.

Some evidence relating to the validity of the experimental test was obtained by product-moment correlations with two outside criteria-standard intelligence test scores and reading achievement test scores taken from the school records. Correlations between the experimental scores and mental age for the twelve age-status cells taken separately distributed about a median of .43 (uncorrected), with ten of the twelve falling between .37 and .65.

TABLE 3

Mean Raw Scores for the Experimental Test by Status Level and Age and
Significant Differences between Status Level by Age

	HIGH STATUS WHITE	LOW STATUS WHITE	LOW STATUS NEGRO	SIGNIFICANCE OF DIFFERENCES (t)			
				High vs. Low White		High White vs. Low Negro	
AGE				Diff.	t	Diff.	t
(1)	(2)	(3)	(4)	(5)	(6)	(7)	(8)
6½	24.80	27.42	21.30	−2.62	1.72	3.50	2.15 *
7½	30.39	30.85	25.98	−0.46	.26	4.41	3.24 **
8½	36.48	36.29	29.82	.19	.12	6.66	4.32 **
9½	41.06	40.12	32.54	.94	.70	8.52	5.60 **

* Significant at .05.
** Significant at .01.

These coefficients indicate a significant and positive, though not high, relationship between the two tests.

Reading achievement test scores were obtainable for nine of the twelve age-status groups.[3] The correlations between achievement test scores and experimental test scores are presented in TABLE 4. These coefficients may be compared with the coefficients between achievement scores and standard tests of mental ability shown in the same table. The usefulness of the two mental tests in predicting reading achievement scores is not significantly different for the two white status

3 N's of some cells were slightly lowered. In no case did this significantly alter the means of the experimental or IQ test scores.

groups if age-status groups are considered separately.

The results of an experimental testing project using a "culture-fair" individual test of mental ability showed marked reduction of the socio-economic differential between high- and low-status groups on standard tests. Individual differences were discriminated by the experimental test, and ability to predict reading achievement test scores within socio-economic status groups was approximately equal to that of standard measures of intelligence. The results emphasize the influence of cultural factors in test performance and suggest that socio-economic differences between high- and low-status samples in this country are exaggerated by standard intelligence tests.

TABLE 4

Correlation Coefficients between Standard Reading Achievement Test Scores and Two Measures of Mental Ability *

	AGE	HIGH STATUS WHITE r	LOW STATUS WHITE r	LOW STATUS NEGRO r
With standard tests	6½	.21		
	7½	.51	.45	
	8½	.51	.35	.74
	9½	.48	.45	.62
With experimental test	6½	.24		
	7½	.54	.38	
	8½	.42	.50	.40
	9½	.51	.44	.16

* Not corrected for attenuation.

J. P. GUILFORD

45. *Potentiality for Creativity and Its Measurement*

"CREATIVITY," like "love," is a many-splendored thing. Small wonder that few have ventured to define it. At a conference on creativity a few months ago, each of the thirty-odd members was asked to write a list of his free associations to the word "creativity." The results were almost as varied as the personalities of those present.

We gain a little bit if we take a first step toward discrimination, namely, the distinction between creative potential and creative production. Creative production, in the popular sense, is the aspect that catches general public fancy because the creative person's output is so frequently in the form of tangible products, such as a poem, a novel, a musical composition, an invention, a painting, a scientific theory, or a philosophical system.

To a psychologist who is interested in the mental operations that lead up to the emergence of the creator's product, the criteria of creative production must be of a different kind. There is agreement that the tangible product must have some novel aspects. The thinking that leads to that product also has novel aspects. In either case, it is these novel aspects that justify the label "creative." We are not concerned here with the operational criteria by which novelty can be gauged. What I wish to point out is that on the way to his final, public product, the creative thinker arrives at numerous *psychological* products. In focusing attention on the public product, we overlook the numerous ideas that the inventor had and discarded. From the psychological point of view, those generated ideas also have many chances of being novel.

In simplest terms, an individual's potential for being creative is his readiness to produce novel ideas or psychological products. In this we should include the production of old ideas in new connections. His readiness depends upon many things. An essential part of his preparation is in the form of specific items of information that are available to him from his memory storage. But, as we know, having the information is not sufficient. It is what the person does with the information that is important. When we speak of creative potential, we usually have in mind the dispositions that enable a person to use his information in new ways. Some of these dispositions are abilities or aptitudes while others are traits of interest, needs, attitudes, and of temperament. The emphasis upon aptitudes in this paper should not be interpreted to mean that these other kinds of traits are thought to be of negligible consequence.

Our investigations of creative potential at the University of Southern California have been directed mainly at the aptitude aspects, in part because they have been conducted in an Aptitudes Project and in part because of the belief that an understanding of the aptitudes will also give us much information regarding the nature of creative thinking itself. From the standpoint of aptitudes alone, creative potential has proven to be considerably more complex than was expected. We did not expect to find a single, universal key to successful creative thinking, but we were not prepared to find so many facets to the subject.

Considering first the interpreted psychological factors found in the analysis of tests with

Reprinted by permission of the Educational Testing Service and the author from the *Proceedings of the 1962 Invitational Conference of Testing Problems*, pp. 31–39.

meaningful, verbal content, the basic traits most clearly related logically to creative thinking include three fluency factors, two flexibility factors, and an elaboration factor. All of these factors are recognized as falling in the same psychological category of divergent-production abilities. They have in common the fact that in measurement of these abilities the tests present the examinee with a certain item, or items, of information and he is to generate from the given information some other items of information. In every case, multiple responses are called for, all different. In many cases, the produced items were probably never previously learned in association with the given information, for example, in a test calling for the activity of forming titles to apply to a given story plot. Information thus comes from memory storage but out of its stored contexts; in other words, by way of transfer. I have elsewhere elaborated on a transfer theory of creative thinking (1).

The fluency factors pertain to *efficiency* of recall under these general circumstances. They differ from one another in terms of the kind of psychological product involved. Ideational fluency pertains to the rapid generation of units of verbal or semantic information— single ideas or units of thought, such as words to fit a described class of meanings. Associational fluency pertains to the rapid generation of semantic units to fulfill a relationship, having given a specified relation (e.g., a relation of similarity, opposition, part-whole, etc.) and a given unit. Expressional fluency pertains to the production of connected discourse, in the form of phrases and sentences. The psychological product involved is recognized as a semantic system.

Flexibility factors have to do with the *lability* or *fluidity* of stored information. The factor first recognized as spontaneous flexibility is now thought to be a matter of flexibility with regard to classes of information. In tests of this kind of flexibility, the examinee must shift his responses readily from one class to another. It has been said that some uncreative people are suffering from a disease known as hardening of the categories. Such a malady may be a matter of low degree of spontaneous flexibility.

The factor first called "originality" was later recognized as a kind of flexibility, described as *adaptive* flexibility. In one test, the examinee who suggests a relatively large number of clever plot titles earns a high score for this factor. To the fable of the fox and the grapes, for example, if he gives the titles "The fox griped about grapes," or "The sweet grapes turned sour," his titles are regarded as clever because he has produced what we call transformations. A transformation is a change or alteration in meaning or interpretation; a redefinition of some kind. Turning old interpretations of information into new ones makes possible new and different uses of what one knows.

Elaboration means building upon given information to round out a structure, to make it more detailed, or to extrapolate in new directions. Proceeding naturally from what is already given is a matter of producing implications. The given information suggests the first step to be taken, and each completed step helps to determine the following ones. The ability to produce a variety of implications is also in the category of divergent production.

We have just seen that the six divergent-production abilities dealing with meaningful, verbal information differ only in the kinds of products of information involved—units, classes, relations, systems, transformations, and implications. These are the kinds of psychological products mentioned early in this paper. They are not restricted to divergent production, but have very general application to intellectual abilities in all other operation categories—cognition, memory, convergent production, and evaluation. It is the relative variety and novelty of the products found in divergent production that links this category of abilities logically with creativity. When we have learned how new products come into existence, how familiar products become transformed, and how known products enter into new connections, we shall know a great deal about creative thinking.

I have mentioned only six divergent-production factors, all pertaining to verbal information. Most likely there are other sets of six, nonverbal, divergent-production abilities parallel to them. One set pertains to (visual) figural information, of which five have been demonstrated. A second set pertains to symbolic information, of which five have also been demonstrated. Thus we have the important general inference that successful creative performance, to the extent that it depends upon aptitudes, is not equally promising in all fields of information. Potential for creative production in the arts is not the same thing as that in mathematics or that in writing, to say nothing of potential for creative handling of problems involving human relations.

It would be incorrect to say that only the divergent-production abilities contribute to success in creative performances. It appears that in the other four operation categories in the structure of intellect (2) we shall find sets of abilities parallel to those in the operation category of divergent production. Thus, in each operation area there is a set of transformation abilities which may contribute to creative potential, particularly in the areas of cognition and convergent production. Convergent production is a matter of generating a single right answer to given information, but it is sometimes necessary to do some searching around or to achieve a transformation in order to arrive at that answer.

In our initial study of creative abilities, we hypothesized and we found a factor interpreted as sensitivity to problems, a factor that has been repeatedly verified. In terms of placement in the structure of intellect, this factor has been recognized as an ability to evaluate implications; for example, seeing the faults in the working of a common appliance or of a social institution. The discovery of a category of evaluative abilities has opened many new possibilities of thinking about thinking. It should have been obvious before that we evaluate just about everything we perceive, or know, or do. Observers of the creative thinking of experts commonly report a terminal period of verification, which, in part, means evaluation. Actually, evaluative operations may occur, and probably do, at any step of the way in thinking, wherever we can gain any feedback information.

Reflection upon the total event of a creative production of some degree of complexity shows how similar that total process is to the commonly held picture of complex problem-solving. The category of problem-solving even applies to the production of objects of art, for the psychoanalysts tell us that in working toward his product, the artist is attempting to solve a personal problem by externalizing a phantasy. The amount of creativity involved in solving any kind of problem is proportional to the amount of novel production the problem solver shows or to the degree of novelty in his solution.

Creative problem-solving involves considerable trial-and-error behavior. Except for instances in which the given information in the problem is sufficient to lead directly to one right answer, every trial is an act of divergent production and the seeing of an error is an act of evaluation. Thus, trial-and-error behavior is an interplay of divergent production and evaluation, ending when some product is evaluated as acceptable. The thinker who can vary his potential solutions easily and extensively has an advantage in getting around to suitable solutions. In everyday life, most problems have no one right answer; there are many answers, a number of which are more or less suitable.

The more able the individual, the more he can produce trial information of high quality, with a higher probability of success. His overall indulgence in trial-and-error thinking is therefore relatively less. But in view of the necessity for at least some trial and error, and the amount of divergent production that this requires, we should give much more attention to facility in this kind of mental activity and its assessment. Certainly, the person who can think of only one possible answer to a problem is much less likely to solve it than the person who can think of several. A number of investigators have found that tests of divergent production account for many cases of so-called over-achieving, when achievement is assessed in terms of standard achievement tests. The same kind of tests may also be found to account for many cases of under-achievement.

Standard tests and scales of intelligence have practically nothing to contribute to assessment of divergent-production abilities. For example, factor analyses of the Wechsler scales have thus far failed to show any such relationships. Recently I indulged in some armchair analysis of the 140 tests in the latest Stanford revision of the Binet scale, from which comes the impression that, in spite of the great surface variety of the tests, there is an overwhelming weighting with tests of cognitive abilities, with some attention to a few of the factors of memory, convergent production, and evaluation. Only five of the 140 tests appear to offer any appreciable divergent-production variance.

Current, standard academic-aptitude tests have been constituted along the lines of intelligence scales. They therefore emphasize much the same factors and neglect the great majority of the intellectual abilities. It cannot very well be claimed that the neglected abilities are of little importance, for there has been little investigation of the relation of most of those abilities to performance in or out of educational institutions. Many of the neglected abilities should be potentially important in connection with various academic subjects and various occupational activities. For example, some recent data that I have seen show that scores from a few divergent-production tests are correlated with criteria of creative performance of public relations personnel and of advertising copy writers (3), with coefficients as high as .60. The criteria of creativity were essentially rankings of personnel by their superiors.

What is the implication of all this for assessment of academic aptitude? Not being as close to this problem as many of you are, I am not as well prepared to draw up an extensive list of implications. I will mention two or three things that I think should be done.

Believing in proceeding on a foundation of research findings, I would urge that extensive efforts be made to discover the phases of academic learning to which each of the basic intellectual aptitudes is relevant and which of the aptitudes are important to development in each academic subject. At USC we are engaged in a two-year investigation of potentially relevant factors for learning ninth-grade algebra. We are planning to follow this with similar studies of other school subjects.

Although some of the neglected intellectual abilities are quite possibly touched upon in current achievement tests, this is on an incidental basis. As rapidly as research findings become available on the relevance of new aptitude factors, there should be appropriate revisions of academic-aptitude batteries. Present batteries should be examined for redundancies, of which I am sure there are a number, replacing parts with measures of new relevant factors. It is well known that current batteries are by no means equally predictive of achievement in all curricula and in all courses of study. Achievement tests may touch upon many of the deficiencies of aptitude batteries, but they cannot do justice to them.

In introducing tests of divergent-production abilities, some technical difficulties will be encountered. Thus far, we have failed to find machine-scorable aptitude tests of these abilities. It is doubtful that any such tests exist, but with application of ingenuity, something may be done about it. Outside the divergent-production area we have employed a few completion tests also, but it is probable that they can be replaced with machine-scorable tests.

Some of you may be alarmed at the possible large number of intellectual factors that may need to be given attention in the assessment of academic aptitude. I suggest that we save such misgivings until we know how many factors are relevant and how much weight needs to be given to them.

Until such time as measures of creative aspects of aptitude can be included in aptitude batteries, something can be done in the way of gathering information regarding creative promise and in the way of predicting creative production of students. Such information could be used less formally than aptitude scores are used and includes certain biographical signs of creative promise, such as self-initiated or spontaneous extra-curricular activities in the form of scientific investigation, writing, or composing. The use of non-aptitude measures is another possibility. Mac-Kinnon and his group at the University of

California have shown that the most creative architects and scientists are distinguished by means of interest and temperament inventories (4). The information they have concerns concurrent validity; presumably predictive validity is also promising.

Thus, although immediate prospects of selecting and placing students with superior creative potential are not certain, future prospects, with the possibilities of using various kinds of information, including aptitude measures, appear to be reasonably bright. The least that we should aim to do is to determine what oversights exist in present aptitude batteries.

REFERENCES

1. GUILFORD, J. P. "Some New Views of Creativity." In H. Helson (Ed.), *Theories and Data in Psychology*. Princeton, N. J.: D. Van Nostrand Co., 1963 (in press).

2. GUILFORD, J. P. and MERRIFIELD, P. R. "The Structure-of-Intellect Model: Its Uses and Implications," *Reports from the Psychological Laboratory*, No. 24. Los Angeles: University of Southern California, 1960.

3. ELLIOTT, J. M. "Advancing our Methods for Measuring Creative Abilities." *Information Service for A.N.A. Members*. New York: Association of National Advertisers, May 1962.

4. MACKINNON, D. W. "Fostering Creativity in Students of Engineering." *Journal of Engineering Education*, 1961, 52, 129–142.

SECTION X

Social Processes

WHAT an individual thinks, feels, and does is almost invariably influenced by the social units to which he belongs (such as his family, his peer group, and his country). Thus many social processes are of interest to the student of general psychology; however, it is especially important that he understand the formation of attitudes because attitudes play such a large part in the determination of individual behavior. We have therefore restricted this section to articles concerning attitudes: how they are shaped by the individual's social environment; how, once acquired, they relate to his behavior; how they operate within his personality and are preserved through defense mechanisms; and how they are modified or maintained by pressure from selected social sources.

Anna Freud and Sophie Dann's "An Experiment in Group Upbringing" describes the effects of three years of concentration-camp living on the emotions and attitudes of six German-Jewish orphans. The paper is interesting not only because it shows the critical impact of early social experiences on general and specific attitudes, but because it concerns people in a real situation—not, like many experiments, a hypothetical situation devised for the purposes of laboratory study.

Once attitudes have been acquired, they interact with other factors to determine behavior. In "Verbal Attitudes and Overt Acts," Melvin L. DeFleur and Frank R. Westie report an experiment comparing subjects' attitudes and overt behavior toward Negroes. The authors suggest that before we can accurately predict behavior from a knowledge of attitudes, we must (1) study the subject's reference groups (the groups to whose standards he refers in deciding what to believe and how to act), and (2) standardize the subject's opportunities for overt action so that his behavior can be "graded."

Attitudes are not formed solely by forces outside the individual; they can also serve important functions within his personality. As they report in "Some Personality Factors in Anti-Semitism," Else Frenkel-Brunswik and R. Nevitt Sanford found that anti-Semites are characterized by personality contrasts (an outward appearance of exaggerated moral strictness, for instance, accompanied by fantasies of extreme aggression and narcissism), and that prejudice against out-groups is used by them to maintain mental balance. When an attitude functions in such a way, defensive behavior usually occurs if the attitude is challenged. In "The Evasion of Propaganda," Eunice Cooper and Marie Jahoda show that when anti-Semites are exposed to anti-prejudice propaganda, they do not, as one might expect, either fight it or give in to it. Instead, using various defense mechanisms, they evade the issue psychologically (and therefore retain their prejudice) by simply not understanding the message.

The influence of social norms on attitude change is illustrated in "Reference Groups, Membership Groups, and Attitude Change," by Alberta Engvall Siegel and Sidney Siegel. The study shows that individuals tend to adopt the attitudes of both the reference groups and the membership groups with which they are identified, even when the membership group is not chosen by the individual.

Societies have different ways of encouraging socially acceptable behavior in their members. Francis L. K. Hsu, in "Suppression Versus Repression," suggests that in individual-centered societies, like Germany and the United States, a person represses the desire to act "wrongly" and feels guilt if he misbehaves, whereas in situation-centered societies, like Japan and China, "wrong" behavior is suppressed and a person who misbehaves feels shame.

ANNA FREUD *in collaboration with* SOPHIE DANN

46. An Experiment in Group Upbringing

THE experiment to which the following notes refer is not the outcome of an artificial and deliberate laboratory setup but of a combination of fateful outside circumstances. The six young children who are involved in it are German-Jewish orphans, victims of the Hitler regime, whose parents, soon after their birth, were deported to Poland and killed in the gas chambers. During their first year of life, the children's experiences differed; they were handed on from one refuge to another, until they arrived individually, at ages varying from approximately six to twelve months, in the concentration camp of Tereszin.[1] There they became inmates of the Ward for Motherless Children, were conscientiously cared for and medically supervised, within the limits of the current restrictions of food and living space. They had no toys and their only facility for outdoor life was a bare yard. The Ward was staffed by nurses and helpers, themselves inmates of the concentration camp and, as such, undernourished and overworked. Since Tereszin was a transit camp, deportations were frequent. Approximately two to three years after arrival, in the spring of 1945, when liberated by the Russians, the six children, with others, were taken to a Czech castle where they were given special care and were lavishly fed. After one month's stay, the 6 were included in a transport of 300 older children and adolescents, all of them survivors from concentration camps, the first of 1000 children for whom the British Home Office had granted permits of entry. They were flown to England in bombers and arrived in August 1945 in a carefully set-up reception camp in Windermere, Westmoreland,[2] where they remained for two months. When this reception camp was cleared and the older children distributed to various hostels and training places, it was thought wise to leave the six youngest together, to remove them from the commotion which is inseparable from the life of a large children's community and to provide them with peaceful, quiet surroundings where, for a year at least, they could adapt themselves gradually to a new country, a new language, and the altered circumstances of their lives.

This ambitious plan was realized through the combined efforts of a number of people. A friend of the former Hampstead Nurseries, Mrs. Ralph Clarke, wife of the Member of Parliament for East Grinstead, Sussex, gave the children a year's tenancy of a country house with field and adjoining woodland, "Bulldogs Bank" in West Hoathly, Sussex, containing two bedrooms for the children, with adjoining bathrooms, a large day nursery, the necessary staff rooms, a veranda running the whole length of the house and a sun terrace.

The Foster Parents' Plan for War Children, Inc., New York, who had sponsored the Hampstead Nurseries during the war years 1940–1945, took the six children into their plan and adopted Bulldogs Bank as one of

[1] Theresienstadt in Moravia.

[2] The camp was organized and directed by Mr. Oscar Friedmann, now an associate member of the British Psycho-Analytic Society, and Miss Alice Goldberger, former superintendent in the Hampstead Nurseries.

Reprinted with abridgment by permission of the International Universities Press, Inc., and the authors from *Psychoanalytic Study of the Child*, 1951, pp. 127–32, 133–34, and 157–68.

their colonies. They provided the necessary equipment as well as the financial upkeep.

The new Nursery was staffed by Sisters Sophie and Gertrud Dann, formerly the head nurses of the Baby Department and Junior Nursery Department of the Hampstead Nurseries respectively. A young assistant, Miss Maureen Wolfison, who had accompanied the the children from Windermere was replaced after several weeks by Miss Judith Gaulton, a relief worker. Cooking and housework was shared between the staff, with occasional outside help.

The children arrived in Bulldogs Bank on October 15, 1945. The personal data of the six, so far as they could be ascertained, [are shown in the chart on page 449.] [3]

Meager as these scraps of information are, they establish certain relevant facts concerning the early history of this group of children:

1. that four of them (Ruth, Leah, Miriam, Peter) lost their mothers at birth or immediately afterward, one (Paul) before the age of twelve months, one (John) at an unspecified date;
2. that after the loss of their mothers all the children wandered for some time from one place to another, with several complete changes of adult environment (Bulldogs Bank was the sixth station in life for Peter, the fifth for Miriam, etc. John's and Leah's and Paul's wanderings before arrival in Tereszin are not recorded.);
3. that none of the children had known any other circumstances of life than those of a group setting. They were ignorant of the meaning of a "family";
4. that none of the children had experience

of normal life outside a camp or big institution.[4]

Behavior Toward Adults on Arrival

ON leaving the reception camp in Windermere, the children reacted badly to the renewed change in their surroundings. They showed no pleasure in the arrangements which had been made for them and behaved in a wild, restless, and uncontrollably noisy manner. During the first days after arrival they destroyed all the toys and damaged much of the furniture. Toward the staff they behaved either with cold indifference or with active hostility, making no exception for the young assistant Maureen who had accompanied them from Windermere and was their only link with the immediate past. At times they ignored the adults so completely that they would not look up when one of them entered the room. They would turn to an adult when in some immediate need, but treat the same person as nonexistent once more when the need was fulfilled. In anger, they would hit the adults, bite or spit. Above all, they would shout, scream, and use bad language. Their speech, at the time, was German with an admixture of Czech words, and a gradual increase of English words. In

3 Nothing has been changed for the purpose of publication except the children's names. According to a Nazi rule, all Jewish children had to bear names out of the Old Testament. These have been replaced here by another set of biblical names.

On immigration the official register of the children contained nothing beyond their names, birth-dates and birthplaces. Some additional information concerning the six Bulldogs Bank children was supplied later by letter by Mrs. Martha Wenger, herself a concentration camp victim who had been in charge of the children in the Ward for Motherless Children in Tereszin.

4 An attachment to a mother substitute is recorded of one child only. Martha Wenger, in the letter mentioned above, writes concerning Ruth: "Ruth was passionately attached to me and maltreated me accordingly. When somebody else had night duty with the children, she slept soundly; when it was me, she would stay awake, cry, and force me to sit with her." No similar relationships are mentioned with regard to the other children. Martha Wenger refers to John as "well liked by everybody" and to Peter as "endearing himself to everybody with his gay, fearless, naughty ways." For the rest she says: "I can very well understand that the Tereszin children have been very difficult on arrival, and are still difficult to handle. There is something wrong with each of them, difficulties which would have been straightened out if they had had a normal life. In Tereszin everybody tried to work as little as possible to make up for the lack of proper nourishment. In the Ward of Motherless Children there was always too much work and too few people to help me. Besides looking after the children we had to see to their clothes, etc., which took time. We looked after the bodily welfare of the children as well as possible, kept them free of vermin for three years, and we fed them as well as was possible under the circumstances. But it was not possible to attend to their other needs. Actually, we did not have the time to play with them. . . ."

NAME	DATE AND PLACE OF BIRTH	FAMILY HISTORY	AGE AT ARRIVAL IN TERESZIN	AGE AT ARRIVAL IN BULLDOGS BANK
John	18.12.1941 Vienna	Orthodox Jewish working-class parents. Deported to Poland and killed.	Presumably under 12 months	3 years 10 months
Ruth	21.4.1942 Vienna	Parents, a brother of 7 and a sister of 4 years were deported and killed when Ruth was a few months old. She was cared for in a Jewish Nursery in Vienna, sent to Tereszin with the Nursery.	Several months	3 years 6 months
Leah	23.4.1942 Berlin	Leah and a brother were illegitimate, hidden from birth. Fate of mother and brother unknown. Brother presumed killed.	Several months	3 years 5 months Arrived 6 weeks after the others, owing to a ringworm infection.
Paul	21.5.1942 Berlin	Unknown	12 months	3 years 5 months
Miriam	18.8.1942 Berlin	Upper middle-class family. Father died in concentration camp, mother went insane, was cared for first in a mental hospital in Vienna, later in a mental ward in Tereszin where she died.	6 months	3 years 2 months
Peter	22.10.1942	Parents deported and killed when Peter was a few days old. Child was found abandoned in public park, cared for first in a convent, later, when found to be Jewish, was taken to the Jewish hospital in Berlin, then brought to Tereszin.	Under 12 months	3 years

a good mood, they called the staff members indiscriminately *Tante* (auntie), as they had done in Tereszin; in bad moods this changed to *blöde Tante* (silly, stupid auntie). Their favorite swearword was *blöder Ochs* (the equivalent of "stupid fool"), a German term which they retained longer than any other.

Group Reactions

CLINGING TO THE GROUP

THE children's positive feelings were centered exclusively in their own group. It was evident that they cared greatly for each other and not at all for anybody or anything else. They had no other wish than to be together and became upset when they were separated from each other, even for short moments. No child would consent to remain upstairs while the others were downstairs, or vice versa, and no child would be taken for a walk or on an errand without the others. If anything of the kind happened, the single child would constantly ask for the other children while the group would fret for the missing child.

This insistence on being inseparable made it impossible in the beginning to treat the children as individuals or to vary their lives according to their special needs. Ruth, for instance, did not like going for walks, while the others greatly preferred walks to indoor play. But it was very difficult to induce the others to go out and let Ruth stay at home. One day, they actually left without her, but kept asking for her until, after approximately twenty minutes, John could bear it no longer and turned back to fetch her. The others joined him, they all returned home, greeted Ruth as if they had been separated for a long time and then took her for a walk, paying a great deal of special attention to her.

It was equally difficult to carry out measures for the children's health, so far as they did not apply to everybody. When the children arrived, they were in fairly good physical condition, though somewhat pale, flabby, with protruding stomachs and dry, stringy hair, cuts and scratches on their skin tending to go septic. All the children were given cod-liver oil and other vitamins which were taken easily and liked by everybody. But it was nearly impossible to keep individual children in bed for small ailments, or for instance to give Miriam and Peter, who needed it, an afternoon nap while the others had no wish to rest. Sometimes those two children would fall asleep exhaustedly in the middle of the noise made by the others. At night, all children were restless sleepers, Ruth being unable to fall asleep, Paul and Peter waking up in the night crying. Whoever was awake, naturally disturbed the sleep of the others. The upset about separation was so great that, finally, children with colds were no longer kept upstairs. The only child who was in bed once, for two days with a slight bronchitis, was Paul. Another time three children had to be isolated for several days with stomatitis. The only other child in need of individual physical treatment was Leah. She had a bad squint, her eyes were treated daily but the operation was postponed for six months to give her time for better adjustment to a renewed separation.

Inability to be separated from the group showed up most glaringly in those instances where individual children were singled out for a special treat, a situation for which children crave under normal circumstances. Paul, for example, cried for the other children when he was taken as the only one for a ride in the pony cart, although at other times such rides were a special thrill to him as well as to the others. On another, later, occasion the whole group of children was invited to visit another nursery in the neighborhood. Since the car was not large enough to take everybody, Paul and Miriam were taken earlier by bus. The other four, in the car, inquired constantly about them and could not enjoy the trip nor the pleasures prepared for them, until they were reunited.

. . . . .

POSITIVE RELATIONS WITHIN THE GROUP: ABSENCE OF ENVY, JEALOUSY, RIVALRY, COMPETITION

The children's unusual emotional dependence on each other was borne out further by the almost complete absence of jealousy, rivalry and competition, such as normally develop between brothers and sisters or in a group of contemporaries who come from normal families. There was no occasion to urge the children to "take turns"; they did it spontaneously since they were eager that everybody should have his share. Since the adults played no part in their emotional lives at the time, they did not compete with each other for favors or for recognition. They did not tell on each other and they stood up for each other automatically whenever they felt that a member of the group was unjustly treated or otherwise threatened by an outsider. They were extremely considerate of each other's feelings. They did not grudge each other their possessions (with one exception to be mentioned later), on the contrary lending them to each other with pleasure. When one of them received a present from a shopkeeper, they demanded the same for each of the other children, even in their absence. On walks they were concerned for each other's safety in traffic, looked after children who lagged behind, helped each other over ditches, turned aside branches for each other to clear the passage in the woods, and carried each other's coats. In the nursery they picked up each other's toys. After they had learned to play, they assisted each other silently in building and admired each other's productions. At mealtimes handing food to the neighbor was of greater importance than eating oneself.

. . . . .

RETARDATION IN MODES OF THINKING

In dealing with the mass of experience which crowded in on them, the children revealed, during the first weeks, some characteristic peculiarities which are worth noting in individuals of their ages.

A first perception of an object, or the experiencing of an event, together with the naming of it, left an impression on their minds far overriding all later ones in strength and forcefulness. This was clearly demonstrated on several occasions.

A pony in the field had been introduced to the children as a donkey by mistake, and the first ducks which they met had been misnamed geese. In both cases it took several weeks to undo the wrong connection between object and word. In spite of repeated efforts at correction, the children clung to the names connected with their first image of the animal.

The first leaf shown to the children was an ivy leaf. For a whole month every green leaf was called ivy leaf.

When the children noticed a plane overhead for the first time and asked where it was going, they were told that it was going to France. "Going to France" remained a fixed attribute of every plane from then onward. During the whole year they called out: "Aeroplane going to France," whenever they heard a plane overhead.

The first time that letter writing had come into the children's lives was on the occasion of Sister Sophie's absence. All later letters, imagined or dictated by them, retained the opening phrases which they had used then: "Dear Sophie in a London in a Miss X's house. Miss X all better," regardless of the fact that Sister Sophie had returned long ago and that the letters were addressed to other people.

The first English song which the children learned in Bulldogs Bank was "Bah bah black sheep." Though they learned and sang many other nursery rhymes during their stay, "Bah bab black sheep" remained in a class of its own. They would sing it when cheerful or as a treat for somebody on special occasions.

When talking of people the children would name them according to their most interesting attribute or possession, or would name these objects after them. Mrs. Clarke, for example, had two small dogs which were the first friendly dogs known to the children and played an important role in helping them to overcome their terror of dogs. In December all children called Mrs. Clarke: "Miss Clarke's doggies." Objects given by her to the children were called by the same name. A big electric stove which came from her house was called by Peter: "Miss Clarke's doggies." Green porridge bowls given by her as a Christmas present were called Mrs. Clarke by everybody.

December 1945—When washing up, John says: "You wash Mrs. Clarke. I dry Mrs. Clarke. Look at that, Mrs. Clarke all dry."

January 1946—Ruth throws Peter's green bowl on the floor. Three children shout: "Mrs. Clarke kaputt, poor Mrs. Clarke all kaputt."

The examples quoted in this chapter reveal primitive modes of thinking which are shown by children in their second year of life. The overwhelming strength of a first link between an object or event and its name is characteristic for the time when children first learn to speak, or—to express it in metapsychological terms—when word representations are first added to the images (object representations) in the child's mind. The inability to distinguish between essential and nonessential attributes of an object belongs to the same age (see example of aeroplanes). Instances of naming where this is directed not to a single limited object but to a whole idea related to it (see example of "Miss Clarke's doggies") are forms of "condensation," well known from the primary processes which reveal themselves normally in dream activity, and continue in the second year of life as a mode of waking thought.[5]

That these infantilisms in the sphere of thinking were not based on a general mental retardation with the children under observation was borne out by their adequate, adapted reasoning and behavior in situations with which they felt familiar (such as household tasks, community affairs, etc.); that they were not merely a function of the reversal in their emotional development is suggested by the fact that they overcame them before their libidinal attachments had changed decisively. That the rapid growth of life experience brought about an equally rapid advance in the modes of dealing with it mentally, suggests rather that it was the extreme dearth of new perceptions and varied impressions in their most impressionable years which deprived the children of the opportunity to exercise their mental functions to a normal degree and consequently brought about a stunting of thought development.[6]

5 See in this respect also H. Werner, *Comparative Psychology of Mental Development* (Follet, Chicago, 1948, p. 58), where he describes these modes of thinking as syncretic phenomena or holophrasis. The term holophrasis is used in connection with language development especially in those cases where a sign stands for a whole related idea or series of ideas, e.g., when a child says "chair" to mean "lift me up."

6 Another instance of this arrest of development in the second year of life, though on the emotional side, concerned the children's attitude to the village people, whom they treated merely as extensions of the adults in their own house. While their aggressive behavior toward the staff was at its peak, the children also spat at the workmen in the house, kicked and pushed passers-by in the road and shouted rude remarks at everybody. When their relations with the staff had become positive, they felt extremely hurt at any lack of interest or affection from strangers. They waved at all passing cars and expected people to wave in return. It was extremely upsetting to them when people ignored their advances. Peter complained on such occasion in December: "Uncle nicht [not] nice, uncle nicht good morning, uncle a shame." Later on they shouted on such occasions: "Naughty driver did not nicht wave." A girl who had not answered their waving in spring but had laughed ironically instead was not forgotten by them for weeks after: "Silly girl, not nice, and she did not wave, she did laugh, she did." It corresponds to the typical mentality of the normal toddler to ignore the difference between strangers and members of the family, to expect the same consideration from both and to extend the same ambivalent attitudes toward both. In the normal family this attitude of the two-year-old is reinforced usually by the parents' inclination to present the most

Fears and Anxieties

THE children had grown up in an atmosphere laden with fear and anxiety. Tereszin was a transit camp, and though some people remained there from their arrest to the end of the Nazi regime, thousands of others, adults as well as children, passed through it on their way to the extermination camps in Poland, their stay in Tereszin lasting days, weeks or months. To be called up for further transport, which was equivalent to a death sentence, was the constant terror of the camp population, from which no inmate was exempt. Arrivals and departures took place continually, especially at nighttime. Inmates who escaped transportation themselves, lost parents, husbands, wives, and children. It was a daily happening for members of the community to disappear, not to be seen again, especially in the last year before the liberation when the camp was cleared of tens of thousands of its inmates in the course of several months. Besides, during the whole time, there was a large death roll owing to epidemics, other illnesses, weakness, and old age, and burials were the order of the day.

There were several thousand children of all ages in Tereszin who lived a comparatively protected life in packed dormitories, cared for by their own compatriots. The Ward for Motherless Children was one of these hostels. Though the workers did their best to shelter the children from the unrest and the miseries of concentration camp existence, the excitements, fears, sorrows and losses cannot but have penetrated into their nursery atmosphere. The children, and the adults who looked after them, lived together in such close proximity that there was no room for privacy. In the yard, the children met the inmates of other hostels, adults and children, and must have heard their talks. Though they had no conscious memories of these matters, some of their attitudes seemed to bear witness to the impressions made on them.[7]

indifferent strangers to the child as "uncles" and "aunties."

7 The recent analysis of another concentration camp child from Tereszin, a boy who arrived in Windermere at the age of four years six months, showed a vast extent of sadistic fantasies which

FEARS BASED ON MEMORIES

Fear of dogs. The only animal of which the children had known in Tereszin was a watchdog which had belonged to one of the German guards and was said to have been feared by the whole population. Whether the children had actually seen or met this dog, or merely heard about it, is not known. But the fact is that all six children were terrified of dogs. They screamed, clung to the adults and went pale whenever a dog came in sight. John would turn completely white and sometimes have tears in his eyes; Ruth, Paul and Peter would tremble with fear. Once, when meeting a strange large dog on a walk, John bit his lip in his terror and thought that the dog had bitten him when it bled. In intensity this fear resembled the dog-phobias which appear so frequently in children of this age. There were, though, certain aspects of it which pointed rather to an external source of danger in the children's past, than to an internal source of anxiety in all of them, or in one of them from whom it might have spread by emotional infection to the others. The fear of dogs played no part except in the presence of the feared object; it did not prevent the children from going out into the danger zones and it was possible to overcome it by letting the children handle friendly dogs. In playing with these harmless small animals ("Miss Clarke's doggies") the children got very excited, half afraid, half enjoying the fact that the dogs were really afraid of them. They stroked them in a somewhat aggressive manner, made "noise at them," chased them, while running away themselves, all attitudes well known from children's animal play and

animal fantasies. While the other children overcame the fear of dogs gradually, with Peter the dreaded dog became a symbol for inner conflicts and dangers toward which he developed a truly phobic attitude.

Fear of feathers. Another fear of similar nature which existed in the children was directed toward feathers. All the children were terrified when they saw a feather, cried with fear, turned white and trembled. Peter called out several times at night "Feder" (feather) and was found trembling with fear. When a dressing for a cut on his head had to be renewed, he cried normally at first. When it came to the point where it hurt badly, he shrieked: "Feder, Feder." Though all the evidence seemed to point to some common experience of their past, it was not possible in this instance to fill the gap in memory.

Fear of the van. The children's great positive interest in traffic and vehicles of all kinds contrasted sharply with Ruth's reaction to a huge dark grey-green van which stopped at the corner of the road one day in May. Ruth stared at it terrified, turning very pale. When John, who was very interested in it, wanted to approach it, Ruth trembled, stamped her feet and screamed in horror: "John, John, du nis go near, come here quickly." She was beside herself with fear, did not listen to reassurance and the children were taken further on their walk as quickly as possible. She continued to sob for some time: "John, nis go near, Ruth stocking, Ruth so stocking!" (meaning: shocking, had a shock). On the way home she peeped round the corner carefully and said with great relief: "Nasty big van is gone." It can be assumed in this case that the van had called up a sudden memory of a gas or transport van in Tereszin, in any case of something which had been an object of terror to the adults of the camp.

Fear of flying. In February Sister Gertrud told the children that she would be going to London for a day. All of them were interested, with the exception of Ruth who looked worried. John began to cry and said: "You nis go in aeroplane, aeroplane will fall down."

---

merged in his mind with memories and tales overheard of soldiers, shooting, the killing of his mother and other atrocities.

A girl who was seven and a half on arrival in Windermere described her first impressions there as follows: "Do you remember, when we came to the house, there were many people crying?" When reminded that it was only the small children among them who cried, that all the grownups were happy to greet the newcomers, she said: "I thought it is a prison and all the people inside shout and cry, because one is going to kill them. . . . You see, I have come from Germany where they put people into prison and killed them and we heard them shout and cry, I didn't know it is different in England."

Sister Gertrud assured him that she would go and return by bus. He cried for some time and then said: "Ich go in aeroplane yesterday—aber—aber—aber—und it made so noise—und ich cry and cry and cry all the time." Gradually the others joined in and said that they too had cried when they were in the plane yesterday. None of them could remember who else was in the plane, or any other details.

ANXIETIES

Apart from these fears which played a big part, the children showed the usual variety of transient individual anxieties which are the manifest expression for the underlying conflicts and difficulties normal for their ages. There were instances of fear of darkness (Miriam), of flies (Paul), of waves (Peter), of crossing bridges, of finding fluff in the bathwater or in the food (Paul). Apart from the fear of dogs, there was no fear of big animals, horses, cows, pigs, etc. Surprisingly enough, these common forms of anxiety were not more noticeable and widespread than with children who grow up under normal conditions; they were, if anything, less in evidence.

It remains an unanswered question why the atmosphere of anxiety and terror in which the children had spent their first years, had not predisposed them to more violent anxiety states of their own. Infants and young children are, as we know, deeply affected by their mothers' conscious and unconscious fears and anxieties. The explanation may be that these young infants, though they lived in closest proximity with their adult guardians, did not have the intimate emotional contact with them which provides the path for the contagion of feeling between mother and child. Perhaps the fact that they had never known peaceful surroundings rendered them more indifferent to the horrors happening around them.[8] A further possible explanation may be connected with the fact that the children possessed strong defenses against anxiety in their close relationship to each other which acted as reassurance and protection. This latter point is borne out by the fact that they became insecure and anxious as soon as they were separated from each other.

A better answer to this question will, the authors hope, be provided in time by the future analysis of these children or others who have undergone experiences of this nature.

Language Problems

WHILE passing through the phases of development as described above, the children had the added task of learning a new language, a necessity which made adaptation more difficult since it rendered them inarticulate in the transition period. They talked German on arrival, mixed with Czech which they had picked up after leaving Tereszin. Ruth's mixture of German and Czech was especially difficult to understand. The members of the staff began to talk English in front of the children and with them after a week and ceased talking German altogether after approximately seven weeks.

Surprisingly enough, there was no violent refusal on the part of the children to adopt the new language. The only outbursts of this kind came from Paul. In October, while repeating English words, which he liked to do, he became furious suddenly: "Is nicht motor car, is Auto, blöde Tante!" "Nicht good morning Paul, guten Morgen Paul!" On the other hand, Paul was the first to realize that the new language was essential to make contact with the village people. At the time when the other children still looked unhappy and withdrawn, he attracted everybody's attention by a very pleasant smile. People smiled and waved at him, though he could only say "hallo" in answer. His first English sentence was spoken in a deliberate effort to make contact:

In December, the children passed one of the cottages whose owner came to the gate and gave flowers to them. Paul said: "Flowers," after

---

8 See an example from October 1945. Miriam finds Ruth's bed empty in the morning. Ruth has been taken to another room during the night so as not to upset the others with her crying. When asked where Ruth has gone to, she shrugs her shoulders, turns up her hands in a typically Jewish gesture and says: "Tot" ("Dead").

some thinking "Lovely flowers," and then "Many lovely flowers, thank you!" The woman was so pleased that she kissed him.

John and Peter followed Paul in using their English words to draw attention to themselves, and soon used more English than German nouns. In a transitional phase they used composite nouns, made up of both languages, such as "auto-car," "doggy-Hund," "dolly-Puppe," "Löffel-spoon," etc. The girls, who were worse speakers altogether, followed much more slowly. The first adjectives and adverbs were used from the fifth week after beginning.

It was of evident concern to the children that the difference in their speed of learning English caused differences between them where there had been unity before. Many of their word battles centered around these points, as the following examples show:

December (at mealtime)

Leah: "Brot."
Ruth: "Is bread."
Leah: "Brot."
Ruth (half crying): "Nis Brot, is bread."
Leah (shouting): "Brot."
Ruth (crying): "Is bread."
Paul: "Is bread, blöder Ochs Leah."
John: "Is nis blöder Ochs."
Paul (shouting): "Is blöder Ochs John."
John (screaming): "Is nis blöder Ochs."
Sister Sophie: "Don't cry, nobody is a blöder Ochs."
Paul (as loud as possible): "Blöder Ochs du, blöder Ochs Sophie."
John: "Sophie is nis blöder Ochs."
Peter (all smiles): "Nis blöder Ochs Sophie."
Paul: "Is hau dich" (turns against Peter).
Peter: "Please bread."
Paul gets bread for Peter and passes it to him.

January (at mealtime)

Paul: "Look, ich big Teller, siehst du?"
John: "Nis Teller, is plate."
Paul: "Oh nein."
John: "Is nis Teller, is in endlich [English?] plate."
Paul (shouts): "Oh nein."
Sister Sophie: "John is quite right, Teller is plate in English."
Paul: "Look, ich big plate."

John: "Clever boy John."
Peter: "No, clever boy Sophie," etc.

These differences disappeared again after January, when the whole group spoke English, among themselves as well as to the adults. They tried to express everything in English, using a picturesque language where the absence of verbs made expression difficult.

January 1946—Peter tries to describe how a young girl had picked hazel-catkins from a high bush: "Sheila and a jump, and a jump, and a jump, and a hazel-catkin."

January 1946—Showing a patch on his mended shoe, Peter says: "This shoemaker's shoe," then showing the old part of the sole: "And this Peter's shoe."

Verbs were used from January onward and presented great difficulties to the children. Instead of using the tenses correctly, they began by using the present participle only: "You writing?" "Doggy barking, we not crying." "You should not nicht talking a lot, you talking awfully much." From April onward they were able to use the present tense correctly but had their difficulties with the imperfect and the past tense: "Sea did make so noise, water did come so nearer, Peter did cry." "I did told you you must not do that." "I did helped in the kitchen, I did cooked the beans." "Die Mr. B. is coming; oh no, she did went away."

There were several wrong uses of words which the children had made habitually in German and which were taken over to English without change. They used "up" and "down," "open" and "shut" the wrong way round. They further used the feminine article and pronoun for men, and the phrases "clever boy," "naughty boy" for females as well as males. "Die John dress herself, clever boy die John." "Die Mr. B. . . ." "Naughty boy, Gertrud." [9]

9 This does not imply that the children were ignorant of the difference between the sexes. The following examples show that their curiosity and theories concerning this subject were normal for their ages:
February 1946—John examines his penis carefully. "Aber, aber, aber, why is it little hole?" Answer: "That is where your wee-wee comes out." John: "Big

For a long time the children clung to the German negation *nicht* (which must have played an overwhelmingly great part in their restricted lives). For some weeks in spring it was used together with its English counterpart as "not-nicht," before it was finally dropped.

The only German word which the children retained throughout the year was *meine* (my). Although the children knew and used the English equivalent, they would revert to the German *meine* when very affectionate: "Meine Gertrud," "Meine dolly."

By August the last German words, with this single exception, had disappeared, though the understanding of the German language as such had ceased much earlier. When a visitor talked German to the children in April, they laughed as if at a joke. In May, a German prisoner of war talked German to Ruth who looked completely blank. In June another visitor who knew the children from Windermere talked German to them; there was absolutely no reaction.

With the adaptation to the new language the children had made a further decisive step toward the break with their past, which now disappeared completely from their consciousness.[10]

Conclusion

"EXPERIMENTS" of this kind, which are provided by fate, lack the satisfying neatness and circumscription of an artificial setup. It is difficult, or impossible, to distinguish the action of the variables from each other, as is demonstrated in our case by the intermingled effects of three main factors: the absence of a mother or parent relationship; the abundance of community influence; and the reduced amount of gratification of all needs, from the oral stage onward. It is, of course, impossible to vary the experiment. In our case, further, it proved impossible to obtain knowledge of all the factors which have influenced development. There remained dark periods in the life of each child, and guesswork, conclusions and inferences had to be used to fill the gaps.

Under such circumstances, no claim to exactitude can be made for the material which is presented here and it offers no basis for statistical considerations. Though an experiment staged by fate, in the sense that it accentuates the action of certain factors in the child's life (demonstrated through their absence or their exaggerated presence), it has little or nothing to offer to the experimental psychologist. What it helps to do is to create impressions which either confirm or refute the analyst's assumptions concerning infantile development—impressions which can be tested and in their turn confirmed or rejected in detailed analytic work with single individuals.

According to the results of child analysis and reconstruction from the analyses of adults, the child's relationship to his brothers and sisters is subordinated to his relationship to the parents, is, in fact, a function of it. Siblings are normally accessories to the parents, the relations to them being governed by attitudes of rivalry, envy, jealousy, and competition for the love of the parents. Aggression, which is inhibited toward the parents, is expressed freely toward brothers and sisters; sexual wishes, which cannot become manifest in the oedipal relationship, are lived out, passively or actively, with elder or younger brothers and sisters. The underlying relationship with siblings is thus a negative one (dating from infancy when all siblings were merely rivals for the mother's love), with an overlay of positive feelings when siblings are used for the discharge of libidinal

---

job aber, aber, aber nis comes out of little hole." Answer: "No, your big job comes out of a little bit bigger hole behind there." John (trying hard to see it): "Wo, is kann nis see."

Apparently he passed on his new knowledge, for a few days later the following conversation between the children was overheard in the evening. Peter: "Peter auch [also] little hole, Paul auch little hole, John auch little hole, Mariam auch little hole." John: "Miriam nis little hole, Miriam aber, aber, aber nur [only] little bit bigger hole."

A fortnight later Miriam has to urinate on a walk. John looks at her and says: "Girls can't do lulu, only big job." When told that they can do it very well, he thinks a bit and then says: "Well, they can do lulu with big job."

10 A year and a half later, when asked by somebody how he ever got to Windermere, Peter replied: "One does not get there, everybody is borned there."

trends deflected from the parents. Where the relations between the children of one family become finally manifestly positive, they do so according to the principles of group formation, on the basis of their common identification with the parents. The rival brother is tolerated as belonging to the mother; in special cases [11] the rival brother even becomes an object of identification as the mother's favorite. The child's first approach to the idea of justice is made during these developments of the brother-sister relationship, when the claim to be favored oneself is changed to the demand that no one should be favored, i.e., that there should be equal rights for everybody. Since contemporaries outside the family are treated like the siblings, these first relationships to the brothers and sisters become important factors in determining the individual's social attitudes.

It is well in line with these views when our material shows that the relations of the Bulldogs Bank children to each other were totally different from ordinary sibling attitudes. The children were without parents in the fullest sense of the word, i.e., not merely orphaned at the time of observation, but most of them without an early mother or father image in their unconscious minds to which their earliest libidinal strivings might have been attached. Consequently, their companions of the same age were their real love objects and their libidinal relations with them of a direct nature, not merely the products of laborious reaction formation and defenses against hostility. This explains why the feelings of the six children toward each other show a warmth and spontaneity which is unheard of in ordinary relations between young contemporaries.

It merely bears out this theory to find that attachments to a mother figure in single instances disturb these positive relations, such as in Ruth's case. Or when John, in his mourning for Maureen, turned against his companions and began to hurt them. In these instances the positive libidinal attachment was directed toward the adult; the other children were thereby changed from the position

of friends and love objects to that of enemies and rivals.

When working with the children of the Hampstead Nurseries, one of the authors has described certain attitudes of helpfulness, co-operation, identification and friendship which appeared in a group of toddlers (between fifteen months and two and one half years of age) who had been temporarily deprived of their mothers' care. The six Bulldogs Bank children, as the observations prove, show these attitudes in excess, the quantitative difference between them and the Hampstead Nursery group corresponding to the difference between total and partial absence of a parent relationship.

The high degree of identification with each other's needs is known from one other relationship in early years, that of identical twins to each other. In a recent study of the subject Dorothy Burlingham demonstrates the emotional importance of twins to each other, the way in which the twin is treated as an extension of the self, cathected with narcissistic as well as object love. Identification with the twin prospers on the basis of common needs, common anxieties, common wishes, in short, on the similar reactions of two beings of the same age living in close proximity under the same external conditions. While in the case of twins the twin relationship conflicts with and has to adapt itself to the parent relationship, the attitude to the companion within our age group of orphans reigned supreme.

That the children were able to attach their libido to their companions and the group as such, bypassing as it were the parent relationship which is the normal way to social attitudes, deserves interest in relation to certain analytic assumptions. In recent analytic work the experiences of the first year of life, the importance of the relationship to the mother during the oral phase and the linking of these experiences with the beginnings of ego development have assumed great significance. Explorations in these directions have led to the belief, held by many authors, that every disturbance of the mother relationship during this vital phase is invariably a pathogenic factor of specific value. Grave defects

11 —which lead to later homosexual attitudes—

in ego development, lack or loss of speech in the first years, withdrawnness, apathy, self-destructive attitudes, psychotic manifestations, have all been ascribed to the so-called "rejection" by the mother, a comprehensive term which includes every disturbance within the mother relationship from loss of the mother through death, permanent or temporary separation, cruel or neglectful treatment, down to lack of understanding, ambivalence, preoccupation or lack of warmth on the mother's part.

The six Bulldogs Bank children are, without doubt, "rejected" infants in this sense of the term. They were deprived of mother love, oral satisfactions, stability in their relationships and their surroundings. They were passed from one hand to another during their first year, lived in an age group instead of a family during their second and third year, and were uprooted again three times during their fourth year. A description of the anomalies which this fate produced in their emotional life and of the retardations in certain ego attitudes [12] is contained in the material. The children were hypersensitive, restless, aggressive, difficult to handle. They showed a heightened autoerotism and some of them the beginning of neurotic symptoms. But they were neither deficient, delinquent nor psychotic. They had found an alternative placement for their libido and, on the strength of this, had mastered some of their anxieties, and developed social attitudes. That they were able to acquire a new language in the midst of their upheavals, bears witness to a basically unharmed contact with their environment.

The authors hope that further contact with these children, or those of similar experience, will give indications as to how such emotional anomalies of early life influence the shaping of the oedipus phase, superego development, adolescence and the chances for a normal adult love life.

12 —though much of these have to be ascribed to the additional material deprivations—

MELVIN L. DE FLEUR *and* FRANK R. WESTIE

47. *Verbal Attitudes and Overt Acts:*
An Experiment on the Salience of Attitudes

I N the face of the steady stream of studies of the verbal dimension of attitudinal behavior, the paucity of investigations of the overt-action correlates of such verbal behavior is indeed striking. Those who have conducted attitude research are not surprised by this one-sided emphasis: overt acceptance-avoidance acts are extremely difficult to isolate and measure. One source of this difficulty lies in the fact that few, if any, standardized situations or instruments have been developed enabling the investigator to quantify, on a positive-negative continuum, an acceptance or avoidance act for a set of subjects, with other conditions held constant.[1]

The present paper reports an attempt to develop an instrument which can readily be used in an interview situation for measuring the "salience" of a person's attitudinal orientations. It also explores the use of reference groups by subjects whose attitudinal salience is being measured. The term *salience* can be defined as the readiness of an individual to translate his (previously expressed verbal) attitude into overt action in relation to the attitude object. The relationship between in-

ner conviction and overt behavior has frequently been discussed in connection with the validity of measures of verbal attitudes. In a thorough summary of the literature, Green [2] comments on this view of attitude measurement validity, pointing out that the validity of an attitude scale is actually the extent to which it truly represents behavior within a particular *attitude universe*. He distinguishes between a verbal attitude universe, from which attitude scale items are drawn, and an action attitude universe, consisting of a variety of overt behavior forms regarding the attitude object. Validity in the measure-mean of an attitude is the problem of determining the degree to which it measures behavior within its appropriate universe; it is not necessarily a problem of determining the extent to which it predicts behavior from one universe to another. In line with this view, the purpose of the present study is not to develop a device for "validating" other attitude instruments. Its aim rather is to provide a simple device which can be used as an "action opportunity" for a subject to give public and overt testimony of his acceptance or rejection of a Negro in a specific action context.

1 There have been several attempts to develop *hypothetical situations tests* as measures of what subjects thought they might do in hypothetical situations which were described to them. Such statements of belief are not conceptually different from other forms of verbal behavior with which verbal attitudes are measured. See, e.g., A. C. Rosander, "An Attitude Scale Based Upon Behavior Situations," *Journal of Social Psychology,* 8 (February, 1937), pp. 3–15. Also: C. Robert Pace, "A Situations Test to Measure Social-Political-Economic Attitudes," *Journal of Social Psychology,* 10 (August, 1930), pp. 331–344.

Studies of Inconsistency

EARLIER studies indicate that a person's verbal acceptance or rejection of minority groups may be quite unrelated to what he

2 Bert F. Green, "Attitude Measurement," in Gardner Lindzey, editor, *Handbook of Social Psychology,* Cambridge, Mass.: Addison-Wesley, 1954, Vol. I, Chapter 9.

Reprinted by permission of the American Sociological Association and the authors, *American Journal of Sociology,* 1958, vol. 23, pp. 667–73.

actually does or would do in overt inter-action situations. For example, in company with a couple from China, La Piere [3] made an extensive tour of the Pacific Coast and transcontinental United States during which they were accommodated by over 250 res-taurants, hotels, and similar establishments. Refusal of service by virtue of the racial characteristics of the Chinese occurred only once. But when La Piere sent each establish-ment a letter and questionnaire requesting a statement of its policy regarding accommo-dating Chinese clients, over 90 per cent of the replies noted that they adhered to a policy of non-acceptance of such minority group members. In these cases, the overt act re-versed the stated intention.

In a more recent study of overt behavior or action attitudes by Lohman and Reitzes [4] 151 residents of an urban neighborhood were located who were also members of a particu-lar labor union. Two conflicting norms re-garding behavior toward Negroes prevailed in these two collectivities. The urban neighbor-hood was predominantly white and was re-sisting Negro penetration; a property owners association (of which the subjects were mem-bers) had been organized for this purpose. In this behavioral area, that is, with respect to having a Negro for a neighbor, the subjects uniformly acted in an anti-Negro manner. However, the 151 subjects also belonged to a labor union with a clear and well-imple-mented policy of granting Negroes complete equality on the job. Here, then, with the same subjects and the same attitude object, were two seemingly opposite action forms. An ex-planation of this situation in terms of indi-vidual verbal attitudes would be inadequate. The authors show that each of the formal organizations (the union and property own-ers association) provided the individual with a set of well-formulated reasons and justi-fications for his actions in each of these spheres. Clearly, action attitudes may be de-termined to a considerable degree by the

extent to which the individual is actually or psychologically involved in social systems providing him with norms and beliefs which he can use as guides to action when *specific* action opportunities arise.

In studying attitude salience, then, it may be predicted that individuals faced with the necessity of making an action decision with regard to Negroes will partially determine the direction of this action by consideration of the norms and policies of social groups which are meaningful to them. Ordinarily, we do not expect subjects to be involved in such well-defined groups, with clearly specified policies regarding action toward Negroes, as those studied by Lohman and Reitzes. Norms and guides to action in more ordinary situa-tions are more likely to be derived from family, friends, or other persons used as ref-erence groups. For this reason, the present paper includes a probe into the reference groups invoked in an action decision made by subjects regarding public involvement with Negroes.

In the larger program of experiments, of which the present report is a part, the sub-jects were studied from the standpoint of the relationship between three dimensions of their attitudinal behavior: verbal, autonomic-physiological, and overt. There were three phases to this research: attitude testing, a laboratory session in which the subjects' autonomic-physiological responses to race stimuli were recorded, and a post-laboratory interview. This paper, however, is concerned only with the relationship between the verbal and overt dimensions and draws its data largely from the post-laboratory interview.

The Summated Differences Scales [5] were

---

3 Richard T. La Piere, "Attitudes vs. Actions," *Social Forces,* 13 (December, 1934), pp. 230–237.

4 Joseph D. Lohman and Dietrich C. Reitzes, "Deliberately Organized Groups and Racial Be-havior," *American Sociological Review,* 19 (June, 1954), pp. 342–348.

5 This device employs the principle of eliciting a response to a white person of a given occupational status and then, many pages later, a response to a Negro of the same occupational status, each por-trayed in the same hypothetical relationship with the respondent. Numerical differences between the responses to whites and to Negroes are then summed. For example, in one item the respondent is asked to respond (from "strongly agree" to "strongly disagree" in five possible categories) to the state-ment "I believe I would be willing to have a *Negro Doctor* have his hair cut at the same barber shop which I have mine cut." Later, after approximately 200 items have been interposed, he is asked to re-spond to the statement, "I believe I would be willing to have a *White Doctor* have his hair cut

administered to 250 students in introductory sociology classes. From the 250 cases, two smaller groups were selected for more intensive study. The distribution of total scores was determined, and from those scoring in the top quartile (indicating the greatest verbal rejection of Negroes) 23 subjects were selected on the basis of eight criteria (noted below). These individuals were carefully matched, by the method of frequency distribution control, with 23 subjects scoring in the lowest quartile (indicating the least verbal rejection of Negroes). The matching process reduced the size of the original group substantially, but 46 subjects were thus carefully selected for their similarity on eight characteristics of their social background. The frequency distributions of the groups were matched according to age, sex (half of each group was male), marital status, religion, social class, social mobility experience, residential history, and previous contact with Negroes. For convenience, we refer to that group showing the

greatest verbal rejection of Negroes as the "prejudiced group," and their counterparts at the opposite end of the verbal scales as the "unprejudiced group."

Method

AFTER each subject had completed a laboratory session in which his autonomic responses to race relations stimuli were recorded,[6] he was conducted to an interview room where a variety of questions, devices, and situations were presented to him regarding his feelings about Negroes. Shortly before the end of this hour-long post-laboratory interview the subject was presented with what may be called an "overt action opportunity." In the laboratory session, and in earlier phases of the interview, each subject had viewed a number of colored photographic slides showing interracial pairings of males and females. Some of these slides portrayed a well-dressed, good looking, young Negro man paired with a good looking, well-dressed, young white woman. Others showed a white man similarly paired with a Negro woman. The background for all of the slides consisted of a table, a lamp, and a window with a drapery, giving an effect not unlike that of a living room or possibly a dormitory lounge. The persons in the photographs were seated beside each other in separate chairs, and were looking at one another with pleasant expressions. The photographer and models had been instructed to strive for a portrayal of cordiality, but not romance.[7] Each of the 46 subjects had given projective interpretations of "what was happening" in these pictures.

---

at the barber shop where I have mine cut." Thus, a respondent may "strongly disagree" to one of these propositions and "agree" to the other. The wide separation between the white and Negro of identical occupation by interposing a great many items provides a concealment factor. The ability of the respondent to remember how he responded earlier is greatly reduced by this control. The difference between the responses is given a numerical value indicating differential acceptance of the white and Negro of the same occupational status in this particular relationship with the respondent. A total of eight occupational categories are involved and a large variety of activities. In all, over 500 responses are elicited from a given subject. The respondent's total score is simply the summated numerical differences between his responses to whites and Negroes of similar occupation in a variety of relationships with the respondent. The total score indicates the extent to which the respondent regards Negroes as objects to be accepted or rejected as compared to whites.

The reliability coefficients of the scales were derived through testing and retesting 99 undergraduate students of Indiana University. The time interval between the test and retest was five weeks. The reliability coefficients were as follows:

Scale I	Residential:	$r = .95$
Scale II	Position:	$r = .95$
Scale III	Interpersonal-Physical:	$r = .80$
Scale IV	Interpersonal-Social:	$r = .87$
	Combined Scores:	$r = .96$

For a detailed discussion of this device, see Frank R. Westie, "A Technique for the Measurement of Race Attitudes," *American Sociological Review*, 18 (February, 1953), pp. 73–78.

6 These autonomic responses to racial stimula are described in some detail in a paper forthcoming in the *Journal of Abnormal and Social Psychology*. Briefly, they consist of galvanic skin responses and changes in finger blood volume occurring when prejudiced and unprejudiced subjects viewed photographic slides portraying Negroes and whites of both sexes shown singly and in all possible pairs. The results indicate that attitudinal responses include changes in the autonomic system which differ for types of subjects classified as prejudiced and unprejudiced.

7 This effort to avoid romantic and sexual connotations was made so that the slides could be used as projective devices in another phase of the research. In spite of these efforts, female subjects tended to "see" these situations as romantic.

To present the overt action opportunity, the interviewer told each subject that another set of such slides was needed for further research. The subject was first asked if he (or she) would be willing to be photographed with a Negro person of the opposite sex, a request which elicited a wide variety of responses, as well as considerable hesitation in many cases. A number indicated willingness, but others refused categorically to be so photographed. Then, regardless of his (or her) stated position, the subject was presented with a mimeographed form and informed that this was "a standard *photograph release agreement,* which is necessary in any situation where a photograph of an individual is to be used in any manner." The photograph release agreement contained a graded series of "uses" to which the photograph would be put (see FIGURE 1), ranging from laboratory experiments, such as they had just experienced, to a nationwide publicity campaign advocating racial integration. They were to sign their name to each "use" which they would permit.[8]

8 In all cases, it was emphasized to the subject that he was free to terminate his participation in the experiment at any time. He was told that he could

---

The directors of the experiment you just participated in need more photographs like you saw on the screen (with Negroes and whites posed together). If you will volunteer to pose for such photographs, please indicate the conditions under which you will allow these pictures to be used by signing the "releases" below. You may sign *some of them, all of them* or *none of them as you see fit.* (It is standard practice to obtain such a signed release for any kind of photograph which is to be used for some purpose.)

If you are not interested in participating in this phase of the study, you are absolutely free to do as you wish. If you do not want to commit yourself in any way on this matter, it is perfectly all right and we will respect your decision. Whatever you do, your decision will be held in the strictest confidence.

I will pose for a photograph (of the same type as in the experiment) with a Negro person of the opposite sex with the following restrictions on its use:

1. I will allow this photograph to be used in laboratory experiments where it will be seen only by professional sociologists.

  Signed.................................

2. I will allow this photograph to be published in a technical journal read only by professional sociologists.

  Signed.................................

3. I will allow this photograph to be shown to a few dozen University students in a laboratory situation.

  Signed.................................

4. I will allow this photograph to be shown to hundreds of University students as a teaching aid in Sociology classes.

  Signed.................................

5. I will allow this photograph to be published in the *Student Newspaper* as part of a publicity report on this research.

  Signed.................................

6. I will allow this photograph to be published in my home town newspaper as part of a publicity report on this research.

  Signed.................................

7. I will allow this photograph to be used in a nation-wide publicity campaign *advocating racial integration.*

  Signed.................................

FIG. 1. Photograph authorization.

In American society, the affixing of one's signature to a document is a particularly significant act. The signing of checks, contracts, agreements, and the like is clearly understood to indicate a binding obligation on the part of the signer to abide by the provisions of the document. The signing of the document in the present study took on additional significance due to the involvement of the racial variable.

The problem of the validity and reliability of this device as a measure of the salience of a subject's attitude toward Negroes can be only partially answered at present. Various approaches to establishing the validity of measuring instruments have been discussed in the literature.[9] The question of acceptable criteria of validity for a particular instrument has received many answers, and the entire issue is currently a controversial one. Such validating techniques as the "known groups" method are unacceptable for measures of salience because the evidence for validity rests upon comparisons of groups on the basis of known *verbal* attitudes. Correlating the instrument with other measures of overt acceptance-avoidance acts would be a useful method, but no standardized instruments exist for such a task.

If the items in an instrument are a reasonably good representation of the items characterizing the attitudinal universe, many investigators would say that the scale is valid by definition, that is, it has *face validity*. The term *intrinsic validity* has been used by Gulliksen to describe this situation.[10] A method which he suggests for at least a preliminary approach to validating an instrument is to employ a group of "experts" to evaluate the items selected for a measuring device.

In a modified version of Gulliksen's procedure, the series of "photograph usages" was submitted in random order to eight judges, who were sociologists of faculty status. The judges were asked to rate the usages, ranking first the use to which they felt the prejudiced person would least object. There was almost complete agreement among their rankings: only one judge reversed the order of a single adjacent pair in the 618 pair-judgments. In the eyes of presumably competent specialists, then, the items of the instrument represent an ordered sample of acts which prejudiced persons would object to in regularly increasing degrees.

The items in the instrument were designed and arranged so that they represent a cumulative series, thereby providing an obvious possibility for scaling. This was not undertaken, however, with the present version of the instrument due to the relatively small number of scale items and subjects. Nevertheless, the response patterns show almost complete transitivity: in only three of the 46 cases were there irregularities in the cumulative feature of the instrument. (In these three instances subjects did not sign an item lower on the scale, selecting one with a higher rank.) This pattern is a rough indication that the reproducibility would be rather good if the items were to be scaled. Such evidence of transitivity, of course, gives only a partial answer to the question of reliability, just as the judgments of experts meet only partially the validity problem.

The subjects uniformly perceived the behavioral situation posed for them as a highly realistic request, and many clearly exhibited discomfort at being caught in a dilemma. Wishing to cooperate with the interviewer, they nevertheless preferred to be uninvolved in a photograph with a Negro of opposite sex. There were a few, of course, who were quite willing to sign the agreement and did so without hesitation.

Verbal Prejudice and Overt Acts

THE purpose of creating this situation was to provide the subjects opportunity to give public and overt testimony of their acceptance or rejection of Negroes. But the data so obtained also allow a test of the hypothesis that individuals with negative or positive verbal attitudes will act in accord with those attitudes in an overt situation.

---

do so without prejudice on the part of the interviewer, and that he would remain anonymous in this decision. No subject took advantage of this opportunity.

9 See, e.g., Harold Gulliksen, "Intrinsic Validity," *The American Psychologist*, 5 (October, 1950), pp. 511–517.

10 *Ibid.*

The results of the photographic release agreement and its relationship to the verbally elicited attitudinal category of the subjects are given in TABLE 1. Subjects were classified as falling above or below the mean level of endorsement. The distribution was such that the mean and median fell at identical points.

In this situation, there was clearly a greater tendency for the prejudiced persons than the unprejudiced to avoid being photographed with a Negro. The relationship is significant, suggesting some correspondence in this case between attitudes measured by verbal scales and an acceptance-avoidance act toward the attitude object. In spite of the statistical significance, however, there were some prejudiced persons who signed the agreement without hesitation at the highest level, as well as some unprejudiced persons who were not willing to sign at any level. Thus, the relationship between these verbal and overt attitudinal dimensions, while significant, is not a simple one-to-one correspondence. These findings are consistent with much of the earlier research, some of which is described above. The factors which account for this seeming inconsistency need careful exploration.

One possibility of explaining the inconsistency in the present study is to assume that prejudiced subjects who signed at the higher levels and unprejudiced persons who refused to sign were misclassified by the original measurement of verbal attitudes. But this explanation is suspect due to the fact that the individuals used as subjects represent the extremes (upper and lower quartiles) of the

TABLE 1

Relationship between Race Attitudes and Level of Signed Agreement to Be Photographed with Negro

SIGNED LEVEL OF AGREEMENT	SUBJECT ATTITUDE	
	Prejudice	Unprejudiced
Below $\overline{X}$	18	9
Above $\overline{X}$	5	14

Chi square = 7.264
$p < .01$

verbal attitude distribution. While this does not eliminate the possibility of error, of course, it reduces it considerably. The inadequacy of an explanation on the basis of error alone is also suggested by the distribution in TABLE 1. Fourteen of forty-six subjects (almost one-third) show behavior patterns in opposition to their verbally elicited attitudes—this is too large a proportion to attribute to measurement errors. The latter, moreover, theoretically are cancelled out by errors in the opposite direction.

The lack of a straight-line relationship between verbal attitudes and overt action behavior more likely may be explained in terms of some sort of social involvement of the subject in a system of social constraints, preventing him from acting (overtly) in the direction of his convictions, or otherwise "legitimizing" certain behavioral patterns. These channelizing influences on behavior have received theoretical attention in terms of such concepts as "reference groups," "other directedness," and "significant others."

Reference Groups

REFERENCE groups were cited earlier as possibly an important influence upon the direction of behavior of individuals confronted with action opportunities regarding attitude objects. This possibility accounts for our hypothesis that the act of signing the photograph agreement involves a conscious consideration of reference groups. Thus the subjects were asked, immediately following their response to the document, "Was there any particular person or group of people (other than the interviewer) who came to mind when you decided to sign (or refused to sign) this document? That is, are there people whom you felt would approve or disapprove?" (Since the entire interview was recorded on tape for later study, it was possible to examine carefully the responses to this question.) The majority of the subjects needed little or no prompting for presumably they had certain key groups or individuals clearly in mind when they made their decisions.

Sixty reference groups were identified as

being influential in the decision-making of the 46 subjects regarding the signing of the photographic release. Nearly three-fourths of them (71.8 per cent) invoked some type of reference group when faced with this problem, while the remaining fourth (28.2 per cent) apparently made an "inner directed" decision. Perhaps significantly, *all* of those who did cite a reference group mentioned some type of peer group, while only a third referred to the family. In all cases the subjects were able to state whether these groups would approve or disapprove of their posing for such a photograph.

Riesman (among others) has discussed the peer group as an important source for behavioral cues and has described the "other-directed" personality, presumably on the increase in American middle class society, as a type for which the peer group operates as a predominant director of behavior.[11] Earlier research, for example the Bennington study,[12] has shown that campus groups function as important influences on attitudes. The present findings are consistent with these conclusions.

In summary, verbally expressed attitudes were significantly related to the direction of the action taken by subjects regarding being photographed with a Negro of the opposite sex. On the other hand, a third of the subjects behaved in a manner quite inconsistent with that which might be expected from their verbal attitudes. Whatever the direction of this action, however, it was a *peer-directed* decision for the majority, with the subjects making significant use of their beliefs concerning possible approval or disapproval of reference groups as guides for behavior.

Conclusions

THE present findings have at least two implications for further research. First, in order to analyze the relationship between the verbal and action dimensions of attitudes, it may be necessary to add to attitude scales a systematic categorization of the system of social constraints within which individual behavior ordinarily takes place. Thus, analysis of the beliefs of an individual about the attitudes, norms, and values held by his reference groups, significant others, voluntary organizations, peer groups, and the like may be essential for better prediction of individual lines of action with the use of verbal scales. This would represent a more distinctly sociological approach.

Second, a systematic development of standardized *overt action opportunities* may be necessary before an individual can be accurately classified on a positive-negative continuum concerning a particular attitude object. That is, standardized opportunities for subjects to make overt acceptance-avoidance acts may provide quantitative assessment of the *salience* of attitudes by classifying overt non-verbal action toward an attitude object. The photograph authorization reported here is a crude attempt to classify such action. Further studies of salience could be based on overt action opportunities in small group settings. For example, individuals could be observed and their behavior categorized when given actual opportunities, say, for physical contact with a Negro, to be seen in public with a Negro in primary group settings, or to use physical facilities used by Negroes. Such behavioral settings could provide standardized ways of measuring the action attitudes of subjects placed in such contexts. They could also provide methods for validating measuring instruments such as the one described in this paper.

Methods which require elaborate or cumbersome physical facilities would have limited utility in the practical measurement of attitude salience. Measuring instruments such as the photograph authorization have the advantage of portability. If it can be shown that these measures correlate highly with overt action in standardized small group behavioral situations, their validity can be established more firmly.

11 David Riesman, *The Lonely Crowd,* New Haven: Yale University Press, 1950, *passim.*

12 Theodore M. Newcomb, "Attitude Development as a Function of Reference Groups: The Bennington Study," reprinted in E. E. Maccoby, T. M. Newcomb, and E. L. Hartley, editors, *Readings in Social Psychology,* New York: Henry Holt, 1958, pp. 265–275.

Further advances in the prediction of overt behavior from attitude measuring instruments may require both systematic measures of the social anchorages of individual psychological orientations and careful studies of their translation into overt social action. These would probably help to clarify the often perplexing relationship between the verbal and overt action dimensions of attitudinal phenomena.

ELSE FRENKEL-BRUNSWIK *and* R. NEVITT SANFORD

48. *Some Personality Factors in Anti-Semitism*

THE present paper is concerned primarily with the personality of some of those to whom anti-Semitic ideology appeals, rather than with the social and economic factors which may be responsible for anti-Semitism as a social movement or social institution. Who are the people that adopt and become active carriers of anti-Semitic ideas? Why do they so readily become—to use a term suggested by Ernst Kris—"scapegoat addicts"? What function, if any, has anti-Semitism in their personality structure? To approach these questions, detailed clinical study seemed necessary.

The major emphasis of the present paper is upon a number of individuals who were found to be extreme—"high" or "low"—in their readiness to accept anti-Semitic statements. Statistical data on the larger groups from which our individuals were selected will be presented as supporting evidence.[1]

The term personality as used here refers both to the behavior patterns and conscious convictions characteristic of a certain person and to the deeper, often unconscious, drives that motivate his behavior. Thus, in studying the personal factors in anti-Semitism it was necessary to use methods which reach different levels of personality: the social behavior and social philosophy, the conscious goals, hopes and fears, as well as the deeper and less rational layers.

The first step preparatory to the clinical

[1] The present writers in collaboration with T. W. Adorno and D. J. Levinson are preparing more extensive publications dealing in detail with a number of the various aspects of the personality correlates of anti-Semitism.

studies was to administer what amounted to a test or scale on anti-Semitism (7) to a group of approximately 100 university students, 76 of them women, members of an elementary course in psychology. The subjects were not asked to sign their names to the test blank. The test was introduced as a measure of public opinion without further specification. This test, a part of a broader questionnaire, was designed to measure the strength of an individual's tendency explicitly to accept or reject anti-Semitic statements and attitudes. The items include statements of common stereotypes about Jews, e.g., that Jews are personally offensive, unpleasant, and disturbing; that they are seclusive, clannish, and foreign; that they are over-assimilative, dangerous, threatening, or corrupting. There are also items suggesting that the Jews be avoided, excluded, and suppressed. Several degrees of agreement or disagreement with the statements are permitted the subject.

A high score on the scale indicates that in terms of the scale items the person in question is highly anti-Semitic on the explicit ideological level. That these high-scoring persons were likely to be actual or potential anti-Semites on the behavioral level, or anti-Semites in the deeper layer of their emotional life seemed confirmed by the interviews and other clinical data considered in the present paper. The terms "high" and "low" anti-Semite as used in this paper are defined exclusively by the responses to this explicit and direct anti-Semitism scale.

Accompanying the anti-Semitism scale was a second set of questions pertaining to public

From the *Journal of Psychology*, 1945, vol. 20, pp. 271–92. Reprinted with permission.

opinion, political adherence, group memberships, etc. This socio-political part of the questionnaire was designed to throw light upon the question of whether anti-Semitism is an isolated attitude or a part of a more inclusive approach to social questions.

Thirdly, the questionnaire included some "projective" items. These questions, especially designed for group studies, provided an indirect approach to the subjects' goals, fears, and identifications. Examples are: "What great people, living or dead, do you admire most?"; "If you knew you had only six months to live, but could do just as you pleased during that period, how would you spend the time?"; "What might cause a person to commit suicide?"; "If you were a parent, what things would you try to instill in your child?" etc.

The subsequent steps in the research program of which this report is a part represent in essence a mutual give-and-take between the questionnaire approach on the one hand and the clinical approach on the other. Selected individuals, chiefly from those obtaining extreme scores on the anti-Semitism scale, were subjected to interviews, the Thematic Apperception Test (see below), and the Rorschach Test. The insights or hunches gained from this more intensive acquaintance with a few extreme subjects were used in revising the three parts of the questionnaire discussed above, in establishing categories for the evaluation of the "projective" part of the questionnaire, and in devising a new section of the questionnaire.

This new part of the questionnaire was a scale composed of items pertaining to such matters as conventionality, aggression and destructiveness, attitude toward the family, superstition, strength of the ego, etc. (A series of examples will be quoted throughout the present paper.) That factors of these kinds were connected with anti-Semitism had already been indicated by an analysis of subjects' responses in interviews, in the Thematic Apperception Test, and in the projective parts of earlier questionnaires. And these "indirect" items have in their turn, when administered to groups of subjects, furnished verification of some of the most basic tentative hypotheses developed in the course of the clinical studies.

Aside from the first group of 76 women, the validating procedures were based in part on the responses of a second group of 140 women students in the Department of Public Speaking at the University of California, to whom the revised and augmented questionnaire had been given. All results reported here are to be considered contingent upon the special character of the student population represented by our sample and are further subject to the particulars involved in the case of our selected extremes.

The scattered *statistical data* referring to the verification of clinical hunches, to be found throughout this paper, are taken from an analysis of the upper and lower extreme 25 per cent—in terms of the direct anti-Semitism scale referred to above—of the various groups that had answered the older or newer forms of the questionnaire. Some of the figures represent *critical ratios of the mean scores of the uppermost and lowermost quartiles* (with the number, n, characterizing the size of the first and the second group mentioned above, 76 and 140 respectively, added in parentheses); another type indicates the *rank of the items in the rank-order of discriminatory power of all items in the list* as based on the differences of the mean scores of the quartiles referred to. A few *correlation coefficients* are also referred to. The shifting from one group to another is due to the fact that partly different items were given to the two groups.

The main source of the present report, however, remains the clinical study of a relatively small group of "high extremes," "low extremes," as well as "intermediates"— in terms of the scale for overtly verbalized anti-Semitism—selected from the various groups taking the questionnaire in its various stages. The present paper is centered around the analysis of the records of 20 female college students, 8 of them high, 8 low, and 4 intermediate on the anti-Semitism scale,[2] with the

2 The subjects of the clinical studies were from the extreme ends and from a narrow region around the mean of the distribution for the anti-Semitism scale. No other consideration entered into their selection.

primary emphasis on the "highs." There is only brief reference to the records of men. The reason for this is the vast predominance of women in the various samples to which the questionnaire had altogether been given. Several techniques were employed in studying the selected subjects. First, these subjects were asked to tell stories about a series of pictures which were presented to them in accordance with a procedure introduced by Murray (8) and known as the Thematic Apperception Test. This test is widely recognized as successful in uncovering such factors as attitudes —conscious or unconscious—toward parental figures and other people and toward one's own sex rôle, the general approach with which one meets the difficulties of life, the content of one's day dreams, and other unconscious fantasy material. We chose six pictures from the Murray set (Nos. 3, 8, and 10, and Nos. F1, F5, and F7). In addition, we presented to our subjects four pictures designed to elicit direct reactions to racial problems. One of them represents "Jewish-looking people" in a poor district, another an older Negro woman with a young Negro boy, the third, a young couple in zoot-suits, and the fourth, a lower class man, apparently in great fear, confronted by a policeman holding a billy-club.

After the stories had been obtained, the subjects were interviewed. These interviews were aimed at the following material: (*a*) Ideology, including such aspects as social and political attitudes, religious affiliations, attitude toward one's profession, social status, money, etc. (*b*) General attitude toward Jews and other minority groups. What spontaneous ideas and formulations on this issue could be elicited? Personal experiences with members of minority groups. We wanted to see how far the general attitude was associated with specific contact. (*c*) Personal data, including as much as possible of the early history, images of father and of mother, goals and aspirations, the pattern of aggression, dislikes, etc.

In line with contemporary psychological insights into personality mechanisms, the interview material was not taken at its face value; but rather, an attempt was made to interpret

it with attention to the different deeper meanings which might be implicit in the same overt response. In our efforts to reconstruct the personality structure, the material from the Thematic Apperception Test was of great help.

To the individuals selected from the later groups of questionnaire subjects, the Rorschach test also was given.

Aside from the clinical records comprising interview, Thematic Apperception Test and Rorschach, some of the responses to the "projective" and "indirect" items from the questionnaire as described above are also quoted in this paper. In this case, however, the material is not only from the small clinical sample but from persons in the entire upper or lower extreme quartiles.

We may begin the discussion of our results with a brief reference to the social outlook of the subjects in our samples as established by the social-political part of the questionnaire as well as by the interviews. Within the limits of our material, subjects with high scores on anti-Semitism were found to be characterized by two major trends. First, they exhibited a kind of conservative attitude; although they showed few signs of having developed an organized social-political outlook, they tended automatically to support the status quo.[3] In some instances this conservatism seems to be not a true conservatism but rather a pattern that is interwoven with tendencies toward change and even violence. Secondly, the approach of these subjects to social issues was found to be characterized generally by "ethnocentrism," that is, a tendency to hold in high esteem one's own ethnic or social group, to keep it narrow, unmixed and pure, and to reject everything that is different. When our more recent data are considered, the correlation coefficient between anti-Semitism and rejection of other minority groups is .75 ($n = 140$). The rejections are

3 Levinson and Sanford (7) found that: "Republicans have higher scores on anti-Semitism than Democrats (Critical Ratio, 2.81). Protestant sectarians and Catholics have higher scores than do the non-religious, the non-sectarian 'Protestants' and our single Unitarian (Critical Ratio, 4.90), and sorority members have higher scores than do non-members (Critical Ratio, 4.57)."

made in the name of what is supposed to be "right" or "good."

The relationship between conservatism and ethnocentrism is, however, by no means perfect ($r = .5$, $n = 140$). But there is apparently one kind of personality structure in which certain aspects of conservatism and certain aspects of ethnocentrism satisfy the same basic personality needs. This will become clear as we turn to our main task, the discussion of one type of personality for whom the social attitudes just discussed have an especial appeal.

The typical anti-Semitic girl differs in her appearance very markedly from those who are against anti-Semitism. Most girls in our limited sample of high extremes were very well groomed, their appearance being in the best middle class social tradition. This is in line with one of the findings of Levinson and Sanford (7) that the higher the income of the father, the greater the proportion of anti-Semites.[4]

The surface of most of these anti-Semitic girls appeared to be composed and untroubled. They seemed to be satisfied with themselves and with their situation generally. Their behavior was conventionally decorous. There are, however, indications that there is at the same time much doubt and feeling of insecurity beneath the surface. The girls were interested mainly in social standing and in an appropriate marriage, and their families tended to be "socially mobile." It was difficult in the interviews to get much material from them. They were sensitive to this encroachment from the outside, resistant to any "prying into their affairs." Aside from a mere resistance to talk about themselves, most of them seemed ill-equipped to do so. They seemed to have little familiarity with their inner lives, but rather a generally externalized orientation.

Our selected anti-Semitic girls declared without exception that they liked their parents. Though there was little concern about political issues, they seemed to take what convictions they did have directly from their parents. This trend is supported by the finding of Levinson and Sanford (7) that anti-Semitic subjects reported less ideological friction with their parents than did those who were not anti-Semitic (Critical Ratio, 4.2). Furthermore, that anti-Semitic girls in general tend to show, at least on the surface, an uncritical devotion to their parents is revealed by the statistically significant inclination of these subjects to subscribe to the statement "No sane, normal, decent person could ever think of hurting a close friend or relative." Likewise, they tend to agree that "He is indeed contemptible who does not feel an undying love, gratitude, and respect for his parents"; the critical ratio between upper and lower quartile is 3.7 (for the second group of 140); both items are from the new indirect questionnaire. Devotion and obedience is not only manifested toward parents, but toward authority in general. Thus our anti-Semitic subjects subscribe readily to the statement "Obedience and respect for authority are the most important virtues children should learn" (Critical Ratio 4.4, $n = 140$).

While aggression is not verbalized toward the ingroups, it comes into the open as far as minority groups are concerned. Mostly without having had much personal experience with Jewish people, our selected anti-Semitic girls tended to regard the Jews as aggressive, dishonest, and dirty.

On all of these points the high extremes stood in contrast to the low extremes. The latter eight girls were predominantly nondescript in appearance, less at ease socially, possessed of varied interests, quite willing to talk about themselves and their situations, and able to make critical appraisals of their parents.

When the fantasy material and the projective responses of our anti-Semitic girls are considered, we find the following main trends that are rather in contrast to what these subjects present on the surface. In view of the fact that anti-Semites seem to be particularly unaware of their underlying motives, the results of these indirect approaches seem of particular importance.

---

4 It should be added that the subjects were students in a State university, and therefore those with the highest income were still for the most part members of the middle class.

1. In the thematic apperceptions of these subjects, *aggressive* themes stand out. Not only is the preoccupation with *destruction* markedly more pronounced than in the productions of the low extremes, but it appears to be relatively extreme by a more absolute standard.[5] And more than this, as will be noted in the examples that follow, it is usually men that are the victims of the aggression and are otherwise shown in an unfavorable light.

In story No. 1, of Case 6 a murder is being committed; in story No. 3, the husband has lost both legs, and the father is mentioned only to tell us that he has been killed; in story No. 4, a man is being foiled and captured; in No. 5, a man has been killed; in story No. 6, the hero is being convicted and severely punished. Very similar are the stories of Case 4: in story No. 3, the father and son are both killed; in story No. 4, the man is a traitor; in story No. 5, he is sent to a concentration camp; in story No. 6, the hero is electrocuted; and in story No. 10, the hero is burned to death and the father killed in battle. Likewise, for Case 7, in story No. 5, the "boy friend" is killed in an accident; in story No. 9, a man is electrocuted; and in story No. 10, the boy "has some kind of physical handicap."

By way of contrast, in the stories of Case 1 and Case 13, both extremely low on anti-Semitism, nobody gets murdered or killed. On the whole, little aggression is manifested. In story No. 5, of Case 1, for instance, the heroine only hurts the feelings of her boy friend and then she has acute remorse. In story No. 3, "The man has a very nice, sensitive face, with a tender expression."

5 To say that a value of a variable is "marked" or "extreme" implies of course a conception of a norm. Unfortunately, empirically established norms for fantasy material are not yet available in print and in this clinical study we are unable to make precise quantitative comparisons. However, both of the authors have had the opportunity to study several thousand stories produced by various types of people, and they have had at hand objectively derived norms for individual pictures, for both sexes and for various age groups. (These latter have been worked out at the Institute of Child Welfare at the University of California.) The authors can only say that in their opinion the frequency and intensity of aggressive themes in the stories of our anti-Semitic girls is markedly above what from their experience they have come to regard as the average.

Furthermore, in response to the questionnaire items referring to "the worst punishments and the worst crimes," the 19 girls in the upper quartile of the first group were willing to set down significantly more cruel and varied crimes and punishments than were those extremely low on anti-Semitism. Similarly, items testing the tendency toward cynicism or a vilification of human nature, such as "Familiarity breeds contempt," or references to the dominating rôle of destructiveness or of personal profit, are subscribed to significantly more often by anti-Semitic subjects than by non-anti-Semites.

2. It is interesting to note that the men in the stories of the anti-Semitic girls are killed in battles and similar situations without any active participation on the part of the heroine. There is thus an emphasis on *externalized and physical causation* in the events described by these girls. They conceive of *fate* not only as threatening, but as providing care, protection, and support in critical situations. A predominantly external focus, as against an internal one, is seen throughout the reactions of the anti-Semites, e.g., their social anxiety, superstition, etc. Here again they stand in contrast to the low extremes.

Thus for the new group of 140 women, there is a Critical Ratio of 4.4 between the upper and lower quartile (in terms of the explicit anti-Semitism scale) on the item "Although many people may scoff, it may yet be shown that astrology can explain a lot of things." Similarly, there is a significantly greater readiness to react in the affirmative to such an item as "It is more than a remarkable coincidence that Japan had an earthquake on Pearl Harbor Day, December 7, 1944," or to statements about the essential limitations of the natural sciences "in understanding many important things." The predominantly external focus is again seen in the reactions to the questions of against what would one protect one's child. The subjects high on anti-Semitism mention significantly more often external dangers like bad people, accidents, etc., whereas those low on anti-Semitism mention ego defects.

3. An external fate or destiny is only one

of the major forces in the world of the anti-Semites. They display at the same time a great amount of *"social anxiety";* there is a *conventional type of conscience,* one that is strict but not fully internalized, not integrated with the rest of the personality. In the picture-stories of these subjects, a sharp differentiation is made between those people who are nice and have money, possessions, and power and who possess the right attitudes and standards, on the one hand, and those who are bad, sinister, morally depraved, and live in slums, on the other. Much use is made of moralistic concepts, e.g., a boy is described as "sinful," reference is made to "a bad part of town," the zoot-suiters are bad because they allow their emotions to dominate. Breaches of this strict, moralistic code have to be severely punished, e.g., in one story a striker gets 50 years in the penitentiary. Anti-Semitic subjects seem to derive their security from subscribing to a conventional moral code. This code contains not only moralistic elements but also seems to include as its counterpart an emphasis on direct striving for social and economic success and prestige. (Ratio of moralistic terms is 67 for highs vs. 13 for lows, $n = 30$.)

In response to the question, "What is the most embarrassing experience?" the girls in the upper quartile mentioned significantly more often than those in the lower quartile violations of manners and conventions in public, and situations in which they were caught and consequently suffered some blow to their prestige or narcissism. Those low on the anti-Semitism scale, however, report self-blame, feelings of inadequacy, failure in achievement and friendship, as the most embarrassing experiences. The Critical Ratio for this difference is 3.4 (referring to the first group of 76 girls). All through the questionnaire, strict conformity to a superficial morality is manifested by the girls high on anti-Semitism. Anything which deviates from this pattern they tend to consider not only as different from themselves but as inferior, low, and immoral.

4. Connected with the conventional moral code is an emphasis on *religion and nationalism as a source of support that could substitute for genuine effort and achievement.*

Examples are: "One could say that this boy has been sinful. . . . He is in bed and sees Christ in his dreams. Maybe it's a vision he has. From then on he is a model boy. . . ." A second girl says, "Oh, I've got it. This woman, a girl of 16 or 19, has had everything she wanted all of her life. She was born with a silver spoon in her mouth. Her family faces financial difficulties. The father dies and the mother becomes a consumptive. The mother dies when the girl is about eight. None of her relatives is interested. One day, being alone, she visits a church and appeals to God for companionship to pull her through these things. This picture shows her appeal to God." A third girl high on anti-Semitism says, "The little boy knows he must die, for there is no way out. He is praying and is getting strength for the ordeal ahead. He will be burned to death."

Those low on the anti-Semitism scale are by no means generally irreligious but religion takes another form. It seems to be experienced on a deeper level and imbued with the character of ethics and philosophy, rather than with the utilitarian touch characteristic of the highs.

In answering the question, "What is the most awe-inspiring experience?" subjects in the upper quartile mention religious and patriotic experiences more often than do those in the lower quartile. The latter mention primarily achievement, beauty, and sensuality. The Critical Ratio (for a total n of 76) is 3.0. Asked to list the great people they admire the most, the upper quartile name patriots, and people with power and control; whereas the lower quartile list humanitarians, artists, and scientists. The Critical Ratio is again 3. It seems generally true, on the basis of the interview material, that those scoring high on the anti-Semitism scale are primarily attracted by the strong man rather than by the political program as such.

5. The high extremes show a certain *aversion against emotionality* or at least against the expression of certain basic needs. These needs are then often projected onto others, especially certain outgroups. In the stories of the high extremes, aggression and sex often appear in infantile forms, isolated from the life of the heroine with whom the girls identify. As was pointed out above, aggression in these cases is not manifested by the

heroine, but is projected into the environment, or destiny, or "lower" people such as proletarians, Jews, Mexicans, etc. These "inferior" people are seen not only as aggressive, but generally as uninhibited. Uninhibited sex life is regarded as a pleasure for a low type of person.

Examples are: "It is a young girl and her boy friend. They are lower class people, and don't know any better than to do this sort of thing. I have an aversion for the things such people do. They are thinking of getting married and are looking forward to a bright future; though I don't believe such people can ever make much of themselves. I don't believe in holding hands in public." Or, to quote another high extreme, "They will get married and will be very happy. They will have lots of little zoot-suiters." A third girl extremely high on the scale tells, "I think they (young couple of zoot-suiters) will marry young but will divorce before long. They allow their emotions to get too much in their way, which is bad in earlier marriage." A fourth says, "This girl and her boy friend are zoot-suiters and I don't approve of them. She goes out to dances, etc. She is finally caught and brought into court." A fifth girl high on the scale says, "I could think of a low grade dance hall or something . . . the girl is the typical type of jitterbug—the kind who hangs around at the U.S.O. The couple has a nice time at the dance; that is in that kind of way." A sixth example is "They are not married and probably won't be. . . . Well, they are more out for the fun of it. That is especially true of him. He doesn't want to be tied down." And to quote a seventh girl, "They are not really married, it's more of a common law affair. Why go through the ceremony, they said. You see, they don't change their ways very much."

These sentences express contempt and at the same time envy for the "lower class sexuality." An important tendency of the girls high on anti-Semitism is thus to keep one's basic impulses repressed, to keep oneself pure and reputable. Primitive needs are rendered ego-alien and projected onto an alien group. The constant repression leads to a distortion of reality, which is chiefly manifested in the projective evaluation of minority groups.[6]

Manifestations of the mechanism of repression can be observed again and again. For instance, in responding to the question "What would you do if you had only six months to live?", the girls high on anti-Semitism never mention sensual pleasures, while the low ones frequently do. "What would drive a person nuts?": The anti-Semites say irritations from without and ideas which keep running in their heads. The fear is expressed that ideas might escape control and become dangerously independent.

Sexual strivings which are kept repressed have acquired a dangerous and sadistic connotation. The fantasies of the high extremes, in contrast to their conventional surface, seem often to be more primitive and cruel. To the picture representing a colored man with a policeman, one of the girls extremely high on anti-Semitism tells the following story: "This man has just been captured for a crime of strong brutality. He has a strong temper and attacked some girl. He beat her, raped her, killed her, and cut her up and threw her in the bushes. . . . He will be convicted and sentenced to a life of hard labor." In this light it is not surprising that the most discriminating item between high and low extreme quartiles on the indirect questionnaire is the following: "Sex crimes, such as rape and attacks on children, deserve more than mere imprisonment; such criminals ought to be publicly whipped," with the high anti-Semites showing a strong tendency to agree.

The fact that a surface of *exaggerated moral strictness* is found in girls who in their fantasies show rather extreme aggression and *narcissism* suggests that the mechanism of reaction formation [7] has had an important rôle in their personality development. For example, heroines of stories in which men have been crippled sometimes dedicate their lives to nursing these unfortunates. The fact

ships brought out in our material have been pointed out independently and in a different context in this fundamental paper by Fenichel.

7 By this psychoanalytic term is meant the reversal into the opposite of an unaccepted instinctual tendency (2). For instance, hostility becomes disguised as overkindness, love for dirt as cleanliness. Exaggeration of the acquired attitude, and breaking

6 The fact that repression is one of the important conditions for the anti-Semitic attitude is also emphasized by O. Fenichel (1). Several other relation-

that kindness, self-sacrifice, and charity are extolled in a context of thinly disguised hostility leads one strongly to suspect that the former is a reaction to the latter, especially so since we have evidence that in their daily lives these girls are definitely not warmhearted. Throughout their projective material the anti-Semitic girls were so insistent about cleanliness, good manners, and honesty as to lead one to raise the question whether these expressed values also were not based upon the inhibition of tendencies of an opposite character as well as upon imitation of social norms, concomitant with their general conventionalism.

All the defense mechanisms described have the very important function of reducing anxiety and conscious guilt. We find very little reference to conscious guilt in the anti-Semites whereas there is a great amount of conscious self-reproach in the low ones.

6. In the thematic apperceptions of the anti-Semitic girls, there is a great deal of material which lends itself to the interpretation that *ambivalent attitudes toward parental figures* are being expressed.[8]

A picture showing an older woman and a younger one was especially suited for eliciting the subject's attitude toward the mother. One girl extremely high on anti-Semitism says: "I think it is an old woman, probably a mother. She is the voice of suspicion. The younger one is trying to look away while she is being talked to by her mother. The younger one is jealous and the old one is adding to her suspicions. She is wondering if everything is like her mother implies. There is a third woman taking away the young woman's husband. The mother is giving advice on how to get rid of the third one. Both are mean and indignant." Another high extreme says: "The mother has just told the daughter a falsehood and is trying to put something over on her. . . . Something to do with a man the mother wants the daughter to marry. He is wealthy and the mother is in on a scheme with him. The daughter is too level-headed though and goes against the

mother's wishes." A third says: "She wants to kill her husband because he doesn't give her enough money. He was ill a lot and she has to take care of him. She would like to murder him" (here we see again the aggression against men), "so that she can marry a wealthy man she has on the string, and live on easy street. She has not a strong enough character to do this, however. The evil looking woman behind her is tempting her. Both are evil and strongwilled. She goes ahead and does the dirty deed. I think the other old woman is her grandmother. She puts her up to this sort of thing. She is convicted and given the death sentence." A fourth high extreme says: "This elderly woman has brought up her daughter to be extremely attractive and polished. . . . This is the way the mother gets a lot of prestige—through the daughter. The mother starts a racket: the mother has the daughter mingle with the rich and sort of act as bait. . . . The mother is a very clever woman and always manages to have all of her schemes work." And a fifth high extreme says in response to this same picture: "This is a lady living in an old house by herself. She heard it was haunted but didn't believe it. This is hard! She doesn't see anything unnatural about the house. The old lady behind her is a spook and will kill her. She turns around and runs from the house. She goes to the police and tells them the house is haunted."

Although the woman in the picture might suggest such unfavorable characterizations, a recent count in 30 subjects strongly indicates that girls low on anti-Semitism see her in a much more favorable light than do the "highs."

That girls who at the conscious level express only admiration and devotion toward their fathers and mothers should in their fantasies put such emphasis on hatred, meanness, jealousy, and suspicion when parental figures are being treated, strongly suggests that the attitudes of these subjects toward their parents are in reality mixtures of love and hate. Death of family members, especially parents, occurs more often in the stories of the "highs" as compared with "lows." The story fragments just given also exemplify what seemed to us another common trend in the fantasies of our anti-Semitic girls, that is, a relative lack of warm human relationships and a tendency to use stereotyped—good or evil—characters. This is another indication

through of the original attitude are some of the cues which make it possible to diagnose whether an attitude is genuine or the result of a reaction-formation.

8 Aside from Fenichel, Ernst Kris has repeatedly stressed that one of the functions of anti-Semitism is to overcome ambivalence by introducing a sharp division between the good and the bad.

that in these subjects the ability to love has been crippled by ambivalence.

In contrast to this pattern is the typical response to the picture of the older and the younger woman by the girls extremely low on anti-Semitism: "This is a young woman with her grandmother. Or it may be symbolic of old age that awaits the young woman. The old woman foreshadows the future for her. The young woman's features are classic— Italian or Greek. The young woman is intelligent and well poised. The young woman will take the old lady's place and the new generation will follow."

7. There is, furthermore, evidence that can be interpreted as in accord with the *possibility of paranoid trends* in our subjects extremely high on anti-Semitism. They agree significantly more often than those low on the scale with the following statements: "To a greater extent than most people realize, our lives are governed by plots hatched in secret by politicians," and "Nowadays when so many different kinds of people move around so much and mix together so freely, a person has to be especially careful to protect himself against infection and disease." It is interesting also to note that when asked to rank a number of activities in the order of their objectionableness, the anti-Semitic subjects often mention "prying" in the first place.

In the stories we hear about the "voice of suspicion" and about haunted houses. There is frequent reference to exceptional mental states like insanity, trance, being under a spell, communicating with the dead, etc.

In connection with the paranoid trends, there is furthermore evidence of confusion about sex rôles.[9] For example, in one story an old woman, after taking off her disguise, turns out to be a nice young man. In other stories men are crippled and have to be taken care of and therefore do not appear in a masculine rôle.

8. The pattern of human relationships as seen by our anti-Semitic subjects is fundamentally a matter of *dominance or submission and the struggle of the two*. This can be seen throughout the stories but especially in the story about the picture of a hypnotist. Anti-Semites generally emphasize the complete subjugation of the hypnotized person shown in the picture, the hypnotist's misuse of his "superhuman" powers in inducing evil or "queer" deeds, getting vital information, etc. By contrast the subjects low on anti-Semitism speak of a "demonstration in class." "This is just an experiment that turned out satisfactorily."

9. The anti-Semitic personality is characterized by *certain typical discrepancies between the overt and the covert layers of the personality*. As was shown above, on the manifest level our anti-Semitic girls express devotion to their parents; in their stories, on the other hand, the parental figures appear in a very unfavorable light. On the surface we find emphasis on high morals, kindness and charity, and these values motivate, perhaps, some of the behavior; but there is much destructiveness in the indirect material. Likewise, there is optimism, on the one hand, and fear of catastrophes, on the other. There is conservatism as well as anarchism. There is the idea that everybody gets what he deserves, as well as doubt and cynicism. Belief in the supernatural is combined with materialistic striving for social status.

Only brief reference shall be made here to a preliminary analysis of a further type of indirect material, the Rorschach-records, of some of our subjects.[10] The following personality trends appear to characterize the high anti-Semitic groups of both sexes as contrasted with the low groups: [11] those high on anti-Semitism tend to be intellectually underproductive, somewhat lower in intelligence, and

10 This analysis was undertaken by Dr. Suzanne Reichard. The present description of the anti-Semitic personality as revealed by the Rorschach Test is quite tentative and based only on inspection, since an insufficient number of subjects were available at the time of writing to make a statistical analysis of the data worthwhile. The records grouped themselves as follows: 11 high anti-Semitic women; 8 low women; 8 high men; 6 low men. Because of the smaller number of men, the results are less clearcut and less reliable for men than for women.

11 For the sake of those interested in the technicalities of the Rorschach Test, the following explanation of the above conclusions is presented: intellectual underproductivity is represented by a

9 The relationship between homosexuality and paranoia, first seen by Freud, has been recently confirmed by statistical observation (3).

lacking in creative imagination. They are less interested in human beings as individuals and show a higher tendency to have hypochondriacal complaints or conversion symptoms. The analysis of the content of their responses suggests that the adoption of an aggressive attitude towards outgroups may stem from frustrations received (mainly at the hands of the mother-figure) in childhood. These frustrations seem to have produced unconscious inferiority feelings centering mainly about the castration complex (symbolized by the number of body parts seen as missing or cut off).

In addition to the above, the following trends were found to occur mainly in the high women: a strong tendency to make crude generalizations, stereotyped and conventional thinking associated with a marked lack of originality. At the same time there was less evidence of pronounced maladjustment than in the low group. The high women seem to be somewhat more troubled by fantasies of a castrating mother-figure (witches), while the low women are more bothered by thoughts of sin and temptation (devils).

The high men, when compared with the low men, on both of whom material is now accumulating, show the following trends: more compulsive traits (preoccupation with symmetry and mid-lines in the Rorschach cards), a critical and disparaging attitude toward the test, more emotional inhibition associated with a basically greater emotional responsiveness.

In reviewing the evidence presented, the most outstanding feature of the anti-Semitic college women, as derived from our small sample, seems to be a restricted, narrow

---

small number of responses; lower intelligence by a smaller percentage of $F+$ and $W+$; lack of creative imagination by lack of M; lack of interest in human beings by lower percentage of human (H) responses; hypochondriacal complaints and conversion symptoms by a higher percentage of anatomical responses; tendency to crude generalization by a high $W\%$ associated with a low $W + \%$; stereotyped thinking by a high $A\%$; conventional thinking by a high number of popular responses; lack of originality by a low number of original responses; maladjustment by a high $F - \%$; emotional inhibition by denial of the influence of color; basically greater emotional responsiveness by a higher percentage of responses to the colored cards.

personality with a strict conventional superego, to which there is complete surrender. It is the conventional superego which takes over the function of the underdeveloped ego, producing a lack of individuation and a tendency to stereotyped thinking.[12] In order to achieve harmony with the parents, with parental images, and with society as a whole, basic impulses, which are conceived as low, destructive and dangerous, have to be kept repressed and can find only devious expressions, as for instance, in projections and "moral indignation." Thus, anti-Semitism, and generally anti-out-groupism, may have an important function in keeping the personality integrated. Without these channels or outlets (if they should not be provided by society) it may be much more difficult, in some cases impossible, to keep the mental balance. Hence, the rigid and compulsive adherence to prejudices.

The type of anti-Semitism we have described might be thought of as "puritanical anti-Semitism." The anti-Semitism found in the leadership of the Nazi party would seem to be definitely not puritanical, or perhaps even anti-puritanical. Certainly there is a striking contrast between the superficial "niceness" of our high extremes and the manifest delinquency and destructiveness of the Nazi party member, or for that matter, of the openly Fascist women on the lunatic fringe in this country. There is indeed some reason to believe that whereas our puritanical anti-Semites project their id impulses onto the Jew, the true Nazi sees in the Jew a representative of a restricting—"plutocratic"—superego or a reasonable—"relativistic"—ego. It should be noted, too, that whereas our anti-Semitic women usually have middle or upper middle class status (since in this country class lines are not so definitely drawn and an individual's status is to such a large degree a frame of mind, it is difficult to be precise in this matter), Nazism in Germany is usu-

---

12 In accordance with what has been reported in the literature dealing with liberalism vs. conservatism, our material suggests a higher grade point average and intelligence for the liberals. It seems thereby, however, difficult to say whether the primary cause has to be sought in intellectual capacity or whether intelligence is itself a consequence of personality structure or of some further common underlying cause.

ally regarded as most typically a lower middle class phenomenon. But this is not to say that German lower middle class anti-Semitism is characteristically anti-puritanical; the anti-puritanical variety may be most largely a matter of individual psychopathology. In any case the type we describe in this paper can well be characterized as the "well-bred" type of anti-Semite (6).

Although the puritanical and the Nazi type of anti-Semitism seems thus to differ with respect to conventionality and inhibition, they seem, however, to have much in common. Primarily they share the authoritarian character, the aggressive undertone, the emphasis on fate, and the externalized superego.

From time to time up to this point we have mentioned some of the ways in which our low extremes stand in contrast to the high extremes. The lows exhibit more psychological perceptiveness, more interest in self-analysis, more direction by "inner" rather than by "outer" or conventional standards, more successful sublimation of id tendencies in realistic achievement drives, in scientific, political and social interests; there is less aggression on the fantasy level, less projection and reaction formation, less ambivalence and less confusion about sex rôles. But this is not to say that our low extremes are closer to the "normal" or that the lower a person stands on our anti-Semitism scale the better off he is from the point of view of mental health. It is a notable fact that the life histories of our low subjects have been less happy or fortunate by ordinary standards than those of our high extremes. In the case of some of these low subjects, it seemed that difficult external circumstances contributed to making them more thoughtful, more introspective and more identified with suffering and with outgroups. It should be emphasized too that whereas our high extremes in their stories made the most frequent use of religious ideas and images, there was ample evidence that the lows of which we speak had religious sentiments and had been profoundly influenced by the Christian ethic. It seemed to us that "the devil" loomed large in the universes of both our high extremes and our low extremes, but whereas in the former he was seen as outside or in outgroups ("I am good and they are bad"), in the latter he was conceived to be inside ("They are no worse than the rest of us"). One might say that subjects of the former group can achieve a sense of well-being at the expense of other people, while subjects of the latter group can make notable contributions to humanity—but this is likely to be at the expense of their own well-being.

The subject who from among the highs showed the most pronounced pathology had many compulsive features in her make-up. She had achieved a superficial security through discipline and order and such devices as touching telephone poles and book pages. She had a fear of being in crowds which seemed to indicate, among other things, instinctual anxiety in a situation where defenses are reduced. The most markedly pathological case from among our lows showed in an extreme degree a pattern that was different from that which we have regarded as most typical of our low extremes. This girl was clearly impulse-ridden. Her ego was lined up with her id, so that sexual perversions, promiscuity and drinking orgies were made to seem permissible to her. This state of affairs had been achieved by means of a general repression of affect. In stating why she liked Jews she gave much the same reasons that the high extremes had given for hating them. This case reminds us that a liberal attitude toward one's own instincts is likely to go with a liberal attitude toward minority groups, but it also shows us that when liberty gives way to license we have something which resembles freedom only superficially. That this low extreme was not free of irrationality with respect to Jews is shown by the fact that her stereotype for the Jews was similar to that of the high extremes: things which repelled the anti-Semites attracted her.

So far only cases extremely high or extremely low on anti-Semitism have been discussed. We do not wish to consider in detail the protocols of the "middle" group. Suffice it to say that they share with the high anti-Semites the conventional moral standards and the sense for social stratification. On the other hand, these subjects show less aggression and more introspection than the high anti-Semitic girls. Their life histories likewise show their intermediate position, perhaps closer to the anti-Semitic picture. Lest it be supposed, however, that a middle position on the scale is an indication of normal adjustment, it may be pointed out that when—in another connotation—the anti-Semitism scale was administered to a group of patients in a psychiatric hospital, the great majority attained middle scores. It was our impression that here, as with many of the middle subjects in our college group, the psychopathic trends had not become connected with ideology.

Due to the war situation, we did not have many male subjects. But our impression from the few we had is that on the whole, the anti-Semitic man shows the same personality structure as the anti-Semitic woman. There is, however, one important difference. The anti-Semitic girls show a conventionally feminine façade and underneath are full of aggression. The anti-Semitic man, on the other hand, tends to conceive of himself as masculine, aggressive, and tough, but has underlying passive and dependent tendencies.

His drive for power makes him long to be "up there with the big boys," and he would satisfy his submissive tendencies at the same time by being on the right hand of some powerful male figure. He tends to project the power drive onto the Jews, whom he characteristically conceives of as a powerful and cohesive group who by always "sticking together" are able to "move in" and "take over" various fields of endeavor. Any appeal for tolerance in the name of humanity is completely lost on him, for the idea of identifying himself with the underdog is what arouses his greatest anxiety. Hitler and his friends did indeed not repress their hostilities but their dependent and feminine passivity.

There can be little doubt but that the personality pattern we have described is a common one in our society. Two basic questions now have to be raised. First, what is the sociological setting in which this pattern develops, and second, what are the conditions under which the generalized disposition found in our high subjects manifests itself in anti-Semitic behavior? Most certainly all of our high extremes belong to the middle socio-economic class; and it is probably not misleading to think of the "well bred" or puritanical anti-Semite as most typically a middle class phenomenon. But if we adhere strictly to objective economic and social criteria in defining status it has to be granted that most of our low extremes also belong to the middle class. What is it that makes the difference? An important clue, we believe, lies in the observation that our high extremes are over-conformist; they adhere rigidly to the middle class values and are made anxious by the appearance, in themselves or in others, of tendencies of an opposite character. This points to insecurity as the condition with which these subjects are struggling. But since the family income in all of our high cases is more than adequate, the insecurity cannot be regarded as economic in any narrow sense of the word. It seems rather to be social—and psychological; a condition that is likely to exist when one's aspirations are much higher than his actual status or when one, or one's family, has recently raised his status to a notable degree. The fear of losing status, in our anti-Semitic girls, seems to be connected not so much with any danger of economic want as with the possibility that with respectability gone they will be tempted to release their inhibited tendencies in the way they believe Jews and proletarians do. Anti-Semitism thus helps them to maintain their identification with the middle class and to ward off anxiety.

Thus it is not so much middle class values themselves that we would call into question, but rather the rigidity with which they are adhered to. And in the individual case this seems to be a result of the manner in which they have been put across. The mischief is done when those trends which are taboo according to the class standards become repressed, and hence, no longer susceptible to modification or control. This is most likely to happen when parents are too concerned and too insistent with respect to their positive aims for the child and too threatening and coercive with respect to the "bad" things. The child is thus taught to view behavior in terms of black and white, "good" and "evil"; and the "evil" is made to appear so terrible that he cannot think of it as something in himself which needs to be modified or controlled, but as something that exists in other "bad" people and needs to be stamped out completely.

A *tendency* to this kind of behavior, it seems to us, springs from the very nature of our society and exists throughout the middle class. It seems most likely to precipitate the manifestations we have described in times of social confusion and unrest. Such times arouse intense but vaguely conceived feelings of insecurity in both parents, with consequent strivings to improve or at least to maintain the social status, and these in turn give rise to unreasoning concern and overaction in the mother and to desperate aggressiveness in the father.

As indicated by the second of the two questions just raised, the kind of disposition to anti-Semitism that we have described does not necessarily manifest itself in overt anti-Semitic behavior. Whether or not it will depends to a large extent upon the individual's situation of the moment—what kind of propaganda he is exposed to, what his friends and exemplars are doing, what scape-goats are available, and so forth. Probably the major factor that brings anti-Semitism out into the open is real economic insecurity, and hence the most effective counter measures will, of course, be those which reduce unemployment and depression. Where these attempts fail, the use of legal force and of psychological devices like associating anti-Semitism with the disreputable are all to the good. But for the basic disposition to anti-Semitism, the only cure would seem to lie in emotional security, self-understanding, and psychological maturity. How to develop these conditions is a major task of applied psychology. There is space here to mention only those points which on the basis of the present study seem particularly important. If the kind of repression which we have seen to be of great importance is to be prevented, there must be less fear of impulses on the part of parents. The parental attitude toward children must be more tolerant and permissive. Parents must learn that the "bad" impulses can be modified and controlled and that it is of crucial importance to invite the child's participation in these processes. To indicate the magnitude of the need for this type of parental education, one has only to recall such findings as that of Pullias (9) that 72 per cent of a group of college freshmen reported they had been taught that masturbation would cause physical damage, or that of Huschka (5) that of 169 cases referred for child psychiatry, over half had had bowel training begun before the 8th month, or that it was more or less officially recommended as late as 10 years ago that such training be begun as early as the end of the first month. Reputable pediatricians were urging all manner of physical restraints to prevent infantile masturbation (4), and so on.

To increase psychological insight and sensitivity, to bring about freedom from repression, throughout the middle class is, of course, a task of tremendous proportions—hence, we should lose no time in increasing our efforts to that end. We cannot hope to psychoanalyze everybody, but education for self-understanding is something that can be tremendously expanded. We should mobilize all possible energy behind a program for increased education about man and society. If one is inclined to regard such a program as hopelessly long-term, let him remember that education is a very durable middle class value, and that the people's appetite for correct information is often greater than the capacity of science to supply it. It is well to remember that the kind of understanding of which we speak has steadily increased during the course of history. Less than 100 years ago, it was still the fashion in science to insist that man was fundamentallly different from other animals, and less than 50 years ago many anthropologists took for granted the white man's superiority to "primitives." The struggle against anti-Semitism is a part of the struggle for enlightenment.

REFERENCES

1. FENICHEL, O. Psychoanalysis of Anti-Semitism. *American Imago,* 1940, 1.
2. FREUD, A. The Ego and the Mechanisms of Defense. (Trans. by C. Baines.) London: Hogarth, 1937.
3. GARDNER, G. E. Evidences of homosexuality in 120 analyzed cases with paranoid content. *Psychoanal. Rev.,* 1931, 18, 57–62.
4. HUSCHKA, M. The child's response to coercive bowel training. *Psychosomat. Med.,* 1942, 4, 301–308.
5. ———. The incidence and character of masturbation threats in a group of problem children. *Psychoanal. Quar.,* 1938, 7, 338–356.
6. The Institute of Social Research (publ.): Research Project on Anti-Semitism. *Stud. Philos. & Soc. Sci.,* 1941, 9, No. 1.
7. LEVINSON, D. J., & SANFORD, R. N. A scale for the measurement of Anti-Semitism. *J. of Psychol.,* 1944, 17, 339–370.
8. MURRAY, H. A. Explorations in Personality. Cambridge: Oxford Univ. Press, 1938.
9. PULLIAS, E. V. Masturbation as a mental hygiene problem—A study of the beliefs of seventy-five young men. *J. Abn. & Soc. Psychol.,* 1937, 32, 216–222.

EUNICE COOPER *and* MARIE JAHODA

49. The Evasion of Propaganda: How Prejudiced People Respond to Anti-prejudice Propaganda

Propaganda Evasion as a Problem

COMMUNICATION research points up the fact that it is difficult in general for a communication to reach people who are not already in favor of the views it presents. It is well known that many people evade points of view which are at odds with their own by the simple expedient of not exposing themselves to such views. Those who most need to be influenced by certain communications are least likely to be reached by them (6, 7).

Thus, the bulk of the listeners to educational radio programs are among the better educated segment of the listening audience. A study of a radio program designed to promote friendship, coöperation, and mutual respect among various immigrant groups showed that a program about Italians was listened to chiefly by Italians, a program about Poles was listened to chiefly by Poles, and so on (5). In the same way, anti-prejudice propaganda is likely to reach or affect a considerably smaller proportion of the prejudiced group in the population than of the nonprejudiced.

This is, of course, not a denial of the value of pro-democratic propaganda. The audience of such propaganda is composed of sympathizers, neutrals, and opponents. Although the opponents may be largely unaffected, the other two groups may still be influenced. Here, however, we are chiefly concerned with the reaction of the prejudiced person to anti-prejudice propaganda. What happens when in an experimental situation they are involuntarily confronted with it?

There are, theoretically, two possibilities: they may fight it or they may give in to it. But our research in this field has shown us that many people are unwilling to do either: they prefer not to face the implications of ideas opposed to their own so that they do not have to be forced either to defend themselves or to admit error. What they do is to evade the issue psychologically by *simply not understanding the message.*

It is true that understanding of communications is related to the amount of education of the audience. However, even among people on the same educational level, those who are prejudiced are more apt to misunderstand a message than the unprejudiced.[1]

This article deals with two aspects of the problem of propaganda evasion: its mechanisms and its cultural basis. The first part is drawn from evidence collected in about a dozen studies of the public's response to anti-prejudice propaganda; the second part is speculative and hypothetical. Considerably more research would be needed to verify our tentative ideas on the motivation of propaganda evasion.

1 There is evidence for this in a number of studies conducted by this Department and by the Bureau of Applied Social Research of Columbia University.

Reprinted by permission of the Journal Press and the authors from the *Journal of Psychology,* 1947, vol. 23, pp. 15–25.

The Mechanisms of Propaganda Evasion

THE evidence for the techniques employed by a prejudiced respondent in order to avoid understanding is, of necessity, inferential. The process of evasion occurs in the respondent's mind some time between the presentation of a propaganda item and the respondent's "final" statement in answer to the interviewer's questions. The mechanisms involved in evasion, although they may be rather complicated and may appear to be deliberate, are in most cases probably unconscious. It is impossible to determine from even depth interview data at what level of consciousness the process occurs, that is, to what extent the respondent is aware of his evasion.

Evidence of the evasion process is often revealed in the course of the interview, if the interview is considered as an integrated whole and individual statements are not accepted in a disjointed, static fashion as isolated answers to isolated questions.

IDENTIFICATION AVOIDED—
UNDERSTANDING "DERAILED"

An example of how a dynamic interpretation of the whole course of the interview reveals evidence of the process of evasion is provided by a recent study of a cartoon series. The cartoons lampoon a character dubbed Mr. Biggott.[2] To bring home the satire of the cartoon, he is shown as a rather ridiculous prudish figure, with exaggerated anti-minority feelings.

What the producers of the cartoon intended was roughly this: The prejudiced reader would perceive that Mr. Biggott's ideas about minorities were similar to his own; that Mr. Biggott was an absurd character; that it was absurd to have such ideas—that to have such ideas made one as ridiculous as Mr. Biggott. He would, then, as the final stage in this process, presumably reject his own prejudice, in order to avoid identification with Mr. Biggott.

The study showed a very different result. Prejudiced respondents who understood the cartoon initially—that is, they went through the first three stages mentioned above—went to such lengths to extricate themselves from their identification with Mr. Biggott that in the end they *misunderstood the point of the cartoon.* To use the phrase of the writers of this report, there was a "derailment of understanding."

Here is an example of one of the ways in which the cartoons were misunderstood: [3] The respondent at first identified with Mr. Biggott, saying, among other things which indicated this identification, "I imagine he's a sour old bachelor—(laughing)—I'm an old bachelor myself." He also seemed to be aware of Mr. Biggott's prejudices. As the interview progressed, in order to differentiate himself from Mr. Biggott he concentrated on proving that Mr. Biggott's social status was inferior, that he was a *parvenu.* This led to a loss of focus on the real problems presented by the cartoons.

Sixth generation American blood. He don't want anything but sixth generation American blood! Ha! That's pretty good.

At this point the man begins to focus on Mr. Biggott's social inferiority and his attention is deflected from the issue of prejudice more and more as the process continues:

Well, you know, *I'm eighth generation myself,* of English descent on both sides. My family settled up on Connecticut, C————, Connecticut, in 1631. A sixth generation American—he's a man of six generations himself. *Maybe less than that. . . .* (What is the doctor thinking?) He's astonished, I guess. He thinks this man has an awful nerve. He looks like a crabby old man. *He may not be the best blood either.*

Mr. Biggott's prejudices have become snobbish pretensions and as the interview con-

2 Several Mr. Biggott studies were done. The one from which the following examples are drawn was conducted for the Department of Scientific Research of the American Jewish Committee by the Bureau of Applied Social Research of Columbia University.

3 In the particular cartoon discussed, Mr. Biggott is shown lying in a hospital bed with a doctor in attendance, and saying that for his blood transfusion he wants only "sixth generation American blood."

tinues, the respondent regards him more and more as a "lower class" symbol:

(Do you know anyone like him?) *No, I have no interest in knowing anyone like that. I've known some like him* up in C——. This particular man was in the Congregational Church —*of course* that's the church to which my family belongs. . . . He made plenty of money as an undertaker too. You know, my father died a few years ago. The burial cost $180. He knew that at the time I didn't have any money. He trusted me, let me pay it gradually. But, you know, he charged me 6 per cent interest. Yes, *that's what he charged me. Even though he knew my family and all that.* . . .

By this time the issue of prejudice has been completely side-tracked. Biggott reminds the respondent only of an old acquaintance whom he considers rather crude. At the end the cartoons become for him only a kind of test for judging personality characteristics:

(What do you think is the purpose of these cartoons?) To get the viewpoint of anyone. From the viewpoint you can form some opinion of that person. You can get different answers—some agree and some say something else. You can compare them and draw some conclusions . . . (What is the artist trying to do?) To get the *viewpoint of people to see if they coincide with the artist's idea of character* and all. Some would, some would differ.

In the same study there were other variations in what might be called the path of the misunderstanding. Some people caricatured Mr. Biggott, made him a target of ridicule; others made him appear intellectually inferior; still others transformed him into a foreigner or a Jew. Regardless of the particular line developed, the process is essentially the same. Whether or not a respondent follows one of these lines rather than another is probably a matter of temperament and character.

Such complicated forms of arriving circuitously at misunderstanding when there is good evidence that spontaneous understanding was present at first are, of course, not the only form of evasion that the prejudiced person takes to escape facing the criticism implied in the message of a propaganda item; but they are the most revealing forms as to the influence of prejudice on comprehension. The conflict about having prejudices must be strong, and at the same time the prejudice must be deeply rooted in the character structure. Under the pressure of this psychological predisposition the respondent takes the roundabout way of first understanding the content of the propaganda item; then identifying with the prejudiced figure, perceiving the criticism of his own position involved in the item; inventing means of disidentification from the special instance of prejudice depicted by the propaganda item; and in the process losing the original understanding of the message. Apparently this process occurs frequently; the unconscious ingenuity of the respondent sets in mainly during the last two steps.

THE MESSAGE MADE INVALID

In other cases the process of disidentification leads to more rationalized argumentation. Understanding has been admitted too openly to permit distortion of the message. The respondent accepts the message on the surface but makes it invalid for himself in one of two ways. He may admit the general principle, but claim that in exceptions one is entitled to one's prejudices; or he may admit that the individual item is convincing in itself, but that it is not a correct picture of usual life situations involving the minority group discussed. There is evidence in our studies of both types.

The first type of distortion occurred as a common reaction to a protolerance propaganda booklet. This was presented in the form of a series of well-drawn comic cartoons exposing the absurdity of generalizations about various groups. It concluded with the Golden Rule, "Live and let live." Prejudiced persons frequently followed the whole story with interest and amusement to the end, accepting the Golden Rule, but added: "But it's the Jews that don't let you live; they put themselves outside the rule."

Perhaps even more frequent is the tendency to accept the isolated story presented in propaganda as "just a story." The need to maintain the attention value of a propaganda item through a human-interest appeal has led many propagandists to exemplify by one outstanding dramatic story the general principle for which they wish to enlist support. This technique was used in a broadcast dramatization, "The Belgian Village," presented on the CBS series, "We, the People." In the story, a Jewish couple in an occupied Belgian Village are saved by the loyal support of the villagers who hide them from the Gestapo. The dramatization was followed by a direct appeal, spoken by Kate Smith, for sympathy and tolerance toward the Jews. Considerably more of the apparently prejudiced respondents [4] than of the others in the test audience refused to admit the applicability of this dramatic story to other situations. They called it an "adventure story," a "war story"; they discussed the dramatic highlights with great interest, but treated the explicit appeal attached to the incident either as if it had not occurred or as an unjustified artificial addition.

CHANGING THE FRAME OF REFERENCE

There remain to be discussed two other forms of misunderstanding by prejudiced persons. One of them is of greater interest than the other: in these cases the prejudiced person's perception is so colored by his prejudice that issues presented in a frame of reference different from his own are transformed so as to become compatible with his own views. Quite unaware of the violation of facts he commits, he imposes on a propaganda item his own frame of reference. This type of response was found in a study of a cartoon depicting a congressman who has native fascist, anti-minority views. The cartoon series seeks to expose and ridicule him so as to focus the readers' attention upon such native anti-democratic movements and to cause them to disapprove of these tendencies. For example, in one cartoon, the Congressman is shown interviewing an applicant in his office. The man has brought a letter of recommendation saying that he has been in jail, has started race riots, has smashed windows. The Congressman is pleased and

says, "Of course I can use you in my new party."

One respondent commented: "It might be anything crooked . . . might be a new labor party. That shady character makes me think so, the one applying for a job."

Another, in response to the second picture in the series, said: ". . . a bunch of men down in Congress that are more interested in keeping their jobs, interested in the votes rather than anything else . . . I never liked Senator Wagner. . . ."

Another: "It's about a strike . . . about trouble like strikes . . . He is starting a Communist party."

The type becomes clearest in the following reply: "It's a Jewish party that would help Jews get more power."

The only clue that these respondents took from the cartoon was the fact that it tried to show up a bad politician. The rest they supplied themselves by identifying the Congressman with whatever appeared to them to be "bad politics." Thus they imposed their own ideology on the cartoon and arrived at an interpretation satisfactory to them—an interpretation which, however, represented a complete misunderstanding of the cartoon's message.

THE MESSAGE IS TOO DIFFICULT

The remaining type of misunderstanding can be dismissed quickly. This takes the same form as misunderstanding by unprejudiced people. Some respondents frankly admit that "they don't get the point." This is most frequently due to intellectual and educational limitations of these respondents or to defects in the propaganda.

These evasion processes have obvious implications for the producers of cartoons (and probably of propaganda in general). Given the tendency to evade opposition propaganda, evasion is facilitated by making the message subtle or satirical. However, simplifying the message may lessen its emotional impact. What seems to be indicated is that the more subtle—and therefore the more easily distorted and misunderstood—forms may be appropriate for neutrals and for inactive sympathizers of the anti-prejudice message: these

---

4 They were rated "conservative" on political attitude questions which have a fairly high correlation with a negative attitude toward minorities.

people do not show evidence of this tendency to *evade* the message although they may misunderstand for other reasons; and the impact of the item may make stronger supporters of them. For the prejudiced person the research suggests that this approach is ineffective.

For a better understanding of the evasion mechanism we must turn to an examination of the motivation underlying it and its rôle in our culture.

Evasion—A Cultural Pattern

A THOROUGH examination of the motivation underlying evasion would require a much more extensive treatment than we can provide here. However, certain cultural features may be mentioned which seem to bear out in other areas the kind of evasion mechanism discussed above.

FEAR OF ISOLATION AND
THE THREAT TO THE EGO

The fear of isolation is a major force in our society, where the majority of people are dependent upon group membership not only for their physical well-being but also for psychological support. They rely upon group codes and group values as guides for their behavior and their ideals. Nearly everyone wants to "belong." At the same time this is complicated by the fact that assembly-line production and the general complexity of modern life tend to drive people into more and more atomistic contacts with their fellow men, thereby increasing the fear of losing identity with the group.

From a psychological point of view, the evasion of a propaganda message with which one disagrees functions as a defense mechanism. Such defense mechanisms come into play whenever an individual senses a danger to his ego structure—that is, whenever his self-confidence hangs in the balance. As we have seen, the steps involved in the evasion process are fairly complicated. However, these complications are obviously negligible compared to the discomfort that would be created by facing the message.

The printed propaganda items that attack prejudice are an attack on the ego of the prejudiced person. Moreover, they constitute an attack made with the authority of the printed word, thus presumably speaking for a large part of the world that disapproves of the respondent. He is confronted with a twofold threat to his security: On the one hand he is an outsider in the world represented by the propaganda item; on the other hand, giving careful consideration to the validity of the propaganda and possibly accepting it threatens the individual's security in the group to which he feels he belongs and which supports his present ideas. The interviewing situation increases the threat to the security of the individual who feels attacked by anti-discrimination propaganda. Interviewers are trained to use an engaging, polite, and friendly manner when approaching a respondent; they are selected, not only for the skill they have acquired, but also for neatness and pleasantness of appearance in order to facilitate their contact with strangers. The respondent, who is on the defensive, probably links the person of the interviewer with that outside world which may disapprove of him. The interviewer's reluctance to voice his own opinion creates the suspicion that he, too, might disapprove of the respondent's attitude.

The emotional nature of prejudice has been well enough established to explain why the prejudiced respondent often does not trust his own capacity for logical argument on the subject. He feels himself attacked in spheres that actually transcend logic. So where possible, he evades the issue. Although there is insufficient evidence on this point, we venture the guess that the less a person has rationalized his prejudices, the greater will be his tendency to evade an attack on them. Those who are most advanced in the rationalization of prejudice will not feel the need for evasion to the same degree as their less ideologically developed supporters. Witness the pseudo-science on race questions developed by the Nazis and their followers in this country. Those, however, who are infected without having made the decisive step over to the "lunatic fringe," and who are only dimly aware of the irrational basis of their particular attitude, will try to weasel out of their

difficulty when confronted with the discon-
certing anti-discrimination message.

THE MULTIPLICITY OF VALUE SYSTEMS

Another dimension must be added to the phenomenon of propaganda evasion before it
can be understood. This dimension is closely
related to that part of our life experience
which involves inconsistencies or contradictions. There exists in our society a culturally
conditioned habit of evasion, a product of the
fact that each individual is compelled to participate in many different groups, each of
which has its own more or less well-defined
value systems. Often, these value systems are
somewhat inconsistent with each other;
sometimes they imply a different hierarchy
of values.

Examples of simultaneous acceptance of
inconsistent value systems abound. The obsequious bookkeeper who assumes a dominant
rôle in political discussions with his barber-
shop cronies is a familiar figure in the modern literature of the western world. We are
not surprised when a store owner who privately champions progressive causes, refuses
to hire a Negro salesclerk on the grounds that
his customers will object. The example of the
bookkeeper illustrates the necessity for flexi-
bly shifting from one social rôle to another.
The storekeeper, too, is involved in a conflict
between his public and private attitudes. He
keeps the solution of this conflict in abeyance
by setting up a special hierarchy of values
for his business rôle: he knows that he is
supported by the generally accepted view
that taking care of one's profits takes precedence over other considerations.

Thus, two possible alternatives are available. These contradictions may either be recognized and resolved; or they may be evaded.
Instead of looking squarely at the inconsistencies, one may divide one's life into so many
little pockets in which behavior is determined
by independent and even contradictory values;
or one may realistically examine and compare
the values involved in his various day-to-day
rôles and then weigh their relative merits as
behavior guides.

Evidence of this was found in a study of
the impact of factory life on children who

had just left school (4). The moral values
they had been taught in school were confronted in the factory with an inflation of the
importance of efficiency to the exclusion of
morality. Nevertheless, the absorption of this
new value system was achieved with incred-
ible speed. But the two systems were not
reconciled, nor was one abandoned for the
other. They coexisted in strictly separate compartments of the personality; the issue of
conflict was evaded by the departmentalizing
of the personality.

OTHER CULTURAL FACTORS IN EVASION

In this context the lack of spontaneity so
characteristic of people living in our culture
must be considered (1, 2, 3, 8). The public
which comprises the audience for the mass
media of communications is entertainment
hungry. Many of them are lulled into boredom and fatigue by their jobs; outside their
jobs they want to have fun. They want to be
entertained without having to think. And they
are encouraged to persist in this mental laziness by the stereotypy of these communications. Not only are they continually confronted with entertainment cast in the same
mold; they are even told how to react to it.
Everything is, as it were, pre-digested for
them. They are informed by advertisements
that a comedy will make them "laugh 'til
their sides ache," that a sentimental love story
will "wring their hearts," to mention only the
most superficial appeals. As one writer has
put it, "they march to their destiny by catch-
words." Ideas are adopted, not as ideas, but
as slogans. Where ideas infiltrate in the guise
of entertainment the habitual shying away
from effort comes to the rescue of the person
who is the propaganda target and helps him
to miss the point of the message. The only
alternative would be to face the implications
of the message and think about them, and
this they neither want nor are habituated
to do.

Also involved but probably less important
in the complex of propaganda evasion is the
factor of recognition-value. Audiences tend
to prefer the things which are familiar to
them. The best-liked music is the music one
knows. What is new is a little suspect, requires

more effort in listening, and has no pre-established associations which prescribe a pattern of response. Hence it is rejected (1). It is quite likely that a similar tendency makes itself felt in the consideration of new (and oppositional) ideas.

WHY EVASION?

Why has evasion become so general? The answer lies partly in the difficulties the individual must face to achieve uniformity in the various areas of his everyday experience. To face the contradictions and try to resolve them would undoubtedly set up disturbing tensions which would in turn involve serious difficulties for most individuals. For example, consider the fact that most people agree with the ideas of their own social group; they are conditioned by the people with whom they live and, in turn, they choose to be with people whose attitudes are compatible with their own. Adopting a conflicting attitude would create antagonisms in inter-personal relationships, requiring considerable adjustment on the part of the individual. Even *considering* an opposing point of view may create great discomfort.

Thus evasion appears as a well-practised form of behavior, which receives encouragement from the social structure in which we live. In connection with response to anti-prejudice propaganda it serves as a defence against group attack. This may partly explain why persons with a poorly developed ego structure tend most frequently to take this easy way out.

REFERENCES

1. ADORNO, T. W. On popular music. *Stud. Philos. & Soc. Sci.,* 1941, 9, 17–48.
2. HORKHEIMER, M. Art and mass culture. *Stud. Philos. & Soc. Sci.,* 1941, 9, 293–304.
3. ———. The end of reason. *Stud. Philos. & Soc. Sci.,* 1941, 9, 366–388.
4. JAHODA, M. Some socio-psychological problems of factory life. *Brit. J. Psychol.,* 1941, 31, 191–206.
5. LAZARSFELD, P. F. (*Ed.*) Radio and the Printed Page. New York: Duell, Sloan & Pearce, 1944.
6. ———. BERELSON, B., & GAUDET, H. The People's Choice. New York: Duell, Sloan & Pearce, 1944.
7. ———, & MERTON, R. K. Studies in radio and film propaganda. *Trans. N. Y. Acad. Sci.,* 1943, 6, 58–79.
8. LOWENTHAL, L. Biographies in popular magazines. In *Radio Research, 1942–1943.* New York: Duell, Sloan & Pearce, 1944. (Pp. 507–548.)

ALBERTA ENGVALL SIEGEL *and* SIDNEY SIEGEL

50. *Reference Groups, Membership Groups, and Attitude Change*

IN social psychological theory, it has long been recognized that an individual's *membership groups* have an important influence on the values and attitudes he holds. More recently, attention has also been given to the influence of his *reference groups:* the groups in which he aspires to attain or maintain membership. In a given area, membership groups and reference groups may or may not be identical. They are identical when the person aspires to *maintain* membership in the group of which he is a part; they are disparate when the group in which the individual aspires to *attain* membership is one in which he is not a member. It has been widely asserted that both membership and reference groups affect the attitudes held by the individual (4).

The present study is an examination of the attitude changes which occur over time when reference groups and membership groups are identical and when they are disparate. The study takes advantage of a field experiment which occurred in the social context of the lives of the subjects, concerning events considered vital by them. The subjects were not aware that their membership and reference groups were of research interest; in fact, they did not know that the relevant information about these was available to the investigators.

The field experiment permitted a test of the general hypothesis that both the amount and the direction of a person's attitude change over time depends on the attitude norms of his membership group (whether or not that group is chosen by him) and on the attitude norms of his reference group.

This hypothesis is tested with subjects who shared a common reference group at the time of the initial assessment of attitudes. They were then randomly assigned to alternative membership groups, some being assigned to the chosen group and others to a nonchosen group. Attitudes were reassessed after a year of experience in these alternative membership groups with divergent attitude norms. During the course of the year, some subjects came to take the imposed (initially nonpreferred) membership group as their reference group. Attitude change after the year was examined in terms of the membership group and reference group identifications of the subjects at that time.

The Field Experiment

THE Ss of this study were women students at a large private coeducational university. The study was initiated shortly before the end of their freshman year, when they all lived in the same large freshman dormitory to which they had been assigned upon entering the university. At this university, all women move to new housing for their sophomore year. Several types of housing are available to them: a large dormitory, a medium-sized dormitory, several very small houses which share common dining facilities, and a number of former sorority houses which have been operated by the university since sororities were banished from the campus. These latter are located among the fraternity houses on Fraternity Row, and are therefore known as "Row houses." Although the Row houses are

Reprinted by permission of the American Psychological Association and the authors from the *Journal of Abnormal and Social Psychology*, 1957, vol. 55, pp. 360–64.

lower in physical comfort than most of the other residences for women, students consider them higher in social status. This observation was confirmed by a poll of students (5, p. 205), in which over 90 per cent of the respondents stated that Row houses for women were higher in social status than non-Row houses, the remaining few disclaiming any information concerning status differences among women's residences.

In the Spring of each year, a "drawing" is held for housing for the subsequent year. All freshmen must participate in this drawing, and any other student who wishes to change her residence may participate. It is conducted by the office of the Dean of Women, in cooperation with woman student leaders. Any participant's ballot is understood to be secret. The woman uses the ballot to rank the houses in the order of her preference. After submitting this ballot, she draws a number from the hopper. The rank of that number determines the likelihood that her preference will be satisfied.

In research reported earlier (5), a random sample was drawn from the population of freshman women at this university, several tests were administered to the Ss in that sample, and (unknown to the Ss) their housing preferences for the forthcoming sophomore year were observed by the investigator. The Ss were characterized as "high status oriented" if they listed a Row house as their first choice, and were characterized as "low status oriented" if they listed a non-Row house as their first choice. The hypothesis under test, drawn from reference group theory and from theoretical formulations concerning authoritarianism, was that high status orientation is a correlate of authoritarianism. The hypothesis was confirmed: freshman women who listed a Row house as their first choice for residence scored significantly higher on the average in authoritarianism, as measured by the E-F scale (1, 2) than did women who listed a non-Row house as their first choice. The present study is a continuation of the one described, and uses as its Ss only those members of the original sample who were "high status oriented," i.e., preferred to live in a Row house for the sophomore

year. In the initial study (5), of the 95 Ss whose housing choices were listed, 39 were "high status oriented," i.e., demonstrated that the Row was their reference group by giving a Row house as their first choice in the drawing. Of this group, 28 were available to serve as Ss for the follow-up or "change" study which is the topic of the present paper. These women form a homogeneous subsample in that at the conclusion of their freshman year they shared a common membership group (the freshman dormitory) and a common reference group (the Row). These Ss, however, had divergent experiences during their sophomore year: nine were Row residents during that year (having drawn sufficiently small numbers in the housing drawing to enable them to be assigned to the group of their choice) and the other 19 lived in non-Row houses during that year (having drawn numbers too large to enable them to be assigned to the housing group of their choice).

E-F scores were obtained from each of the 28 Ss in the course of a large-scale testing program administered to most of the women students at the university. Anonymity was guaranteed to the Ss, but a coding procedure permitted the investigators to identify each respondent and thereby to isolate the Ss and compare each S's second E-F score with her first.

To prevent the Ss from knowing that they were participating in a follow-up study, several procedures were utilized: (a) many persons who had not served in the earlier study were included in the second sample, (b) the testing was introduced as being part of a nation-wide study to establish norms, (c) the test administrators were different persons from those who had administered the initial tests, (d) Ss who informed the test administrator that they had already taken the "Public Opinion Questionnaire" (E-F scale) were casually told that this did not disqualify them from participating in the current study.

The Ss had no hint that the research was in any way related to their housing arrangements. Testing was conducted in classrooms as well as in residences, and all procedures and instructions were specifically designed to avoid any arousal of the salience of the housing groups in the frame of reference of the research.

The annual housing drawing was conducted three weeks after the sophomore-year testing, and, as usual, each woman's housing ballot was undertood to be secret. In this drawing, each S had the opportunity to change her membership group, although a residence move is not required at the end of the sophomore year as it is at the end of the freshman year. If an S participated in this drawing, the house which she listed as her first choice on the ballot was identified by the investigators as her reference group. If she did not, it was evident that the house in which she was currently a member was the one in which she chose to continue to live, i.e., was her reference group. With the information on each S's residence choice at the end of her freshman year, her assigned residence for her sophomore year, and her residence choice at the end of her sophomore year, it was possible to classify the subjects in three categories:

A. Women (n = 9) who had gained assignment to live on the Row during their sophomore year and who did not attempt to draw out of the Row at the end of that year;

B. Women (n = 11) who had not gained assignment to a Row house for the sophomore year and who drew for a Row house again after living in a non-Row house during the sophomore year; and

C. Women (n = 8) who had not gained assignment to a Row house for the sophomore year, and who chose to remain in a non-Row house after living in one during the sophomore year.

For all three groups of Ss, as we have pointed out, membership group (freshman dormitory) and reference group (Row house) were common at the end of the freshman year. For Group A, membership and reference groups were identical throughout the sophomore year. For Group B, membership and reference groups were disparate throughout the sophomore year. For Group C, membership and reference groups were initially disparate during the sophomore year but became identical because of a change in reference groups.

As will be demonstrated, the Row and the non-Row social groups differ in attitude norms, with Row residents being generally more authoritarian than non-Row residents. From social psychological theory concerning the influence of group norms on individuals' attitudes, it would be predicted that the different group identifications during the sophomore year of the three groups of Ss would result in differential attitude change. Those who gained admittance to a Row house for the sophomore year (Group A) would be expected to show the least change in authoritarianism, for they spent that year in a social context which reinforced their initial attitudes. Group C Ss would be expected to show the greatest change in authoritarianism, a change associated not only with their membership in a group (the non-Row group) which is typically low in authoritarianism, but also with their shift in reference groups, from Row to non-Row, i.e., from a group normatively higher in authoritarianism to a group normatively lower. The extent of attitude change in the Ss in Group B would be expected to be intermediate, due to the conflicting influences of the imposed membership group (non-Row) and of the unchanged reference group (Row). The research hypothesis, then, is that between the time of the freshman-year testing and the sophomore-year testing, the extent of change in authoritarianism will be least in Group A, greater in Group B, and greatest in Group C. That is, in extent of attitude change, Group A < Group B < Group C.

Results

GROUP NORMS

FROM the data collected in the large-scale testing program, it was possible to determine the group norms for authoritarian attitudes among the Row and the non-Row women at the university. The E-F scale was administered to all available Row residents (n = 303) and to a random sample of residents of non-Row houses (n = 101). These Ss were sophomores, juniors, and seniors. The mean E-F score of the Row women was 90, while the mean E-F score of the non-Row was 81.

TABLE 1

Frequencies of E-F Scores Above and Below Common Median for Row and Non-Row Residents

	RESIDENTS OF NON-ROW HOUSES	RESIDENTS OF ROW HOUSES	TOTAL
Above median	36	166	202
Below median	65	137	202
Total	101	303	404

The E-F scores of the two groups were demonstrated to differ at the $p < .001$ level ($\chi^2 = 11.1$) by the median test (6, pp. 111–116), a nonparametric test, the data for which are shown in TABLE 1.

ATTITUDE CHANGE

The central hypothesis of this study is that attitude change will occur differentially in Groups A, B, and C, and that it will occur in the direction which would be predicted from knowledge of the group norms among Row and non-Row residents in general. The 28 Ss of this study had a mean E-F score of 102 at the end of their freshman year. The data reported above concerning authoritarianism norms for all women residing on campus would lead to the prediction that in general the Ss would show a reduction in authoritarianism during the sophomore year but that this reduction would be differential in the three groups; from the knowledge that Row residents generally are higher in authoritarianism than non-Row residents, the prediction based on social group theory would be that Group A would show the smallest reduction in authoritarianism scores, Group B would show a larger reduction, and Group C would show the largest reduction. The data which permit a test of this hypothesis are given in TABLE 2. The Jonckheere test (3), a nonparametric k-sample test which tests the null hypothesis that the three groups are from the same population against the alternative hypothesis that they are from different populations which are ordered in a specified way, was used with these data. By that test, the hypothesis is confirmed at the $p < .025$ level.

TABLE 2

Freshman-Year and Sophomore-Year E-F Scores of Subjects

Group	End of Freshman Year	End of Sophomore Year	Difference
	108	125	−17
	70	78	−8
	106	107	−1
	92	92	0
A	80	78	2
	104	102	2
	143	138	5
	110	92	18
	114	80	34
	76	117	−41
	105	107	−2
	88	82	6
	109	97	12
	98	83	15
B	112	94	18
	101	82	19
	114	93	21
	104	81	23
	116	91	25
	101	74	27
	121	126	−5
	87	79	8
	105	95	10
	97	81	16
C	96	78	18
	108	73	35
	114	77	37
	88	49	39

Discussion

SUBSTANTIVELY, the present study provides experimental verification of certain assertions in social group theory, demonstrating that attitude change over time is related to the group identification of the person—both his membership group identification and his reference group identification. The hypothesis that extent of attitude change would be different in the three subgroups of Ss, depending on their respective membership group and reference group identifications, is confirmed at the $p < .025$ level; in extent of change in authoritarianism, Group A < Group B < Group C, as predicted.

Another way of looking at the data may

serve to highlight the influence of membership groups and reference groups. At the end of the freshman year, the *S*s in Groups A, B, and C shared the same membership group and the same reference group. During the sophomore year, the *S*s in Group A shared one membership group while those in Groups B and C together shared another. From membership group theory, it would be predicted that the extent of attitude change would be greater among the latter *S*s. This hypothesis is supported by the data (in TABLE 2): by the Mann-Whitney test (6, pp. 116–127), the change scores of these two sets of *S*s (Group A versus Groups B and C together) differ in the predicted direction at the $p < .025$ level. This finding illustrates the influence of *membership* groups on attitude change. On the other hand, at the conclusion of the sophomore year, the *S*s in Groups A and B shared a common reference group while those in Group C had come to share another. From reference group theory, it would be predicted that attitude change would be more extensive among the subjects who had changed reference groups (Group C) than among those who had not. This hypothesis is also supported by the data (in TABLE 2): by the Mann-Whitney test, the change scores of these two sets of *S*s (Groups A and B together versus Group C) differ in the predicted direction at the $p < .05$ level. This finding illustrates the influence of *reference* groups on attitude change. Any inference from this mode of analysis (as contrasted with the main analysis of the data, by the Jonckheere test) must be qualified because of the non-independence of the data on which the two Mann-Whitney tests are made, but it is mentioned here to clarify the role which membership and reference groups play in influencing attitude change.

The findings may also contribute to our understanding of processes affecting attitude change. The imposition of a membership group does have some effect on an individual's attitudes, even when the imposed group is not accepted by the individual as his reference group. This relationship is shown in the case of Group B. If the person comes to accept the imposed group as his reference group, as was the case with the *S*s in Group C, then the change in his attitudes toward the level of the group norm is even more pronounced.

Methodologically, the study has certain features which may deserve brief mention. First, the study demonstrates that it is possible operationally to define the concept of reference group. The act of voting by secret ballot for the group in which one would like to live constitutes clear behavioral specification of one's reference group, and it is an act whose conceptual meaning can be so directly inferred that there is no problem of reliability of judgment in its categorization by the investigator. Second, the study demonstrates that a field study can be conducted which contains the critical feature of an experiment that is usually lacking in naturalistic situations: randomization. The determination of whether or not a woman student would be assigned to the living group of her choice was based on a random event: the size of the number she drew from the hopper. This fact satisfied the requirement that the treatment condition be randomized, and permitted sharper inferences than can usually be drawn from field studies. Third, the test behavior on which the conclusions of this study were based occurred in a context in which the salience of membership and reference groups was *not* aroused and in which no external sanctions from the relevant groups were operative. This feature of the design permitted the interpretation that the E-F scores represented the *S*s' internalized attitudes (4, p. 218). Finally, the use of a paper-and-pencil measure of attitude and thus of attitude change, rather than the use of some more behavioral measure, is a deficiency of the present study. Moreover, the measure which was used suffers from a well-known circularity, based on the occurrence of pseudo-low scores (1, p. 771; 5, pp. 221–222).

Summary

IN the social context of the lives of the subjects, and in a natural social experiment which provided randomization of the relevant condition effects, the influence of both membership and reference groups on attitude change was assessed. All subjects shared a common reference group at the start of the period of the study. When divergent membership groups with disparate attitude norms were socially imposed on the basis of a random event, attitude change in the subjects over time was a function of the normative attitudes of both imposed membership groups and the individuals' reference groups. The greatest attitude change occurred in subjects who came to take the imposed, initially nonpreferred, membership group as their reference group.

REFERENCES

1. ADORNO, T. W., FRENKEL-BRUNSWIK, ELSE, LEVINSON, D. J. & SANFORD, R. N. *The Authoritarian Personality.* New York: Harper, 1950.
2. GOUGH, H. G. Studies of social intolerance: I. Some psychological and sociological correlates of anti-Semitism. *J. soc. Psychol.,* 1951, 33, 237–246.
3. JONCKHEERE, A. A. A distribution-free *k*-sample test against ordered alternatives.

Biometrika, 1954, 41, 133–145.
4. SHERIF, M., & SHERIF, CAROLYN W. *Groups in harmony and tension.* New York: Harper, 1953.
5. SIEGEL, S. Certain determinants and correlates of authoritarianism. *Genet. Psychol. Monogr.,* 1954, 49, 187–229.
6. SIEGEL, S. *Nonparametric statistics: For the behavioral sciences.* New York: McGraw-Hill, 1956.

FRANCIS L. K. HSU

51. Suppression Versus Repression:
A Limited Psychological Interpretation
of Four Cultures

THE word "repression" is used here in the Freudian sense, namely "the exclusion of painful and unpleasant material from consciousness and from motor expression." [1] According to this definition, materials that are repressed are buried deep in the unconscious. The word suppression is used here in the common everyday sense: namely, the restraint from certain actions because of external circumstances, the thought of such actions, however, not being necessarily excluded from consciousness. As a rule the materials that are suppressed are not buried in the unconscious and can be called forth very readily and unwarped. The much-discussed feeling of guilt, which according to Freud is traceable to the infantile sexuality of the person in relation to one or another of the parents, is an illustration of repression. On the other hand, the fact that many motorists drive within specified speed limits because of police patrol or fear of accidents may be a case of suppression. After long years of driving, a motorist may appear to obey automatically the various road signs;

1 William Healy, A. F. Bronner, and A. M. Bowers, *The Structure and Meaning of Psychoanalysis;* New York, A. Knopf, 1930; p. 218. The use of the word "unpleasant" in this connection has been criticized by Robert R. Sears in "Survey of Objective Studies of Psycho-analytic Concepts" [Social Science Research Council Bull. No. 51 (1943); 156 pp.; see p. 105]. However, the criticism has no vital importance to the present paper in which one could just as well substitute the word "certain" for "unpleasant."

but few motorists, when directly questioned, will fail to see the relationship between speed limits, the law, possible accidents, and the unfortunate consequences which might result from unwise actions.

Every society is bound to impose some restraint on its members, whether in the earlier years of the individual or later. Since no individual is fully conscious of all the restraints of his society that are applicable to him and since repression usually begins as suppression, it is evident that, in the normal course of events, the individual in every society is subject to some forces of suppression and some of repression. However, some cultures employ more suppression as a mechanism of socialization, while others employ more repression for a similar purpose. In a culture which emphasizes suppression as the mechanism of socialization, external controls will be more important to the individual than internal controls. In a culture which emphasizes repression as the mechanism of socialization, internal controls will be more important than external controls. In the former the basic pattern of life tends to be situation-centered. In the latter the basic pattern of life tends to be individual-centered.

It will be clear at once that this thesis is somewhat similar to that advanced by the late Dr. Benedict in her book on Japan:

True shame cultures rely on external sanctions for good behavior, not, as true guilt cultures

Reprinted by special permission of The William Alanson White Psychiatric Foundation, Inc., and the author from *Psychiatry*, 1949, vol. 12, pp. 223–24 and 233–42.

do, on an internalized conviction of sin. Shame is a reaction to other people's criticism. A man is shamed either by being openly ridiculed and rejected or by fantasying to himself that he has been made ridiculous. In either case it is a potent sanction. But it requires an audience or at least a man's fantasy of an audience. Guilt does not. In a nation where honor means living up to one's own picture of oneself, a man may suffer from guilt though no man knows of his misdeed and a man's feeling of guilt may actually be relieved by confessing his sin.[2]

Three things will, however, make the present paper materially different from Dr. Benedict's treatment of the subject. First, Dr. Benedict speaks of a contrast between Japan on the one hand and America or the West on the other, while in the present paper four cultures will be selected for analysis: Germany and the United States are selected as examples in which repression as a mechanism has greater weight than suppression; Japan and China are selected as examples in which the order of the two mechanisms [is] reversed. Furthermore, it will become plain later that there are differences—between Germany and America on the one hand and between Japan and China on the other—which cannot be explained on the basis of her theory. Second, it will be shown that shame or guilt [is] only symptomatic of the basic socialization processes undergone by the individual. The total range of facts may be more adequately covered by the concepts of suppression versus repression, leading respectively to greater sensitivity on the part of the individual to external sanctions or to internal controls. The behavior of an individual brought up under a primary emphasis on suppression may range from using different kinds of language for different occasions—which are not necessarily contradictory one to another—to so much shame that he has to commit suicide; just as the behavior of an individual brought up under a primary emphasis on repression may range from all kinds of internally satisfying rationalization within himself to an actual feeling of guilt. Thirdly, the social origin of the Japanese character en-

visaged by Dr. Benedict, though superior to that envisaged by Dr. Gorer,[3] is inadequate and even wide of the mark. For, as the ensuing analysis will show, what accounts for a large part of the basic Japanese character must also be applicable to that of the Chinese, and Dr. Benedict's picture of growing up in Japan does not fit China.

. . . . .

Religion and Other Aspects of Culture

FROM the point of view of any modern anthropologist, the origin of certain religions, such as Christianity, Mohammedanism, or Buddhism, is a historical problem and cannot, therefore, be reasonably accounted for in personality-psychological terms. However, the influence and spread of one or another form of religion in given cultures—provided that there is agreement that forms of religions are subject to scientific treatment—are very much dependent upon their acceptability or unacceptability according to the personality characteristics generated by the pre-existing cultural norms. From an analysis of novels it is apparent that there are certain differences between the two camps in the approach to sex. The actual differences are, however, far wider in scope. If the differences in Eastern and Western novels can be characterized, it might be said that the latter usually emphasize introspection or searching for the soul as well as the inner meaning of life, while the former usually interest themselves in the opposite direction, namely, the external equilibrium or searching for the individual's proper places in the most appropriate social situation. From this point of view it is easy to see why Christianity has taken much deeper root in Europe and America than in either Japan or China. The personality-culture pattern which is developed out of repressive mechanisms emphasizes the individual, which in turn looks for one all-pervasive god. The personality-culture pattern which is developed out of suppressive mechanisms emphasizes

2 Ruth Benedict, *The Chrysanthemum and the Sword;* Boston, Houghton Mifflin Co., 1946; p. 223. [Reprinted with permission.]

3 G. Gorer, "Japanese Character Structure and Propaganda," New Haven (mimeographed), 1942; and "Themes in Japanese Culture," *Trans. N. Y. Academy of Science* (1943), 2:106–124.

the external relationship of the individual which in turn looks for satisfactory adjustments with a number of gods, each for a specific purpose.

In the same way it becomes easy to see why Protestantism had to replace Catholicism in Western Europe. Catholicism, with its many saints and a priestly hierarchy as well as numerous and complicated rituals which are considered necessary parts of the total function of individual worship, is less soul-searching and less introspective—in a sense much closer to polytheism than monotheism—than Protestantism, with its simplified rituals, absence of saints, and emphasis on direct communication with God. Furthermore it is no accident that Christianity, in spite of many centuries of Western missionary work and a desire on the part of the East to imitate the West, has made scarcely any headway. Up to the present less than one percent of the Chinese population is nominally Christian, while roughly the same proportion is reported for Japan.[4] Furthermore, the most interesting thing is that of the about 3,000,000 to 4,000,000 Chinese Christians, only about 400,000 are Protestants and the rest are Catholics.[5]

Thus repression versus suppression translated into the realm of religion may also be seen to be related, respectively, to religious intolerance versus religious tolerance. In Anglo-Saxon-Teutonic cultures religion is a matter exclusively of individual souls; in China and Japan it is a matter primarily of the spiritual station of the individual. In the West the search for inner peace and balance is primary; in the East the search for suitable rapport with the world of spirits is primary. In the West religion concerns itself with individual guilt and salvation; in the East it concerns itself with group responsibility and individual salvation within the group. For this reason condemnation to hell is believed to be irreversible in the West, while the misfortune of the dead in China may be alleviated by the good deeds of those family members who are alive.[6]

Let us next examine certain basic psychological attitudes in the two types of cultures. The best exposition of this is that of Dr. Benedict on guilt and shame. To quote:

> The strong identification of circumspection with self-respect includes, therefore, watchfulness of all the cues one observes in other people's acts, and a strong sense that other people are sitting in judgment. 'One cultivates self-respect (one must jicho),' they say, 'because of society.' 'If there were no society one would not need to respect oneself (cultivate jicho).'
>
> True shame cultures rely on external sanctions for good behavior, not as true guilt cultures do, on an internalized conviction of sin. Shame is a reaction to other people's criticism. A man is shamed either by being openly ridiculed and rejected or by fantasying to himself that he has been made ridiculous. In either case it is a potent sanction. But it requires an audience or at least a man's fantasy of an audience. Guilt does not. In a nation where honor means living up to one's picture of oneself, a man may suffer from guilt though no man knows of his misdeed and a man's feeling of guilt may actually be relieved by confessing his sin.[7]

Dr. Benedict was, of course, speaking only of Japan when she spoke of shame culture. In terms of the present paper, guilt occurs most readily in a culture that is obviously based upon repression as the chief mechanism of social control; while shame occurs most readily in a culture that is obviously based upon suppression as the chief mechanism of social control. One does not have to go far to look for evidence of guilt in Anglo-Saxon-Teutonic cultures. Even the recent House bill which changed immigration laws affecting Japanese was passed in terms of retribution for a wrong committed by the United States.[8]

On the other hand, in China and Japan, shame, an embarrassment arising out of the

4 Douglas Haring, "Japan and the Japanese" in Ralph Linton (ed.), *Most of the World;* New York, Columbia Univ. Press, 1949; p. 858. John Embree's figures are higher, about less than half of one percent of the population (*The Japanese Nation;* New York, Farrar, 1945; p. 218).

5 In Japan the proportion of Catholics is the smaller of the two, being about one-fourth of the Protestants. See John Embree, reference footnote 22; p. 219.

6 For a discussion of Chinese religion and its main differences from Christianity, see F. L. K. Hsu, *Under the Ancestors' Shadow;* New York, Columbia Univ. Press, 1948. See also Hsu, "China," in Linton, reference footnote 22; pp. 775–785.

7 Benedict, reference footnote 2; pp. 222–223.

8 See report in Chicago *Tribune,* March 2, 1949.

fact that one is suddenly out of tune with one's social relationship, is very much in evidence. The sense of shame is applicable to a wide range of life's activities. It applies to national affairs no less than it does to personal affairs. It applies to serious business relations no less than it does to casual social encounters. The appropriate clothes for the appropriate occasion, the suitable manners for the suitable situation, the commonly recognized deference and subordination between superiors and inferiors—a mistake in any of these or other conventions—may be a grave cause for the rise of the sense of shame. A traditional Chinese scholar who has misused or given the wrong stroke to a word in a public document or even a letter, will have a hard time living the experience down. In the same way a slip of tongue in public is a much more serious matter in Japan than in the United States.

It is in this sense of shame that one must look for the meaning of the concept of "face." It is a popular misconception that "face-saving" is peculiar to China and Japan. Anybody who has made even a cursory observation on American public and private affairs will realize that this is untrue. On numerous occasions "face" and "face-saving" are equally an American concern. But what distinguishes "face" in the East from that in the West is that it is much more inclusive in the former than in the latter. A person brought up in a culture with suppression as the major mechanism of social control tends to concern himself much more with what he does in the presence of others, and in many more connections, than a person brought up in a culture with repression as the major mechanism. For this reason form has much greater meaning and importance in the East than in the West. For the same reason the relationship between superiors and inferiors, such as male and female, bureaucrat and commoner, employer and employee, conqueror and conquered, tend to be more rigid and more without humor in the East than in the West.

Using the same key of suppression versus repression certain new light could be thrown on the so-called "racial problem." Race prejudice has been explained on the basis of a frustration-aggression theory,[9] but such a theory alone cannot explain why such prejudice is a common problem in Germany and the United States, but nonexistent in China and Japan, or at least not in the form which is found in the West. In a culture which is based upon suppression and therefore a satisfactory external relationship, the different statuses are adequate for the purpose of handling the situation involving contact between two ethnic groups. The Chinese traditionally called all non-Chinese groups barbarians but as barbarians they were to be left alone, once the acknowledgement of political superiority was made. In fact the conquests against non-Chinese groups in Chinese history were chiefly done at the whim of the autocratic emperors. Once the conquest was accomplished, the people had little interest in the conquered. Many aboriginals in China achieved distinction in the imperial examinations and bureaucracy. This group and their descendants were at once accepted because of their statuses in the existing scheme of things. They were respected or laughed at according to their literary achievement, the same as if they were Chinese scholars.

The treatment of conquered peoples like Koreans, Chinese, Europeans, and Malays in modern times by Japan has often been exceedingly harsh at first, when the battle dust was still not settled. The Japanese, because of their treatment in the first place in the hands of Westerners, wanted revenge and also wanted to show that they were far above the other Asiatics. They usually wanted the conquered peoples to show them extreme external signs of subordination. Take Korea for example. At first, extreme external obedience was exacted from all Koreans. There were many forms and instances of harsh persecution of the Koreans in Korea. But as the Japanese position in Korea became more secure, the Koreans who took over Japanese clothing, language, and manners were more and more accepted by the Japa-

9 J. Dollard, N. E. Miller, L. W. Doob, O. H. Mowrer, and Robert Sears, *Frustration and Aggression;* Institute of Human Relations, Yale Univ. Press, 1939; pp. 151–156. See also J. Dollard, *Caste and Class in a Southern Town;* Institute of Human Relations, Yale Univ. Press, 1937.

nese. Many Koreans I know complained about the fact that some upper class Koreans would rather be Japanese than Koreans. Many of them did make the change, including marriage to Japanese women.[10]

This is not the case in Germany or the United States. In each of these cultures, because of its emphasis on repression as a mechanism and therefore on inner balance, external passive accommodation between the dominant and the subordinate castes—Jews in Germany and Negroes in the United States —is not enough. Negroes who are "uppity" in the South have been lynched. In spite of isolation in ghettos or otherwise restricted spheres, the Jews in Germany were continuously objects of pogroms.

It is true that there were outstanding Negroes who were not only accepted but also nearly idolized by British society in the eighteenth century,[11] but it took less than half a century for various forms of prejudice to rise.[12] There was also the Chinese Boxer Rebellion of 1911 in which the chief objects of attack were European missionaries and later all Europeans. However, in discussing the racial problem of the Anglo-Saxon-Teutonic world one has to remember that the direction of persecution in each culture was first of all given by its historical background. In the United States it is only the Negro who is an object of nation-wide persecution, while the other minorities such as Chinese, Japanese, Mexicans, Indians, and so on, are not so historically related to the mass hysteria. Furthermore, many American landladies and restaurant-keepers have been known to accommodate Negroes from Jamaica and elsewhere, while at the same time refusing to have anything to do with Negroes with a southern accent, who are their compatriots.

10 John Embree has given an excellent account of Japanese national attitudes towards various foreign groups (reference footnote 22; pp. 237–258). Some discriminatory attitudes and measures against native peoples in Japan, Korea, China, and so on, have been described, but the over-all picture one gets is consistent with the present thesis. Only one large scale outburst against Koreans in Japan has been reported. That was during the 1923 earthquake (p. 246).

11 K. L. Little, *The Negroes in Britain;* London, K. Paul, Trench, Trubner, 1948; pp. 199–202.

12 Reference footnote 29; pp. 207–209.

In Germany, persecution only befell the Jews and not other groups. Britain of the eighteenth century simply had no historical condition for racial prejudice against the Negroes. The Chinese Boxer Rebellion against European missionaries must be understood as a temporary mass hysteria under conditions of general poverty, ignorance, obvious Western encroachment, and misconduct on the part of many missionaries. It was certainly neither deliberately planned or carried out, and it did not last. Furthermore, the hysteria only hit the north and west. In a number of southern provinces the governors rigidly forbade the activities of the Boxers, and the movement did not spread. Lastly, the movement was not only against European missionaries but also against Chinese ministers and Christians in general. All in all the outbursts—whether the object was racial or otherwise—in the Eastern cultures lacked the deliberation and permanency which such outbursts had in the Western cultures.

China vs. Japan, and America vs. Germany

FROM the foregoing analysis it may have seemed that there is a complete similarity between Chinese and Japanese culture on the one hand and American and German culture on the other. Nothing would be further from the truth. The similarity appears only because one factor has been examined: suppression or repression as the chief mechanism of social control. When a second factor is added, the picture at once changes. This second factor is the presence or absence of a unified loyalty to the wider society or state. When this factor is added it will be seen that there are vast differences between Japan and China, and again between Germany and the United States.

Here again the analysis must be begun with the understanding that the origin of German loyalty to the abstract symbol of the state and Japanese loyalty to her emperor are both historical facts the origin of which cannot be explained simply on the basis of the projective system of the individual. However, given this loyalty or its lack, combined with the mechanism of repression or suppression, certain features will tend to appear in one or another culture in given situations, such as constructive effort in peace, or revitalization after defeat.

The presence or absence of a strong sense of a unified loyalty to the wider symbol of state could largely be held to account for the differences in modernizing developments in Japan and China. Although both Japanese and Chinese societies emphasize suppression and therefore proper external relationship of the individual as the goal of life, the existence of a strong sense of loyalty to the emperor means that each individual attempts to fulfill his obligations not only in his immediate but also the widest possible social environment under the emperor. This makes for a smooth and thorough national organization which is capable of effective and quick action. Japanese industrial and military advances in modern times, with no change in her traditional social and political structures, is an outstanding illustration of this point.[13]

In defeat, once the situation is clarified, the Japanese, because of the traditional emphasis on proper stations under the emperor, will have overwhelming and genuine enthusiasm and love for their conquerors. The individual has merely changed his object of loyalty a bit, especially when the old nominal symbol has not been altered. There will be no sense of shame any more. All the individual

13 A similar observation has been made by both Dr. Hu Shih ["The Modernization of China and Japan," in Ruth Nanda Anshen (ed.), *Freedom, Its Meaning;* New York, Harcourt, Brace & Co., 1940; pp. 114–121] and Dr. Ruth Benedict (reference footnote 2; pp. 78–79 and later chapters of the book). The argument presented here is, however, closer to that of Dr. Hu and further from that of Dr. Benedict. The latter emphasized the fact that the rapid advances of Japan were "rooted in traditional Japanese character" the main attribute of which was "taking one's proper station" (Benedict, p. 79). From the analysis presented so far, it becomes apparent that that which Dr. Benedict regarded as "traditional Japanese character" was generally common to traditional China as well. If one follows Dr. Benedict's argument entirely, he would expect the Chinese to make comparable advances in industrial and military fields, as Japan did during the last century. This, however, China failed to do, and in my view it was the lack of a traditionally sanctioned symbol of loyalty to the wider society in China which made the difference.

has to do is to accommodate to a new situation with somewhat modified statuses. Because of the individual conditioning to suppression as a mechanism of social control, the changed situation, once established, causes no deep resentment, simply because the individual is not psychologically hurt. A conditioning to proper external relationship merely calls for a readjustment of that external relationship when the necessity comes. Because of the loyalty to a wider national symbol, the Japanese are not likely to be so resistant to such customs as social dancing (as the Chinese will, regardless of what happens), if the custom is endorsed by the new conquerors, which is the power behind the throne. Once the conqueror-conquered statuses are clarified and well established, what is good for the wider nation will be good for the individual.

The case of China is similar to Japan in one respect and different in another. Chinese culture emphasizes suppression as a mechanism of social control, but China traditionally has no permanent symbol of loyalty to the wider state. It is significant that while in Japanese history there has been only one dynasty which claimed its descent from the Sun Goddess, who in turn was the creator of the universe, in Chinese history there have been nearly twenty dynasties which were unrelated and which replaced one another. Certainly none would be considered as the ornator of the universe, or even of Chinese society as a whole. The emperor, though equipped with absolute power while the dynasty lasted, was nevertheless regarded by the people functionally and could be removed by revolt. In place of a permanent loyalty to the emperor and his descendants, the Chinese believe in permanent affiliation to a kinship group. The descendants of emperors of a fallen dynasty were soon forgotten by the people; but among the ordinary families even the remotest kin member would be traced in genealogical books. Many wealthy and powerful families boast of descent from some famous ministers, legendary or real, who supposedly existed in Chow or Chin dynasty, about two thousand or more years ago.

This being the case, when the need for modernization arose in China as it did in

Japan, China was unable to take quick and effective action in order to meet the challenge of the West, because the organization of the wider society was neither smooth nor thorough. The loyalty of the individual was to the family group, and the most important goal of an individual was in achieving proper status within that group. As a result Chinese large-scale industrial enterprises, which started more or less at the same time as large-scale Japanese industrial enterprises, and with equal advantage in capital and equipment, deteriorated into nonentity, while their Japanese counterparts went ahead by leaps and bounds. The respective histories of the Chinese Merchant Navigation Company and the Japanese Nippon Yosen Kaisa provide us with one of the many illustrations on this point.

In defeat and under conditions of conquest, the Chinese, like the Japanese, will not be deeply resentful, because the individual is psychologically unhurt; but the allegiance to kinship ties will cause the average person to be without enthusiasm for the new regime set up by the conquerors. In this respect the Chinese will be unlike the Japanese. Furthermore the conquerors of China will be opposed if they do not leave the people alone. Throughout Chinese history those alien dynasties which remained in power the longest were those that knew how to leave the Chinese alone. On the other hand indigenous dynasties were shortlived if they did not leave the people alone. The opposition of Chinese to conquest is more likely a result not of any deep-seated feelings against the new rulers but of hatred for external inconvenience.

If left alone, the average Chinese attitude toward conquest or a new regime will be one of indifference. They will not effectively form large non-kinship groups, or participate actively in such groups, unless the basic kinship pattern has been in some way modified. So far whatever modification there has been in kinship pattern has usually occurred in large urban centers and even there slowly.[14] New elements of culture from the West, especially

14 F. L. K. Hsu, "The Family in China," in R. N. Anshen (ed.), *The Family: Its Function and Destiny;* New York, Harper & Bros., 1949; pp. 81–92.

where it pertains to the virtues involving kinship groups, will be accepted, if at all, with reserve.

Germany and the United States present two different combinations of the factors analysed in this paper. German culture emphasizes repression as a mechanism of social control, and therefore, individualism; but this individualism is combined with a desire for loyalty to the widest possible culturally defined group, the state. This flair for some wider structural framework of reference is clearly seen in German scholarship for the last several hundred years. Germany is, as far as I know, the only Western European society in which, as in Japan, the sanctity of the family and the female sexual function could be exploited to suit the purposes of the state without serious opposition from the people. Nevertheless, because of the fact that this emphasis on the wider social and political framework is combined with repressive mechanisms and individualism, in German culture there has always been a conflict between these two poles. It was no accident that Hegelian dialecticism, with its thesis and antithesis, first arose and gained popularity in Germany.

This extreme emphasis on the place of the individual with reference to the state enables the German people to make smooth and thorough organization on a large scale for effective and quick action in time of peace and stress. The fact that Germany, a comparative late-comer in the Industrial Revolution, should have been able to catch up with England, in terms of expansion, output, and productivity, is good evidence for this observation. Once defeated, and subject to a situation of conquest by alien rulers, the German will not only have no enthusiasm for the conquerors but will intensely hate the outsiders, because his internal emotional balance is badly hurt. Before a new political and social framework is established, the individual, because of lack of any real social anchorage, will feel lost and aimless; but he will soon converge toward anything which will suggest the rise of a wider framework with an indigenous German appearance: this may be Naziism or its modified form; anti-Semitism; or something new. The important thing is that the new framework desired will have to be wide, on a state scale, and it will also have to look German. In this connection it is very interesting to contrast the external attitudes of Japan and Germany toward conquerors. The Japanese, as a whole, are afraid that the United States will leave; they find comfort in having United States support and authority for, at any rate, an indefinite period of time. On the other hand, Germans, as a whole, are anxious for the departure of the controlling powers. Recent reports show that Western Germans are suspicious of the new German government set up there, because it is not sufficiently German. In both cases the desire for a wider allegiance is present; but the people brought up in a culture which emphasizes internal emotional balance cannot react in the same way as another people brought up in a culture which emphasizes external harmony with the powers that be.

America represents a situation different from any of the foregoing three, because here the cultural tradition emphasizes no unified allegiance by the individual to any single group, from family to the state. As aptly observed by many scholars, Americans are suspicious of any single group exerting overwhelming control, and the entire constitution as well as the power structure of the various levels of government are based upon the principle of check and balance. The social groups claiming allegiance of the individual are many, but most of them are neither permanent nor necessarily in harmony with the whole. As a matter of fact the typical picture of American social groups is one in which there are all kinds of inconsistencies, contradictions, conflicts as well as accommodation. The over-all cultural emphasis is still stark individualism, based upon repression as the chief mechanism, and the age-old philosophy that if each works for his own good the end result will be the most good for the largest number.

In time of peace the constructive efforts will be slow. In spite of her superabundance of resources, tremendous mechanization and the highest standard of living in the world—floods, droughts, the dust bowl, hurricanes, tornadoes, poorly equipped and staffed schools, and so on will continue to affect one sector or another of the American nation. There will be little or no coordinated effort to deal with some of these basic problems and the colossal production and economy will move on with tremendous waste.

In time of national distress, of defeat, and under conditions of conquest—from which Americans have fortunately never suffered—the American people would be deeply disturbed and would resist the conquerors, regardless of whether the latter left them alone or not. There would certainly be no enthusiasm for any alien regime, not even a passive acquiescence. Allegiance to idealism would make any external accommodation with conquerors very difficult. The individual in such a situation would have less feeling of being lost or aimless like the Germans, but would be able to look around for some positive lines of action, simply because Americans have been used to managing for themselves and not to being told to do one thing or another. The lack of any permanent traditional allegiance to any single group, such as the Chinese kinship structure or the German and Japanese state, coupled with historical experience of organization from chaos, would enable an American to enter into much wider associations of resistance, and with much greater speed than, for example, the Chinese.

A Discussion on Origin

THE foregoing analysis is really only a first approximation of the problem. In a paper of this kind it is impossible to treat the subject exhaustively. Furthermore, any discussion of the wider national issues in personality terms is bound to be limited in application and value. However the question of the origin of the patterns of suppression or repression in the two types of cultures must also be examined, and the personality characteristics correlated with each.

In Dr. Benedict's attempt to explain the origin of the Japanese character, which from the Western point of view is full of contradictions, she says:

The contradictions which all Westerners have described in Japanese character are intelligible from their child rearing. It produces a duality in their outlook on life, neither side of which can be ignored. From their experience of privilege and psychological ease in babyhood they retain through all the disciplines of later life the memory of an easier life when they 'did not know shame.' They do not have to paint a Heaven in the future; they have it in their past. They rephrase their childhood in their doctrine of the innate goodness of man, of the benevolence of their gods, and of the incomparable desirability of being a Japanese. . . .

Gradually, after they are six or seven, responsibility for circumspection and 'knowing shame' is put upon them and upheld by the most drastic of sanctions: that their own family will turn against them if they default. The pressure is not that of a Prussian discipline, but it is inescapable. In their early privileged period the ground has been prepared for this development both by the persistent inescapable training in nursery habits and posture, and by the parents' teasing which threatens the child with rejection. These early experiences prepare the child to accept great restraints upon himself when he is told that 'the world' will laugh at him and reject him. He clamps down upon the impulses he expressed so freely in earlier life, not because they are evil but because they are now inappropriate. He is now entering upon serious life. As he is progressively denied the privileges of childhood he is granted the gratifications of greater and greater adulthood, but the experiences of that earlier period never truly fade out. In his philosophy of life he draws freely upon them. He goes back to them in his permissiveness about 'human feelings.' He reexperiences them all through his adulthood in his 'free areas' of life.[15]

This lucid theory, which would account for contradictions in Japanese personality by the sharp contrast between early and later childhood experiences, is inadequate simply because it fails to apply to China. In many respects Chinese culture does not carry as many or as extreme contradictions as does Japanese culture. But from the Western point of view Chinese personality is equally full of contradictions. What can be more contradictory than for an educated and respected bureaucrat-scholar to talk earnestly on the evil of

licentiousness, while he himself may have a thoroughly good time with his male friends at a brothel with no qualms at all? What can be more contradictory than for a people to forget about various gods until the occurrence of an emergency like a cholera epidemic?[16] Yet the same discontinuity in training between early and later childhood which Dr. Benedict observed for Japan does not hold true in China.[17] Furthermore, a kind of sharp discontinuity between earlier and later experiences is very evident in the life of an American.[18]

That there is no consistent correlation between infant care and personality in all cultures studied thus far has been admirably demonstrated by Orlansky.[19] On the other hand, I believe that the factors responsible for, or correlated with, the basic contrast in the mechanism of socialization—suppression versus repression—between the two Eastern and two Western cultures may be sought in the broader aspects of the family life. These factors are considerably different from those given by Dr. Benedict for Japan alone.

If one looks at the family in China and Japan on the one hand, and Germany and the United States on the other, he sees that there are quantitative as well as qualitative differences. First the quantitative differences: The family in China and Japan is, as a whole, the larger joint family with more than one married couple and more than two generations living under the same roof. In contrast the family in Germany and the United States is, again as a whole, the smaller conjugal family with only a married couple and their unmarried children as the sole occupants of one unit of the living quarters. This being the case, it is obvious that the Chinese and Japanese individual in the proc-

15 Ruth Benedict, reference footnote 2; pp. 286–287.

16 For a description and analysis of measures taken by a rustic community against a cholera epidemic, see F. L. K. Hsu, *Magic and Science in Western Yunnan;* New York, Institute of Pacific Relations, 1943.

17 For child training in China, see Hsu, *Under the Ancestors' Shadow;* reference footnote 24.

18 F. L. K. Hsu, "American and Chinese Adolescence: Their Theoretical Implications," unpublished paper, read at Toronto meetings of the American Anthropological Association, 1948.

19 Harold Orlansky, "Infant Care and Personality," *Psychological Bull.* (1949) 46: 1–48.

ess of growing up, as compared with the German and American individual in the same condition, is likely to have a much larger number and more categories of persons who have meant something to him from every period of life. This could mean in terms of the present suppression-versus-repression theory, two things. First, in the mind of the developing Chinese or Japanese child the parental image, in the normal course of events, is likely to be adulterated with that of a number of other relatives who, in one way or another, enter into the picture. This means a more diffused source of disciplinary power from the very start. The reverse, again in the normal course of events, is true of the developing American or German child. Second, because of the much larger family unit, the child in the two Eastern cultures early learns to appreciate the importance of different categories of relatives who mean something to him and to his parents. This sets the beginning of the sensitivity to external harmony, because, not only the child's life but the parents' attitude and behavior tend to be more or less seriously influenced by the presence or absence of one or another of the members of the joint family. The American and German picture is again the reverse.

However, compared with the qualitative differences, these quantitative differences are of minor importance. For if the average size of a family in the two Eastern cultures is compared with that in the two Western cultures, it is at once clear that the differences are not as tremendous as one would imagine. While there are many families in China of 30 or more people, the average size of the Chinese family is only 5.3 while that of America is between 3 and 4. The average family size in Japan is equally not tremendous. But if one examines the ideal and even actual patterns underlying the behavior of the individuals of the family in the two kinds of cultures, the differences are found to be truly great. First, even in premodern times, the family in Europe and America tended to atomism—except that modern America has carried the trend farther than the rest. The basic pattern of the Euro-American conjugal family is that each new generation ruthlessly replaces the old. And as the old no longer has any place in the existing scheme of things they, among a few other classes of people, are the ones who will suffer the greatest amount of psychological misery. On the other hand, China and Japan, even in modern times, emphasize loyalty to the family group as a whole, except that in China the picture is much more complicated and uneven. The basic pattern of the family is that age leads to new and more respected statuses and greater significance. True psychological misery does not, therefore, befall the aged. Misery is the lot of those who have no descendants or are otherwise without place in any existing kinship structure.

The matter goes beyond a mere question of atomization versus loyalty to the whole. Probably as a result of the tendency to atomization, and the stark fact that each new generation ruthlessly replaces the old one, parents of the Anglo-Saxon-Teutonic family tend to exert complete control over their children, the other relatives having no disciplinarian importance even if they live in the family. In such a family a person has little escape from parental control before maturity. On the other hand, lacking such motivation, parents of the Japanese-Chinese family have less determination to exert complete control over their children. Even if they wanted to do so, other family members like grandparents, aunts, and in-laws can exert effective interference with their authority in one way or another.

The implications of these differences are, in terms of the present theory, both far-reaching and obvious. The more exclusive and severe parental control in the Western family is consistent with the importance of repressive mechanisms in socialization and therefore with greater or more severe internalization of the parental imago and other restraining forces in the individual. The less exclusive and severe parental control in the Eastern family is consistent with the importance of suppressive mechanisms in socialization and therefore with smaller or less severe internalization of the parental imago and other restraining forces in the individual. As pointed out at the beginning of this paper, although both suppressive and repressive mechanisms are present and operative in an average person regardless of his culture, the individual in the two Western cultures discussed here tends to look more to internal forces for guidance of his actions, while the individual in the two Eastern cultures tends to look more to external circumstances for guidance. This makes the difference between guilt and shame. This also makes the difference between individualism and what in the absence of a better term may be termed situationalism. Finally, it is easier for the individual to tolerate contradictions in the external situation by treating each situation more or less separately, than for the individual to reconcile contradictions in the internal psyche —since the functioning mind has to be much more closely knit than the functioning society or culture; thus the behavior of the Eastern individual is, from the point of view of that of the West, naturally rife with obvious contradictions.

Summary

THE present paper is primarily an attempt at explaining certain culturally determined aspects of personality in terms of suppression-versus-repression theory, in two types of cultures. Four cultures have been selected for analysis: Japan and China represent the cultures in which suppression is the more important mechanism of socialization of the individual; America and Germany represent the cultures in which repression is the more important mechanism of socialization of the individual. Certain serious differences between Japanese and Chinese cultures and also between American and German cultures are explained on the basis of an additional factor— namely, loyalty to a wider political framework, state or the throne. No claim is made that these factors—suppression or repression, and loyalty to the wider state or the lack of it —explain the whole of the four cultures. They only explain a number of selected phenomena which are, I think, essential to these four cultures.

In the same way no all-inclusive claim is made that the quantitative and qualitative differences between the family patterns in the two types of cultures can explain the origin of everything. I have tried to demonstrate the possible connection between the Chinese-Japanese type of family and suppression as the major mechanism of socialization; and the possible connection between the American-German type of family and repression as the major mechanism of socialization. But these family differences will not explain the origin of loyalty to the wider state of Germany and Japan, or the lack of such loyalty in America and China. In fact I believe that factors bearing on the latter differences certainly must be sought in a wider field, including historical developments.